Music and Context

ESSAYS FOR JOHN M. WARD

Music and Context

Essays for John M. Ward

EDITED BY ANNE DHU SHAPIRO
ASSISTANT EDITOR: PHYLLIS BENJAMIN

DEPARTMENT OF MUSIC
HARVARD UNIVERSITY
1985

Editorial Committee

David G. Hughes
Rulan Chao Pian
Christoph Wolff

Library of Congress Cataloging-in-Publication Data
Main entry under title:

Music and context.

  "Bibliography of the works of John Milton Ward": p.
  1. Music and society—Addresses, essays, lectures.
2. Ward, John M. (John Milton), 1917–   . I. Ward,
John M. (John Milton), 1917–   . II. Shapiro, Anne
Dhu, 1941–
  ML3795.M77   1985   780'.07   85–8472
ISBN 0-674-58888-6

Table of Contents

Foreword

JOHN WARD HAS TOUCHED all of us with the magic wand of his boundless curiosity concerning the music of this world, in the most all-inclusive meaning that 'music of this world' could have."

So writes one of John Ward's many students, who came to the Harvard Music Department set on a particular course but found himself changed forever by the teaching of the man to whom this volume is dedicated, and by that man's curiosity and respect for all music.

Born in Oakland, California, in 1917, John Milton Ward was active in musical affairs throughout his undergraduate years, first at San Francisco Junior College and then at San Francisco State College, where he studied harpsichord, sang in madrigal groups, and organized a four-day festival of Tudor music and drama. It was also during these years that he developed an interest in folk music, inspired by his study of Elizabethan keyboard music.

As a graduate student he was drawn to professors whose interests ranged from Medieval and Renaissance music to that of the Native Americans. Among his first mentors was Otto Gombosi at the University of Washington, where he received an M.M. in 1942, with a thesis on the use of trumpets in Elizabethan and early Stuart theaters (see Bibliography). While still in California, he studied composition with Darius Milhaud at Mills College; after moving to New York City to continue graduate work, John became a member of the ISCM Forum, which performed some of his piano and vocal compositions. He continued his graduate work in musicology with George Herzog, Erich Hertzmann, and Paul Henry Lang at Columbia, and with Curt Sachs and Gustave Reese at New York University. He earned his Ph.D. from N.Y.U. in 1953, with a dissertation entitled "The Vihuela de Mano and Its Music, 1536–1576," in which he emphasized, among other things, popular music as an important thread in the fabric of instrumental art-music—early proof of his broad perspective on the discipline of musicology.

During his early graduate years at the University of Washington, John met Ruth Neils, also a graduate student in music, and after a short time in New York, he came back to marry her, in 1945. She has been his indispensable companion ever since.

John began his teaching career in 1947 as an instructor at Michigan State University, where he remained until 1953. From then until 1955, he taught at the University of Illinois as an assistant, and then an associate, professor. He came to Harvard University in 1955 as an associate professor and in 1961 was appointed William Powell Mason Professor of Music, a post from which he retires in June of 1985. In 1983 he was elected an honorary member of Phi Beta Kappa, Alpha Chapter of Massachusetts, and an Honorary Foreign Member of the Royal Musical Association.

In both teaching and scholarship, John Ward has dealt with an exceptionally wide range of musical periods, genres, and styles. The bibliography at the end of this volume attests to his numerous publications in Renaissance instrumental music and English popular and folk music. To graduate students, it is Music 200, Introduction to Musicology, that has earned him the praises—sometimes at a few years' remove—of generations of Harvard Ph.D.'s. It can be fairly said that no one who goes through "the Music 200 experience" emerges unchanged. John Ward is exacting, demanding, and unsparing with the red pencil, which he liberally applies to everything from a disorganized argument to a misspelled word. All-important to him is the development of the student's ability to think critically, speak concisely, and write with clarity and grace. "What's the point?" becomes the rallying cry of each new Music 200 group. But as sharp as he is with his red pencil—and occasionally his tongue—all students who come to him seriously for help are assured of his time and attention.

Perhaps less well known, except by his Harvard colleagues and students, is his lively involvement in music outside the European art-music tradition. His interest, not only in the structure of music, but also in the ways music is used and what it means to the people of a given culture, has led to many innovative course-offerings. Among the courses he has created at Harvard are Music and Ritual, Music and Narrative, and Music and Dance; in each of these, music has been defined as variously as mankind has created it. "Saturday Night at the Rain Dance," the affectionate nickname given to Music and Ritual on the undergraduate grapevine, evokes the excitement of traversing strange new territory under John Ward's enthusiastic guidance. The many graduate students who have assisted him in these courses through the years could not have had a better training in ethnomusicology. It was natural that eventually a seminar on ethnomusicology came into being that would face the issues of the discipline more directly. Even here he never stopped exploring and experimenting with new approaches.

In whatever courses he has taught, John Ward has broadened the views of his students, as is shown by the variety of subjects for Ph.D.

theses that he has directed. All such investigations—from music of the Bushmen to music for the silver screen, from Renaissance lutenists to jazz pianists—have found their initial inspiration in John Ward's provocative teaching, his constant questioning, and his open-minded, inquisitive approach to the astonishingly varied forms of musical expression the world over.

—Isabel Pope Conant
Lorna Jean Marshall

Preface

THE ESSAYS THAT FOLLOW show some of the many directions taken by
John Ward's students and colleagues, whose lives he has touched
through both professional contact and personal friendship. In keeping
with his own central concern, the authors have sought to relate the music they discuss to its surrounding context—hence the organization of
the volume into cross-disciplinary sections, and its title, Music and
Context. In juxtaposing, for example, the essays of Craig Wright, David
Hughes, and Frank D'Accone on Medieval and Renaissance liturgy
with Thomas Vennum's revelation of the origins of an Ojibwa ritual,
the Editorial Committee has followed the pedagogical practice of John
Ward himself, in the hope that the reader will find stimulation not only
in the range of topics but also in their surprising parallels. Thus the essays are placed in categories that reflect underlying conceptual similarities, rather than historical or geographic relationships.

Musical composition reflects not only an individual composer's
training and tastes, but also expresses more widely held societal values.
The thorny issue of the cultural bias with which music is made and
received underlies essays by Howard Brown, Nicholas Tawa, and James
Haar; Laurence Berman reviews the cultural and aesthetic world of
nineteenth-century Romanticism to understand a facet of Debussy's
music.

Musicology in some sense always treats history. Yet Claude Palisca's investigations into the influence of the music of the French Revolution on Beethoven's Eroica, and Eileen Southern's study of a Renaissance noblewoman who enjoyed an unusual reputation as a dancer,
take us beyond music history into social and cultural fields. Nino Pirrotta's essay on the Italian trecento links detailed musical analysis with
the broader issues of patronage and politics.

Several articles focus on the conjunction of music and other art
forms. Rulan Pian discusses the mixture of dramatic and narrative elements in a Chinese dance and song form, the Twirling Duet; Colin
Slim scrutinizes the art of Caravaggio for its depictions of Renaissance
music. Curtis Price, Daniel Heartz, and John Wiley examine the interplay of music and popular culture in the theaters of London, Paris, and
St. Petersburg in the seventeenth through nineteenth centuries.

The dialectic between the notated and the unwritten has long been at the center of John Ward's own research; facets of this opposition are explored in the essays on Renaissance lute music by Edward Kovarik and Arthur Ness. Bell Yung draws on both ancient literary sources and modern fieldwork to illustrate a technique of Chinese instrumental performance; and Albert Lord shows how stanzaic structure in Yugoslav folksong effects a compromise between the musical and the textual impulse.

The final group of essays in the volume focuses on the topics of change and persistence. My own essay documents continuity of Scottish song-style, despite linguistic change; Ivan Waldbauer analyzes patterns of formal change in selected works of Bartók; and Robert Provine traces variation in the long-term performance history of a Korean farmer's drum piece. In the closing essay, Wainwright Love renders a Samoan farewell, complete with metaphorical allusions to the dedicatee of this volume.

The Afterword is a gift from two of John Ward's Asian friends: a former student at Harvard, Masakata Kanazawa, now teaching at the International Christian University in Tokyo, and Shigeo Kishibe, a former colleague at Harvard. Through their personal reminiscences the reader may feel even more clearly the impact of John Ward as man and as teacher on generations of scholars.

Thanks are owed to all these distinguished contributors for their cooperation in promptly completing articles and proofs—and then patiently awaiting publication; to the Editorial Committee for level-headed advice in all phases of the process; to Ruth Ward for her assistance in getting information and in keeping secrets; to Wainwright Love for his meticulous proofreading and work on the Bibliography. My special thanks go to the assistant editor, Miss Phyllis Benjamin, doctoral candidate in Musicology, whose incredible combination of long-honed editorial skills, musical expertise, and devotion to the task at hand were largely responsible for seeing this volume to completion.

—Anne Dhu Shapiro

Cambridge, Massachusetts
January, 1985

Aside from the support of the Harvard Music Department, the following people have helped make possible the publication of this book:

Isabel Pope Conant	Roland J. Wiley
Lorna Jean Marshall	Anonymous I
A. Tillman Merritt	Anonymous II
Nino Pirrotta	Anonymous III
Eileen Southern	Anonymous IV

ABBREVIATIONS

BAMS	*Bulletin of the American Musicological Society*
CMM	*Corpus Mensurabilis Musicae*
IMSCR	*International Musicological Society Congress Report*
JAFL	*Journal of the American Folklore Society*
JAMS	*Journal of the American Musicological Society*
MGG	*Musik in Geschichte und Gegenwart*
MLA NOTES	*Notes: The Quarterly Journal of the Music Library Association*
MQ	*The Musical Quarterly*
New Grove	*The New Grove Dictionary of Music and Musicians*
RISM	*Répertoire international des sources musicales, Receuils imprimés, XVIᵉ–XVIIᵉ siècles*

The Feast of the Reception
of the Relics
at Notre Dame of Paris

CRAIG WRIGHT

ONE DAY MANY YEARS AGO, when I was privileged to be a graduate student at Harvard under the tutelage of John Ward and his colleagues, there suddenly and inexplicably appeared on the wall of the Loeb Music Library a cartoon that obviously had been fabricated by one of my fellow students. It depicted a cemetery in the center of which was a tombstone that bore the inscription *Johannes Dowland Requiescat in Pace*. There, digging furiously toward the bones of Dowland, was a figure that looked suspiciously like our mentor, John Ward, and above him was the caption "Let us return to the primary sources!" Acknowledging his wisdom and the wisdom of this injunction—to return to the primary sources and the bare bones of fact—the following brief essay on saintly relics is offered to John with respect and affection.

It is difficult for us today, given the spirit of scientific skepticism that dominates our age, to comprehend fully the importance of saints and saintly relics within medieval society.[1] As tangible objects of divine power, the physical remains of the heroes of the Christian story influenced all aspects of human existence. They were the intermediaries by which the spiritual will was manifested in the material world, and their presence provided explanations for mundane occurrences when no other answers could be found. Remnants of the apostles, of hundreds of martyrs, confessors, and matrons of the Church, of the

---

[1]The hagiographic bibliography is enormous. Among the studies drawn upon for this paragraph are the following: Patrice Boussel, *Des reliques et de leur bon usage* (Paris, 1971); Peter Brown, *The Cult of the Saints: Its Rise and Function in Latin Christianity* (Chicago, 1981); Patrick J. Geary, *Furta Sacra: Thefts of Relics in the Central Middle Ages* (Princeton, 1978); H. Leclerq, "Reliques et reliquaires," in *Dictionnaire d'archéologie chrétienne et de liturgie*, ed. F. Cabrol, H. Leclerq, and H. I. Marrou, vol. XIV (Paris, 1948), cols. 2294–2359; and Heinrich Schauerte, *Die Volkstümliche Heiligenverehrung* (Münster, 1939).

1

True Cross, of the raiments of the Virgin, and of the Lord's circumcision and of His passion all became objects of devotion. Sometimes veneration was given to objects that to the modern mind appear bizarre or even macabre: drops of milk of the Virgin or beads of sweat of St. Anne, drops of the Lord's blood, His fingernails, umbilical cord, and even His foreskin (at least fourteen of them were claimed by churches in France, Italy, and Germany),[2] to list just a few. Whether real or fictitious, the remains of the holy were thought to possess causal powers. They could stop a plague or generate a bountiful harvest; they could bring rain in times of drought or sunshine in times of flood; and they could heal the sick, cure the lame, give sight to the blind, or exorcise the devil. Seen in terms of the evolution of religious thought, the cult of relics provided a necessary bridge between the immediate naturalism of the ancient religion and the theocentric abstractions of the new Christianity. On a more practical level, particular relics gave a sense of local identity to the community, and, to the extent that they served as a goal for pilgrimage or aided in raising money for new constructions, they promoted the economic vitality of the region. Thus relics provided both a focus and a stimulus for many of the spiritual and commercial activities of the religious community. Often encased in richly jeweled reliquaries, the sacred souvenirs were usually placed within or displayed behind the main altar of the church at the east end of the choir, where they could be viewed by the faithful who gathered in the ambulatory to gaze through the perforations in the choir screen. When need arose, the reliquaries were taken down from their niches near the altar and, with the encouragement of both ecclesiastic and civil authorities, paraded around the town in order to inspire popular devotion and elicit divine favor.

Notre Dame of Paris was not immune from the hagiolatrous fever that swept Western Christendom in the Middle Ages. One of the earliest manuscripts of the cathedral, a tenth-century sacramentary, contains a list of the most sacred relics that the clergy of Notre Dame had to that moment been able to accumulate.[3] While some of these saints were certainly mythical and soon fell into obscurity, others such as Denis, Germanus of Paris, Germanus of Auxerre, Genevieve, Stephen, Eligius, and Marcel were of special importance to Paris and became,

---

[2]A list of these churches is given in Boussel, *Reliques*, p. 106.

[3]Paris, Bibliothèque nationale (hereafter cited as BN, MS Latin 2294, fol. 97v). The original Latin of this list of relics can be found in Léopold Delisle, "Notice sur un sacramentaire de l'église de Paris," *Mémoires de la Société imperiale des antiquaires de France*, 3rd series, vol. III (1857), p. 169; and B. Guérard, ed., *Cartulaires de l'église Notre-Dame de Paris*, vol. III (Paris, 1850), p. 375. The transliteration in the latter source is somewhat defective.

along with the Virgin, the principal saints of the cathedral. It is they who gave the liturgical books of the church an indigenously Parisian stamp, and it is in their honor that much of the polyphony of Leonin and Perotin was composed. The final item on the list is indicative of the almost magical powers of good and evil that the populace and clergy attributed to relics of this sort:

> These relics [are found] in the reliquary of Holy Mary
> A great part of the head of the martyr St. Denis
> Part of the knee of St. Denis
> Part of the raiment of St. Denis
> Part of the hair shirt of St. Denis
> Part of the beard of St. Germanus [of Paris]
> Part of the hair shirt of St. Germanus
> Part of the hair shirt of St. Eligius
> Part of the spoon of St. Genevieve
> Relics of St. Amanda
> Part of the candle of St. Genevieve
> Part of the sepulchre of the Lord
> Relics of Saints Martin, Anian, Avitus, Brice, Priscus, Cottus, Amand, Aunaarus, [and] Desiderius
> The entire hair shirt of St. Denis
> A stone from the lapidation of St. Stephen and
> A necklace which St. Germanus of Auxerre sent to St. Genevieve
> The entire hair shirt of St. Germanus [of Auxerre?] and his knee bone
> Hair and ashes of a certain saint
> Balm of St. Marcel
> Relics of St. Eutropius and St. Florentius
> Vestments of St. Germanus [of Paris], which vestment Vuineradus, deacon, brought into the treasury in the forty-second year of the reign of King Clotharius (ca. 626) . . .
> A small reliquary with the relics of St. Germanus [of Paris]
> Unknown relics which no one should dare to see, for anyone wishing to see them will lose the sight of his eyes.

In the course of the next three centuries, from roughly 1000 to 1300, other relics were piously believed to have been added to this collection. Among the more important of these were the head of St. Gendulph, parts of the arms of St. Julian of Le Mans, of St. Simeon, of St. Eligius, and of the Apostle Andrew, three teeth of St. John the Baptist, a part of the crown of thorns, a finger of St. Nicholas and one of St. Blaise, a part of the True Cross, a rib of St. Louis, and a lock of hair of the Virgin. Such hallowed debris reinforced the importance of existing festivals or, as in the case of the fragment of the True Cross carried from Jerusalem by canon Anselm in 1120, caused yet new feasts to come into being. But that was not all. Just as "new" relics could be brought to the cathedral or monastery from elsewhere, those already existing *in situ* could be "lost" and then "rediscovered" in a transparent attempt to intensify popular religious fervor and reaffirm the oral tradition that assigned a specific identity to a particular relic.

Such was the case for a succession of unusual events that transpired in Paris in the late twelfth century and that gave rise to the feast of the Reception of the Relics (Susceptio reliquiarum) at Notre Dame. Sometime during the early construction of the present cathedral, several important relics were removed from Notre Dame and placed in another church for safekeeping. These included a lock of hair of the Virgin, three teeth of St. John the Baptist, some stones from the lapidation of St. Stephen, the cranium of St. Denis, and an arm of St. Andrew.[4] Later these sacred mementos were "rediscovered" and given to King Philip Augustus (1179–1223), who then returned them to the cathedral with all due liturgical pomp. Precisely when these important relics were lost, when and where they were found, and when they were given back to the cathedral are questions that have been debated sporadically from the early fifteenth century down to the present day.[5] We need not enter here into the sometimes tedious particulars of the dispute. Suffice it to say that the relics were most likely removed from the church around 1163 when construction of the new cathedral was begun, were housed in a church under the patronage of St. Stephen (likely St. Etienne des Grès, one of the dependency churches of the cathedral situated on the Left Bank), and were probably rediscovered and then returned to the cathedral by Philip Augustus in the 1180s.[6] It is in this decade that the choir of the church was completed, the main altar dedicated, and the new choir stalls set in place.[7] At this same time liturgical services were being celebrated in the new sanctuary; these undoubtedly included at least some of the organa then being written by Magister Leoninus,

[4]The first extant document to list these relics is apparently the mid-thirteenth-century necrology of Notre Dame, Paris, BN, MS Latin 5185CC (fol. 126v).

[5]The issues are discussed thoroughly in H. François Delaborde, "Le procès du chef de Saint Denis en 1410," Mémoires de la Société de l'histoire de Paris et de l'Ile-de-France, 11 (1884), 297–409. They have been taken up again more recently by William M. Hinkle in "The King and the Pope on the Virgin Portal of Notre-Dame," The Art Bulletin, 48 (1966), 4–5. I am grateful to Prof. Rebecca Baltzer for having brought this latter source to my attention.

[6]The chronicler Robert de Torigni includes the following remark among his list of important events that transpired in the year 1186: "Apud urbem Parisiorum, in quodam monasterio sancti Stephani protomartyris, inveniuntur reliquiae de capillis sanctae Mariae XXXII, brachium sancti Andreae apostoli, caput sancti Dionysii martyris, ejusdem urbis episcopi." He gives no indication as to when they were returned to Notre Dame (Robert de Torigni, Chronique, ed. Léopold Delisle [Rouen, 1873], p. 136). In the fifteenth century the canons of Paris believed this occurred in 1218 (Delaborde, "Procès," p. 372).

[7]See, for example, Marcel Aubert, Notre-Dame de Paris (Paris, 1920), chap. 2.

canon of Notre Dame, in what came to be called the *Magnus liber*. The reposition of the relics at Notre Dame and the institution of a feast in honor of this event to be celebrated annually on December 4 was likely a concomitant of this spirit of architectural and liturgical renewal at the cathedral of Paris in the last decades of the twelfth century.

It is difficult to say with certainty how much time passed between the return of the relics to Notre Dame and the institution of a feast to commemorate this *repositio*. In the Middle Ages the number of years that elapsed between a religious event, such as the canonization of a saint or the transfer of his relics, and the instauration at a particular church of an observance to mark that occasion varied greatly from church to church.[8] The feast of the Conception of the Blessed Virgin, for example, was celebrated in parts of England in the eleventh century but did not become widespread on the Continent until the end of the thirteenth;[9] similarly, the feast of Corpus Christi was insinuated into the liturgies of certain churches in the area of Liège in the 1240s, but only after Pope John XXII ordered its adoption throughout the Roman Church in 1317 did it enjoy universal currency.[10] Within a single church, one feast might be introduced into the liturgy rather quickly while another might go unobserved for several decades, depending upon the volition of the local clergy. At Notre Dame of Paris, for example, the feast of St. Bernard did not become part of the liturgical year until 1207, although he had been canonized shortly after his death in 1174;[11] on the other hand, the clergy of the cathedral was not only celebrating, but celebrating with organum, the feast of the translation of St. Thomas of Canterbury around 1228, only a few short years after his remains had been moved to a new shrine at Canterbury in 1220.[12] Since the obvious purpose of the seemingly well-planned *repositio* of the Parisian relics at Notre Dame was to rekindle there the intensity of the cult of the local saints, it is likely that the annual feast commemorating this translation was instituted contemporaneously with the event.

[8]For an excellent general discussion of this subject, see R. W. Pfaff, *New Liturgical Feasts in Later Medieval England* (Oxford, 1970), chap. 1.

[9]See Edmond Bishop, "On the Origins of the Feast of the Conception of the Blessed Virgin Mary," *Liturgica Historica: Papers on the Liturgy and Religious Life of the Western Church* (Oxford, 1918), pp. 238–59.

[10]C. Lambert, "L'office de la Fête-Dieu: Aperçus nouveaux sur ses origines,' *Revue bénédictine*, 54 (1942), 61–123; and L. M. J. Delaisse, "A la recherche des origines de l'office du Corpus Christi dans les manuscrits liturgiques," *Scriptorium*, 4 (1950), 220–239.

[11]Victor Leroquais, *Le bréviaire de Philippe le Bon* (Brussels, Paris, New York, 1929), pp. 95–96; and Guérard, *Cartulaires*, vol. I, p. 430.

[12]Paris, BN, MS Latin 5185CC, fol. 105; printed in Guérard, *Cartulaires*, vol. IV, p. 105.

Soon the *Susceptio reliquiarum* was entered into the calendars and service books of the cathedral. It first appears among the extant sources of the Parisian rite in Bibliothèque de l'Université, MS 1220, a breviary dating ca. 1200–08.

By whose authority was this new feast instituted? Medieval canon law empowered the local bishop to make additions to his diocesan calendar.[13] At Notre Dame of Paris it appears that the feast of the *Susceptio reliquiarum* was introduced bilaterally by the bishop and the chapter of canons. Several entries in the capitulary acts of Notre Dame affirm that only the will of the bishop and the consent of the chapter were necessary to effect a change in Parisian usage.[14] Indeed, in the Middle Ages each church and monastery enjoyed considerable freedom in formulating the constituents of its devotional ritual; and not until after the Council of Trent, under Popes Pius V, Clement VIII, and Paul V, did the Court of Rome attempt to arrogate to itself the power to unify and standardize fully the liturgy of the Western Church.[15] Prior to that time, the arbiters of the liturgical services were mainly the local clergy, and they were swayed in their judgments by such considerations as local ecclesiastical history, the presence of relics, the preference of the prelate or wealthy benefactors, and the popular piety of the region.

Once the bishop and chapter of Notre Dame had determined that a feast was to be celebrated annually on December 4 to honor the relics, it was incumbent upon them to fashion a service to that end; that is to say, it was necessary to assemble prayers, lessons, psalms, antiphons, responsories, hymns, and other chants to form an appropriate Mass and office. This was not the first time the clergy of Notre Dame had been faced with such an exigency. Between 1150 and 1300 at least twenty new feasts were added to the calendar of the cathedral, and the growth of the Parisian *sanctorale* continued undiminished into the sixteenth century. For some festivals, such as Corpus Christi and the *natale* of Thomas of Canterbury, the clergy of Paris borrowed wholesale a liturgy that was already in common circulation in the West.[16] Other offices

---

[13]William R. Bonniwell, *A History of the Dominican Liturgy* (New York, 1944), p. 98; and Victor Leroquais, *Les sacramentaires et les missels manuscrits des bibliothèques publiques de France* (Paris, 1924), vol. I, p. xxviii.

[14]Archives nationales, LL 105, p. 127; and L 538, no. 3.

[15]Theodor Klauser, *A Short History of the Western Liturgy*, trans. John Halliburton (London, 1969), pp. 117–119; and Aimé-Georges Martimort, *The Church at Prayer: Introduction to the Liturgy*, trans. Robert Fischer *et al.* (New York, 1968), p. 61.

[16]Regarding the feast of Corpus Christi, compare the studies cited in fn. 10 and, for example, Paris, BN, MS Latin 861, fols. 428–433. The Parisian form of the office of St. Thomas of Canterbury is discussed by Heinrich Husmann in "Zur Überlieferung der Thomas-Offizien," *Organicae Voces: Festschrift Joseph Smits van Waesberghe* (Amsterdam, 1963), pp. 87–88.

were newly created by the Dominicans of Paris and then adopted, wholly or in part, for use at the cathedral, namely those for the Reception of the Crown of Thorns (Susceptio coronae, 1239) and for the feast of St. Louis (1297), both of which were composed as rhythmical offices.[17] Finally, there were other newly instituted festivals whose formularies were nothing more than reproductions or rearrangements of offices already in use at the cathedral. A precedent for this sort of liturgical duplication could be found in two earlier universal feasts, the commemorations for All Saints and for All Souls, which drew heavily upon the offices of the Common of Several Martyrs and of the Dead, respectively. When the Reception of the Cross was introduced at Notre Dame (1120), it merely duplicated the ritual used on the feast of the Exaltation of the Cross; similarly, when a liturgy was assembled for St. William of Bourges (1218), patron saint of the University of Paris, it proved to be simply a composite of chants taken from the Common of a Bishop Confessor.

A careful examination of the service of the Susceptio reliquiarum shows that, in a fashion similar to the office of All Saints' Day, it too was cut wholecloth from pre-existing liturgical material. At first Vespers, for example, the antiphons for the (ferial) psalms are drawn from the Common of Several Martyrs, as are the prolix responsory Concede nobis, the hymn Sanctorum meritis, and the antiphon Dic nobis quando for the Magnificat. Matins similarly commences with material from the Common of Several Martyrs (for the antiphon to the Invitatory Psalm and for the hymn, again Sanctorum meritis), but it then proceeds to commemorate individually the saints whose relics were honored that day. The antiphons, lessons, and responds of the first nocturn are devoted to the Virgin. Those of the second nocturn are distributed equally, first to John the Baptist, then to St. Andrew, and finally to St. Stephen. And the chants and readings of the third nocturn exclusively honor St. Denis, the apostle to Gaul and first bishop of Paris. Again, the office of All Saints' Day may have provided the liturgical paradigm for the new observance, since at Matins it too presents a logical succession of lessons and responsories in honor of various saints and heavenly powers, a series that duplicates the order of the saints invoked in the Litany.

[17] Concerning the feast of the Reception of the Crown of Thorns, see Bonniwell, History, p. 114; and compare the Dominican source London, British Library, MS Additional 23935, fols. 332ff with the Parisian, Paris, BN, MS Latin 10482, fols. 478ff. On the adoption of an office for St. Louis, see Jacobus Quetif and Jacobus Echard, eds., Scriptores Ordinis Praedicatorum Recensiti, vol. I, part 2 (Paris, 1719), p. 409; and Edmund Martene and Ursini Durand, eds., Veterum Scriptorum et Monumentorum Historicorum, Dogmaticorum, Moralium, Amplissima Collectio, vol. VI (Paris, n.d.), p. 463; and Bonniwell, History, pp. 201–203.

RESPONSORIES OF MATINS ACCORDING TO PARISIAN USAGE[18]

ALL SAINTS' DAY
1. *Benedicat nos deus* (Trinity)
2. *Felix namque* (Blessed Virgin Mary)
3. *Te sanctum* (Archangel Michael)
4. *Inter natos* (St. John the Baptist)
5. *Cives apostolorum* (Common of Apostles)
6. *O constantia* (Common of Several Martyrs)
7. *Sint lumbi* (Common of Several Confessors)
8. *Audivi vocem* (Common of a Virgin)
9. *Concede nobis* (Common of Several Martyrs)

RECEPTION OF THE RELICS
1. *Missus est gabriel* (Blessed Virgin Mary)
2. *Ave maria gratia plena* (Blessed Virgin Mary)
3. *Suscipe verbum virgo* (Blessed Virgin Mary)
4. *Inter natos* (St. John the Baptist)
5. *Vir iste in populo* (St. Andrew)
6. *Ecce iam coram* (St. Stephen)
7. *In hoc ergo loco* (St. Denis)
8. *Per beatum dyonisium* (St. Denis)
9. *Vir inclitus dyonisiu* (St. Denis)

For the office of Lauds the compiler of the new service of the *Susceptio reliquiarum* pursued his eclectic bent. The first antiphon, *Benedicta tu in mulieribus,* was taken from Lauds of the feast of the Annunciation; the second, *Inter natos,* from the feast of St. John the Baptist (antiphon at second Compline); the third, *Biduo vivens,* from St. Andrew (third antiphon at Lauds); the fourth, *Lapides torrentes,* from the *natale* of St. Stephen (second antiphon at Lauds); and the fifth, *Et sancta est comes,* from the *natale* of St. Denis and his companion martyrs (fifth antiphon at Lauds). And so the adoptive process was employed throughout the various lesser hours and even for the Mass of the day. Each and every one of the chants incorporated in the feast of the *Susceptio reliquiarum* can be shown to have existed in the liturgy of Paris prior to the institution of this new observance. Popular devotion was thus renewed and

[18]The following antiphoners and breviaries were consulted. They are listed here in approximate chronological order: Paris, Bibliothèque de l'Université, MS 1220; *idem,* MS 178; Charleville, Bibliothèque municipale, MS 86; Paris, Bibliothèque Mazarine, MS 343; Paris, BN, MS Latin 749; *idem,* MS Latin 1023; *idem,* MS Latin 10482; *idem,* MS Latin 13233; *idem,* MS Latin 15181; *idem,* MS Latin 15613; Paris, Bibliothèque Ste. Geneviève, MS 2618; Paris, BN, MS Nouv. Acq. Lat. 3095; *idem,* MS Latin 745; *idem,* MS Latin 1024; Paris, Bibliothèque Mazarine, MS 341; *idem,* MS 342; Paris, BN, MS Latin 10485; *idem,* MS Latin 1264; *idem,* MS Latin 746A; *idem,* MS Latin 1291; *idem,* Réserve, B. 538.

the authenticity of the relics reasserted by the wholesale use of familiar musical and textual materials.

Once the formulary for the canonical hours of the Reception of the Relics had been established sometime toward the end of the twelfth century, it remained unchanged for almost five hundred years, until the compilation of the new breviary of Paris in the mid-seventeenth century. Stated more specifically, the same chants, readings, and prayers appear in the same order of succession in the printed sources of the sixteenth and early seventeenth centuries as they do in the earliest manuscripts of Parisian usage containing the service, namely those of the early thirteenth century. The only exception to this rule are the readings at Matins, for these display discrepancies in both content and length within the various manuscripts and prints.

For the Mass, however, the situation is different. Here liturgical uniformity appears not to be the rule. While the melodies of the Ordinary of the Mass comprised an invariable set (the present Roman Mass IV), the chants of the Proper initially differed from source to source. For the present study thirty-one missals, graduals, and ordinals of Parisian usage were examined. Nine of these did not contain the feast of the Relics; these are manuscripts that were compiled in the late twelfth or very early thirteenth centuries or that are unrevised copies of exemplars from that period.[19] Among the twenty-two later sources that do preserve the *Susceptio reliquiarum*, three different formularies for the Proper of the Mass are found.[20]

BN LATIN 1112, 16317 and 15615	BN LATIN 9441	ALL OTHER SOURCES
Introit: *Gaudeamus omnes*	*Gaudeamus*	*Gaudeamus*
Gradual: *Timete*	*Gloriosus*	*Timete*
Alleluia: *Sancti et justi*	*Judicabunt*	*Judicabunt*
Offertory: *Letamini*	*Letamini*	*Mirabilis*
Communion: *Gaudete*	*Gaudete*	*Gaudete*

[19]Listed in approximate chronological order: Paris, Bibliothèque Ste. Geneviève, MS 93; Rome, Biblioteca Casanatense, MS 1695; New York City, General Theological Seminary, MS 55757; Bari, Chapel of St. Nicholas, MS 1; Paris, Bibliothèque de l'Université, MS 177; Paris, BN, MS Latin 862; *idem*, MS Latin 15616; *idem*, MS Latin 830; and London, British Library, MS Additional 38723.

[20]Listed in approximate chronological order: Paris, BN, MS Latin 1112; *idem*, MS Latin 16317; *idem*, MS Latin 15615; *idem*, MS Latin 9441; *idem*, MS Latin 860; *idem*, MS Latin 861; *idem*, MS Latin 1099; Paris, Bibliothèque de l'Arsenal, MS 110; Paris, BN, MS Nouv. Acq. Lat. 2649; *idem*, MS Latin 8884; Paris, Bibliothèque de l'Arsenal, MS 203; London, British Library, MS Additional 16905; Paris, BN, MS Latin 1337; Paris, Bibliothèque de l'Université, MS 705; Paris, Bibliothèque Mazarine, MS 411; *idem*, MS 409; *idem*, MS 407; Baltimore, Walters Gallery, MS 302; Paris, BN, MS Latin 858; *idem*, MS Latin 15280; Paris, Bibliothèque Mazarine, MS 410; and Paris, BN, Réserve B. 159.

Significantly, the four manuscripts that contain the variant formularies are the four earliest extant sources to include a Mass for this feast. Bibliothèque nationale Latin 1112 can be dated ca. 1212–18 on the basis of its *sanctorale:* it contains the feast of St. Bernard, which was entered in the Parisian calendar in 1207, and that of the translation of St. Eligius, which commemorates the transfer of an arm bone of that saint from Noyon to Paris in 1212;[21] on the other hand, it lacks the feast of William of Bourges (1218) and the translation of the relics of St. Thomas of Canterbury (1220). The ordinal Bibliothèque nationale Latin 16317 undoubtedly dates from only a few years later, since it is generally similar to Latin 1112 but also lists a Mass for William of Bourges. The two other missals, Bibliothèque nationale Latin 9441 and 15615, possess an almost identical *sanctorale;* they both contain the feast of St. Francis (canonized in 1228) and the reception of the Crown of Thorns (1239) but lack the festival of St. Omer (ca. 1250) and St. Peter of Verona (canonized 1253) as well as other feasts introduced into the Parisian calendar in the second half of the thirteenth century. Thus these two missals likely date 1240–50. All the remaining sources were written in the second half of the thirteenth century or later.

How do we account for the presence of three different formularies for the same feast within a single liturgical usage? Likely in the following way: although the chants, readings, and prayers for the canonical hours were set forth in explicit detail from the very beginning, it appears that some latitude was allowed the diocesan cantors in the selection of chants for the Proper of the Mass. As long as the text of the Propers extolled the virtues of an unspecified collection of martyrs, then liturgical propriety would have been met. By the end of the thirteenth century, however, a single formulary had emerged and was to remain the norm for this feast within the diocese of Paris for centuries: the Gradual *Timete*, the Alleluia *Judicabunt*, and the Offertory *Mirabilis* were set between the Introit *Gaudeamus* and the Communion *Gaudete*.

The process evident in the evolution of a single formulary for the Proper of the Mass of the *Susceptio reliquiarum*, one that exhibits a movement from liturgical diversity to fixity, is manifest in other feasts of the Parisian calendar as well. The Mass for Holy Trinity, for example, ceased to be exclusively a votive Mass and was entered into the *temporale* of the church year at Notre Dame of Paris in the mid-thirteenth century. The Alleluia *Benedictus es*, which had been used in the votive Mass, was gradually replaced by two alleluias, one with the verse *Benedicamus* and the other with *Verbo domini*, as the Trinity liturgy was

[21]Leroquais, *Bréviaire*, pp. 95–96; and Paul Perdrizet, *Le calendrier Parisien à la fin du Moyen Age* (Paris, 1933), p. 161.

annexed to the end of Paschaltide.[22] Yet several mid-thirteenth-century sources list all three alleluias for Trinity Sunday,[23] suggesting that the cantor was at liberty to choose two of the three chants. By the fourteenth century, however, only the latter two melodies are specified, and this pair remains rigidly in place for several centuries thereafter.

Thus the Parisian formulary for the Proper of the Mass of the Reception of the Relics and, to a lesser extent, that of Trinity Sunday were initially characterized by liturgical diversity, but by the end of the thirteenth century they had evolved into fixed cycles that subsequently remained inviolate. The evolutionary process evident in the development of these two newly instituted observances contrasts sharply with the observable history of the commemoration of All Saints at Paris. Although four of the five chants of the Proper of the Mass for All Saints' Day are also present in the Mass of the *Susceptio reliquiarum* in its final form, the former feast reveals not the slightest liturgical variation in the missals and graduals of Parisian usage. From the time of the very earliest manuscripts, such as the twelfth-century missal Bibliothèque Sainte Geneviève MS 93, until the seventeenth century, the celebration of All Saints' Day at Notre Dame of Paris employed an invariable formulary: Introit *Gaudeamus*, Gradual *Gloriosus*, Alleluia *Judicabunt*, Offertory *Mirabilis*, and Communion *Gaudete*. All Saints' Day, of course, was an ancient observance, one that had entered the Parisian calendar by at least the tenth century. Although it had many of the same chants in common with the Reception of the Relics, the older feast had assumed an invariable formulary while the younger one had not, at least during the early years of its existence. Through this comparison we again see the truth of a venerable liturgical law, one observed in various contexts and expressed in different ways by liturgists such as Frere, Baumstark, Hesbert, and Delalande:[24] variation within

---

[22]It is the alleluia for the votive Mass, Alleluia *Benedictus es*, that was set in two-voice organum by Leonin in the *Magnus liber*. As for the feast of the Reception of the Relics, there appears to have been no polyphony written specifically for this observance, probably because it was introduced into the Parisian liturgy shortly after Leonin completed his great book of organa. The Alleluia *Sancti et justi*, which is specified in the earliest sources of the feast, is nowhere to be found in the *Magnus liber*. The possibility remains that the Alleluia *Judicabunt* came to be the preferred alleluia for this Mass during the second half of the thirteenth century precisely because a two-voice organum, one originally written for the Common of Several Martyrs, already existed for this chant.

[23]See, for example, Bari, Chapel of St. Nicholas, MS 1, fol. 80; and Paris, BN, MS Latin 830, fol. 162.

[24]Walter Frere, ed., *Graduale Sarisburiense* (London, 1894; rpt. 1966), p. x; Anton Baumstark, *Liturgie comparée: Principes et méthodes pour l'étude historique des liturgies chrétiennes* (Chevetogne, 1955), chap. 3; René-Jean Hesbert, *Antiphonale Missarum Sextuplex* (Brussels, 1935), p. xxxi; and Dominique Delalande, *Le graduel des Prêcheurs* (Paris, 1949), p. 22.

liturgical ceremonies is characteristic of more recent feasts; and, conversely, absolute fixity is suggestive of liturgical antiquity.

In the Middle Ages there were many feasts in the calendars of the Western church to honor the transfer and reception of saintly relics. Several of these were celebrated on a specific day universally, even though the remains of a particular saint reposed only at a single church. Thus the translations of Saints Nicolas (May 9), Martin (July 4), Thomas of Canterbury (July 7), and Benedict (July 11) were observed on identical days at such diverse institutions as the cathedrals of Erfurt, Chartres, and Salisbury, though only shrines in Bari, Tours, Canterbury, and Fleury-sur-Loire, respectively, could claim the honor of possessing at least the greater part of their relics. Yet there were other *translationes* that were not widely observed but were particular to a single diocese, and sometimes only to a single church. The feast of the Reception of the Relics as celebrated on December 4 was unique to the cathedral of Paris and to the parish and collegiate churches under its authority. The Benedictine, Cluniac, Dominican, and Franciscan houses within this ecclesiastical territory felt no compulsion to incorporate the festival and did not do so. Nor was it adopted by the Augustinians of St. Victor and Ste. Geneviève in Paris, a fact particularly significant since these two monasteries patterned their liturgies closely after that of Notre Dame. Thus any service book prescribing a feast of the relics on December 4 can only belong to the liturgical usage of the secular churches of the diocese of Paris.

Examples of this sort can be multiplied at length. At the Sainte Chapelle of Paris, the relics of the Passion housed in that collegiate church were venerated annually on September 30;[25] elsewhere in the Western Church, even at the nearby cathedral of Notre Dame, a commemoration for St. Jerome was celebrated that day. At the cathedral of Rouen a collective feast for the *translatio reliquiarum* was observed on December 3.[26] Yet that same day at the monastery of St. Pierre at Blandigny near Ghent, the reception of two local saints, Gudval and Bertulf, was honored.[27] At Chartres, and apparently only within that diocese, the translation of St. Aignan, erstwhile bishop of Chartres, was observed on December 7.[28] Similarly, the translation of Renobert (September 3)

---

[25]Perdrizet, *Calendrier*, p. 230. For a list of these relics, see Boussel, *Reliques*, pp. 55–56.

[26]Abbé A. Collette, *Histoire du bréviaire de Rouen* (Rouen, 1902), p. 192.

[27]London, British Library, MS Additional 29253. Ms. M. Jennifer Bloxam kindly brought this feast to my attention.

[28]Yves Delaporte, ed., *L'ordinaire Chartrain du XIIIe siècle*, vol. XIX of the *Mémoires de la Société archéologique d'Eure-et-Loir* (Chartres, 1953), p. 63.

seems to have been particular to the diocese of Bayeux,[29] just as the *repositio* of the relics of St. Firmin (November 16) was unique to Amiens.[30] Only the Augustinian monks of Ste. Geneviève in Paris celebrated an octave (November 4) of the translation of their patron (also the patron saint of the city), thereby giving special honor to a transfer of the relics of St. Geneviève piously believed to have been effected by St. Eligius in 630.[31] These and countless other local *translationes reliquiarum* not only offer insights into the religious history and popular devotion of a region, but provide the liturgist with a useful tool by which to identify the diocese and sometimes even the church of origin of the liturgical manuscripts that contain them. The feast of the Reception of the Relics instituted at Notre Dame at the end of the twelfth century was unique only to the extent that this particular collection of relics was venerated on December 4 nowhere but in the diocese of Paris. Seen in the context of many such feasts, it proves to be a typical manifestation of the universal idolatry of saintly relics within the medieval Christian Church, just as it provides a clear example of the way in which a liturgical office might enter the world as a patchwork of previously used chants and readings.

[29]Ulysse Chevalier, *Ordinaire et coutumier de l'église cathédrale de Bayeux (XIIIe siècle)* (Paris, 1902), p. 245.

[30]Georges Durand, ed., *Ordinaire de l'église Notre-Dame cathédrale d'Amiens par Raoul de Rouvroy (1291)* (Amiens and Paris, 1934), p. 483.

[31]Paris, Bibliothèque Ste. Geneviève, MS 1259; and Joseph Van Heck *et al.*, eds., *Acta Sanctorum Octobris Tomus Duodecimus* (Brussels, 1884), p. 411b.

Another Source for the Beauvais
Feast of Fools

DAVID G. HUGHES

I⊤ IS A COMMONPLACE THAT IN THE medieval liturgy music served
above all as a means of enhancing splendor and solemnity, in a fashion
similar to, but on a higher level than, rich vestments, multitudes of
large candles, and other ritual objects. If we were to search for the apex
of such liturgical and musical splendor, we should probably think first
of a Papal Mass for Christmas or Easter, or perhaps of an episcopal Mass
in one of the great northern cathedrals. Although that idea might well
be correct, there is no documentary proof for it. The most elaborate liturgical use of music for which we have written evidence is rather to be
found in partly parodistic services conducted for, and in part by, the
lower orders of the clergy on the days just after Christmas.[1] These are
the four famous clerical *tripudia,* each one given over to one of the four
orders: priests, deacons, choirboys, and subdeacons. The members of
the celebrating order became masters of the day, usually electing a
"bishop" or even a "pope" from among their number.[2]

It is not entirely clear why these festivities, often so rowdy that they
were condemned and forbidden by the Church, should have generated
such elaborate liturgies. The usual explanation—and probably the correct one—is that with so much ritual to organize and so much music to
rehearse and perform, the celebrating clerics would have neither time
nor energy to get into serious trouble. On this reading, the surviving
liturgies would be both a legitimation and a reform of existing (and rep-
rehensible) customs. It should also be noted, however, that the most
important feasts of the calendar already had large quantities of music
especially composed for them (tropes, prosae, versus, and other post-
Gregorian genres). The calendrically less important days of the tripudia
would have needed ingenious adaptations of materials designed for

---

[1] As pointed out by Ruth Steiner in *New Grove,* XI, 776, s.v. Mass, I, 5.
[2] A full account, together with abundant bibliography, is given in E. K. Chambers,
The Medieval Stage (Oxford, 1903), vol. I, 275–335.

other purposes in order to achieve a suitable degree of magnificence. For a splendid Christmas Mass the cantor had only to consult a book already on his shelf—a proser or troper, among others; for an equally splendid Mass for the octave of the Epiphany (on which the subdeacons' feast was in some places celebrated), he would have needed to construct the ceremony from the ground up, as it were, using the same books, but in a much more complex and selective fashion. He might well have had the result written out as a convenience for the next year.

The four tripudia are often indiscriminately referred to as the "Feast of Fools," but that designation is strictly proper only to the subdeacons' feast, held either on the octave of Christmas (then the Feast of the Circumcision, but originally a Marian commemoration), or on the octave of the Epiphany. The subdeacons seem to have been the worst of the lot, older than the choirboys but not wiser. Their abuses have been abundantly documented.[3] Whether because the subdeacons caused so many problems, or because their order was the only one lacking a natural patron saint (the priests had St. John, the deacons St. Stephen, and the choirboys Holy Innocents—a concatenation that must have figured largely in the origin of the tripudia), almost all of the surviving manuscript material pertains to the true Feast of Fools and is thus for the subdeacons. The sources, all well known, are as follows:

Laon, Bibliothèque municipale, MS 263. Late 12th century. Material for each of the tripudia, but far more for the subdeacons than for any other order.[4]

Le Puy, 16th-century copy of an earlier manuscript for the subdeacons' office.[5]

Sens, Bibliothèque municipale, MS 46 A. Early 13th century. Complete Office and Mass for the subdeacons.[6]

London, British Library, MS Egerton 2615. Copied 1227–34. Complete Office and Mass for the subdeacons.[7]

[3]Chambers gives a wealth of detail (above, fn. 2).

[4]This manuscript has not been fully studied. The only part published is the material for the deacons' feast in my "Music for St. Stephen at Laon," *Words and Music: The Scholar's View* (Harvard University Department of Music, Cambridge, Mass., 1972), pp. 137–159.

[5]Text published by Ulysse Chevalier, *Prosolarium ecclesiae Aniciensis*, Bibliothèque liturgique V_1 (Paris, 1894). The copy contains music, but I have not seen it.

[6]Text and music published in an exemplary edition by Henri Villetard, *Office de Pierre de Corbeil* (Paris, 1907).

[7]Text and music published, also in exemplary fashion, by Wulf Arlt, *Ein Festoffizium des Mittelalters aus Beauvais*, 2 vols. (Cologne, 1970). For the date, see the *Darstellungsband*, p. 29. The date given above is the traditional one, based on the absence from the *laudes regiae* of names for the queen of France and for the local bishop. This has been taken to require a date prior to the marriage of Louis IX in 1234. Arlt correctly observes that the same logic would require a time during which the see of Beauvais was

A further Beauvais manuscript for the subdeacons' office must have existed, although it is now lost. It is briefly described by the Beauvais historian Pierre Louvet, with enough detail to make both its origin in Beauvais and its early date (c. 1160) certain.[8] Some years ago I showed that still another Beauvais source for the subdeacons had once been available. This survives only in the form of a précis or synopsis, made in the seventeenth century by an unknown Beauvais historian and now preserved in the Collection Bucquet-Aux Cousteaux, an immense collection of documents, copies, and notes gathered by local scholars at Beauvais in the eighteenth century.[9] The following pages are concerned primarily with this last source and its relation to the other subdeacons' offices from Beauvais.

The two leaves on which the synopsis are written are in very poor condition. The bottom right corners have been eaten away by dampness, and some of the remaining paper is so badly stained as to make the writing illegible. The hand—by no means distinguished for clarity even under good conditions—appears to be of the seventeenth century, and is certainly French.[10] In general, the synoptist merely lists in order the incipits of pieces to be said or sung through the entire day (January 1), with the important exception of the Mass. He occasionally quotes brief rubrics, and sometimes adds comments of his own (in French), invariably about the absence from his source of certain pieces that are all present in Egerton 2615. A few texts are given in extenso, rather than merely by incipit, but no music is provided or even mentioned. The last page is blank in its bottom quarter, and its verso is wholly blank; since the synopsis begins with a formal title, we can thus be sure that what we have is all that the synoptist intended to write.

---

vacant (only a few days in 1234). It is my belief, however, that the *laudes* here were addressed not to the real bishop, but rather to the *Dominus festi*—the elected "bishop" of the subdeacons—and that the absence of a name results merely from the annual change of that office-holder.

[8]An account of what is known about this lost manuscript may be found in Arlt, *Darstellungsband*, pp. 30–31, and in the article cited in the next footnote.

[9]This source is first mentioned and briefly described in my article, "The sources of *Christus manens," Aspects of Medieval and Renaissance Music* (New York, 1966), pp. 432–433. This volume of the collection, like many others, is in such bad condition that it can be consulted only via photocopies. What follows is based on a microfilm kindly supplied by the Bibliothèque municipale of Beauvais, where the entire collection is preserved.

[10]I am indebted to Professor Gary Rodgers, formerly of the Department of Romance Languages and Literatures, Harvard University, for sharing with me his paleographic expertise, and for valiantly tackling some of the more obstinately illegible words. His suggestions made possible the recovery of several passages that would otherwise have eluded me. As will be seen, material can also in some cases be recovered by comparison with Egerton 2615 and, less often, the Sens Office.

The provenance of the synoptist's manuscript seems reasonably certain. The synopsis itself is contained in a collection of documents concerning Beauvais, and there is nothing to hint that its original came from somewhere else. Moreover, as will be seen, its content agrees so closely with that of both Egerton 2615 and Louvet's manuscript that an origin outside of Beauvais seems hardly possible. In the case of Egerton 2615, the agreement extends to the sharing of unica and near-unica, and to agreement in otherwise unique readings in some of the pieces that the synoptist gives in extenso. It is also evident that the synoptist actually had before him both his own manuscript and Egerton 2615 as he wrote. Shortly after the beginning, the synoptist writes, "Veni sancte spiritus," then "vel ve," then crosses out the "vel ve." This makes sense only if we imagine the synoptist's eye straying to Egerton 2615, which in fact has the rubric "vel Veni doctor previe" following *Veni sancte spiritus*, then returning to the other source, which does not have this alternative. After two syllables, the writer realizes he has made a mistake, and promptly stops writing to cross out the error (the process must have been instantaneous, not a later editorial change, since the deleted syllables do not make up a complete sense unit).

The connection with Egerton 2615, which was kept in the Beauvais cathedral library at least through the fifteenth century, and in the city of Beauvais through the seventeenth,[11] helps to establish the provenance of the synoptist's manuscript. The date is another matter: there are virtually no clues. The internal evidence merely shows that the synoptist's office is much less elaborate and more severe than Egerton 2615, but it would be idle to infer from this an early date. The authorities may have been (or may have become) conservative at any time.

There are two faint indicators. The synoptist entitles his précis "Ancien antiphonier in festo stultorum." The word "ancien" surely pushes the source back to the fifteenth century, and possibly even further: anything later would hardly be "ancien" to a seventeenth-century scholar. But there is a more enigmatic liturgical oddity. Just before the end of the post-Vespers procession to the altar of the Virgin, the synoptist has "redeundo [in chorum] dicatur R[esponsorium] de Sancto Ecclesio." This

---

[11]Henri Omont, *Recherches sur la bibliothèque de l'église cathédrale de Beauvais* (Paris, 1914). Item 28 on p. 21 and item 76 on p. 41 must refer to Egerton 2615: the words cited in these fifteenth-century catalogues as beginning the second and the penultimate folios match the words found there in Egerton 2615. A letter from the Beauvais canon Foy de Saint-Hilaire in 1697 cites material from a manuscript having a lacuna at just the same point where the missing gathering occurs in Egerton 2615; hence here too the identification is assured. See Paul Denis, *Lettres autographes de la Collection de Troussures* (Publications de la société académique de l'Oise, III; Beauvais, 1912), pp. 311–312. No surviving records of the cathedral library refer to anything that might be either Louvet's manuscript or the synoptist's source.

is clearly written, and the final letter of the last words is unquestionably "o." The synoptist knows too much Latin to make an elementary mistake in gender; and in any event even a "responsory of the holy church" would make no better sense. Moreover, there really was a St. Ecclesius,[12] for whom any one of a number of responsories from the Common of Saints could have been used or adapted. His cult, however, appears to have been wholly restricted to Ravenna, where he had lived. His name is not mentioned in any other Beauvais manuscript or calendar known to me (nor have I seen it in any French source). That he should be so prominently honored in the synoptist's manuscript can only be the result of the intervention of someone who had both authority at Beauvais and, at the same time, some connection with Ravenna. No one can be proved to fulfill both of these conditions; but Bishop Milon de Nanteuil, who occupied the see of Beauvais from 1217 to 1234, is at least a likely candidate.

Milon spent much time in Italy, and in 1229–30 was in charge of the duchy of Spoleto, which then extended well into the Adriatic side of the Apennines. In 1238 he journeyed from Beauvais, intending to go to Rome, but fell ill and died in the town of Camerino, which lies on the Eastern slopes of the Apennines. Almost the only imaginable reason for such a peculiar route would have been the desire to visit—or revisit—some city in eastern Italy. If that city were Ravenna, the mention of St. Ecclesius would find a reasonable explanation.[13] Thus the synoptist's manuscript would have been compiled during Milon's episcopate, and would be roughly contemporary with Egerton 2615.

This dating would at first seem to raise a problem—an excess of manuscripts for the same purpose—but in fact it solves one instead. Egerton 2615 prescribes, in its copious rubrics, many elaborate visual and spatial effects within the liturgy. The present cathedral had yet to be built,[14] and the episcopal church was at that time the pre-

[12]Biographical material regarding Ecclesius is available in any of the larger Lives of Saints. I have used the article by Giovanni Lucchesi in the *Bibliotheca sanctorum* published by the Istituto Giovanni XXIII, vol. IV ([Rome], 1964), pp. 897–898.

[13]The information about Milon is taken from [François-Antoine] Delettre, *Histoire du diocèse de Beauvais* (Beauvais, 1842–43), vol. II, 163, 237–40, 252, 272, 307. Delettre is not generous in his citation of sources, but his account appears to be reasonably accurate. The ultimate source for the assertion that Milon died at Camerino is the thirteenth-century chronicle of Albericus, a monk of Châlons-sur-Marne. Albericus merely inserts the mention of Milon's death in the midst of unrelated material, in typical chronicle fashion (Gottfried Leibniz, *Accessiones historicae*, vol. II, *Alberici monachi trium fontium chronicon* [Leipzig, 1698], p. 554).

[14]The generally accepted chronology of the cathedral—commencement about 1226, first use in 1272—may be found in Gustave Desjardins, *Histoire de la cathédrale de Beauvais* (Beauvais, 1865), pp. 5–8. The usual assumption is that a Romanesque cathedral had once existed but had been destroyed by fire before the present building was begun. Extensive excavations carried out in Beauvais in recent years suggest that no

Romanesque basse oeuvre, only 28 by 22 meters in size. Hence the liturgy of Egerton 2615 almost certainly had to be celebrated somewhere else (perhaps in the nearby church of St. Michel, now destroyed, or in the larger St. Etienne). The synoptist's manuscript may have been intended for the basse oeuvre (in which its much simpler liturgy could easily have been executed), hence, by inference, for the bishop himself. That an exuberant and partly parodistic manuscript could have been made for a public celebration and a more restrained one for the bishop and his entourage is hardly beyond belief. Only at the end of this study will we be in a position to return to the question of date, and—at least conjecturally—support an origin early in the thirteenth century for the synoptist's manuscript.

In any event, we now have remains from three Beauvais Circumcision Offices, of which one survives as a real manuscript (Egerton 2615, hereafter E), another in a brief and cursory description (Louvet's manuscript, hereafter L), and the third in a detailed synopsis (Bucquet-Aux Cousteaux, hereafter B). Although comparisons among such diverse documents are difficult, it is at once evident that the Beauvais tradition for the Feast of Fools was extremely consistent. Not only liturgical items, but also proses and other extraliturgical pieces appear in precisely the same places in all three sources. For example, at the beginning of first Vespers (described rather fully by Louvet and hence a good point for comparison), one finds:

E	L	B
Lux hodie	Lux hodie	Lux hodie
Orientis partibus	Orientis partibus	
Hec est clara dies	Hec est clara dies	Hec est clara dies
Salve festa dies	Salve festa dies	Salve festa dies
Letemur gaudiis	"Deux autres proses"	Letemur gaudiis
Christus manens		Christus manens
Ecce annuntio	Ecce annuntio	Ecce annuntio

Romanesque cathedral ever existed, since no remains have been found that could reasonably be associated with such a structure. See Philippe Bonnet-Laborderie, *Cathédrale Saint-Pierre: Histoire et architecture* (Beauvais, 1978), p. 25. The dimensions of the basse oeuvre in the thirteenth century are not certain. The building was severely damaged by fire in 1225 (presumably the event that prompted construction of the "nouvel-oeuvre"—the present cathedral). Some time thereafter it was provided with a new choir, so that episcopal services could be continued during the construction of the present cathedral and after the collapse of the latter's vaults in 1284. This new choir was then razed to make way for the present cathedral transepts, built in the sixteenth century. Bonnet-Laborderie at one point gives the date of construction of the choir as 1225 (p. 26), but later (p. 35) qualifies that with "vraisemblablement." In any event, however, the fire had destroyed only the chevet of the basse oeuvre: even if the new choir had not been completed, the bishop would doubtless have had available some part of the building for the celebration of the liturgy.

Since all of these pieces except the last are non-liturgical, and since the "deux autres proses" of L were quite probably the same as those of E and B, we have here an exactness of agreement that only a continuing tradition could produce. (The exception, *Orientis partibus*, is in all probability missing from B because B regularly avoids any reference to pieces connected in an obvious way to the Feast of Fools.) This agreement can be further confirmed by comparing B with those parts of L that are described, and with E throughout. Since the Beauvais tradition is easily accessible in Arlt's edition of E, the chief interest of B lies in those areas where it appears to differ from the tradition, and in those where it can supply material missing from E.

The usefulness of B in the latter context is somewhat limited. E is complete except for one lost quaternion, the pages of which originally contained an extraliturgical ceremony after Lauds, then Prime, Terce, and the beginning of Mass. Since Mass is lacking in B, for reasons unknown, and since any ceremony after Lauds is also lacking (almost certainly because the ceremony in E was at least potentially scandalous and hence foreign to the austere tone of B), the primary utility of B for reconstruction lies in the important service of Prime and the lesser one of Terce. Unfortunately, these services occur near the bottom of p. 400 of the synopsis, where the corner of the page has worn away entirely: even what remains is not always possible to read. Hence even this modest reconstruction cannot be complete.

Prime begins with the hymn *Jam lucis orto sidere*. After citing the first two words of the hymn, the synoptist adds the rubric "per singulos versus mutatur cantus." No doubt only a few of the nearly forty preserved melodies for this hymn[15] were known and used at Beauvais at any one time, but it is reasonable to assume that two or more were available. This rubric would direct the singers to use one melody for the first stanza and another for the second. Thereafter, either these two melodies would alternate, or one or more further melodies would be used in some sort of rotation for the remaining stanzas (five in all).

There follows the antiphon *O admirabile* (as expected, since the Little Hours use the antiphons of Lauds, one per service, in order), and the psalm *Deus in nomine tuo*. As was normal at the time, the following Symbolum Athanasianum is also treated as if it were a psalm, with its own antiphon, here *Quem vidistis*. The synoptist then passes over the capitulum and short responsory that would normally follow (these items are present in the parallel services of Sext and Nones in E and are given for Terce and Nones even in B; there seems to be no reason for their omission here), and prescribes *Exurge pie Domine*. This is a free

---

[15]John R. Bryden and David G. Hughes, *An Index of Gregorian Chant* (Cambridge, Mass., 1969), I, 238–239, and the pages there referred to in Bruno Stäblein, *Hymnen (I)* (Monumenta monodica medii aevi, I [Basel, 1956]).

poetic expansion of the verse and response "Exurge Domine [in the modern rite: Christe] adjuva nos; Et libera nos propter nomen tuum," that would normally follow the responsory. It is similar in technique to the widely known *Deus in adiutorium . . . laborantium* of second Vespers, but *Exurge pie* is otherwise known only from the offices of Laon[16] and Le Puy,[17] both of which use it at this same point in Prime.[18]

Following *Exurge pie* there appears *Exurge Domine nostra redemptio*. Its placement here may result from the similarity of its first line to that of *Exurge pie*. In fact, the Sens Office uses *Exurge Domine* at Prime in place of *Exurge pie*.[19] Since Arlt has shown that Sens depends ultimately on L,[20] we may assume that L must have contained *Exurge Domine*. Since that piece represents a step further away from the liturgical text—a step more easily understood if *Exurge pie* were present as an intermediate station—L, like B, may well have had both. The Sens Office would then merely have selected one out of two pieces appropriate for this liturgical moment.

There follows the Kyrie *Pater cuncta qui gubernas . . . sede sedens* (not the much rarer *Pater . . . summa servans*, which uses the same melody). To judge from the sources collated by the *Analecta hymnica*, this Kyrie was fairly widely disseminated.[21] The same Kyrie appears at Compline in the Sens Office; hence it is at least likely that it was used at some point in L. Sens gives only an incipit, but the synoptist gives the full text, in a version comparable to other North French sources of the period. *Pater cuncta* also occurs in Laon 263 (fol. 29), in a version differing sharply from that of B. Such divergence in this piece (and in others as well) indicates that while Laon shares many rare works with the Beauvais sources, there is no direct dependence.

The Credo and Pater noster come next, both expanded internally. Each phrase of the authorized texts is followed by the supplication "Miserere rex, miserere; agnum rogo filium" (at its first appearance, after "in celis" of the Pater noster, this phrase is preceded by the word "eleison"). This formula is not known to me from other sources, although the single-refrain principle may be found in both the Sens and Le Puy Offices, in which the phrase "fulget dies" is intercalated between the stanzas of the hymn *Jam lucis* at Prime.[22]

The synoptist entered Terce and Sext at the extreme bottom of p.

[16]Laon 263, fol. 113v.

[17]Chevalier, *Prosolarium*, p. 34.

[18]Laon uses the piece for Innocents', not the Circumcision, and omits the capitulum and response, while drastically shortening the Symbolum.

[19]Villetard, *Office*, pp. 105, 158.

[20]*Darstellungsband*, p. 32, *Editionsband*, p. 193.

[21]*Analecta hymnica* XLVII, 63. See also Margareta Melnicki, *Das einstimmige Kyrie des lateinischen Mittelalters* (Erlangen, 1954), melody 58.

[22]Villetard, pp. 104, 157; Chevalier, p. 34.

400, and there now remains little that can be clearly read. Although the first words of Terce are illegible, one may immediately thereafter make out "-o natus. ps. Legem. cap. Apparuit gratia." Again using the principle that the Little Hours use the antiphons of Lauds in order, there can be no doubt that this once read, "Ad tertiam, ant. Quando natus," and so on. What follows is no more than a succession of some legible words and syllables alternating with a rather larger number of illegible ones. Other sources are here of no help, since the legible words cannot be fitted into any text known to me. Given that the Little Hours end with a versiculus, and given also the amount of space involved, the lost text is doubtless another versiculus. Since B and E agree in prescribing otherwise unknown versiculi for both Sext and Nones, it is likely that this lost text was also in the missing gathering of E. Now, however, this versiculus appears to be permanently lost, and our reconstruction of the missing hours of E is necessarily incomplete.

We may turn now to those areas in which B differs from the other Beauvais sources. The most striking of these is its omission of the numerous pieces of the versus or conductus type. As has been observed, the synoptist underlines the omission by adding comments in French: "Manque le conductus Eva virum dedit in mortem. Manque aussi le conductus Ex ade vitio," and several similar remarks. These comments come at the ends of Nocturns, and, by way of exception, near the beginning of first Vespers, where, as has been noted, the conductus *Orientis partibus* does not appear. The impression given is one of restraint in the manuscript itself, and of interest on the part of the synoptist (this is of course another indication that the synoptist either had E before him, or, less likely, that he had memorized its contents). It would be unwise to use the diminution in the number of conductus as an argument for an early date; at both first and second Vespers B calls for at least some conductus and Benedicamus poems in the developed rhymed style of the later twelfth century.

Another difference must remain probable rather than certain. Both E and L call for polyphonic music, the former by the explicit rubric "cum organo," and the latter almost certainly in the same way. Louvet actually writes "auec le ieu des orgues," but this is a natural seventeenth-century interpretation of the Latin "cum organo." Nothing of the sort is mentioned in the synopsis, and it seems reasonable to conclude that polyphony was not required by the manuscript. It is possible, however, that the synoptist saw but ignored "cum organo" rubrics: in fact he gives few rubrics of any kind, although there may well have been more. He may have seen his job as merely noting what was sung, not how it was performed. The evidence given by the pieces in the manuscript is inconclusive. Some works known only in polyphonic settings are omitted in B (e.g. the motet *Veni doctor previe* and the conductus *Salvatoris hodie*); but some sung polyphonically in E are given in B without performance instructions (e.g. *Et honore virginali*). Naturally, if polyphony was absent from B, it would be consistent with the tendency of that source towards simplicity and austerity.

The remaining differences between B and the other Beauvais sources are specific rather than general. What follows is necessarily selective: the differences vary in importance and interest, and a number of them are connected with more general issues concerning the nature of the Feast of Fools—issues whose discussion would require more space than is available here.

There is a minor difference between B and E in the procession at the end of first Vespers. In E the procession is fused into the end of Vespers itself, so that Magnificat is not sung until the procession is under way. In B Magnificat is contained within Vespers in the normal way, and the service concludes with the Benedicamus-Deo Gratias poems *Corde patris genitus* and *Super omnes alias benedicta*. Then the procession begins (as in E) with the responsory *Gaude Maria* embellished with proses, followed by further Marian material (normal for January 1). In E, the return of the procession to the choir is in part given over to music for St. Peter, no doubt because the cathedral, whether or not it was in actual use, was dedicated to him. In B, the Petrine material is replaced by the responsory for St. Ecclesius. Obviously there is no question of a Beauvais building dedicated to that saint, but the implicit analogy between Ecclesius and the local patron certainly enhances the importance of the former for the liturgy of B.

There are more substantial differences between E and B, notably at second Vespers. These are most conveniently observed in tabular form.

E	B
Deus . . . laborantium	Deus . . . laborantium
Hymn: A solis ortu	
Ant. O admirabile	Ant. O admirabile
Ps. Dixit	Ps. Dixit
Ant. Quando natus	Ant. Quando natus
Ps. Confitebor	Ps. Confitebor
Ant. Rubum	Ant. Rubum
Ps. Beatus vir	Ps. Beatus vir
	Capitulum: Verbum caro
Alleluia: Multipharie	Alleluia: Multipharie
Prosa: Christi hodierna	Prosa: Christi hodierna
Ant. Germinavit	
Ps. De profundis	
Ant. Ecce Maria	
Ps. Memento	
Capitulum: Verbum caro	
R. Descendit de celis	

Prosa: Hac clara die
V. Qui scis infirma   V. Qui scis infirma
Ant. O beata infantia   Ant. O beata infantia
Magnificat   Magnificat

The synoptist has here omitted both the hymn, as he regularly does, and the last two antiphons (in fact he gives only three antiphons for Lauds as well, but this seems to be a different sort of problem).[23] In E the antiphon series is interrupted at just this point by a sort of irregular liturgical interlude, consisting of the *Alleluia: Multipharie* and the prosa *Christi hodierna*. This intrusion of pieces from the Mass into Vespers may derive ultimately from Vespers of Easter Week, into which such migration is fairly common.[24] Nevertheless, since almost all of the tripudia use the idea of farsing Vespers in some such way, it is likely that sources such as E and B are modeled not directly on an Easter prototype, although the idea doubtless came from there, but rather on their own predecessors—in this case, L.

It is possible to formulate a complex hypothesis, postulating the loss of two leaves from the synoptist's manuscript, that would bring E and B into substantial agreement.[25] But since the synoptist has entered the capitulum *Verbum caro* immediately after the last of his antiphons, it seems more likely that he merely omitted the last two antiphons,

---

[23]In the case of Lauds, the synoptist's first two antiphons are those of the normal Circumcision series (Dom R. Le Roux, "Aux origines de l'office festif: les antiennes et les psaumes de matines et de laudes pour Noël et le 1er Janvier," *Études grégoriennes*, 4 [1961], especially the table following p. 170). The third, *Natus est nobis hodie*, is not an antiphon at all but a capitulum, given as such (with notation) in E. The closest antiphon text is *Natus est nobis Deus*, and this is a German piece (Le Roux, p. 160). It is possible that the words "natus est," occurring in *Quando natus est* also, caused the synoptist to skip over the three antiphons. In any event, while it is curious that both Lauds and second Vespers appear to have only three antiphons, the causes are clearly different.

[24]Andrew Hughes, *Medieval Manuscripts for Mass and Office: A Guide to their Organization and Terminology* (Toronto, 1982), pp. 50, 215.

[25]In brief, the hypothesis may be stated as follows. The prosa *Christi hodierna* contains the words "Intra uteri claustra porta." The prosa *Hac clara die* contains the similar phrase "Intra tui utera claustra portas." In E, these two phrases are separated by exactly two pages. Assume that B was ruled and written in about the same way as E (very likely, of course, since the two were doubtless the product of the same scriptorium), and further assume some sort of arrangement of the pieces that would place both of the similar phrases on the first line of recto pages, two pages apart (it is not difficult to formulate arrangements of this sort). Then if two pages of the manuscript had in fact been lost before the synoptist came to his work, only the most careful scrutiny would have made the synoptist aware that anything was missing: the sense begun at the bottom of one surviving page would have flowed smoothly into that of the (apparently) next page, and the liturgical abnormality of second Vespers as a whole would have masked the irregularities that resulted.

transforming what is in E an interlude between antiphons into a post-lude after them, and perhaps as a result omitting the by now redundant postlude of E (the responsory *Descendit* with the prosa *Hac clara die*). Once again, the resulting service would be a simplification of the analogous service in E, whether one accepts the hypothesis of the missing pages or assumes inadvertent omission on the part of the synoptist.

The last difference between B and E to be discussed here concerns the end of the liturgical day—that is, the material that follows second Vespers, hence following directly upon the group of pieces just examined. In this case, a tabular comparison is not especially useful, since the differences are far more important than the similarities. Instead, it is preferable to examine each complex separately with a view towards determining its purpose.

In E the nature of the concluding material is not at once apparent. The rubrics, up to this point numerous and instructive, here become mere indications of category (although of course even that much is helpful). The sequence of pieces is as follows:

1.	Benedicamus	Super omnes alias creaturas
2.	Benedicamus	Dei sapientia
3.	Responsory	Styrps iesse
4.	Prosa	Ave Maria
5.	[Antiphon]	Alma redemptoris
6.	[Prosa]	Alle resonent
7.	Benedicamus [?]	O regina virginum
8.	Deo gratias	Virgo gemma virginum
9.	Benedicamus	Patrem parit filia
10.	Benedicamus	Dies ista celebris
11.	Conductus	Regis natalitia
12.	Conductus	Alto consilio

The large number of Benedicamus poems need cause no alarm: a rubric at the end of the Laon office (Laon 263, fol. 141v) seems to indicate that the subdeacons there might sing as many such poems as they wished. The sole Deo gratias, *Virgo gemma virginum*, has the same melody as *Super omnes alias* (transposed down a fourth for *Virgo*). These two poems are explicitly joined in a Benedicamus-Deo gratias pair in other sources.[26] Whether the scribe of E was aware of this pairing or not, he should have observed the melodic identity: items 1–8 in the

[26]Madrid, Biblioteca nacional, MS 289, fols. 131–132v, MS 288, fols. 166v–167v. These are two of the group of Norman-Sicilian manuscripts preserved in the Biblioteca nacional. Apart from some sharing of repertoire, there is no connection between these and the sources of the subdeacons' Office. Their testimony regarding the pairing of these pieces may therefore be accepted as uncontaminated. See Arlt, *Darstellungs-band*, pp. 153, 178.

list above form a unit, and the content of that unit—especially its inclusion of a responsory and an elaborate antiphon—strongly suggests that
it was in fact a procession,[27] similar to but rather richer than the procession following first Vespers.[28] The overwhelmingly Marian content of
these eight pieces may indicate that the destination of the procession
was the altar of the Virgin (the goal of the procession at first Vespers);
but since January 1 is a day of Marian commemoration in any event, it
is possible that the subdeacons merely processed out of the church. The
final three items are not helpful: *Dies ista* and *Alto consilio* both refer
to the "baculus," the staff symbolizing the authority of the elected ruler
of the subdeacons for the day; and *Regis natalitia* mentions (heavenly)
feeding; but all of these references are quite unemphatic. Thus while it
is possible that these poems were sung at the refectory (where the subdeacons went at the comparable point in the Sens Office) during some
sort of acclamation of the Dominus festi, it is at least equally likely that
these simply were the final songs of the day, after which the subdeacons
might presumably amuse themselves as they saw fit.

   In any case, it seems clear enough that in E second Vespers ends with
Magnificat and is followed by a procession, which in turn is followed by
something unspecified. In B, on the contrary, there are only four pieces
after Magnificat:

1. [Benedicamus]	Super omnes alias
2. [Prosa]	Kalendas ianuarias, etc. [sic]
3. [Conductus]	Nostri festi gaudium
4. [Benedicamus?]	O regina virginum

Here the lack of a Deo gratias poem is somewhat disturbing, since as
the series as it stands contains no true conclusion for Vespers (as noted,
these pieces follow directly upon Magnificat). The synoptist writes out
Super omnes alias in full: had its mate, *Virgo gemma virginum*, been in
his manuscript, he could hardly have missed it. Even if the second
poem had lacked a characteristic initial—had looked, that is, like no
more than a continuation of *Super omnes alias*—the synoptist would
have had either to copy it as a continuation or recognize it as a new
item; since he did neither, and since he surely knew that a Deo gratias
was needed, we may assume that neither *Virgo gemma virginum* nor an
analogous piece was present in his manuscript.

---

[27]As also proposed by Arlt, *Darstellungsband*, p. 156.

[28]As at first Vespers, there is a certain amount of interlocking between the end of
the service and the beginning of the procession. At first Vespers, the collect was postponed until the procession had got well under way. Here there is (inexplicably) no collect at all, and the first Benedicamus does double duty, as the conclusion of Vespers and
the beginning of the procession, its proper Deo gratias being postponed until the end of
the latter.

The three remaining pieces are less difficult. In the Sens Office, *Kalendas ianuarias* is a "conductus ad poculum." Here in B it is used earlier, as one of the few conductus at Matins; this creates a problem relating to the Feast of Fools, which cannot be pursued here. The gratuitous insertion of "etc." creates yet another problem, for which I have no solution at all. *Nostri festi gaudium* is an intrinsically functional poem. Its last line reads, "Cuius Deus portio/legatur in gaudio/lectio"; for it to make sense, a lection must follow immediately. Taken together, these two pieces suggest that the party (the bishop and his entourage, on my reading) proceeded directly—that is, without a formal procession—to the refectory. If the services had been conducted in the basse oeuvre, this would have been a matter of only a few minutes, as the present-day episcopal palace (the core of which dates back to the twelfth century) is just across the street from the basse oeuvre, and its thirteenth-century predecessor probably occupied the same location. *Kalendas* would have accompanied the sharing of a ceremonial cup, as at Sens (in this case also the poem is functional, if marginally so: the third stanza does indeed refer to a "poculum," although in the event, the reference is to the chalice, not to a secular cup), and *Nostri festi* the conventional lection at supper.

The last piece is rubricated "Benedicamus" in E, but it is not a Benedicamus poem in any discernible sense. It seems to be known only from its appearances in E and B. It refers several times to the act of feeding, and, given that and its position here, may well have served as a conductus ad or post prandium. In the Sens Office, the conductus ad prandium is the *O crucifer bone lucis sator* of Prudentius.

These last paragraphs have shown that in the one area in which E and B disagree almost totally, the differences are the result of different purposes. The end of E is primarily occupied by a procession, that of B by a modest embellishment of the evening meal. We may compare these closing sections with that of Sens:[29]

1. Benedicamus   Super omnes alias
2. Deo gratias   Virgo gemma virginum
3. Conductus ad   Novus annus hodie
   bacularium

---

[29]In actual fact, the items listed are not literally the end of the Sens Office: there follow three farsed epistles, one for each of the three post-Christmas feasts (Villetard, pp. 123–127, 188–194). The purpose of these is not clear. Perhaps they were sung during the evening meal, as commemorations during the octaves of these feasts; or perhaps each was sung on the actual octave day, the scribe entering them here as a convenient place for material otherwise hard to classify. In any case, the epistles have no analogue in any of the other subdeacons' Offices, and hence may be disregarded in the present context.

| 4. Conductus ad poculum | Kalendas ianuarias |
| 5. Versus ad prandium | O crucifer bone lucis sator |

Obviously this is rather closer to the series in B than to that of E. Now Sens is known to be a descendant of Louvet's manuscript, as is E, and B probably is also. Thus the material common to B and Sens is likely to have been present in L also (how else to account for the agreement of the later sources?): *Super omnes alias, Virgo gemma virginum* (assuming that its omission from B is an error of some sort), and *Kalendas ianuarias.* Does not the agreement between E and B with respect to *O regina virginum* prove that this too was present in L? Perhaps, but it is also possible that E and B, if they were in fact roughly contemporary, were more intimately related to each other than to any archetype—that one of them was a reworking of the other. More generally, this returns us to a more fundamental question: where does B stand within the complex of Circumcision Offices from (or derived from) Beauvais? Or, to put the matter more concretely, what is the relation between L, E, B, and the Sens Office? Since external and (as we shall see) internal evidence both suggest that Sens was an isolated source (it was made, after all, for a different city, even a different diocese), and since Sens is earlier than E, one part of the stemma is already clear: the Sens Office descends independently from L.

But this still leaves two possibilities: all of the sources may have derived independently from L, or E and B may be interrelated with each other more closely than either is with Sens. The latter is intuitively likely in any event, and is overwhelmingly supported by the internal evidence. Where differences occur among the sources, by far the commonest—almost the only—pattern is S:LBE (or more often S:BE, since the description of L is so fragmentary that it can only rarely be used for detailed comparison). This remains true even when all those differences that might reasonably be attributed to diocesan custom (e.g. choices of specific liturgical pieces to be sung at any moment in a service) are disregarded. Thus either still another lost manuscript may once have existed, from which both E and B derived, or the latter two are related in a filial pattern, or E and B were both copied independently from L.

Surely the postulation of yet another hypothetical intermediary is repugnant as well as unnecessary: the assumption of independent or filial relation is preferable on all counts.

Each possibility must be considered in turn. It is, I believe, fair to assume that B is not the earliest of the Beauvais sources. There is no evidence that it predates L, and its content—notably the numerous poems in modern fully rhymed style—does not encourage the idea. We may then consider the two remaining choices. The scribe of E must have had available to him at the time of making his manuscript the following: L (naturally in its complete form, whatever that may have looked like) and some source of polyphonic music in more modern style.[30] His purpose was to create an up-to-date version of the subdeacons' feast, for which the older manuscript L had for some reason become no longer appropriate. There is no reason that compels us to suppose that he also had B available; the latter contains nothing he could not have gotten from L, and it is fair to assume that a scribe uses no more exemplars than are absolutely necessary.

The scribe of B, whenever he may have worked, had a quite different object. His aim was to produce a liturgy for the Feast of the Circumcision, purged of all elements directly connected with the Feast of Fools but consistent with the liturgical tradition of that day in Beauvais. This purpose could also have been achieved by basing the work either on L or E—now, however, abridging and omitting rather than elaborating and expanding. (The omission of the Mass—whether by the manuscript itself or by the synoptist—poses a problem for which I have no ready solution.) Two clues point in the direction of L as the source for the scribe of B. The first depends on the one occasion where the synoptist notes a textual variant. At the very beginning of his work he enters the first piece of first Vespers thus: "Lux hodie etc. . . . revomendus erit." "Revomendus" is of course not a real word; the synoptist has made an error and has failed to note it. But why enter an internal word in any case? Because there are two readings for the only place in the text that could generate "revomendus":

Sens, L: quisquis erit removendus erit
E: quisquis erit renovandus erit

The synoptist's non-word must be an error for "removendus."

Since his other comparative remarks all refer to E, it is certain that here too he is calling attention to a reading in his source that differs from E. The variant pattern here, then, is E:LBS, which, by any conceivable method of textual criticism, excludes E as an intermediary between any of the other sources—and thus excludes E as a possible source for B. There remains of course the possibility of some sort of conflation: B got Lux hodie from E but for some reason corrected its reading from L; but there seems absolutely no reason to assume a process at once complex and purposeless. (Admittedly there is still a problem: in a second variant later in the same piece, Sens and L agree against E in having "asinaria" instead of "presentia." B does not give the complete text,

---

[30]See my "Liturgical Polyphony at Beauvais in the 13th Century," *Speculum*, 34 (1959), 189–191.

so its reading cannot be ascertained; but if B was in fact copied after L, it too should have had "asinaria," and the synoptist ought to have noted this variant as well. He might merely have missed it, or B might have made the change independently as part of its purpose in avoiding references to the Feast of Fools.)

The second clue concerns the position of the "prose" *Kalendas ianuarias*. In L it is specifically cited as one of the nineteen proses sung at Matins ("dixneuf proses . . . dont l'vne d'icelles se commencoit par ces mots. Calendas Ianuarias solemnes Christe facias etc."). It does not occur during Matins in E, but its incipit is given just before the last gathering—at the end, that is, of Lauds. In B, however, it appears as one of the proses during first Nocturn, as well as in the concluding ceremonies after second Vespers. Once again, L and B agree against E, suggesting that the latter was not the source for B. Again, the pattern might conceivably be fortuitous: the scribe of B, having *Kalendas* available anyway, might have added it somewhere to Matins; but this is also most unlikely.

While either of these indications taken alone might well be considered insufficient evidence, the two together seem to show with reasonable certainty that the synoptist's source depends on the other lost manuscript of the Beauvais tradition, that described by Louvet. What are the implications of this dependence for the otherwise unascertainable date of B? Only inferential, I believe. If E was in fact made as an up-to-date replacement of the much earlier L, anyone intending to make still another manuscript would presumably turn to E, rather than the source it replaced, as an exemplar. That the scribe of B did not do so might well be taken as evidence that E was not in existence when B was inscribed, and that B must therefore date from before 1220 or so. It is also possible, however, that the two manuscripts were made concurrently or nearly so—that they were two different phases of the modernization of the subdeacons' office, one for the use of the celebrating order, the other for the bishop and his party. There is not much basis on which to choose between the two hypotheses until the earlier problem concerning St. Ecclesius is remembered. Since Milon de Nanteuil was the bishop most likely to have ordered the insertion of the responsory for that saint, and since he occupied the see from 1217 to 1234, to assume that both B and E were copied in his episcopacy solves two problems rather than one.

The same assumption also helps with the final problem—what happened to deprive us of two out of the three subdeacons' manuscripts from Beauvais? The fate of L is fairly easy to guess: it was redundant as soon as E had been made. While it survived long enough for Louvet to see and describe it, it was not kept in the cathedral library in the fifteenth century, while E was (see note 11 above). Presumably it was discarded. It is likely enough that B met the same fate. The restraint and conservatism of its content suggest that it may have been modest in appearance as well. It too is absent from the cathedral library catalogues. There is no reason to suppose that any later bishop would have shared Milon's devotion to St. Ecclesius, nor could the manuscript compete with E as a practical document for a public celebration. That it should have survived as long as it did—long enough for a seventeenth-century scholar to write down his tantalizing summary of it—is perhaps matter enough for astonishment.

Updating the Style: Francesco Corteccia's Revisions in His Responsories for Holy Week

FRANK A. D'ACCONE

For Francesco Corteccia the publication of his *Responsoria omnia* at Venice in 1570 was the realization of a long-cherished dream. Here, in a handsomely printed collection dedicated to his patron and sovereign Duke Cosimo I de' Medici, were his settings of the responsories, canticles, versicles, and psalms for the Tenebrae services of Holy Week. The collection had long been in the making. It was in 1544 that Corteccia first mentioned his responsories in print when he announced, in the dedication of his first book of madrigals, that he intended to send them, together with his Lamentations, motets, and hymns, to the printer and that he would soon be making a gift of all of these works to the Duke.[1] Corteccia, however, was unable to keep his promise, and it was not until a quarter of a century later that he was finally able to begin the long-delayed publication of his sacred works with the *Responsoria omnia*. Two books of motets for five and six voices followed in 1571; but the composer's death just prior to their publication effectively put a halt to his ambitious aspirations.

In the dedicatory letter that precedes the *Responsoria omnia*, Corteccia states that he was publishing his responsories first because very few polyphonic settings of the texts were then available in Florence. Although he does not say so, we can be sure that there was a demand for such music, because the city's major churches, and many of its smaller ones also, traditionally observed the solemn rites of the *Triduum sacrum* with elaborate performances of polyphony. At Corteccia's own

---

[1]Portions of the dedication have been reprinted a number of times, most recently in Emil Vogel, Alfred Einstein, François Lesure, and Claudio Sartori, *Bibliografia della musica italiana vocale profana*, vol. I, pp. 414–15 (?Geneva, 1978). A facsimile of the entire text and an English translation appear in Vol. VIII of my "Music of the Florentine Renaissance," Francesco Corteccia, *The First Book of Madrigals for Four Voices* (Rome: American Institute of Musicology, 1981).

church of San Lorenzo, which normally did not maintain a polyphonic choir, it had been customary since 1517 to hire a group of singers especially for Holy Week. So much importance was attached to the performances that supervision of the group was entrusted to one or more of the canons or chaplains, among whom, in certain years, was Corteccia himself.[2]

In those days, as until quite recently, Tenebrae services, i.e., the offices of Matins and Lauds, were anticipated on the evenings preceding each of the last three days of Holy Week. The principal polyphonic items at these services were the Lamentations of Jeremiah; the responsories—twelve for each day, including a repetition of the third, sixth and ninth ones; the versicle "Christus factus est," distinguished by the addition of a new portion of text each day; the Canticle of Zachary, "Benedictus Dominus Deus Israel"; and the 50th psalm, "Miserere mei, Deus." Musical and documentary sources make it clear that not all of these items were always sung in polyphony in the Florentine churches. Polyphonic settings of the Lamentations and of the first three responsories, for example, might be followed by chanted performances of all but one or two of the remaining responsories, and more often than not, the various verses of the canticles and psalms were sung in alternation with the chant.

This latter practice is reflected in the way that Corteccia's music for Holy Week appears in print. It was brought out in two volumes of unequal size. The larger one, the *Responsoria omnia*, contains responsories and versicles as well as the odd-numbered verses of canticles and psalms. The smaller volume, entitled *Residuum Cantici Zachariae*, has the even-numbered verses of the canticles and psalms. Thus, three possible ways to perform the canticles and psalms are provided: odd-numbered verses alternating with chant; even-numbered verses alternating with chant; and complete polyphonic performances.[3]

Although two canticles and one versicle can be traced back to Cor-

---

[2]See my "Singolarità di alcuni aspetti della musica sacra fiorentina del Cinquecento," *Musica e spettacolo/Scienza dell'uomo e della natura*, "Firenze e la Toscana dei Medici nell'Europa del Cinquecento," vol. II (Florence, 1983), 517.

[3]As for the settings themselves, with few exceptions, the verses of the canticles utilize portions of the chant as a cantus firmus, while the psalms are no more than settings in *falsobordone* of the traditional tones. The responsories and versicles are freely composed, the former mixing imitative, chordal, and other textures, the latter in a predominantly familiar style. The responsories follow the familiar form of the chant, with the respond itself being divided into two principal sections (ab), the second of which is repeated after the verse (c). All the pieces in the collection are for four voices, save for one canticle à 5. Contrast is obtained by setting the verses of the responsories and the even-numbered verses of the canticles for fewer voices, in different combinations. The Lamentations, also mentioned earlier by Corteccia, were apparently never published and have not come to light thus far.

teccia's early years, the remaining ones and the psalms were composed long after the responsories, perhaps even as he began formulating his final plans for printing his Holy Week music. Corteccia indicates as much in his dedicatory letter to Duke Cosimo, where he also mentions some of the reasons that caused him to put off publication for so long:[4]

Although I decided and resolved in my own mind some time ago, O Most Serene Grand Duke, to publish certain sacred songs—commonly called motets, before bringing out these responsories which we customarily use to fulfill our duties to Christ our Saviour on those three Holy Days, it happened that because of the lack of printers I had suddenly to put aside the plans I had made after so much deliberation. Nevertheless, beseeched by many men solicitous of my own interests, indeed, urged to such an extent by them, I at last and at my own not inconsiderable expense prepared these same responsories for the press, and this because practically nothing else exists here [in Florence] except for those most ancient ones by a certain Arnolfo . . . [and] those composed by Bernardo Pisano. . . .

After due consideration I have added to them the Canticle of Zachary, the 50th psalm of David, and that versicle "Christus factus est" adapted for those three days, and I have composed different settings [of them] for each of the three days so that variety may obviate satiety. In this way have I thought not only to accede to the entreaties of my friends but also to satisfy you in some measure and to discharge myself of my obligation, since those things that I promised so long ago have never escaped my memory.

Thus, I beg you, O Grand Duke who can never be sufficiently praised, to take up the defense of this little work of mine with a joyful and complacent spirit so that under your protection it will not be reviled by malicious and invidious people. For in fact at times men are so spiteful and abusive by nature that whenever a work of some value is produced through the ability of others, they immediately—what worse can be said of them?—harass it with every manner of reproach, with slanderous, not to say, shameless, words, and they pluck at it and tear it to pieces with complete cruelty, and they hiss and hoot it right off the world's stage, even if its faults are minimal and unimportant, forgetting totally and imprudently that it is man's fate to err . . . The virtue of excellent men is worthy of imitation, not of envy, and this has always been my conviction. But so as not to keep you any longer, I shall tell you only that as soon as permission to print those songs [motets] has been granted, I shall immediately take care to send to you what has already been pledged to you. . . .

[4]The original Latin and a complete English translation appear on pp. 110–14 of Vol. 1 of Ann McKinley's "Francesco Corteccia's Music to Latin Texts," 2 vols. (Ph. D. dissertation, University of Michigan, 1962). The translation given here is slightly abridged, and differs in several places from the generally excellent one provided by McKinley.

Certain statements in the dedication require comment. For example, Corteccia's assertion that he was unable to follow through with the publication of his sacred music because there was no music press in Florence was, of course, true, but it had not prevented him from publishing his secular works. He simply sent them to the Venetian printers—to Scotto in 1544 for the first volume, and to Gardane in 1547 for a new edition of the same volume and two others.

Corteccia also mentions, though almost in passing, that the *Responsoria omnia* were being brought out at his "own not inconsiderable expense," a statement which can only mean that the enterprise was not supported by the Florentine court. This is surprising in view of the composer's excellent relations with Duke Cosimo, who, it seems logical to suppose, must have previously subvented the publication of his secular works. Corteccia was, after all, the only musician of note then in the Duke's service, and his madrigal books contained a good many pieces with texts that praised Cosimo and extolled the virtues of Medici rule. In the intervening period, however, the number of ducal retainers had grown. Cristofano Malvezzi and Alessandro Striggio were among the newer musicians appointed to Cosimo's household, and as more and more people vied for ducal support, there were more claims on the court's financial resources.

Under the circumstances it is easy to imagine that the *Responsoria omnia* might have been deemed unworthy of subvention by the Duke's advisors, who were perhaps more inclined to favor newer works that could be explicitly connected with the Medici. This is speculation, but it would help explain why Corteccia felt compelled to ask Cosimo to take his "little work" under the ducal wing. Indeed, how else are we to interpret his vehement outburst against unseen enemies, who, it seems clear, had spoken ill of the work even before it appeared? The situation leaves one with the impression that the "internecine bickering" that is said to have typified relations among Florentine artists and men-of-letters also extended to various musical factions associated with the court.[5] Certainly we know this to have been the case later, during the time of Caccini, Cavalieri, and Peri.

In the dedication of his 1571 volume of motets, Corteccia said that he had been working on those pieces for more than thirty years.[6] Although he made no such statement in the *Responsoria omnia*, he might well have done so, for three of the manuscript sources that antedate the

[5]The words are Eric Cochrane's. For a lively account of the Florentine artistic and intellectual community at this time, see his *Florence in the Forgotten Centuries, 1527–1800* (Chicago and London, 1973), pp. 73–78.

[6]The original and an English translation are also in McKinley's dissertation, cited in fn. 4, vol. I, pp. 121–25.

1570 print offer ample evidence that he revised his responsories a number of times over the years.[7] The three manuscript sources are dated and thus provide a chronological context for Corteccia's revisions. They furnish rare and important examples from the sixteenth century of a composer's second thoughts about music he had already written, and show how he set about incorporating changes within existing musical frameworks.[8]

A few remarks about the sources will be useful before discussing the revisions in detail. Florence, Opera del Duomo, MS 49, the earliest of the three, is a moderately sized volume of 66 folios. The complete set of responsories, copied by one hand, appears anonymously on folios 1ᵛ– 62ʳ.[9] I have not yet been able to identify the copyist, although I cannot

[7]In all, there are five manuscripts that preserve the responsories in whole or in part. Two of them are peripheral to the points I wish to make regarding the chronology of Corteccia's revisions, but I shall cite them here for the sake of completeness. They are: Florence, Opera del Duomo, MS 45, and Pistoia, Archivio del Duomo, MS 215. Neither shows signs of having been altered, and both their readings agree, except for a few small details, with the 1570 print. The Florentine source contains a cycle of music for Holy Week and is the work of several scribes. (See Charles Hamm and Herbert Kellman, *Census-Catalogue of Manuscript Sources of Polyphonic Music, 1400–1550*, vol. I [Rome: American Institute of Musicology, 1979], p. 241.) Ten of Corteccia's responsories, without attribution, were copied into the volume at folios 81ᵛ–95ʳ by Michele Federighi, mentioned below. While certain portions of the manuscript may date from c. 1559 (the date suggested in the *Census-Catalogue*), the evidence assembled in this study leaves no doubt that Corteccia's pieces were copied after 1562 or later. It also renders untenable Mario Fabbri's assertion that the inclusion of the responsories in MS 45 furnishes the necessary proof that the volume is the one commissioned by Corteccia himself in 1559. (See his "La vita e l'ignota opera–prima di Francesco Corteccia, musicista italiano del rinascimento," in *Chigiana*, 22 [1965], 210–11.) The Pistoia manuscript was compiled a decade or more after the 1570 print. It, too, contains a number of items for Holy Week, chief among which is the complete set of responsories, without ascription. They were first identified by Mario Fabbri in his "Una preziosa raccolta di musica sacra cinquecentesca: il Codice 215 dell'Archivio del Duomo di Pistoia," *Collectanea Historiae Musicae*, 4 (1966), 103–123.

[8]Evidence of a similar sort is offered by Carpentras's *Liber Lamentationum Hieremiae Prophetae* (Avignon, 1532). Carpentras wrote his Lamentations for Leo X, between 1513 and 1521, revised them for Clement VII, c. 1524–30, and had the final version of the set printed in 1532. For a discussion of manuscript sources that may preserve remnants of the first version, see pp. xv-xxix of Albert Seay's Introduction to his edition of the Lamentations in Elziarii Geneti (Carpentras), *Opera Omnia*, vol. II (Rome: American Institute of Musicology, 1973). See also H. Colin Slim's *A Gift of Madrigals and Motets*, vol. I, p. 97 and vol. II, pp. 203–27, for a discussion and transcription of Claudin de Sermisy's "Quare fremuerunt," a part of which was apparently revised for publication.

[9]The remaining folios, copied perhaps by as many as three scribes, contain two more responsories and several settings of the 50th psalm in *falsobordone*, all without attribution. The latter, though varying in a few details, appear to be Corteccia's. On folio 1ʳ a later hand has written: "Responsi del Corteccia/49."

doubt that he worked closely with the composer. Whoever he was, he took pains to date a few of the responsories as he copied them out. The earliest date, "1553," is on folios 7^v and 8^r; a more complete one, "in dì primo di Marzo 1553," does not occur until folio 17^r. The year in this case should be understood as 1554, because the Florentine new year did not begin until March 25. It is possible that the previous date also stands for 1554, which suggests that the copyist began his work earlier that year. He must have put the volume aside, however, for the next date, "3 Aprile 1555," on folios 27^v and 28^r, is from more than a year later. "1555" is given again toward the end of the set, on folio 53^r.

At one time MS 49 must have contained many of the settings Corteccia referred to in the preface to his 1544 madrigals. But ubiquitous signs of revision, making the music conform to the 1570 print, leave no doubt that only a fraction of the responsories remain in their original state.[10] Rare is the folio that does not exhibit an erasure or cancellation or which does not contain new writing over the old. At times an entire system has been pasted over with a freshly copied one, and on occasion the eye is struck by a group of notes crowded into an otherwise evenly spaced and neatly executed manuscript. The revisions were made by the original copyist, and other considerations, discussed below, suggest that he did so at various times between 1562 and 1570, or even somewhat later.

Florence, Archivio Parrocchiale di San Lorenzo, MS N, consists of two separate collections of music for Holy Week that were bound as a single volume in the early seventeenth century.[11] The first, which is given over principally to Bernardo Pisano's responsories, need not concern us. The second contains Lamentations and other items for Tenebrae which are for the most part without attribution. Concordant sources reveal many of these pieces to be the work of Carpentras, Pisano, Verdelot, Layolle, Morales, and, in the case of six of the responsories, Corteccia. MS N comes down to us without any later revisions. It was commissioned by San Lorenzo's prior from Ser Braccio Baglione, a chaplain at San Lorenzo and singer in the Florentine chapel under Corteccia. He is recorded as having received payment for his work on May 29, 1559, and the collection is mentioned in San Lorenzo's inventories of 1560, 1581, and 1593.

The last of the manuscript sources, also from San Lorenzo, where it is now designated as MS C, is a composite volume of 84 folios. The first 52 contain the complete set of responsories, again without attribution. They were copied by Michele Federighi, who inscribed his initials, his

---

[10]About a third of them seem not to have been altered.

[11]The manuscript is described briefly on pp. 517–22 of my study, mentioned above in fn. 2.

full name, and several dates at various points in the manuscript. Folios 1^v–2^r contain the first responsory, dated "MDLXI," and folios 51^v–52^r the last, where the inscription "Laudetur Deus, 3 Marzo 1561" [1562] appears.[12]

Michele Federighi, whom Corteccia called "my pupil" ("mio creato") in his last will and testament, was first a canon and then prior of San Lorenzo from March 1574 until his death on May 31, 1602.[13] He was on intimate terms with the composer, who named him executor of his estate and charged him with seeing the rest of his works through the press—a charge that Federighi was unable to fulfill. He was the principal copyist of Corteccia's works in the composer's later years and doubtless had immediate access to any and all revisions. Interestingly, MS C, which was Federighi's personal copy, shows signs of later alterations (also in his hand) to bring it into conformity with the 1570 print, though these are not so numerous as the ones in MS 49. It is likely that he revised his copy before November 16, 1576, when he made a gift of it to San Lorenzo's Chapter. The volume is subsequently listed in the inventories of 1581 and 1593. The latter inventory was compiled by Federighi himself, who states that he personally donated four of the volumes of music in San Lorenzo's library, among them, "a large folio volume of Corteccia's responsories, copied in pen."[14]

Although MS N contains only six of the thirty-six responsories, its readings are particularly valuable because they appear in a dated source that shows no signs of alteration. As such, they can be used in conjunction with evidence supplied by the two other sources to date some of the revisions with greater precision. A comparative analysis of readings in the three sources will take the following points into account: (1) no holograph copy of the responsories is extant, so it is impossible to know whether the earliest surviving versions are in fact the original ones mentioned by Corteccia in 1544; (2) pieces entered into MS 49 in 1554–55 were in most cases subsequently altered to conform to a later version, generally the one in the 1570 print; and (3) changes were made to

[12]The remaining folios contain an incomplete copy of Corteccia's first Canticle of Zachary, also in Federighi's hand, and a few other Holy Week pieces, in as many as three different hands.

[13]Portions of Corteccia's last will and testament, including the reference to Federighi, have been published by Mario Fabbri on pp. 202–3 of his "La vita e l'ignota opera-prima di Francesco Corteccia," cited above in fn. 7. This bit of information about Federighi is given in Domenico Moreni's *Continuazione delle memorie istoriche dell'ambrosiana imperial basilica di San Lorenzo di Firenze*, vol. I (Florence, 1816), pp. 330, 354. Volumes of Corteccia's works which were copied by Federighi include: Florence, Opera del Duomo, MS 46, and Florence, Biblioteca Medicea Laurenziana, Palatino 7. (See p. 241 of the *Census-Catalogue*, mentioned in fn. 7.)

[14]The document is quoted on p. 519 of my study, cited in fn. 2.

the pieces in MS C for the same purpose, though these are far fewer in number.

Feria V, Resp. 1 "In monte Oliveti"

In MS 49 added and altered notes, which obscure earlier material, reveal that the relevant folios were later revised. Those in MS C have no signs of alteration. The readings in both sources agree completely with the 1570 print, while the one in MS N is substantially different from it. These facts indicate that an early version, in use in 1554 as MS 49 was begun, was still current in 1559, when MS N was compiled. This was reworked between 1559 and 1562, when a new version was copied into MS C. The new version was subsequently printed and also superimposed over the earlier one in MS 49. The sources thus leave no doubt about the existence of a second version of the piece by 1562 and show that it underwent no further revision for the 1570 print.

Feria V, Resp. 2 "Tristis est anima mea"

Several passages in MS 49 are palimpsests and point unmistakably to a revision of an earlier setting. MS C again gives no evidence of alteration. Both sources agree in substance with the print, though both have common variants with it. MS N differs from the print in quite a few places, the same ones that show signs of revision in MS 49. These circumstances reveal an additional step in the sequence of events inferred from the first responsory. An early version was in circulation between 1554 and 1559. A new one, which retained some of the passages still found in MS N, was made before 1562, when MS C was copied. This version, too, was subsequently revised, and it is the second revision that appears in the print. The latest changes, however, were not entered into either MS 49 or MS C. In this case, then, three versions of the piece can be documented before 1570: one originally entered into MS 49 and still present in MS N; another copied into MS C and superimposed over MS 49; the last, from after 1562, printed in 1570.

Feria V, Resp. 3 "Ecce vidimus eum"

Corteccia originally set this responsory without the words "propter iniquitates nostras," which come at the end of the first part of the respond. The three sources indicate that this shortened text setting (mm. 1–30)[15] was current through 1562. MS 49 and MS C have pasteovers in

---

[15]In my transcriptions I have reduced original note values by one half. References to measures are thus to be read as references to breves. Eight of the responsories have been

all parts to accommodate four new measures of music and text; MS N does not. MS 49 was extensively revised in spots other than those where the new text was added, as for example in mm. 12–13; unfortunately, the original readings are no longer visible. The only remaining trace of the earlier version is a variant in the tenor at mm. 19–21. This variant is present in MS N, which, save for another variant at the same place in the alto, agrees with the print through m. 30. The version in MS C has been altered only to receive the additional four measures; otherwise it agrees with MS N, including the variants in mm. 19–21. Thus, three versions are again documented, but in yet another sequence. The original shortened text setting was revised between 1554 and 1559, as shown by MS N, and the revised version was still current in 1562, when it was copied into MS C. Between that year and 1570 the second version itself underwent changes, including the addition of four new measures of music and text, and this was the form in which the piece was printed. There is no way of ascertaining when the new measures were appended to the readings in MS 49 and MS C; but when they were, those portions of the revised shortened text setting that did not clash with the latest changes were allowed to remain.

Feria V, Repetitio Resp. 3 "Ecce vidimus eum"

This setting also originally lacked the full text of the respond. As before, MS 49 shows signs of revisions—in this case recoverable—other than those occasioned by the newly added portions of music and text. Again, the changes indicate that an earlier shortened text setting was revised by 1559, when MS N was copied. Here, however, the sequence of revisions varies from that seen in the preceding responsory. MS N, while lacking the four new measures, agrees with the print. So does MS C, though it has been altered to include them. It is clear, then, that apart from the additional measures composed after 1562, it was the second version of 1559 that was retained for the print.

Sabbato Sancto, Resp. 3 "Plange quasi virgo"

Extensive changes are evident in MS 49. Nevertheless, it now agrees with the print except for a different chord in m. 2. MS N, while in general agreement with the print, also has the different chord as well as a few other variants. Except for the different chord, MS C now agrees

---

published in modern edition by Ann McKinley in vol. II, pp. 37–56 of her dissertation, mentioned fn. 4. Three of these also appear in her edition of Francesco Corteccia, *Eleven Works to Latin Texts,* "Recent Researches in the Music of the Renaissance," vol. VI (Madison, 1969), pp. 23–29. My edition of the complete *Responsoria omnia* is forthcoming as vol. XI of "Music of the Florentine Renaissance."

with the print, although it shows signs of having been altered in those places where the variants occur in MS N. These facts leave no doubt that there was a revision of the earlier version by 1559 and that this was still in use in 1562. It, too, underwent changes and the resulting third version was printed in 1570. The latest changes, except for the different chord in m. 2, were then incorporated into MS 49 and MS C. Thus although three different versions are again documented, it is only the print that has the completely revised final version.

Sabbato Sancto, Repetitio Resp. 3 "Plange quasi virgo"

Alterations to MS 49 and to MS C and the version in MS N indicate a sequence of revisions similar to that in the preceding responsory. In this case, however, no remnants of the earlier readings remain in MS 49 and MS C, and except for MS N, all sources now preserve the third version.

In summary, half of the pieces (the third, fifth, and sixth) extant in all three sources show the same chronological sequence of revisions—a 1554–55 version, a first revision by 1559, and a second revision by 1570—thus making three versions within a fifteen-year time span. Three versions are also documented during the same years for the second piece, but in a different sequence: a 1554–55 version, a first revision by 1562, and a second revision by 1570. The first piece exists in two versions only, the one from 1554–55 and a 1562 revision. The fourth is also represented by two versions, the one from 1554–55 and a revision from 1559, but with the difference that new measures were added to the second version after 1562.

Although it is possible to determine the number and date of revisions this precisely in only a handful of pieces, the physical condition of MS 49 and MS C leaves no doubt that Corteccia revised many more of the responsories during the same period. The exact nature of all of his changes is not always discernible because often only the faintest trace of an original reading remains. The revisions seem to have been made for both pragmatic and aesthetic reasons. His underlying practical concern was to bring the texts of the responsories into line with current liturgical use as reflected in the new breviary, incorporating Tridentine reforms, that was issued by Pius II in 1568. Altogether there are sixteen instances where Corteccia's responsories originally differed from those of "the restored form of the Roman breviary."[16] The variants, though not earth-shaking, as can be seen from the following list, run the gamut

---

[16]The phrase *(Iuxta Breviarii Romani Formam restitui)* is Corteccia's, from the full title of the *Responsoria omnia.* Three places in Corteccia's responsories do not agree with texts found in present-day chant books. These variants, however, represent noth-

from simple misspellings and incorrect wordforms to omissions of whole words or, in one case mentioned above, of a whole phrase.

1 *Feria V, Resp. 3:* originally lacked "propter iniquitates nostras"
2 *Feria V, Resp. 3, Repetitio:* same as (1)
3 *Feria V, Resp. 5:* originally gave "fuerat" for "erat"
4 *Feria V, Resp. 6:* originally gave "veh" for "vae"
5 *Feria V, Resp. 6, Repetitio:* same as (4)
6 *Feria V, Resp. 6:* originally gave "fuerat" for "erat"
7 *Feria V, Resp. 6, Repetitio:* same as (6)
8 *Feria V, Resp. 8:* originally gave "qui" for "quid"
9 *Feria V, Resp. 8:* originally gave "ut non intretis" for "ne intretis"
10 *Feria VI, Resp. 1:* originally gave "percutiens" for "percutientes"
11 *Feria VI, Resp. 4:* originally gave "comprendere" for "comprehendere"
12 *Feria VI, Resp. 6:* originally lacked "dilectam"
13 *Feria VI, Resp. 6, Repetitio:* same as (12)
14 *Feria VI, Resp. 8:* originally lacked "eum"
15 *Sabbato Sancto, Resp. 2:* originally lacked "et"
16 *Sabbato Sancto, Resp. 4:* originally gave "dirupit" for "disrupit"

Not all of the textual emendations required recomposition. In nos. 4, 5, 8 and 16, for example, Corteccia (or his copyist) had only to write in the correct form of the word. The others contain musical modifications, none of them very extensive except for no. 15. The simplest, such as nos. 3, 6, and 7, merely entailed replacing the chordal pattern of dotted quarter-, eighth- and half notes that originally set "fuerat" with a pattern of two half notes for "erat." In no. 14 (Ex. 1), where two syllables were added rather than eliminated, half notes were split to accommo-

---

ing more than readings from the 1568 breviary that were modified by later popes. They are:

　　1. *Feria V, Resp. 1:* the phrase "fiat voluntas tua" appears at the end of the first section of the respond

　　2. *Feria VI, Resp. 7:* at the beginning of the verse "in" is used in place of "adversum"

　　3. *Sabbato Sancto, Resp. 3:* "veniet" is given for "venit"

　　4. *Sabbato Sancto, Resp. 3, Repetitio:* same as (3)

Curiously, these variants and the sixteen listed above also appear in the set of responsories composed between 1511 and 1520 by Bernardo Pisano, Corteccia's teacher and predecessor as chaplain at San Lorenzo. Both composers obviously used a common source. In an attempt to locate it I consulted several Florentine chant books, among them the "Libro corale" of the Curia arcivescovile, Florence, perhaps the oldest one extant in the city, and MS G n° 22, a fifteenth-century antiphonary now in the Opera del Duomo. Both these manuscripts have some but not all of the variants; the conclusion I draw is that both composers probably used a source from their own church of San Lorenzo, one that is either lost or has not yet been identified. I take this opportunity to thank Dom Jean Claire of the Abbaye Saint-Pierre de Solesmes for his invaluable assistance as I attempted to track down the source of Corteccia's textual variants.

Example 1. Feria VI, Resp. 8

date the extra text, and the underlay and rhythm were adjusted where necessary to maintain the proper word accent.[17] The harmony, save for a shift at one place from first inversion to root position of the same chord, remains unchanged. Similarly, in no. 10 (Ex. 2), apart from the addition of a repeated chord on G, the original harmonies were kept, and the rhythmic pattern was adjusted to fit the extra syllables.

The revision in no. 12 (Ex. 3) is slightly more elaborate. Corteccia originally set the opening phrase "Animam meam dilectam tradidi in manus iniquorum" without the word "dilectam." When he corrected the passage, he retained the first two measures of his original setting through the "me-" of "meam" and, with the exception of a new chord on the first "di-" of "tradidi," the rest of the phrase beginning with that word. In between he replaced the half-note chord on the "am" of "meam" with a quarter-note chord and inserted a five-beat succession of chords for "dilectam." In all, the alteration entailed the addition of no more than one-and-a-half measures of new music and changed neither the shape of the original phrase nor the clarity of its harmonic movement.

Both MS 49 and MS C show signs of alteration here and in all of the other places just mentioned, so it is clear that the majority of Corteccia's revisions were not made until after 1562. The same is true of the

---

[17]In this and the following examples the version at top is from MS 49 and MS C, that at bottom from the 1570 print.

Example 2. Feria VI, Resp. 1

Example 3. Feria VI, Resp. 6

responsories numbered (1) and (2) in the above list. In the final versions of both of these pieces, the only alteration demanded by the addition of the new words was the replacement of the final cadence with transitional material that led to the added musical phrase.

The remainder of Corteccia's revisions were made purely for aesthetic reasons. In these instances his intention was to improve upon the textual declamation by changing certain musical passages. To be sure, even in their earlier versions his pieces exhibit a concern, so typical of the Florentine attitude, for clear enunciation and proper accentuation of the text; but the revisions always show a greater sensitivity to the finer points of textual declamation. It is possible to document sixteen such passages, although there are many others that show traces of revision but cannot be reconstructed because the original readings in MS 49 and MS C can no longer be read. In any case, the traceable revisions clearly show that Corteccia's conceptions of good textual declamation sharpened with the years, as he absorbed the musical lessons of Willaert and the practical advice of Lanfranco and Zarlino.

As before, Corteccia's revisions extend from a single measure to several, from a brief rhythmic substitution to the addition of a few chords, from changes in a single part to changes in all parts. I shall limit this discussion to a few examples that illustrate his methods as he applied them in increasingly complex situations. An elementary example is furnished by the opening words of Feria V, Resp. 4 (Ex. 4). The compression of "-mi-cus" to allow the first syllable of "meus" to fall a half measure earlier—a simple revision in itself—gives the phrase a fluency that was only barely hinted at before.

The first five measures of the revised verse of Sabbato Sancto, Resp. 7 display slightly more extensive changes (Ex. 5). Although a semblance of the original point of imitation has been retained, even emphasized

Example 4. Feria V, Resp. 4

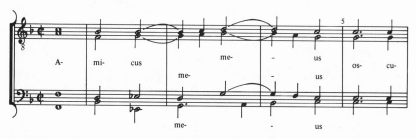

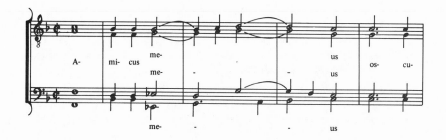

Example 5. Sabbato Sancto, Resp. 7

through the early entrance of the bass, each of the parts now develops more freely, so as to correct both the oblique motion and some of the perfunctory, though correct, declamation. As a result, the phrase is shortened by a measure, the proper accentuation of each word is enhanced, and the parts move to their natural climax on "gentes" without recourse to textual repetition as before.

Feria V, Resp. 1 is the only piece that has revisions in all of its sections. The earlier version, preserved in MS N, was reworked between 1559 and 1562. In the revision, Corteccia retained the same number of measures at the opening of the respond; but by prolonging the tonic harmony in m. 3 and recasting the existing melodies in m. 4, he ensured better enunciation of the word "Oliveti" (Ex. 6). By anticipating the tenor's final syllable in m. 5 he was also able to begin the descending fourth

Example 6. Feria V, Resp. 1

motive on "oravit" a half measure earlier. This, and a shift forward by a
half measure of the upper parts in the following passage, provided a
more properly accented setting of "oravit" in all voices. Remodeling
the final phrase then allowed him to stress more fully the first syllable
of "Patrem."

The revision of a passage in the second part of the respond (Ex. 7) also

Example 7. Feria V, Resp. 1

involved prolonging a tonic harmony, recasting some of the original melodies, and shifting old material a half measure forward. Subsequently, a half measure of dominant harmony was added to the existing one at m. 33, thus enlarging the section by a full measure. The formerly abrupt setting of "caro autem" has been replaced with one that affirms the strong syllables of each word; the slight rhythmic alterations in the cantus, tenor, and bass improve the accentuation on "fiat voluntas," while retaining the point of imitation.

The verse section has a number of minor changes, none involving structural alterations. More than any of the others, however, this responsory strikingly illustrates Corteccia's new attitude toward textual declamation as well as the changes in text placement that he must have made throughout the set as he prepared his responsories for publication. The opening of the verse (Ex. 8) is representative. In m. 40 of the tenor the original melisma on "la" of "vigilate" is broken; the new phrase for the repeated word is modified slightly in order to accommodate better the following words, "et orate." The last syllable of "orate" is now extended so that the tenor's next phrase, "ut non intretis," no longer duets with the bass but rather with the cantus, a full measure later; this brings out the cantus-bass imitation more clearly. The one change in the cantus, shifting the emphasis on "la" of "vigilate" to a melisma on "te," is not only in accord with contemporary advice regarding proper text placement in such passages but assuredly makes the words easier to sing. The bass has little more than a few rhythmic changes in mm. 42–43, which allow better enunciation of "et orate." All in all, the simplicity of these alterations is disproportionate to the effect achieved, for there is no doubt that the revisions make the old phrases breathe more naturally while unmasking the potentially excellent declamation of the original.

The last example I shall cite is furnished by Sabbato Sancto, Resp. 2 (Ex. 9) which, as mentioned above, originally lacked a word. The earlier version, for reasons that are not clear, still survives in MS C, an indication that the piece was not revised until after 1562. Although the changes it underwent then were both practical and aesthetic, it was undoubtedly the need to make the piece liturgically correct that provided the initial impetus. The text originally available to Corteccia omitted the conjunction "et" between the principal and subordinate clauses of the verse. This led him to read it as "Deduc quasi torrentem lacrimas/ per diem et noctem non taceat pupilla oculi tui,"[18] which he set as two phrases of unequal length. The first, slightly longer one, comes to a Phrygian cadence on A after an extended melisma in the cantus on the

---

[18]"Let your tears flow like a torrent/day and night let there be no repose for your eyes."

Example 8, Feria V, Resp. 1

"la" of "lacrimas" (m. 30). The second consists of two subsections, one leading from a cadence on F directly into the other, which lights fleetingly on the tonic g before being repeated and extended by a full cadence at the very end.

When he emended the text, Corteccia could have made the revision easily enough by changing a rhythm or two or by adding a few more beats to his original setting, as he had done in other such cases. But he realized that with the addition of "et" before the subordinate clause, the words of the principal clause were now modified, and it was neces-

Example 9. Sabbato Sancto, Resp. 2

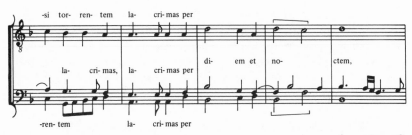

(continued)

Example 9, continued

sary to reflect the change musically.[19] Accordingly, he added two measures to the end of the first phrase and brought it to a full cadence, replete with suspension, on B♭. He then introduced a slight melisma on
the final syllable of "noctem" to connect it with the second phrase,
which he began with a half-note chord on F for the added "et." Apart
from some minor rhythmic and melodic changes (alto, m. 36; bass, m.

[19]"Let your tears flow like a torrent day and night, *and* let there be no repose for your
eyes."

36; cantus and alto, mm. 39–40), the new second phrase is nothing more than the second subsection of the older version. Noteworthy are the harmonic changes, which, though minimal, give the setting a firmer tonal foundation. Clearly, the new authentic cadence on the relative major (mm. 37–38) strengthens the G mode much more than the previous inconclusive one on the supertonic. By beginning the second phrase with repeated harmonies on F, Corteccia affirms the relative major and makes the ensuing passage to the tonic seem less abrupt than before. So much for what may be termed structural changes, all of them occasioned by the emended text and accomplished within the same number of measures as the earlier setting.

The few changes within the first phrase were obviously made with a view to better text declamation. The original setting of "lacrimas" in the cantus had a somewhat forced, awkward rhythmic pattern on its first appearance, one that was barely redeemed by the lovely melisma in the repetition. In the new version Corteccia made a slight rhythmic and melodic change so as to replace the first "lacrimas" with a repetition of "quasi torrentem" and to move on from there to a new setting of "lacrimas," which he now made coincide with the first and only statement of the same word in the bass. Simultaneously, he dropped the alto's melisma in m. 30 and replaced it with a repetition of "lacrimas," set to the same rhythm as the outer parts. By shifting to a chordal texture here, Corteccia made a smooth transition to the new measures that set "per diem et noctem"; and he joined the words so gracefully and effortlessly that we have the impression of their having been conceived that way from the start. I must confess that I find it a masterly stroke. But rather than insist upon the merits of the piece, and in the spirit of Corteccia's own attitude in these matters, I shall refrain from further comment and, in his words, "let those who are expert in musical matters judge whether or not" I am correct.[20]

---

[20]"Quod quantum ipse praestiterim, illorum qui Musice rationis ignari minus habentur, sit iudicium," from the dedication of the 1570 print.

The Ojibwa Begging Dance[*]

THOMAS VENNUM, JR.

Many cultures celebrate calendar customs of masked ritual solicitation, in which community members ostentatiously make their way in groups from one dwelling to the next to solicit goods, food, or money. Whether Nova Scotian belsnickles or Norwegian *julebukker* at Christmastime, Zinacantecan bull-chasers before the Feast of San Sebastian, Sonoran Faroseos during Lent, or American Halloween "trick-or-treaters," begging parties tend to exhibit unusual behaviors, expressed through costuming or performance antics.[1]

North American Indians practiced a wide variety of such activity, almost all of it accompanied by music. Ponca Ȋskáiyuha Society members would dance before lodges of the wealthy to receive presents; Cree ritual beggars, wearing masks with long noses, would pretend to stalk and shoot at the food put out for them as they sang and danced from tent to tent; during the Taos Pueblo deer dance the Black Eyes collected food from each house, shouting, gesturing, and singing as they went; men of the Stars and Wolfmen warrior societies of the Gros Ventre, mounted on their horses and aided in singing by their wives, would perform begging songs before the lodges of leaders of the opposite society.[2]

The begging dance of the Ojibwa Indians is a complex example of

---

[*]An abbreviated version of this paper was presented at the annual meeting of the American Folklore Society, Minneapolis, October 1982.

[1]See Roger W. Abrahams and Richard A. Bauman, "Ranges of Festival Behavior," in *The Reversible World: Essays in Symbolic Inversion*, ed. Barbara Babcock (Ithaca, 1978), pp. 193–208; Evon Vogt, *Tortillas for the Gods* (Cambridge and London, 1976), pp. 155 ff.; Homer Sykes, *Once a Year: Some Traditional British Customs* (London, 1977), p. 91; Elsie Clews Parsons and Ralph Beals, "The Sacred Clowns of the Pueblo and Mayo-Yaqui Indians," *American Anthropologist*, 36 (1934), 500. Other begging rituals described in Sykes's publication include The Hobby Horse (p. 21), Helston Furry (p. 64), Burry Man (p. 122), and the Norn Dance (p. 122).

[2]Alanson Skinner, "Ponca Societies and Dances," *Anthropological Papers of the American Museum of Natural History*, 11 (1915), 786; J. A. Teit, *The Salishan Tribes of the Western Plateaus*, Forty-Fifth Annual Report of the Bureau of American Ethnology, 1927–1928 (Washington, D.C., 1930), p. 389; Parsons and Beals, "The Sacred Clowns," p. 496; Regina Flannery, *The Gros Ventre of Montana*, Catholic University of America Anthropological Series, no. 15, I (1953), 41. For other American Indian beg-

54

such solicitation, and its decoding helps to provide interpretations missing from previous studies of American Indian clown rituals.[3] Ritual begging in the area that is now Wisconsin and Minnesota was cited as early as the eighteenth century in reports of travelers and government officials. Some form of the Ojibwa begging dance is suggested by Jonathan Carver's experience around 1767 on the Mississippi River near Lake Pepin. Objecting that it occurred "at so late an hour," Carver described the approach of twenty dancing Indians in war paint. "At every ten or twelve yards they halted, and set up their yells and cries." Moving right into his tent, they struck its poles with their warclubs and refused the peace pipe, but accepted the "ribands and trinkets" that Carver took from his chest. These gifts, he noted, "seemed to stagger their resolutions. . . . Soon after they took up the presents . . . and appearing to be greatly pleased with them, departed in a friendly manner."[4] In the summer of 1826, at the American Fur Company's Fond du Lac post, Superintendent of Indian Affairs Thomas McKenney encountered forty Ojibwa who arrived one day by canoe from their island at the west end of Lake Superior. Forming a noisy procession led by singers with hand drums, they danced their way in double file to McKenney's quarters, all the time emitting shouts and war whoops. They continued to dance, now in a circle, outside his building; during pauses in the music, warriors would relate their various battle exploits. McKenney astutely discerned the nature of this ritual and gave it its proper name:

This was a pipe dance, a dance of ceremony, or rather as it ought to be called, *a begging dance* [italics McKenney's]. Their object was to get presents; and it would have been deemed most ungracious not to have

---

ging rituals see Clark Wissler, "Societies and Dance Associations of the Blackfoot Indians," *Anthropological Papers of the American Museum of Natural History*, 11 (1913), 460; Robert H. Lowie, "Dances and Societies of the Plains Shoshone," *Anthropological Papers of the American Museum of Natural History*, 11 (1915), 834; typescript notes on Hopi songs recorded by Samuel A. Barrett in 1911 in the archives of the Department of Anthropology, Milwaukee Public Museum, pp. 21, 73; Frances Densmore, *Northern Ute Music*, Bureau of American Ethnology, Bulletin 75, (Washington, D.C., 1922), 188–90.

[3]See Julian H. Seward, "The Ceremonial Buffoon of the American Indian," *Papers of the Michigan Academy of Science, Arts, and Letters*, 14 (1931), 187–207. Seward's distribution map, p. 188, shows the Plains and Southwest to have strongly developed clown rituals. By contrast, the Woodlands area is represented as a "weakened complex," although Seward admits inadequate data are partly responsible for this impression. This had led him to stress the "amusement" characteristic of Woodlands' begging rituals without probing their deeper significance.

[4]Jonathan Carver, *Travels Through the Interior Parts of North America*, 3rd ed. (London, 1781; facsimile edition, Minneapolis, 1956), [pp. 279–82]. It is conceivable that Carver's evening visitors were eastern Sioux (he does not name them), as Lake Pepin was in the contested zone between them and the Ojibwa at the time.

given them. We put out a mocock [birchbark container] filled with to-
bacco, and some whiskey, (the chief object of their visit) well diluted
with water. They drank each a wine-glass of this beverage. . . .[5]

The presents were accepted by a special Indian attendant called a
machinewa,[6] whose discretion in their distribution, noted McKenney,
was not to be challenged. After receiving the gifts, the Ojibwa fired off a
gun, reformed their double line, and marched off, dancing their way towards the Captain's quarters to repeat their solicitation. Word of the
donors' generosity seems to have spread quickly, for McKenney wrote
in his journal that another begging dance was performed two days later,
this time by a delegation from Sandy Lake.[7]

Nine years later, some 100 miles east of Fond du Lac, I. I. Ducatel
witnessed similar rituals. The occasion was the 1835 annuity payments at La Pointe on present-day Madeline Island, at that time the
headquarters of the American Fur Company:

> During the period of the payment the performance of the pipe-dance, to-
> gether with the war-dance, is a very frequent exhibition with them; and
> as they resort to it for the express purpose of levying a contribution upon
> the merchants and traders of Lapointe, it has been more significantly
> called the "begging-dance."[8]

Describing the dancers as wearing war paint and their songs as accompanied by a kettle and bells, Ducatel also noted that few if any Indian
women were present, even as spectators. His general depiction of this
performance is consistent with McKenney's account, except that the
libations offered the Indians at La Pointe were nonalcoholic:

> The dance being over, the party is usually at the factory treated with
> some crackers and cheese; and a pail of sweetened water into which has
> been poured a bottle or two of essence of peppermint, is brought out to
> which they help themselves at discretion. They are very fond of this sort
> of mint julep, which they call *mahkahwahgomik*.[9]

Both nineteenth-century accounts above mention the pipe dance,
the war dance, and the use of war paint by the dancers. Ducatel's obser-

---

[5]Thomas L. McKenney, *Sketches of a Tour to the Lakes* (Baltimore, 1827; repr.,
Minneapolis, 1959), pp. 284–86.

[6]McKenney probably heard this term incorrectly. Cf. Friedrich Baraga, *A Dictionary of the Otchipwe Language, Explained in English*, rev. ed., Albert Lacombe (Mon-
treal, 1878 and 1880; repr., Minneapolis, 1966), s.v. "*mijinawe*, steward, administrator
of a property, manager." McKenney notes that the *machinewa* is a sort of attendant
and that every chief has one.

[7]McKenney, *Sketches*, p. 299.

[8]I. I. Ducatel, "A Fortnight Among the Chippewas of Lake Superior," in *The Indian
Miscellany*, ed. W. W. Beach (Albany, 1877), p. 366.

[9]Ibid, p. 367.

vation of the pipe dance as marked by the physical contortions of its performer conforms to later, more detailed descriptions of it in the literature.[10] Apparently, by around 1825–35 the Ojibwa had combined elements of the pipe and war dances to perform their ritual begging. It seems also that the dance could be initiated spontaneously if the targets for solicitation were white merchants and traders. By the turn of the century, however, most reports of the begging dance associate it principally with the spring maple sugar harvest, when those solicited were fellow Indian campers. This is generally reflected in the texts of begging-dance songs collected at the time, such as: "Maple sugar is the only thing that satisfies me," or "I wish he would give me food, corn meal with sugar spread over it." Frederick Burton, living at the eastern end of Lake Superior, described the springtime begging ritual of the Desbarets (Ontario) Ojibwa in his *American Primitive Music* (1909). At that season the Indians were customarily settled in larger social aggregates to tap the maple trees, following their wide dispersal for hunting and trapping during the winter months:

> As evening comes on and all are resting, the young men take empty pans, and, headed by a drummer, dance grotesquely from one family shelter to another, singing this song ["We look as if we could eat"]. They hold out their pans for contributions of syrup or sugar, and though their words are not explicit their actions say "give, or we will take by force." Usually the contributions are forthcoming good humoredly, but when they are not, the young men invade the shelters of the niggardly, drive out or overpower the occupants, and take as much sugar as they think will teach the owners to behave more hospitably in the future.[11]

Burton provided a transcription of only one begging-dance song in his publication, without assigning it to any particular genre or giving it a name. It remained for Frances Densmore to discover the wide distribution of this ritual, not only among the Ojibwa but also among the Menominee and Teton Sioux. Her monographs on the musics of these tribes, published by the Bureau of American Ethnology beginning with *Chippewa Music* in 1910, are the first to indicate that begging-dance songs comprised distinct genres. She appears also to have been the first scholar to investigate the beliefs concerning the origin of the dance.

Densmore's first exposure to an Ojibwa begging dance was during a July 4th celebration on the Red Lake Reservation in northern Minnesota in 1908. She recalled that in the early evening,

[10]For the pipe dance, see Frances Densmore, *Chippewa Music—II*, Bureau of American Ethnology, Bulletin 53 (Washington, D.C., 1913), 293–96. See also McKenney, *Sketches*, p. 311.

[11]Frederick R. Burton, *American Primitive Music, With Especial Attention to the Songs of the Ojibways* (New York, 1909), pp. 223–24.

a crowd from the camp was moving toward an old store, Nae'tawab'
leading and the drum in the midst. Before this building they stopped and
began to dance around the drum, all singing the high droning melody of
the "begging dance." Soon a shifting of the crowd showed that they were
going toward the Chippewa trading store. Nae'tawab' was the leader,
dancing and waving a little flag. Standing before the store he faced the
Indians, dancing with all his might and urging them to sing louder and
louder. Soon the trader brought out a box of oranges which he distributed; then the melody changed slightly to the "thanks-for-a-gift" song,
and the crowd passed on to another store.[12]

At the time, she persuaded William Prentice and Wabezic' each to record a begging-dance song for her on wax cylinders; Wabezic' also recorded two songs used to express thanks for donations.

It was not until Densmore extended her fieldwork to Wisconsin reservations, however, that she unearthed her most significant information about the begging dance. While recording at Lac du Flambeau in
northern Wisconsin, Densmore collected six more begging-dance
songs, from Mec'kawiga'bo (Joe Kobe) and Ĕ'niwûb'e, her two principal
singers on that reservation. There she gathered her principal ethno-
graphic data concerning the origin of the ritual and its traditional performance contexts.

By the time *Chippewa Music-II* (1913) was published, Densmore had
augmented her Red Lake data sufficiently to provide the Ojibwa name
for the dance—*bagosañ'ninge'nimiwĭn'*[13]—and to give a general description of the ritual:

A begging dance could be started at any time, a leader and a small company going from one wigwam to another, dancing and singing. If the occupants of the wigwam were asleep the dancers entered and danced
around their fire. The people then arose and gave them food, for those
who danced the begging dance were never refused. If the people had no
cooked food, the visitors took such provisions as they had, placing them
in a birchbark bag which an old woman carried for the purpose.[14]

Participants in the begging dance were never refused provisions, according to Densmore's informants, and so in this way the tribe's poor
were fed. Still, the custom also provided a form of amusement, particularly by forcing stingy members to give or by embarrassing those who
were caught short. (Densmore recalled one woman chasing after a begging party with a pail of sugar that she had been unable to find when
they visited her tent.)

[12]Frances Densmore, *Chippewa Music,* Bureau of American Ethnology, Bulletin 45
(Washington, D.C., 1910), 171.
[13]Cf. Baraga, *A Dictionary,* s.v. *pagossêndjige,* "I beg, pray, ask."
[14]Densmore, *Chippewa Music–II,* pp. 228–29.

Apparently the Ojibwa had shared this custom with their Siouan and Algonquian neighbors for some time, occasionally even joining them in it. More than 150 years ago, the painter George Catlin watched "the beggar's dance" performed by Sioux and Ojibwa in front of the Agent's Office at Fort Snelling, Minnesota, also during Fourth of July festivities.[15] Densmore found that the Menominee indulged in ritual begging not only in the sugar bush, as did the Ojibwa, but also at any large gathering. During the sugaring season the leader of the begging party solicited maple sugar, while several other members carried bags in which to take it away. This normally took place at the end of the season, and if they were unable to cover the whole camp in one evening, they completed their rounds the next.[16]

From Ĕ'niwûb'e at Lac du Flambeau Densmore learned the origin of the dance. Her curiosity had been aroused by the text of one of his begging-dance songs, "The dogs will accompany me." The origin of the ritual was attributed to the Assiniboin Sioux and explained to Densmore as follows: The Sioux customarily put their newborn boys outside the dwelling in the place where the dogs would lie so that the dogs, encircling the infant, would keep him warm with their breath. The child was not permitted to enter the dwelling until he could creep into it on all fours in the manner in which dogs entered. The begging dance originated when a certain boy received the song performed by Ĕ'niwûb'e from the dogs he lived with. The dogs did not actually sing it to him but rather "willed" him to learn it. When the boy was older he went from camp to camp with his dogs, performing the song, in reward for which both he and the dogs were fed. Because of this belief, it is said that the members of a begging party "represent themselves as dogs, using the term (ogi'tcĭda'dog [warriors]) which dogs are supposed to use towards their masters."[17] Conforming to his symbolic role as a dog, Ĕ'niwûb'e preceded the performance of his begging-dance song with whining and barking (see Example 1).[18]

Following Densmore's studies, little information was published on

[15]George Catlin, *Letters and Notes on the Manner, Customs, and Condition of the North American Indian* (New York, 1841; repr., Minneapolis, 1965), vol. II, p. 135. Catlin also sketched a beggar's dance of the Sioux at the mouth of the Teton River, vol. I, Plate 103, and one of the Sauk and Fox, vol. II, Plate 293. In both instances the dancers were said to petition for the poor of their respective tribes.

[16]Frances Densmore, *Menominee Music*, Bureau of American Ethnology, Bulletin 102 (Washington, D.C., 1932), 187.

[17]Densmore, *Chippewa Music–II*, p. 230.

[18]Cf. Densmore, *Chippewa Music–II*, p. 229, cat. no. 403; the original recording is in the Library of Congress, Archive of Folk Culture, AFS 10,5486. The Ojibwa belief expressed in this story that dogs were capable of communicating with infants may be shared with other Great Lakes peoples.

Example 1. Ojibwa Begging-Dance Song

(Translation: "The dogs will go with me.")

the Ojibwa begging dance, probably because the practice began to be abandoned. This is generally consistent with the gradual reduction in the number of song genres when their contexts disappeared as traditional Ojibwa culture experienced a sharp decline, beginning about 1915.[19] However, vestiges of the begging dance survived in some Ojibwa communities until recently. William Bineshi Baker, Sr. of Lac Court Oreilles Reservation remembers organizing begging groups about 1924 to petition merchants in nearby Hayward, Wisconsin, for bread and baloney as they carried their large drum by four straps from store to store; the merchants willingly complied, as the spectacle attracted business. In conjunction with this solicitation, the begging group sometimes performed a dance in a parking lot, where they spread a blanket onto which bystanders could deposit money. (Baker recalls earning as much as $25 in one day for himself.) When asked if they performed begging-dance songs, Baker discounted the existence of this genre per se, saying that one simply used a war-dance song, preferably one that "sounds mournful." At Red Lake, Minnesota, a form of the ritual was continued during the annual Fourth of July powwow into the late 1960s, though it has since been discontinued. On the morning of the powwow, trucks were loaded with drums, singers, and the powwow princess to begin a caravan. It was led by someone holding the tradi-

[19]See Thomas Vennum, Jr., Southwestern Ojibwa Music, (Ph.D. dissertation, Harvard University, 1975), vol. I, pp. 34-39.

tional feather flag—exactly the type of banner carried by the leader of the Sandy Lake begging party that visited McKenney in 1826. Like the event Densmore witnessed on the same reservation in 1908, the Red Lake parade made stops at the hospital and grocery stores for the participants to disembark and dance in order to receive such provisions as soft drinks and potato chips (see Plates 1 and 2). It is noteworthy that Red Lakers called the ritual a "shivaree," a folk term used mostly in the South and defined as "a noisy mock serenade to a newly married couple who are sometimes expected to furnish refreshments to silence the serenaders."[20]

Whether the story told to Densmore about the origins of the begging dance was widely accepted is not known. What is significant is that some Ojibwa, at least, had seized upon the dog as the appropriate animal to be represented in the begging dance. All evidence shows the dog to occupy a highly ambivalent position in Ojibwa culture, being treated with both cruelty and respect. Under traditional Ojibwa attitudes, dogs function alternately as profane and sacred beings and are thus not easily classified; they fall into neither the pet nor wild animal categories with any regularity. Ojibwa dogs are in that borderline area that Edmund Leach has defined in his study "Animal Categories and Verbal Abuse;" as marginal creatures they are very powerful indeed.[21]

Those with traditional European-American standards assumed the inconsistent Ojibwa treatment of dogs to represent a peculiar racial trait. Superintendent McKenney, while touring the Great Lakes in 1826, summarized the Ojibwa attitudes toward dogs in relating the interrogation of a Lac du Flambeau Indian to discover the murderer of a white:

> Another Indian declared that he knew he was innocent. The Governor said, will you put your hand on your breast, and say that in the presence of the Great Spirit? The moment the interpreter put this question, he looked him full in the face, and answered, *"am I a dog that I should lie!"* This reply is somewhat remarkable. . . . In the first place, there is hardly any thing on which an Indian sets so high a value as he does upon his dog. This is proverbial. Yet he is constantly referred to as an object of contempt! Indians never swear—I mean until they learn it of their white brothers—and their most degrading epithet is to call their opponents *dogs.* Here is a strange union of respect and contempt. But further. A dog is considered the best offering to their enraged manito [spirit], and often in a storm is one thrown overboard to appease him. Yet they kill him and

[20]*Webster's Third New International Dictionary* (1971), s.v. "shivaree."

[21]Edmund Leach, "Anthropological Aspects of Language: Animal Categories and Verbal Abuse," in *New Directions in the Study of Language*, ed. Eric H. Lenneberg (Cambridge, Mass., 1964), pp. 23–63.

Plate 1. Ojibwa dancing to solicit donations at Red Lake, Minnesota, July 4, 1969. Adult dancers, left to right: William Bineshi Baker, Sr., Lac Court Oreilles, Wisconsin; William Dudley, Red Lake, Minnesota; Sam Yankee, East Lake, Minnesota.

Photo by Charles Brill

Plate 2. Ojibwa singers in pickup truck, Red Lake, Minnesota, July 4, 1969, with soft drinks given by local merchants for their "shivaree" performance. Lead singer, far right, Peter Seymour, Kenora, Ontario. Photo by Charles Brill

eat him, and consider a feast greatly enriched when this animal, which they so highly respect as never to be without them, makes part of it.[22]

McKenney correctly assessed the value the Ojibwa placed upon his dog. Not only were these animals relied upon for hunting, but before Woodlands Indians had horses, dogs were used as beasts of burden. Because of their usefulness, dogs were believed to be gifts of the Great Spirit. In 1855 when the German traveler Johann Kohl inquired why the La Pointe Indians killed dogs for religious purposes, he was told:

> The dog was created in heaven itself, and sent down expressly for the Indians. It is so useful to us that, when we sacrifice it, this must be considered as a grand sign of piety and devotion.[23]

Companions in everyday life, dogs accompanied an Ojibwa wherever he went, even when he traveled by water. Ducatel's general impression was that the animal received much the same treatment from Lake Superior Ojibwa as he did from the white man:

> The [Ojibwa] is also fond of his dogs; whenever a canoe is met coasting the shores of the lake, the sire is at the helm, the squaw and grown up boys or girls are paddling, the helpless children and a pack of dogs are the steerage passengers. The dogs have their litter in the wigwam. . . . The Indian pets them, as the white man does the lamb, and feeds them to gratify his [sic] appetite.[24]

Such fond attention was so exaggerated by an Ojibwa recluse named Maguesh that he became a topic of conversation. In place of a wife and children, he kept twenty dogs in his wigwam; ". . . he nursed [them] like children, shared his breakfast with them every morning, often held a dialogue with them, and warned them like children to behave properly and not quarrel." His notoriety became widespread when in 1811 he presented each dog with a bearskin.[25]

Newborn puppies were divided among the children of the family, each receiving a pet.[26] Thereafter, apparently, the allegiance of one's dog was so important that there were charms to make him faithful (Plate 3). The dog's indispensability was stressed in the narrative of John Tanner, a white captive who lived among the northern Ojibwa on and off for thirty years in the early nineteenth century. Tanner makes it clear that only under dire circumstances, such as the threat of starvation, did he resort to killing any of his dogs. Once when his best dog

[22]McKenney, *Sketches*, p. 325.

[23]Johann G. Kohl, *Kitchi-Gami: Wanderings Round Lake Superior* (London, 1860), p. 39.

[24]Ducatel, "A Fortnight," p. 371.

[25]Kohl, *Kitchi-Gami*, pp. 407–8.

[26]Ibid., p. 39.

Plate 3. Ojibwa Charm to make a dog faithful, courtesy of the American Museum of Natural History

frightened away a moose he was stalking to feed his family, he called the dog, told him it was his fault, killed him, and fed him to his family in place of the moose. At another time when provisions were depleted, Tanner and his companions ate a dog of his who had died, and later also killed his last dog for food.[27]

Normally Tanner was a staunch defender of the beast. When the Shawnee prophet came to the Ojibwa around 1810, among the changes he demanded were that the people stop drinking and beating their wives and children, and that they kill their dogs. Tanner spoke out against this, saying, "Has not the Great Spirit given us our dogs to aid us in procuring what is needful for the support of our life, and can you believe he wishes now to deprive us of their services?" Although many killed their dogs in compliance with the prophet's wishes, gradually the Indians lost faith in his teachings and returned to their old ways, including raising dogs.[28]

Despite the high value placed on dogs, by non-Indian standards their treatment was excessively abusive. Ducatel, at LaPointe in 1835, described the unruly behavior of "a parcel of idle boys" in the Indian camp who were "teazing a whole gang of half-starved dogs that bark and growl."[29] Fifteen years later, in the same community, Kohl found the miserable condition of these "very seedy" looking creatures unchanged:

> Their great object in life is to crawl into the huts and carry off something eatable; but they are continually driven out by the women and children, and recommended, by a smart blow, to satisfy themselves with the fish and beaver bones thrown out for them.[30]

[27]Edwin James, *A Narrative of the Captivity and Adventures of John Tanner* (New York, 1830; repr. Minneapolis, 1956), pp. 202, 263.

[28]Ibid., p. 144 ff.

[29]Ducatel, "A Fortnight," p. 362.

[30]Kohl, *Kitchi-Gami*, p. 37.

So lowly was their status that dogs were considered to have a disturbing, even contaminating effect on sacred events. Consequently, in the late nineteenth century dogs found entering a drum-dance enclosure were customarily killed, although by 1911 they were simply chased out of the ring and whipped.[31] Because of dogs' disturbing potential, before the sucking doctor began his cure, he would send his assistant outside to see that none were around; their barking would frighten away the spirit helpers.[32] When a dog was sacrificed for a Grand Medicine ceremony, the killing took place away from the lodge. The body was placed at the lodge entrance for the congregation to step over it upon entering; it was then removed and cooked, again away from the *mitewikan*.[33] Such attitudes have persisted until recently. When Robert Ritzenthaler attended a shaking-tent rite at Sand Lake, Wisconsin, in 1942, the juggler, John King, insisted that dogs not be allowed near the *jizikan* (shaking tent), so they were shut in the house.[34]

Despite their physical abuse, dogs functioned as sacred mediators for the Ojibwa. Archaeological evidence shows that dog sacrifice was formerly widespread among many tribes. The articulated skeletons of dogs have been found in pits and ossuaries in Wisconsin and Michigan, areas occupied by the Ojibwa and their neighbors.[35] After contact, Europeans, believing animal sacrifice to be heathen, almost always described those they encountered. Often reported in the literature is one method the Indians used: strangling or clubbing dogs to death and then suspending them from "medicine" or "offering poles." Almost always, the animals chosen for this purpose were white; the Ojibwa appear to have shared this preference with other tribes. During a sugar harvest in 1763, when a child accidentally fell into a vat of boiling sap, among the sacrifices presented to the spirits for her recovery were dogs "killed and hung upon the tops of poles, with the addition of stroud blankets and other articles."[36] In the spring of 1867, Frank Folsom witnessed

[31]Samuel A. Barrett, "The Dream Dance of the Chippewa and Menominee Indians of Northern Wisconsin," *Bulletin of the Public Museum of the City of Milwaukee*, 1 (1911), 258–59.

[32]Joseph B. Casagrande, "John Mink, Ojibwa Informant," *Wisconsin Archeologist*, n.s. 36 (1955), 116.

[33]Densmore, *Chippewa Music*, p. 37. See also Ruth Landes, *Ojibwa Religion and the Midewiwin* (Madison, Milwaukee, and London, 1968), p. 138.

[34]Robert Ritzenthaler, "Chippewa Preoccupation with Health," *Bulletin of the Public Museum of the City of Milwaukee*, 19 (1953), 202.

[35]George I. Quimby, *Indian Culture and European Trade Goods* (Madison, Milwaukee, and London, 1966), pp. 123, 135. Quimby's dates for the historic period in the Upper Great Lakes are 1610–1820.

[36]Alexander Henry, *Travels and Adventures to Canada and the Indian Territories* (New York, 1809), p. 150. For a Seneca example, see Samuel Crowell, "The Dog Sacrifice of the Senecas," in *Indian Miscellany*, p. 329.

(through his spyglass) a funeral on the opposite shore of Big Wood Lake (Wisconsin). In front of the wigwam containing the deceased, the Ojibwa had put up an offering pole with a crossbar from which was suspended a dead white dog and a dirty calico shirt.[37]

Dogs were also thrown into lakes and rivers to appease the spirits. Folsom continued his description of the Big Wood Lake funeral by noting that the following day the mourners crossed the lake, dropped the dog overboard, having weighted him down with a rock around his neck, dug a grave on the shore, built a small house over it and erected a wooden pole with an owl effigy on it—the traditional form of burial in the *mitewiwin*. Clearly unsympathetic to Indian music, Folsom was relieved when the ceremony ended: "They continued making all the hideous noises possible during these proceedings and finally in the afternoon their demonstrations ceased."

White dogs were preferred for drowning sacrifices as well as for hanging ones. William Dudley, a convert to Christianity, indicated recently that such customs were still followed on the Red Lake Reservation:

[Traditional practitioners] will sacrifice animals, they are still doing it. Has to be an animal without a blemish. . . . The most valuable sacrifice that you can give now, as I remember here years back ago, would be a white dog without a spot . . . About 30 years ago now we was very close to this old man. He says, 'I'm looking for a dog,' he says, 'a white dog . . . without a spot. Going to sacrifice one, drown it in the lake. . . .' That's the way they talked with their god, the heathen people.[38]

Not only the sacrifice of dogs to the spirits, but also the ritual consumption of dog meat once held high ceremonial value for the Ojibwa.[39] This was also true for most Algonquian and Siouan peoples adjacent to them, particularly among their military societies. The

[37]Frank W. Folson, letter dated 1874 from Taylor's Falls, Minnesota, Folsom Papers, Minnesota Historical Society, A.F670. See also Lucy R. Hawkins, "A Chippewa Indian Idol," *Wisconsin Archeologist*, 6 (1927), 84.

[38]Microfiche transcripts of the University of South Dakota American Indian Oral History Project (Sanford, N.C., 1979), part II, tape 253, p. 4. Henry, *Travels and Adventures*, p. 108, also mentions a dog thrown overboard en route to Michilimacinac Island to calm an approaching storm.

[39]Albert B. Reagan, "Some notes on the Grand Medicine Society of the Bois Fort Ojibwa," *Americana*, 26 (1933), 519. Dogs were required as ceremonial food by most groups practicing the medicine dance. Carver, in 1766–68, found this true of the "Naudowessies," probably the eastern or Santee Dakota: "I was informed that at all their public grand feasts they never made use of any other kind of food. For this purpose, at the feast I am now speaking of, the new candidate provides fat dogs, if they can be procured at any price." See Carver, *Travels*, [p. 278]. The Ojibwa dog feast is discussed fully in Thomas Vennum, Jr., *The Ojibwa Dance Drum: Its History and Construction*, Smithsonian Folklife Studies, No. 2 (Washington, D.C., 1982).

Thunder gens of the Fox Indians, for example, went through an elaborate preparation and eating of dogs prior to unwrapping their sacred war
bundle.[40] Because dogs were considered such potent creatures, the Fox
entrusted their killing only to warriors; others, particularly those with
expectant wives, were afraid to kill dogs lest their children be born crip-
pled.[41] Similarly, the Winnebago sacrificed a dog to Disease-giver and
ate him in their war-bundle feasts.[42]

While Ojibwa traditionalists continued to partake in such feasting,
about the turn of the century attitudes appear to have changed, and dog
consumption was generally discontinued. This may reflect the influence of missionaries, or else simply the abandonment of old practices during the reservation period, due to pressures to conform to "civilized" social patterns. Before its decline, however, the practice of eating
dogs received some early impetus when the Ojibwa adopted a form of
the grass dance from the Sioux around 1880. That ceremonial complex
featured an elaborate dog feast with a large repertoire of songs and sub-
rites, including a belt dance during which former warriors ate bits of
cooked dog. This practice, which spread with the general diffusion of
the grass dance over the Plains, had its precursors in the so-called "hot
dances" of warrior societies, in which men demonstrated bravery in
various fire ordeals. Typical was the Siouan ritual described by Daniel
Leasure while visiting the Standing Rock Agency in July 1875, where a
dog was cut into four parts and boiled in kettles, around which braves
danced. They would reach into the kettles to pull out a piece of meat,
"taking out the scalding mess and eating it till the skin of the hands,
lips and mouth hang loose in whitened shreds, and all this time no sign
of pain or discomfort finds an expression on any face. . . ."[43]

Despite Woodlands peoples' acceptance of the general ritual outlines
of the dog feast, there is evidence of some reluctance on their part actually to eat dog meat. For instance, not just any camp dog was considered
acceptable for a ceremonial feast. The Menominee Helen Wynos
echoed William Dudley's observations at Red Lake in noting that special dogs were reserved for such occasions:

They used to have a certain [kind of] dog. Like a newborn dog; well, that

[40]Truman Michelson, *A Sacred Pack Called A'penäwänä'a Belonging to the Thunder Gens of the Fox Indians*, Bureau of American Ethnology, Bulletin 85 (Washington,
D.C.: Government Printing Office, 1927), 107–10.

[41]Truman Michelson, *Notes on the Buffalo-Head Dance of the Thunder Gens of the
Fox Indians*, Bureau of American Ethnology, Bulletin 87 (Washington, D.C.: Government Printing Office, 1928), 4.

[42]Paul Radin, *The Winnebago Tribe*, Thirty-Seventh Annual Report of the Bureau
of American Ethnology, 1915–1916 (Washington, D.C., 1923), p. 380.

[43]Daniel Leasure, "A Visit to the Standing Rock Agency," in *Indian Miscellany*, pp.
389–90.

dog's got to be clean; he's got to eat everything that's clean. Not the way a regular dog eats; eats slop and everything else. This kind's got to be clean, kept clean. And that's the kind they used to raise for that purpose in them days [to eat during the dog feast of the drum dance.][44]

Not all were receptive to eating dog flesh; many considered the practice abhorrent. In fact the Sioux, who regularly ate dog, were sometimes given the derogatory epithet "[dog] roasters" by the Ojibwa, their traditional enemies.[45] For their dog feasts the Ojibwa and Menominee began to substitute wild animals such as porcupine or raccoon, or even pork and beef, and the ceremonial food server came to be called Bullcook. If a dog were in fact used, the Menominee referred to the animal euphemistically as a "white raccoon," and permitted those who did not wish to partake of the meat to hire a former warrior to do so for them.[46] A distaste for the practice lingers today. Ojibwa at a recent powwow in Sisseton declined the stew offered them by their Siouan hosts, as the rumor had spread among them that it was *animoshwabo* (dog soup). (There is an in-joke current among the Ojibwa that the sentence "See Spot run" in grade-school primers refers to a dog of the Sioux about to be butchered.)

Beyond its ceremonial value, the dog was accorded a high place in the legends and visions of the Ojibwa, and extraordinary powers were attributed to him as well. Paul Radin related two eastern Ojibwa stories in which dogs played fabulous roles. In one a certain small boy was transformed into a dog and disappeared underground. The other story was published in its entirety as follows:

> Certain Indians who went hunting had a fine, handsome dog. One evening this dog jumped up from the house, ran out, and barked. Finally it rose up in the air. They heard it barking and they continued to hear it barking in the sky. Then all the dogs barked.[47]

Generally attentive to all animal sounds, the Ojibwa believed that dogs, like owls, were capable of forewarning them of impending events. Shamans could convert themselves into dogs to spy on events, and a

[44]James S. Slotkin, "The Menomini Powwow: A Study in Cultural Decay," *Milwaukee Public Museum Publications in Anthropology*, no. 4 (1957), p. 129.

[45]See William W. Warren, *History of the Ojibwa* (St. Paul, 1885; repr. Minneapolis, 1957), p. 36. Warren gives "Ab-boin-ug" as meaning "roasters," the name given the Sioux, he claims, in reference to their alleged burning of captives. Ives Goddard informs me that this is really folk etymology, and that the word is an old one meaning "our principal enemies."

[46]Alanson Skinner, "Menominee Associations and Ceremonies," *Anthropological Papers of the American Museum of Natural History*, 13 (1915), 181; loc. cit., fn. 1. Also, Slotkin, *The Menomini Powwow*, loc. cit.

[47]Paul Radin, "Ojibwa Ethnological Chit-chat," *American Anthropologist*, 26 (1924), 514.

dog's howling near a wigwam warned of sorcery. Such a notion was described by Paul Buffalo at Leech Lake in Minnesota in 1969:

> And then you may have . . . a dog lying there, and he'll get up and he'll
> howl, cry, just a howl cry. And generally will run away, he'll run off a
> distance. That's a warning too, that's bad. . . . There's trouble ahead or
> there's a bad sign before you, bad warning. Maybe death, maybe trouble,
> maybe somebody's injured. That's why [the Ojibwa] used to get
> alarmed.[48]

Conversely, a "bear-man," having sacrificed eight dogs for the power to
destroy an adversary, causes his victim's dogs to fall asleep as the bear-
man approaches, thus keeping them from barking to warn their master.[49]

The Great Spirit is thought sometimes to have used dogs to communicate with humans. A young girl, Maggie Quarters, had a series of visions at Lac Court Oreilles around 1909 in connection with drum-
dance practices in her community of Whitefish. Because another visionary, Steve Grover, had been ridiculed for relating similar messages,
the Great Spirit had brought Maggie to Heaven, instructing her to relay
them once again:

> [The Great Spirit] also spoke bitterly of the disbelief of the people and
> complained that the people refused to believe him when he sent his mes-
> sages through adults and said that he had decided to try talking through a
> baby, meaning of course this little girl. He further declared that if the
> people did not heed him when this message was sent in this manner he
> would next try a dog as messenger. After this she was returned to the
> earth as miraculously as she had been carried away.[50]

All of our data connecting dogs with the Ojibwa begging dance were
collected after 1900. While none of the earlier reports includes the animalistic performance described to Densmore by Ĕ'niwûb'e and others,
they at least mention the pipe dance, which involved physical contortions, or otherwise depict the dancing style as grotesque. Clearly, then,
some sort of unruly behavior was associated with begging parties before
the dog element was introduced. The question remains, however, of
how the canine association came about and why.

As mentioned, the Ojibwa not only shared the begging dance with
Siouan neighbors to the west, but also credited them with its origins.
Furthermore, the origin story specifically describes dogs as beggars
moving from camp to camp, while referring to their masters as warriors. Since the dog feast was adopted about 1880, together with the

drum dance, it seems likely that at about that time any previous association of dogs with warrior groups was reinforced.

It is very likely that the representation of a beggar by a dog was a Plains concept which acculturated the Ojibwa, perhaps in the manner Alan Merriam has proposed for the Flathead, a Salish people northwest of the Plains.[51] Merriam has shown that the Flathead were already acquainted with the begging behavior of Plains tribes, possibly through the Cree. We know that various "dog societies" on the Plains had special food privileges; the research of Lowie and Wissler has shown this for the Blackfoot, Mandan, Hidatsa, and Teton Sioux.[52] These societies are frequently reported to have long exhibited unusual, clownlike behavior. For instance, Wissler learned from Woman Dress, an Oglala, that a cult known as "the dogs" formerly existed among her people; they were considered *wakan* (sacred) but acted as peculiarly attired ritual fools to make people laugh.[53] Perhaps partly to amuse, dog societies sometimes even imitated the actions of dogs when they went to various lodges for food, which they often took by force. Such animalistic behavior was noted by Maximilian Nuwied in depicting the ritual feeding of the Ruhptare "dog band," four of whom were known as "the true dogs, who, when a piece of meat is thrown into the fire, are bound immediately to snatch it out and devour it raw."[54]

Although information about Flathead dog societies was scant, Merriam was nevertheless able to reconstruct the probable connection of dog behavior to their ritual begging. Certain unarmed Flathead warriors had dogs as guardian spirits who protected them in battle. Citing Turney-High, Merriam notes that music and doglike actions were ritually combined by these men during the winter hunt. When they reached the Plains, those with dog spirit guardians "sang their songs and romped and barked dogwise in front of the column."[55]

The Flatheads' description of their begging ritual in fact approximates the Ojibwa performance, except that it was carried out on horseback rather than on foot and accompanied by rattle rather than by drum. Two singers riding double on a horse, but without any special costuming, formed the begging party:

[51]Alan P. Merriam, *Ethnomusicology of the Flathead Indians* (Chicago, 1967), pp. 103–7.

[52]See the articles by Lowie and Wissler cited in fn. 1.

[53]Clark Wissler, "Societies and Ceremonial Associations in the Oglala Division of the Teton-Dakota," *Anthropological Papers of the American Museum of Natural History*, 11 (1912), 99.

[54]*People of the First Man*, ed. Davis Thomas and Karin Ronnefeldt (New York, 1976), p. 199.

[55]Merriam, *Ethnomusicology*, p. 104.

When these two people hit the camp, they sing this special Dog song and
they will not let anything interrupt them. They are dogs, and they cannot talk. People make presents to them, and they tie these presents to
their clothes or to the bridle or saddle of their horses. They do this just for
fun. They are not poor people.[56]

The horse was trained to remain standing at the doorway of the tipi and
not to leave until some gift was tied to it or to the riders. The introduction of this begging ceremony was attributed to one Jim Sapeel, who
initiated it at the first Fourth of July ceremony in about 1890. In this
manner the dog song became attached to ritual begging among the Flathead, although by the time Merriam collected his information, the
practice had been discontinued.

We know, then, that the Ojibwa warriors in the past practiced ritual
begging, forming raucous parties moving from one trader to the next,
and that such activity was perhaps emulated in the sugar camp by
young men. We know also that in soliciting, both groups exhibited unusual behavior, either with elements of the pipe dance or other grotesque
forms of dancing. But how do we explain the accretion of dog symbolism in the later version of the begging dance? And why would the singers incorporate barking sounds into their songs? The explanation, I believe, lies in a general understanding of the meaning behind animal
sounds in Ojibwa song performance—that they are a form of masking
and as such accompany a variety of unusual behaviors.

Early accounts of American Indian music invariably mention its
"barbaric" qualities. One characteristic performance practice that Europeans found particularly objectionable was the interpolation of various extraneous nonmusical sounds into songs, such as yells, war
whoops, and the like—hardly up to the standards of bel canto singing.
Even those who had come to appreciate Indian music as a valid cultural
expression continued to take exception to these particular aspects of
performance. They awaited their inevitable refinement, which, they
were certain, would emerge from contact with the superior musical
culture of Europe. Still, such collectors as Frances Densmore deliberately suppressed such sounds from many of their recordings in order to
preserve "the actual melody." Despite Densmore's attempts, her early
cylinder recordings have preserved on them, in addition to the singers'
yells, their spoken interpolations, peculiar sounds associated with
healing and power transference, and imitations of animal cries.

A great variety of animal noises were at one time part of the Ojibwa
vocabulary; when honoring any animal, the Ojibwa traditionally performed the sound associated with it. For example, during the crow
feast, already extinct when Peter Jones described it in 1861, the partici-

[56]Ibid., p. 105.

pants would make crow noises while "gormandizing."[57] When songs were created to accompany such activities, the animal sounds were apparently transferred to them, and thus became one means of recognizing the song's origin and use. The old men of the tribe, for instance, would make cattle sounds while preparing a special protective medicine to be carried on the warpath. Singers later used cattle medicine songs in war dances and included the cattle sounds in the performance of them. Similarly, the Ojibwa once had songs containing buffalo bellows. Typically, the buffalo song had its origins in a dream, and its transfer to the Ojibwa was similar to that of the begging-dance song "willed" to the Siouan infant: A man, while fasting, heard sounds which at first seemed to come from a gathering of Indians. Soon he came upon a herd of buffalo, "walking in a circle knee-deep in mud, with swaying heads and lashing tails; all were singing as they walked around. The Indian joined the herd and thereupon became a buffalo. For this reason they gave him the song which they were singing." The text of the song commemorates the incident: "I join the buffalo as they stand in a circle."[58]

Similarly, deer sounds appear in Ojibwa songs for those animals which, like the buffalo songs, had dream origins and were used when hunting. Those that have been recorded include an imitation of the bleat an adult male uses in pursuit of a doe; a high-pitched honking sound that represents the bleat used by a fawn in danger to communicate with its mother; and blowing sounds that probably represent the snorts of an adult deer, frequently emitted as an alarm signal while pawing the ground.[59] Because the Ojibwa relied for subsistence on the Virginia, or white-tailed, deer above all other game animals, it is to be expected that any hunter would be totally familiar with the full vocabulary of such sounds. In fact, the Ojibwa had even manufactured a trumpet-shaped deer-call lure from birchbark.

But why would singers include animal sounds in a song, and why would Ě'niwûb'e bark between the strophes of his begging-dance song? An explanation can be found, I believe, by reviewing the function of sound communication in traditional Ojibwa ontology. Their spiritual affinity with animals dates back to early tribal history, when the Ojibwa were an amalgamation of social groups distinguishable by totemic clans. Animal-mime dances are still an important part of the repertoire, and animal impersonations abound in Ojibwa beliefs and are

---

[57]Peter Jones, *History of the Ojebway Indians* (London, 1861).

[58]Densmore, *Chippewa Music–II*, p. 203.

[59]The deer sounds may be heard on Archive of Folk Culture, Library of Congress, cat. nos. AFS 10,548a3, 10,548a4a, 4b, 10,548b3. I am indebted to Marshall White of the Wildlife Department, University of California, Berkeley, for their identification.

reflected in the folktales. In one story, Wenebozho, the trickster-hero, after tempting Toad Woman to doctor him in order to learn her secrets and songs, kills her, skins her, and dons the toadskin to impersonate her, thereby gaining access to Chief Snake's house to do away with him. This story is a prelude to the lengthy legend of the flood and creation of the new world, which is filled with animal characters—each given its separate voice, songs, and cries.

Through constant exposure to such stories from childhood on, the Ojibwa gradually places more emphasis on auditory than on visual forms of communication, particularly if the communication takes place within the supernatural sphere, where animals and humans freely intermingle.

Consider, for instance, the conspicuous absence from Ojibwa ceremonialism of one means of visual communication: zoomorphic costuming. Although a number of their mime dances simulate animals—the fish dance or the snake dance, for instance—the visual communication is restricted to the rehearsed figures of a group of dancers. There are none of the special costumes worn in dances of other tribes, such as the feather wings and headdresses of the Pueblo eagle and buffalo dances. While the Ojibwa priest entering the medicine lodge represents Bear or Otter, he is dressed in ordinary or Sunday clothes, the only Indian costuming being beaded knee garters and bandoleer bags. In the drum dance, except for the special feather bustle assigned to the Belt Man, the others wear everyday clothes.

The stress on the audible over the visible world is also evident in the Ojibwa attitude toward metamorphosis. While the ability to change into animal forms is commonly believed to be a capacity of sorcerers and conjurers, the metamorphosis is never witnessed. In the celebrated bearwalk, for instance, an old woman would change herself into a bear to commit murder, then change back again and be seen lurking about the vicinity in human form; or a shaman might transform himself into a hawk to catch the departing soul of a dying man, but on his return would be seen once again in human form, holding the soul in a matchbox. By contrast, metamorphoses frequently manifest themselves audibly. The conjurer in the shaking tent frees himself in Houdini fashion from the ropes binding him by turning briefly into a snake; though hidden from view by the tent, his efforts to wriggle loose can be heard. Similarly, there is a story of an old, starving woman who, on being refused food by her people, changed into an owl to haunt them and could be heard hooting incessantly thereafter in the neighborhood.

The important role of auditory communication among the Ojibwa may result partly from the high value Woodlands peoples place on an acute sense of hearing. To provide subsistence for his family, a hunter must keep his ear finely attuned to the noises of the forest to direct him to game. This is one reason that his vocabulary of animal sounds is so great. Furthermore, the persistent threat of ambush in former times required his remaining alert to telltale noises of another's approach; constant attention to his own sounds enabled him to move quickly either to capture game or to escape danger.

The audible world of the Ojibwa, however, extends beyond the empirical happenings of daily life to include the spiritual world as well, for it is their belief that spiritual power travels through the air and, in doing so, manifests itself in one of several familiar sounds. A. Irving Hallowell goes so far as to state: "The only sensory mode under which it is possible for human beings to directly perceive the presence of souls of *any* category, and then under certain conditions only, is the auditory one."[60] There are many reports, for example, of shaking-tent rituals, where each entry of a spirit through the hole in the top of the tent is indicated to the audience by a whistling sound followed by a loud thud on the floor; his particular identity is then recognized by a special vocal characteristic—the turtle, for instance, speaking in a high squeaky voice. Ghosts are said to use a whistling form of speech, and children are therefore admonished not to whistle.[61] In the Grand Medicine ceremony, immediately prior to the shooting ritual, priests would blow on their medicine bags. As some Ojibwa have described this as "loading the gun," it is clear that the action of blowing is also seen as infusing the bag with spiritual power. Other spiritual sounds that move through the air are the hissing and whistling sounds of the sucking doctor as he attempts to remove the cause of some affliction.

There is reason to believe that animal noises used in songs were also meant to contain spiritual power and thus functioned as a form of supernatural speech. The Ojibwa beliefs concerning the role of dream songs may help explain why animal sounds were incorporated into hunting songs. The Ojibwa goal was the achievement of what was called *bimadisiwin*, which meant a long life free of sickness and bad luck.[62] The most traditional means of obtaining *bimadisiwin* was through the vision quest, embarked upon in boyhood during a fast. Christopher Vecsey points out that during this experience the supplicant was cast in a begging relationship with the spirits:

The Ojibwa youths in vision fasts felt pitiful because they were powerless, talentless, helpless and devoid of permanent identity, as indicated

[60]A. Irving Hallowell, *Culture and Experience* (New York, 1967), p. 180. Although Hallowell's fieldwork was principally among the northern Ojibwa or Saulteaux, his observations are generally also valid for the southwestern Ojibwa, the focus of this paper.

[61]Ibid., p. 158.

[62]Ibid., p. 104.

by their state of hunger. Their ontological emptiness was symbolized by the emptiness of their stomach; they were begging the manitos to fill both voids. They correlated a full belly with self-esteem and sought both food and identity in the same vision quest.[63]

It was said that if a man dreamed well, he would achieve a good life; consequently, one sought through dreams direct contact with the powers controlling the universe. During his vision or dream, the boy also received a song. This dream song subsequently certified to the community that the grown man had a spiritual source of power, while the song itself served its owner, whenever he invoked it, as a means of reenacting a part of the dream and thereby reestablishing his original contract with the spirits.

Hallowell provides an excellent example of how this power contract operates to explain success or failure at hunting. It is believed that every species of game is owned and controlled by a leading or "boss" animal spirit. To hunt well, it is not sufficient simply to have the proper traps or firearms; one must also be on good terms with the boss spirit of the particular animal hunted, in which case he will help you by sending game to your traps or within your shooting range. One must be careful not to offend the boss spirits, which is why we find the Ojibwa apologizing to a bear before killing it. Since all men are presumed to be equal in knowledge of hunting and possession of equipment, and game is evenly distributed throughout the forest, if someone is unlucky in hunting, it is a clear indication that he has somehow offended the boss *manito*, or spirit. A special hunting song communicated in a dream is therefore a powerful means of maintaining favor with the boss spirit and avoiding his displeasure. Possibly, then, by imitating the sound of the animal he hunts, the singer/hunter increases his efforts to pay special tribute to the hunted species, and perhaps even flatters his boss *manito* by using the sounds the spirit uses to communicate with his earthly congeners. The Ojibwa clearly recognize that the sounds of animals, and indeed of all nature, communicate meanings as readily as does human speech. Hallowell recounts the story of a couple once startled by a thunder clap: "What was said?" asked the man, to which his wife replied, "I'm sorry, I didn't catch it."[64]

While begging-dance songs do not appear to be dream-given, Ĕ'ni-wûb'e's story nevertheless explicitly assigns a supernatural origin to the ritual. It should also be evident that, like hunting songs, their intended use is to obtain provisions. Now, while a begging party is said to

[63]Christopher Vecsey, *Traditional Ojibwa Religion and Its Historical Changes,* Memoirs of the American Philosophical Society, no. 152 (Philadelphia, 1983), p. 135.

[64]See A. Irving Hallowell, "Some Empirical Aspects of Northern Saulteaux Religion," *American Anthropologist,* 36 (1934), 389–404.

represent a pack of dogs, there is nothing in the literature describing the dance to indicate that its participants attempt to communicate that representation visibly. They neither dress to look like dogs, nor do they incorporate characteristic canine motions in the dance. The only indications that dogs are represented are the audible messages: the references in the texts of some begging-dance songs and the barking of the singers during a performance.

The best explanation of the barking is that it is a masked form of communication used to accompany a ritual, the begging dance, whose purpose seems clearly to sustain traditional tribal attitudes toward ownership and charity. Such songs became particularly important in the reservation period, when these attitudes were increasingly undermined by the emulation of the social patterns of white entrepreneurs.

The Ojibwa begging dance itself exhibits a form of behavior that is abnormal in Ojibwa culture, although similar behavior is condoned and often institutionalized elsewhere in the world—for example, the Nova Scotian tradition of belsnickling, which in many ways parallels the begging dance.[65] The belsnickles are a group of young men who disguise themselves on Christmas Eve in various anthropomorphic, zoomorphic, and transvestite costumes and move noisily from house to house, blowing horns and ringing bells to request entrance. Unless they are too frightening to the children of the house, they are generally permitted to move into the kitchen, where they perform clumsy dances to a mouth harp or drum. In return for their antics, they receive treats that have been prepared for them in advance, which are taken away and eaten by the group at the end of the evening. While in the kitchen, they ask each child of the house if he has been good all year, rewarding an affirmative answer with candy.

At least superficially, belsnickling and the begging dance have the following features in common: a group of younger males constituting only a small part of the total community organizes at specified times of the year to proceed from one dwelling to the next, where they perform raucously to musical accompaniment in return for gifts of food. While belsnickling traditionally takes place at Christmas, the begging dance occurred principally on two occasions—the maple sugar harvest and the Fourth of July, both of which were times of large social assemblies among the Ojibwa. The Fourth of July—still a large gathering for a powwow—roughly coincided in time with an aboriginal feast called *abita nibin*, or "halfway through the summer." At some point the two events were combined in one celebration, possibly with the encouragement of the federal government.

Because Ojibwa state that the goal of a begging party was to feed the

[65]See Abrahams and Bauman, "Ranges of Festival Behavior," cited in fn. 1.

poor of the tribe, or at least to ridicule stinginess and lack of prepared-
ness to share, the dance functioned symbolically as a means of sustain-
ing the traditional Ojibwa attitude toward ownership, just as the belsnickles helped socialize children by rewarding good behavior with
candy. Due to the severity of the Woodlands climate, the general welfare of the tribe was dependent upon sharing. Misers were despised, and
men who had plenty to eat while others went hungry could be and often
were "starved out" by bad medicine. When some stranger appeared in
an Ojibwa wigwam, he was immediately fed and his other needs cared
for without question. As Kohl noted, "They are almost communists,
and hence there are no rich men among them."[66] The emphasis on giving was so strong that it became celebrated in a number of rites: giving
away the ceremonial dance drum, the gift exchange in the woman's
dance, the requisite distribution of goods in the Grand Medicine initia-
tion. During these and other rituals, special songs were performed to
accompany the act of giving as well as to express thanks for special
gifts, such as ponies and bandoleer bags.

When the Ojibwa were settled on reservations, poverty assumed
new proportions. Their former freedom to hunt, fish, trap, and cultivate
sugar and rice over large areas of land was now restricted, and they were
forced to compete with non-Indians who were licensed by state agen-
cies for many of these activities. Thus, traditional sharing has become
even more important to them. Whereas many other song genres could
be expected to have disappeared, having lost their purpose, the begging
dance, if anything, would assume greater significance, which probably
accounts for its vestigial practice until recent times.

The only feature generally associated with solicitation rituals but
notably absent from the Ojibwa begging dance is the symbolic inversion provided by costumes and masks, which by disguising the individual identities of the participants permits their rude and disorderly behavior as a group. It seems, however, that a singer's barking in the
course of a begging-dance song serves the same purpose, as an audible
rather than visible sort of masking. By resorting to the supernatural
communication represented by animal sounds, the Ojibwa singer momentarily casts himself in the powerful but ambivalent sacred/profane
position of the dog. Thus disguised, he is permitted actions not ordinarily condoned in Ojibwa behavior: to beg, barking and whining like a
lowly dog; or if necessary, as a superhuman agent, to take forcibly from
those who do not conform to traditional modes of Ojibwa sharing.

[66]Kohl, *Kitchi-Gami*, p. 66.

Ambivalent Trecento Attitudes Toward Music: An Iconographical View

HOWARD MAYER BROWN

Music, the ineffable art fit to adorn the most solemn religious ceremonies as well as the sublime science better able than any other to teach medieval university students the rational principles that underlay the workings of the universe, nevertheless aroused negative reactions in some medieval thinkers, who realized its power to charm and to seduce. Saint Augustine's poignant affirmation of music's capacity to lead men's thoughts astray impresses us, especially because of its tone of personal conviction:

> So oft as it befalls me to be more moved with the voice than with the ditty, I confess myself to have grievously offended: at which time I wish rather not to have heard the music. See now in what a state I am! Weep with me, and weep for me, O all you, who inwardly feel any thoughts, whence good actions do proceed.[1]

Moreover, the Church Fathers unanimously and vehemently condemned musical instruments, which were associated in their minds with immorality and with pagan rites, as James McKinnon has pointed out.[2]

Such negative attitudes toward music surface time and again in later societies, especially among those Christian moralists whose prejudices derived from the polemics of the Church Fathers. Even in fourteenth-century Italy, where secular music flourished as never before, and mu-

---

[1]Quoted after the *Confessions* of Saint Augustine in Oliver Strunk, *Source Readings in Music History* (New York, 1950), pp. 74–75.

[2]James McKinnon, "The Meaning of the Patristic Polemic Against Musical Instruments," *Current Musicology* (Spring, 1965), pp 69–82. See also William M. Green, "The Church Fathers and Musical Instruments," *Restoration Quarterly*, 9 (1966), 31–42, a summary of McKinnon's dissertation, "The Church Fathers and Musical Instruments," Columbia University, 1966.

sical instruments could be heard at every court and in every patrician house as well as in less socially respectable places, writers and artists sometimes used music as a symbol for immorality, or at least they acknowledged its power to seduce and flatter the senses. To be sure, music was thought to be a noble and dignified way to pass the time, if it were cultivated with moderation and modesty. The poet and jurist Francesco da Barberino, for example, in his treatise on the education and deportment of women, written early in the century, makes clear that music was considered a desirable social accomplishment.[3] Well-born young ladies could sing (so long as they sang decorous songs softly in the manner he called "camerale"), dance (so long as they danced seemly dances and did not leap about immodestly), and play instruments (so long as they were instruments such as the psaltery, fiddle, and harp—he calls them "mezzo cannone," "viuola," and "arpa"—that were not associated exclusively with professional minstrels).

And some artists seemed to regard music as a worldly pleasure appropriate for the elegant pastimes of the upper classes. At least, I assume that Francesco Traini intended no strongly negative value judgment in his fresco in the Camposanto at Pisa, *The Triumph of Death* (Plate 1), in which he shows a group of wellborn ladies and gentlemen entertaining themselves with a pet dog and a hawk and by telling stories to one another and playing instruments, as they are about to be cut down by the angel of death, who swoops toward them.[4] Almost as though he were illustrating Francesco's treatise, Traini gave to his musical lady a quadruply-strung thirteen-course *mezzo-cannone*, which she is apparently holding with her left hand and playing with a plectrum held in her right hand (so she is presumably performing a single line of melody), while her companion, with his back to the viewer, bows a fiddle. His multicolored cloak and his position, slightly separated from the main group, may suggest that he is in fact a *giullare*. The two musicians seem to be playing together without a singer—the lady standing between them does not in any case appear to have her mouth open—so that we may infer that they are performing either a mono-

[3]See Francesco da Barberino, *Del reggimento e costumi di donna*, ed. Conte Carlo Baudi di Vesme (Bologna, 1875), pp. 30–31 and 52–53, an edition more faithful to the original than that by G. E. Sansone (Turin, 1957). On Francesco's *Reggimento*, see also G. B. Festa, *Un galateo femminile del trecento* (Bari, 1910). On Francesco's treatment of music, see Giuseppe Vecchi, "Educazione musicale, scuola e società nell'opera didascalica di Francesco da Barberino," *Quadrivium*, 7(1966), 5–29. On the life and works of Francesco, see Antoine Thomas, *Francesco da Barberino et la littérature provençale en Italie au moyen age* (Paris, 1883) and Ramiro Ortiz, *Francesco da Barberino e la letteratura didattica neolatina* (Rome, 1948).

[4]On Traini's fresco, see Millard Meiss, *Painting in Florence and Siena After the Black Death* (Princeton, 1951), pp. 74–75 and 171, and the literature cited there.

Plate 1. Francesco Traini. The Triumph of Death. Pisa, Camposanto

phonic instrumental piece or instrumental version of a song (perhaps heterophonically or with some sort of drone) or else a polyphonic piece, perhaps with the fiddle taking the more ornate top line and the psaltery accompanying it with a slower diatonic tenor. It is not obvious that Traini intends us to disapprove of their activities. He merely presents us with an especially vivid *memento mori*. Even in the midst of life we are threatened by death.

But music was also explicitly associated in fourteenth-century Italy with sin and wantonness. Even the bawdy story-teller Boccaccio sounds almost like a Church Father in his treatise on famous women when he equates music with immorality and lust. St. Ephraim's statement that "where kithara playing and dancing and hand clapping find place, there is the beguiling of men, the corruption of women, the sorrow of angels and a feast for the devil"[5] seems almost to be echoed in Boccaccio's claim apropos Sulpicia that "if a woman is to be considered completely chaste . . . she must avoid singing and dancing as arrows of lasciviousness, and attend to temperance and sobriety."[6] Boccaccio passes an even harder judgment on the Roman Sempronia, who "with dancing and singing, which are instruments of sensuality, . . . turned to wantonness. Burning with lust, she discarded all womanly honor and reputation, and to satisfy that lust she sought men more often than they sought her."[7] But Boccaccio's attitude toward music in his chapter on Sempronia is ambivalent and not wholly negative, for he has already described her as a cultivated and elegant woman, who knew Latin and Greek, could write verse, and by her eloquence could affect her audience's behavior; among her virtues, wrote Boccaccio, "she also knew how to sing and dance elegantly, and these skills are perhaps the most commendable in a woman, so long as they are used properly."[8] It was Sempronia's improper use of music, not the fact that she cultivated it, that drew Boccaccio's wrath. This ambivalence toward music distinguished his views from the unrelievedly harsh and austere censures of the early Church Fathers, and characterizes him as a worldly and sophisticated man of the trecento.

Like literary witnesses, some trecento pictures also express either a wholly negative or a somewhat ambivalent attitude towards music. At first sight, the music makers in Andrea da Firenze's famous *Way to Salvation* or *Via Veritatis*, painted between about 1366 and 1368 in the Spanish Chapel at Santa Maria Novella in Florence, seem to be just

[5]Quoted, after McKinnon, in Green, "Church Fathers," pp. 37–38.
[6]Giovanni Boccaccio, *Concerning Famous Women*, trans. Guido A. Guarino (New Brunswick, N.J., 1963), p. 147.
[7]Boccaccio, *Famous Women*, p. 173.
[8]Ibid.

such a dignified group of wellborn ladies and gentlemen entertaining themselves as appeared in Traini's *Triumph of Death*. One of the ladies plays a fiddle, and several groups of smaller (hence more plebeian) girls dance to the sound of the tambourine. There is also a bagpiper, of ambiguous social status.[9] These pleasure seekers, though, appear on the sinister side of Christ, among the heretics and unbelievers; they are not to be associated with the defenders of the Church below Christ's right hand, who stand guard before the image of the cathedral of Florence. The merry-makers have not yet found the redemption of the Church, nor the way to salvation. They are sinners, and Andrea has associated them with music in order to make his message clear.[10]

About the same time Andrea painted his great fresco in Florence, the more modestly talented Andrea da Bologna was asked to decorate the chapel dedicated to Saint Catherine of Alexandria, commissioned by the Spanish Cardinal Egidio Albornoz—Johannes Ciconia's patron—for the lower church of the basilica of Saint Francis in Assisi in 1362, but not completed until five or six years later, after the cardinal had died.[11] Andrea's cycle of frescoes shows the principal scenes in the life of the saint: her conversion to Christianity, her mystical marriage to Christ, her refusal to worship the idol of the Emperor Maxentius, her dispute with the philosophers assembled by the Emperor to discredit her, the

[9]Just what the bagpiper is supposed to be doing Andrea does not make quite clear. On the one hand, his size suggests that he is to be associated with the upper register of wellborn youths; but on the other hand he can hardly be accompanying the fiddler, and he stands on the same level as the dance. Perhaps he is meant to be standing alone, without relating in any way to either of the other two groups.

[10]On Andrea da Firenze's fresco, see Meiss, *Painting in Florence and Siena*, pp. 94–104, and the literature cited there. Meiss offers the interpretation of the musicians as unredeemed sinners on p. 98.

Andrea da Firenze used music again in the 1370s as an exemplification of sinful worldliness in his frescoes for the Camposanto in Pisa, depicting the life of the city's patron, Saint Ranieri. In one fresco, the young saint is shown playing a demi-trapezoidal psaltery—a *mezzo cannone*—with both hands (the right holding a plectrum, the left apparently plucking with the middle finger) while four girls dance in a circle. The instrument, shown with fifteen quadruple courses, is strapped around the saint's neck. A lady standing behind him exhorts him to give up his life of worldliness. The right side of the fresco shows him converted to a holy life by Saint Albert. The section of the fresco showing Saint Ranieri playing dance music is reproduced, among other places, in Mario Bucci and Licia Bertolini, *Camposanto monumentale di Pisa. Affreschi e sinopie* (Pisa, 1960), figs. 58–59 (see also pp. 72–73).

[11]On Andrea da Bologna's fresco, see Francesco Filippini, "Andrea da Bologna miniatore e pittore del XIV secolo," *Bollettino d'arte del Ministero della Pubblica Istruzione*, 5 (1911), 5–50; Raimond van Marle, *The Development of the Italian Schools of Painting*, vol. 4 (The Hague, 1924), pp. 184–86; Emma Zocca, *Catalogo delle cose d'arte e d'antichità d'Italia: Assisi* (Rome, 1936), pp. 41–43; and Francesco Arcangeli, *Natura ed espressione nell'arte Bolognese-Emiliana* (Bologna, 1970), pp. 141–43.

martyrdom of the philosophers, the visit of the Empress Faustina and the soldier Porphyrus to her in prison, the martyrdom of Faustina, the threatened torture of Saint Catherine on the wheel and the punishment of her torturers, and finally, the martyrdom of the saint and the translation of her body to Mount Sinai by angels. By the middle of the fourteenth century some or all of these scenes, with or without other events in her life, had become the traditional way of representing the saint.[12]

The precise way Andrea chose to depict the third of these scenes, Catherine's appearance before the Emperor Maxentius (Plate 2), was highly unusual, however, because of the presence of musicians. The saint is shown with her arms raised, between the Emperor and his idol, while his advisers look on rather fearfully. On the left, two trumpet players suggest the pomp and ceremony of the imperial presence in the temple, and below them people shepherd the various animals brought to be sacrificed. The lower right-hand corner of the picture is almost completely filled by five or six men and women standing in a circle holding hands, and by two instrumentalists. They are evidently temple dancers, performing to the accompaniment of two instruments: a portative organ with 20–25 pipes (apparently flue pipes) and two rows of buttons to serve as a keyboard, strapped (rather inefficiently) to the girl who plays it; and a seven-string (four-course?) fretted gittern, played with a plectrum by a larger, and hence presumably older, minstrel.

The events depicted are spelled out in the caption that runs across the bottom of the picture: "Quomodo beata katerina audiens mugitus animalium et sonitus instrumentorum et timorem indens Christianorum accessit ad templum in quo Maxentius ydole faciebat sacrifiam" ("How Saint Catherine hearing the bellowing of the animals and the sound of instruments causing fear among the Christians approached the temple where Maxentius was making sacrifice to an idol"). The sentence recalls a passage in the story of Saint Catherine as told in the thirteenth-century collection of saints' lives and other legends associated with feast days throughout the church year that served so many artists as a source for their images, The Golden Legend by Jacobus de Voragine. Jacobus, however, wrote that Catherine had heard the sound of singing, and not musical instruments, coming from the temple:

[12]For an overview of images of Saint Catherine in Italian art, see George Kaftal, Iconography of the Saints in Tuscan Painting (Florence, 1952), pp. 226–34; Kaftal, Iconography of the Saints in Central and South Italian Schools of Painting (Florence, 1965), pp. 257–67; and Kaftal, Iconography of the Saints in the Paintings of North East Italy (Florence, 1978), pp. 189–202.

For an overview of images of Saint Catherine in other countries, see Lexikon der christlichen Ikonographie, ed. Wolfgang Braunfels, vol. VII (Rome, 1974), pp. 289–97.

Plate 2. Andrea da Bologna. Saint Catherine before the Emperor Maxentius. Assisi, Basilica of Saint Francis, Lower Church

The time came when the Emperor Maxentius convoked all, rich and poor alike, to Alexandria, to offer sacrifice to the idols; and when the Christians refused to obey him, they were punished. Then Catherine, who at the age of eighteen had been left alone in a palace filled with riches and servants, hearing the roaring of the beasts and the ringing of the chant, sent a messenger to find out speedily what all this might mean. When she learned this, she armed herself with the sign of the cross, took with her some of her household, and went to the scene of the torture, where she saw many Christians driven to offer sacrifice by the fear of death.[13]

In spite of the similarities in wording between the picture's caption and the account in the *Golden Legend*, Andrea's source must have been some other version of Saint Catherine's life, perhaps some variant of the twelfth- or thirteenth-century legend that described Catherine, in the palace of her father, hearing "ex templo idolorum hinc sonus animalium et tibicinum, hinc multimodum genus organorum."[14]

It is perhaps not surprising, therefore, that Andrea's painting, with its circle of temple dancers and accompanying minstrels, remained so isolated in the history of trecento art, since it translates a slightly unfamiliar version of Saint Catherine's life and not that of the *Golden Leg-*

[13]*The Golden Legend of Jacobus de Voragine*, trans. Granger Ryan and Helmut Rippenberger (New York, 1969), p. 709. The original Latin, published in *Legenda aurea*, ed. Johann Georg Theodor Graesse, 3rd ed. (Bratislava, 1890), chap. 172, p. 790, reads:

Cum autem Maxentius imperator omnes tam divites quam pauperes ad Alexandriam convocaret, ut ydolis immolarent, et christianos immolare nolentes punitet, Catherina, cum esset annorum decem et octo et in palatio divitiis et pueris pleno sola remansisset, audiens animalium diversorum mugitus et cantantium plausus misso illuc nuntio inquiri jussit celeriter, quid hoc esset. Quod cum didicisset, assumtis aliquibus de palatio signo crucis se muniens illuc accessit ibique multos christianos metu mortis ad sacrificia duci conspexit.

[14]Quoted in Herman Knust, *Geschichte der Legenden der h. Katharina von Alexandrien und der h. Maria Aegyptiaca nebst unedirten Texten* (Halle a. S., 1890), p. 238, after London, British Library, MS Caligula A. VIII, which contains a twelfth- or thirteenth-century version of the legend of Saint Catherine. Knust also prints a thirteenth-century French translation and a fourteenth-century Spanish translation of the legend. In the French version, Catherine hears "les sons des corneurs et des estrumenz de mout de manieres," and in the Spanish version "las tronpas e los estrumentos."

One of Jacobus de Voragine's principal sources of information was Vincent of Beauvais's encyclopedic *Speculum historiale*, written in the thirteenth century. Vincent, too, wrote only that Catherine heard "tumultus animalium, et vox cantantium" coming from the temple, according to Vincent of Beauvais, *Bibliotheca mundi seu speculi maioribus*, 4 vols. (Douai, 1624), vol. IV, p. 508 (Bk. 13, chap. 5). In the late fifteenth-century collection of the lives of saints, *Sanctuarium seu vitae sanctorum*, comp. Bonino Mombritius (Paris, 1910), vol. I, p. 284, the sacrifices took place with "una canentes cum tybiis et cytharis: et pluribus instrumentis et plaudentibus manibus," and Catherine heard "strepitum tybiis et aliis instrumentis canentium."

end, the text trecento artists would have been most likely to use as a source for their pictures. Andrea's musical scene in the foreground of the painting seems not to have been adopted by later painters, nor does it appear to have been taken from any earlier representations of Catherine before the emperor. I know of only one other obscure trecento painting that makes the same association, and with apparently the same meaning, even though the disposition of the figures within the painting differs radically from Andrea's composition, and the musicians do not play for dancers. Two shutters from a tabernacle painted by an anonymous Umbrian or Abruzzese artist about 1350 or even before, now in the Museo nazionale at L'Aquila in the Abruzzi, show six scenes from the life of Saint Catherine.[15] In the first of the six, the saint again stands between the emperor and his idol (Plate 3). But here the musicians are all gathered on the balcony. To the left of the four trumpeters stand a gittern player and a fiddler; and to their right appears a more heterogeneous collection of instrumentalists, minstrels playing pipe and tabor, tambourine and shawm.

Music at the temple of Maxentius can only be understood as representing the vanity and idleness of the heathens, who passed their days in dancing and sacrificing to idols rather than in doing good works and worshiping the one true God. Like the Church Fathers, Andrea da Bologna and the anonymous painter both associated musical instruments with pagan worship, and the presence of music makes the painters' moral judgment vivid and compelling.

Catherine is much more often seen in trecento paintings with the Christians kneeling at her feet, with no musical instruments present, as in the version painted by Altichiero da Zevio for the Oratorio di S. Giorgio in Padua.[16] Since neither Andrea da Bologna nor the anonymous painter seems to have been following a fixed convention, and since neither borrows from the other the disposition of the musicians, the nature of the musical ensembles, or the composition of the picture as a whole, I can only surmise that the pictures might actually reflect social reality—not, to be sure, the music in heathen temples in

[15]Described and reproduced in Mario Moretti, *Museo nazionale d'Abruzzo nel castello cinquecentesco dell'Aquila* (L'Aquila, 1968), p. 27.

Music does appear occasionally in St. Catherine cycles, but, so far as I know, no other painting shows so varied a collection of instruments. One scene of St. Catherine refusing to worship idols, which Spinello Aretino painted in the 1390s for the Oratorio di Santa Caterina in Antella (near Florence), shows merely two men playing trumpets, the conventional accompaniment to a royal or imperial presence. Spinello's fresco is described and a brief bibliography of references to it given in Miklòs Boskovits, *Pittura fiorentina alla vigilia del Rinascimento, 1370–1400* (Florence, 1975), p. 436.

[16]Reproduced in Gian Lorenzo Mellini, *Altichiero e Jacopo Avanzi* (Milan, 1965), fig. 179.

Plate 3. Anonymous Umbrian or Abruzzese Painter. Saint Catherine
before the Emperor Maxentius. L'Aquila, Museo nazionale d'Abruzzo

fourteenth-century Italy, but rather, through association with the Emperor Maxentius, the sort of musicians and musical ensembles that could have been seen and heard at a prince's court at that time. The artists quite possibly give us some graphic impression of a courtly musical establishment, or at least what they imagined such an establishment to be.[17] To be precise, it seems to me reasonable to suppose that a

[17]The testimony of Andrea da Bologna's fresco and the anonymous panel painting in L'Aquila is not contradicted—it is even supported—by other kinds of evidence about the instruments heard at trecento courts. To cite but two early fourteenth-century literary examples, both the allegorical poem *L'Intelligenza*, sometimes attributed to Dino Compagni, and the onomatopoeic poem by the *giullare* Immanuel Romano beginning "Del mondo ho cercato" cite similar groups of instruments in use at court.

The anonymous author of *L'Intelligenza* comes upon a room in the palace he is describing, filled with people singing and playing musical instruments "Di nuove cose ch'i'non vidi mai,/Si come a grande corte si pertiene." His list of instruments is more extensive than the representative samples shown in the pictures. Among stringed instruments, he mentions harp, fiddle ("viuola"), the mysterious "gighe," hurdy-gurdies ("ciunfonie"), gitterns ("chitarre"), various kinds of psaltery ("cannon," "mezzi cannon" and "salter"), lute, rebec ("ribebe"), and possibly citole ("ceterare"). And among wind instruments he mentions organ (presumably portative organ, but possibly positive organ, since the lady playing the instrument may be producing more than one melodic line: "Qui v'era una donzella c'organava/Ismisurate dolzi melodie,/Colle squillanti boci che sonava,/Angelicali, e dilettose, e pie"), trumpets, shawms ("cennamelle"), pipes and tabors ("sufoli, con tambur bene accordanti"), and bagpipes (if that in fact is what "otricelli" are). The "cembali alamanni" he also mentions may well be tambourines. The anonymous author does not make clear how these instruments are used or for what repertory. Apparently he heard singing, possibly even in polyphony ("E audivi dolzi boci e concordanti,/E nobili stormenti e ben sonanti"). The lady playing harp was singing to it a *lai* (presumably monophonic) on the death of Tristan. The gitterns were playing dances and "caribi" (presumably dancing songs). And the shawms, or trumpets and shawms, may also have been engaged in polyphony ("E trombe, e cennamelle in concordanze"). The complete poem is printed in Dino Compagni, *La cronaca fiorentina . . . e L'Intelligenza*, ed. Domenico Carbone (Florence, 1871); the passage on music appears on pp. 196–97.

Immanuel Romano's bizarre rhymed account of life at the opulent court of Can Grande della Scala, to which the poet was attached after 1312, describes the wonderful hubbub there: the crowds of fascinating foreigners, the life of busy activity, the hunting parties, the soldiers, the exotic animals kept as curiosities, and the stimulating debates about astrology, philosophy, and theology. Not least, he exclaims over the musical instruments: not only the ubiquitous trumpets and drums, necessary accoutrements, as we have seen, to embellish the ceremonial occasions in every aristocratic household, but also the voices and instruments that accompanied the more elaborate courtly music, gitterns and lutes and fiddles and flutes ("Chitarre e liuti/viole e flatùi/voci alt'ed acute,/qui s'odon cantare"), as he writes. And for good measure, he adds his version of how they sounded: the trumpets ("Tatim tatatim" or "Bobò bobobò"), the drums ("Dudu dududu . . . sentirai naccherare"), the lutes ("Tatam tatatam . . . gli liuti tubare"), the pipes and tabors ("Stututù ifiù . . . tamburar, suffolare") and the dancers ("Intarlatitim . . . ghirbare e danzare"). Immanuel's *Bisbidis* is printed, among other places, in Maurizio Vitale, ed., *Rimatori comico-realistici del Due e Trecento*, 2 vols. (Turin, 1956), vol. II, pp. 103–12.

gittern and organetto could have played together in the performance of
a fourteenth-century Italian courtly dance, and that Italian fourteenth-
century courtiers could have heard, besides the ubiquitous ceremonial
trumpets, combinations of fiddle and gittern, as well as players of the
pipe and tabor, the tambourine, and the shawn, playing either singly or
just possibly in some combination. In short, in translating the texts of
old legends into modern terms, these painters focused their disapproval
of courtly behavior on music and musicians and gave us thereby invaluable evidence of what one segment of life in fourteenth-century Italy
was really like.

The relationship between image and reality is equally indirect but
also compelling in another trecento picture that associates music with
behavior unacceptable to pious God-fearing Christians, an illuminated
page from an incomplete treatise on the vices, written by a member of
the Cocharelli family of Genoa, now in the British Library (Plate 4).[18]
The artist, presumably the otherwise unknown Genoese miniaturist
Cybo, the monk of Hyères, has dulled the picture's reality but sharpened its meaning by offering so obviously a racist point of view. The
page shows a Tartar Khan guzzling food, surrounded by his servants, his
dogs, and his musicians.

In the bottom register, the conventional trumpets and drums proclaim the Khan's authority. The piquant detail that a blackamoor carries the nakers around his neck and at the same time plays cymbals
may or may not be merely an exotic Oriental effect, but certainly the
positive organ offers rare evidence of the nature of that instrument in
fourteenth-century Italy and even rarer testimony of its association
with secular music-making. The top register, with its heterogeneous
group of trumpet, psaltery, and fiddle, may only serve as ornamental
heading to the whole page—as a kind of title—or it may extend the
courtly music makers from the immediate environs of the ruler, who
was entertained, then, both by a pair of courtly *giullari* playing double
recorder and fiddle and by a pair playing psaltery and fiddle.

A few other musical instruments appear in the manuscript. On folio

---

[18]London, British Library, MS Add. 27695, fol. 13. The page is reproduced in E. A.
Bond and E. M. Thompson, *Facsimiles of Manuscripts and Inscriptions*, 1st ser., vol. II
(London: Paleographical Society, 1873–83), Pls. 149–50. On this manuscript and other
manuscripts in the British Library by Cybo, see also R. Flower, "Two Leaves from the
Book of 'The Monk of Hyères,' " *British Museum Quarterly*, 8 (1934), 128–30; Otto
Pächt, "Early Italian Nature Studies," *Journal of the Warburg and Courtauld Institutes*, 13 (1950), 13–47 and esp. 20–22; and A. C. Crombie, "Cybo d'Hyères: a
fourteenth-century zoological artist," *Endeavour*, 11 (1952), 183–87. According to Pietro Toesca, *La pittura e la miniatura nella Lombardia* (Milan, 1912), p. 411, the page
illustrating gluttony was not painted by the artist responsible for the other pages in the
manuscript.

Plate 4. Cybo of Hyères. ? The Sin of Gluttony. London, British Library, MS Add. 27695, fol. 13

1^v a tiny angel plays the trumpet within Christ's mandorla while a crowd of fallen angels plummets downward toward Hell's mouth. The margins of several folios are decorated with indistinct figures of ambiguous nationality, although most of them seem to be Oriental. The marginalia have been so worn away by the ravages of time—or perhaps they were never very clearly drawn—that one can scarcely make out what the figures are doing; but some of them are clearly making music. In one roundel near the top of folio 2, a hooded figure certainly plays a fiddle or, more likely, a rebec. On folio 4 (Plate 5), two clearly Oriental grotesques, half men and half animals, play non-Western instruments: a three-stringed long-necked fiddle and a pair of cymbals. And on folio 4^v (Plate 6), a European plays a fiddle. These pictures, especially those on folio 4, must be among the earliest European witnesses to contemporary musical practices outside Europe. The presence of these non-Western instruments may merely testify to the active trade Genoa had with the Orient. Certainly, the pictures reinforce our impressions that this enigmatic artist had some knowledge of Oriental miniature paintings, as Otto Pächt has pointed out. And the images of long-necked Eastern fiddles and cymbals surely affect our assessment of how well the full-page illumination of the Tartar Khan reflects specifically Italian practices. However, since most of the minstrels at the Khan's court look European; since the artist did not include any unambiguously Oriental instruments, even though we know he knew what they looked like; and, perhaps most important, since there seems to be no well-established artistic tradition in the trecento for representing the sin of Gluttony, the artist may well have painted the scene from real life, or, more probably, from his fantasies about the style of life enjoyed at an Italian court, the nationality of the main protagonist notwithstanding.

The page illustrates the sin of Gluttony, as its heading (not visible in the reproduction) attests: "Capitulum VI. De Gula." The fragments of the treatise that survive make no mention of music.[19] But the meaning of the picture is nevertheless clear: it could as easily be seen as an illustration of the better-known treatise on vices and virtues by the late thirteenth-century Florentine Bono Giamboni, who describes in one passage the differences between a good meal (when you satisfy the needs of your body), a bad meal (when you gorge yourself with unnecessary luxuries), and a perfect meal (when you nourish your soul with spiritual happiness).[20] The luxurious banquet is bad not only because

[19]It is not listed in Morton W. Bloomfield, "A Preliminary List of Incipits of Latin Works on the Virtues and Vices, Mainly of the Thirteenth, Fourteenth, and Fifteenth Centuries," *Traditio*, 11 (1955), 259–379.

[20]The chapter on the bad meal ("De la cena rea") appears in Bono Giamboni, *Il libro de'vizî e delle virtudi e il trattato di virtù e di vizî*, ed. Cesare Segre (Turin, 1968), pp.

Plate 5. Cybo of Hyères. Marginalia. London, British Library, MS Add. 27695, fol. 4

Plate 6. Cybo of Hyères. Marginalia. London, British Library, MS Add. 27695, fol. 4ᵛ

the quantity and variety of food exceed one's needs, but also because on such occasions tongues are unbridled, people tell lies and scoff, women are loose, and there are songs and the sounds of instruments. The attitudes that inspired Giambono's strictures against high living and excessive consumption; Cybo's emphasis on the musical accompaniment to the sin of Gluttony; and even Cybo's implication that it is especially heathen foreigners who indulge in such excesses, can all be found as well in the writings of the early Church Fathers. McKinnon quotes Clement of Alexandria, for example, from a chapter on how to conduct oneself at banquets:

> If people spend their time with auloi, psalteria, dancing, and leaping, clapping hands like Egyptians, and in other similar dissolute activities, they become altogether immodest and unrestrained, senselessly beating on cymbals and drums, and making noise on all the instruments of deception.[21]

Cybo's gluttonous Khan seems designed to provoke the same sharp rejection of the pleasures of this world that we find in the early Church Fathers and in such trecento pictures as Andrea da Firenze's *Way to Salvation* and Andrea da Bologna's view of Saint Catherine before the Emperor Maxentius.

The last set of trecento pictures on which I should like to comment—the illustrations for Francesco da Barberino's curious didactic and allegorical poem *I Documenti d'amore*—expresses an altogether more complex and more truly ambivalent attitude toward secular music. *I Documenti* dates from the first decades of the fourteenth century. Most of it was written between 1309 and 1314, but Francesco may have begun work on it as early as 1296, and he may not have finished the elaborate Latin gloss on the original Italian poem until about 1325.[22] In it Love presents to Eloquence a lengthy series of moral

---

41–43. The passage that mentions music reads: "Anche è ria, perché quivi la lingua isfrenatamente favella; quivi si dicono bugie e parole di scherne; quivi ha canti e stormenti; quivi sono le femine di sozze cose richieste, e sono spesso volte concedute; quivi hae ogni cosa disfrenata."

[21]Quoted in McKinnon, "The Meaning of the Patristic Polemic," p. 71.

[22]The complete poem and its Latin gloss are published in *I Documenti d'amore di Francesco da Barberino secondo i manoscritti originali*, ed. Francesco Egidi, 4 vols. (Rome, 1922–27). On the *Documenti*, see also Thomas, *Francesco . . . et la littérature provençale*, pp. 51–66. For a more extensive treatment of music in the *Documenti*, see Vecchi, "Educazione musicale." Francesco's own drawings in the Vatican Library, MS Barb. lat. 4077, and the copies in MS Barb. lat. 4076 are explained and reproduced in Francesco Egidi, "Le miniature dei codici Barberiniani dei 'Documenti d'Amore,' " *L'Arte*, 5 (1902), 1–20 and 78–95; and in Bernhard Degenhart and Annegrit Schmitt, *Corpus der italienischen Zeichnungen, 1300–1450*. Part I: *Süd- und Mittelitalien*, 3 vols. (Berlin, 1968), vol. I, part 1, pp. 31–38, Catalogue no. 13, and vol. I, part 3, fig. 30.

and philosophical statements about twelve ladies who personify aspects of love: Docilità, Industria, Discrezione, Pazienza, Speranza, Prudenza, and so on.

Music figures only in the third section of *I Documenti,* on Constanza or Constantia, Constancy or Fidelity.[23] Like the other personifications, Constanza is pictured at the beginning of the section devoted to her. In the manuscript copy now in the Vatican Library as MS Barb. lat. 4077, a copy presumably prepared by Francesco himself and decorated with his own drawings, Constanza is shown surrounded by personifications of four qualities that might lead her astray (Plate 7).[24] Francesco has labeled each figure and he explains briefly in his poem and its gloss who they are. Constanza herself (labeled "constantia") holds a book in which we can read "in vanum laborant qui querunt mentem meam" ("they labor in vain who seek my mind"). She is assailed by *corruptor* (corrupter or briber), who offers her an apron full of coins (the poem, though, explains that she can be bribed either by money or by power); *superbus* (arrogance or pride), who stands on the left side of the picture threatening her with a sword; *consanguinea* (consanguinity or, perhaps better, sisterliness), who kneels at her feet and is explained in the poem as "disordered benevolence" ("non ben ordinata benvogliença"); and, finally, by *blanditor* (flatterer or tempter), who stands behind her playing a gittern.

Without Francesco's labels it might not have been so easy to associate each of the figures with their correct attributes, even though they are explained in the poem and the gloss. When *I Documenti* was recopied, for example, into Vatican Library, MS Barb. lat. 4076, the same characters appear, painted by a professional artist, but no identifying tag helps us associate each individual with the attributes explained in the poem (Plate 8). And without knowing of the existence of this picture, with its elaborate explanation, we might be puzzled about the true meaning of one of the illustrations in one of the early copies of the encyclopedic work *Il Tesoro* by Francesco's friend Brunetto Latini. Book VI of *Il Tesoro* deals with virtue, including *constanza.* But notwithstanding the fact that Latini explains *constanza* in terms completely different from those used by Francesco, the chapter is illustrated with virtually the same miniature as that in the copies of *I Documenti d'Amore* (Plate 9).[25] The four figures surrounding Constanza are not identified at

[23]On Constantia, see *Documenti,* ed. Egidi, vol. 2, pp. 303–46.

[24]Vatican Library, MS Barb. lat. 4077, fol. 46, and MS Barb. lat. 4076, fol. 57, reproduced in Egidi, "Le miniature," p. 14, and discussed there, pp. 78–81. See also Degenhart and Schmitt, *Corpus,* vol. I, part 1, pp. 31–38, and vol. I, part 3, fig. 30.

[25]The miniature appears in Florence, Biblioteca Medicea Laurenziana, MS Plut. 42.19, fol. 47ᵛ. It is reproduced in Richard Offner, *A Critical and Historical Corpus of*

Plate 7. Francesco da Barberino. Constanza, from I Documenti d'A-more. Vatican Library, MS Barb lat. 4077, fol. 46

Plate 8. Anonymous illuminator. Constanza, from Francesco da Barberino, *I Documenti d'Amore*. Vatican Library, MS Barb. lat. 4076, fol. 57

all in Latini's manuscript. Thus the only way to know who they are is to have previous knowledge of Francesco's poem.

But what, in fact, is the true meaning of the gittern player standing behind Constanza? What resonance would such a picture have in the mind of a trecento reader? And why should temptation appear specifically in the form of a single gittern player? Part of the answer to these questions has, of course, already been given, for we have seen that music—at least secular music with instruments—appears in various

Florentine Painting, Section 3, vol. VI (New York, 1957), Plate 1, as the work of the Biadaiolo Illuminator. See also Degenhart and Schmitt, *Corpus*, vol. I, part 1: Catalogue no. 15. The miniature illustrates the chapter "Della constanza" printed in *Il Tesoro di Brunetto Latini volgarizzato da Bono Giamboni raffrontato col testo autentico francese*, ed. P. Chabaille and Luigi Gaiter, 3 vols. (Bologna, 1878–80), vol. III, pp. 127–29.

trecento pictures as the exemplification of the pleasure-loving, sinful life of the upper classes castigated by Christian moralists. A single musician, then, effectively conveyed the notion *blanditor* to Francesco's readers, or rather a single musician of a kind regularly employed as a minstrel to sing and play for the entertainment of the wellborn; for we have already seen that Francesco himself approved of the cultivation of music and dancing, so long as it were done with modesty, and so long as the ladies did not play instruments associated with *giullari.*

Francesco's objection to playing minstrels' instruments reflects an upper-class or genteel contempt for professional musicians, different from the Christian moralists' strong stand against lascivious secular music in general and instrumental music in particular. Prejudices against *giullari* surface from time to time in late medieval literature. A clear example of such disdain appears, for instance, at the very beginning of Andrea da Barberino's novel *L'Aspramonte*, in which the minstrels employed by various princes fight among themselves about who is the greatest lord in the world. Andrea scathingly points out that envy and hatred are characteristic of these *buffoni*, who have little *virtù*, "buffoons without learning, trumpet players, drummers and other persons who torture themselves in order to earn money, such as acrobats and string players, rope walkers and shawmists. And you will know that all the above-named sorts of people have more envy and hatred than other sorts of people, and are usually distinguished by three qualities: irreverence, wantonness, and gambling."[26]

That gittern players could be associated with this professional class seems clear from the career of a man like Cenne de la Chitarra, from his name apparently a performer who specialized on the instrument.[27] His rude, satirical sonnets, parodying the *dolce stil nuovo* of Folgore di San Gimignano, give us some insight into the literary interests—and the very real literary accomplishments—of one member of this disreputable group of entertainers. And trecento paintings suggest that gittern players were almost invariably minstrels, as, indeed, we have already

[26]Andrea da Barberino, *L'Aspramonte*, ed. Luigi Cavalli (Naples, 1972), p. 39. The passage reads in Italian: "e questi sono buffoni senza scienza, trombetti, tamburini e altre persone che loro straziano per guadagnare, come giocolari di mano e alla corda, cioè al canapo, e pifferi. E poni mente che tutta questa spezie di gente sottosopra hanno più invidia e odio che altra spezie di gente e hanno tre cose per consuetudine: bocca, lussuria e dado."

For a similar statement about fourteenth-century German minstrels, condemning those who use their ability for financial gain, see Christopher Page, "German Musicians and their Instruments: A 14th-century Account by Konrad of Megenberg," *Early Music*, 10 (1982), 192–200, and esp. 195.

[27]His career is summarized and some of his poems printed in Vitale, *Rimatori comico-realistici*, vol. II, pp. 173–96.

Plate 9. Anonymous illuminator. Constanza, from Brunetto Latini, *Il Tesoro*. Florence, Biblioteca Medicea Laurenziana, MS Plut. 42.19, fol. 47ᵛ

seen in Andrea da Bologna's representation of Saint Catherine before the Emperor Maxentius. Surely it was a minstrel who accompanied Salome's dance at the court of Herod. While most trecento paintings show Salome dancing to the sound of a single fiddle, the fresco of the Feast of Herod, attributed to Taddeo Gaddi or his assistants, in the chapel of the Castle of Poppi near Casentino supplies her with a gittern player as accompanist, identified as a minstrel by his particolored costume.[28] Orpheus, who was, after all, a professional musician, sang to the gittern before the court of Hell, according to a fourteenth-century Italian copy of Seneca's tragedies now in the Biblioteca governativa in Naples.[29] And gittern and double recorder formed an instrumental duo, contrasted with a vocal trio, at court when St. Martin was knighted by the emperor, according to the well-known fresco of Simone Martini in the lower church of the Basilica of St. Francis in Assisi.[30]

Perhaps the best example for our purposes of the professional trecento gittern player appears in a fresco in the Sanctuary of the Madonna di Ghirli near the small town of Campione in northern Italy. Signed by the little-known Milanese painter Franco de Veris and by his son Filippolo, and dated 1400, the painting contrasts the joys of the blessed and the torments of the damned at the Last Judgment, one of the subjects most often treated by medieval and early Renaissance painters. One of the most charming and unexpected details of the painting is shown in Plate 10.[31] A wonderfully supercilious and elegant young trecento dandy evidently sings to his lady love, for he is accompanied on the git-

---

[28]The fresco is briefly discussed in Osvald Sirén, *Giotto and Some of His Followers,* 2 vols. (Cambridge, Mass., 1917), vol. I, p. 156, and reproduced there, vol. II, Pl. 137.

At least two other trecento pictures show a single instrumentalist, possibly playing a gittern, entertaining at banquets: a Feast of Herod in the Contini Bonacossi Collection of the Palazzo Pitti, Florence, by Giovanni del Biondo, reproduced, among other places, in Richard Offner, *A Critical and Historical Corpus of Florentine Painting,* 16 vols. (New York, 1930–81), vol. IV, no. 4, pp. 112–14, Pls. 25 and 25⁹, and in *Gli Uffizi. Catalogo generale* (Florence, 1979), p. 303 (fig. 753); and a Feast of Ahasuerus, in Paris, Bibliothèque de l'Arsenal, MS 593, reproduced in Bernard Berenson, "Due illustratori italiani dello Speculum Humanae Salvationis," *Bollettino d'arte* (1926), p. 50 (fig. 50). In both pictures, the neck of the instrument is not shown, so the artists have left unclear whether they intended to depict a gittern or a lute.

[29]Naples, Biblioteca governativa dei Gerolamini, Codice CF 4.5. The picture is reproduced in Flavio Testi, *La musica italiana nel medioevo e nel rinascimento,* 2 vols. (Milan, 1969), vol. I, p. 147.

[30]Reproduced, among other places, in Georg Kinsky, *Album musical* (Paris, 1930), Pl. 50/2; Karl Michael Komma, *Musikgeschichte in Bildern* (Stuttgart, 1961), Pl. 123; Giovanni Paccagnini, *Simone Martini* (Milan, 1955), Pl. 24 and fig. 61; Enzo Carli, *Sienese Painting* (Greenwich, Conn., 1956), Pls. 28 and 32; and Curt H. Weigelt, *Sienese Painting of the Trecento* (Florence, 1930; repr. New York, 1974), Pls. 51 and 52.

[31]Described and reproduced in Stella Matalon and Franco Mazzini, *Affreschi del Trecento e Quattrocento in Lombardia* (Milan, 1958), no. 7, fig. 56. See also Francesco

Plate 10. Franco and Filippolo de' Veris. Detail from The Last Judgment.
Campione, Sanctuario della Madonna dei Ghirli

tern by his rather older and less attractive *giullare*. The painting belongs to the tradition that condemned high living, as exemplified by singing wanton love songs and playing musical instruments. The courtly scene appears on Christ's left-hand side, along with the damned, and the consequence of the young man's actions is visible in the fresco, to the right of the detail shown in the reproduction: the young man lies dead, and his lady love laments over his body.

In short, Francesco da Barberino's gittern player, seen in Plate 7, representing *blanditor* attempting to lead Constanza astray, might well be labeled "Temptation in the Form of a Professional Musician." But what is especially fascinating about Francesco's attitude toward music concerns the only other musical illustration in *I Documenti d'Amore*, which appears at the end of the section on Constanza. It shows her being taken up into heaven by angels, where she is received by Christ and the Virgin Mary. In Francesco's own drawing she is accompanied by three angels playing tambourine (or small frame drum), psaltery, and gittern (Plate 11); and in the professional reworking of Francesco's

---

Malaguzzi Valeri, "Campione," *Rassegna d'arte*, 8 (1908), 167–74 (the dead singer and his despairing lady are reproduced on p. 169).

The pictures cited here and in notes 28–30 are typical in showing the gittern in the hands of minstrels; it was evidently one of the instruments, then, that Francesco da Barberino would have said well-bred ladies should not play. Nevertheless, a few bits of evidence suggest that the rich and the noble did sometimes play the gittern in the fourteenth and fifteenth centuries. In the romance *Meliadus*, written in French by Rustichello da Pisa, the king Meliadus in one episode writes a *lai* for the queen of Scotland, with whom he is in love. It is sung to the harp at King Arthur's court, in the queen's presence, by an associate of Meliadus, a knight. The episode is summarized in E. Löseth, *Le roman en prose de Tristan, le roman de Palamède et la compilation de Rusticien de Pise* (Paris, 1891), pp. 444–45. The "harpeor" is illustrated in London, British Library, MS Add. 12228, fol. 223, a manuscript written and illuminated in Naples in the 1350s or 1360s, by a man playing a gittern at court. The miniature is reproduced in Roger Sherman Loomis, *Arthurian Legends in Medieval Art* (London, 1938), fig. 309.

In the fifteenth century, Leonello d'Este, marchese of Ferrara, knew how to play the *chitarino*, doubtless the gittern, according to Lewis Lockwood, "Pietrobono and the Instrumental Tradition at Ferrara in the Fifteenth Century," *Rivista italiana di musicologia*, 10 (1975), 118. Pietrobono (who was normally described in documents as "Pietrobono del chitarino") taught the *chitarino* to a Venetian nobleman, Hieronymus Bondi, in 1465 (or, rather, he was engaged to teach Bondi to play seven songs on the *chitarino*), according to a contract printed in Enrico Peverada, "Vita musicale nella cattedrale di Ferrara nel quattrocento," *Rivista italiana di musicologia*, 15 (1980), 6. For a more extensive consideration of Pietrobono as gittern player, and some discussion of the playing technique and repertory of the gittern, see my forthcoming essay "St. Augustine, Lady Music and the Gittern in Fourteenth-Century Italy." On the gittern in general, see Laurence Wright, "The Medieval Gittern and Citole: A case of mistaken identity," *The Galpin Society Journal*, 30 (1977), 8–42. Wright established the current term for the small lute that used to be called in musicological literature the "mandora."

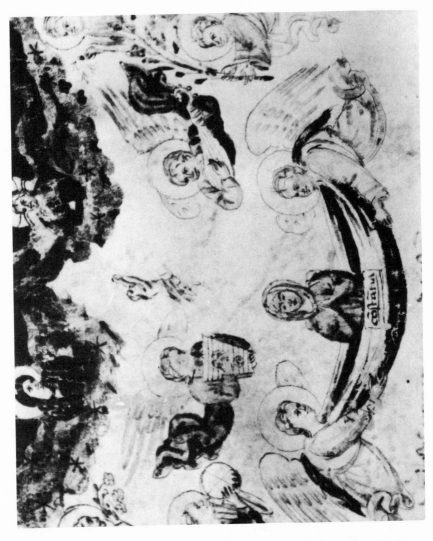

Plate 11. Francesco da Barberino. The Ascent of Constanza to Heaven, from *I Documenti d'Amore*. Vatican Library, MS Barb. lat. 4077, fol. 49

drawing, angels play the same three instruments plus a shawm or a recorder (Plate 12).[32] The instrument that represented *blanditor* on earth
is nevertheless worthy of accompanying Constanza on her assumption
into heaven. Music, Francesco seems to be telling us, is not altogether a
wicked thing, but only when it is misused.

Some trecento artists, in other words, had a more ambivalent attitude toward music than others. Andrea da Firenze, Andrea da Bologna,
Cybo of Hyères, and Franco and Filippolo de'Veris offer sharply negative views of the wantonness of secular music. It is not clear that Francesco Traini intended a negative value judgment about his aristocratic
young pleasure seekers, and Francesco da Barberino offers the same
mixed point of view as Boccaccio.

Cybo painted his gluttonous Khan late in the century, presumably
quite some time after 1368, when Andrea da Bologna was commissioned to produce his cycle of the life of Saint Catherine. That year was
also about the time Andrea da Firenze completed his *Way to Salvation,*
created under the direct impact of the plague that had decimated Italy.
But before we jump to the conclusion that these three pictures signal a
widespread rejection of music as a result of the feelings of guilt, penance, and religious rapture that swept the country after the plague,[33] we
should remember that the genre of treatises on vices and virtues existed
long before the onslaught of the plague, and that the second half of the
century witnessed a significant increase in the amount of secular polyphony being written, and even in the introduction of new genres—or
at least newly elaborated older genres—such as the polyphonic ballata.
It seems more reasonable to suppose that artists (and presumably also

---

[32]Vatican Library, MS Barb. lat. 4077, fol. 49, and MS Barb. lat. 4076, fol. 60. The
illustrations are reproduced in Egidi, "Le miniature," p. 15, and discussed there, pp.
78–81. See also Degenhart and Schmitt, *Corpus,* vol. I, part 1, pp. 31–38.

The instrument on the extreme right in MS Barb. lat. 4076 certainly looks like a
recorder rather than a shawm, although it is very difficult to tell the difference between
the two instruments, especially in so sketchy an artistic style. If it is a recorder, it is one
of the very few pictures of the instrument from fourteenth-century Italy, and all the
more remarkable for appearing so early in the century, albeit illustrating a work written by a man who had spent considerable time in France.

When the author of *I Documenti* asks the angels what happened in Paradise after
Constanza arrived, one of them responds with a poem in three stanzas, explaining that
everyone at the heavenly court greeted her with song ("di canti"). Francesco may have
intended that the angel sing her answer ("respondit" could as easily mean "responded
in song" as "responded by speaking"), but even so, it seems unlikely that the angel's
answer can have been accompanied by the instruments shown in the illustration. They
play while Constanza ascends; and in any case, the angel does not frame her reply in the
form of a madrigal or a ballata, the two poetic forms most closely associated with music. The entire poem is given in Egidi, "Le miniature," p. 80.

[33]See Meiss, *Painting in Florence and Siena,* pp. 74–94; his chapter on Andrea da
Firenze's fresco is called "Guilt, Penance, and Religious Rapture."

Plate 12. Anonymous illuminator. The Ascent of Constanza to Heaven, from Francesco da Barberino, *I Documenti d'Amore*. Vatican Library, MS Barb. lat. 4076, fol. 60

writers and thinkers) in the second half of the century reacted to the troubled times in extreme ways. Christian moralists rejected sharply the pleasure-loving life of the upper classes, while some musicians evidently found a new impetus for the continued and even expanded exploration of the possibilities of polyphony.

The more ambivalent attitudes toward music expressed by Francesco da Barberino, Boccaccio, and Traini (whose *Triumph of Death* may well have been painted about 1350, possibly under the impact of an epidemic that preceded the Black Death) may then reflect a slightly happier or more confident time in Italy, before the onslaught of the plague.[34] Or it may only be that Christian moralists always strongly condemned what seemed to them the wantonness of courtly behavior, whereas the more sophisticated men of the world, such as Boccaccio and Francesco da Barberino, understood, like St. Augustine, the very real pleasures of music as well as its power to seduce the senses.

Whatever the truth, these few pictures not only expand our view of what fourteenth-century Italians thought about the proliferation of secular music they heard around them, but also offer valuable information about trecento performance practice. Whereas Francesco da Barberino's angels may no more reflect social reality than the angels who can be seen in countless pictures of the period offering songs of praise to the Virgin Mary, the gittern-playing *blanditor* apparently shows us a figure familiar to trecento courtiers; and the combinations of instruments portrayed by Traini, Andrea da Firenze, Andrea da Bologna, and Cybo of Hyères may well have been those actually played by upper-class or courtly musicians, professional and amateur, for their own amusement or for the entertainment of others.

---

[34]Several paintings come to mind that demonstrate the more positive attitude toward music and dancing earlier in the century. I think immediately of Ambrogio Lorenzetti's *The Effects of Good Government* in Siena, Palazzo pubblico, reproduced, among other places, in George Rowley, *Ambrogio Lorenzetti*, 2 vols. (Princeton, N.J., 1958), vol. I, Pl. VII (in color) and vol. II, Pl. 157, in which girls—ordinary citizens rather than members of the power elite—dance in the streets (to a dancing song, possibly a ballata but more likely some sort of *canzone a ballo*, sung by one girl playing the tambourine). Obviously, dancing in the streets is here intended to be a good thing, one of the positive effects of living under a good government. And Giotto's series of vices and virtues (now badly eroded) in the Arena chapel in Padua includes a figure of Justice with a painted frieze below her showing people hunting, riding horseback, and dancing (a couple dances to the song sung by a woman playing a tambourine). The three groups demonstrate "the benefits of life under Justice and contrast vividly with the scene of rape and robbery under the figure of Injustice" (James H. Stubblebine, ed., *Giotto: The Arena Chapel Frescoes* [New York, 1969], p. 89; the two figures are reproduced there, figs. 62 and 63).

Early Democratic Song and the Representation of an American Arcadia

NICHOLAS E. TAWA

T HIRTY-THREE YEARS OF SOCIAL, ECONOMIC, and political turmoil began in 1828 when Andrew Jackson, after his election to the presidency of the United States, set upon an upper class whose strengthening prerogatives threatened to undermine the rights of ordinary citizens. The militant promotion of majority rule and the destruction of aristocratic privilege became principal tenets of Jacksonism. Monetary crisis and economic depression accompanied the activation of the policy. In addition, this era, which would terminate with the Civil War, saw the rapid increase of tensions over other issues such as slavery, industrialization, large-scale immigration, and the incessant movement of rural Americans westward or into the burgeoning cities. A sense of anomie afflicted the thousands of men and women passing through or living in alien surroundings. Without their former support system of tradition and neighborliness, they felt disoriented, uneasy, and isolated. They wondered if human existence could have meaning, given the utter confusion and the contrariety of the times.[1]

The serious popular song of the antebellum period, even as it mirrored its confusion and exposed its polarizations, helped resolve people's anxieties. It explained them to be necessary concomitants of a fully explored life. It placed them within a philosophic structure that delineated Everyman's spiritual passage from the innocence of childhood through the conflicts of adulthood to the recovery of happiness and serenity in death. The themes were consistent, not so much be-

---

[1] J. Perry Leavell, Jr., "Introduction," to James Fenimore Cooper, *The American Democrat* (New York, 1969), p. xxi; Sydney E. Ahlstrom, *A Religious History of the American People* (New Haven, 1972), p. 475; Norman Ware, *The Industrial Worker, 1840–1860* (New York, 1974), pp. x–xi, 1; Rowland Berthoff, *An Unsettled People* (New York, 1971), pp. 177, 189–95; Arthur M. Schlesinger, Jr., *The Age of Jackson* (Boston, 1945), pp. 92, 218–19, 264.

cause the lyricists and composers made them so, as because the public chose to sponsor only those compositions it found to contain the greatest meaning and the most attractive melody.[2]

At the core of the meaning of song was the assurance that suffering, however acute, was passing, and that humans, born unacquainted with evil and sorrow, might regain purity of heart and joy after they shook off the dross of self-interest and ambition, which came with adult worldliness. Thus, popular song's frame of reference for humankind's beginning was invariably an unblemished rural paradise. This was elicited in song as a dream of the past envisioned by an "I," an ordinary person, convulsed by present pain and grief. Arcadia was a "hallowed archetypal dream" that helped reconcile the singer to a reality full of misery and evil, where life was "a battleground" and nobody was "even sure that . . . good" would "overcome evil, or joy defeat pain."[3]

For the troubled, American song was "the balm for the bosom when dreary." "Sweetest Come Sing to Me," "words and music by an amateur" (c. 1840), tells of this therapeutic need for song:

When in my solitude haunted by sorrow,
  Banish the fiend from me with thy guitar,
Song can put off the dark day 'till tomorrow,
  Chasing the clouds by its murmurs afar.

Stephen Foster, in "The Voice of By Gone Days" (1850), hears that voice "come back again":

Whispering to the weary hearted many a soothing strain.
  Youthful fancy then returns, childish hope the bosom burns,
Joy that manhood coldly spurns, then flows in memory's sweet refrain.

The voice "murmurs to my brain/'till the cherish'd forms departed seem to live again."

Sometimes the dream is elicited by an object connected with the Arcadian past—an old Bible, chair, flower, or whatever. One of the most famous of such songs is "The Old Oaken Bucket" of Samuel Woodworth, who wrote the lyrics around 1818. (The music was added around 1835 by an author of uncertain identity.) The "I" says that seeing the "moss-covered vessel" brings back the "dear . . . scenes of my childhood," which include "every lov'd spot which my infancy knew." He names an orchard, meadow, wood, pond, mill, waterfall, and "the

---

[2]A thorough examination of all of these aspects of popular song occurs in Nicholas E. Tawa, *A Music for the Millions: Antebellum Democratic Attitudes and the Birth of American Popular Music* (New York, 1984).
[3]Carl Jung, *Man and His Symbols* (New York, 1968), pp. 74–75.

cot of my father." The bucket is treasured because, in recalling these memories, it changes into "the emblem of truth overflowing."

Another famous song, "Woodman! Spare that Tree!" (1837), words by George P. Morris, music by Henry Russell, begs that an ancient tree standing before the former home of the singer be spared the axe. Why? Because "my forefather's hand . . . placed it near his cot"; "in youth it sheltered me"; "here, too, my sisters played"; "my mother kiss'd me here"; and "my father press'd my hand" beneath "its grateful shade." Nostalgic evocations such as these proved irresistible to antebellum audiences.

In the dream of yesterday, exemplary humans dwelt in a lovely rural area that nineteenth-century men and women yearned to reach but discovered, as Emerson says, "always to be only a dream, a song, a . . . vision of living."[4] The vision was fleeting and ended with an awakening to the doubtful ambience of the here and now. Like Emily Dickinson, the commonalty might say: "I think of the perfect happiness I experienced . . . as of a delightful dream, out of which the Evil One bid me wake."[5] For a valued moment, the "I" (representative of the thousands of Americans who sang and listened to popular music) had found a fellowship of caring companions who could calm his mind and raise his spirits.

Arcadia, in the eyes of nineteenth-century Americans, was not an uncharted, pathless land. Nor was it inhabited by the uncivilized natural men romanticized by Jean Jacques Rousseau and James Fenimore Cooper. It was a garden spot set off from the wilderness of strife and ambition. Typical are the images that "Ben Bolt" conjures up: "the green sunny slope," the colorful flowers, the "wide spreading shade" of a great tree, the rhythmic "click of the mill," the school and its "master so kind and so true," and the "clear running brook" of yesteryear. "O Give Me a Home 'Neath the Old Oak Tree" envisions "a sweet retreat,/ From the tumult of men in the noisy street,/From the city's trade—the hum of the crowd."[6]

In lyric after lyric, the narrator muses on a "lowly cot," a "humble church," a "little schoolhouse," a "cultivated field," an "old mill"—all of which symbolize man's handiwork and union with a loving God. These commonplaces of popular song represent domesticity, worship, learning, and labor under optimum conditions, as life should be but is

---

[4]Ralph Waldo Emerson, *The Journals and Miscellaneous Notebooks*, ed. Merton M. Sealts, Jr. (Cambridge, MA, 1973), p. 10.

[5]Emily Dickinson, *Letters*, ed. Thomas H. Johnson (Cambridge, MA, 1965), p. 30.

[6]"Ben Bolt," music by Nelson Kneass, from an old German melody (Louisville, 1848); "O Give Me a Home 'Neath the Old Oak Tree," music by Isaac B. Woodbury (New York, 1855).

not. Often a stream or a sea bounds the parkland, setting limits to it; for Arcadia is a place where Everyman stays temporarily before departing on "life's stream" or "the sea of life" to experience the next stage of existence. The water is there to bear him away from Arcadia and toward the "distant shore," the eternal paradise of Heaven.

This distant shore is the only place where the ordinary American can regain happiness and serenity. While he lives on earth, he knows, as does the "I" in Stephen Foster's "Old Black Joe" (1860), that youth, gaiety, and friends are gone. All that's left is grief "for forms now departed long ago." Consolation of sorts comes when the "I" hears "their gentle voices calling," inviting him to join them in death.

George Root, in "Departed Days" (1857), mentions "mem'ries dear, of loved and long departed days." He hears "sweet voices from the spirit land," belonging to family and friends he sees no more. He lives as a stranger oppressed by "long and weary days," during which he walks "in the throng . . . alone." Welcome, therefore, are the voices of "beloved ones from the distant shore." Since he cannot go back to Arcadia, he continues to endure with a "sorrowing heart"; but the expectation is implicit that death will end his travail and gain him entrance into a paradise peopled with loved ones.

For the time being, however, the "I" consoles himself with thoughts of a past Arcadia. It is saturated with benign light, even after nightfall: "In the sky the bright stars glittered/On the grass the moonlight shone," or " 'Tis midnight hour, the moon shines bright,/The dew drops blaze beneath her ray,/The twinkling stars their trembling light/ Like beauty's eyes display."[7]

Love is essential to the scene—not as passion or sexual urge but as mutual warmhearted regard and attentive nurturing. The singer of the song is surfeited with the lonely, loveless world of reality. He cries out for true companionship. He does not bring Arcadia to mind merely for the sake of its natural beauty; it has to be inhabited by loved and loving maidens, mothers, fathers, friends, and all other living things to whom he is utterly committed and who tender commitment in return. Love thus understood is a rallying force when "the heart" feels "sorrow" and "the bright sunny moments are flown."[8]

J.R. Thomas's "Blue-Eyed Jeannie" (1856) sings of the unclouded "days of long ago," when "the light that shone around me . . . was love's own light;/When hand in hand I strayed, with a young and rosy maid." The maid is the Jeannie "I shall see ne'er again." Those "happy days . . .

---

[7]"When I Saw Sweet Nelly Home," music by P. S. Gilmore (Boston, 1856); " 'Tis Midnight Hour," music by an amateur (Boston, 1843).

[8]"Love Now," words by Dr. L., music by R. C. Clarkson (Philadelphia, c. 1844).

one long summer-time of love" are gone. Of Jeannie and the love for her, however, he says: "I would not, if I could, forget."

In mid-nineteenth-century popular song, woman is the idealized personification of affection. She is humankind's spiritual center expressed in archetypal terms—the Jungian *anima* representing the psyche, in contrast to the *animus* representing the outer self.[9] The genre portrays woman as the subservor of God. Delicate, gentle, and retiring, she nevertheless compels attention, owing to her moral excellence and selflessness. She is Stephen Foster's little Ella, an "earthly cherub coming nearest to my dreams of forms divine." Her "bright presence" brings "solace"; her "spontaneous love restrains" the "I" from doing "a thousand selfish things."[10]

She is John Ordway's "queen of night," blessing the "I" and filling "darkest space with loveliness."[11]

Stephen Foster's "Jeanie with the Light Brown Hair" (1854) depicts her as once "tripping where the bright streams play" and warbling melodies with "a merry voice." But her melodies are of the past, her smile has vanished, and her image now is "flitting like the dreams that have cheered us and gone." He can only sigh "like the night wind" and "long for Jeanie," the "lost one that comes not again."

Woman is found explaining the Bible, hymning chaste ditties, and inducing proper behavior in lover, husband, and child. If pictured as a maiden, she is a simple country girl, unconscious of her physical beauty and capable of loving only an upright youth, however impoverished his circumstances.[12] The suitor looks into her "bonny blue eyes" and discovers there truth, affection, intellect, hope, and Heaven. She stands before him without "fleck or flaw, a diamond in love's diadem."[13]

A number of songs show the maiden asleep, unaware that the "I" stands outside entreating her to awaken. Stephen Foster, in "Ellen Bayne" (1854), has the singer whisper to the sleeping maiden:

Soft be thy slumbers, rude cares depart,
    Visions in numbers cheer the young heart.
. . . .
Gentle slumbers o'er thee glide,
    Dreams of beauty round thee bide.
. . . .

[9]Jung, *Man*, p. 17.

[10]"Little Ella," words and music by Stephen C. Foster (New York, 1853).

[11]"Twinkling Stars Are Laughing, Love," words and music by John P. Ordway (Boston, 1855).

[12]See "Song of the Little Heart," music by O. R. Barrows (Boston, 1856); "Jenny Lane," words and melody by R. Bishop Buckley (Boston, 1850).

[13]"Bonny Blue Eyes," words by Joana Tyler of Leominster, Mass., music arr. J. Gib-

Scenes that have vanished smile on thee now,
    Pleasures once banished play round thy brow,
Forms long departed greet thee again,
    Soothing thy dreaming heart, sweet Ellen Bayne.

At times, in vision quest, she moves gently through infinity to touch the stars, to skirt death, and to preview the spiritual life beyond. The "I", struck with wonder, can only murmur:

Linger in blissful repose,
    Free from all sorrowing care, love;
While round thee melody flows
    Wafted on pinions of air, love,
Let not thy visions depart,
    Lured by the stars that are beaming,
Music will flow from my heart
    While thy sweet spirit is dreaming,
Dreaming, dreaming, unfettered by the day,
In melody, in melody I'll breathe my soul away.[14]

Yet his happiness depends on her opening her eyes and coming to him. He remains incomplete so long as she is absent from his side,[15] grows most complete when she becomes his wife, and is devastated if she dies (a frequent occurrence in these songs).

Fortunately, the "I" has recourse to another kind of love: maternal affection. The mother loves the "I" unconditionally, for no other reason than that he lives and is hers. She cares for him despite his transgressions; she pleads with God to forgive him; she alleviates the suffering he brings on himself or that is inflicted upon him. This is the mother delineated in Isaac Woodbury's "There's Music In a Mother's Voice" (1847). In John Baker's "My Trundle Bed" (1860), the "I" remembers "the music of my mother's voice in song" and the prayers she taught him. The memory guides his steps as he copes with the disturbances in his present world.

John Hewitt, in "Welcome, Mother!" (1834), describes how the "I" has "long'd to meet" her again. Over the years, "I have often traced thine image in my dreams" and "cherish'd—dearly cherish'd all the lessons given me./Every prayer my bosom nourish'd has been fraught with love to thee."

---

son (Boston, 1849); "Annie Law," words by W. W. Fosdick, music by J. R. Thomas (New York, 1857).

[14]"Linger in Blissful Repose," words and music by Stephen C. Foster (New York, 1858).

[15]See "Wake! Dinah, Wake!," words and melody by S. C. Howard (Boston, 1854); "Sweetly She Sleeps, My Alice Fair," words and music by Stephen C. Foster (New York, 1851); "Dream No Longer, Maiden Fair," music by Isaac B. Woodbury (New York, 1849).

Normally the Arcadian child is portrayed as "a laughing boy" whose "young heart could beat to praise/And every pulse respond to joy"; whose "every word was of the heart/When every feeling was sincere."[16] The child is what the democratic man imagined himself to have been before experiencing the relentless crush of adult existence. He could not accept the notion of original sin; his debasement was entirely of this world. It comforted him to believe that God's chastisement would sear away his own earthly vileness, that irreproachable loved ones were interceding for him, and that after living through his own hell on earth, he would recover his former innocence. Nowhere in his thoughts is space given to the predestined damnation and corruption of most of mankind, an idea that had haunted the Puritans of earlier times.

Popular song's Arcadian child, therefore, is born guiltless. As Andrew McDonall's "Years Ago" (1842) makes clear: "Years ago—oh, I was free from sin and care," "loved and loved again," "happy"; it was a time when his heart was "the shrine of truth."

His surroundings, "like the abode of the blessed," appear harmonious. His life is not yet tainted by materialistic desires. He exhibits the same purity of heart as do the maidens and mothers already mentioned. Therefore, he can also receive intimations of the immortality promised to humanity. This is the message of songs such as Bernard Covert's "The Child's Dream" (1848), H.D. Munson's "The Child's Wish" (1851), and John Baker's "Years Ago" (1857). The anonymous "Oh, the Merry Days When We Were Young" (1840) tells of "the hill and forest glen," where "we chas'd the shadows." With childhood has disappeared

Those sunny hours with all the joys that youth could bring.
  And now in wintry bow'rs we sigh to lose our happy spring,
When love and friendship smil'd and careless hope beguil'd,
  Ne'er shall we others see like the merry days when we were young.

The child's rustic home provides protection; its walls symbolize security. Within its sanctuary, as Donald Mitchell explains in his book *Dream Life* (1854), there is a "protecting power that no castle walls can give to your maturer years. Aye, your heart clings in boyhood to the roof-tree of the old family garret, with a grateful affection, and an earnest confidence that the after years . . . can never recreate. Under the roof-tree of his home, the boys feels SAFE: and where, in the whole realm of life, with its bitter toils, and its bitter temptations, will he feel *safe* again?"

The home in William Mason's "The Cot with the Sanded Floor" (1854) is small, pleasant, and scoured clean. It contains a small table, a

[16]"My Boyhood Days," music by John C. Baker (Boston, 1849).

few cups and plates, wicker chairs, a corded bed—all bathed in warm sunshine. The song closes with: "Now we have houses, gold, and lands with cares unknown before;/But call to mind with longing our cot with sanded floor."

A thirsting for the venerable home of bygone days began in the 1820s with the extraordinary popularity of "Home! Sweet Home!" (music by the Englishman Henry Bishop and lyrics by the American John Howard Payne). Later came the equal success of Stephen Foster's "Old Folks at Home" (1851). From the late twenties on, hundreds of songs eulogized the lowly cottage that sheltered healthy and happy children, rocklike fathers, and saintly mothers.

Not surprisingly, several of the American singing groups that traveled the country performing these songs introduced the Arcadian concept into their own personal backgrounds as an additional way to attract large audiences. The Hutchinson Family, possibly the most popular of these groups, had come from a farm near Milford, New Hampshire. "The Cottage of My Mother" (1848), "written by Jesse," "music by Judson," and "sung by Abby Hutchinson," told audiences:

I live among the hills in the cottage of my mother,
    My bonnie playmates are a sister and a brother;
The hills are ever green and blooming are the flowers,
    O, who has ever seen more happy home than ours.

The little stream runs near from purest fountains springing,
    And every morn we hear its silvery echoes singing;
The little birds are free as they play among the fountains,
    While their notes of liberty run o'er the distant mountains.

On each returning spring, when snow has gone and sleighing,
    We hear the blue birds sing and see the young lambs playing;
'Tis then our hearts are gay and merrily pass the hours,
    As to the fields we stray and gather sweet May flowers.

Here are all the accoutrements of a blissful and bucolic paradise.

Edgar Allan Poe once wrote of the "four unvarying laws, or rather elementary principles of Bliss"—which consisted of wholesome activity in the open countryside, love of woman, the elimination of ambition, and the constant treasuring of highly spiritual objects. Significantly, the land where this bliss is realized is denominated "a landscape garden."[17] The popular songs of Poe's day assuredly embraced these principles of bliss, and created images of them as intrinsic to their concept of the landscape garden—Arcadia.

---

[17]Edgar Allan Poe, "The Landscape Garden," Works, IV (New York, 1856), p. 337.

As for the music meant to accompany the vision of Arcadia, it was intended to steady and reanimate the listener. In the words of William Cullen Bryant, speaking in 1856: "The effect of music is to soothe, to tranquillize; a series of sweet sounds, skillfully modulated, occupies the attention agreeably and without fatigue; it refreshes us like rest."[18]

A beautiful melody, in particular, stimulates the listener to feelings of happiness and to remembering the moral lessons of the lyrics, according to William Porter, in his *Musical Cyclopedia*. Porter adds that it is the experience of most persons, when "delighted with a new air which rivets their attention," that the melody "will haunt them for days" and will continually call to mind the "good moral words" with which it is associated. In this way, songs become "their companions through life, giving them consolation in times of affliction and trial, furnishing them with rational amusement for leisure hours," and providing a "warning" to "deter from temptation and danger."[19]

Music provides models of loveliness untarnished by mundane matter. This is Christopher Cranch's meaning when he writes: "Music is an attempt to paint on the black canvas of the present . . . the soul's ideal reminiscences of the scenery of its native clime."[20] By embodying man's incorporeal essence, it makes audible what the inner self craves to have known but cannot in any other way.[21] When words and music are wedded in the minds of listeners, the lyrics clarify the particular ideas represented, and the melody eliminates the limitations that words impose on ideas and endows them with dimensionless implications.

Victor Zuckerkandl, a twentieth-century thinker who has written extensively on the nature of music, states: "Singing man reaches back deeper into himself, reaches out farther, and thus also gets farther out, penetrates deeper into things, than speaking man. . . . The tone of the singer adds to the word, does not cancel out the word, but rather gives it the sharpest edge, makes it vibrate with the highest frequency, so that it penetrates things to a greater depth. . . . Singing man reaches a new depth of the world, and by the same token a deeper level of himself."[22]

The successful melody of popular song is invariably described as sweet-sounding—pleasant and gently flowing. Its valued traits in-

---

[18]William Cullen Bryant, *Prose Writings*, II (1884, repr. New York, 1964), p. 203; see, also, Nicholas E. Tawa, *Sweet Songs for Gentle Americans* (Bowling Green, Ohio, 1980), pp. 36–38.

[19]William S. Porter, *The Musical Cyclopedia* (Boston, 1834), s.v. "Ear."

[20]E. Douglas Branch, *The Sentimental Years, 1836–1860* (1962, repr. New York, 1965), p. 184.

[21]Porter, *Cyclopedia*, s. v. "Expression."

[22]Victor Zuckerkandl, *Man the Musician*, trans. Norbert Guterman (Princeton, 1971), p. 50.

clude primarily conjunct motion, interspersed with comfortable skips; limited range; and carefully balanced phrases. In keeping with the style of music meant to be readily understood by a general public, pleasing melody is diatonic, free of ornamentation, and, therefore, close to the "pure celestial song" heard from "angel voices."[23]

Most Americans who enjoyed these songs rarely had any affection for melody that attempted to capture the specific meanings of the text. Since music lovers found elaborate accompaniment to be obtrusive, the songs of greatest popularity usually have plain accompaniments that are entirely supportive of the melody and have no importance of their own. Originality had no significance for these music lovers. The melody had to please and move them; who composed it was a matter of indifference. Nor did they care if the songwriter was deficient in musical skill and composed awkward and error-filled harmonic progressions. So long as the melody was smooth, elegant, and easily fitted to the text, they forgave the rest.

One of the most popular songs of the antebellum period was "If I Were a Voice" (1850), music by Judson Hutchinson (Ex. 1). The text succinctly explains the hoped-for effect of melody on the listener. The hauntingly beautiful melody was a "persuasive voice" that penetrated the hearts of contemporary Americans—as evidenced in the accounts praising Abby Hutchinson's renditions, in the many requests for it at Hutchinson concerts, and in the brisk sale of sheet-music copies over several years. One must remember that during any given concert night, the audience would have heard several songs on the distant Arcadia and the emptiness of present life. They would gaze on the cherubic Abby, whom Walt Whitman praised as one of the most wholesome-looking singers he had heard in his younger years, and remember the Hutchinsons claimed to be Arcadians. Then the words united to music would accomplish all that was intended in a mid-nineteenth-century popular song.

The musical phrases of the Hutchinson song in Example 1 are less predictable than those of the typical popular song of the day. More representatives of the norm is the melody to Foster's "Happy Hours at Home" of 1862 (Ex. 2). The phrases are regularly 4 measures long, group themselves into three 8-measure strains, and use but a few melodic motives, frequently repeated. Not a single accidental appears anywhere. All melodic skips are confined to the tones of the tonic, subdominant, and dominant seventh chords. The composer has removed every barrier to the ready understanding of the music. It is a quintessential example of how early democratic song represented the American Arcadia.

---

[23]"There's Music in the Air," music by George Root (Boston, 1857).

Example 1. "If I were a Voice" by Judson Hutchinson, 1850, courtesy of the Harris Collection, Brown University

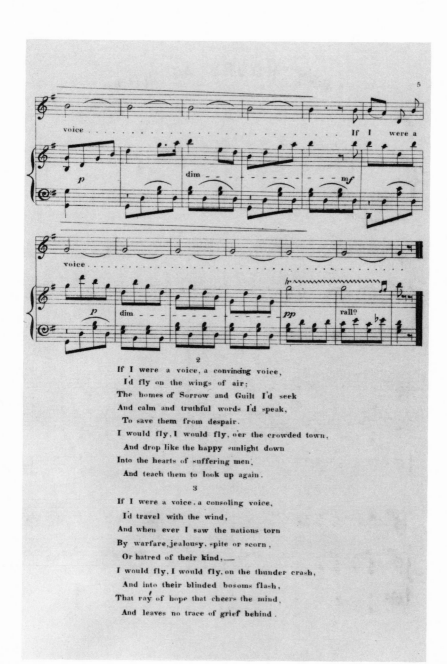

2

If I were a voice, a convincing voice,
    I'd fly on the wings of air;
The homes of Sorrow and Guilt I'd seek
And calm and truthful words I'd speak,
    To save them from despair.
I would fly, I would fly, o'er the crowded town,
    And drop like the happy sunlight down
Into the hearts of suffering men,
    And teach them to look up again.

3

If I were a voice, a consoling voice,
    I'd travel with the wind,
And when ever I saw the nations torn
By warfare, jealousy, spite or scorn,
    Or hatred of their kind,——
I would fly, I would fly, on the thunder crash,
    And into their blinded bosoms flash,
That ray of hope that cheers the mind,
    And leaves no trace of grief behind.

Example 2. "Happy Hours at Home" by Stephen Foster, 1862, courtesy of Foster-Hall Collection, University of Pittsburgh

Stephen Foster was elevated to the position of "the ballad-writer of America" on the basis of his "easy, flowing melody, the adherence to plain chords in the accompaniments, and the avoidance of intricacy in the harmony, or embarrassing accidentals in the melody."[24] An unassuming Foster ballad could surpass an elaborate Italian operatic aria that gloried in the singer's art and a subtle German art song that sensitively reflected the text—at least in the eyes of contemporary American song lovers.

Foster's "Happy Hours at Home" is but one of many songs by this composer that describe Arcadia and its inhabitants in the simplest terms, juxtapose it to Everyman's troubled present, and clothe it in sound so beautiful to nineteenth-century ears that it could be appreciated "wherever men sing. In the cotton fields of the South, among the mines of California and Australia, in the sea-coast cities of China, in Paris, in the London prison; everywhere in fact, his melodies are heard. . . . All his compositions are simple, but they are natural, and find their way to the popular heart." This claim, made by an unidentified writer in *Dwight's Journal of Music*, March 21, 1857, might have been more than a little exaggerated, but the songs cited as having the most immense followings throughout the United States are all on the Arcadian theme, from the standpoint of the joyless present: *The Old Folks at Home*, *My Old Kentucky Home*, and *Old Dog Tray*.

Assuredly, songs such as these held great meaning for the troubled Americans of the antebellum years. They not only entertained their listeners, but also told them who they were, whence they had come, and where they were going, in terms comprehensible to music lovers from every walk of life.

---

[24]John W. Moore, "Appendix," *Complete Encyclopedia of Music* (Boston, 1880), s.v. "Foster, Stephen C." The 1880 edition is a reprint of the original publication of 1854, with the Appendix added to it.

Music of the Renaissance as Viewed by the Romantics

JAMES HAAR

During the first half of the nineteenth century musical historiography made great strides. Assemblage of source materials, begun by Padre Martini and Gerbert, was continued but tended to focus on particular figures (Baini on Palestrina), places (Caffi on Venice), or periods (Winterfeld on sixteenth-century sacred music); straightforward chronicles, such as those of Hawkins and Burney, were succeeded by works including elements of historically grounded critical judgment, forming as in the case of Kiesewetter's study of the Franco-Netherlandish school the prototype for much later work on the period. Not long after Jacob Burckhardt's seminal volume on the Italian Renaissance came the first great modern synthesis of historical thought about music, A. W. Ambros's *Geschichte der Musik*.[1] The thoroughness with which Ambros treated the music of the fifteenth and sixteenth centuries, and the multiplicity of detail with which he illustrated his points, made his work a model for future scholars; Gustave Reese's *Music in the Renaissance* (1954) might be said to be the most distinguished but by no means the only twentieth-century continuation of Ambros's method. The work of Ambros, when compared with that of Burney, Hawkins, or Forkel, shows how much scholars had learned about the period in question between 1760 and 1860; in many of its essential outlines the musical history of the Renaissance had been rediscovered.

The accumulation of knowledge that made Ambros's work possible

---

[1]Burckhardt's *Die Kultur der Renaissance in Italien* was published in 1860; the first volume of Ambros's *Geschichte der Musik* appeared in 1862 (the volume on the 15th and 16th centuries was published in 1868; the later 16th century in Italy is covered in vol. IV, which appeared posthumously in 1878).

For a survey of the character and influence of later 18th-century musical historiography see Elizabeth Hegar, *Die Anfänge der neueren Musikgeschichtsschreibung um 1770 bei Gerbert, Burney und Hawkins* (Strasbourg [1932]). The work of Kiesewetter is summarized in Herfrid Kier, *Raphael Georg Kiesewetter (1773–1850), Wegbereiter des musikalischen Historismus* (Regensburg, 1968).

was of course gradual, if not always steady; but through much of the early nineteenth century there seems to have been no clear general picture of Renaissance music, and many individual aspects of the period were curiously, sometimes comically distorted. Much was corrected by Ambros and his contemporaries. Much but not all; some of the misapprehensions of the Romantics about Renaissance music lingered well into the twentieth century, and a few may not yet have been eradicated; for example, the importance, even uniqueness of stature given to Palestrina by the Romantics—as, to a lesser degree, by their predecessors—has only recently begun to be viewed critically, and we still do not perhaps have a truly balanced picture of this undoubtedly great but hardly unique figure.[2]

Ambros, like Burney and some other earlier historians, treats the history of music by national and regional schools as well as in chronological order. In another respect he also follows the precedent of eighteenth-century historians; the one-and-a-half volumes devoted to music of the fifteenth and sixteenth centuries are not subtitled "The Renaissance." In avoiding this classification Ambros escaped facing the problem of what "Renaissance" means in music. Some of us might be grateful for this, and even wish that later musicologists had followed him here; but the problem, once scholars began to see it as such, has remained with us and will not go away. Yet Ambros's work shows that the lead set by Burckhardt in conceptualizing the Renaissance as a period of cultural as well as political history was not immediately followed by music historians; when we blame historians of culture for being slow to include music in their work, we might remember that musicologists were themselves slow in approaching a definition of the Renaissance in music.

While Burckhardt was establishing his view of the Renaissance as a period sharply distinct from what preceded it—a view that was to become both familiar and generally accepted, though not to remain un-

---

[2]On the growth of the Palestrina legend see K. G. Fellerer, *Der Palestrinastil und seine Bedeutung in der vokalen Kirchenmusik der achtzehnten Jahrhundert* (Augsburg, 1929); Joseph Müller-Blattau, "Die Idee der 'wahren Kirchenmusik' in der Erneurungsbewegung der Goethezeit," *Musik und Kirche*, 2 (1930), 155–60, 199–204; Otto Ursprung, "Palestrina und Deutschland," *Festschrift Peter Wagner zum 60. Geburtstag*, ed. Karl Weinmann (Leipzig, 1926), pp. 196–221. The publication of Giuseppe Baini's *Memorie storico-critiche della vita e delle opere di G. P. da Palestrina* (Rome, 1828) was an event of central importance in 19th-century growth of Palestrina worship. Baini's work was made known in Germany through F. S. Kandler's *Ueber des Leben und die Werke G. P. da Palestrina* [with a foreword by Kiesewetter] (Leipzig, 1834) and Carl von Winterfeld's *J. P. da Palestrina. Seine Werke und deren Bedeutung für die Geschichte der Tonkunst, mit Bezug auf Baini's neueste Forschungen* (Breslau, 1832).

challenged,[3] historians of music were still regarding the art of the Renaissance as a continuation of medieval musical culture.[4] Thus Adrien de La Fage spoke in 1844 of "la seconde partie du moyen-âge ou la renaissance."[5] This view had fateful consequences. Josquin, even Palestrina were seen as belonging to a "Gothic" tradition in music, a tradition ended only by the rise of monody and opera. If one considered this a kind of Huizingesque antidote to a Burckhardtian view of music history, there might be a lot to be said for it; but such was not the case. Although the high polish and full sonority of Palestrina's polyphony was of course seen to differ from earlier music, Palestrina was thought to fit into the picture of medieval music as Romantic historians saw it, indeed to complete and round off the picture by being the perfect embodiment of Christian piety in music. Going along with a view of history that stressed the religious piety of the Middle Ages was the notion that the highest achievement of medieval music was the "wahre Kirchenmusik" of the sixteenth century, cultivated with almost unblemished seriousness by Palestrina.[6]

Admiration of Palestrina was not new; but the increasingly romanticized view of the Middle Ages was. Total seriousness and simplicity of religious faith characterized for the Romantics medieval man at his best.[7] The art of Palestrina and a few of his contemporaries was thought to capture this seriousness and simplicity perfectly.[8] Josquin, on the other hand, was seen—by means of a few anecdotes handed down by eighteenth-century historians who drew ultimately on Glareanus—as having a jesting, frivolous side that all but spoiled his art; this was Baini's view, and it is in strong and telling contrast to the unqualified admiration of Josquin seen in Burney's history.[9] The constructivist

---

[3]See Wallace K. Ferguson, *The Renaissance in Historical Thought* (Boston, 1948), chapters 8–11, for the *Rezeptionsgeschichte* of Burckhardt's work.

[4]For this view on the part of men such as Friedrich Rochlitz and Raphael Kiesewetter, see Tibor Kneif, "Die Erforschung mittelalterliche Musik in der Romantik und ihr geistesgeschichtliche Hintergrund," *Acta Musicologica*, 36 (1964), 130–31.

[5]*Histoire générale de la musique et de la danse*, 2 vols. (Paris, 1844), foreword, p. xiii, cited by Kneif, "Die Erforschung," p. 131. For La Fage, the period from the time of Guido [d'Arezzo] to the rise of opera was one epoch.

[6]On the view that Palestrina's music stood, from the 1760s at least, for "wahre Kirchenmusik" to be admired, revived, and cultivated in Protestant as well as Catholic circles, see Müller-Blattau, "Die Idee der 'wahren Kirchenmusik.' "

[7]To what extent this was a real belief of the Romantics, as opposed to a standard set up for their own age to emulate, is hard to determine; but it may be thought of as primarily a historicist view rather than a genuinely historical one.

[8]Nearly every writer of the Romantic period stressed these elements in Palestrina; see below, and fn. 11. An eloquent statement to the point is that of E. T. A. Hoffmann in "Alte and neue Kirchenmusik," *Allgemeine musikalische Zeitung*, Jahrg. 16 (1814), 577–84, 593–603, 611–19, especially 581–83.

[9]Baini, *Memorie storico-critiche*, vol. II, 407–11. Baini recognizes "gradevoli melo-

techniques of the "Netherlanders," Ockeghem and Josquin pre-eminent among them, were also thought to interfere with the purity of religious music; even Palestrina was criticized for his occasional use of such artifices as canonic technique or abstract cantus firmi.[10] Use of secular tunes as the basis for sacred compositions was of course frowned upon; scholars and dilettantes of the Romantic period, whether Catholic or Protestant, seem to have imposed on themselves a strict Counter-Reformation point of view when judging the music of the whole of the fifteenth and sixteenth centuries, and to have done so as a result of a one-sided and humorless view of medieval culture.

What did the sacred music of the sixteenth century sound like to the Romantics? For Abt Vogler the polyphony of Palestrina and his successors was simple, natural, unaffected, unadorned—a Rousseauesque vision.[11] To Anton Thibaut, the earnest champion of the frequent and precisely executed performance of old music, Josquin's *Stabat Mater* had greater moral strength than Pergolesi's; Senfl's *Sieben Worte Christi* was stronger and purer than Haydn's setting; in Palestrina he heard mastery of the old modes and of music in "reinen Dreyklange."[12] To E. T. A. Hoffmann Palestrina was "simple, true, childlike, pious, strong and powerful—truly Christian in his works, like Pietro da Cortona and our own old Dürer in painting."[13] Alexandre Choron thought

die" in Josquin, and admits that he sometimes exclaims "bello" over a passage, but he concludes that "Jusquino era uomo nato non per cultivare la musica sagra, siccom' ei fece; ma per divertire le liete brigate con suoni scherzevoli. . . ." Traces of this attitude persist in Ambros even as he terms Josquin (*Geschichte* IV, 48) "dieses genialsten unter den Tonzetzern der Vor-Palestrinazeit."

On Burney as an enthusiastic admirer and thorough student of Josquin, see Don Harrán, "Burney and Ambros as Editors of Josquin's Music," *Josquin des Prez*, ed. Edward E. Lowinsky (London, 1976), pp. 148–77.

[10]See, for example, Baini's treatment of Palestrina's "artificial" style (*Memorie*, p. 423).

[11]K. G. Fellerer, *Der Palestrinastil*, pp. 328 ff; cf. Müller-Blattau, *"Die Idee der 'wahren Kirchenmusik,' "* p. 200, where similar views on the part of Schubart (*Ideen zu einer Aesthetik der Tonkunst*, 1787) are cited. An early French statement on the "naturalness" of Palestrina's art is that of J.-J. de Momigny, *Cours complet d'harmonie et de composition*, 3 vols. (Paris 1803–06), vol. I, "Discours préliminaire," p. 15. I am grateful to Ian Bent for referring me to Momigny's work.

Some writers of the time set up Palestrina's "naturalness" in opposition to what they saw as the affectedly and artificially dramatic style of the sacred music of their own day; this is true of Vogler and certainly of Hoffmann.

[12]A. F. J. Thibaut, *Ueber Reinheit der Tonkunst* (1825), 3rd ed. (Heidelberg, 1851), p. 53. On the strict criteria by which old music was judged and the severely serious atmosphere in which Thibaut's performances were conducted, see Wilhelm Ehrmann, "Der Thibaut-Behaghel Kreis. Ein Betrag zur Geschichte der musikalischen Restauration im 19. Jahrhundert," *Archiv für Musikforschung*, 3 (1938), 428–83; 4 (1939), 21–67.

[13]"Alte und neue Kirchenmusik," p. 583. This passage is cited in Lewis Lockwood, ed., *G. P. da Palestrina. Pope Marcellus Mass* (New York, 1975), pp. 134–35.

that proper performance of Palestrina's music would produce "un effet extraordinaire, qui a réellement quelque chose de surnaturel"; and indeed Victor Hugo, Alfred de Vigny, and Théophil Gautier were all much moved, or said they were, by Choron's renditions of Palestrina.[14] Joseph Mainzer, hearing the Sistine choir in the early 1830s, was not enamored of what he called the "brouillamini" of imitative polyphony, but he greatly admired a Victoria Passion, for the enjoyment of which he thought one's experience of modern music was but inadequate preparation; he loved the sublime simplicity of Palestrina's *Improperia* and of chant sung in *falsobordone* or in parallel tenths.[15] A few dissident opinions were heard from time to time. Anton Reicha thought Palestrina's music had little to say to nineteenth-century ears; Stéphen de la Madelaine, though he admired Renaissance counterpoint, admitted that its real existence was only in scholars' libraries, and he likened the historical concerts of Choron and Fétis to "séances archéologiques"; Berlioz, while admitting that Palestrina's music could induce in the listener a trancelike state that was not without charm, thought that the music was little more than chord progressions lacking in individuality or power.[16] But these are exceptions; perhaps many early nineteenth-century listeners were pleasantly bored by Renaissance music, but nearly everyone who described hearing it did so in terms of glowing if vague admiration.[17]

[14]See Willi Kahl, "Zur musikalischen Renaissancebewegung in Frankreich während der ersten Hälfte des 19. Jahrhunderts," *Festschrift Joseph Schmidt-Görg zum 60. Geburtstag*, ed. Dagmar Weise (Bonn, 1957), pp. 164–67.

[15][Joseph Mainzer], "La Chapelle Sixtine à Rome," *Gazette musicale de Paris*, 1 (1834), 12f, 22f.

[16]Hans Eckardt, *Die Musikanschauung der französischen Romantik* (Kassel, 1935), p. 37. For Madelaine's remark, made in passing in a historical tale, see *Revue et Gazette musicale*, 4 (1837), 158. Reicha's views on music history, given in the introduction to his *Traité de haute composition musicale* (Paris, 1824–26; translated into German in Carl Czerny, *Vollständiges Lehrbuch*, 4 vols. [Vienna, 1832]), were attacked by Fétis and by Baini, who devotes several pages (ii, 363 ff) in his *Memorie* to bitter criticism of Reicha's unhistorical approach to counterpoint. Berlioz's views on Palestrina may be seen in David Cairns, trans., *The Memoirs of Hector Berlioz* (London, 1969), pp. 182–84. Berlioz was here writing of the *Improperia* so admired by Mainzer (presumably the "German" he mentions); but he extends his criticism to include all of Palestrina's works, which he thinks of as less striking than the harmonies made by an Aeolian harp in the wind, and "no one has ever thought of numbering the makers of aeolian harps among the great composers."

[17]Only rarely does one find a balanced view such as that given by Edouard Fétis, "La Musique d'autrefois et la musique d'aujourd'hui," *Revue et Gazette musicale*, 14 (1847), 22; "Roland de Lattre, Crequillon, Jean Mouton, Ciprien de Rore, Josquin-des-Près, avaient du génie; ils n'en avaient pas moins que Beethoven, que Rossini, et que Weber. Ils le manifestaient sous une autre forme, à l'aide de moyens que comportait l'art de leur temps, et dans la proportion des besoins de leurs contemporains; voilà toute la différence."

This music seemed appropriately religious to its authors, and in its tranquil beauty it suited their often rather sentimentalized—to one writer, "perfumed"—notions of an old and pure faith.[18] It also sounded picturesque; for example, Mainzer thought the "antique" sound of the music he heard in the Sistine Chapel was increased by the frequent flatting of the leading tone.[19] In the opinion of Carl Dahlhaus, the Romantics, even though they continued to use the Palestrina-Fux style for technical exercises, were unable to hear sixteenth-century music objectively; they considered the modes to be picturesque variants of major and minor tonality, and the music was for them a tonal reminder of a forgotten past, speaking to them with an unmistakable "Sehnsuchtston."[20] If this was true even for genuine admirers of old music, it was all the more so for the greater number of Romantic critics who used Renaissance polyphony as a stick with which to beat the "degenerate" church music of their own time. Palestrina was thus for many of the Romantics less a real musical figure than a symbol, representing a lost Golden Age that ought somehow to be recovered. The hyperbolic and usually, sometimes wildly, anachronistic comparisons—Palestrina was the Homer, even the Christ of music, but above all its Raphael—seem ridiculous when we consider the composer and his work as we understand it today.[21] Yet the pinnacle on which Palestrina was placed, and the religio-aesthetic trance his music induced in listeners, are significant as indications of Romantic sensibility, of a way of hearing music that, at least in the West, was new and was to affect composers as well as listeners during the course of the nineteenth century.[22]

[18]Eckardt, *Die Musikanschauung*, p. 35.

[19]*Gazette musicale*, 1 (1834), 13.

[20]Carl Dahlhaus, "Traditionszerfall in 19. und 20. Jahrhundert," *Studien zur Tradition in der Musik. Kurt von Fischer zum 60. Geburtstag*, ed. H.H. Eggebrecht and Max Lütolf (Munich, 1973), p. 183. As early a work as Kiesewetter's *Die Verdienste der Niederländer um die Tonkunst* (1829) considered old folk music to be major-minor as opposed to the deliberately archaic use of modes in polyphony (p. 45).

[21]See Thibaut, *Ueber Reinheit*, p. 55, where Palestrina is called the Homer of Music, a view echoed in Winterfeld, *Palestrina*, p. 34. According to Choron "Palestrina c'est le Racine, c'est le Raphael, c'est le Jésus-Christ de la musique," a remark cited in Monika Lichtenfeld, "Zur Geschichte, Idee und Aesthetik des historischen Konzerts," *Die Ausbreitung des Historismus über die Musik*, ed. Walter Wiora (Regensburg, 1969), p. 42. Lasso was thought to be receiving high praise when he was called the "Palestrina du Nord" (*Revue et Gazette musicale*, 3 [1836], 329, in an article entitled "Souvenir de voyage. Munich").

Nearly everyone equated Palestrina with Raphael; perhaps little Counter-Reformation painting was known, but it is more likely that even for serious scholars aesthetic and religious affinities outweighed the chronological discrepancies.

[22]For a telling example of this kind of reaction to Palestrina on the part of a later 19th-century composer, see the remarks of Wagner cited in Lockwood, *Pope Marcellus Mass*, p. 137.

In the early Romantic period there was not very much Renaissance music available for performance; historians such as Padre Martini and Burney transcribed and published a good deal for their own purposes, but others often relied on second-hand information or on what little music earlier scholars had transmitted.[23] During the first half of the nineteenth century a large amount of music was scored, and sometimes—though not always—published, by Choron in Paris, Ett in Munich, Thibaut in Heidelberg, Commer in Berlin, and Proske in Regensburg, to name but a few.[24] A thorough study of early nineteenth-century editions of Renaissance music sounds like something one would like to palm off onto a complacent robot; I have certainly not made such a study, but from what I have seen it would appear that most editions were simply scorings of the parts without editorial interference. Attitudes toward performance of this music were not, however, completely neutral. We have seen that an effect of the ineffably religious was aimed at. How was this realized? Choron's advice was as follows:

> As for the style of performance [of Palestrina's music], I will limit myself to saying that all this music must be sung in legato and sustained sound, very softly, with precision, in a moderate, even way, very simply but with much sweetness and tenderness.[25]

This of course sounds ineffably dull, and probably was; one thinks of Madelaine's remark about "archeological" concerts. Not everyone shared Choron's views; Kiesewetter, Gustav Billroth, and Otto Nicolai were all proponents of a more varied, less "Cecilian" style of performance for sixteenth-century music.[26]

There is some evidence of a more specific nature about one style of

---

[23]In 1810, according to Choron, neither the Conservatoire nor the Bibliothèque impériale had any works by Palestrina; see Kahl, "Zur musikalischen Renaissancebewegung," p. 160.

[24]The fullest bibliography of early publications of Renaissance music remains Robert Eitner's *Verzeichniss neuer Ausgaben alter Musikwerke aus der frühesten Zeit bis zum Jahre 1800* (Berlin, 1871). For a survey of early 19th-century collectors and collections of old music in Germany see Willi Kahl, "Öffentliche und private Musiksammlungen in ihrer Bedeutung für die musikalische Renaissancebewegung des 19. Jahrhunderts in Deutschland," *Bericht über den internationalen musikwissenschaftlichen Kongress Bamberg 1953*, ed. Wilfred Brennecke et al. (Kassel, 1954), pp. 289–94.

[25]Cited in Eckardt, *Die Musikanschauung*, p. 29.

[26]See Wiora, *Die Ausbreitung des Historismus*, p. 52, a contribution by Herfrid Kier to the article by Lichtenfeld, "Zur Geschichte . . . des historischen Konzerts," cited above, fn. 21. La Fage also opposed the notion of a subdued style—what he termed "chanter en timbre obscur"—for performance of this music; see his "Avis sur l'exécution de la musique palestrinienne," *Miscellanées musicales par J. Adrien de la Fage* (Paris, 1844), p. 504.

performance of Renaissance music by nineteenth-century enthusiasts. Franz Xavier Witt, a protegé and friend of Proske in Regensburg, left detailed sets of instructions for performance of certain works of Palestrina and Lasso. Witt's pupil Anton Walter printed two of these with admiring comments on Witt's prowess as a conductor of old music, adding that Witt's mode of performance was strongly in the Proske tradition; we may thus assume that these directions are descriptive of how Palestrina and Lasso were sung in the 1840s.[27] The two works chosen were Lasso's *Missa Qual donna attende* and Palestrina's *Missa Papae Marcelli*, the latter being described in greater detail. Witt was strongly critical of what he called a mechanical way of conducting this music, with tempi set for each movement by prearranged convention (Kyrie slow, Gloria a little faster, etc.) rather than according to the character of the individual work.[28] His own method was hardly mechanical; in the *Missa Papae Marcelli* there are in Witt's version almost as many internal changes of tempo as in Artur Schnabel's edition of a Beethoven sonata. The tempi range from $\downarrow = 46$ for the Benedictus (though on consideration Witt decides that this was really too slow for the singers to manage) to $\downarrow = 132$ for the Amen of the Credo. Here is the Kyrie of the Pope Marcellus Mass in Witt's version:

> One should open the *Kyrie* not *forte* but sweetly, the first four measures <*mf*>; in the ninth bar a *forte* can be introduced, in some parts rising yet a degree higher in volume, in others subsiding to *mf*. If one begins with $\downarrow = 72$, the tempo should soon pick up, going to as fast as $\downarrow = 88$. By the third-to-last measure before the *Christe* in any event, one should be singing *ff*; the *ritardando* occurs only at the next-to-last bar.
>
> The first section of the *Christe* comprises the first eight bars; these can be taken more quietly and tenderly, about $\downarrow = 76$. From bar nine on there is a gradual increase in tempo and rise in dynamic level. Bars 18–19 are the top of this rise. One can establish the following as a rule (the first exception occurs at the *Et incarnatus est*): all six-voice passages are to be sung in a louder, fierier, more accented way—and are so to be conducted—than the three- or four-voice passages; for the composer draws upon the full six voices in order to make a crescendo, to expand the importance, the weight of tone and volume. Here the six-voice passages are bars 18–19 and 24–26. The *Christe* can be sung by half the chorus, or a double sextet. The choir director can let *Kyrie* II begin $\downarrow = 92$ and gradually and in certain places increase to $\downarrow = 100$.[29]

The other movements are treated similarly, with many *fortissimo*

---

[27]Anton Walter, "Dr. Witts Zeugnis für Palestrina und Lasso," *Kirchenmusikalisches Jahrbuch*, 9 (1894), 48–59; the remark about the Proske tradition is made on p. 53.

[28]"Dr. Witts Zeugnis," p. 54.

[29]*Ibid.*, p. 53.

passages and much alteration of tempi. In the Agnus Dei individual
figures are singled out; a frequently used cambiata figure is to be sung
quietly and tenderly, while the motive for "qui tollis," full of skips, is to
be done strongly and with a crescendo. In general, Witt concludes, this
Mass can because of the breadth of its motives be taken much faster
than most of Palestrina's later Masses.[30] Witt's use of the quarter note
for metronome markings, and his admission that although Proske usually performed the Mass in C he transposed it to B♭, suggest that he was
using a "performing" edition. Proske's own edition of the Mass, published in 1850, gives it in original note values, untransposed, and without tempo or dynamic markings.[31] An edition of the kind Witt was using does survive from this period, in Stephan Lück's *Sammlung* of
1859.[32] In this edition there are shortened note values, a transposition
down a tone, and tempo, dynamic, and expression marks; they are not
always identical with what Witt calls for, but the similarities are frequent and striking enough to suggest that this edition comes out of the
same performing tradition.[33]

If faster than most other sacred pieces by Palestrina, the *Missa Papae
Marcelli* in Witt's version is still rather slow by our standards, and the
music is of course romanticized; it is an example of "wahre Kirchenmusik" as a general aesthetic type rather than an attempt at recaptur-
ing sixteenth-century musical style. This is how listeners, singers, con-
ductors, even scholars thought of Renaissance polyphony; and
composers wishing to create new works in *a cappella* style must have
been strongly influenced by it, just as they were by contemporary
modes of performing Bach's instrumental and concerted polyphony.[34]

[30]*Ibid.*, p. 54.
[31]Proske's edition, published in Mainz in 1850 (*Missa Papae Marcelli triplici con-
centu distincta . . . juxta editiones principes fidelissime in partitionem redegit . . .
publicavit Carolus Proske),* includes the four-voice arrangement of the work by Anerio
and the eight-voice version by Suriano. It preserves original clefs as well as note values.
For other early editions (from the 1840s and 1850s) see Eitner, *Verzeichniss*, p. 152.
The Masses of Anerio and Suriano have been edited by Hermann J. Busch, *Two Settings
of Palestrina's* Missa Papae Marcelli (Madison, Wisc., 1973).
[32]Stephan Lück, *Sammlung ausgezeichneter Compositionen für die Kirche,* 2 vols.
(Trier, 1859). I consulted the second edition (Leipzig, 1884), which is so far as I know an
unaltered reprint of the music in the first edition. The Mass is printed in vol. I, pp. 149–
99.
[33]On Lück see Hugo Riemann, *Musik Lexikon,* 12th ed., ed. Willibald Gurlitt
(Mainz, 1961), *Personenteil* II, 107. La Fage's directions for performing Palestrina (*Miscellanées musicales,* pp. 499–504) outline a less extreme but generally similar approach, with one exception: he advocates (p. 503) a constant *mezzoforte* for a chant
cantus firmus "tandis que chacuns des autres parties nuancera convenablement."
[34]On this point see Erich Doflein, "Historismus in der Musik," *Die Ausbreitung
des Historismus,* pp. 36–37.

We think of the study of historically accurate performance practice as a twentieth-century development, as indeed it is. But there is no reason why scholars in the early nineteenth century could not have begun such a study; no reason except that they felt no need for it. Just as they saw old church music as both a resuscitated ideal and a living reproach to the effete sacred music of their own time, so the Romantics were content to give it a "timeless" mode of performance, hence, paradoxically, one grounded specifically in the performance practice of their own time. The historicism of musicians in the nineteenth century was thus as eclectically conceived and motivated as that of painters or architects—perhaps more so.

Eclecticism in nineteenth-century culture is too well known a phenomenon to need emphasis here, but citation of a few parallel instances might be relevant. In Vienna in the 1780s, at the height of the neoclassical movement in all the arts, Baron van Swieten's historical concerts of Baroque music, following the precedent set by Reichardt in Berlin, took place; during the same decade the "re-gothicizing" of Austrian churches was begun.[35] It is perhaps only natural then that Carl Maria von Weber, writing in 1821, should say that Bach built in his music a "wahrhaft gothischen Dom der Kunstkirche."[36] Classical, Gothic, Renaissance, even Romanesque building styles were mixed in the ambitious rebuilding of central Munich undertaken in the reign of Ludwig I (1825–68), just the years when Kaspar Ett was performing the works of Lasso along with those of Baroque polyphonists in that city.[37] The Paris of the historical concerts given by Choron, then by Fétis, themselves a mix of styles and periods, is summarized wittily by Alfred de Musset:

> Our century has no style of its own; we have not given the stamp of our own time to our houses, our gardens, or anything else. One sees in the streets men with beards trimmed in the style of Henri III, others clean-shaven; some with their hair arranged as in a portrait by Raphael, others as if these were the times when Christ was alive. And the houses of the wealthy are curio-cabinets: the antique, the gothic, the taste of the Renaissance, that of Louis XIII—all is mixed together. We have something out of every century but our own, a thing never seen before. Eclecticism

---

[35]Herfrid Kier, "Musikalischer Historismus im vormärzlichen Wien," *Die Ausbreitung des Historismus*, p. 58.

[36]Doflein, "Historismus in der Musik," p. 12. The remark is in a biographical-critical notice on Bach, printed in C.M. von Weber, *Ausgewählte Schriften*, ed. Wilhelm Altmann (Regensburg, 1928), p. 294. On the preoccupation of the German Romantics with Gothic architecture (beginning with Goethe's essay on the Strasbourg Cathedral), see Brian Plimma, "Unity and Ensemble: Contrasting Ideals in Romantic Music," *19th Century Music*, 6 (1982), 105 f.

[37]Doflein, "Historismus," p. 13. On the career of Ett see Kahl, "Öffentliche und private Musiksammlungen," p. 290.

is our taste; we take up everything we come upon—this for its beauty, that for its convenience; one thing for its antiquity, still another for its very ugliness—to the extent that we live as it were among debris, as if the end of the world were near.[38]

In this milieu it is no surprise that Louis Niedermeyer should proclaim, in the opening number of Le Maîtrise (1853), "Pour le plainchant, nous disons Saint Grégoire; pour le musique sacrée, nous disons Palestrina; pour l'orgue, nous disons J.-S. Bach."[39] It is a well-known but none the less telling fact that renewed interest in Palestrina coincided with the beginnings of the Bach revival; the master of Counter-Reformation Catholic polyphony and the master of late Baroque Protestant church music were both viewed as "Gothic" musical saints and were both transplanted, like the historically costumed people of Musset's remark, into nineteenth-century surroundings.[40]

One indication of this growing eclecticism of culture is the choice of subjects for opera libretti. Although eighteenth-century operas were occasionally based on "medieval" chivalric topics descending from Ariosto and Tasso, serious opera at any rate continued to use classical myth and ancient history for its subject matter through the third quarter of the century. After this all kinds of exotic subjects were chosen, and in the early nineteenth century a strong preference for medieval and Renaissance subjects can be seen; the most popular source was of course the novels of Walter Scott. The pages of Loewenberg's Annals are full of such titles, and there must have been many more. An example of an opera on a Renaissance topic, one not reported by Loewenberg, is François Ier à Chambord, a two-act opera of unknown authorship premiered in Paris in 1830. The "historical" plot of this work is about Leonardo da Vinci's mistress, whose life is saved by Francis I at Marignano; the king brings her to Chambord, but on her confession of love for Leonardo the king gives her to the artist and the lovers are

---

[38]La Confession d'un enfant du siècle (1836), p. 89, in A. de Musset, Oeuvres complètes en prose, ed. Maurice Allem and Paul-Courant (Paris, 1960). Musset writes in the persona of a young man afflicted with mal de siècle; but his observation has the ring of truth about it. (The translation given here, like those elsewhere in this paper, is my own.)

[39]Cited in Eckardt, Die Musikanschauung, p. 43.

[40]Sometimes there were attempts at a distinction between the nature of Bach's music and that of Palestrina. Thus Friedrich Rochlitz, "Ueber der zweckmässigen Gebrauch der Mittel der Tonkunst," Allgemeine musikalische Zeitung, 8 (1805–06), cols. 49, 56, 193, 199, using terminology common in the late 18th century, calls Palestrina's art an example of the "sublime" ("Erhabene"), while Bach's that of the "great" ("Grosse"), differing from the earlier master in its greater complexity and more dramatic character. On the other hand Rochlitz does indulge in an unhistoric comparison of his own, calling (col. 199) Bach the "Albrecht Dürer der Musik."

united.[41] This libretto is of course not history but a *nouvelle* or *feuilleton* of the type that was beginning to appear in the Parisian press; and there were, as we shall see, *contes historiques* on topics in Renaissance musical history at this time.

It has been pointed out that nineteenth-century Italian libretti on historical subjects were concerned with character and situation, showing little respect for fidelity of historical detail.[42] Many French operas were similarly casual; but Scribe in his libretti paid much greater attention to the facts as they were known, and in productions of these operas there was real concern for historical accuracy in sets and costumes.[43] Not so with the music, of course, and this anomaly was occasionally remarked. In Fétis's *Revue musicale*, an account of a ball at the Opéra asks whether it is not a serious anachronism to see dancers representing the courtiers of Francis I or Charles IX perform to the music of Rossini and Meyerbeer.[44] To most people it evidently was not; and in fact this situation has lasted, with few exceptions, up to our own day in costume dramas on film or television. Opera composers certainly did not try to write in antique style, nor could they have; the only old music that was known to them by more than name was the sacred polyphony of the *stile antico*. An occasional prayer scene in pious chords or a ballad with some slight archaicism of detail might be used, but that was about all. Even Meyerbeer, nothing if not eclectic, seems not to have reached beyond the Lutheran chorale, harmonized in "neo-Gothic" style, in the direction of old music. It is of course possible that we might miss something heard as intentional historicism at the time. For example, Meyerbeer wrote a setting of a ballad of Marguerite of Valois, a poem said to have been published in 1540.[45] The song, a strophic setting in syllabic style, alternating in Schubertian manner between major and minor but with no archaicisms that I can see, was reviewed thus:

> The ballad of Marguerite de Valois, grandmother of Henri IV, was published in 1540; the melody to which she sang it has not, so far as I know, come down to us. But M. Meyerbeer has so beautifully grasped the color of medieval melodies, there is in his music such a flavor of old tales, that one would think himself hearing one of those epics that Blondel sang at the court of Richard Coeur-de-Lion. . . . The beginning, "Pour être un

---

[41]A review of this work appears in the *Revue musicale*, 7 (1830), 210ff.

[42]Patrick Smith, *The Tenth Muse. A Historical Study of the Opera Libretto* (New York, 1970), pp. 211–12.

[43]*Ibid.*, pp. 212, 221.

[44]*Revue musicale*, 13 (1833), 403. The reviewer, probably the editor himself, takes the opportunity to praise the old dance music performed at Fétis's historical concerts.

[45]The song was published in Giacomo Meyerbeer, *Quarante mélodies à une et à plusieurs voix avec acc‡. de Piano* (Paris, n.d.).

digne et bon chrétien," is especially remarkable for its gothic naiveté, further emphasized by the style of the accompaniment and by the mixing of major and minor modes.[46]

Note that Middle Ages and Renaissance are characteristically mixed together as "Gothic," that in 1540 one was assumed to have sung in the style of the late twelfth century. The reviewer was, by the way, Hector Berlioz, who knew how to use an occasional scent of "parfum antique" himself.[47]

From the eclectic use of historical novels and plays—themselves often not pedantically close to historical fact—for libretti, it is but a short step to the historical *nouvelle*, a genre popular in France and Germany in the early nineteenth century. Following the precedent of E.T.A. Hoffmann, a number of writers turned to musical subjects for historicist fiction, especially in France. The early years of the *Gazette musicale de Paris* (1834–35) and its successor the *Revue et Gazette musicale* feature these stories quite regularly. Particularly interesting for us here are the stories contributed by Stéphen de la Madelaine during the years 1835–38, and the single but vivid contribution by Berlioz to the genre, a story on the creation of the first opera by Alfonso della Viola in the mid-sixteenth century, about which I have written elsewhere.[48]

Madelaine also wrote a story about opera in the sixteenth century, with the figure of Lambert de Beaulieu as hero and with a loose connection to what was then known about the *Balet comique de la Royne*.[49] In this tale Beaulieu goes to Florence, where he hears a new opera, *Endymion*, by "Horace Vecchi," who "laid the foundations of comic opera in 1595." The music to *Endymion* is lost, but Madelaine is able to say that

it was written after the models provided by Emilio Cavalieri, Mei, and Caccini. In addition the composer made use in his work of the happy innovations with which Claude Goudimel had enriched harmony; and he

[46]*Gazette musicale*, 2 (1835), 351.

[47]See, for example, the "Roi de Thulé," subtitled "Chanson gothique," in the *Damnation de Faust*, as well as Berlioz's fanciful attribution of *L'Enfance du Christ* to one Pierre Ducré, "maître de chapelle of the Saint-Chapelle," said to have written the work in 1679. See Jacques Barzun, *Berlioz and the Romantic Century*, 3rd ed. (New York, 1969), vol. I, 486–87; vol. II, 90.

[48]"Berlioz and the 'First Opera,' " *19th Century Music*, 3 (1979), 32–41. The story, "Le Premier Opéra: Nouvelle du passé, 1555," first appeared in the *Revue et Gazette musicale*, 4 (1837). For Stéphen de la Madelaine, whose career was spent as a civil servant but whose avocation was music—he was a friend of Berlioz, a singer, an editor of the *Univers musical* and of musical *feuilletons* for the *Courrier français*, see F.-J. Fétis, *Biographie universelle des musiciens et bibliographie générale de la musique, Supplément et complément publiés sous la direction de M. Arthur Pougin*, vol. II (Paris, 1880), 68–69.

[49]"Comment l'opéra fut introduit en France," *Gazette musicale*, 2 (1835), 377–84.

substituted the *récitatif* invented by Vincenzo Galilei for the too-monotonous forms of counterpoint. Finally, choruses were introduced as finales for each act, just as Peri had provided examples of in his *Euridice*.

All this music, though full of variety for the time, was excessively simple in form and mediocre in execution. But its style was pure, and its naive expression had a core of truth that our tormented melodies and our inflated instrumentation do not always achieve.[50]

A pretty full description of a lost score; and the historical bits read like a substandard student examination essay. Madelaine is here as elsewhere vague about chronology; as we shall see, he allowed the most glaring inconsistencies to pass, or perhaps he simply scribbled away, a journal deadline before him, and never looked back. He was certainly not writing history, and his stories must have been intended primarily as diversions. One of his main purposes, seen here at the end of the passage just cited, was to attack the present by extolling the past, something he did consistently in writing about sacred music. Still, he did know some facts, gathered from the survey provided by Choron and Fayolle, from other general histories available to him, and certainly from his association with Fétis, whom he appears to have known fairly well.[51] What is perhaps most interesting about his musical tales is that they show elements of knowledge, however casually handled, about the Renaissance filtering down from scholars to the reading public, which was clearly expected to find them picturesquely intriguing.

Stéphen de la Madelaine wrote two more pieces about early opera: "Francesca," a tale about a real musician, the gifted daughter of "Jules Caccini, l'un des pères de la musique dramatique," and "La Jeunesse de Bassini," a tale set in the 1630s about a personage Madelaine seems to have invented or compiled out of several real Bassanis.[52] His most extraordinary contribution to the genre of the musical *nouvelle* is, however, a series of three interrelated stories on Dufay, Josquin, and Mouton.[53] In the first of these tales, the aging and absent-minded Dufay

---

[50]*Ibid.*, p. 380.

[51]Choron and Fayolle's *Dictionnaire historique des musiciens . . . précédé d'un sommaire de l'histoire de la musique*, 2 vols. (Paris, 1810–11), pp. i, lv, has a good deal of the basic information used by Madelaine. The bit about Goudimel is Madelaine's own; one should remember, however, that at this time Goudimel was commonly thought to have been Palestrina's teacher. The first volumes of Fétis's *Biographie universelle* appeared in the mid-1830s, just before Madelaine wrote his *contes historiques*.

[52]"Francesca," *Revue et Gazette musicale*, 4 (1837), 37–44; "La Jeunesse de Bassini," *ibid.*, 157–60, 166–69, 181–85.

[53]"La Vieillesse de Guillaume Dufay," *Revue et Gazette musicale*, 3 (1836), 453–60; "Les Psaumes de Josquin," *ibid.* 4 (1837), 109–13, 129–34; "Le Maître de Chapelle de François Ier, Chronique du XV[e][sic] siècle," *ibid.* 5 (1838), 245–49, 253–57.

roams the streets of Paris pondering the mysteries of musical science, after finishing a conversation with some respectful young students to whom he reveals his recent discoveries "sur l'harmonie tonale."[54] Entering the wrong house by mistake, Dufay meets by sheer accident the daughter of an old friend of his, now dead; he adopts the young woman and her illegitimate child, and makes them known to his favorite pupil Josquin, the son of his physician Grégoire Desprez. In an unfortunate household accident the infant dies; his mother Hélène is inconsolable and spends her time singing lullabies to an empty crib. Dufay, at the worst of moments always a musician, notes that the two lullabies sung by Hélène are somehow related; he and Josquin sing them together and in that happy moment—in the year 1465—"le contrepoint venait d'être découvert!" In the speedy dénouement Hélène recovers and ends by marrying the young Josquin, at this time maître of the chapel at Saint-Denis.

The second of these stories is set in the Paris of 1510, an ominous place full of spies and assassins. In a modest dwelling on the Left Bank the "savant Josquinus, le favori de messire Apollo," now maître of the Sainte-Chapelle, is literally burning the midnight oil while putting together his "combinations de la science." He is then seen playing "savantes modulations" on the organ while his wife Hélène (Dufay's adopted daughter) sings. Josquin is poor; he runs into debt by paying much of the expense for the brilliant wedding music for Louis XII and Anne de Bretagne—music consisting of "fragments de symphonies et même plusieurs morceaux à deux voix qui constituaient de véritables choeurs." The composer "qui instruisait l'Europe musicale" further ruins himself by keeping up a carriage; he is reduced to giving "leçons de plain-chant" to court ladies and to fulfilling their trivial commissions. At one point, sick of all this, Josquin sits down to write a piece for himself; the result is *Coeli enarrant gloriam Dei*, "en contrepoint et canon à quatre parties, savante composition," a work admired by Padre Martini and even by LeSueur, who in setting the same text was, says Madelaine, reluctant to compete with Josquin.[55] Josquin receives a

---

[54]Compare the remarks of Fétis, *Traité de la théorie et de la pratique de l'harmonie* (Paris, 1844), on how he resolved musical problems and found the truth while walking "dans un chemin solitaire" (Preface to the third edition [Paris, 1849], p. xi).

[55]Josquin's *Coeli enarrant gloriam Dei* was published in J. N. Forkel, *Allgemeine Geschichte der Musik*, vol. II (Leipzig, 1801), 580. I have not found Martini's reference to the work. The other pieces by Josquin mentioned in Madelaine's story are all cited by Choron and Fayolle, *Dictionnaire historique*, vol. II, 357–58; their ultimate source is Glareanus.

LeSueur did indeed write a setting of *Coeli enarrant*, a clangorous C major setting for chorus and orchestra, published in *Deux Psaumes . . . Composées par LeSueur* (Paris, n.d.). Whether LeSueur knew Josquin's piece would be hard to determine from his own composition.

benefice in Meulan; he suspects the donor, a certain "comte de Meulan," of designs on his wife, but is relieved when the count reveals himself to be Louis XII. Josquin lives to a ripe old age, dying in the early seventeenth century; among the "déplorations et contrepoint" written for him is one by "Jean Mantou," *maître de chapelle* of Francis I.

This wonderful mélange of fact and fiction, supremely indifferent to matters of chronology, is followed by the tale on Mouton (his name now spelled correctly). The young Mouton, an instrument maker, lodges in Paris with a woman whose favorite music is, prophetically it would seem, the *De Profundis* of Goudimel. At a religious celebration Mouton hears Josquin singing in one of his own Masses, and is so overcome that he falls into a fever, saying in his delirium "Josquinus ego sum, Josquinus musicorum princeps." He is cured by Josquin himself, who teaches Mouton the secrets of counterpoint. Mouton ends by becoming the first maître of the royal chapel, starting a tradition that ends only—by reason of the unfortunate political circumstances in nineteenth-century France—with LeSueur and Cherubini.

These stories were of course not meant as serious history;[56] still, their whimsicality and fast-and-loose treatment of fact make the fabled errors of Fétis pale into insignificance. Madelaine tired of or was discouraged from continuing in this vein; his name disappears from the masthead of the *Revue et Gazette* in 1839, and although he continued to write on music he did not, so far as I know, compose any more musico-historical *contes*.[57] Contributions of a historical nature in the pages of the *Revue et Gazette* from 1840 on are of a much more sober and technical nature, typified by the serious work of La Fage rather than the fantasy of Madelaine; this may well be a sign of changing attitudes, mid-nineteenth-century scholarship displacing Romantic tale-telling.

Chronological oddities were not peculiar to Madelaine; some of the most serious of his contemporaries fell, or leaped, into them. For example, Thibaut tells (or retells, from a source unknown to me) of a dream experienced by the painter Correggio (d. 1534) in which the artist died and on arrival in paradise met the awesome figure of Palestrina (b. ca. 1525).[58] The insistent coupling of Palestrina with Raphael, still met

---

[56]They resemble Berlioz's tale of the "first opera" in making their protagonists typical 19th-century Frenchmen. It is possible that Madelaine was in these stories giving veiled portraits of contemporary musicians (Dufay = Fétis?), but one can only guess at who they might be.

[57]In 1840 Madelaine published his *Physiologie du chant; Théories complètes du chant* followed in 1852, and *Etudes pratiques de style vocal* was issued in 1868. He also wrote a long series of novels of an educational Christian tone; see the entries of his work given in the *Catalogue générale des livres imprimés de la Bibliothèque nationale*, vol. 103 (Paris, 1930), cols. 179–82.

[58]*Ueber Reinheit*, p. 67.

with in the pages of Ambros, is further evidence of the Romantics' attitude toward the Renaissance: the end of the Age of Faith was all one to them. This is a matter less of insouciance than of a dreamlike conceptualizing of the past as an *Engelkonzert* in which matters of chronological sequence were of no importance, or as an inconographic representation of aesthetic religious belief. To hear Bach fugues sounding in the background of such a picture was no anomaly. The errors were gradually weeded out; shortly before Madelaine wrote his account of Beaulieu hearing Vecchi's "Endymion," Fétis presented a corrected account of the career and oeuvre of Vecchi.[59] And in the rising generation of scholars such as Robert Eitner and Emil Vogel there was great if not uniformly successful emphasis on factual accuracy; but by this time the Romantic glow had faded. Ambros deplored the inaccuracy of popular histories of the preceding generation, citing the enormities to be found in works such as Müller's survey, where Ockeghem is said to have been a papal singer in Rome and to have discovered his pupil Josquin while on a visit to Prato.[60] And as early as 1836, Bottée de Toulmon, librarian of the Conservatoire in Paris, lamented the inaccuracy of most histories of music, saying that not only was it difficult to uncover the facts but that since music was thought by most people to be "uniquement un art d'agrément" it was thought useless, even ridiculous, to study it in a scientific way.[61] But for as long as Romanticism held sway, it would seem that music of the past was either a monolithic reproach to the frivolous present—as for Madelaine[62]—or a thing too perfect to investigate in a detached way.

One further anomaly in the Romantic view of Renaissance music may be touched on here. We have seen that the music of Palestrina and of selected figures among his contemporaries, successors, and predecessors was looked upon as a thing of otherworldly purity and detachment,

---

[59]*Revue musicale*, 3 (1828), 443f. This is followed, unfortunately, by a biography of Vicentino in which the latter is said to have had a talented pupil named Willaert. . . .

[60]Ambros, *Geschichte* III, iii, 477 n., cites a work by W. C. Müller, *Uebersicht einer Chronologie der Tonkunst mit Andeutungen allgemeiner Civilization und Culturentwickelung*. This is actually a kind of subtitle for Müller's *Aesthetisch-historische Einleitungen in die Wissenschaft der Tonkunst* (Leipzig, 1830); but Ambros reports the passage in question accurately enough. This book, intended as a text-book (Müller is described on the title page as "Lehrer an der Hauptschule in Bremen"), is a typical summary of what was known at the survey-text level about early music in the 1830s.

[61]"Discours pronouncé par M. Bottée de Toulmon," *Revue et Gazette musicale*, 3 (1836), 65–71, especially p. 66. Bottée does pay some tribute to the seriousness of purpose of Fétis, in whose journal he was writing.

[62]In a straightforwardly polemical essay, "De la musique réligieuse," *Revue et Gazette musicale*, 3 (1836), 121–24, Madelaine calls for a revival, under government patronage, of church music of a serious and exalted nature.

and the musicians themselves on the whole as figures of saintly remove from their surroundings—an analogy, deliberate or unwitting, to the notion of Romantic artistic alienation. Their work was consistently viewed as the sublimely tranquil culmination of the long centuries of the Age of Faith. This does not fit at all with the picture of the Renaissance drawn by historians such as Burckhardt; it is even more out of joint with the use made of the Renaissance in the literature of the late eighteenth and early nineteenth centuries. For poets and dramatists of the *Sturm und Drang* period the Renaissance was a violent and godless period, with conspiracy and murder—sometimes but not always an idealistically motivated *Tyrannenmord*—its distinguishing characteristics. Florence under the Medici, from the Pazzi conspiracy of the 1470s through the end of the sixteenth century, was a favored location.[63] In general a "Gift und Dolchromantik" colored German Romantic treatment of the Renaissance in literature. Machiavellian intrigue and Cellinesque unbridled egoism and opportunism were prime subject material; in the case of Cellini the artist himself was a violent and irreligious type.[64]

Music (and doubtless religious painting as well) seemed to the Romantics to stand apart from all this. Opera libretti could stress violent aspects of the Renaissance, but it was as if sixteenth-century men, when they were in a secular mood, made music in nineteenth-century style. Occasionally one reads of the music that might accompany a scene of robbers (the *Räuberroman*, often set in the distant past, was a favorite early Romantic genre) or smugglers in action; but the music for such a scene, sounding like thunder or wind in the trees, would be a contemporary piece, not one by a Renaissance or Baroque composer.[65] The kind of vision that enabled Goethe to see both classical repose and tempestuous violence in Renaissance culture was denied to, or deliber-

---

[63]Poets, novelists, and playwrights—among them F.M. Klinger, T.Berger, J. Ch. Brandes, Wilhelm Heinse, and even the young Schiller—writing in the 1770s and 1780s were much preoccupied with this view of the Renaissance as a period of violent upheaval of every sort. See Walther Rehm, *Das Werden des Renaissancebildes in der deutschen Dichtung vom Rationalismus bis zum Realismus* (Munich, 1929), chapters 4 and 5.

[64]The quoted phrase is from Rehm, *Das Werden*, p. 91. Goethe, who translated Cellini's memoirs, was fascinated by the latter's "terribiltà" (Rehm, pp. 103, 110).

The libretto of Berlioz's *Benvenuto Cellini* in its final form was much toned down; for Berlioz's view of Cellini, his story of the artist, and his relationship to the musician, Viola, cited above, fn. 48, is much more revealing. Viola, an exceptionally vivid portrait of a Renaissance musician, is of course Berlioz himself.

[65]See the review by Carl Loewe of Beethoven's Sonata Op. 27, no. 2, in the *Berliner Allgemeine musikalische Zeitung*, vol. 14, no. 4 (1827), p. 27, in which the third movement is compared to the creaking of an old storm-tossed tree or the sound of robbers in a mountain hideout—all "Stoff zu einem Scherzo."

ated avoided by, musicians interested in the past.[66] They chose to isolate one aspect of Renaissance art, and in so doing they exaggerated and distorted its significance. Thus the study of music as an integral part of Renaissance culture was ignored, and it has taken a long time for the distorted image created by the Romantics to be corrected; indeed, we can hardly see the process of correction as completed today.

Thus in one way the straightforward chronicles of eighteenth-century historians such as Hawkins and Burney, despite their adherence to the aesthetic prejudices of their own time, are more direct ancestors of modern musical scholarship than the work of most of the Romantics, which in a way disrupted the forward march of scholarly inquiry. The Romantics, in looking at the Renaissance, often tell us more about themselves than about the subject they were writing about. This is of course a phenomenon interesting in itself. And further, Romantic enthusiasm provided an impetus for scholarly work, as the achievement of Ambros shows. The scholarly work which we, ever so cautiously and soberly, cultivate in the field of Renaissance music continues on occasion to reflect the glow cast upon the subject by the Romantics. It would be too bad to try to extinguish it altogether.

[66]On Goethe's ambivalent attitude toward the Renaissance, whose violence appealed to him at the same time as its classicism and its relationship to antiquity, see Rehm, *Das Werden*, pp. 103, 110, 117–18, 128.

Claude Debussy, Melodramatist

LAURENCE BERMAN

THE ABOVE TITLE IS AN exaggeration. As such, it means to be in keeping with the subject it announces (or more precisely, the latter half of the subject). Equally in keeping is the shock value of a misalliance: what can the reticence of Debussy possibly have to do with the high voltage of melodrama? While I mean to give this question my full attention, I am perhaps even more concerned with the matter of restoring melodrama's good name. Legitimate artistic categories being in short supply, we cannot afford to lose one to a value judgment. And value judgment is largely what has befallen melodrama: "melodramatic" has come more and more to be a convenient label that critics attach to whatever does not conform to certain current preconceptions of good art ("balance," "formal integrity," "emotional sincerity," etc.), even though in their more clearheaded moments, these same critics must recognize that the valid distinction to be made is not between melodrama and good art, but between bad and good melodrama.

In the present essay, I aim to follow the lead of a few literary scholars who, in their efforts to enhance the fortunes of melodrama, have linked the genre with a literary name reputed for extreme subtlety and complexity of psychological analysis: Henry James. This link is encouraged by James's professed admiration for Balzac, the long-recognized and oft-maligned exponent of every trick of the melodramatic trade. Peter Brooks takes James's interest in Balzac to signal the "melodramatic tenor" of James's own imagination.[1] Describing that imagination, Theodora Bosanquet, the author's secretary, once wrote:

> When he walked out of the refuge of his study into the world and looked about him, he saw a place of torment, where creatures of prey perpetually thrust their claws into the quivering flesh of the doomed, defenceless children of light.[2]

---

[1]Peter Brooks, "The Melodramatic Imagination," in *Romanticism*, ed. David Thorburn and Geoffrey Hartman (Ithaca, 1973), p. 203.

[2]*Ibid.*, p. 203.

Bosanquet's description is very apt in characterizing a hyperactive way of looking at the world. If this was James's way—and one has no reason to believe that it was not—it is hardly betrayed by James's literary style, the epitome of courtliness and discretion. James's use of language seems directly calculated to cover up violent emotion, or perhaps more precisely, to let it peek through just enough for us to see it as the undercurrent running through his work. In the direct tradition of courtly manners, *The Golden Bowl* is an object lesson in how a most exquisitely artful self-control exerted by each of the four protagonists succeeds in preventing the total shattering of their lives, even as it seals their unhappiness for all time. Few will deny that James's language of suggestion is a brilliant solution for his own purposes. But in the final analysis, suggestion runs counter to the melodramatic mode: the Jamesian novel provides resolution but not that full-blown, no-holds-barred release which is the mark of true melodrama. What James seems to have effected is a change in balance amounting to a paradox, for even as melodramatic expression has been discarded, melodramatic content has been preserved. If this is so, we may have a clue as to how to interpret certain developments taking place in late nineteenth-century France, notably among the Symbolists.

Critical judgment against melodrama comes in a variety of forms, some more subtle than others. In a study of Shakespearean tragedy entitled *Fools of Time*, the eminent critic Northrop Frye argues:[3]

> We began this discussion by establishing a distinction between authentic tragedy and melodrama. By melodrama I mean a dramatic vision that confirms the audience's stock moral responses, that achieves comedy primarily by applauding the hero and tragedy primarily by punishing the villain. Such a dramatic vision is aesthetic in the perverted Kierkegaardian sense of externalizing man's ethical freedom. In a sense it is anti-tragic providing as it does a justification for a tragic action that comes from something outside tragedy, and so, really, explaining tragedy away.

Finely reasoned as this statement appears, its reference to tragedy as "authentic" must inevitably cast a suspicion of inauthenticity on melodrama. In another place, Frye has called melodrama "a type of comedy without humor."[4] But whether linked with tragedy or comedy, the unique features of the genre are less likely to emerge than if they were examined independently of other categories. Where Frye has at least made some interesting and valid distinctions, others have summarily dismissed melodrama as dealing in unrelieved exaggeration. If,

[3]Northrop Frye, *Fools of Time* (Toronto, 1967), pp. 115–16.
[4]Northrop Frye, *Anatomy of Criticism* (Princeton, 1957), p. 40.

as we suspect, what such critics mean by exaggeration is the practice of literary melodrama to represent supposedly normal, everyday people acting in a manner far more violent and emotional than they would act in everyday life, the answer is simple enough: melodramatic expression is indeed highly charged, highly colored expression, but that is because the basic obligation of melodrama, as with any authentic art, is to be faithful not to "everyday life" but to "inner life," which is a reality not actually seen, but envisioned. Melodrama is, just as Frye says, a "dramatic vision," and that vision, in order to be true to itself, demands to be dramatized in hypervivid terms. Melodrama *is* antitragic—again, just as Frye says—though not necessarily for the reasons he gives; far from being a subform of tragedy, it is rather based on assumptions almost diametrically opposed to those underlying tragedy. Its central vision is excitement, while that of tragedy is suffering.

The formalist emphasis in present-day aesthetics *(ars gratia artis)* has done much to obscure the alternate conception of art as symbol. It is therefore increasingly difficult for us to understand (to take the particular example at hand) how melodrama as an artistic genre corresponds to something that originates in the everyday human imagination, something born in the seat of primitive human desire. Whenever we suffer an affront, or feel betrayed or merely inconvenienced, our melodramatic impulse sets to work and produces a scenario designed to rectify the supposed wrong. The most minor irritant, from a surly petty functionary to a jaywalking pedestrian to a neighbor's stereo blaring forth the latest hard-rock gem, is usually enough to touch off in our minds a melodramatic episode, in which the offending party is cast as the villain against our own immemorial role as virtue personified. Usually, these episodes do not get beyond the imaginal stage, the censor of reason stepping in to prevent further developments. There is, however, a type of personality with a distinct taste for overt melodrama—for creating conflicts that others find unnecessary and exhausting, if not genuinely painful. Examples of the type are easy to find in settings involving any extended partnership, personal or professional. In these examples we discover the very positive character the subject attaches to conflict, as if conflict were the only means by which life could take on meaning and excitement and the subject himself become an object of surpassing interest.

So far we have defined the "melodramatic component" of human psychology as part fantasy, part neurosis. But if fantasy and neurosis are, as we believe today, undeniable presences in human nature, any activity that purports to study human nature at close range cannot afford to pass them by. Western literature is such an activity; yet the history of Western literature shows that melodrama was a latecomer to the pantheon of recognized literary genres and that it has enjoyed comparatively little prestige. One reason for this must be that fantasy and neurosis, until very recently, have not been considered edifying emotions. They may shed light on human motivation, but on its more ephemeral and trivial, if not baser, aspects; by the standards of tragedy, they have no "ethical" value. Aeschylus' famous lines in the *Agamemnon* about the acquisition of self-awareness through suffering do not mean merely that man learns to know himself only when he is hit by tragedy; they tell us also that tragedy teaches us how to endure, thus, to grow, to become more human.[5] In Sophocles' dramas on the Oedipus story, the hero's healing experience at Colonnus is what redeems the catastrophe at Thebes. But in fact, this central idea of fifth-century tragedy—that suffering is a specifically human possession and not to be despised—is already prefigured in Homer; in a number of places and in varying degrees of explicitness, he delivers the stunning insight that the gods are inferior to men because they are ethically superficial, having been protected from crisis through their immortality and so never having been truly tested.[6]

Great tragic art presents terrible dilemmas for which there are no final answers. By comparison, melodrama, with its sharply drawn antagonisms and neat solutions, looks like a quick release to blocked desire, a glorified safety-valve, a vicarious means of escaping pain by romanticizing it and turning it into dangerous charm. I do not mean to leave the impression that melodrama is therapy rather than art, but from the viewpoint of tragedy it may seem so; and that alone does much to explain why melodrama was so long in coming into its own. Still, the impulse of melodrama is alive in a great deal of art where it would not be suspected, much less identified, by the practitioners themselves: Hellenistic sculpture, for instance, or Baroque painting and music. The evolution from Classical poise to Baroque restlessness is usually described as representing a tendency away from ethical toward pathetic expression. While this is generally true, I would propose the following modification: pathos is not an elemental conception, but rather a curious admixture of ethos and melodrama, marking a point somewhere between those conceptual extremes. As an aesthetic principle, pathos concentrates on *arousal* of emotion—Monteverdi's La Musica sings of "inflaming the iciest hearts"—and thus pulls away

---

[5]*Agamemnon*, Opening Chorus, Strophe 3.

[6]See Charles Rowan Beye, *Ancient Greek Literature and Society* (Garden City, New York, 1975), pp. 66–77, for an illuminating discussion of this point. I should add that my reading of *Oedipus at Colonnus* comes closer to Beye's than to that of Walter Kaufmann, who thinks that the notion of this play as expressing humane and life-affirming sentiments is totally "misguided." See Kaufmann, *Tragedy and Philosophy* (Princeton, 1968), p. 281.

from the more Classical notion of *purgation* or *catharsis*. Behind the aesthetic notion of arousal lies the impulse to see the world as fundamentally vibrant and exciting: Milton's reference to "gorgeous tragedy" suggests that something has been added to the original Aristotelian conception of confronting suffering soberly—with, so to speak, "all passion spent."[7] We have been conditioned to treat tragedy as a focal point of Western thought and to look upon pathos as tragedy's major effect, but it may clarify matters to place pathos at the center of Baroque thought and to think of tragedy as the major vehicle by which pathos makes itself felt. This would at least confirm the generally held contention that the Italians of the early Baroque were willing to sacrifice a measure of "dignity" (i.e., sobriety) of expression for an increase in vehemence.

The word *pathos* has come to have at least two connotations— suffering and passion—which are in dialectical tension with each other. The modern association of suffering with pain and of passion with romance is greatly due, I believe, to the positive feeling the Baroque period attached to passion. In the aesthetic of the Baroque, "noble rage" is the root cause of dynamic growth, the creative energy that sets things in motion and inspires heroic action. A "heroic effort" is one that transcends the normally human, that distinguishes itself in action we call "extraordinary." Such an effort requires passion; without passion there can be no aspiration to greatness, to *gloire*. But this passion, in order to work toward the desired end, must be properly channeled and directed. If the qualities of directedness and sustained growth are particularly felt in works of art of the mature Baroque period, it must be because those works realize a vision of passion not merely subjected to control but made manifest and grandly effective through such control.

Here we may detect the chief distinguishing feature between ethos and pathos. The courtly ethic of the hero-leader is common to them both; but while ethos emphasizes sobriety and composure, pathos concentrates on excitability and rage. Yet the element of control implicit in the ideal "*noble* rage" reminds us that passion, in the Baroque view of things, will lead to a triumphant end only when it is accompanied by manifest signs of discipline and dignity. In this context we are able to see what distinguishes, in the Baroque mind, pathos from tragedy: the central content of Baroque pathos is not suffering, but—though it may seem like a contradiction—passion triumphant. Tragedy, of course, does have a place in Baroque thought; indeed, it appears at just those moments when the Baroque ideal of passion controlled (thus, trium-

---

[7]Milton's epithet appears in the Penseroso section of *L'Allegro ed il Penseroso*, "Sometime let Gorgeous Tragedy in Scepter'd Pall come sweeping by." Handel's setting of these lines (1740) takes the form of an aria in moderate $\frac{3}{4}$ time in F♯ minor.

phant) is upset. Tragedy, in short, is the direct outcome of an *excess* of passion. Discussing the drama of Racine, Wilfrid Mellers underlines the "evil" of unruly passion:[8]

> The intensity of passion in [Racine's] characters, especially Phèdre, sometimes breaks down the conventional norm; but it is only because of the existence of the norm that the effect of the passion is overwhelming. The sudden glimpses of an unsuspected world in the dark reaches of the mind which the imagery and movement reveal to us, are the more terrible because they appear against the background of "les bornes de l'austère pudeur."

"Les bornes" are precisely those limits beyond which healthy passion does not venture; the very formality of Baroque manners is designed to keep passion from running out of control, from becoming tragic and destructive. Melodrama, however, recognizes no such limits. Where passion is concerned, it is melodrama's mission to reach for the ultimate.

It is common knowledge that with the advent of the Renaissance, modern European art made a conscious effort to reinstate the ancient principle of mimesis, that is, the action by which an artwork imitates its contents through its material attributes. It is also true that the importance of mimesis grew proportionately with the growing conviction that it was a revelation of human nature; if human emotions had become the central object of artistic interest, artists must find the imitative means at their disposal to render those emotions in all their diversity and drama. The particular interest of Baroque pathos in excited emotion comes out plainly in Monteverdi's claims to having found the musical means of imitating the affection he calls *concitato*. But *concitato*, which I believe is better translated as "noble rage" than as "agitation," corresponds exactly to the Baroque view of passion discussed above.[9] As children of an age whose assumptions have been greatly

[8]Wilfrid Mellers, *François Couperin and the French Classical Tradition* (New York, 1968), pp. 38–39.

[9]In the English version of Monteverdi's preface to the *Madrigali Guerrieri ed Amorosi* of 1638 that appears in Strunk, *Source Readings in Music History*, ed. Oliver Strunk (New York, 1950), pp. 413–415, *stile concitato* is translated as "agitated style." My choice of "noble rage" is prompted by a moment from the prologue of Monteverdi's *Orfeo* of 1607 (already referred to above in another context), in which La Musica sings: "Et hor di nobil' ira et hor d'amore poss'infiammar le più gelate menti" (And with noble rage and with love I can inflame the iciest hearts). Those who are familiar with this passage will remember that the composer, in an effort to make the music closely imitate the sense of the text, sets the words "Et hor di nobil' ira et hor d'amore" to a flurry of thirty-second notes. In other words, he renders them in just that excited "Pyrrhic rhythm" which, thirty years later, in the 1638 preface, he will describe as being the essence of *concitato* expression. Although it is true that the most memorable and developed examples of this excited speech are found in the *Combattimento di Tancredi e Clorinda* of 1624 (see *Historical Anthology of Music*, ed. Archibald T. Davison and

shaped by the experience of Romanticism, we are inclined to equate Baroque and Romantic versions of passion by defining them both from the Romantic perspective. But we should bear in mind that in all courtly thought lies the inevitable balance between feeling and behavior, the tension between how a man acts (affect) and how he should act (ethos). Romanticism predicates the notion of *unqualified* emotion, and thus dispenses with the constraints on feeling imposed by behavior. In encouraging the *stile concitato*, Baroque pathos shows more than a passing sympathy for melodramatic excitement; but only with Romanticism does melodrama have the chance to emerge as the primary content of European expression—in short, to assume its place as the quintessential Romantic mode.

It is difficult to know which is uppermost in Romantic aims, knowledge of unknown power or ecstatic sensation. Even the early German Romantics are vague—perhaps deliberately so—as to the primary direction of their gaze: is it fixed on the self and the burning question of personal freedom, or does it look out toward an incommensurable and mysterious beyond? Hoffman says of Beethoven's Fifth Symphony that it leads "the listener imperiously forward into the spirit world of the infinite";[10] Herder refers to "the dark abyss of your soul."[11] The intermingling of "my soul" and "immeasurable space" described by Phillip Otto Runge in the following statement comes close to Schopenhauer's realization that the distinction between the psychological and the ontological—between "inner" and "outer" being—is negligible, by reason of the infiniteness of both:

> When the sky above me teems with innumerable stars, the wind blows through the vastness of space, the wave breaks in the immense night . . . then my soul rejoices and soars in the immeasurable space around me, there is no high or low, no time, no beginning and no end.[12]

Runge's testimony is the raw material of mysticism, the sensation of

---

Willi Apel, vol. II, No. 189), this fleeting passage from *Orfeo* is testimony to the fact that Monteverdi intuitively understood the expressive possibilities of *stile concitato* long before he gave them a name and consciously went about methodizing them in the *Combattimento*.

This last point is worth noting, but my main point still concerns the translation of the word "concitato" itself. If I insist on *"noble* rage," it is because the Baroque perception of passion is not of any kind of rage—not what a later period would call "frenzy" or "agitation"—but of a rage powerfully directed and focused, calculated to have an imposing and authoritative effect. In short, noble rage is the passion of a leader.

[10]E. T. A. Hoffmann: "Beethoven's Instrumental Music", in *Source Readings*, p. 778.

[11]Herder's statement is quoted in Friedrich Blume, *Classic and Romantic Music*, trans. M. D. Herter Norton (New York, 1970), p. 13.

[12]Quoted in Hugh Honour, *Romanticism* (New York, 1979), p. 73.

terror and joy that Cassirer calls the "momentary god" and Otto the "wholly other"—rightly so, because the sensation itself appears to the sentient subject as an unmistakable sign of contact with something nonhuman and ultimate.[13] This mystical experience, however, is sporadic and momentary; it needs a sustained and steadily pursued program to give it more permanent meaning. Traditionally, this was supplied by religious doctrine and the *askesis* of monastic life. Romanticism proposes instead the sensuousness of art.

The effect of Romanticism's innovation is still with us today. In the minds of many, art continues to stand superior to religion and philosophy as a means of achieving ultimate significance. Art, of course, has always relied on the sensuous image to reveal its contents, but the idea forwarded by Romanticism that the senses can be engaged in the pursuit not only of *ethos* and *pathos*, but also of *logos*—even more, that the only kind of human sensibility prepared to apprehend the transcendent is the artistic kind—extends the capacities of art beyond any prior conception. Among all the arts, the place of music in the hierarchy of human activities is the one most radically affected by this development. Because music is imagined to operate on a level of consciousness where intellect and the senses are absorbed into a unity, and subject and object are no longer distinguishable, it is the modality supremely equipped to embody the Romantic vision of transcendence. We may say that Romantic music imitates the experience the individual undergoes in reaching for the "spirit-world," and, in so doing, means to become that experience.

The history of Romantic music shows this imitative process to have taken a number of distinct forms. For the purposes at hand, however, we must limit ourselves to considering only that category of Romantic art that operates under the direct initiative of melodrama. Melodrama is less high-minded than Romanticism, dedicated merely to the psychological reality we call excitement, or the promise of desire fulfilled. But the precise nature of that reality lends to Romantic expression a unique character, one that we associate in particular with a musical style prevailing between 1830 and 1880. To consider for a moment an earlier style: we can accept Hoffmann's view of Beethoven as a Romantic in the sense that Beethoven's music aims at (and indeed achieves) transcendent feeling. But Beethoven's illuminations are too meditated, his exhilaration too much the product of struggle and breakthrough to

---

[13]Ernst Cassirer's discussion of the "momentary god" is found in *Language and Myth*, trans. Susanne K. Langer (New York, 1953), pp. 17–23. Rudolf Otto's concept of the "holy other" is the central theme of his once extremely influential book, *The Idea of the Holy* (London, 1936), a translation by J. W. Harvey of *Das Heilige: Ueber das Irrationale in der Idee des Göttlichen und sein Verhältnis zum Rationalen* (Breslau, 1917).

have any connection with melodrama. The essential quality of melodramatic emotion is its suddenness, the effect it gives of having come
from nowhere; in that respect, it corresponds to the mystical sensation
referred to above as the "momentary god." We are reminded by
Nietzsche that Dionysian ritual was the ancient Greek way of re-
creating the original, spontaneous mystical experience by inducing
trance (or, to use Nietzsche's word, "intoxication"). The final objective
of this practice—union with the god—could be effected only through an
ec-stasis, a surrendering of (a "stepping-out-from") the self. By virtue of
this example, one realizes that to live "at the brink of emotion" means
to give oneself up to one's emotion totally and unqualifiedly. Romantic
rapture, like the ancient ecstasis (though realized through art instead of
ritual), is the feeling of total release, acquired through the surrendering
of all control.

In musical terms, melodrama gets expressed in three distinct image-
types. First, there is the *agitato* image such as we find at the beginning
of the Chopin Scherzo in B♭ minor, where the sharp juxtapositions of
high and low, forte and piano, full and spare textures bear analogies to
the clashes of the "forces of light and darkness" of literary melodrama.
Second, there is the imitation of rapture in process, the wave of heav-
ing, rolling, surging, billowing sound by which the experiencing subject
is transported to a final peak of excitement and permanent release. The
"Funeral March" Sonata of Chopin (Ex. 1) provides a consummate example, as does, of course, the Liebestod of *Tristan*. Finally, there is the
music of evocation and reverie, which, rather than lifting up the listener and carrying him away, steals over him and wraps him in a man-
tle of velvet sonority. In the seventh and fourteenth nocturnes of
Chopin, the dark harmonic coloring is at the same time so soft and so
iridescent, that what in an earlier style would have been taken as a
tragic image seems, in the new context, a symbol of seductive and exciting mystery. The masterpieces of Chopin and Wagner leave us with
the sense that the pain of darkness has been exchanged for the enigma
of darkness. The sultry aura of such music seems to correspond to the
enigmatic source itself, where life's pain and pleasure have been tran-
scended and no distinction remains between the demonic and the divine. Similarly, the opposition has been removed between the self-
centeredness of melodramatic wish-fulfillment and the "giving up of
the self" embodied in the aesthetic emotion of *ecstasis*. In this particular action, great melodramatic music truly realizes the central Romantic prophecy of art as transcendence; for what in everyday life would
have remained a permanent contradiction is—and could only be—
reconciled through the very seductiveness of the artwork. The natural
symbiosis of melodrama and Romanticism is thus confirmed.

Recent criticism has taken to replacing Debussy's traditional

Example 1. Chopin Sonata in B♭ minor, op. 35, mvt. 1, mm. 61–81

status of "colorist" with that of "structuralist." Along with this revision has grown the tendency to downplay his associations with Impressionism. Jean Barraqué, for instance, has gone so far as to speak of "the myth of Impressionist music"—"a rather vague notion," he writes, "which was to serve, for close to fifty years, to cover up the Debussyan revolution with a screen of pink smoke."[14] Merely to reverse an earlier trend, however, is not necessarily to create a more balanced picture. If only in terms of stylistic innovations—the blurring of figure and ground, the tendency toward subtle shiftings of color and away from sharp oppositions, the breaking up of line and mass to create effects of buoyancy and shimmer—the parallels between Debussy and Impressionist painting are too striking to be ignored. But beyond technique and style, works such as the song "L'échelonnement des haies" and the piano pieces "Jardins sous la pluie" and "Reflets dans l'eau" seem to embody the basic values of Impressionism, its original spiritual impulse. In the words of Werner Hofmann, "Impressionism is the 'voice' of the spirit of the liberal bourgeoisie which withdrew from its public duties and sought to create an earthly paradise within its private world."[15] If Hofmann is right, Impressionism in its most intuitive phase is an updating of the Arcadian pastoral, which seeks out the idyllic and the gently civilized in an effort to express the ideals of peace, intimate community, and cultivated well-being. Pastoral, then, would be the art of *ethos* in the most orthodox Platonic sense; and in that respect, Claude Debussy, Impressionist, would seem to have as much to do with melodrama as Louis XIV with tap-dancing.

The significance of Impressionism, however, does not stop with the idyll of pastoral art. It is true that Impressionist painting concentrates on nature as a harmony, a blending of diverse shapes and forms. But along with that cheerful vision comes the more ambiguous one of nature as a field of change: Impressionism earns its name honestly in the sense that it is concerned with the fleeting impression, the momentary sensation destined for oblivion. The monochrome effect of Monet's *Impression: View of Le Havre* (the result of nuanced differentiations of gray rather than color) and its confusion of figure and ground connote shadowiness and ephemerality; the fleeting image becomes the symbol not only of our capacity to enjoy the experiences of this world but also of our incapacity to hold on to such experiences and find in them some enduring character.[16] Typically, Impressionism offers only the artwork

[14]Jean Barraqué, *Debussy* (Paris, 1962), p. 106. The translation is mine.

[15]Werner Hofmann, *The Earthly Paradise* (New York, 1961), p. 346.

[16]Monet's painting of Le Havre was first exhibited in 1874, and its title apparently suggested to a critic present at the exhibition the name "Impressionism." One of the most frequently reproduced Impressionist paintings, it has been used recently as the cover illustration for the Dover publication of Debussy's piano music.

itself, "capturing" the fugitive event as a kind of tentative insurance against impermanency. Nature and light are the primary symbols of the Impressionist painter, because they stand for what is *known* about the world—what is confined to time and space and can be experienced through the senses. In those paintings where gray haze predominates, there may be more than a suggestion of light's opposite, but Impressionists typically do not explore beyond natural limits; in later nineteenth-century France that function is left to the Symbolists.

Symbolism, too, begins with "transient facts"; but, as Rémy de Gourmont writes, it means to "attend to the permanent meaning" of those facts, to "seek the eternal in the diversity of shifting forms."[17] At its most ambitious and high-minded (the poetry of Mallarmé, the drama of Maeterlinck, the painting of Odilon Redon), Symbolism is turned toward the unknown: Redon is described as a "poet of the night," Maeterlinck confesses to having a "passion for the beyond."[18] Symbolism is thus a visionary art—the first since Romanticism; and like Romanticism, it feels art to be society's only promise, the only road to ultimate understanding. But while the Romantic travels this road in something of a state of exhilaration, the Symbolist is more ambivalent: behind the mystery may be concealed total significance—the sublime—or nothing but a void.

This alternation between hope and dread is presented in particularly acute form in the late sonnets of Mallarmé. The sonnet, a tight design under normal circumstances, undergoes an extreme compression in Mallarmé's hands, as if to convey the intense struggle waged by the artist in wresting a few precious drops of meaning from the impenetrable darkness. Not only the form of the typical Mallarmé sonnet, an intricate system of sense/sound relationships that might well fall apart or explode were one detail to be changed, but also the imagery—a swan caught helpless in an icy lake, the earth ("this festive planet") found flickering in an otherwise "hideous emptiness of time"—continually proclaim the life-and-death character of the modern poet's condition. The poem is his only hope of salvation, or perhaps more realistically, the only means of staving off an eternity of nothingness.[19]

Debussy's associations, both personal and artistic, with Mallarmé and Maeterlinck are well documented. The influence of Mallarmé on Debussy has its most specific outlet in the *Prelude to the Afternoon of a*

[17] Quoted in *French Symbolist Painters*, ed. Geneviève Lacambre (London, 1972), pp. 166–167.

[18] Maeterlinck attributes his "passion for the beyond" to Poe; see Edward Lockspeiser, *Debussy: His Life and Mind* (New York, 1962), vol. I, p. 196.

[19] The poems in question are "Le vierge, le vivace, et le bel aujourd'hui" and "Quand l'ombre menaça de la fatale loi."

Faun (1892–94), though the deeper lessons of Mallarmé may have been learned later.[20] The impact of Maeterlinck's *Pelléas and Mélisande*, which I will discuss below, cannot be overestimated. It is easy to see the charming ambiguity of Impressionism merging imperceptibly into the more sustained hiddenness of Symbolism. And Debussy's status as a Symbolist is as natural and self-evident to modern critics as his affinities with Impressionism were to an earlier generation. Still, this last fact is hardly adequate reason to link Debussy to *melodrama;* on the contrary, Symbolism would remove itself from melodrama just to the extent that it looks upon terrifying experience as painful instead of seductive.

If there is any justification for the title of this essay, it must be looked for in a larger context than Symbolism can supply. We must consider what it was to be an artist in France in the last two decades of the century and to live through the first stages of a crisis that is still with us. That crisis took shape in the conscious realization of a discrepancy— the discrepancy between an implicit belief in art as the ultimate revelation and the uncertainty as to what there was left to reveal. To the avant-garde artist of c. 1890, Wagner's monumental work could be more an obstacle than an inspiration; for if one believed that Wagner had said it all, then there was nothing more to say. On the other hand, the encyclopedic certainty of Wagner provoked sincere misgivings in those who saw reality as something less whole than Wagner had pictured it and sublimity as something less palpable. The fragmentary and ambiguous effect of Symbolist art is not an isolated event in fin-de-siècle France; it is indicative of a generally questioning and ironic mood. Such a welter of post-Romantic fallout as is represented by Aestheticism, Decadent Art, Pre-Raphaelism, and Art Nouveau (in addition to Impressionism and Symbolism) attests, perhaps more than any other factor, to a disintegration of shared belief, a splintering of values.

The Symbolist solution to this predicament was to proclaim uncertainty itself as the central theme. In terms of the theme of the present essay, however, the examples of Decadence and Aestheticism may be more pertinent; for the artists who fall loosely under these two rubrics are, unlike the Symbolists and the Romantics, no visionaries. They see the world not in ontological terms, but as a projection of their own psychological needs. In that respect, Aestheticism and Decadence are the logical descendants of melodrama, all three art-classes motivated by the promise not of ultimate revelation, but of ultimate ecstasy. This motivation is pointedly expressed in a letter from Wagner to Liszt writ-

[20]In my article *"Prelude to the Afternoon of a Faun* and *Jeux:* Debussy's Summer Rites" in *19th Century Music,* 3 (1980), 225–238, I try to show how *Jeux* (1913) bears closer comparison than the Prelude with Mallarmé's procedures.

ten in 1854, in which he says that since he has never felt true love, he will write an opera in compensation.[21] If Wagner's remark causes us some uneasiness, it is first because he seems to sell himself short—the chief intimation of his remark being that had he actually experienced true love, he would never have felt the compulsion to write *Tristan*—and second, because the conception of art as sublimation finds little favor today in critical circles. This last fact explains in part why Aestheticism and Decadence have been relegated to the byways of art history, and why *Tristan*, by contrast, is an "edifying" landmark, insofar as Wagner is able to convince us that revelation and sublimation—or, more precisely, the ecstasy that proceeds from sublimation—are one and the same thing.

But there is another reason why Aestheticism and Decadence are typed as secondary art-movements: the sublimations they create are of a very particular and restricted sort—dream-images alongside which those of melodrama emerge the very picture of health. The wish-fulfillment of Aestheticism is prompted by a revulsion for the ugliness of everyday urban life, hence the urge to find refuge in an artworld of fairy wonder and physical loveliness.[22] Decadence seeks not so much to retreat from the everyday world as to revolt against it; images of sacrilege, debauchery, and rich voluptuousness, such as we find in Flaubert's *Salammbô* or numbers of paintings of Moreau, are designed, at least in part, to *épater les bourgeois*.[23] What Aestheticism and Decadence have in common is an obsession with the senses: a hypercivilized dependence on physical beauty in the case of the former, a near-compulsive worship of carnality in the case of the latter. The excitement of Romantic melodrama, by contrast, while containing a generous measure of the sensual, does not exclude the spiritual. When Wagner refers to "true love," he is speaking, of course, of the kind of love that is consummated in the sexual act; but the ecstasy to be derived from that act can never be ultimate and enduring unless the love is *true*—unless, in other words, desire has been intense and unswerving, and the souls of the lovers have been previously knitted together. It

---

[21]*Briefwechsel zwischen Wagner und Liszt* (Leipzig, 1900), vol. II, p. 46.

[22]The following quotation from Oscar Wilde is fairly representative of the wish-fulfillment element in the Aestheticist mentality: "And when that day dawns . . . we shall lay our hands upon the basilisk, and see the jewel in the toad's head. Champing his gilded oats, the Hippogriff will stand in our stalls, and over our heads will float the Blue Bird singing of beautiful and impossible things, of things that are lovely and that never happen, of things that are not and that should be" (*The Decay of Lying*, 1889).

[23]Flaubert as a whole would not be classified as a Decadent, but the Decadent elements in *Salammbô* and *La Tentation de St. Antoine* are unmistakable. Huysmans's *A Rebours* remains the best statement about Decadence.

is precisely the spiritual component in melodrama that permits it to be "elevated" by Romanticism.

Melodrama, then, is *erotic* art in the purest and most complete sense of the term. By erotic, however, I mean something more than the feeling that is normally associated with sexual love, though in the same breath I admit that sexual love is the most intense image of the erotic there exists, and thus the best way we have of grasping the principle of Eros. Freud defines Eros as the life-force and contrasts it with Thanatos, the death instinct, which is not a wish for literal death, but the will to reach what James Hillman has described as the "state below and after the actions of life and . . . deeper than they—that is, what is symbolically attributed to death."[24] As another author writes:[25]

> Classical Indian philosophy has always followed the Thanatos principle and rejected the principle of Eros; the ideal state, the goal, is the reintegration of the self into the perfect whole, the 'release' of the individual life force from the debasing influence of the senses so that it may be reabsorbed into the undifferentiated god-head. This is the 'blowing out of the flame' *(nirvana)*.

Applied to everyday experience, Thanatos, like Eros, is *desire*—but a kind of desire pointed toward the ontological and archetypal, toward meaning free of personal and sensory implication. Thanatos would lead to what we traditionally think of as *logos;* while Eros would lead to *pathos*, because it is inextricably tied up with life and the distinguishing features of life, namely the senses and the individual self. The revolution that Romantic melodrama performs on this traditional view is to propose the possibility of arriving at *logos* by way of Eros.

Earlier, it was said that melodramatic excitement comes from the anticipation of individual desire being fulfilled. But individual desire is the very nature of Eros, which is neither mere sensual desire nor a pure reaching out to the "spirit-world," but rather a titanic yearning for unconditional individual freedom, to be realized in that mixed, imperfect, sensual/spiritual way which we think of as being specifically "human." In one respect, melodrama goes one step beyond Romanticism; for more than predicating the sensuousness of art as the imitation of its vision (which, in any case, is the factor common to all mimetic art), melodrama holds sensuality itself to be a fundamental content of that vision. If melodramatic art means to imitate the action of the individual in his effort to realize Eros—if it means to provide us with an experience of what it is to live and find fulfillment as much through the

---

[24]James Hillman, *Re-Visioning Psychology* (New York, 1977), p. 173.
[25]Wendy Doniger O'Flaherty, ed. and trans., *Hindu Myths* (Harmondsworth, England, 1975), p. 13.

senses as through the spirit—then melodramatic images must in themselves be pungent and alluring; they must have the power to seduce and
intoxicate, to take over our senses, to put us under a spell. In short, they
must be erotic.

Space will not allow us to examine in any detail how and to what
degree Debussy's music is erotic. For those who have any doubts on the
matter, I suggest beginning with the relatively early songs on the Verlaine love poems, "Green" and "En Sourdine," and comparing them to
the Fauré settings. (Fauré's songs, in their combination of tonal irides-
cence and supple, yet confined, rhythms, offer a far more restrained—
one might say dignified—conception of love than is customarily associated with the period.) Simultaneously with the composition of these
and other Verlaine songs (1888), Debussy is busy setting to music a
French translation of Dante Gabriel Rossetti's poem *The Blessed Damozel*. In a recent article entitled "Debussy and the Pre-Raphaelites,"
Richard Langham Smith explains why *Pelléas* was almost predestined
to follow on the heels of *The Blessed Damozel*. He shows the strong
presence of Pre-Raphaelite thought in the development of
Maeterlinck's thinking: "a Rossettian opposition of innocence and violence," "the visionary quality of the idealised woman," "the idea of silence as indicating a profound 'knowing.' "[26] All the links Langham
Smith draws between Rossetti and Maeterlinck are absolutely convincing. I would add only that Maeterlinck carries the Pre-Raphaelite conception of silence, to a point beyond that of the Pre-Raphaelites, and
produces a qualitative difference. In the final analysis, the Pre-
Raphaelites are wedded to their personifications—specifically, to their
image of the "ange-femme." Silence, in Rossettian terms, is the background *against* which human action takes place or *with* which human
emotion vibrates sympathetically. The genius of Maeterlinck is to have
created in *his* "ange-femme," Mélisande, not simply the embodiment
of silence, but the instrument through which silence flows. Silence in
Maeterlinck's hands becomes a force independent of personification: it
becomes nothing less than the "eternal ground of being," or what
Wordsworth a hundred years before (with an uncanny penchant for
thinking pantheistically) had described as "A motion and a spirit that
impels/All thinking things, all objects of all thought/And rolls through
all things."[27]

It is rare to be able to identify a distinct event in an artist's experience
as being the turning point of his creative life. Yet this is the precise
function of Debussy's encounter with Maeterlinck's play: if *Pelléas* did

---

[26]Langham Smith's article appears in *19th-Century Music*, 5 (1981), 95–109.
[27]William Wordsworth, *Lines Composed a Few Miles Above Tintern Abbey* (1798),
lines 100–102.

not set Debussy on a new course, it set him firmly on the course he had been groping for. Maeterlinck's conception of silence provides the vehicle enabling Debussy to make a breakthrough to his mature style, and thereby resist Wagner. For of all the avant-garde artists of late nineteenth-century France, Debussy had the most to fear about being swept away in the Wagnerian current. Lockspeiser and others have written at length on Debussy's ambivalence with regard to Wagner, on his struggles with "old Klingsor" even during the writing of *Pelléas*.[28] What Maeterlinck does for Debussy is to take the two fundamental elements of Romantic melodrama—Eros and the "ultimate mystery"— and change definitively the balance between them. The tumult of Wagner's music is the dynamic action of Eros as it reaches for the ultimate mystery and finally achieves it in a heroic synthesis of body and spirit. For Maeterlinck, the mystery—the undifferentiated whole, the static principle—is the *given*, not the endpoint; Eros becomes a secondary element, a force attached to the dualistic nature of the world, working in contention with the unity, even though born of it.

To match the stillness of Maeterlinck's play, Debussy invents a music that approaches literal silence—a silence broken only, but then paroxystically, by Golaud's outbursts of violence, as in the scenes where Yniold is held up to the window and Mélisande is dragged along by her hair. In *Pelléas*, then, Eros is represented chiefly as an evil, as human passion disruptive and out of control; out of control precisely because it does not know how to give up asserting its own will and yield to the will of destiny. In Debussy's works after *Pelléas*, Eros is an almost constant presence, though it need not always carry the same tragic implications. In *Sirènes*, its significance, personified in the sirens themselves, is an ambiguous cross between destructiveness and alluring beauty; at the end of the first movement of *La Mer*, Eros, symbolized in the sun rising to its zenith, is the life-force triumphant.

In all of these cases, Eros is signalled in musical terms by *paroxysm*—a momentary release of energy that can no longer be contained "beneath the surface," so to speak, but which, having pierced the surface, is dispelled as suddenly as it rose up. Paroxysm becomes a habit, if not a formula, in Debussy's later works. We find its effect not only in the pieces just mentioned but also in the second movement of *La Mer*, *Jeux*, *Pagodes*, *Voiles*, the *Étude pour les tierces*, the Sonata for flute, viola and harp. Paroxysm becomes Debussy's way of simultaneously compressing reality into little blinding flashes of truth and giving shape to his larger-scale musical designs. He prepares for the outbursts by laying down that blanket of static harmony, animated by an interac-

[28]See Lockspeiser, *Debussy*, p. 191.

tion of microscopic motifs, which we have come to think of as the typical Impressionistic texture (Ex. 2a). Yet, in view of the above discussion, the confusion of figure and ground that this texture represents
may be more expressive of Symbolist silence than Impressionist quiet.
To paraphrase Rémy de Gourmont, Debussy is perhaps more interested
in the eternal aspect of shifting forms than in their diversity. Nevertheless, both static and dynamic principles are alive in this interplay of motif and harmonic ground; the motifs themselves contribute their part to
the overall sonorous hum, yet they are not submerged in that hum to
the extent of losing their identity and thus forsaking the opportunity to
emerge at a later time and claim center stage. Perhaps no motif is more
expressive of this last action than the figure emitted *sotto voce* by the
horns and mezzo-sopranos at the opening of *Sirènes* and then reappear-
ing in all its untrammeled splendor in the strings at m. 76 (Ex. 2a and
2b).

Example 2a. from *Sirènes*, piano reduction by Gustave Samazeuilh

Example 2b. measures 76–83

In paroxysm Debussy's melodramatic longings find their proper fulfillment. Clearly, a Symbolist artist, true to his vision of the world as ambiguity and uncertainty, could not engage in the extended raptures of a Chopin or a Wagner. But *ecstasis* was too imperious a demand in Debussy's artistic nature to be ignored altogether; he was attracted to Chopin and Wagner no less than James was to Balzac. Indeed, his ambivalence regarding Wagner is not from lack of feeling but from too much feeling: it is Stravinsky rather than Debussy who had nothing to fear from Wagner, because he was, from the very outset, impervious to Klingsor's charms.[29] Both James and Debussy liberate themselves from pure melodramatic expression through understatement, though Debussy's style, in following Maeterlinck's path toward stasis and "a failure to say," probably represents a more far-reaching solution than James's elaborately allusive speech. Of course, the language of both artists is often described as being distinctly "antimelodramatic"; but if the choice of this adjective is a correct one, then it means all the more that their respective arts were forged out in the context of melodrama itself.

No discussion of Debussy and melodrama could be considered adequate without a reference, however brief, to Poe. Poe's overwhelming influence in later nineteenth-century France has always to some degree mystified the American intellectual community, which sets much greater store by Hawthorne and Melville. Nonetheless, every artistic movement in France of the period—with the notable exception of Impressionism—claims Poe as its spiritual ancestor. Decadence and Pre-Raphaelism, especially, are inconceivable without Poe's conception of beauty equated with death, reflecting the tendency of the erotic sensibility to be so overwhelmed by the experience of great physical beauty that such beauty must in the final analysis belong not to nature, but to the dark and secret realm beyond. Debussy's obsession with Poe most clearly manifests itself in his persistent, yet abortive, attempts to make operas of two of Poe's tales, *The Fall of the House of Usher* and *The Devil in the Belfry*. The first of these, with its murky atmosphere and paroxystic *dénouement*, would seem obvious material for Debussyan treatment. Andrew Porter suggests that this may have been just the problem. In more than one place Debussy makes clear his intentions of working out a totally new manner in setting *The Fall of the House of Usher* to music, and he is particularly concerned not to write another *Pelléas*.[30] But as Porter quite justly remarks:[31]

> How could an opera set in an ancient castle where the air seems stifling, where the action passes into subterranean vaults, where a pale, mysterious maiden suffers, fail to recall "Pelléas" in subject or atmosphere?

It was indeed unlikely that a composer who, by a great effort of will, had escaped one tradition, namely the Wagnerian, could escape a sec-

[29]*Ibid.*, p. 94.
[30]Andrew Porter, "Fragments of the House of Usher," *New Yorker Magazine,* March 14, 1977, p. 133.
[31]*Ibid.*

ond tradition, namely his own.[32] Porter gives further reasons why Debussy might not have been able to bring the Poe projects to a proper conclusion. He is not alone: a number of other commentators have done their part to add to what is now a fast-growing collection of hypotheses. At the risk of flooding the market, I would like to advance two hypotheses of my own. The first concerns Debussy's perception of the character of Roderick Usher. In one account of his intentions, Debussy speaks of his opera as a "progressive expression of anguish," a characterization that suggests that he saw Poe's hero essentially as a tragic figure. But Usher's "anguish" has nothing of the nature of tragic suffering; it is a kind of dread that goes hand in hand with hallucination and sensuality, and thus deliberately avoids the business of arousing pity. *Pelléas* has moments of true tragedy, but Poe's tale is steeped in melodrama. Debussy might have found the emotional substance of *Usher* resistant to a tragic setting, if that, in fact, is what he wanted to provide it. This brings us to my second hypothesis. Being melodrama, Poe's work was facing a rapidly developing problem of communication in the Paris of 1910. Debussy may have been dimly aware of this. He may have realized that in spite of his own delicious absorption in *Usher*, the revolutions being fomented in the art worlds of 1910 were day by day consigning Poe to protracted, if not terminal obsolescence. Melodrama would continue to thrive as the stuff of popular art, but it had effectively ceased to function as a content of serious significance and inspiration. Indeed, far from being a content of serious significance, melodrama was soon to become, not only in artistic circles but also in the sectors of scholarly and public criticism, the easy butt of ridicule and scorn.

[32]This irony did not slip by Debussy himself, who writes to André Caplet on December 22, 1911: "I haven't yet managed to finish the two little operas of Poe. Everything strikes me as being so deadly dull. For a single bar that I write that may be free and alive, there are twenty stifled by the weight of what is known as tradition, the influence of which I consider to be hypocritical and despicable. Observe, if you please, that I am little concerned about the fact that it may be my own tradition we are talking about" (Lockspeiser, II, 148).

Back to Ars Nova Themes

NINO PIRROTTA

WHEN, AS A NOVICE MUSICOLOGIST, I first got acquainted with the manuscript Florence, Biblioteca Nazionale Centrale, Panciatichi 26, it was through a few negative photographs—white on black, the kind we used before the advent of microfilms—provided to me by my dear friend Ettore Li Gotti. Today, already almost half a century later, access to this central source of fourteenth-century Italian polyphony has been made easy and comfortable by the publication of its facsimile, pertinently sponsored by the Centro di Studi sull'Ars nova italiana del Trecento of the town of Certaldo.[1] Were the season right, I could take the facsimile with me and peruse it "sedendo all'ombra d'una bella mandorla" ("under the shade of a pretty almond tree"); nor would I feel in danger of falling asleep "su la man e'l gonbito" ("resting on hand and elbow")!

Both of these poetic images come from a madrigal set to music by Giovanni da Firenze (more precisely from Cascia, near Reggello),[2] another good friend who I hope may have condoned some wrongs I have unwittingly committed against him. Among these is my having understated the fact that Panciatichi 26 (hereafter FP; see fn. 2 for a key to manuscript sigla used in this article) is as important a source for his

---

[1]F. A. Gallo, ed., *Il codice musicale Panciatichi 26* (Florence, 1981).

[2]See Giovanni's madrigal "Sedendo all'ombra d'una bella mandorla," namely its incipit and third line "Ond'io dormetti 'n su la man e'l gonbito." For the latter I quote the version of Lo (see below for this siglum), which I prefer to the one given by G. Corsi in *Poesie musicali del Trecento* (Bologna, 1970), p. 21. The sigla I will use for the manuscripts are the following:

FC: Florence, Biblioteca del Conservatorio, D 1175
FL: Florence, Biblioteca Medicea Laurenziana, Palat. 87 (Squarcialupi Codex)
FP: Florence, Biblioteca Nazionale Centrale, Panciatichi 26
Lo: London, British Library, Add. 29987
P: Paris, Bibliothèque Nationale, fonds ital. 568
PR: Paris, Bibliothèque Nationale, fonds nouv. acq. frç. 6771 (Codex Reina)
Rs: Roma, Biblioteca Apostolica Vaticana, Rossi 215

works as for those of Landini.[3] In fact, it contains a higher percentage of Giovanni's works than it does of Landini's: eighteen out of his known corpus of nineteen pieces, including seven unica. More precisely, it contains fifteen of his sixteen extant madrigals (missing is "Fra mille corvi," an unicum in FL; but "Deh come dolcemente," "In sulla ripa," "Per ridd'andando ratto," and "Quando la stella" are unica in FP), and it is the only source of his three cacce.

I edited all these works in the first volume of the series *The Music of Fourteenth-Century Italy*,[4] not a particularly lucky volume, due to inadequate proofreading; yet I consider still valid my attempt to stress there, at least for some pieces, the divergences in readings provided by different sources.[5] I propose now to go back to such differences, typical of the oldest composers and most pronounced in Giovanni, and try to assess their meaning.

The most conspicuous variations occur in those pieces that were notated in *octonaria* or *duodenaria* measures in some sources, but in others in *quaternaria* measures, two or three of which replace, respectively, one *octonaria* or *duodenaria* of the former. It is generally agreed that the resulting pseudo-modal *Longanotation* (which also implies a reduction of the *quaternaria* according to a *sesquitertia* proportion)[6] is

---

[3]The first half of FP is entirely dedicated to Landini's works; see J. Nádas, "The Structure of MS Panciatichi 26 and the Transmission of Trecento Polyphony," *JAMS*, 34 (1981), 393 ff. For Giovanni and Piero (the latter's name is preserved only in FP), the importance of the manuscript essentially derives from the likelihood that its compilers had access to old materials, probably coming from northern Italy, that were becoming outdated; see Nádas, pp. 412–13 and fig. 7.

[4]Nino Pirrotta, ed., *The Music of Fourteenth-Century Italy*, vol. I, Corpus Mensurabilis Musicae, 8 (Rome: American Institute of Musicology, 1954)—hereafter cited as *MFCI*, I. The volume was published at the time of my first move to the United States and is affected by a number of minor errors which I should have eliminated in the process of proofreading.

[5]See my attempts to show the most important variants in the versions of No. 3 ("Appresso un fiume chiaro"), No. 9 ("Nascoso el viso"), No. 12 ("O tu, cara scienza"), and No. 15 ("Quando la stella"). The double versions in W. Thomas Marrocco, ed., *Italian Secular Music by Magister Piero, Giovanni da Firenze and Jacopo da Bologna* in *Polyphonic Music of the Fourteenth Century*, vol. VI (Monaco, 1967) are less effective because they juxtapose one text from a single source (Lo, usually the least accurate) with an editorial conflation of all the other sources; nor is the comparison helped by the placement of the two versions on different pages.

[6]In the Italian system, the "quantity" of the *novenaria*, both *senariae*, and the *quaternaria* is determined by the number of minims each contains. Exceptions are the *duodenaria* and *octonaria*, which are used as the equivalent of, respectively, *novenaria* and *senaria imperfecta*. Accordingly, a *quaternaria* measure needs to be diminished in a *sesquitertia* proportion when taken to represent a *semibrevis maior* of either *duodenaria* or *octonaria*. This is the intended meaning of the sign at the beginning of Gherardello's *Gloria* (P, fols. 131ᵛ–132ʳ), where the sign of *modus perfectus* is accompanied by the reversed half circle, indicating *tempus imperfectum* in *sesquitertia* pro-

a refashioning of an original *Brevisnotation* in *octonaria* or *duodenaria;* but I cannot take for granted the assumption, first suggested by Johannes Wolf and later supported by Kurt von Fischer,[7] that such refashioning is related to French influence, hence the custom of styling the two types as "Italian" and "French" notation.[8] Although the time of the notational change probably coincided with a growing awareness of French models, French influence always invited technical and notational complexity; but in this case it would have worked paradoxically, in the direction of simplicity. Nor was the *quaternaria* a foreign element to the Italian system; what was new was only a growing need to clarify all the ambiguities inherent in the Italian measures for their use of several kinds of semibreves *(maiores, minores, minimae)*, and for the several ways in which they could be expressed in musical figures.[9] This need in turn resulted from a change in the way to approach a pre-existing composition, from an intuitive grasp and inventive re-creation of its musical substance to an analytical consideration intent on the faithful reproduction of all details. The first approach had been typical of a few performers who were themselves composers; the second was spreading in a new category of "receptive users" (performers, scribes, and readers, occasionally coexisting in one single person).[10]

Transcriptions of Giovanni's madrigals into *Longanotation* occur twice in FP ("Appress'un fiume chiaro" and "Nascoso el viso," in both

---

portion. In the foreword to Pirrotta, *MFCI,* I, ii, I adopted $\frac{3}{4}$* and $\frac{2}{4}$* for the transcription of *duodenaria* and *octonaria*, and $\frac{1}{4}$* (regrouping the measures as $3 \times \frac{1}{4}$* or $2 \times \frac{1}{4}$*) when it seemed likely that the *quaternaria* replaced earlier notations in *duodenaria* or *octonaria.*

[7]See Johannes Wolf, *Handbuch der Notationskunde* (Leipzig, 1913), vol. I, 296 ff., and Kurt von Fischer, *Studien zur italienischen Musik des Trecento und frühen Quattrocento* (Bern, 1956), pp. 111–12.

[8]See E. C. Fellin, "The Notation-Types of Trecento Music," *L'Ars nova italiana del Trecento,* vol. IV (Certaldo, 1978), pp. 211 ff., as well as Nádas, "Panciatichi 26." The latter's perceptive reconstruction of the assemblage of the manuscript is a felicitous complement to the facsimile edition.

[9]Let us remember that a semibreve with a downward tail *(maior)* had a "normal" value of four minims, eight in the case of alteration, and eleven when followed by a single semibreve with an upward tail *(semibrevis minima).* Semibreves without a tail were usually *minóres* (with the value of two minims, or four when altered); but they assumed the value of *semibreves maiores* when in groups of no more than three between *puncti divisionis,* and could assume the value of *semibreves minimae* when in groups of five to eight in *octonaria,* or of seven to twelve in *duodenaria.* In addition to the number and shape of the notes, their graphic arrangement was also used to suggest their rhythmic grouping.

[10]The way in which various scribes worked together or alternated in FP (or in any other similar source) suggests that such manuscripts were copied and assembled in monasteries, whose members, still the main depositaries of *ars musica,* may have been performers or even composers. Anyway, the art of notation consisted more of general criteria, apt to be variously interpreted, than of precisely defined, binding rules.

cases with ·*q*· measures replacing ·*d*· measures of the other sources),[11] and twice in FL ("Più non mi curo" and "Nel mezzo a sei paon," with the ·*q*· measures replacing, respectively, ·*d*· and ·*o*· measures). *Longanotation* also appears briefly in ritornelli: those of "Nel mezzo a sei paon" and "Sedendo all'ombra" in FL, of "Togliendo l'una all'altra" in FL and P. Quite peculiar is the case of "Nel mezzo a sei paon," which indicates that transcription was not necessarily the product of French influence: the passages of its first section that are notated in ·*q*· in FL correspond to ·*o*· notations in FP and PR; but while the ·*q*· measures of FL correspond to half an ·*o*· measure of FP, each ·*o*· measure of FP in turn corresponds to half an ·*o*· measure of PR.[12] The *Longanotation* (presumed French) of FL simplifies the Italian *Brevisnotation* of FP, which in turn simplifies the Italian *Brevisnotation* of PR.

Giovanni's works are affected only to a limited extent by this kind of notational variation.[13] More pervasive, although less easily perceived, are other variants related to the composer's habit of making frequent shifts from one mensuration to another. Such changes, it would seem, were only sporadically indicated by the pertinent letters, even less so when the changes occurred between equivalent measures (·*d*· and ·*n*·, or ·*o*· and ·*si*·, the members of each pair having equal total value and main division; or ·*si*· and ·*sp*·, having equal total value and the same number of minims). Evidently the composer and the successive copyists of his works relied partly on the reader to grasp the number and grouping of

---

[11]According to Nádas, "Panciatichi 26," p. 397, the two madrigals appear to have been copied on consecutive pages of FP by scribe C.

The following are the letters traditionally used for the various *divisiones* of the Italian system:

·*q*·   quaternaria
·*sp*· senaria perfecta
·*si*· senaria imperfecta
·*n*·   novenaria
·*o*·   octonaria
·*d*·   duodenaria

[12]There is an allusion to this relationship in E. C. Fellin's cryptic remark ("Notation-Types," p. 222, fn. 12) that the first section is in augmentation.

[13]The same applies to the other older composers, Iacopo da Bologna and Piero. *Longanotation* becomes a conspicuous phenomenon in the works of slightly younger Florentine composers such as Gherardello, Lorenzo, Donato, and the adoptive Florentine Niccolò da Perugia, although versions of the same works in *Brevisnotation* are either extant or likely to have existed. My tentative explanation is that the works by the younger composers were still in current use at a time (possibly late fourteenth century) when embarrassment with the older notations and the need to refurbish them were most urgently felt, and performing and copying works of the older composers had become less common. *Longanotation* does not affect the works of Bartolino da Padova (nor, in general, the versions of North Italian sources like PR) for which other ways to solve the ambiguities of *Brevisnotation* were found.

notes between *puncti divisionis.* The consequences of their attitude are nowhere better exemplified than in the three readings of Giovanni's madrigal "Nascoso el viso," of which the version in FP is transcribed in *Longanotation.*[14]

I shall not dwell on the minor differences among the three versions in the first section of "Nascoso el viso," where the basic rhythm is ·*d*· (or its equivalent, the alleged perfect *modus* of FP) alternating with a few passages of ·*n*·.[15] The discrepancies are much more pronounced in the ritornello, however, resulting in substantial alterations. In the oldest version, that of Rs (which I assume to be nearest to the original),[16] the ritornello begins in ·*n*· and changes to ·*d*· after four measures for the next six measures, up to the final *longa* of the first line of text; but the letter indicating the change to ·*d*·, duly marked in Rs, must have been missing in the sources from which FL and FP were copied. The resulting confusion was undoubtedly aggravated by the presence in the original of two features that are present in Rs, namely, certain supernumerary rests (*suspiria*, which have no mensural meaning but rather suggest phrasing and breathing)[17] and the virtual absence of *semibreves minimae* in the ·*d*· measures.[18] FL continues in ·*n*· for three more measures, corresponding to four of Rs, and then reverts to ·*d*·, compressing the last two measures of Rs into one.[19] FP begins conventionally with four ·*n*· measures, changes to ·*si*· for the next four measures, and shifts to ·*sp*· for the last two measures. In this way, the rhythmic design of Rs is closely reproduced but compressed into ·*si*· and ·*sp*· measures that should last only two-thirds as long as the ·*d*· measures of the original.[20] Analogous phenomena are present in the second line of the ritornello: five ·*d*· measures of Rs (mm. 54–58) are compressed into two of FL,[21] while the

[14]All three versions are reproduced in Pirrotta, *MFCI,* I, 20–24.

[15]The change from ·*n*· to ·*d*· (m. 20 in Rs and FP) is delayed until m. 22 in FL (while the tenor, as in the other sources, remains in ·*d*·). At m. 26, both FL and FP change to ·*n*·, reverting to ·*d*· at m. 31., while Rs continues in ·*d*· throughout.

[16]Yet diverging from it, as it will later appear.

[17]Such *suspiria,* not easily distinguished from normal semibreve rests, appear almost exclusively in such florid monophonic ballate of Rs as "Che ti zova," "Lucente stella," and "Non formò Cristi." Out of all the madrigals, they occur only in "Nascoso el viso."

[18]Minims are present only in mm. 40 and 44 of Rs.

[19]The altered readings of FL and FP were also influenced by the way in which the ·*d*· measures of Rs are internally arranged so as to result in a slow $\frac{6}{8}$.

[20]In the Italian system, as applied in practical documents, ·*si*· has the value of two-thirds of ·*n*·, which has the same total value as ·*d*·. See the foreword to Pirrotta, *MFCI,* I, xi.

[21]As a result of this compression, the text is recited at a rate of one syllable per *semibrevis minima,* a declamation pattern never found in a ·*d*· mensuration in other madrigals by Giovanni.

same measures plus m. 59 are compressed into as many ·sp· measures of FP.[22]

"Nascoso el viso" is an extreme case; but anticipated, delayed, or altogether missing mensural changes are frequent occurrences in those madrigals by Giovanni in which the old measures ·d· and ·o· are the basic rhythmic frames; as a consequence, minims or even *semibreves minores* needed to be rearranged and regrouped to fit the new rhythmic interpretation. Such variants, doubtless unintentional, are often coupled with such other variants as the change or omission of a few auxiliary tones, or the addition of a few passing ones,[23] which may have been unintentional as well. Other variants, however, seem to be deliberate, to fill in the static rhythm of certain passages—for instance, the richer version of Rs at m. 2 of "Nascoso el viso," or the melismas at m. 6 of the same piece, which are present in FP and FL but lacking in Rs.[24] We may also identify as "intentional" variants the increased motion of the tenor at mm. 5 and 20 of the FP and FL versions, and its reduced activity in FP at mm. 24 and 29).[25] One might be tempted to see a progression in the addition of rhythmic motion from Rs to FL to FP, except that in m. 2, the earliest source gives the most complex reading.[26]

*   *   *   *   *

[22]·*Sp*· measures, being equivalent in length to ·*si*·, also have two-thirds the value of ·*n*· and ·*d*· measures.

[23]Comparison is easily possible for the madrigals mentioned in fn. 5 above. I regret having given only one composite version (cantus of Rs and tenor of FP) of "La bella stella," the most widely represented of Giovanni's madrigals in the sources.

[24]Similar variants may be seen in my edition at m. 13 of "Appress'un fiume," mm. 1, 3, 16, and 29 of "Più non mi curo," and mm. 1, 18–19, 37, and 42 of "Sedendo all'ombra."

[25]The variants in the tenor, more often than those in the cantus, seem dictated by a desire to modify the counterpoint. In m. 20 of "Nascoso el viso" the tenor of FL avoids clashes of a second and an augmented fourth, while the augmented fifth it introduces functions as an appoggiatura. In the same measure of FP, by contrast, the tenor runs quickly away from the clash of a second to fall on a major sixth, greatly emphasizing the cadence.

[26]Whatever the date we think of assigning to FL, it is generally agreed to be the latest of the Florentine sources of the Ars Nova period; nevertheless, some of its readings seem to reflect an older stage of notation than those of previous manuscripts. The same can be said of some of the works in Lo, whose scribe or scribes tended to reproduce uncritically what was in the models. The question of the relationship between sources and models is a central point of the article by Nádas cited above, and I shall be most interested in the results of his investigation of sources other than FP. To think that everything in one source (occasional mistakes aside) derives from its model eludes the question of intentional changes; yet the recognition of personal habits, preferences, and deliberate intentions of certain scribes cannot completely negate the importance of the models from which they copied.

I realize I am becoming involved in minute details of notation, the natural outcome of dealing with a facsimile. Since I do not want to displease my readers, but rather entertain them with what I have learned by coming back to Giovanni and his music, let us recall what we are told about him by Giovanni Villani in his chapter "De plerisque Musicis florentinis qui in ea arte egregie floruerunt et praesertim de Francischo Cecho viro mirabili."[27] Giovanni da Firenze visited the court of the Veronese "tyrant" Mastino della Scala, where, enticed with gifts from the despot, he took part in a competition with "a Bolognese most expert in the art of music." Villani's words find confirmation in a group of madrigals by Giovanni, Iacopo da Bologna, and an elusive figure named Piero (although he is not mentioned by Villani), all dealing with recurrent themes: a tree ("perlaro") abloom on the bank of a majestic river ("presso un fiume regale"), and a lady named Anna.[28] Evidently, the competition was not restricted to this cycle; in other texts we find Iacopo and Piero each praising a Margherita, while both Giovanni and Piero set the same caccia text describing a hunt on the banks of the river Adda.[29]

According to Villani the competition involved, along with "mandrialia plura" ("a number of madrigals"), also "sonos . . . multos et ballatas . . . mire dulcedinis et artificiosissime melodie, in quibus Johannes quam magna et quanta doctrina fuerit in arte manifestavit" ("many soni and ballate of admirable sweetness and most artful melody, in which Giovanni showed the extent and greatness of his skill in the art [of music]").[30] We have no soni or ballate left among the works of the three masters,[31] although Villani's distinction between "plura" (the

---

[27]The text given in F. Villani, *Liber de origine civitatis Florentiae et ejusdem famosis civibus*, ed. Galletti (Florence, 1847), p. 34, and reprinted in L. Ellinwood, *The Works of Francesco Landini* (Cambridge, MA, 1939), pp. 301–3, is not entirely reliable. The versions of the two main manuscript sources are rechecked and compared in Ettore Li Gotti, "Il più antico polifonista italiano del Trecento," *Italica*, 24 (1947), 196–200, especially p. 198.

[28]On this subject see Ettore Li Gotti, "Anna o dell'amor segreto," *Accademia* 1, No. 1 (1945), 9–11, and my short addendum, "Note ad 'Anna' o dei dispetti amorosi," *Accademia* 1, No. 2 (1945), 7.

[29]For Margherita, Iacopo set the madrigals "Lucida petra, o Margherita cara" and "Si come al canto"; Piero also set the latter. Both Piero and Giovanni set the caccia text "Con brachi assai," introducing amusing variants in the ritornello.

[30]A *sonus* was a lyrical song in ballata form, while the term "ballata" applied to certain songs "quia ballantur" ("because they are danced"). See Nino Pirrotta, "Ballate e 'soni' secondo un grammatico del Trecento," *Saggi e ricerche in memoria di Ettore Li Gotti*, vol. III (Palermo, 1962), pp. 42–54.

[31]It is possible that some are preserved among the five anonymous ballate of Rs. I might suggest the *sonus* "Lucente stella" in Pirrotta, *MFCI*, II (1960), 43, whose melodic style recalls that of Giovanni's madrigals.

madrigals) and "multa" (the *soni* and ballate) seems to indicate that the latter were more numerous. They still belonged to the monophonic repertory, and were therefore less likely to have been written down than polyphonic pieces,[32] and at the same time more likely to have been performed by their own composers. We may then envisage a situation in which Piero, Giovanni, and Iacopo acted not merely as composers of polyphonic music but also as singers of monophonic songs. Perhaps they can be related to the kind of high-ranking minstrels described in a slightly earlier text also connected with the Scala family:[33]

> ... Qui bon cantori
> con intonatori,
> et qui trovatori
> udrai concordare ...

("... Here [in Verona, at the court of Cane della Scala] you will hear good singers with *intonatori*, as well as *trovatori*, all consorting ...") This passage might be one of those in which words are strung together for the sake of sound and rhyme. Yet the text clearly refers to a group of musicians more refined than others described elsewhere in the poem; the lines here seem to make a distinction between the good singers, the authors and singers of polyphonic music *(intonatori)*, and those continuing the old troubadour tradition of monophonic song.[34]

Apparently, Giovanni never returned to Florence.[35] Villani's survey

---

[32]Polyphony required precise notation of pitch and rhythm to ensure the harmonious concordance of all voice parts, while monophonic music, more easily memorized and freer in rhythm, was usually committed to oral tradition. On the few extant monophonic ballate, see my old article "Lirica monodica trecentesca," *La Rassegna Musicale,* 9 (1936), 317–25.

[33]From "Bisbidis di Manoello Giudeo a magnificenza di messer Cane della Scala," a minstrel song in V. De Bartholomaeis, *Rime giullaresche e popolari d'Italia* (Bologna, 1926), pp. 68–70. *"Intonato"* is the adjective used in Sacchetti's autograph collection of his poems to identify which madrigals, cacce, and ballate had been set to music, usually in polyphony. If the *"intonatori"* were to be identified with composers of polyphony, this text would give evidence of polyphonic performances in Verona before 1329, the year of Cane della Scala's death.

[34]In the previous twelve lines, trumpet sounds, guitars, lutes, viols, loud shrill voices, drum, and pipes are referred to, sometimes with onomatopoeic evocations. See fn. 33 for the possible meaning of *"intonatori."*

[35]We have no documentary evidence on Giovanni beyond Villani's text. He seems not to have been a clergyman. (The miniature from FL reproduced in the article "Giovanni da Cascia" in *New Grove* 7 (London, 1980), p. 400, does not portray our Giovanni at all, but rather a younger "Magister Jouannes horganista de Florentia," i.e., Giovanni Mazzuoli). Neither can we identify Giovanni with a "ser Giovanni degl'Organi," whose visit to the monastery of S. Trinita in Florence in January of 1360 is recorded in a document published by Frank D'Accone, "Music and Musicians at the Florentine Monastery of Santa Trinita, 1360–1363," *Quadrivium,* 12 (1971), 131 ff.

of Landini's predecessors in Florence includes Bartholus, because of a Credo whose novelty had attracted crowds in S. Reparata, and Lorenzo, possibly because he had been Landini's teacher; but Giovanni is recalled only for his exploits in northern Italy, and Villani's praise is mixed with blame for Giovanni's having attended the tyrant's "atria" for the sake of profit ("questus gratia").[36] In the eyes of the people Giovanni must have been a courtly musician in the troubadour tradition, seen mainly as a performer.[37] He must have performed his monophonic *soni*; and the unusual number of variant readings of his polyphonic works suggests that he may have performed some of his own madrigals too.[38] Compared to the relatively fixed repertoire transmitted by his competitors, Giovanni seems to have left many aspects of the performance to improvisation.

Judging from the polyphonic works, one can say that Giovanni's fluent vocalization does not merely rely on the momentary appeal of its floridity, but is always subservient to the broad shape of extended melodic lines. His melodies, interspersed as they are with pauses from which they easily rebound, always have a feeling of continuity within their variety. These melodic traits may be seen in "La bella stella," transcribed here in its entirety, both because it is transmitted in six sources and in order to give a different version (that of P) from the one adopted in both my edition and Marrocco's.[39]

The first melodic phrase descends from *d* to *G*, rekindles its interest

[36]The setting of "La bella stella" seems to indicate Giovanni's continued presence in northern Italy after the death of Mastino della Scala in 1351. F. A. Gallo, in "Antonio da Ferrara, Lancillotto Anguissola e il madrigale trecentesco," *Studi e problemi di critica testuale* No. 12 (April, 1976), pp. 40 ff., quotes the following lines of a sonnet addressed to Lancillotto Anguissola by Antonio da Ferrara: ". . . e questo ven da la terza fasella/celeste, la cui forma e'l cui dolzore/fa sì vago el sovran al bel tenore/del vostro madrial 'La bella stella' "; from these lines Gallo convincingly deduces Anguissola's authorship of the text and a date of about 1353 for the music.

[37]At this time musical composition and authorship were still concepts with which only a few were familiar.

[38]A late testimony to the performance of polyphonic pieces by one singer accompanying himself on a stringed instrument is provided by Simone Prodenzani in sonnet No. 25 of his *Saporetto*: ". . . Una arpa fo addotta assai reale/ove Solaço fe' 'La dolce cera,'/'Ucel di Dio' con 'Aquila altera,'/ 'Verde buschetto' et puoi 'Imperiale,'/'Agniel so' bianco' et anco 'l 'Pelegrino' . . ." The madrigals mentioned are: Giovanni's "Agnel son bianco"; Bertolino's "La douce cere" ("La dolce cera" in Lo) and "Imperiale"; and Iacopo's "Aquila altera" (a three-voice polytextual madrigal whose tenor, "Uccel di Dio," but not the "cantus secundus," is also mentioned in the sonnet). See S. Prudenzani, *Il "Sollazzo" e il "Saporetto" con altre rime*, ed. S. Debenedetti; *Giornale Storico della Letteratura Italiana*, Supplemento No. 15 (Turin, 1913).

[39]Both Pirrotta, *MFCI*, I, 18–20, and Marrocco, *Polyphonic Music*, VI, 40–41, give a transcription in which the cantus of Rs is combined with the tenor of FP. The madrigal appears in Rs (cantus only), FP, FC (cantus only), P, FL, and in the fragment Rome, Vatican Ottoboni 1790 (only a small section of the tenor).

with a leap of an augmented fourth (indicated as such in all the sources), and descends again in a new rhythm. The second phrase begins even higher, on g, and goes down a full octave, but then reascends with a recitative section and a short melisma. Phrase three has but a short ascending melisma on its first syllable; the line then fluctuates before coming to a temporary rest on c♯, gains new strength with another upward leap of a diminished fourth and a new change of rhythm, and ends by descending slowly but purposefully to A. The ritornello is faster in delivering its two lines of text. The first is framed by two short melismas; the second, while lacking an initial melisma, ends with a long one that recalls the final melisma of the first section, especially in the way that an ascending leap coincides with a change of rhythm. In both phrases of the ritornello, the descent to the tonic A starts on high a.

Of course, no verbal description can render the feeling of coherent variety, the sudden changes giving new impetus to lines that seemed near their conclusion, the careful balance between phrases of different length, or the reflection of this balanced coherence in the smaller melodic details. Any reader tempted to go through the melodies of "La bella stella," or any other of Giovanni's madrigals, will find, whatever version he selects, that their coherence and natural fluency are unaffected by the addition, subtraction, or modification of melismas. It could be just because of his clear perception of the essentials of melodic development that Giovanni did not care to give too precise an intimation of all details. Or else, thinking of himself as the performer, he might have noted down only what he would need to recreate the spirit of his works, leaving to himself (and to other eventual performers) the freedom to adjust details in accordance with the occasion of a given performance.

We may better appreciate the quality of Giovanni's music by comparing it with pieces of his competitors. For this purpose nothing could be more apt than the above-mentioned madrigals for Anna, five by Iacopo, three by Giovanni, and two by Piero.[40] Iacopo's "Un bel perlaro"[41] and Giovanni's "Appress'un fiume chiaro"[42] belong to the smiling phase of a love story and are similar in their description of Anna, a radiant beauty seen among dancers against the background of the blooming tree and the river. The descriptions in Piero's "Sovra un fiume regale" and "All'ombra d'un perlaro"[43] are only slightly different

[40]Iacopo's madrigals are included in Pirrotta, *MFCI*, IV (1963); Piero's madrigals in Pirrotta, *MFCI*, II (1960). Of course, all the works of Giovanni, Iacopo, and Piero are also included in Marrocco, *Polyphonic Music*, VI; yet I will refer only to my own edition to avoid confusion over measure numbers (which differ in the two editions due to different systems of barring).

[41]Pirrotta, *MFCI*, IV, 30–31.

[42]Pirrotta, *MFCI*, I, 8–11.

[43]Pirrotta, *MFCI*, II, 6–7 and 1–2.

(in the latter the lady is also a singer). Iacopo must have taken the first round of competition lightly, for he wrote a short madrigal almost without melismas, flat in its recitation and only slightly enlivened by running minims in the tenor. Piero's "All'ombra d'un perlaro," scarcely more generous in melodic effusion, resorts to canon (the composer's forte) in the ritornello, thereby bringing into prominence the lady's name in the ritornello's opening line ("A nnascere del suo vis'el parecchio"). However, in "Sovra un fiume regale," Piero attempts to imitate Giovanni's floridity (but for his more pedantic use of sequential repetition). The imitation is also evident in Piero's dramatic upward leap of a diminished fifth (mm. 44–45 of the ritornello), coinciding with a change of rhythm from ·n· to ·d·. Giovanni's "Appress'un fiume chiaro" displays the author's characteristic melodic fluency and his taste for unusual melodic intervals (m. 7); the rhythmic change from ·d· to ·n· (mm. 16–17) happily coincides with the words describing the dancing girls. The influence of the competition, more precisely of Iacopo, is felt in the minims of the tenor (mm. 22, 26, and 40).

There are other signs of each composer's awareness of the works of his competitors. The pieces of both Iacopo and Giovanni make a pretense of keeping secret the name of the lady, while actually stressing it at the beginning of the ritornello: Iacopo's "A nnave, a nnave! le donne cantando" and Giovanni's "Annamorar mi fa el so viso umano" are both underlined in the music by repetitions playing on f' and a'.[44] Each composer reiterates the pun in the later phase of complaining, Iacopo with "Ahi, lasso mi, non vol venir più a nnave" (ritornello of "O dolce appress'un bel perlaro fiume") and Giovanni with "Ahi, lasso a me, non vol più annamorarmi" (ritornello of "O perlaro gentil").[45] Furthermore, neither of the "complaining" texts consists of the usual tercets plus ritornello; rather, both have the ABABCC DD metrical structure of the so-called madrigale-rispetto.[46]

In the music of this second round, it was Giovanni's turn to resort to a relative conciseness, yet with some unusual features;[47] the wordplay

[44]Do we have here an early case of a "soggetto cavato dalle parole" (fa-la = Anna)? Although we lack definite evidence, it seems likely that the composers were often the authors of their texts.

[45]Pirrotta, MFCI, IV, 18–19, and Pirrotta, MFCI, I, 26–28.

[46]Whatever their real relationship with the rispetto, and in spite of Giovanni's rearranging the lines of "O perlaro gentil" into the usual scheme of two tercets and a distich (in this case ABA BCC DD), the madrigali-rispetti cannot all be reduced to the usual scheme, as G. Corsi argues in Poesie musicali del Trecento (Bologna, 1970), pp. 24–26. Actually, the first six lines of Iacopo's "O dolce" and Giovanni's "Donna già fu' " are through-composed; in the case of Iacopo's "Sotto l'imperio" we even have a double rispetto plus ritornello (Corsi's scheme, Poesie, p. 47, should be emended).

[47]I refer to m. 22 of the cantus. I regret to have given only the version of FP in my edition, because the fanfare-like motif is repeated more times in other sources.

on "Anna" is now delayed to the middle of the first line of the ritornello. Iacopo's highly contrapuntal "O dolce appress'un bel perlaro fiume," through-composed in its first six lines of text, is much more assertive. The beginning of each line of the first section is marked by staggered entrances, with the tenor almost equal to the cantus in floridity (and even surpassing it in speed of text recitation). Things return to normal in the ritornello with the simultaneous recitation of the text in the two voices, which only separate in order to emphasize Anna's name.

After the phase of courtship and radiant smiles and that of complaining arrives the time of bitterness and reproach. The lady in the beautiful garden encircled by the river has become a venomous adder in Iacopo's "Nel bel giardino che l'Adice cinge."[48] Nonetheless, the composer adopts Giovanni's placid style, framing each line of text with extensive vocalization (if not exactly melismas) spiced with hocket. Iacopo's "Posando sopra un'acqua" is similarly florid, except that the meter is changed from ·o· to a brisk ·si· in both sections of the madrigal.[49] Giovanni participates in this phase with "Donna già fu' leggiadra annamorata," a rebuke in defense of the lady. While maintaining the wordplay on "*anna*morata," she recognizes that she has become an adder; it is for just cause, however, for she has been offended. Even so, she ends with a promise of mercy:[50]

> Com'io di tormentarlo sia ben sazia
> tornerò donna, renderoll'in grazia.

("As soon as I've had enough of tormenting him/I'll change again into a woman and readmit him to grace.") The text is again a *madrigale-rispetto*,[51] which Giovanni duly set this time with a through-composed first section plus ritornello. Stressing the tendency of the lines to group into twos rather than threes, he framed the first two lines with the usual melismas; suppressed the melismas and accelerated the text declamation in the next two lines; and reverted to a more relaxed mood for the final couplet. Several atypical features suggest a possible wish to emulate Iacopo: the absence of rhythmic changes (the whole first section is in ·o·, the ritornello in ·d·); the melismatic passage in the tenor (m. 6); the lack of full stops at the end of the second, third, and fourth lines; and the hocket passages at mm. 18, 31–33, and 35.

---

[48]Pirrotta, *MFCI*, IV, 14–15. Except for a few minims, the tenor is quite subdued, and the cantus is not as florid as in Giovanni at his best. The madrigal is exceptional among Iacopo's because of the relatively high number of variants provided by its four sources (P and FC are less ornate than FL; FP is richest in melismas).

[49]Pirrotta, *MFCI*, IV, 21–22.

[50]Pirrotta, *MFCI*, I, 12–14.

[51]See fn. 46.

For all we know, Iacopo had the last word. He undoubtedly overwhelmed his competitors with the lengthy text of "Sotto l'impero del possente prinze," a three-voice double *madrigale-rispetto* with the metrical scheme ABABCC DEDEFF GG. The work is rightly considered one of his masterpieces,[52] for it emphasizes Iacopo's best stylistic traits: the rhythmic variety within a constant mensuration (·*o*· in the first section, ·*sp*· in the ritornello);[53] the rapid, deft declamation (often reaching the rate of one syllable per minim); and, above all, the great rhythmic and contrapuntal independence of the three voices. There is occasional imitation between the two upper parts, set off by the tenor (actually a contratenor bassus),[54] whose rhythms are slightly smoother.

All five of Iacopo's madrigals must have been composed within a limited span of time; yet such is the difference between "All'ombra d'un perlaro" and "Sotto l'imperio del possente prinze" that one might easily be tempted to assign the former to an early stage of the composer's career, the latter to his full maturity. There could be no more vivid warning against any attempt to establish chronology on the mere basis of style, without the support of documentary evidence.

Despite occasional borrowing arising from the unusual circumstance of a competition, the three masters taking part in the Veronese contest remained faithful to their individual stylistic profiles. The statistically dominant composer is Iacopo, represented in the Anna cycle by five madrigals—as many as the combined total of his competitors. His high rate of preservation reflects the esteem in which he was held by his contemporaries and immediate successors, surpassed only by the glory of Francesco Landini in a later generation. Iacopo certainly deserved his reputation as the most daring, most resourceful, most artful of the composers of his own generation and the next. Not only was he active in the fields of both madrigal and motet, but the imitative openings of his three-voice works (such as the polytextual madrigal "Aquila altera") probably established a model that would continue to exert an influence down to the era of Ciconia's motets. Yet I feel that the high quality of each individual measure tends to be an end in itself, so that Iacopo's music aligns itself in a series of similarly refined details but seldom achieves a spontaneous, convincing continuity.

---

[52]Pirrotta, *MFCI*, IV, 26–27. It cannot be a mere coincidence that "Sotto l'imperio" is given first position in the entire manuscript of P and among Iacopo's works in FL; in PR it is preceded only by "Lo lume vostro," probably because a full opening (fols. 1ᵛ–2ʳ) was required for the three voices of "Sotto l'imperio."

[53]The transition from ·*o*· to ·*sp*·, though quite unusual for Iacopo, is fairly frequent in the works of Giovanni.

[54]The two upper parts are harmonically self-supporting, while the so-called tenor is abundantly interspersed with rests, as if it had been added after the interplay of the other voices had been established.

Piero is the most poorly represented of the three composers, both in the Anna cycle (only two madrigals, both belonging to the early phase) and in the size of his known corpus (only seven works, in which the cacce are not clearly distinguished from the madrigals). The dearth of surviving pieces may result from the discontinuity of the northern tradition (which makes all the more impressive Iacopo's success in overcoming it). Except where Piero's assiduous cultivation of canonic imitation results in a natural expansion, his music tends to be a gentle, simple, somewhat miniaturistic art.[55]

Last but not least is Giovanni da Firenze. I do not need to restate my admiration for him as a natural, convincing melodist whose works were a model for succeeding generations of Florentine composers.

* * * * *

I do not know how many readers will have had the patience to follow me through several scores of Ars Nova madrigals; but I trust that my nostalgia for a musicological first love, and for an Ars Nova edition that I once started and no longer envisage completing, will be appreciated by the dear friend to whom this essay is addressed, and whose dedication to and keen understanding of all cultural endeavors I have come to know and admire during the many years of our friendship. And as I have been comforted in my brooding by the tangible presence of the Panciatichi facsimile and the ideal shadow of an ancient almond tree, thus I shall ask Giovanni's help to sum up my nostalgia. From his "O tu, cara scienza, mia musica,/o dolce melodia con dolci canti" ("O you, dear science, my music, o sweet singing of sweet songs") I shall borrow my last line: "Però ritorno a te, musica cara" ("This is why I am back to you, my dear music").

---

[55]A marked preference for canonic imitation often induced Piero to through-compose the first section of his madrigals, thus producing works which are an important step in the transition from madrigal to caccia.

APPENDIX

The following version of Giovanni da Firenze's madrigal "La bella stella" is transcribed from P, ff. 19ᵛ–20ʳ, following the criteria for transcription and barring that I set down in the foreword to *The Music of Fourteenth-Century Italy*, vol. I. As an additional proviso, I have bracketed all signs of mensuration that are not explicitly indicated in the source but can be deduced from the context. I have transcribed just what is in this one source, deliberately ignoring other text versions of other sources; more particularly, I have remained faithful to a given mensuration (ignoring changes present in other sources) as long as the notation was compatible with that mensuration.

Compared with the version given in *The Music of Fourteenth-Century Italy*, vol. I, pp. 18–20, the present transcription differs in the following details of mensuration: Measure 7: Cantus changes to ·*si*· one brevis later (no real change in the musical substance). M. 10: Cantus reverts to ·*o*· for one brevis. M. 17: Cantus reverts to ·*o*· for three breves. M. 23: Cantus continues in ·*si*·. M. 32: Cantus reverts to ·*o*·. M. 34: Cantus changes to ·*si*·. M. 36: tenor changes to ·*si*·. M. 38: Both versions change to ·*sp*· (mistakenly indicated as $\frac{3}{4}$* in the older transcription). Mm. 42–47: Cantus and tenor continue in ·*sp*· instead of ·*si*·. Mm. 52–57: Cantus and tenor continue in ·*sp*· instead of ·*si*·.

Giovanni da Firenze, "La bella stella"

A Prima Ballerina of the Fifteenth Century

EILEEN SOUTHERN

Mᴏᴅᴇʀɴ ɪɴᴠᴇsᴛɪɢᴀᴛɪᴏɴs ᴏF ᴛʜᴇ dance in quattrocento Italy have centered primarily on dance masters and their manuals, to the general neglect of the dancers for whom these manuals may have been written. The reason for this neglect is that little is known specifically about Italian dance-performance practice in the fifteenth century, despite numerous contemporary reports on the *"gran balli"* that were an essential part of festive occasions at court. The aim of this essay is to assemble the sparse data available in scattered sources with a view to illuminating one small area of this subject.[1] The heroine of my story is Ippolita Sforza, a beautiful, learned, and charming princess of the mid-fifteenth century, who was noted for her graces in the dance.

Ippolita Maria Sforza was born on April 18, 1445, at Jesi, a small town in northeastern Italy near Ancona; she was the second child and first daughter of Francesco Sforza (1401–1466) and Bianca Maria Visconti Sforza (1425–1468).[2] At that time Francesco was known primarily as the celebrated *condottiere* who had fought in the service of Filippo Ma-

---

[1]The studies of the Italian dance manuals I found most useful for the present essay are: Otto Kinkeldey, "A Jewish Dancing Master of the Renaissance: Guglielmo Ebreo," *Studies in Jewish Bibliography and Related Subjects in Memory of Abraham Solomon Friedus* (New York, 1929; repr. New York, 1966), pp. 328–72; and Artur Michel, "The Earliest Dance Manuals," *Medievalia et humanistica*, 3 (1945), 117–131.

[2]Ippolita was not born at Pesaro, as stated in some sources. Since another of my aims is to correct some of the factual errors that have crept into accounts about Ippolita, hereafter this will be done without calling attention to the errors in print. In regard to Ippolita's place of birth, see W. Terni de Gregorj, *Bianca Maria Visconti, Duchessa di Milano* (Bergamo, 1940), p. 213. Fifteenth-century sources do not agree on whether she was born on the 18th of March or the 18th of April. The most reliable sources of information about the Sforzas are: Cecilia Ady, *A History of Milan Under the Sforza* (London, 1907); Lacy Collison-Morley, *The Story of the Sforzas* (London, 1933); Caterina Santoro, *Gli Sforza* (Milan, 1968). A useful biographical sketch of Ippolita is Alfredo Baccelli, "Ippolita Sforza: Duchessa di Calabria," *Rassegna Nazionale*, 52 (1930), 21–32.

ria Visconti, fourth Duke of Milan (1392–1447). But Francesco also had fought against Filippo, and he had been in the employ of Cosimo de' Medici and, for a brief period in 1449, the Ambrosian Republic (i.e., Milan), among others. In 1450 Francesco took over Milan and founded his own dynasty, which was destined to rule for almost a century—basing his fragile claim to the Duchy on his marriage to Filippo's only child, Bianca Maria.[3] Ippolita's older brother, Galeazzo Maria (1444–1476) would become renowned as a patron of the arts during his rule as the fifth Duke of Milan (1466–76), and a younger brother, Ludovico Maria (1452–1508), called "il Moro," would inaugurate a golden age of splendor at Milan beginning in the 1480s.[4]

Life at the Sforza court during Ippolita's childhood was relatively simple and, in comparison to some places, perhaps even frugal. As late as 1463, for example, Duchess Bianca Maria had only four ladies-in-waiting, and Ippolita had only one. The family lived primarily in the Castello at Pavia, although they occasionally used the ducal palaces at Abbiategrasso and Vigevano. The Visconti palace at Milan had been destroyed during the fighting in the 1440s, and although Francesco began to repair it as early as 1451, it was used chiefly as a fortress during his lifetime. It was not until late in 1468, when Galeazzo moved his court from Pavia to Milan, that the Castello of Milan became the physical setting for the brilliant court of the Sforzas.

The Sforza children received a superior education, especially in languages and the literary and fine arts. Ippolita studied Greek with the grammarian Constantine Lascaris of Byzantium, who came to the Sforza court after the fall of Constantinople in 1453 and remained there eleven years.[5] Another of Ippolita's tutors, Baldo Martorelli, remained with her throughout her youth, then became her secretary after she married. Both Galeazzo and Ippolita attracted attention as children for their command of Latin. Ippolita was only fourteen years old when she delivered beautifully an oration in Latin for Pope Pius II at the Congress of Mantua in 1459. We do not know the name of Ippolita's music teacher, but obviously she began lessons at an early age. When René,

---

[3]Bianca Maria, illegitimate daughter of Filippo and Agnese del Maino, was betrothed to Francesco when she was eight years old; they were married in 1441. The dowry she brought to Francesco included the town of Cremona.

[4]Ludovico was named Duke of Bari in 1479 after the death of his brother Sforza Maria, who formerly held the title. Ludovico actually assumed control of Milan in 1480 when he took over the regency for his nephew, Gian Galeazzo; but he became Duke only in 1494.

[5]Lascaris (1434–1501) dedicated his Greek grammar, *Erotemata* (Milan, 1476), to Ippolita, presumably because it was written for her use; it was the first Greek book printed in Italy.

Duke of Anjou, visited the Court at Pavia in the fall of 1453, Galeazzo and Ippolita sang French songs for his entertainment.

But it was as a dancer that Ippolita became most noted. In 1454, the courtier and dance master Antonio Cornazano of Piacenza (c.1430–1484) entered the service of Francesco as "consigliore, segretario, o ciamberlano."[6] His most important responsibility, however—at least insofar as history of the dance is concerned—was that of "direttore di ballo" to Ippolita, and she soon became a star pupil. In 1455 he dedicated his *Libro dell'arte del danzare* to her, opening it with a sonnet that acclaims her graces:[7]

Amaçonia nympha, inclyta diua,
    di leda figlia non, ma di diana,
    nel cui materno exempio, honesta e piana,
    infinita belleça aggionge a riua.
Giusto amor m'ha costrecto ch'io vi scriua
    che l'arte già insegnata non sia uana,
    poi che compresi quanta altiera, humana,
    in sì giouinil cor virtù fioriua
La più matura età che'n uoi s'expecta,
    col studio di questa opra, ch'io ui noto,
    ui farà dea fra l'altre donne electa.
Intenderete qui il legiadro moto
    de' piedi in ballo: et se 'l mio dir s'accetta,
    in quanto io uaglio, a voi tutto m'auoto.

We shall return later to a discussion of Cornazano's treatise.

---

[6] The definitive biographical study of Cornazano is in Cristoforo Poggiali, *Memorie per la storia letteraria di Piacenza*, 1 (Piacenza, 1789), 64–130. See also Ingrid Brainard, *New Grove*, s.v. "Cornazano." The quoted titles applied to Cornazano are from Poggiali, *Memorie*, p. 80.

[7] Cornazano's treatise is reprinted in Curzio Mazzi, *La Bibliofilia*, 17 (1915–1916), 1–30. A reproduction of the title page of the 1455 copy, including the sonnet, is on page 8. The following translation is by Massimo Ossi.

Amazon nymph, glorious goddess,
    daughter not of Leda but of Diana,
    in whose maternal example, virtuous and simple,
    infinite beauty is attained.
Just love compels me to write to you
    so that the art already taught will not be in vain,
    since I understood what lofty and human
    virtue flowered in such a youthful heart.
The full maturity that you are yet to reach
    with the study of this work, which I commend to you,
    will make you a goddess chosen from among other women.
You will learn here the graceful motion
    of the feet in dance: and if my few words are accepted
    for what I am worth, I pledge myself to you.

As the Sforza children grew older, they became increasingly involved in the frequent festivities that took place when visitors came to the court or when family events were celebrated, and the presence of Cornazano undoubtedly placed a high priority on the dance. But Cornazano was not the only dancing master with whom Ippolita came in contact. In the spring of 1455 the famous *ballarino* Domenico of Ferrara (d.c.1470) was called to Milan to organize dances for festivities associated with the marriage of Beatrice d'Este (1427–1497) to Tristano Sforza (1422–1477), Francesco's illegitimate son.[8] According to a contemporary report, Domenico directed several large-scale ballets that were "ingeniously and subtly contrived."[9]

Regarded as the founder of the Lombard school of dance, Domenico was the first in Italy to write a dance manual, entitled *De arte saltandi e choreas ducendii* (c.1420), and was the teacher of the two most celebrated dance masters of the mid-fifteenth century, Cornazano and Guglielmo Ebreo da Pesaro (c.1425– after 1480). Guglielmo's treatise on the dance, *De pratica seu arte tripudi vulgare opisculum*, which is extant in six versions, includes autobiographical data as well as dance melodies and choreographies composed by himself and others, among them his teacher Domenico.[10] It is generally felt by dance historians that Guglielmo and Giovanni Ambrosio da Pesaro were one and the same person because of the marked similarities—even agreement—among the extant copies of the dance manuals.[11] One of the copies at Paris

[8]For biographical information about Domenico see Brainard, *New Grove*, s.v. "Domenico"; and Michel, "Dance Manuals," p. 119. Brainard is preparing an edition of Domenico's dance treatise for publication. Beatrice d'Este, natural daughter of Niccolo d'Este and sister of Duke Borso d'Este, was first married to Niccolo da Corregio (in 1448).

[9]Gabriele Paveri-Fontana, a professor at the university in Milan, wrote an account of the festivities in a 1455 letter to the Milanese envoy in Venice. See Michel, "Dance Manuals," p. 119. There is also discussion of the wedding in Emilio Motta, *Nozze principesche* (Milan, 1894), but that book was not available to me.

[10]Biographical information about Guglielmo appears in Kinkeldey, "Jewish Dancing Master"; Brainard, *New Grove*, s.v. "Guglielmo."

[11]The copies at Siena (Communal Library, L.V.29) and Modena (Biblioteca Palatina, VII.A.82) carry no author identification. A copy at Paris (Bibliothèque nationale, fonds. ital. 476) is ascribed to Johanni Ambrosii pisauriensis. And three copies identify the author as Guglielmo hebraei (or ebreo) pisauriensis: those at Florence (Magliabechiana, Class.XIX.9.8), Paris (Bibl. nat., fonds. ital. 973), and New York (Public Library, *MGZMB—Res. 72–254).

Some of the choreographies in the New York copy, which dates from the years 1465–75, are ascribed to "Giovan Abrogio *ebreo*" and some to "Giovan Abrogio *che fu ebreo*," which seems to support the premise that Guglielmo might have become a Christian at some time during the late 1460s. The New York Public Library has microfilms and photographic enlargements of the Paris and Siena copies of the Guglielmo manuscript (formerly in the Toscanni collection).

(fonds. ital. 476), which was copied for Francesco Sforza in 1463 by one Paganus Raudensis (Pagano da Rho), includes a charming miniature depicting three dancers, a man between two women, holding hands and moving slowly to the music of a harpist. (Plate 1) The copy at New York also includes a reference to Francesco.

If Guglielmo and Ambrosio are one and the same, the change of name would have occurred after 1463, the date of the manuscript copied for Francesco. It has been suggested that perhaps the dancing master converted to Christianity and thereafter identified himself as Giovan Ambrogio. He was active at several courts of the time; it is not known when he first went to the Milanese court, but certainly he was there in 1465, along with Domenico, "a fare moresche e molti balli" for Ippolita's nuptial festivities.[12]

It was in 1455 that Ippolita began to receive public attention from outside her small, self-contained world in the Castello at Pavia—a

Plate 1. Anonymous miniature of three dancers from Johanni Ambrosii pisaurensis, *De practica seu arte tripudi vulgare opusculum*, Paris, Bibliothèque Nationale fonds. Ital. 476.

[12]Quoted from Brainard, "Domenico."

result, in part, of political events. The continuous struggling for power that had existed during the first half of the fifteenth century among the five major city-states in Italy—Milan, Venice, Florence, Rome, and Naples—ceased temporarily with the Peace of Lodi in 1454 and the establishment of the Italian League of States, which later admitted smaller states to membership. For a period of fifty years thereafter, the peninsula enjoyed relative peace and prosperity, and with that came an unprecedented cultivation of the arts and of learning.[13] Humanism in Italy reached its zenith during this period.

Francesco Sforza had long maintained a close alliance with Florence through Cosimo de' Medici (1389–1464) and with Naples through King Alfonso V the Magnanimous of Aragón (1396–1458), who became King of Naples in 1442 and transferred his court there permanently in 1443. Now Francesco sought to bind Naples and Milan even closer. In October 1455, he concluded an agreement with Alfonso that promised a double marriage alliance between the two city-states: Ippolita was to marry Alfonso's grandson, also named Alfonso (1448–1495); and her younger brother, Sforza Maria (1451–1479), would marry Alfonso's granddaughter Eleonora (also called Leonora, 1450–1493).[14] Although Ippolita was only ten years old at the time of her betrothal, thereafter in contemporary literature she frequently was referred to as the Duchess of Calabria, the title she would carry after her marriage in 1465.

Ippolita and the Balli

Despite the vagueness of the reports that have come down to us about Ippolita as a dancer, some data are included that gives insight, however limited, into her relationship to dance practice of the period. There is, for example, the occasion of the wedding of Beatrice d'Este and Tristano Sforza in 1455. As stated above, Domenico organized the dances for the wedding festivities and undoubtedly saw to it that the bride occupied the center of attention, for Beatrice was widely acclaimed for her skills as a dancer and for her grace. Cornazano praised her as "la regina della feste" and quoted a Ferrarese proverb that asserted, "He who would see Paradise on earth, should see Madonna Bea-

---

[13]This is not to imply that fighting ceased in Italy, but only that pressure from foreign forces was successfully resisted until 1494, when Charles VIII invaded Italy (with assistance from some Italians).

[14]The Neapolitan archives do not identify the children by name—see Camillo Riccio, "Alcuni fatti di Alfonso di Aragonia dal 15 Aprile 1437 al 31 di Maggio 1458," *Archivio storico per le province napoletane*, 6 (1881), 437—which may account for some confusion in the literature as to whether it was Galeazzo or Sforza who was betrothed to Eleonora. But see *Dispatches of Milanese Ambassadors, 1450–1483*, vol. I, prepared by Paul Murray Kendall and Vincent Ilardi (Athens, Ohio, 1970), p. 181.

trice in the dance."[15] It was no small honor to participate in a ballo with such a paragon of the dance. And yet that is precisely the honor that came to Ippolita when she was only ten years old. According to a contemporary report, the high point of the festivities was a danza performed by eight persons, of whom Ippolita was one. Ballarino Domenico led the dance with Duchess Bianca Maria as his partner. We do not know how the other dancers were paired, but it may be assumed that Ippolita's partner was her eleven-year-old brother Galeazzo. The other dancers were the bride, Beatrice d'Este; Alessandro Sforza, Francesco's brother; the Marchioness Barbara of Mantua; and the Marquess Guglielmo of Monferrato.[16]

Although this report is slight, it does at least inform us that one kind of court dance—perhaps a typical one—involved a small group of eight dancing in pairs. And we learn that Ippolita must have been an excellent dancer by the time she was ten years old, if she was allowed to dance in a ballo with the celebrated Beatrice d'Este. Add to this Cornazano's dedication of a dance treatise to her before she was eleven, and one begins to appreciate how graceful and skilled she must have been. Cornazano also praised Ippolita's dance artistry in the introduction to his *Vita di Maria Virgine,* which he dedicated to her.[17]

Cornazano's original dance treatise is now lost. In a later copy, which he dedicated to Ippolita's half-brother, Sforza Secondo (1433–1492), Count of Borgonuovo, Cornazano made some changes in the text, although he did not specify precisely what the changes were. The title page of the original treatise, with its dedicatory sonnet to Ippolita, was included in the later copy, but there is no date for this copy. Clues to a possible date, 1465, may be found, however, in verses 24–27 of the dedicatory poem to Sforza Secondo, where Cornazano refers to the sister who traveled [the length of] Italy to be wed and thus became related to a king:

E cosí, riuerente a' uostri piedi	And thus, bowing at your feet,
mando copia di quel ch' all' excellente	I send [you] a copy of that which
uostra Sorella intitulato diedi:	to your notable sister I dedicated:
I' dico di quell'una che al presente	I speak of the one who recently
ha trauersata Italia a tôr marito	crossed Italy to wed,
et ha el bisson d'un re facto parente.	and has become a relative of the king's son.

---

[15]Cornazano in Mazzi, *La Bibliofilia,* p. 10.
[16]Michel, "The Earliest Dance Manuals," p. 120.
[17]Poggiali, *Memorie per la Storia letteraria di Piacenza,* p. 80:
 E siccome più volte io v' ho provata
 porgervi man, se v' ho conducta in ballo
 e dare orecchie a chi vi havea insegnata.

This obviously is a reference to Ippolita, who journeyed from Milan to Naples in 1465 to be married to Alfonso, Duke of Calabria and son of Ferrante (also known as Ferdinand) of Naples (1424–1494). Ferrante, illegitimate son of Alfonso V, had become King of Naples upon the death of his father in 1458.[18]

Ippolita's bridal journey has been called "uno dei più famosi viaggi del quattrocento."[19] While a detailed discussion of the journey is beyond the confines of the present essay, it will be helpful to outline its prominent features. Thanks to contemporary writers, we have many details about the persons who were involved and their activities.[20] In March 1465 King Ferrante sent his youngest son, the thirteen-year-old Federigo (1452–1504), to escort Ippolita to Naples for the wedding ceremony. On March 3 Federigo set out for Milan accompanied by a large company of noblemen (some say as many as 600), soldiers, and others. About mid-April he arrived at Pisa, where Lorenzo de'Medici (1449–1492) met him and escorted the company to Florence on April 17. There the cortège rested for a time. The Florentines noted that the Neapolitans were in mourning because of the recent death of Federigo's mother, Queen Isabella of Naples. On April 25 the wedding company arrived at Bologna, where Giovanni and Ginevra Bentivoglio were their hosts; they then moved on to Pavia, arriving there in late April or early May.

The Castello at Pavia was the scene of two wedding celebrations in the spring of 1465. In March, Duchess Bianca Maria gave an entertainment for Francesco's illegitimate daughter Drusiana (1437–1474) in celebration of her marriage in 1464 to Jacopo Piccinino (d. 1465), a famous *condottiere* who had fought for both her father and King Ferrante of Naples. Next it was Ippolita's turn to be feted. Although there was a week of feasting and dancing, few details about the dances have come down to us. We do know, however, that one of the dancers was Lorenzo de'Medici, who had been sent by his father, Piero, to represent the Re-

---

[18]See further about the royal family of Naples in Ernesto Pontieri, *Per la storia del regno di Ferrante I d'Aragona, re di Napoli* (Naples, 1968).

[19]Quoted from Ruggero Palmieri, "Con Ippolita Sforza da Milano a Napoli," *Storia*, 1 (1938), 394–399.

[20]The most useful accounts for the present discussion were Allegretti di Allegretto, *Diarium Senense* in Ludovico Muratori, *Rerum italicarum scriptores*, vol. 23, cols. 771–772; Giovan Pietro Cagnola, *Cronache Milanesi: Dall anno 1023 sino al 1497* in *Archivio storico italiano*, 3 (1842); *Cronica di Bologna* in Muratori, vol. 18, col. 758; Ludovico de Raimo, *Istoria di Napolitana* in Muratori, vol. 23, col. 233. See also Palmieri, "Con Ippolita Sforza"; Cecilia Ady, *Lorenzo dei Medici and Renaissance Italy* (London, 1955), p. 21; Ady, *The Bentivoglio of Bologna: A Study in Despotism* (London, 1937), p. 141; Edward Armstrong, *Lorenzo de' Medici and Florence in the Fifteenth Century* (New York, 1914), pp. 53–54, 71.

public of Florence, and that Lorenzo and Ippolita at that time formed a close friendship that proved to be long-lasting.

Finally the bridal party left Pavia and set out for the long trek southward, with plans to stop at the important courts of the time along the way, where there would be entertainment offered by lords and princes of the realm. It was a huge cortège; one report states the number to have been over a thousand. Ippolita's immediate escorts included Federigo, soon to be her brother-in-law, with his immense company, and her two brothers, Filippo Maria and Sforza Maria.[21] Lorenzo was not a member of the group; he had rushed back to Florence in order to help prepare for the reception to be given Ippolita when she arrived there later. But dance-master Cornazano did travel for a time in the procession and made note of some of the most memorable occurrences.[22]

The first stop was Reggio d'Emilio, where Duke Borso d'Este (1413–1471) of Modena and Reggio gave the company a "grande honore." Next came Bologna, where Ippolita and her party were entertained royally for two days by the Bentivoglios. On June 19 the bridal cortège left Bologna for Florence, arriving there on the feast day of St. John the Baptist (June 24), patron saint of the city. The festivities in Florence were unusually elaborate, undoubtedly because of the close ties between Milan and Florence and the warm personal relationship between Lorenzo and Ippolita. On June 29 the bridal cortège entered Siena, and it was there that contemporary writers offered, for the first time, details of an entertainment staged in Ippolita's honor.[23] Organized by the Sienese Corporation of the Arts, the entertainment consisted of a moresca performed in the Piazza della Signoria by twelve young men and women dressed in elaborate costume and one dressed as a nun—the dance performed to a song that included the following text:

Non vogl'essere piu Monica;	I don't want to be a nun
arsa le sia la Tonica,	Burn the habit
chi se la veste più, &c.	Of whoever keeps wearing it.

Ippolita was ready to continue her journey on July 4th, but political events dictated otherwise. Her new brother-in-law, Jacopo Piccinino, who had been imprisoned in Naples by King Ferrante on June 24, was subsequently strangled. When Francesco Sforza received word of the murder, he was furious; he commanded the wedding party to remain in Siena until further notice and even threatened to call off the wedding.

---

[21]The betrothal of Sforza Maria and Eleonora d'Aragon in 1455 was later rescinded by Ferrante, who gave Eleonora in marriage to Duke Ercole I of Ferrara. In 1464 Ferrante made Sforza Maria the Duke of Bari.

[22]Palmieri, "Con Ippolita Sforza," p. 396.

[23]Ibid., p. 398, and Allegretto in Muratori, Rerum italicarum, col. 772.

After various persons, including King Ferrante and Pope Pius II, had re-
monstrated with him, he finally relented, allowing Ippolita to leave Siena. She had been forced to remain there for two months. The story of
the murder and the circumstances surrounding it was retold again and
again in courtly literature as well as popular literature and song of the
quattrocento.

Finally, on September 14, Ippolita and her company made their triumphant entry into Naples, where a week was given over to the wedding festivities before she finally was settled in her new home, the Castello Capuano. Much has been written about that exhilarating week,
but regretfully no one has given details about the balli that took place.[24]
We may assume, however, that the graceful and beautiful bride attracted the attention of all present for her skill in the dance.

There were other times when Ippolita would have been "on stage" as
a prima ballerina of court circles. In 1460, for example, her cousin Battista Sforza, daughter of Alessandro Sforza, was married to the celebrated *condottiere* and patron of the arts Federico da Montefeltre of Urbino. Since Battista grew up with the Sforza children in Pavia and
studied with their tutors, she was regarded as a member of the family.
There would have been much feasting and dancing when she left to be
married, and Ippolita would have been in the midst of it all. In December 1467 Ippolita returned north to visit her mother and to represent
King Ferrante (and herself) at the wedding of her brother Galeazzo to
Bona of Savoy in May 1468. This, too, obviously was an occasion for
great festivity.

Marriage and raising a family seem not to have interfered at all with
Ippolita's dancing. She was a mother of two children in 1470 when it
was reported that her father-in-law, King Ferrante of Naples, "had no
other pleasure, and nothing seemed to him more like Paradise than to
see her dancing and singing."[25] The report came from ballarino Ambrosio (= Guglielmo), who had been sent by the Duchess of Milan, Bianca
Maria, to the Court of Naples to teach the latest balli of Lombardy to
the princesses there—Ferrante's daughters Eleonora (1450–1493) and
Beatrice (1457–1508). Moreover, as Ambrosio wrote in his letter to
Bianca Maria, Ippolita had composed two dances herself to the music of
French chansons, which she sang as she danced. What were the French

---

[24]See Alessandro Lisini, *Le Feste Fatte in Napoli in 1465 per la matrimonio di Ippolita Sforza Visconti con Alfonso duca di Calabria* (Siena, 1898), which includes reprints of letters that Ippolita's brothers wrote to their father, Francesco, describing the
wedding festivities. This small book (thirty-nine pages) was presented by Lisini to his
friend Alessandro Mocenni as a wedding gift.

[25]"La Maesta de Re non ave altro piacere nei altro paradiso non parel che trove se
non quando la vede danzare e anche canthare." The letter is reprinted in Emilio Motta,
"Musica alla corte degli Sforza," *Archivio storico Lombardo*, 14 (1887), 61–62.

tunes? Were the choreographies of her dances preserved? At present there are no answers to those questions.[26]

In addition to the regular court activities at Naples in which Ippolita would have participated, there were at least two events of the 1470s that would have called for grand celebrations. Early in June of 1473 Eleonora left Naples to travel to Ferrara, where on July 4 she was married to Ercole d'Este (1431–1505), Duke of Ferrara and Modena. Contemporary writers, who left brilliant descriptions of the entertainment given Leonora in stops along the way of her bridal journey and of the elaborate wedding festivities, are silent about the sendoff Leonora must have received from the Neapolitan court. And yet it is improbable that Ferrante would have allowed his eldest daughter to leave home without giving special entertainments in honor of her marriage. Two years later Beatrice set out on her wedding journey to Hungary, where she was married at Buda in December, 1476, to King Matthias Corvinus. Again, it is inconceivable that her father would not have made arrangements to celebrate her approaching wedding at court before she left. And it is unthinkable that the wedding celebrations in both instances would not have included dancing, and that Ippolita would not have been centrally involved in the planning and performing of the balli.[27]

A final reference in contemporary literature to Ippolita and the dance comes in 1479. In December of that year Lorenzo de' Medici went to Naples as an accredited envoy from Florence to pursue peace between the two city-states, and during the three-month period of negotiations, his friend Ippolita entertained him sumptuously with balls and banquets.[28]

The Dance at Siena and Its Music

The description of the moresca performed for Ippolita at Siena is unique in the story of her involvement with the dance. Despite the meagerness of the report, it does inform us of several things. Here is an example of the moresca performed as a dance-spectacle, as distinguished from a social dance; to the accompaniment of a song, rather

[26]We know that Domenico used a French melody, "Hellas, la fille Guillemin," for choreographic purposes. See Dragan Plamenac, "The Two-Part Quodlibets in the Seville Chansonnier," *The Commonwealth of Music, in Honor of Curt Sachs*, Gustave Reese and Rose Brandel, ed. (New York, 1965), p. 166. The tune appears in a quodlibet, "A Florence la joyeuse," in a manuscript at El Escorial (Bibl. nat., IV.a.24, f. 119v–120r). As for extant choreographies of non-professionals, the New York copy of the Guglielmo/Ambrosio manuscript includes two dances composed by Lorenzo de' Medici, titled *Venus* and *Lauro*.

[27]I am hopeful that further research will uncover information about the balli that must have been danced at the Neapolitan Court during the 1470s.

[28]See Ady, *Lorenzo dei Medici*, pp. 77–78.

than of instruments; by a group of young professionals or semi-professionals. As pointed out earlier, the "moresche" directed by Domenico and Ambrosio for Ippolita's wedding festivities were performed by aristocratic amateurs at court.

Dance historian Curt Sachs has observed that in the fifteenth century the term *morisca* applied not only to the dance of Moorish origin but as well to choral dances, which used a double-file formation.[29] And there are references in contemporary literature to choral dances being accompanied by the singing of ballatas—the dancing group singing the refrain at the beginning and a leader singing the stanza verses, after each of which the group comes in with the refrain or a part of it.[30] Now the song used for the moresca at Siena is a ballata. Did the girl dressed up as a nun take the role of a leader and sing the stanza verses? Did the group of twelve youths and maidens sing the refrains as they danced? There are extant at least two texts of the ballata in contemporary manuscripts and at least one musical setting of the text (see the Appendix for examples). Although we would need much more information in order to re-create the little ballet that Ippolita saw in June 1465, we can imagine at least the setting.

The present brief essay of course neglects Ippolita Sforza's position as one of the most illustrious women of the early Renaissance in Italy, distinguished for her learning and her promotion of the cultural arts at Ferrante's Neapolitan court. Her influence upon the development of the young princesses at Naples cannot be overstated—first, there were her sisters-in-law Eleonora and Beatrice, who contributed enormously to the development of the cultural arts at their own courts after their marriages; then there was Eleonora's daughter Beatrice d'Este, who lived during the years 1477–1485 with her grandfather Ferrante at Naples, where she came under Ippolita's influence; and finally there was Ippolita's own daughter Isabella, who married her cousin, Gian Galeazzo Sforza, and became the Duchess of Milan in 1489. History confirms that Ippolita passed on to her young charges a love of the cultural arts and the kind of thorough humanistic training she herself had received. I rather suspect that she also prided herself on how beautifully her charges could dance.

Ippolita Maria Sforza, Duchess of Calabria, died on August 20, 1488, at Naples.

[29]Curt Sachs, *World History of the Dance*, English edition (New York, 1937), p. 335.

[30]In regard to a fifteenth-century choral dance performed to the singing of a ballata at Bologna on the feast day of St. John the Baptist, see Maurice Bowra, "Songs of Dance and Carnival," *Italian Renaissance Studies: A Tribute to the Late Cecilia M. Ady* (London, 1960), pp. 329–330. See also Sachs, *World History*, pp. 278, 286, 289–290. Sachs comments on a fresco in the Town Hall of Siena, dating from about 1340, that depicts a choral dance with nine aristocratic women hand in hand, and a tenth leading the singing and playing a tambourine (p. 272).

Appendix: Music and Text for the Moresca at Siena *

53. Hora may che fora son

Ora may che fora son	Since I am out
Non uolio esser monica	I don't want to be a nun anymore
Arsa li sia tonicha	Burn the habit
A chi se la uestera piu.	Of whoever keeps wearing it.

Staua in quelo monastero	I stayed in that monastery
como una cosa perduta	Like a lost thing
senza refrigerio alcuno	Without any comfort
non uedea ne era ueduta	Not seeing nor being seen.
Ora may che ne son insuta	Since I have rebelled
Non uolio esser piu monicha	I don't want to be a nun anymore
Arsa li sia tonicha	Burn the habit
A chi se la uestera piu.	Of whoever keeps wearing it.
Sorela mia tu ay rasone	Sister mine you are right
e ben dici la uerita	And speak the truth
ch'el non e pezor presone	[When you say] that there is no worse prison
che perder la liberta	Than to lose one's freedom
in poter de queli frati	At the hands of those friars
se piu ci stava era morta	Had I stayed there longer I would have died
quando batiaō a la porta	When they knocked at the door
apri che fra piero son.	"Open up—it's Fra Piero."
Quando uano per la via	When they go in the streets
domandando la carita	Begging for charity
cum la uoce humile e pia	In humble, pious voices
dati del pane ay fra	"Give some bread to the monks."
tanto ne azo pietado	I pity them
e uoriali con piacere	And would like to accommodate them
mi che habiamo absoluere	Me whom they should absolve
non me acolierano piu.	They will never again allow in.
Sorela mia poy che noy siamo	Sister mine, now that we are
suti fora de quelo inferno	out of that hellhole
demozi festa e godiamo	Let us rejoice and enjoy
bona uita bon governo	Good life and good rule.
se scampasse in eterno	
Non uolio esser . . .	I don't want to be . . .
E fazando tal vita	And leading such a life.
non e melior paradiso	There is no better paradise
ben amata e ben servita	Well loved and well provided
Cum solazo zoza e riso	With solace, joy, and laughter
lo zurato e impromeso	I have sworn and promised
Non uolio esser . . .	I don't want to be . . .

Sorela mia uo che te dica	Sister mine, let me tell you
preti oy frati oy seculari	Priests or monks or worldly men
chi me uolia per amicha	Whoever wants me for a sweetheart
se conuen che habia dinari	Had better have money
che me uolio maritare	Because I want to marry
Non uolio esser . . .	I don't want to be . . .
Sorela mia uolio uenire	Sister mine I want to come
ala casa doue stay	To your house
uolio usire de tanti guai	I want to leave all those troubles
e pensarme de galdere	And think of enjoying myself.
uolio stare al mio piacere	I want to live at my pleasure
Solazar a la mia uolia	Amuse myself at will
che sia morta de una dolia	I could have died of pain
Mader mia soy zoueneta	Mother mine I am young
questo mondo uolio godere	I want to enjoy this world
piu non uolio essere sozeta	I no longer want to be a prisoner
ne monastero piu seruire	Or serve in a monastery
che durasse sti martire	Putting up with the tortures
de leuar de meza note	Of getting up in the middle of the night
prego dio che mala morte	I pray God strike me dead
possa far sen entro piu.	If I ever go back there
la madre maritare	Mother would like to marry me off
me uoria se io podesse	If it were possible.
ma sey senza dinari	But without money
non se po cantar le messe	You can't sing a mass
ora maychi scrisse scrisse	By now, let those who would write, write
Non uolio esser piu monicha	I don't want to be a nun anymore
Arsa li sia tonicha	Burn the habit
A chi se la uestere piu.	Of those
	who would keep wearing it.

*The music is reprinted from *Anonymous Pieces in the Ms El Escorial IV.a.24*, ed. Eileen Southern (American Institute of Musicology, 1981), p. 69. This text is a reprint from the transcription of the original by Antonio Ive without any alterations, such as addition of punctuation or capitalization, except that I have changed the spacing so as to indicate the four-line stanzas of the ballata and point up the refrains. See A. Ive, "Poesie Popolari: Tratte da un Ms. della Biblioteca Nazionale di Parigi," *Giornale storico della letteratura italiani* 2 (1883), 153–155. Translation is by Massimi Ossi. A description of the manuscript (fonds. ital. 1069), which was unavailable to me, is given on p. 149.

French Revolutionary Models for Beethoven's *Eroica* Funeral March*

CLAUDE V. PALISCA

THE PART NAPOLEON BONAPARTE played in Beethoven's thoughts in the composition, dedication, intitulation, and publication of the *Eroica* Symphony has been a subject of both speculation and research. There is firm documentary evidence for Beethoven's original plan to dedicate the symphony to Napoleon and for his continuing desire to name it for him after it was completed. Eventually Napoleon's name was omitted from the title in favor of a more universal designation, "Heroic Symphony . . . composed to celebrate the memory of a great man," when it was published in 1806 with a dedication to Prince Lobkowitz. But this did not erase evidence in the music itself of Beethoven's desire to please the original intended dedicatee. Little has been said of this evidence in the literature about the work's genesis. Most modern students of the *Eroica* have been content to let its relationship to Napoleon rest along with much of the mythology that has surrounded the work. But de-mythification may have gone too far in this case.

Traces of the composer's preoccupation with Napoleon as the hero celebrated in the symphony are concentrated in the second movement, the *Marcia funebre*. They take the form of allusions to musical genres, styles, and even clichés practiced in the public memorials honoring heroes of the French Revolution, Directoire, and Consulate. These allusions must have been introduced in part to flatter Napoleon, and to stir his memories of the many civic festivals that he must have witnessed and the music he would have heard there. They established a link be-

*Much of the research for this article was accomplished in 1966–67 as part of a curriculum development project sponsored jointly by Yale University and the Cooperative Research Program of the Office of Education, United States Department of Health, Education and Welfare. Although no findings were reported in the scholarly organs, they were incorporated into the teacher's and student's manuals for the course, "An Approach to Musical Understanding," which was widely distributed, though never commercially published. See my report, "A Curriculum for Understanding Music Through Discovery and Discussion: The Yale Music Curriculum Project," *College Music Symposium*, 9 (1969), 36–47.

tween the music with which Napoleon was associated (and presumably familiar) and the unfamiliar idiom of this symphony, thus making this difficult work more palatable. At the same time the heroic references locate their subject in place and time, for Beethoven not only destined the work for Bonaparte but admitted that he wrote the symphony "on" or "about" him.

One of the myths concerning the symphony that should have been laid to rest long ago is the belief that Beethoven put Napoleon out of his mind as the subject of the symphony when he heard that the First Consul had become Emperor. The story told by Ferdinand Ries that Beethoven became enraged upon hearing that Napoleon had proclaimed himself Emperor and tore up the title page that bore the general's name seems to rest on good grounds. It has tended, however, to discredit any further association of the symphony with the person of Napoleon. The Ries story has to be balanced against other documents that attest to Beethoven's continued intention of dedicating the symphony to Bonaparte, or at least naming it after him. Scholars have recently begun to restore this balance, thanks to the wealth of documentary material that has come to light.[1] Maynard Solomon devoted an entire article in 1968 to examining the facts surrounding the dedication and intitulation of the symphony and to Beethoven's attitudes toward the Emperor Napoleon.[2] Joseph Schmidt-Görg and Hans Schmidt, in their pictorial biography, also note the conflicting evidence of Ries's account and Beethoven's correspondence.[3] The incident that Ries witnessed would have happened in May 1804.[4] On October 22, 1803, he had written to Nicolaus Simrock that Beethoven "desires very much to dedicate it [the symphony] to Bonaparte himself. However should Lobkowitz wish to have it for half a year for 400 [ducats], then it will be called Bonaparte."[5]

On the covering page of Beethoven's own copy of the symphony, preserved in the library of the Vienna Gesellschaft der Musikfreunde, appears the title "Sinfonia grande/intitolata Bonaparte" ("Grand Symphony/entitled Bonaparte"), followed by the date "1804 im Au-

---

[1]Almost all of the known documentary material, translated into English, was included in the Student Manual for Unit IV, "The Symphony," and put before high school and college students in the curriculum mentioned in footnote 1, inviting them to review the Beethoven-Napoleon question.

[2]"Beethoven and Bonaparte," *The Music Review*, 29 (1968), 96–105. This was reprinted in Solomon's *Beethoven* (New York, 1977), pp. 132–42.

[3]*Ludwig van Beethoven* (New York, Washington, London, 1970), pp. 36–39.

[4]Elliot Forbes, *Thayer's Life of Beethoven* (Princeton, 1967), p. 349.

[5]That is, for 400 ducats the symphony would be dedicated to Lobkowitz but named after Bonaparte. Georg Kinsky, *Das Werk Beethovens* (Munich-Duisburg, 1955), p. 131.

gust." But the words "intitolata Bonaparte"[6] are partly rubbed out and replaced with Beethoven's hand-penciled notation "Geschrieben auf Bonaparte" ("composed on Bonaparte").[7] Beethoven's own letter to Breitkopf & Härtel of August 26, 1804, offers the firm "a *new grand symphony*," which he wishes to have first published in score rather than parts. He adds this clarification: "The title of the symphony is really *Bonaparte* [Beethoven's emphasis]. . . ."[8]

The symphony was first published, not in score but in parts, neither by Simrock nor Breitkopf & Härtel but by the Bureau of Arts and Industry in Vienna in 1806. Dedicated to Prince Lobkowitz, it bore the title "Sinfonia Eroica . . . composta per festeggiare il sovvenire di un grand Uomo."[9] Clearly, Beethoven never denied the existence of a live hero under the nameless cloak of "grand' uomo."

Beethoven's apparent fascination with French revolutionary music has received some attention from scholars. Einstein noted Beethoven's adoption of the marchlike first movement of the French violin concerto, and he remarked that the First Piano Concerto "should have earned Beethoven, like Schiller, an honorary citizenship in the French Republic."[10] Boris Schwarz gave a list of works other than concertos with a strong military character, noting: "Beethoven's two 'heroic' funeral marches (in Op. 26 and in the Third Symphony) bring to mind the two great funeral compositions of the French Revolution—the *Marche lugubre* by Gossec (for Mirabeau's funeral in 1791) and the *Hymne funèbre* by Cherubini (in memory of General Hoche, 1797)."[11] Arnold Schmitz dedicated part of the chapter "Zur Auffassung des Heroischen" in *Das romantische Beethovenbild* to Beethoven's relationship to French civic music; he cites parallel passages from works of Rodolphe Kreutzer, Cherubini, Catel, Gossec, and Méhul, although he neglects the *Marcia funebre*.[12]

[6]The word is clearly "intitolata," and not "dedicata," "intitulata," or "intitolato," as some have read, for it is all legible; but the name "Bonaparte" has been partly obliterated. In the full-color facsimile in Schmidt-Görg and Schmidt, *L. van Beethoven*, the "Bona" of "Bonaparte" is barely visible, but the "rte" is clearly there. Of the "pa" only the descender of the "p" remains. Black-and-white facsimiles are in Robert Bory, *Ludwig van Beethoven, His Life and Work in Pictures* (New York, 1960), p. 108, and H. C. Robbins Landon, *Beethoven, A Documentary Study* (New York, 1970), p. 175.

[7]This is not visible in the facsimiles. See the line-by-line analysis of this title page in Solomon, "Beethoven and Bonaparte," p. 98.

[8]Emily Anderson, *Letters of Beethoven* (London, 1961), Letter no. 96.

[9]See the facsimile of the title page in Schmidt-Görg and Schmidt, *L. van Beethoven*, p. 36.

[10]*Essays on Music* (New York, 1956), p. 247.

[11]"Beethoven and the French Violin School," *MQ*, 44 (1958), 438.

[12]Arnold Schmitz, *Das romantische Beethovenbild* (Berlin and Bonn, 1927), pp. 159–76.

While he was a violist in the theatre orchestra in Bonn, Beethoven had an opportunity to participate in performances of the works of a number of French composers such as Dalayrac, Grétry, and Monsigny. Even before Beethoven left Bonn, in November 1792, he must have been aware of the republican festivities in Nancy and Strasbourg, barely 150 miles away, not to mention those in Paris. He may even have heard some of the music. Rouget de Lisle recalls in his *Essays en vers et en prose* (1796) that after the first performance of his *Hymne à la liberté*, with music by Ignace Pleyel, in Strasbourg in 1791, the text was translated into German, and the song was heard across the Rhine in Breisgau.[13] Perhaps the most famous march to issue from the body of revolutionary music was Gossec's *Marche lugubre*, from which Beethoven quotes—or so it seems—a passage in the Funeral March. It was first performed to honor the victims of the sedition in Nancy on September 20, 1791 and again on several other occasions: the funeral of Mirabeau, April 4, 1791; to accompany Voltaire's burial procession to the Pantheon, July 11, 1791; for the ceremony honoring Simoneau on June 3, 1792; for the victims of August 10, 1792; and still later for the funerals of General Hoche, October 1797, and Joubert, September 6, 1799.[14]

The function of the music in these commemorations may be gathered from descriptions of the ceremony to honor General Hoche, ordered by the Directoire and held on the Champs de Mars in Paris. Cherubini's *Marche funèbre* accompanied the procession. After an address by the president of the Directoire, forty young students of the Conservatoire, dressed in white, with narrow bands around their hair, came forward and gathered around the mausoleum to sing the first strophe of Cherubini's *Hymne funèbre sur la mort du général Hoche* on a text by M.-J. Chénier. Their part, for unison sopranos, represented the voices of young girls. After a eulogy pronounced by Daunou, a group of alto voices, representing old men, sang the second strophe in unison, accompanied by trombones, horns, bassoons, and serpents. The third strophe was sung in unison by baritones (haute-contre), representing soldiers, accompanied by flutes and muted trumpets. Finally all the men's voices united in a choir à 3 accompanied by a wind band made up of two petites flûtes, two clarinets, two horns in E^b and two in C, two bassoons, serpent, three trombones, two trumpets in C, and timpani, and an orchestra made up of strings in four parts, two flutes, piccolo, two oboes, two clarinets, two horns in E♭ and two in C, two trumpets in C, three trombones, two bassoons, and timpani.[15]

---

[13]Constant Pierre, *Les Hymnes et chansons de la révolution* (Paris, 1904), p. 217.
[14]Pierre, *Les Hymnes*, p. 843.
[15]Pierre, *Les Hymnes*, p. 402.

The marches were usually in binary form, with each section repeated. Beethoven instead patterned the *Marcia funebre* on his more usual march-and-trio layout. Of the two components of the *Eroica's* second movement, only the march, marked *Minore* on its return, is akin to the revolutionary *marche funèbre*. The trio, marked *Maggiore*, is in spirit closer to the revolutionary hymn. This will be evident in our analysis.

Beethoven's *Minore*, the *Marcia funebre* proper, borrows a number of devices from the French revolutionary funeral march. The thirty-second notes in the strings, particularly when marked pianissimo or piano, were obviously intended to imitate the sound of muffled drums, the *caisse roulante voilée*, called for in a number of the sets of parts of the French funeral marches, as in Gossec's *Marche lugubre*.[16]

The most striking parallel with the French repertory is the virtual quotation of a phrase from this very march of Gossec. At m. 19 of the E♭ major section of the *Minore*, Beethoven seems to parody a passage in Gossec's second period (Example 1):

Example 1.

a: Gossec, *Marche lugubre*

b: Beethoven, *Marcia funebre*

[16]See the list of parts in Pierre, *Les Hymnes*, pp. 840–41. For a score made from the original parts, see C. Palisca, ed., *Norton Anthology of Western Music*, vol. II, no. 113, (New York, 1980), pp. 84–87. The parts, which were printed, are in Paris, Bibliothèque nationale, in the folder H/2-143, formerly belonging to the Conservatoire national. Only the tam-tam part was not printed, and it is handwritten in this set on the folio marked 143q and cued to the first clarinet part. There is an unfortunate error in the early printings of the *Norton Anthology*. The tam-tam in mm. 6-9 should play on the first half of the measures and rest on the second half rather than vice versa.

The examples have in common the descent by semitone-tone-semitone, spanning a diminished fourth—doubled at the unison and octave in Gossec, harmonized in Beethoven; followed by two loud chords—diminished sevenths in Gossec, dominant sevenths in Beethoven; then silence, punctuated in Gossec, however, by the gong. The subsequent semitone descent E♭-D-C♯ in the second oboe and alto trombone in Gossec is paralleled by the semitone motion in the first violin of the Beethoven. Gossec then approaches a German sixth chord by a series of syncopations, whereas Beethoven reaches a similar chord directly. The augmented sixth chord, common enough in this period, always strikes one as a bold effect in the spare simplistic harmony of the revolutionary music. Beethoven draws attention to it with a sforzando followed immediately by piano.

Gossec's phrase culminates in a sequence of orchestral unisons. Beethoven reserves his unisons for a more strategic location, just before the entrance of the *Maggiore,* and again at its conclusion, before the return of the *Minore.* Orchestral unisons are a cliché borrowed from the choral revolutionary hymns, where they never fail to make a strong impression, as an ensemble that has been singing part-music suddenly converges into unisons and octaves on a hymn's key words. This is illustrated in the *Chant triomphal* of Johann Paul Aegidius Martini for the holiday of the first of Vendémiaire, year VII (1798; Example 2a).[17] Sometimes, as in Beethoven's return to the *Minore,* the effect was combined with the Neapolitan sixth harmony (Example 2b).

Example 2

a: J.P.A. Martini, *Chant triomphal*

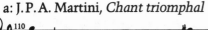

(Instrumental accompaniment omitted.)

(continued)

---

[17]Constant Pierre, *Musique des fêtes et cérémonies de la révolution française* (Paris, 1899), p. 159.

Example 2, continued

b: Beethoven, *Marcia funebre*

The main theme of Beethoven's *Minore* section itself owes some of its characteristic turns to the French hymn repertory. Both the antecedent and consequent two-bar phrases of the opening C minor melody end in the telltale feminine pattern of many French songs. The alto part of Gossec's three-voice a cappella *Hymne à la liberté* (Example 3a) illustrates this penchant for the feminine cadence at line ends at "Patrie" and "chérie." At m. 17, where the alto voice sings alone, we find the turn Beethoven uses in the first measure of the march. The continuation of the march melody in the earliest sketch in the so-called *Eroica* Sketchbook (MS Landsberg 6, p. 6, staves 4–5; see Example 3b) bears some resemblance to the continuation of this alto line, but this is probably fortuitous.[18] A later sketch of this opening in the same manuscript (p. 42, staff line 5; see Example 3c) shows the melody starting on C, as in Gossec's alto solo. The haute-contre, or top voice, at the words "Règne, règne" (Example 4a) is also suggestive of a passage (Example 4b) in Beethoven's *Minore*, the melody of the transition from E♭ major back to the main theme in C minor at mm. 25–27. But this likeness too may be purely accidental.

[18]I am indebted to Professor Lewis Lockwood for the loan of a film of this still relatively inaccessible source, formerly in the Preussische Staatsbibliothek. Concerning its present location in the Biblioteka Jagiellonska, Krakow, see the communication, "The Berlin Manuscripts Recovered," by P. J. P. Whitehead, *Notes*, 36 (1980), 773–76.

Example 3

a: Gossec, *Hymne à la liberté*

O Dé- i- té de ma Pa-- tri- e. Li- ber- té. des Fran- çais ché- ri- e. ché- ri- e. Rè- gne [etc.]

b: Beethoven, Sketchbook Landsberg 6, p. 6

c: Landsberg 6, p. 42

Example 4

a: Gossec, *Hymne à la liberté*

Rè- gne. rè- gne sur notre

b: Beethoven, *Marcia funebre*

The E♭ major theme also has the ring of a revolutionary hymn; indeed, the incipit matches the *Hymne à l' Égalité* with text by "citoyen" Malingre and music by "citoyen" Beauvarlet-Charpentier fils (see Example 5).[19]

[19]Pierre, *Les Hymnes*, no. 1432, p. 701.

Example 5
a: *Hymne à Egalité*

O   fil- le de l'Ê- tre su- prê-   me

b: Beethoven, *Marcia funebre*

c: Gossec, *Le Triomphe de la Republique*

The repetition of the theme in m. 19 of the Beethoven is preceded by a run that is another of Gossec's favorite devices. A gesture perhaps inherited from the baroque French overture, it is used several times in *Le Triomphe de la République* (Example 5c).[20] Throughout these passages we have not so much evidence of borrowing as of Beethoven's having assimilated the idiom of the popular patriotic songs.

The *Maggiore* section, although in the same tempo and meter as the march proper, has the character not of a march but rather of a hymn punctuated by fanfares and drumrolls. Comparison with the march of the piano sonata Op. 26, no. 3 in A♭ (1800-01), entitled *Marcia funebre sulla morte d'un eroe* and dedicated to Prince Lichnowsky, is illuminating in that its trio, also in the parallel major, consists entirely of imitations of drum rolls alternating with fanfares. In the *Eroica* Beethoven highlighted a lyrical hymnlike theme in the oboe and flute, while he assigned to the fanfares and drumrolls a transitional and cadential role. The idiomatic French elements are arranged as follows:

Hymn	Fanfare over Drumroll	Hymn	Fanfare over Drumroll	Unisons
69	76	80	96	101

Both the opening melody and the accompaniment exhibit traits of the French hymn repertory. As in the *Minore*, the opening statements dis-

---

[20]Gossec, *Le Triomphe de la République ou Le camp de Grand-Pré, Divertissement lyrique en un acte, représenté à l'opéra le 27 janvier l'an 2me* (Paris: Mozin, J. H. Naderman [gravé par Huguet], p. 117). [Yale Music Library Mq20 G695t.]

play the French feminine ending and two-bar phrasing. Triadic C major melodies such as that which opens the *Maggiore* were especially popular among composers of revolutionary hymns. The opening of Ignace Pleyel's *Hymne à la liberté* (1791), on a text of J. Rouget de Lisle, is representative of the genre (Example 6a). Both the thematic arpeggiation of the tonic chord and the frequency of the key of C major are attributable to the use of trumpets in C. Pleyel's accompaniment, reduced in Example 6a, exploits fanfare motives, even though the original scoring was for string orchestra with clarinets, horns, and bassoons, but without trumpets.[21]

Example 6

a: Pleyel, *Hymne à la liberté;* reduction from Pierre,
Musique des fêtes, p. 131

b: Beethoven, *Marcia funebre*

Alberti-bass accompaniment, like that of Example 6b, appears occasionally in the hymns, as in Gossec's *Hymne guérrier.*[22] Beethoven had used an Alberti bass throughout the trio of the March, Op. 45, no. 1, another piece with a Gallic flavor. Finally, the fanfare that follows the

[21]Scoring described by Pierre, *Les Hymnes*, p. 216. For other triadic C major themes see Méhul, *Le chant du retour*, in Pierre, *Musique des fêtes*, pp. 404, 406; Devienne, *Hymne à l'éternel*, ibid., p. 243; and Gossec, *Choeur à la liberté*, ibid., p. 351.
[22]Pierre, *Musique des fêtes*, p. 91.

lyrical section of the *Eroica* march may be indebted also to Gossec, for it is found in his *Aux mânes de la Gironde* (1795), from which Beethoven may also have taken the theme of the last movement of the Fifth Symphony.[23] Gossec's fanfare appears at the end of this *hymne élégiaque* (Example 7a), in a position similar to Beethoven's.

Example 7

a: Gossec, *Aux mânes de la Gironde*; reduction from Pierre, *Musique des fêtes*, p. 325

b: Beethoven, *Marcia funebre*

Could Beethoven have written the Funeral March without knowing any of the French repertory? And could he have known this repertory without being present at any of the festivities? The answer to the first question must be negative. To the second question there can be at present no precise answer.

The republican music traveled throughout France, which in 1795 extended to cities such as Antwerp and Cologne; some of the music reached beyond. The works mentioned in this article were all published, most of them by the Magasin de musique à l'usage des fêtes nationales, which was organized by the Institut national de musique to propagate the music of the public festivities, so that they might "promptly circulate throughout the Republic."[24] The Magasin issued variously instrumental parts, scores, and reductions for voice and

---

[23]See David Charlton, "Revolutionary hymn," *New Grove*, vol. 15, 777–78, and, therein, example 2.

[24]Pierre, *Les Hymnes*, p. 122.

figured bass. The printings were quite large, particularly of the hymns, which were distributed in as many as 18,000 copies. It is not unlikely that copies of the best known hymns and marches drifted to Vienna. Some of the noble families there maintained wind bands, and a piece that had the reputation of Gossec's *Marche lugubre*, which was published in parts by the Magasin de musique, though without the gong (tam-tam) part, would have been a desideratum for their bands' libraries. It is said that a crowd gathered every evening to hear the regimental bands at the Imperial Palace for the changing of the guard.[25] Their directors could not have ignored the novel French repertory.[26] French-style marches and choruses, moreover, abounded in operas produced in Vienna. Among the stage works of Méhul produced in Vienna between 1795 and 1803 were *Euphrosine, L'Irato, Une Folie* (as *Die beyden Füchse*), *Le Trésor supposé*, and *Héléna*. The best evidence of Beethoven's acquaintance with the French Republican repertory, however, lies in the music itself of works such as the *Marcia funebre*.

One would not venture to call the parallels and resemblances that have been displayed here borrowings. Rather, aside from the passage from the *Marche lugubre*, these examples bear witness to Beethoven's sensitivity to the French republican style, to his having assimilated it so thoroughly that the characteristic phrases and clichés poured forth effortlessly. Beethoven's *Marcia funebre* is surely greater than the sum of the parts sampled here. Although they were enough to lead a listener acquainted with French revolutionary music to recognize the style, certainly the work as a whole would have struck such a listener as unlike any of the models; it is a synthesis and idealization of the commemorative march and hymn, lifted to their ultimate heights.

[25]Michel Brenet [pseud. for Marie Bobillier], *La musique militaire* (Paris, n.d.), p. 63.
[26]More research is needed in this area. Constant Pierre reports in *Les Hymnes*, besides holdings of Parisian and French provincial libraries, only those of the British Library and Berlin Staatsbibliothek.

The Twirling Duet: A Dance Narrative from Northeast China

RULAN CHAO PIAN

In 1957, Maa Kee, in his book *Talks on Music Among the Chinese People*,[1] described a kind of singing and dancing performance found in Northeast China, called *Ell Ren Juann*, The Twirling Duet:

> The sound of clappers reaches the sky, Ai-hai-ya——! As soon as people hear this familiar sound, they rush to the scene and gather around into a circle—not too large and not too small—forming a most convenient stage where the spectators can watch from all angles, and share the mood intimately with the performers.
>
> There are only two dancers. The one who plays the part of the "Maid" *Dann* wears a colorful skirt and holds a handkerchief in one hand and a paper fan in the other. The performer flutters these two props up and down while dancing, like a colorful butterfly. The other, who plays the part of the "Clown" *Choou* is dressed more simply: a black outfit with a cap, an apron around the waist. In his hands are two pairs of bamboo clappers. As he waves his arms and capers about, gyrating his body, he clicks out a complicated rhythmic pattern that also sparkles with a variety of tone colors.
>
> Behind the dancers three or four men are sitting. This is the backstage, as well as the orchestra. Together with the dancers these make up the entire troupe. The orchestra is simple enough: a wooden-faced fiddle, an *ell-hwu* fiddle, and a woodblock. Each man is basic and indispensable to the whole ensemble. The player of the wooden fiddle, at lively moments, also doubles as the double-reed suoonah blower.
>
> Against the sustained tone of the suoonah, the actors begin to sing:
> . . .
> "That's 'Meeting at Blue Bridge'!" the spectators whisper knowingly, nodding at each other. It is a familiar tale, all right. Still, the minute the people are certain of the story they are about to hear, they eagerly wait for the performance as if it were all a pleasant surprise. . . .

NOTE: A Glossary of characters for Chinese terms is on page 230.
[1] Maa Kee, *Jonggwo Minjian Inyueh Jeanghuah* (Peking, 1957), pp. 81–96.

The words they have just sung consist of only four phrases. Yet the melody can extend to thirty-two bars. No one would complain that it is too long. On the contrary, some might even find it too short. The reason is that along with this rhythmically impelling melody that they are singing, the two performers are also doing an intricate dance, weaving back and forth like two shuttles. The Maid spins her kerchief and throws it in the air. Then, after twirling around several times, she nimbly catches the kerchief again. The Clown, with his bamboo clappers, creates sounds like metal and stone, which seem to shoot out of his body from head to toe. He puts one hand on his partner's shoulder, the other hand around her waist, turning left, twisting right, now backing away, now coming together. It is the joy of spring with emotions full and compelling. Who says this is too long?

The question is, do we not find some contradiction between such joyous singing and dancing, and the tragic content of the story, "Meeting at Blue Bridge" [which is about two ill-fated lovers]? I do not think so. People do not necessarily always look upon their unfortunate lives fatalistically. It could be an expression of their enduring optimism, confidence, praising those who dare to rebel against a benighted society. . . .

The account quoted above contains some very interesting facts about this art. In the first place, this is a complicated performance that involves simultaneous dancing, singing, and storytelling. Second, an obvious dichotomy exists between the mood of the presentation, which is lively and gay, and the mood of the story, which in this case is sad. The account also leads to some intriguing questions. In what manner is the story told? Is it, for example, in the third-person narrative mode or the first-person dramatic mode? With two performers assuming characters, dialogue can occur; thus, potentially a drama can be created. However, when the story involves more than two characters, exactly how are the roles shifted from one to another, and in what way are they divided between the two performers? Finally, given the realistic acting (or gesturing) of a narrator, how is it combined with the seemingly irrelevant dance movements?

Studies have recently been conducted in China on the origin, definition, and development of the Twirling Duet.[2] Its close relationship, in choice of tunes and style of dancing, with the seasonal farmer's dance

---

[2]Many works that I am citing appear in the following collections:

a. *Ell Ren Juann Jyi-jiuh Wenjyi* [*Collected Essays on the Twirling Duet and the Jyilin Opera*]. The Jyilin Institute of Regional Opera Studies (Charngchuen, Jyilin, 1980), 322 pp. Articles dated from 1956 to 1980.

b. *Ell Ren Juann Shyyliaw* [*Source Materials on the Twirling Duet*], vol. III, ed. Wang Keen. The Jyilin Institute of Regional Opera Studies (Charngchuen, Jyilin, 1980), 351 pp. Mainly interviews of old performers by field workers.

c. *Shihjiuh Yanjiou Tzyliaw* [*Journal of Sources for the Study of Drama*], vol. III (Charngchuen, Jyilin, 1979), 81 pp.

songs in North China—the *Iangge*, "Rice Sprout Songs" (or, more freely, "Rice Planting Songs")—is unquestioned.[3] However, the assumption that there is an inevitable evolutionary process from the narrative arts to the dramatic-operatic arts (all Chinese traditional drama is musical) is still open to debate. The prominent writer Lao Sheh once remarked that the Twirling Duet should be considered a dramatic form, using a very special and economic means of presentation. To him, people are doing an injustice to the art by calling it a narrative form (*Cheu yih*).[4] More recently, scholars such as Wang Keen, while considering the Twirling Duet an intermediate stage in the evolution from the narrative to the dramatic art, nevertheless admit that the special character and appeal of the Twirling Duet comes precisely from its having stubbornly retained a character halfway between the two.[5]

During the summer of 1981, I had occasion to videotape a performance of the Twirling Duet in the city of Sheenyang in Liaoning Province, Northeast China, one of the centers where this art flourishes. For the present investigation, I have made a complete translation of the text of the performance (see Appendix), and will examine exactly what is happening in the performance and how the performers handle the telling of the story. Furthermore, I will describe and roughly catalogue those movements of the performers that seem relevant to the content of the story.

---

[3]The name *Ell Ren Juann*, literally meaning "two persons twirling," actually came into existence only in the early 1950s. Previously, the genre had many other names, some considered derogatory (here marked with *), e.g., *Dongbeei Dueykoou* (Singing Duet of the Northeast), *Dueykoou Lianhuanleh* (Happy Song Duet), *Benq.benq* or *Dih Benq.tz* (The Hopping [Show]), *Shuang Wanyell* (A Game of Two Players), etc. At present, all of these names except the last one have been replaced by the term *Ell Ren Juann*. This art shares many features with other genres of rural North China, one of which, called the *Lianhualaw* (The Lotus Lai) can be traced back to the mid-18th century. Hence it is generally accepted that the art is about 200 years old (See article by Wang Keen in *Ell Ren Juann Jyi-jiuh Wenjyi*, p. 194). The Twirling Duet is often performed at New Year's and during festival seasons. According to a 1948 report by Jih Ming, the total repertory at the time was about 35 pieces (*Benq.benq Music of the Northeast* [Peking]). Jang Lin, in "Ell Ren Juann Chii Yuan Chu Tann" [A preliminary Investigation into the origins of the Twirling Duet] has discussed the sources of such elements as the tunes, the dance steps, the story, the verse form, etc., of the genre (in *Cheu Yih Yih Shuh Luenn Tsorng* [Collected Essays on the Art of the Narrative Genres], 1981, no. 2).

See also article by Jang Chyr in *Ell Ren Juann Jyi-jiuh Wenjyi*, p. 220. In *Jiuh Been* [Journal on Drama], 2 (1983), 91, Wang Keen has an article, "The Rustic Twirling Duet," on the latest summary of the art. See also his discussion in *Ell Ren Juann Shyyliaw*, p. 36, on the origin of the Twirling Duet.

[4]Correspondence by Lao Sheh in *Ell Ren Juann Shyyliaw*, p. 151.

[5]Ibid., p. 152.

The performance was an invited presentation at the Sheenyang Academy of Music.[6] It took place in a large classroom (with chairs and desks pushed aside in the corners). The spectators, who sat at one end of the room, were on the same level as that of the performers at the opposite end. Such a stageless indoor performance of the Twirling Duet is a common thing, although Maa Kee's account quoted above shows that it is also done outdoors.[7] The two dancers were students of the Sheenyang School of Narrative Arts. The Clown was played by Yang Woei, a twenty-five-year-old male student, and the Maid was played by Chern Lihjiun, a nineteen-year-old female student. The orchestra consisted of a double-reed suoonah, a yangchyn (dulcimer played with bamboo hammers), a pyiba (a four-string lute), four two-string fiddles,[8] a mouth organ, a woodblock, and a Western cello. The audience that evening consisted mainly of faculty members of the Academy. The twenty-minute Twirling Duet performance was the last item of a series of numbers on the program, which extended well over two hours.

The costumes of the performers were not specific to any one character. The Maid wore a long pink dress with a flowing skirt and a shoulder coverlet with embroidered ornaments. She had earrings with long pendants. Her long hair was tied at the base, partly forming a bun on top and partly hanging in the back. The Clown wore a two-piece blue outfit, which had a black collar and black trimmings on the sleeves. He wore a black broad-brimmed hat with the front rim turned up, and a black sash around his waist. Each performer held a big floppy fan in the right hand and a colorful kerchief in the left hand. Of the performances that I have

[6]President Ding Ming, of the Sheenyang Academy of Music, and Mr. Jwu Feng, associate condutor of the Central Chinese Orchestra in Peking, made the videotaping of the performance possible. Ms. Maa Lih and Prof. Yang Yeh of the Sheenyang Academy, Ms. Jang Tzuuwuu of the Jyilin School of Art, and Prof. Tarng Lihmin of the Dalian Institute of Technology have provided me with numerous reference materials and various other aids for the present study. Mr. Doong Goangsheng, the musical arranger for the present work, provided me with a copy of the text during a 1982 interview. I also wish to thank Prof. J. R. Hightower, who helped me with the translation of the text in the Appendix, and carefully read through this paper and offered various suggestions.

[7]The one public (commercial) performance of the Twirling Duet that I attended was held indoors in August of 1982, in Sheenyang. The hall held nearly 200 people and had a slightly elevated dancing area, which was even smaller than the classroom of the Academy.

During the 1940s, according to recollections of Mr. Heh Torngren, a native of Northeast China whom I met in 1983, the Twirling Duet was regularly performed indoors during the New Year's season.

[8]One of these could have been a wooden-faced fiddle (called *baan-hwu*) as mentioned by Maa Kee, which uses soft wood instead of snakeskin to cover the face of the soundbox. The orchestra for this performance was obviously larger than the traditional kind.

witnessed over the past three years[9]—one in a commercial theatre—none of the dancers held clappers as described in Maa Kee's account.

The terms *Dann* and *Choou* (literally, "Female Role" and "Comic Role"), which I have here translated as "Maid" and "Clown," are used today by all Chinese artists and writers on the subject, and are probably borrowed from dramatic terminology, which emphasizes the role-type rather than a specific character. This will be further discussed later.

The story of the piece, *Yang Ba Jiee You Chuen* ("Sister Yang No. 8 Goes for a Spring Outing"), is one of numerous episodes about the various members of the famous Yang family (some of whom are known to have been historical figures of the tenth century).[10] Many of these episodes still appear today in various narrative and dramatic forms. The present work concerns the beautiful daughter, Sister No. 8, who goes for an outing with Sister No. 9 and encounters the Emperor Ren Tzong of the Sung Dynasty. The Emperor is struck by her beauty and wants to take her in as an imperial concubine. He sends a message of proposal to the mother. Mother Yang, a proud matriarch who has already lost her husband and all her sons in one way or another while they were defending the country against evil ministers and invading foreigners, is reluctant to give her daughter to the frivolous monarch. Realizing that she cannot refuse directly, she writes down a list of requests for the bride's dowry that are impossible to fulfill. The Emperor is annoyed, and at the suggestion of the evil minister, Liou Wen Jinn, he sends a troup to the Yang house to kidnap the girl. However, he is defeated by the Yang women warriors and has to give up.

Sequence of Presentation and Division of Roles

An instrumental prelude is played while the two dancers stand with their backs to the audience. Toward the end of the prelude, they turn around and begin to twirl their fans and kerchiefs and to sing. It is an

[9]The works include "Pigsey Tills the Soil," performed in Charngchuen by the Association of the People's Art of Jyilin in 1981; this same work, plus "The Romance of the Western Chamber," was performed in Heilongjiang, in June 1983, by the Twirling Duet Association of Shuangcherng County.

[10]These episodes are often collectively called *Yang Jia Jianq Yean Yih*, which means "Stories of the Yang Family Warriors." By the late Ming period, at least two collections appeared in printed novel form: (1) the *Beei Sonq Jyh Juann (Stories from the Northern Sonq)*, which is also called *Yang Jia Jianq Yean Yih*; and (2) *Yang Jia Fuu Yean Yih (Stories of Members from the Yang Mansion)*, dated 1606. Critical editions of both books were published in 1980. In the 20th century, various abridged editions, especially of the first version, also came into existence. Although many of these episodes are extremely popular and have lasted for centuries, the printed novel versions are not regarded as works of high literary value, nor do they include many of the well-known episodes. The present episode is a case in point.

introductory piece—a lyrical song about jasmine flowers in the garden—and is completely unrelated to the main story. The dance movements are mostly abstract, with only an occasional suggestive gesture. For example, when the Maid sings, "I wish to pick a blossom, and wear it in my hair, . . ." she gently touches her head with her fingers.

After the song, everything comes to a halt, and the Clown speaks to the audience:

> What we just sang was a Prelude piece [*Sheau Mawl*, literally, a "Small Cap"]. Let us now sing about "Sister Yang No. 8 Goes for a Spring Outing."
>
> [The Maid answers:] Fine!

Ordinarily this section, called *Shuo koou* or "Spoken Dialogue," lasts much longer; it can be a very important part of the whole performance. It is similar to the Comedian's Crosstalk (*Shianq. Sheng*) in that there is much joking and horseplay. Like the introductory song, the content is hardly relevant to the main performance that follows. Frequently the Clown flirts with the Maid, and invariably some off-color jokes are told (these features remind us of similar ones in seasonal celebrations of many other cultures.)[11] This type of humor must have been a persistent feature in the Twirling Duet, as again and again we find writings in China condemning the genre for this very reason. Historians also frequently mention efforts by puritanical authorities to clean up or proscribe its performance.[12]

The two performers then recite alternately, in a declamatory manner, the following seven-syllable lines, pausing on the fourth syllable in each line. These four lines summarize the whole story:

> Maid: The Ruler of Sung——is out of his mind;
> Clown: He forgets his country——all for a girl.
> Maid: A daughter of Yang——he wants for a bride;
> Clown: Old Lady Yang resists, and——
>   Together: Names—her—price!

The main story of Sister Yang No. 8 is divided into six sections. Except for the first section, which incorporates three different tunes, each other section has one individual tune, used in a way similar to the treat-

---

[11]See Violet Alford's *Sword Dance & Drama* (London, 1962), or Alan Brody's *The English Mummers & Their Plays* (Philadelphia, 1969), for some interesting comparisons.

[12]See account cited by Her Ge in *Ell Ren Juann Jyi-jiuh Wenjyi*, p. 80, and criticisms by present-day writers such as Sonq Jenntyng in 1964, in *Ell Ren Juann Jyi-jiuh Wenjyi*, p. 10. According to Heh Torngren (see fn. 7), sometimes women and children were asked to leave the room during such Spoken Dialogue passages.

ment of established tunes in the Medley Song of the Peking and Tient-
sin areas.[13] Like most Chinese popular genres (including the Peking Opera), such a tune, with a title of its own, typically consists of a two-line
strain, set to the two-line structure (the couplet form) of the text.[14]
Within each section of the story, the couplet structure, as well as the
tune, can be repeated as many times as necessary. There are constant
variations in the detail of these tunes, due to formal constraints, prosodic features, and meanings of the text, as well as to purely musical
considerations, but not to the extent that the identity of the tune is
lost.[15]

The present work has a total of 116 couplets (see Appendix), distributed among the six sections in groups of various sizes:

Section I. This section begins with the tune called *Hwu.Hwu
Chiang.* The general setting of the story is given in five couplets, describing the weak character of the Emperor and the meritorious deeds
of the Yang family. Neither the Maid nor the Clown assumes a specific
role in this section; both describe the scene in the third person. As in
the previous recitation, they alternate their lines, so that the Maid sings
line one of a couplet and the Clown sings line two. The description is
moralizing in tone, and the narrator's presence in both singers is clear.
In the middle of this section, the melody first switches to a fast version of *Hwu.Hwu Chiang,* then to another short tune, *Ia Ba Sheng,*
which is followed by a portion of a third tune, *Dah Jiow Jiah,* with a long
refrain section.[16]

Section II. In the second section begins the real narration. The Emperor, holding court, decides to go for a ride in the country. In a switch
to another scene, the Yang Sisters No. 8 and 9 tell their mother that
they are bored sitting in their room and wish to go for an outing. This
section has nineteen couplets (numbers 6 to 24). The tune used is called
Wuu Hai.Hai.

[13]See my transcription and study of the Medley Song in *CHINOPERL Papers* (Cor-
nell University), nos. 8 and 9 (1979, 1980).

[14]At present there are about ten basic tunes that are regularly used (though not always all used in one piece), plus another ten-odd supplementary basic tunes, which are
also used fairly often. Both categories are of the two-strain structure. A third category,
which can number up to two or three hundred, is used for specific stories and consists
mainly of tunes borrowed from traditional songs and ballads, which often have a four-
line structure. In the present work, all sections make use of basic tunes, except Section
1, which has two additional supplementary basic tunes. For lists and comments on this
subject, see the article by Nah Biingchern in *Shihjiuh Yanjiou Tzyliaw,* pp. 52–73. For
lists with musical examples, see Jih Ming, *Dongbeei Benqbenq Inyueh [Music of the
Hopping Show of Northeast China]* (Peking, 1950).

[15]In "Text Setting with the Shipyi Animated Aria," *Words and Music: The
Scholar's View . . . in Honor of A. Tillman Merritt* (Cambridge, Mass., 1972), pp. 237–
270, I have tried to construct a list of causes for various kinds of melodic changes.

[16]For the complete version of this tune, see Maa Kee's transcription of "Meeting at
Blue Bridge" in *Jonggwo Minjian Inyueh,* p. 83.

In this section, regardless of the length of the text, the Maid sings all the lines pertaining to the Emperor, while the Clown sings all the lines that have to do with the ministers—first Liou Wen Jinn, who suggests the outing to the Emperor; then Minister Bau, who volunteers to accompany him. Both performers sing only partly in the first person. Invariably each begins with the narrator's point of view to introduce the character, then continues singing in the character's role. At Couplet No. 8, for example, the Clown sings:

> Behold, the evil Liou Wen Jinn kneels before the King;
> "Hail, Your Majesty, the Virtuous One."

Couplet No. 10 provides a second example. Here the Maid sings:

> Hearing this, the Lord of Sung says, "A fine idea;
> Who will be my guard as I go out the gate?"

Another frequently used device that gives the performance a nondramatic quality is the dividing of a single line between the two singers. As a rule, regardless of the content, the Maid begins with the first half of the line, while the Clown finishes with the second half. This line-splitting technique is most often used for descriptive passages, e.g., the court scene in the beginning, the Emperor setting out for the countryside, or Sisters No. 8 and 9 sitting in their boudoir feeling bored.

Section III. This is a short lyrical passage, sung to the *Wen Hai.Hai* tune, which describes the beautiful outdoor scenery that the sisters are enjoying. In their own words, the sisters enumerate what they see. The lines are all split, with one exception: in the last couplet, the Maid sings alone, in the voice of the narrator, "Let us continue with the story about the Emperor." As the section ends, the music returns to the previous *Wuu Hai.Hai.*

Section IV. Here the encounter between the girls and the Emperor occurs. The atmosphere becomes tense, and the tempo is fast. A new tune, called *Baw Baan,* is introduced; it is set to words in a much more syllabic style than previously. It takes only a short time to cover eighty-six lines (Couplets 29 to 71). Each singer also tends to sing a much longer section without interruption, as opposed to the earlier alternation every half line.

The meaning of the tune name *Baw Baan* is literally: "Grasping the Clappers." Formerly, the dancers played their own clappers while singing and dancing (see Maa Kee's description); however, when they came to the section using this tune, the vocal delivery became so fast (because the plot situation at this point is usually so tense) that it was impossible to continue playing complicated rhythmic patterns with the clappers. Hence the performers stopped playing the clappers altogether; they simply grasped their clappers in their hands and concentrated on their singing.

The scene of the encounter and the description of the beauty of Sister No. 8 are all told by the Maid alone, first in the third person, then continuing with the Emperor's thoughts in his mind, and finally speaking in the role of the Emperor:

"My Dear Minister, who is she? . . ."

The Clown sings:

[Minister] Bau Jeeng quickly makes his reply:
"Why, they are Sisters No. 8 and 9, out for a ride."

The Maid continues to describe the Emperor's decision and his preparations for a proposal to the Matriarch, Mother Yang. She then recounts the proposal in detail as written by the Emperor.

The Clown becomes very busy, assuming different roles in quick succession. He describes how Minister Bau sets out to bring the message to the Yang Mansion. In Bau's character, he orders his horse to be saddled. He describes the trip, his arrival at the gate of the Yang Mansion, and his exchange with the guard. Then immediately he assumes the role of the guard, who turns around and reports to the Matriarch. The Maid takes over momentarily, singing in only one couplet (in the third person) that the Matriarch has come out to greet Minister Bau. Regardless of whether the story is in the third person or in the first person, the Clown and the Maid take over whatever line is relevant to the character(s) each is assuming, even though that character may not actually be speaking at a given moment.

There follows an exchange between the Matriarch and Minister Bau. The Matriarch sizes up the situation and comes to a decision. Next comes a brief moment (the only one in the entire performance) in which the characters speak on their own without the preliminary words of introduction. As a gesture of defiance against the Emperor, the Matriarch decides to make a list of impossible demands for her daughter's dowry. The music stops completely. Speaking, rather than singing, in a slow and deliberate tone, the Matriarch orders her servant to bring her the writing equipment. The four lines of exchange between the Matriarch and the servant (assumed by the Clown), between Couplets 71 and 72, are brief but effective. The situation is clear. The decisive tone of the Matriarch's voice, her posture, and the obedient attitude of the servant are unmistakable; there is no need to explain who is speaking and why. The contrast in the sudden change from singing to pure speech also highlights the drama.

Section V. The long list of gifts requested by Mother Yang is dramatically the most static moment in the whole story, although the listing of the fantastic items can be highly entertaining in itself. The tune used is called *San Jye Baan,* a moderately-paced lyrical piece. In this section there is an almost constant splitting of the lines between the two singers, even though they are all supposed to be the words of the Matriarch. For example, at Couplet 74 Mother Yang sings:

If you wish to marry my daughter—
  [The Clown continues:] Sister Yang No. 8;
[Again the Maid sings:] I request that some presents—
  [The Clown continues:] Be brought to our house.

While in the previous section there seems to be an effort to discriminate between roles in the narration assigned to each singer (even in the third person), here we see complete nondiscrimination in that the two singers share, in the first person, a single sentence belonging to one character. The only possible explanation for this seeming contradiction is that in neither case is realism the primary concern; instead, it is liveliness in presentation that is most important. Whenever there is an excuse, or even without an excuse, alternate singing is preferable to an extended solo. This is especially true in the last example, where the story is at a static moment and the speed is moderate. Possibly for the sake of relief from the splitting, there is also alternate singing of full lines at Couplets 81 and 82, with a few single lines (line one of Couplets 72, 75, 77, 80, and 87) sung by the Maid alone. The last line of Couplet 91 is entirely taken over by the Maid, effectively introducing the refrain, which is continued on to the end by both performers.

Section VI. After the recitation of Mother Yang's requests, the messenger takes the letter to the Emperor. Excitement begins to build. The fast *Baw Baan* tune reappears here and continues to the end. Many different characters are involved in this section. The Maid sings all the lines relating to the Emperor or the old Matriarch, either assuming the roles or just describing their action. The Clown handles all the other characters: Minister Bau, who brings back the list of requests; the evil Minister Liou Wen Jinn, who suggests the kidnapping; and eventually also the lines of the female warriors of the Yang household, who clamor to fight against the royal guards. In despair, old Mother Yang agrees to repel the guards and march on the palace herself. The last three couplets are neither spoken nor sung, but delivered in a kind of rhythmic recitation.

To sum up a few points about the sharing of lines, we have seen that at relatively calm moments with little action, or in descriptive passages, the two performers sing alternately, either by splitting a couplet or by splitting a single line. Such playful patterning for its own sake, without regard for dramatic realism, is carried to the extreme with the Clown coming in at the second half of a line in the middle of a syntactic word: e.g., at Couplet No. 17, the name "Tian Po" is ungrammatically separated from "-Fuu", a bound word meaning "Mansion (of)-."

In contrast to the splitting format is the unison singing or declaiming of the latter portions of a line by the two performers. Some examples are contained in the general descriptive passages, such as the final phrase in the introductory poem, "Names—her—price!", or at Couplet 24b, "They gallop out of the city." At Couplet 91b this device is most fitting. Here the two sing a refrain together with the syllables "Ai-ai-ai-ai . . ." following the Matriarch's list of requests. However, sometimes the unison singing is just as unrealistic as the split lines. In a way it resembles the use of the responsorial chorus (as in the Swatow or Szechwan operas), which serves to reinforce the latter half of a solo singing line. Such is the case of the example already mentioned at Couplet 17b, where the Clown is really joining the Maid in unison for the incomplete phrase, "Mansion's Family of Yang." At 71b, the Matriarch sings, "I'll demand some presents that are—" and the Clown joins her in unison: "Nowhere to be found!" Again at Couplet 116b, the very end of the work, he joins her in uttering together the words of the Matriarch, "See that Crazy King!" In the present work, these unison utterances are a formal device marking the end of a large or small section.

The assigning of the roles to each singer is relatively consistent. Of course, with split lines, where the words of one single character in the story are shared by two singers, the role assignment could become slightly more vague. The Maid assumes all the parts referring to the Emperor, the sisters, and the Matriarch, including descriptive passages, while the Clown plays both the good and the evil minister, the servant in the Yang household, and, toward the end, the Yang family lady warriors. Only the role of the Matriarch is played by both singers—by the Maid usually, but at one point by the Clown instead, while the Maid sings the words of Sisters No. 8 and 9.

The roles are not divided by sex. Both the Maid and the Clown play male and female roles. A difference between the two performers, however, is that the Maid usually takes over the leading role of the moment—first the Emperor, then the sisters, and later on the Matriarch—while the Clown, hovering around the Maid, plays various kinds of supporting roles. The only scene where the Clown occupies center stage (Couplets 52–63) is during the delivery of the Emperor's proposal to the Matriarch. Here the Clown plays, in succession, Minister Bau, the servant Yang Horng, and then Minister Bau again.

During the singing, whenever there is couplet splitting or line splitting, the Maid consistently sings the first line of the couplet, or the first half of a single line, while the Clown sings the second part of the couplet or line. From the prosodic or the musical point of view, the Clown, who sings more often the rhyming words and the cadential melodic segments, occupies no less important a position than that of the Maid. The traditional technical terms for the part of the Maid, *Shanq Juanq*

(The Upper Mummer), and for the Clown, *Shiah Juanq* (The Lower Mummer), show a certain degree of abstractness in the dualism between the two performers.[17] Actually the place where the male-female relationship is really significant is in the comical dialogue section (see p. 215 above), where the Clown tells jokes, often with sexual connotations, in which case the Maid usually takes the brunt. It is also the only point in the performance where the Clown really takes over the lead.[18]

The two performers not only play many different roles, but also present the story through different narrative modes. At times the straight third-person narrative is used. More often, however, one begins with the description of a character, and then the same singer proceeds to assume the role of that character and begins to speak in the first person. At times, but far less often, the singers become characters without the self-introduction, as in the end of Section IV. The versatility of the performers, and this kind of quick shift from one mode of storytelling to another, has been noted by the writers and actors themselves. Such shifting in the narrative modes is technically called "entering into character" or "stepping outside the character."[19]

Physical Movements and Gestures

The difference in modes of presentation also has its parallel in the physical movements of the performers. I should first say a word about the movements accompanying the change of roles. Throughout the piece, the two performers never go offstage. As a rule a performer simply takes a few steps away from the center of the stage, with or without circling around, comes back, and assumes the posture of a new character. This is done smoothly, quickly, and quite inconspicuously, when the other person is momentarily occupying the center of the stage. A good example is at Couplet 10a, where the Clown, acting as Minister Liou, kneels before the Emperor, acted by the Maid, and suggests that the Monarch go out for a ride. As the Emperor responds favorably to the idea, the Clown gets up, walks to the other side of the Emperor, becomes Minister Bau, and then volunteers to accompany the Emperor on his trip.

Another example of such physical movement occurs when the Matriarch (again acted by the Maid) finishes her list of requests and hands

---

[17]See report by Yu Yeongjiang in *Ell Ren Juann Shyyliaw*, pp. 115 and 325, on the relation between the Upper and the Lower Mummer. The Maid is also referred to as the *Bautour*, one who wears a wrap around the head.

[18]See article by Her Ge in *Ell Ren Juann Jyi-jiuh Wenjyi*, p. 80.

[19]According to an interview of Cherng Shiifa by Yu Yeongjiang in *Ell Ren Juann Shyyliaw*, p. 170, and comment by Wang Keen, "The Rustic Twirling Duet" in *Jiuh Been [Journal on Drama]*, 2 (1983), 92.

it to Minister Bau to take back to the palace. While Bau describes his approach to the palace (Couplets 93–95), the Maid assumes the majestic stance of the Emperor waiting for the minister's return.

Although the moments of true dramatic dialogue are few, one-sided, realistic dramatic action without words of self-introduction or description are slightly more frequent. While one performer sings, the other quietly moves about or shows facial expressions in the role of another character. For example, the Maid, in the role of the Emperor, listens attentively to Minister Liou while the latter makes his suggestions (9b) about the outing. Later on the Maid, in the role of the Matriarch, bends over like an old woman listening to the guard announcing the arrival of Minister Bau (59a-b). The Clown, as Minister Liou kneeling before the Emperor (101b), or as Yang Horng, the servant obediently bringing the imaginary writing equipment to the Matriarch (72b), performs actions that need no words of explanation or introduction.

Far more frequently the action illustrates the words being sung. The movements may be specific or vague. They can also operate on a purely symbolic level. To give an example of the most concrete type: When the Maid sings that Sisters 8 and 9 are coming downstairs to see their mother (20a), she lifts up her skirt, carefully stepping as if descending the stairs. At 52b, the Clown describes how Minister Bau takes the Emperor's message and tucks the letter in his belt as he gets ready to leave. He mimes this action as he describes it; likewise at 93b, when Minister Bau is secretly pleased as he looks at the Matriarch's list of demands.

At times, when a particular gesture is repeated over and over again, the movement becomes stylized. One example is the continuous up-and-down stepping and dipping motion of the performers with their hands raised, holding the fans and kerchiefs in the air, as they sing of the two girls going out riding and enjoying the scenery. At Couplet 85, where the Matriarch specifies that during the wedding ceremony two gods should beat the gongs and four heavenly spirits should carry the bridal sedan, the two dancers turn the repeated motions of gong-beating and sedan-carrying into a dance.

The examples listed above mostly accompany words describing simultaneous action. The last example, however, serves to demonstrate visually the narrator's words. Some gestures are addressed directly to the audience. At the second half of line 26a, the sisters describe what they see out in the open during their ride. As they mention the green grass, the two performers dip down and flutter their fans in a sweeping motion from left to right. At 27b, when they mention the blue sky, they flutter the fans, making circular motions in the air. These gestures assist the narrator in localizing his or her words. Another good example occurs in the scene where the Emperor comes upon the girls in the countryside. As the Maid describes (through the eyes of the Emperor)

Sister No. 8's appearance—her hair, her clothing, etc.—she points with both hands to her own head, chest, waist, and skirt (36a–b).

At Couplets 75b through 91b, where the two performers sing the list of demands, we find further examples of symbolic gestures. The Maid sings:

[75b:] I want three ounces of cool breeze—
[Clown:] And four ounces of cloud.
[Maid, 78a:] Of four-cornered chicken eggs—
[Clown:] I would like seven.

In both cases the Clown underlines his words with his hand, reaching out to the audience with fingers forming the numbers "4" or "7." At 91a, as the Maid sings, "My daughter when small," and the Clown continues, "Had her fortune told," we find an extreme example of symbolic gesture by the Clown. He imitates the shaking of a bell—something a fortune teller traditionally carries as he wanders on the street, going from door to door. Such gestures could be considered either to be directed at the imaginary Emperor, or, more likely, simply an elaboration for the benefit of the audience.

Among the performers' many gestures that are meaningless by themselves but are used for emphasis, such as any speaker might, is one in which the performer reaches a hand out to the audience with one finger vaguely pointing upward, usually on a downbeat or a stressed syllable. This gesture simply captures the listener's attention. For example, at 18b, after the Maid sings:

They are none other than Sisters No. 8 and 9—

the Clown points and continues:

The two young Mistresses.

Another example is at 28b, where the Maid sings with a similar pointing gesture:

Let us continue with our story about the Emperor.

Just as in normal speech, such emphatic but nonillustrative gestures are also used when the speaker wants to show something impressive. We see the pointing gesture again in 82b, when the Clown sings:

I want a washing basin that will stretch across the earth.

Or at 79a–b, where both singers use such gestures while singing:

[Maid:] I want the hearts of flies—
[Clown:] And mosquito galls.

The above movements are in some way related to words, either as specific illustrations or as abstract gestures; but there are also many dance movements in this work that are entirely independent of the content of the words sung. For example, we find various kinds of rocking movements of the two performers in time with the music: at the very beginning of the story (2a–b), at the Emperor's departure for his ride (13–14), while the girls admire the scenery (25a), and even while the Matriarch demands a red coat made of cricket wings for her daughter (80a). Similarly, at 88a, the Clown jumps into the air and lands squatting down, in a movement that has nothing to do with his singing about the Matriarch's demand that a money tree has to be planted along the gold-paved road.

The fan and the kerchief, which frequently serve as all-purpose props such as a writing instrument or a letter, are more often used to create various kinds of abstract movements. The twisting, shaking, and quick fluttering of the fans accompany the singing from the very beginning. While the story continues at 2a, the fans are swung about in time with the music. The opening of the big floppy fan with a sudden jerk—always a spectacular gesture—is used repeatedly with no particular meaning of its own except to punctuate the lines (for example, at 5a–b and 51b).

The kerchief is a colorful piece of octagonal-shaped cloth that is decorated with sparkling ornaments and has weights sewn in the corners. It is used in an even more playful manner than the fan. It is spun like a top with one finger supporting it in the middle (done by both performers at 27b), and it is at times thrown in the air and caught again (26b). Such juggling acts certainly add to the gaiety of the atmosphere in the description of the pleasant outdoor scene. With the exception of the tense moments of the *Baw Baan* (Grasping Clappers) in Sections IV and VI, such playful acrobatic acts and gestures are used throughout in the process of telling the story.

Finally, there are certain movements that typically function as formal markers. To begin or end a singing passage, the Clown strikes a pose with one leg bent and body leaning slightly forward. At 27b, the end of the description of the country scene, the two performers strike such a pose together. While the Clown sometimes stands balanced on one foot, the Maid more often slowly lowers herself into a half-kneeling position and rises again.

Another frequent formal marker used by both dancers is the quick wrapping of the kerchief around the wrist with a flip. It is an abstract gesture that usually precedes another, more meaningful, movement. For example, at 41b, the Clown, in the role of Minister Bau accompanying the Emperor as he prepares to go back to the palace, precedes his action with such a gesture. At 73a, this little preliminary flourish is again executed by the Clown before he salutes, as he sings, ". . . Humbly, humbly I bow." The most elaborate single abstract gesture for such formal use in this performance is the elaborate spin done by the two performers together to conclude the entire performance.

To summarize, there are basically three types of movements of the performers: one, movements that by themselves illustrate the dramatic situation or the relationship between the characters portrayed, as in a real drama; two, movements that accompany the words of a narrator, ranging from specific illustration to symbolism and abstract gestures performed for emphasis; and three, stylized movements and pure dance that have nothing to do with the content of the words.

Real dramatic action appears rather infrequently. As mentioned before, it can serve to facilitate the quick change of characters when one actor impersonates a character while the other sings. However, when one person sings for a considerable length of time, a problem is created for the other person. In this performance, when such cases arise, the Clown simply stands aside while watching the Maid attentively (e.g., when the Maid is describing the encounter scene). The Maid is seldom idle for long; one rare moment is when the Clown describes his delivery of the Emperor's letter of proposal to the Matriarch. During his description, she circles to the rear of the stage area and stands with her back to the audience, remaining this way until it is her turn to sing again. This is a convention one often sees in the Peking Opera.

The movements of categories two and three are both common. In fact, the line between the two is difficult to draw, since there are various shades of stylized gesture that blend easily into pure dancing. The whole work is a continuous performance of song, dance, and gesture, subtly blending with different degrees of realistic acting. The only break in the musical continuity is the brief dialogue at the highpoint of the drama, a deliberate pause for effect.

Music

Space does not allow a complete transcription and thorough discussion of the music. Therefore, to illustrate my points, I will only make some general remarks relevant to the discussion above, and present a short excerpt of the work in transcription as it was performed (see below). This passage shows several features typical of the whole work.

The music of the Twirling Duet has often been described as rustic, vigorous, passionate, etc.[20] The tunes, as the music example shows, often have a wide range. There are frequent upward or downward skips of

[20]See article by Keh Jyi in *Ell Ren Juann Jyi-jiuh Wenjyi*, p. 278; also see fn. 25 below.

Excerpt from Twirling Duet: *Yang Sister No. 8*

fourths and fifths, and angular melodic progressions that remind us of other genres from North China, such as the Peking Drum song.[21] Strong and clear rhythm is very important in music for dance. The frequent short syncopations actually reinforce the basic steady beat. In order to give weight to the beats, the singers frequently insert extra vocables such as *a, ai, ia, ua,* or *na* between meaningful words to fill in the spaces that have extra melodic flourishes. Here and there, even a single syllable is broken into two parts for the sake of accommodating two musical notes; thus *jinn* becomes *ji-enn* (4a), *chyan* becomes *chy-an* (5a), and *tzuoh* becomes *tzu-oh* (6a).

Also characteristic of songs sung along with dance is the use of extended refrains with vocables. A good example is the *Dah Jiow Jiah* in Section II, one of the supplementary basic tunes (see note 14).

I have mentioned above that the Twirling Duet is structurally similar to *Dan Shyan,* the Medley Song, from the Peking area, in that both have a series of different tunes presented one after another. However, the traditional way of presenting the Medley Song is to insert a section of plain speech between the singing passages, either to explain and anticipate or to review and expand the content of the singing passages, thus creating constant breaks in the music.[22] In the Twirling Duet, music is practically continuous throughout, because it must accompany continuous dancing. As a result, one sometimes finds sudden modulations in key or mode, or both, as the different tunes are closely juxtaposed. Such examples can be found at the second half of line 5a, and between the end of 5b and the beginning of 6a.

Another important musical feature typical of the Twirling Duet, which did not appear in this particular performance but was described in great detail by Maa Kee, is the use of a backstage chorus either to sing the refrain sections or to join in at the latter half of a line sung by the performer (see also discussion above p. 220). These singers are often simply the members of the orchestra.[23]

---

[21]See Rulan C. Pian, *Feng Yeu Guei Jou* ["Boat Return in the Rain"], a transcription with commentary, in *Dong Bang Hak Chi [Journal of Far Eastern Studies],* 2 (Seoul, 1980), 389–403.

[22]This kind of alternate singing and speaking pattern is clearly illustrated in Tsaur Baoluh's performance of "Wuu Song and Pan Jinlian" (videotaped in Peking in 1981). The recorded version of the Medley Song "The Courtesan's Jewel Box," as performed by Shyr Hueyru (see Pian, *CHINOPERL Papers,* no. 8, pp. 161–206), has eliminated the spoken sections for the recording; however, the demarcation between the sections by means of instrumental interludes is still very clear. According to Wey Shiikwei, the spoken sections have been omitted regularly since the early 1950s.

[23]See Maa Kee, *Jonggwo Minjian Inyueh,* pp. 90–92. I did witness the use of such a chorus (although it was very short) at the Changchuen performance. Wang Yeefu, in *Ell Ren Juann Jyi-jiuh Wenjyi,* p. 86, complains about the dwindling of this aspect of the art and speaks nostalgically of the effect of the chorus's singing on the audience. Wang

Conclusion

The present analysis shows that the Twirling Duet is essentially a narrative art using an elaborate set of visual and aural means to enrich the performance. It is clear that such a performance is far from a dramatic presentation. The verbal aspect is essentially narrative; the movements consist mainly of a combination of narrative gestures and pure dance. Aside from the practical considerations of economy of means, the attraction of the narrative art hardly needs defending. Subtler characterization and fuller description are both easier than in the dramatic mode. Dancing and singing, which are, after all, the main attractions of the art, combine more easily with a story in the narrative mode, so that one can ensure a continuous flow throughout. Finally, as Wang Keen has pointed out, the narrative mode of presentation also brings the performer closer to the audience, since there is direct communication between the two.[24]

It has been stated that the Twirling Duet is intimately related to rural life. All the performers used to be farmers, and before 1949 both dancers were male. For various reasons, the dance met with disdain by the literati, and proscription by the authorities, in the past.[25] Today protagonists of the Twirling Duet believe that while it is an art of the com-

---

Chaurwen, in *Ell Ren Juann Jyi-jiuh Wenjyi*, p. 130, describes how the chorus—which is sung by the instrumentalists—responds to the heroine's mood and urges her to pour out the grief in her heart. He also notes that at exciting moments, even the audience participates in the choral support (ibid., p. 122). An interesting comparable situation of narrative with dance and choral refrain in the Faroe Islands is described by George McKnight in the article "Ballad and Dance," in *The Critics and the Ballad* (Carbondale, Ill., 1961), p. 35. The choral convention of the Twirling Duet is also carried over to the new operatic form of Jyilin, the *Jyi-jiuh* (see Wang Chaurwen in *Ell Ren Juann Jyi-jiuh Wenjyi*, p. 183).

[24]Wang Keen, "The Rustic Twirling Duet," p. 93. Jang Boryang, in "Tarn Dan Shyan Pair·tzyy Cheu de Shuo Bair" [On the Speech Sections of the Medley Song], uses the same reason to justify the spoken sections in the Medley Song performance (see *Cheu Yih Yih Shuh Luenn Tsorng [Collected Essays on the Art of the Narrative Genres]*, no. 1, 1981).

[25]Reports of its condemnation by the authorities go back to the Ching dynasty and the early Republican period (see *Ell Ren Juann Jyi-jiuh Wenjyi*, p. 48). The latest proscription was during the Cultural Revolution, from the mid-1960s to the mid-1970s (ibid., p. 22). Critics of the art have often described it as crude, vulgar, lascivious, etc., and believed that the stories and scenes were of low taste and selected simply for sensationalism.

Wang Chaurwen gives a rather touching account of certain underground performances during the Cultural Revolution, at which members of the audience volunteered to stand on guard outside the theater, prepared to give warnings should there be raiders from the authorities (see *Ell Ren Juann Jyi-jiuh Wenjyi*, p. 121).

If we include farmer's dances (*Iangge*) in general, reports of its proscription go further back to the earlier Ching period in the 17th century (see Wang Kehfen, *Jonggwo Guuday Wuudao Shyyhuah [Talks on the History of Ancient Dances in China]* (Peking, 1981), pp. 75–76.

mon people, thus deserving protection, it does need to be cleaned up, refined, and stripped of its superstitions.[26] It is not the purpose of the present study to argue against or in favor of such criticisms; however, the issue sometimes adds to the confusion about the relative merits of the narrative and dramatic forms.

As I have previously mentioned, some writers believe that the narrative art is part of an inevitable evolutionary process that leads to truly dramatic forms. The fact that so many narrative genres are still alive and well in China today shows that this is an enduring medium of artistic expression. Of course, any art will change with the times, if the fashion and the public demand it (e.g., a cello has been introduced into the orchestra, or some dance movements resembling ballet steps appear, as we see in the Sheenyang performance). Since the late 1950s, there have indeed been efforts to create a new drama, the *Jyi-jiuh* (Opera of Jyilin). This drama makes use of some dance movements of the Twirling Duet, borrows tunes from it to create new aria types, and at the same time incorporates dramaturgical devices from the Peking Opera, such as the percussion pattern.[27] Nevertheless, such creation is not part of a necessary evolutionary process. On this point, Maa Kee is one of the few writers who see the Twirling Duet as a self-sufficient, independent art form, rather than a mere transition from one genre to another.[28]

The fact that the narrative arts in China were known much earlier than true drama (which appeared around the fourteenth century) need not imply a sequence of development. Actually, we can see the mutual influence of the narrative art and the dramatic art very clearly in the present-day Peking Opera and the Peking Drum Song.[29] The evolutionary view carries a value judgment, suggesting that the narrative performance is somehow immature, having not yet evolved into the "higher" form of drama. One sees a reflection of this attitude in Lao Sheh's defense of the Twirling Duet when he says that it is "unfair" to call it a narrative performance. Such defense of the Twirling Duet, or Maa Kee's effort to rationalize the sensual enjoyment of it, as well as the repeated condemnations by the authorities—all serve as proof of the people's acceptance of this art as it is.

[26]It seems that in the past, the performance was sometimes used in association with the worship of certain deities (see *Ell Ren Juann Jyi-jiuh Wenjyi*, p. 5). On suggestions of reform of the Twirling Duet, see Bor Wanncherng's 1962 essay in *Ell Ren Juann Jyi-jiuh Wenjyi*, pp. 70–75.

[27]On the adoption of percussion patterns from the Peking Opera for this new opera form, see the 1959 article by Shian Cherng in *Ell Ren Juann Jyi-jiuh Wenjyi*, pp. 264–268.

[28]Maa Kee, *Jonggwo Minjian Inyueh*, p. 96.

[29]See articles by the leading Peking Opera actors: Mei Lanfang, "On the Artistic Creation of Liou Baochyuan, the King of the Peking Drum Song," *Cheu Yih [The Journal of Narrative Arts]*, 2 (1962), 2–19; and Maa Lianliang, "Remembrances of the Master Liou Baochyuan," *Cheu Yih*, 6 (1962), 43–46.

Glossary of characters for Chinese terms.

1. Baan-hwu 板胡
2. Bair Wanncherng 白万程
3. Bau (Jeeng) 包拯
4. Bautour 包頭
5. Bau Wen Jenq 包文正
6. Baw Baan 抱板
7. Beei Sonq Jyh Juann 北宋志傳
8. Benq.benq, Dih Benq.tz 蹦蹦, 地蹦子
9. Charngchuen 長春
10. Chern Lihjiun 陳麗君
11. Cherng Shiifa 程喜發
12. Cheu Yih 曲藝
13. Choou 丑
14. Dah Jiow Jiah 大救駕
15. Dalian 大連
16. Dan Shyan 單弦
17. Dann 旦
18. Ding Ming 丁鳴
19. Dong Banq Hak Chi 東方學志
20. Dongbeei Benq.benq Inyueh 東北蹦蹦音樂
21. Dongbeei Dueykoou 東北對口
22. Doong Goangsheng 董廣生
23. Dueykoou Lianhuanleh 對口聯歡樂
24. Ell-hwu 二胡
25. Ell Ren Juann 二人轉
26. Ell Ren Juann Jyi-jiuh wenjyi 二人轉吉劇文集
27. Ell Ren Juann Shyyliaw 二人轉史料
28. Feng Yeu Guei Jou 風雨歸舟

29. Heh Torngren 賀同仁
30. Heilongjiang 黑龍江
31. Her Ge 禾歌
32. Hwu.Hwu Chiang 胡胡腔
33. Ia Ba Sheng 压巴聲
34. Iangge 秧歌
35. Jang Chyr 張馳
36. Jang Tzuuwuu 張祖武
37. Jih Ming 寄明
38. Jiuh Been 劇本
39. Jonggwo Guuday Wuudao Shyyhuah 中國古代舞蹈史話
40. Jonggwo Minjian Inyueh Jeanghuah 中國民間音樂講話
41. Jwu Feng 竹風
42. Jyi-jiuh 吉劇
43. Keh Jyi 克吉
44. Lao Sheh 老舍
45. Lianhualaw 蓮花落
46. Liaoning 遼寧
47. Liou Baochyuan 劉寶全
48. Liou Wen Jinn 劉文晉
49. Maa Kee 馬可
50. Maa Lianliang 馬連良
51. Maa Lih 馬力
52. Mei Lanfang 梅蘭芳
53. Pyiba 琵琶
54. Ren Tzong 仁宗
55. San Jye Baan 三節板

56. Shanq Juang　上裝

57. She (The Matriarch)　余

58. Sheau Mawl　小帽儿

59. Sheenyang　審陽

60. Shiah Juang　下裝

61. Shian Cherng　先程

62. Shianq.sheng　相聲

63. Shihjiuh Yanjiou Tzyliaw　戲劇研究資料

64. Shuang Cherng　双城

65. Shuang Wanyell　双玩意儿

66. Shuo Koou　說口

67. Shyr Hueyru　石慧儒

68. Sonq Jenntyng　宋振庭

69. Suoonah　哨吶

70. Tarng Lihmin　唐立民

71. Tian Po Fuu　天波府

72. Tsaur Baoluh　曹宝祿

73. Wang Chaurwen　王朝閗

74. Wang Keen　王肯

75. Wang Kehfen　王克芬

76. Wang Muu　王母

77. Wang Yeefu　王也夫

78. Wen Hai.Hai　文咳咳

79. Wuu Hai.Hai　武咳咳

80. Wuu Song & Pan Jin Lian　武松与潘金蓮

81. Yang Ba Jiee You Chuen　楊八姐遊春

82. Yangchyn　楊琴

83. Yang Horng　楊洪

84. Yang Jia Fuu Yean Yih　楊家府演義

85. Yang Jia Jianq Yean Yih　楊家將演義

86. Yang Woei　楊偉

87. Yang Yeh　楊叶

88. Yu Yeongjiang　于永江

Appendix

Yang Sister No. 8 Goes for a Spring Outing
(A Twirling Duet from Northeast China)

M = The Maid
C = The Clown

I. (In the *Hwu.Hwu* Tune)

   1. M: Emperor Ren Tzong of the Great Sung is holding court;
(Interlude)
        C: All his ministers are in attendance.

   2. M: Here stand the civil officers who have brought peace to the country;
        C: There stand the great generals who have proven their loyalty to the state.

(In fast *Hwu.Hwu* Tune)

   3. M: In Tian Po Mansion the Yang generals lived;
        C: They protected the nation, the glorious land.

(In the *Ia Ba Sheng* Tune)

   4. M: But there is still the evil minister, Liou Wen Jinn;
        C: Who cheats the Emperor and rules over his peers.

   5. M: Alas, the unprincipled Ren Tzong is bringing chaos to the nation;
(A segment of the *Dah Jiow Jiah* Tune) Ai-ai-ai-ai . . .
        C: Hear me sing the story of Sister No. 8 Going for a Spring Outing. Ai-ai-ai-ai . . .
        M: Ya-na-yi-hu-hai-hu-hai,   C: Ya-na-yi-hu-hai-hu-hai;
        Both: Ai-ai-ai-ai-ai . . .

II. (In the *Wuu Hai.Hai* Tune)

   6. M: On this day the Emperor Ren Tzong—
                        C: Sits on his golden throne;
        M: Addressing his ministers, he says—
                        C: "My Dear Officers.

   7. M: If any of you have business, speak up quickly;
             Otherwise, let's roll the curtain and dismiss the court."

   8. C: Behold, the evil Liou Wen Jinn kneels before the King;
             "Hail, Your Majesty, the Virtuous One.

   9.   It is now the Third Moon, the height of spring;
             Why doesn't my Master go out for a ride?"

  10. M: Hearing this, the Lord of Sung says, "A fine idea;
             Who will be my guard as I go out the gate?"

  11. C: Hardly has he finished his words;
             His Excellency Bau of the South Ministry kneels before him.

12.   "If my Master wishes to go enjoy the scenery;
Your servant is happy to be your guard outside the gate."

13. M: Hearing this, the Emperor is pleased;
He steps down from his—
C: Ornate throne.

14. M: Outside the main gate—
C: He boards the royal chariot;
M: Behind him follows—
C: The Minister Bau.

15. M: The avenues and the streets—
C: Are decorated bright;
M: Yellow sand is scattered—
C: Three inches deep.

16. M: Before you know it, they're out—
C: In the open;
M: The spring scenery—
C: Fills one with joy.

17. M: The Emperor of Sung—
C: Let us leave aside;
M: We shall tell about Tian Po—
Both: Mansion's Family of Yang.

(Interlude)

18. M: Sitting in the Western Pavilion—
C: Are two young maidens;
M: They are none other than Sisters No. 8 and 9—
C: The two young mistresses.

19. M: Facing each other they sit—
C: Feeling very bored;
M: They finish their toilet—
C: And say, "Let us go out."

20. M: Tripping lightly, they descend the steps of the Western Pavilion;
In the White Tiger Hall they greet their mother.

21.   Approaching the Matriarch, they bow with a flourish;
"Dear Mother, your daughters wish to enjoy the sights of spring."

22. C: The Matriarch says, "Go and come back early;
Don't stay out too late and make your mother worry."

23. M: Hearing this, Sister No. 8 says, "Why, yes, of course."
Bidding goodbye, they go off together.

24. M: The two girls mount their—
C: Peach-red horses;
M: Waving their whips—
Both: They gallop out of the city.

(Interlude)

III. (In the *Wen Hai.Hai* Tune)

25. M: It is spring, the Third Moon—
                      C: The scenery is fair;
     M: Red flowers and green willows—
                      C: The grass is soft.

26. M: Sister No. 8 sighs, "Here is another spring, and the grass is
          green;"
                      C: *(Simultaneously):* Hey!
          Sister No. 9 replies, "Ten miles of apricot blossoms—
                      C: Makes one intoxicated."

27. M: The birds play on the branches—
                      C: Singing about the spring;
     M: Blue sky is clear for ten thousand miles—
                      C: Dotted with a few clouds.

   (In the *Wuu Hai.Hai* Tune)

28. M: Now these two girls—
                      C: We'll leave for a moment;
     M: Let us continue with our story about the Emperor.

(Interlude)

IV. (In the *Baw Baan* Tune)

29. M: While the Lord of Sung is enjoying the spring scenery;
          He hears the galloping sounds of horses' hooves.

30.   Sitting in his royal carriage, he blinks his royal eyes;
          He sees two young maidens drawing near.

31.   Both girls riding on peach-red horses;
          Pretty girls, handsome horses, it was quite a sight.

32.   Her hair is blacker than pitch-black coal;
          Bright ribbon neatly tied at the base.

33.   Ingot-shaped ears left and right;
          A face like peach blossoms, matching red lips.

34.   Willow-leaf eyebrows beautifully arched;
          A pair of almond eyes with spirited gaze.

35.   Gall-shaped nose and cherry-shaped mouth;
          Her white teeth are like grains of corn, full and even.

36.   Above she wears a red over-jacket;
          Around her waist an eight-paneled green skirt.

37.   What a youthful, lovely maiden;
          She is like a fairy descending to earth.

38.   I've looked and looked, I've made up my mind;
                I'll summon her into the Palace to be my bride.

39.   My Dear Minister, who is she?
                My eyesight is dimmed, I can't make out too well.

(Interlude)

40. C: Bau Jeeng quickly makes his reply:
                "Why, they are Sisters No. 8 and 9, out for a ride."

41. M: Hearing this, the Sung Monarch says, "Excellent;
                Here is my order: turn the carriage, we're going back home."

42.   The Lord of Sung seats himself on the golden throne;
                A seven-inch bamboo brush he holds in his hand.

43.   Above he writes the words: Hear Ye the Emperor speaks;
                Below he writes: To the Matriarch *She*, of the Yang Family of
                   Tian Po.

44.   When I was out today, enjoying the sights of spring;
                I came upon two young maidens of your household.

45.   Sister 8 is truly beautiful;
                I wish to make her my royal consort.

46.   If the Matriarch agrees to this proposal;
                On the whole Yang family I'll confer honors.

47.   Your three-year-old youngsters can wear an officer's cap;
                Your seven-year-old lassies may put on the royal phoenix skirt.

48.   One man from each generation will be appointed a chief council-
                 lor;
                From each two generations, two ministers.

49.   If you find this still not enough;
                I can split the country and give you half.

50.   With flourishes and dots he composes his letter;
                He calls in his favorite, Minister Bau.

51.   "Go quickly to the Tian Po Mansion;
                When you get there, present this proposal."

52. C: Says Bau Jeeng: "I quickly kneel down low";
                Taking the message, he tucks it inside his coat.

53.   Right away he leaves the Royal Palace;
                To his attendant he gives his order.

54.   "Hurry up, saddle my horse!"
                He dashes away, leaving a cloud of dust.

55.   Before you know it, he arrives at the Tian Po Mansion;
                He calls out old Yang Horng, the family servant.

56.   "Hurry, hurry, go inside;
             Report to the revered Matriarch.

57.   Just say that I, Bau Jeeng, am here;
             I am carrying a message from the throne."

58.   Old Yang Horng dashes straight away;
             In the White Tiger Hall he meets the great Dame.

59.   "His Lordship Bau is at the gate;
             He says he is carrying a message from the throne."

60. M: The Matriarch, carrying her dragon-head cane;
             Goes out to meet His Lordship Bau.

61. C: Bau Jeeng quickly addresses her;
             "My Dear Godmother, pray listen:

62.   If Godmother is well, your Godson is well;
             If Godmother is fine, your Godson is relieved.

63.   Today I cannot bow low at your feet.
             I am carrying a message from the throne."

64. M: She taps three times her dragon-head cane;
             That is her salute to the Emperor of Sung.

65.   "It is too windy outside, we cannot talk;
             Come into the White Tiger Hall so we can chat."

66. C: In the White Tiger Hall he hands over the letter;
    M: The old Matriarch takes it in her hand.

67.   From top to bottom she reads it through;
             "What an insane ruler!" she exclaims to herself.

68.   "A hundred thousand miles of our country you care not for;
             Instead you have your eyes fixed on a lass in my house.

69.   If I should give him Sister No. 8;
             Would not the Yangs become slaves to the throne?

70.   I do not want to give him Sister No. 8;
             But who has the audacity to resist the Emperor?"

71.   Lowering her head, she ponders; "Ah, I have it!
             I'll demand some presents that are—
                                    Both: Nowhere to be found!"

        M: (Spoken): Yang Horng!
        C: (Spoken): At your service!
        M: (Spoken): Bring me the Four Treasures of the Study.
        C: (Spoken): Right away.

(Prelude)

V. (In the *San Jye Baan* Tune)

72. M: I order Yang Horng to fetch me the Four Treasures of the Study;
         A seven-inch bamboo brush—
                C: I hold in my hand.

73. M: On top I write, "I bow humbly—
                C: Humbly, humbly I bow;
    M: I bow to the reigning—
                C: Monarch of Sung.

74. M: If you wish to marry my daughter—
                C: Yang Sister No. 8;
    M: I request that some presents—
                C: Be brought to our house.

75. M: I want from you an ounce of stars, I want two ounces of the
         moon;
         I want three ounces of cool breeze—
                C: And four ounces of cloud.

76. M: five ounces of sparkling flames—
                C: six ounces of air;
    M: seven ounces of charcoal smoke—
                C: eight ounces of zither tune.

77. M: Of sun-dried snowflakes I want two and a half pecks;
         Ashes of burnt ice cubes—
                C: Give me eighty pounds.

78. M: Of four-cornered chicken eggs—
                C: I would like seven.
    M: Cow's hair three-spans around—
                C: Nine would be enough.

79. M: I want the hearts of flies—
                C: And mosquito galls;
    M: Horns of rabbits—
                C: And scales of toads.

80. M: Wings of crickets made into a big red coat;
         Wings of flies—
                C: Woven into a green gauze skirt.

81. M: I want a hunk of jade as big as the Taishan Mountain;
    C: I want a strip of gold as long as the Yellow River.

82. M: I want a dressing mirror that will cover the sky;
    C: I want a washing basin that will stretch across the earth.

83. M: All these presents—
                C: Are only part of my requests;
    M: I want to use the Heavenly Court—
                C: To hold the wedding feast.

84. M: I want the Queen Wang Muu—
                        C: To perform the ceremony;
     M: I want the Jade Emperor—
                        C: To entertain the guests.

85. M: Let the Nuptual Gods Ho and Ho—
                        C: Beat the gongs;
     M: Tell the four Spirits of the Gate—
                        C: To carry the bridal sedan.

86. M: The Twenty-eight Constellations—
                        C: Will serve as escorts;
     M: The fairies of the high heavens—
                        C: Shall be the choir.

87. M: From Tian Po Mansion to the Palace is fifteen miles;
         The road should be paved with gold bricks—
                        C: Three inches deep.

88. M: For every single step—
                        C: You should plant a money tree;
     M: For every second step—
                        C: You must place two treasure bowls.

89. M: On each money tree—
                        C: You should tie a golden horse;
     M: In each treasure bowl—
                        C: You must place a golden boy.

90. M: Each golden boy should hold in his hand—
                        C: Four big characters;
     M: Saying: The rhinoceros gaze at the moon—
                        C: The hippocampus looks up at the clouds.

91. M: Oh yes, my daughter when small—
                        C: Had her fortune told;
     M: Before she is ninety-nine she cannot be married;

         Both: Ai-ai-ai-ai . . .

VI. (In the *Baw Baan* Tune)

92. M: With flourishes and dots, the Matriarch finishes the list;
         She hands it straightaway to His Lordship Bau.

93. C: Bau Jeeng takes it in his hand;
         He carefully reads the contents and is secretly pleased.

94.   Stepping out of the White Tiger Hall;
         He hastens back to the Emperor of Sung.

95.   Outside the Palace gate, he gets off his horse;
           Approaching the golden throne, he kneels on the ground.

96.   The list of requests he submits to the Emperor;
    M: The Lord of Sung takes it in his hand.

97.   From top to bottom he reads it through;
           "Why, Madame *She!*" he exclaims to himself.

98.   "If you refuse, I am not angry;
           Why must you make such demands that embarrass me?"

99.   The Lord of Sung is indeed annoyed;
    C: Then comes the wicked minister, Liou Wen Jinn.

100.   Approaching the golden throne, he quickly kneels down;
           Three times he calls, "Long live the King, My great Master.

101.   That old Matriarch is making fun of Your Majesty;
           To rebel against a superior is none other than treason.

102.   If you do not punish her right away;
           How can My Lord be the Master?

103.   Give your servant some men and horses;
           I shall go to Tian Po Mansion and carry off the bride."

104. M: Hearing this, the Emperor is overjoyed;
           "My Dear Minister, that's just what I had in mind."

105.   From the throne the Emperor issues an order;
           He calls forth three thousand royal guards.

106.   Soon they come and surround the Tian Po Mansion;
    C: Startling all the ladies in the house.

107.   Wang Hwai Neu rattles her sabre, which flashes against the light;
           Yang Pai Feng raises her club that whirls through the clouds.

108.   Muh Guey Ing swings her silver spear that catches the sun and
           the moon;
           Sister No. 8 is ready to slaughter the invaders with her sword.

109.   The ladies enter the White Tiger Hall;
           With a flourish they bow to the Matriarch.

110.   "Let's rebel, let's rebel!
           That unscrupulous ruler is going too far!"

111. M: The grand old lady looks toward the Palace, bursting with anger;
           "You crazy King!" she mutters under her breath.

112.   "All the country's burdens that you should bear;
           Eight parts out of ten were carried by us Yangs.

113.   You reject honest advice and listen to villains;
            You neglect the state to dream about pretty girls.

(In rhythmic speech)

114.   His Late Majesty awarded me this dragon-head staff;
            It is the time for me to give this Monarch a lesson."

115.   The dragon-head staff she holds in her hand;
            The women warriors of the Yang family she summons together.

116.   "Come, all of you, let's be on our way;
            We're marching to the Palace to—
                              Both: See that Crazy King!"

Musical Inscriptions
in Paintings by Caravaggio
and his Followers

H. COLIN SLIM

For students of Michelangelo Merisi da Caravaggio and his followers, Benedict Nicolson's *The International Caravaggesque Movement* (Oxford, 1979) is what Claude Simpson's *The British Broadside Ballad and Its Music* (New Brunswick, 1966) is for students of folklore and popular tunes. Augmented by John Ward's review and article,[1] the riches of Simpson's book are self-evident. Those of Nicolson's book are not. In order to be useful to music historians, they require considerably more mining than space allows here. For of the one hundred forty painters whom Nicolson lists, no fewer than thirty-seven painted one or more canvases containing scenes with music. Ten such paintings are discussed below.

The compositions used by Caravaggio (1571–1610) himself in two of his four "musical" paintings have so far eluded identification, in each case for a different set of reasons. His so-called *Concert Party of Youths*, painted about 1595 for his patron, Cardinal Francesco Maria del Monte (1549-1626), and now in the New York Metropolitan Museum,[2] is "in ruined condition" and "badly preserved."[3] Three people are singing in the picture: a central figure tuning a seven-course lute with seven frets, a background figure holding a cornetto, and the far right figure holding a partbook. Two other partbooks appear in the lower foreground. The boy in the left background originally had wings, and a quiver with arrows over his right shoulder, thus making the *Concert Party* an allegory of love.[4]

---

[1]*JAMS*, 20 (1967), 131–34 and 28–86.

[2]No. 52.81; canvas, 92 x 118.4 cm.; reproduction in Maurizio Marini, *Io Michelangelo da Caravaggio* (Rome, 1974), Plate 8.

[3]Alfred Moir, *Caravaggio and His Copyists* (New York, 1976), p. 123, note 183, and Nicolson, *The International Caravaggesque Movement* (Oxford, 1979), p. 34.

[4]Richard E. Spear, *Caravaggio and His Followers*, 2nd ed. (New York, 1975), p. 70.

The badly damaged uppermost partbook, in oblong format, has a majuscule Roman B within an ornamental border, followed by four staves (perhaps in an alto clef with one flat) of only intermittently readable music. Below the first staff is "En prio di na [?]." A violin rests on the second partbook, in which nothing is readable. Below this a third partbook has a majuscule Roman P within an ornamental border.[5] Its four staves seem to be in a G clef with one flat. No text is visible.

The location is not known for any of the three copies of this painting. A catalogue photograph of the first copy, sold in Berlin in 1901, is not readable, except to suggest that the music had no text.[6] A second copy, formerly in a private collection in Florence, may now be in Siena.[7] Without text, it shows that the partbook under the violin had music. Photographs of a third copy, which appeared at the Chelsea (London) Art Fair in 1955—the painting is now in London in a private collection—are in the Metropolitan Museum.[8] Utilizing photographs of this copy (which also lacks text), and the few notes still visible in the original in New York, allows some reconstruction of the music, but the lack of any clear textual incipit prevents identification.

Caravaggio's *Love as Conqueror* at Berlin-Dahlem,[9] painted about 1602 for Marchese Vincenzo Giustiniani (1564–1637), includes an open oblong partbook (the verso of which is folded) next to a violin and bow, and a lute with seven double courses and five visible frets—perhaps the same instrument as depicted in New York. There are two known copies of this painting.[10]

Though the notation on four staves is reasonably clear in both the

---

[5]See also Volker Scherliess, *Musikalische Noten auf Kunstwerken der italienischen Renaissance* (Hamburg, 1972), p. 30 and *idem,* "Zu Caravaggios 'Musica,' " *Mitteilungen des Kunsthistorischen Institutes in Florenz,* 17 (1973), 141–48.

[6]*Werthvolle Oelgemälde von Meistern des XV. bis XVIII. Jahr. 17. April 1901 u. folg. Tag* (Berlin, 1901), no. 1265, lot 74, attributed to Niccolò dell'Abbate; 96 x 138 cm.; reproduction on plate VI and in Moir, *Caravaggio and His Copyists,* Plate 17.

[7]Reproductions in Scherliess, *Musikalische Noten,* Plate 30 and *idem,* "Zu Caravaggio's 'Musica,' " p. 143, Plate 2, and in Carlo Volpe, "Annotazioni sulla mostra Caravaggesca di Cleveland," *Paragone,* 23, no. 263 (1972), Plate 13.

[8]See Moir, *Caravaggio and His Copyists,* p. 85, no. 7b and Plate 18. Moir confused this copy with the one cited in fn. 7, above.

[9]No. 369; canvas, 156 x 113 cm.; reproductions in Edwin Redslob, *The Berlin-Dahlem Gallery* (New York, 1967), Plates 100–101 (with detail of music) and in Benvenuto Disertori, *La Musica nei Quadri Antichi* (Calliano [Trent], 1978), p. 145 (detail); transcription in Susan Guess Welcker, "Aspects of Music in the Early Paintings by Michelangelo Merisi da Caravaggio" (M.A. dissertation, University of Illinois, 1967), p. 101, example 14.

[10]Listed by Marini, *Michelangelo,* p. 397, but not cited by Moir, *Caravaggio and His Copyists,* p. 96.

verso and recto, neither page has any text. The fold in the verso prevents transcription, as well as hiding its clef and possibly also an initial letter. Opening with a majuscule Roman V (unornamented), the recto is notated throughout in a C clef; whether it is a mezzo-soprano or soprano clef is difficult to ascertain. The musical style suggests a source earlier than the painting.

Problems of poor condition, lack of text, and illegible music do not plague us in Caravaggio's *Boy Lutenist* at the Hermitage, painted about 1596 for Cardinal del Monte.[11] Even if they did, an excellent copy at Badminton in the collection of the Duke of Beaufort would lead us to the same conclusions that the original does.[12] On a table, in front of a lute with six double courses and eight frets, a violin and bow rest on an open partbook in oblong format, below which is another (closed) oblong partbook, marked "Bassus." The five-staved open partbook includes three madrigals, the first and third with textual incipits.[13] On the verso appears almost all of "Chi potrà dir" by Jacques Arcadelt (c.1505–c.1568), preceded by a large majuscule Roman C within an ornamental border. This madrigal concludes on the fourth staff. Though the violin hides the opening of the next madrigal, the fifth staff initiates Arcadelt's "Se la dura durezza," which concludes on the facing recto, staff three. The last two recto staves, beginning with a large majuscule Roman V within an ornamental border, contain the opening $19^1/_2$ breves of Arcadelt's "Voi sapete." Behind this recto appears the end of the first staff on the next recto. The two notes visible are sufficient to identify its music as Arcadelt's "Vostra fui."[14]

While these four madrigals appear together in Arcadelt's *Libro primo a quattro voci* from its earliest surviving edition of 1539 through many

[11]No. 45 (217); canvas, 94 x 119 cm.; reproduction in S. Vsevolozhskaya and I. Linnik, *Caravaggio and His Followers* (Leningrad, 1975), Plates 1–4 (including detail of music).

[12]See Moir, *Caravaggio and His Copyists*, p. 85, no. 8g, and Plate 20.

[13]Aided by Nanie Bridgman, Germain Bazin (ed.), *Musée de l'Ermitage; les grands maîtres de la peinture* (Paris, 1958), pp. 61, 67–70, and Plate 42, identified "Voi sapete"; three madrigals are identified by Welcker, "Aspects of Music," p. 99, example 12. I owe my knowledge (since 1972) of three Arcadelt madrigals to Thomas Bridges; see his "The Publishing of Arcadelt's First Book of Madrigals" (Ph.D. dissertation, Harvard University, 1982), pp. 55–56.

[14]In February 1981, I announced at Cambridge University the discovery of the fourth madrigal, independently of Franca Trinchieri Camiz and Agostino Ziino, whose report was made at the Congresso della Società Italiana di Musicologia in November 1981 and appeared as "Caravaggio: aspetti musicali e committenza," *Studi Musicali*, 12 (1983), pp. 67–90. I wish to thank them for sending me proofs in advance of publication. The four madrigals are in Jacob Arcadelt, *Opera Omnia*, ed. Albert Seay (Rome, 1970), vol. II, nos. 9, 52, 58, and 60, respectively.

later editions up to 1566, only "Se la dura durezza" and "Voi sapete" ever appear successively in the order depicted by Caravaggio.[15] That his source was perhaps an unknown print by Antonio Gardane is hinted at by the similarity of Caravaggio's large ornamental C and V to majuscules sometimes used by Gardane,[16] including Arcadelt's *Primo libro* of 1539.

Unfortunately, identification of the texts to Arcadelt's four madrigals reveals next to nothing about Caravaggio's motive for including them. Moreover, one bass partbook lying atop another need not have much relevance for the lutenist. Although he surely would not play just a bass part, perhaps he would improvise a lute accompaniment from it while singing by heart another line from the madrigal. Or are the partbooks, one conspicuously marked "Bassus," present to clarify the sex of the androgynous youth, who by the late seventeenth century was already being described as "una donna?"[17] Did Caravaggio choose the two partbooks at random from among music belonging to his patron, Cardinal del Monte, who apparently had a large library?[18] If so, then the partbooks would be mere studio props, much like the celebrated pair of wings and Capuchin's frock which Orazio Gentileschi (1562–1647) reported in 1603 that Caravaggio had borrowed.[19]

The music in Caravaggio's *Rest on the Flight into Egypt*—painted about 1595, hung in Prince Pamphili's house in Rome, and still in the Doria-Pamphili collection—can now be identified.[20] No direct copy exists, nor is one needed, for the painting is in excellent condition and the music perfectly legible throughout, though it lacks any text. While the Virgin and Child sleep, an angel violinist plays from a five-staved partbook in large oblong format, held up by Joseph. There are three compositions, each in a G clef. On the verso, a large Gothic majuscule Q begins a work that ends on stave four. Joseph's fingers hide the beginning of the second piece, which, commencing on the fifth staff, concludes on

[15]Emil Vogel et al., *Bibliografia della musica italiana vocale profana pubblicata dal 1500 al 1700* (Pomezia, 1977), I, s.v. "Arcadelt," nos. 98–113, 117; and II, s.v. "Willaert," no. 3000.

[16]See Mary Stuart Lewis, "Antonio Gardane and His Publications of Sacred Music, 1538–55" (Ph.D. dissertation, Brandeis University, 1979), vol. 1, pp. 68–77.

[17]Walter Friedlaender, *Caravaggio Studies* (Princeton, 1955), pp. 155–56, and Marini, *Michelangelo*, p. 358.

[18]Christoph Luitpold Frommel, "Caravaggios Frühwerk und der Kardinal Francesco Maria Del Monte," *Storia dell'Arte*, 9 (1971), 12–13.

[19]Friedlaender, *Caravaggio Studies*, pp. 278–79.

[20]No. 384; canvas, 133 x 162 cm.; reproductions in Friedlaender, *Caravaggio Studies*, Plates 8, 8B (detail of music) and in Disertori, *La Musica*, pp. 50–52 (with transcription); transcription in Welcker, "Aspects of Music," p. 94, example 9.

the facing recto, staff two. A third composition, preceded by a Gothic majuscule G, begins on the third staff of the recto and presumably closes on the fifth staff or on the following folio (not depicted).

Whereas the angel's arm obscures most of the second and third compositions, the first one is almost complete, except for several notes below Joseph's finger at the beginning of Caravaggio's fourth staff. Disertori, calling it a "ninna nanna," published it with regular barring in duple meter.[21] Nothing in it resembles musical style around the time of the painting, neither the jaunty rhythms in groups of sixes and threes, the internally repeated phrases (breves 7–10 and 10–13), nor the extensive opening section repeated at the close.

The key to identifying the work lies not in its musical style but in its typography. Similar gothic letters, clefs, and custodes appear in Petrucci's late prints and in Roman prints of about 1520–30. The first composition, on the verso, is the superius part of a four-voice motet by Noel Bauldeweyn (c.1480–1530), "Quam pulchra es et quam decora"; the second composition is its *secunda pars*, "Veni dilecte mi."[22] Both parts of Bauldeweyn's motet were first printed as no. XV in Petrucci's *Motetti de la corona. Libro quarto* (Fossombrone, 1519), which survives in two variant issues. While both issues have similar G clefs, only one has a gothic Q similar (although not identical) to that in the painting. However, the motet's position in Petrucci (opening in the superius on the fourth of his six staves) and the style of his custodes in both issues eliminate Petrucci as the painting's direct source. On the other hand, although the reprint of *Libro quarto*, financed by Jacomo Giunta (Rome, G. G. Pasoti and V. Dorico, 1526), begins "Quam pulchra es" on the first of five staves (as in the painting) and has an identical gothic Q and custodes, it cannot be Caravaggio's source either, because Giunta places the entire motet on a single recto. And the reprint of "Quam pulchra es" by Berg and Neuber, no. XI in their *Selectissimae symphoniae* (Nuremberg, 1546), is entirely unrelated to the appearance of the motet in the painting.

Petrucci, Giunta, and Berg and Neuber do not omit breves 26/2–32/3 of the motet as does the painting; and none of them follows this motet,

[21]Disertori, *La Musica*, p. 52; presumably the source of Frommel's "Wiegenlied," a characterization disputed by Scherliess in "Zu Caravaggio's 'Musica,' " p. 147.

[22]Independently discovered by Camiz-Ziino and by me, the former aided (Summer 1982) by John Hill in Rome. See Edgar H. Sparks, *The Music of Noel Bauldeweyn* (New York, 1972), Plates I–II, which are reversed, as pointed out by Stanley Boorman in "The 'First' Edition of the *Odhecaton A*," *JAMS*, 30 (1977), 190, note 16. This motet, a processional antiphon to the Virgin, is transcribed in David Maulsby Gehrenbeck, "Motetti de la corona: A Study of Ottaviano Petrucci's Four Last-Known Motet Prints (Fossombrone, 1514, 1519), with 44 Transcriptions," (Dissertation Doc. Sac. Mus., Union Theological Seminary, New York, 1970), vol. IV, pp. 1796–1801.

as does Caravaggio on his recto, with another work in a G clef headed with a gothic G. The style of this letter is nearly identical to that of the G in Bauldeweyn's motet "Gloriosus Dei Apostolus Bartholomaeus," printed in Giunta several folios earlier as no. XI.[23] Caravaggio shows two minims at the beginning of the second staff of this motet (fourth staff, recto in painting), which correspond to the two minims that open staff four in Giunta's edition of "Gloriosus Dei." Thus, if Caravaggio was copying a printed book, he was working from a source that is no longer known. It was probably printed in Rome in the 1520s by someone associated with Giunta, and contained, near its close, Bauldeweyn's motets "Quam pulchra es" and "Gloriosus Dei," in that order.

In 1642 Carlo Magnone (1620–1653) received payment for having copied Caravaggio's *Boy Lutenist* for Cardinal Antonio Barberini (1607–1671).[24] Until 1950, the copy was in the Palazzo Barberini, attributed to Carlo Saraceni (1585–1620).[25] It is now in a private collection in New York, with a copy in a private collection at Catania.[26] For Caravaggio's vase of flowers and fruit, Magnone substituted a birdcage and a spinettino. He added a recorder, changed the position of the violin bow, and brought Caravaggio's six-string lute up to date by adding a seventh double course, making it similar to Caravaggio's lutes in the Metropolitan and Berlin paintings, though Magnone depicted no frets.

Here the modernization ceased. Almost fifty years after the original *Boy Lutenist*, Magnone simply replaced Caravaggio's four madrigals with two different ones, omitting the texts of both. Neither has been identified before now. Magnone's verso, headed "XXXII," has a majuscule Roman L within an ornamental border. Appearing on five staves, ending on the first staff of the facing recto, which is headed "XXXIII," is the bass part to "Lasciar il velo" by Francesco de Layolle (1492–c.1540).[27] On the second staff of the recto, a majuscule Roman P within

[23]Edited (after Petrucci) in Gehrenbeck, "Motetti de la corona" vol. IV, pp. 1634–44. Camiz and Ziino, "Caravaggio: aspetti," note 30, explain Caravaggio's missing breves as an error in copying "Quem pulchra es."

[24]Marilyn Aronberg Lavin, *Seventeenth-Century Barberini Documents and Inventories of Art* (New York, 1975), p. 9, document 78.

[25]Canvas, 129.5 x 101.5 cm.; reproductions in Ernst Benkard, *Caravaggio-Studien* (Berlin, 1928), Plate 22 (paintings reversed); in *The Connoisseur*, 145 (April, 1960), 203, no. 4; in the *Enciclopedia [Ricordi] della musica* (Milan, 1964), 3, Plate XV; in Scherliess, *Musikalische Noten*, Plate 50; and in Moir, *Caravaggio and His Copyists*, Plate 19.

[26]Marini, *Michelangelo*, p. 359.

[27]See Arcadelt, *Opera omnia*, II, no. 27, and Francesco Layolle, *Collected Secular Works for Four Voices*, ed. Frank A. D'Accone (American Institute of Musicology, Rome, 1969), no. 10. These identifications were not made in Camiz and Ziino, "Caravaggio: aspetti" (see fn. 14).

an ornamental border initiates thirty-two breves of the bass part to "Perchè non date voi" by Jacquet de Berchem (c.1505–c.1565).[28] As with Caravaggio's four Arcadelt madrigals, no known printed edition places these two madrigals in succession, let alone as nos. XXXII and XXXIII. For example, in a 1546 edition "Lasciar il velo" appears on page XXXII, but "Perchè non date voi" is on page XXXV.

Although the earliest extant edition of Arcadelt's *Primo libro* (1539) assigns these two madrigals to Layolle and Berchem, subsequent editions from 1541 to 1557 give them to Arcadelt. From 1558 to 1566, editions of Arcadelt include only "Lasciar il velo," which they attribute once again to Layolle. Thereafter the attribution varies.[29] The 1642 edition (the year of payment to Magnone) includes neither madrigal.

The Barberini cardinals owned, as did Cardinal del Monte, a large library of printed and manuscript music.[30] Thus one wonders whether Magnone, in replacing Caravaggio's Arcadelt madrigals, conscientiously painted in what he believed were two by Arcadelt, having selected them from some now unknown edition of Arcadelt owned by the Barberini, in which the madrigals appeared as nos. XXXII and XXXIII. With the exception of the choice of Bauldeweyn's "Quam pulchra es et quam decora" for Caravaggio's *Rest on the Flight into Egypt*, the little evidence we have suggests that both Magnone and Caravaggio chose their madrigal books either as studio props or perhaps to reflect the tastes of their patrons, rather than for any specific relevance of their texts to the subject matter of their paintings.

A *Still Life with Violinist* in a private collection at Lecce, attributed by Carlo Volpe to Giovanni Battista Crescenzi (1577–1660) and by Nicolson to an unknown, Roman-based Caravaggesque painter, was subsequently altered to a later owner's taste.[31] According to Volpe and Nicolson, the violinist in the background was added later and by a different hand to the original still life of fruit (left), vegetables (right), and three recorders and two partbooks (center), all set out on a table.

The open upper partbook in large oblong format is slightly covered by a recorder. Both rest on the title page of the lower partbook, which is supported by two other recorders. Painted with photographic exactitude on five staves of the verso of the open partbook is the cantus of

[28]See Arcadelt, *Opera Omnia*, II, no. 39.

[29]See the editions cited above, fn. 15.

[30]Frederick Hammond, "Girolamo Frescobaldi and a Decade of Music in Casa Barberini: 1634–1643," *Analecta musicologica*, 19 (1981), 107–9.

[31]Carlo Volpe, "Una proposta per Giovanni Battista Crescenzi," *Paragone*, 24, no. 273 (January, 1973), 29, Plates I and 5; and Nicolson, *International Caravaggesque Movement*, p. 38.

"Anchor che col partire" by Cipriano de Rore (1515/16–1565).[32] Typographical features, such as the large initial Roman majuscule A within an ornamental border and the page number "11" and "CANTO" in the running head, indicate that the open verso is from one of Antonio Gardano's editions of Rore's *Primo libro a quattro voci* issued from the 1560s on.[33]

The familiar lion-and-bear printer's mark on the title page of the lower partbook confirms the identification. The upper decorative border upon which Antonio Gardano superimposed the indication of voice-part first appears in surviving editions of Rore's *Primo libro* from 1564 (bass only extant) and continues in editions of 1565, 1569, 1575, and 1582, the latter two issued by Angelo Gardano. For some reason (perhaps to save space?), the artist deleted the verso's blank sixth staff, which appears in these editions. Unfortunately, neither of the two available reproductions of the painting makes clear the date of the edition—its last two numerals are probably "69"—or which partbook (presumably alto, tenor, or bass) is intended. A gathering indication, "X," appears in the lower right-hand corner. Since the title pages of the bass partbooks in editions of 1564, 1565 (?bass is lacking), 1569, 1575, and 1582 are signed "K," we may suppose that the artist erroneously painted "X" for "K."

The placement of three recorders of various sizes around "Anchor che col partire" in the painting suggests instrumental performance of the madrigal. Indeed, printed arrangements of "Anchor che col partire," and sets of diminutions on it for voice, winds, and stringed instruments (above all for viola bastarda), were first published in 1584, and continued to appear until 1624.[34] The enduring popularity of the madrigal in instrumental form during the first quarter of the seventeenth century both explains the original painter's choice of music for what was, after all, a *Still Life with Three Recorders and Two Partbooks*, and hints at the date of the painting. It also explains why some later owner (perhaps himself a violinist?) had the violin player added: he must have felt how appropriate a fourth instrument—and a stringed one at that—would be for instrumental performance of this four-voiced madrigal.

The subject matter of a painting called *Musicanti con natura morte di uva e strumenti musicali* by Volpe, who attributed it jointly to Barto-

[32]Cipriano de Rore, *Opera omnia*, IV, ed. Bernhard Meier (American Institute of Musicology, Rome, 1969), 31.

[33]Listed in Vogel, *Bibliografia*, II, s.v. "Rore," nos. 2380–82 and 2384–85. On the typographical features, see Lewis, "Antonio Gardane," vol. I, pp. 65–77.

[34]See Ernest T. Ferand, "Anchor che col partire. Die Schicksale eines berühmten Madrigals," *Festschrift Karl Gustav Fellerer*, ed. Heinrich Hüschen (Regensburg, 1962), pp. 146–50.

lomeo Cavarozzi (c.1600–1625) and Crescenzi, was not further eluci-
dated by Nicolson, who titled it *Two Musicians (Girl with Flute-
Playing Boy)* and attributed it to an unknown Caravaggesque,
Roman-based painter, possibly from the Crescenzi circle.[35] The original painting is at Bergamo in the Perolari collection. Nicolson refers to a
variant copy at Naples, in the Franco Piedimonte collection, and a second copy in the Louvre. He does not list a third copy, which was formerly in New York, in the Dorothy Wanderman collection, and was
sold there in 1968,[36] or a fourth copy, reported in 1964 (not further described) as being in London in a private collection.[37] Aside from size of
canvas and quality of execution, the chief divergence from the original
among the copies of it is that the copy sold in New York lacks the left
hand of its central figure.

In all the versions a shepherd lad at the left, wearing a laurel wreath,
plays a recorder. On a table in front of the second (central) figure
(whether boy or girl is hard to tell), whose right hand rests on a tambourine, an open partbook in oblong format lies facing the viewer, next to a
violin and bow. At the top of the verso of the partbook appears "Prima
parte." Following a majuscule Roman D within an ornamental border
are five texted staves of music in mezzo-soprano clef, which begin "Dolor che si mi"; a sixth staff is blank. At the top of the facing recto appear
"parte" and "17," followed by two staves of music and text; the remaining four staves are hidden by the body of the violin. Underneath the
verso a treble clef and three notes of the preceding verso's sixth staff are
visible.

The music and text on the facing verso and recto are a virtual photo-
copy of the cantus of "Dolor, che sì mi crucii" and "Bello è dolce
morir," the first and second parts respectively of a madrigal by Erasmo
Marotta (1578–1641). This madrigal appears on pages 16 and 17 of his
*Aminta musicale. Il primo libro de madrigali a cinque voci, con un
dialogo a otto* (Venice, Angelo Gardano, 1600).[38] The few notes visible
on the preceding verso in the painting are from the first part of the preceding madrigal by Marotta, on page 14: "Mentre madonna il lasso
fianco posa. Sopra l'aria del Passo e mezzo siciliano."

Many years ago, Einstein located in Tasso's Play *Aminta* (1573) the

---

[35]Canvas; 88 x 113 cm.; see Volpe, "Una proposta," p. 33 and Plate 9, and Nicolson,
p. 38 and Plate 12.

[36]Sotheby Parke-Burnet sale, November 27, 1968, lot 110: "Two young Musicians.
A young man [sic] leaning . . . with a second youth playing a recorder." Canvas, 30 x 39
inches (76.3 x 99 cm.). A photograph from the Wanderman collection is in the Fototeca
at the Harvard University Center for Italian Renaissance Studies, Villa I Tatti, Florence.

[37]See the exhibition catalogue, *La Natura Morta Italiana* (Milan, 1964), p. 36.

[38]See Vogel, *Bibliografia,* I, s.v. "Marotta," no. 1726. The unique surviving copy
lacks alto and tenor parts.

seven passages selected by Marotta, pointing out that Marotta's "Mentre madonna" is not from the drama.[39] However, this poem shares many phrases with the authorized edition of Tasso's sonnet "Mentre madonna s'appoggiò pensosa." Although Marotta's text is not identical to Tasso's, it is the same poem that Gesualdo (a personal friend of Tasso's) set for five voices in 1594.[40] Marotta probably obtained it from the Gesualdo print.

Marotta signed his dedication to Cardinal [Girolamo] Mattei (1546–1603) on January 1, 1600. The dedication reveals not only that he had been in Mattei's service for some considerable, though unspecified, period of time, but that he had composed his *Aminta* madrigals in Mattei's house.[41] Written when he was no older than twenty, these madrigals are among Marotta's earliest surviving compositions. Only one other madrigal had appeared previously, in a 1598 collection dedicated to Caravaggio's patron, Cardinal del Monte.[42] Except for that one, all of Marotta's madrigals are on texts by or derived from Tasso.[43]

Not only Marotta's "Dolor che sì mi crucii," but the painting itself echoes Tasso. Chosen from the close of Act III, scene ii (lines 1417–38), the madrigal's text follows on from Aminta's faint, the hero having just learned that his beloved Sylvia has been devoured by seven wolves. In "Dolor," Aminta bitterly vents his grief to the nymph Daphne. His friend Thyrsis has presaged Aminta's outburst of agony by recalling, at the close of Act III, scene i (lines 1319–20), Aminta's habit of solacing his bitter suffering by playing his bagpipe:

> Raddolcir gli amarissimi martiri
> Al dolce suon de la sampogna chiara.

A woodcut from a 1590 Aldine edition of the play—wrongly assigned

---

[39]"Ein Madrigaldialog von 1594," *Zeitschrift der Internationalen Musikgesellschaft*, 15 (1913–14), 204–5, note 3. It is unrelated to either of the *arie ciciliane da cantar* in the recently discovered *Balletti moderni* (Venice, Angelo Gardano, 1611) for lute, discussed by Charles P. Coldwell at the Annual Meeting of the American Musicological Society, Boston, 1981. On Marotta, see Lorenzo Bianconi, *New Grove*, XI, p. 697.

[40]This discrepancy is not noted either by Glenn Watkins, *Carlo Gesualdo: The Man and his Music* (London, 1973), p. 14, or by W. Weismann and Watkins, eds., Carlo Gesualdo, *Sämtliche Werke* 1 (Hamburg, 1957), 31. I am grateful to Professor Watkins for assistance in this matter.

[41]Unfortunately, the archives of the cardinal, who lived in a palace on the Via delle Botteghe Oscure (now Via Gaetano), are lost. For this information, I am grateful to Gerda Panofsky, whose study, "Zur Geschichte des Palazzo Mattei di Giove," *Römisches Jahrbuch für Kunstgeschichte*, 11 (1967–68), 109–188, concerns Girolamo's brother Asdrubale. Further, see Frommel, "Caravaggios Frühwerk," p. 9, note 31.

[42]See RISM, I, 1598[8].

[43]See Lorenzo Bianconi, "Sussidi bibliografici per i musicisti siciliani del Cinque e Seicento," *Rivista italiana di musicologia*, 7 (1972), 28.

by Adriano Cavicchi to the concluding chorus of Act III—depicts a
shepherd playing a bagpipe while a standing figure, who leans on his
staff, listens dejectedly.[44] In the 1590 edition this woodcut follows "Dolor che sì mi crucii." The artist not only intended to depict Aminta
playing his bagpipe to Thyrsis, but, by placing it after Aminta's great
lament, sought to intensify it by making the reader recall lines 1319–
20.

Something similar, although even more intense, takes place in the
painting (which replaces Aminta's bagpipe by the contemporary recorder). Thyrsis (the ambiguous central figure) sadly listens while leaning on a tambourine, which, along with the violin, is probably a reminder of livelier, happier occasions. The painter chose "Dolor" from
Marotta's *Aminta*, rather than some other madrigal from the collection, precisely for its image of Aminta's desperate state.

In this regard, we should note that the play's prologue (lines 85–88)
apostrophizes Love's supreme achievement of rendering wind instruments (rustic bagpipes) similar to stringed instruments (the most
learned lyres); that is, Love raises pastoral poetry, in elegance and dignity, to the level of learned poetry:[45]

> ... e questo è pure
> Suprema gloria e gran miracol mio:
> Render simili a le più dotte cetre
> Le rustiche sampogne ...

Cavicchi has demonstrated that the woodcuts in the 1583 edition of
Tasso's *Aminta* derive from the mise-en-scène of productions of the
play at Ferrara between 1573 and 1583; these are supplemented by the
same artist's woodcuts in the 1590 edition.[46] One might even speculate
that the painting records a scene from a production of *Aminta* a decade
later at Rome, in Cardinal Mattei's palace, with incidental madrigals by
Marotta.

A *Crowning of Saints Cecilia and Valerian* by Antiveduto Gramatica (c.1570–1626), dated c. 1615 and sold in London in 1975,[47] de-

---

[44]Adriano Cavicchi, "La scenografia dell'*Aminta* nella tradizione scenografica pas-
torale ferrarese del secolo XVI," *Studi sul teatro veneto fra rinascimento ed età
barocca*, ed. Maria Teresa Muraro (Florence, 1971), p. 61 and figure 37.

[45]Torquato Tasso, *Aminta*, ed. Giorgio Cerboni Baiardi (Urbino, 1976), p. 8, and
Emanuel Winternitz, *Musical Instruments and their Symbolism in Western Art* (New
York, 1967), p. 79.

[46]Cavicchi, "La scenografia," pp. 58–62.

[47]Christie's sale, November 28, 1975, lot 1: canvas, 140 x 108 cm.; reproduction in
Richard E. Spear, "Bolognese Painting in Florence," *The Burlington Magazine*, 117
(July, 1975), 505, figure 113; dated by Spear on p. 507.

picts a familiar subject stemming from the sixth-century Acts of St. Cecilia.[48] Having just been baptized at Cecilia's request, Valerian, her fiancé, returns to find her in prayer. An angel holds above the pair two crowns of flowers destined for them. Representations of this scene with the addition of musical instruments (usually an organ) first appear in the fifteenth century, and reach great frequency in the early seventeenth century.[49] In Gramatica's painting a second child angel, perhaps singing, holds a wicker basket at the lower right. The basket contains a violin and bow, the instrument covered by an open partbook in oblong format. On three staves each of the verso and facing recto, Gramatica depicts the bass part to an unidentified polyphonic liturgical work. Virtually the entire text and most of its music is visible:

Example 1. Diplomatic transcription from Gramatica, *Crowning of Saints Cecilia and Valerian* (c. 1615)

The text, which appears with two different plainchant melodies as early as the twelfth century (where the final word is "vacabat"), is an antiphon for second Vespers in the Office of St. Cecilia (November 22).[50] Gramatica's bass part does not paraphrase either plainchant. Nor does it resemble polyphonic settings by such contemporary composers as Giovanni Francesco Anerio (c.1567–1630) or Urban Loth (?–1637), published in 1613 and 1616, respectively.[51] Among many different polyphonic settings of this text (and of others closely related to it) between 1539 and 1556,[52] only one of the two settings by Thomas Crec-

[48]See James W. McKinnon, "Cecilia," *New Grove*, IV, p. 45.

[49]See Albert P. de Mirimonde, *Sainte-Cécile: Métamorphoses d'un Thème Musical* (Geneva, 1974), Plates 1 and 4–10.

[50]See *Paléographie musicale*, XII (Tournai, 1922), 405–6.

[51]RISM, I (Munich, 1960): 1613[4] and *Musa melica. Concertationes musicas* (Passau, 1616).

[52]See RISM 1532[11] (Paignier and Pieton); 1539[10] (Carette, Hugier, and Manchicourt); 1547[6] (Clemens); 1548[2] (Crecquillon); 1554[15] (Canis); and 1556[6] (Baston).

quillon (c.1490–1557), first published in 1554, shows any melodic similarity whatever with Gramatica's music.[53] The frequent sets of four reiterated *fusae* in the painting suggests seventeenth-century music much more than that of the sixteenth century. Though we do not know Gramatica's musical source, there can be no question that he chose music and text to enhance the iconography of his painting.

Plate I. Gramatica, Cittern-playing angel

[53]RISM 1554[8]; the motet appears in H. Lowen Marshall, ed., *The Four-Voice Motets of Thomas Crecquillon*, II (New York, 1971), no. 9.

A painting incorrectly titled *An Angel Playing a Lute* (see Plate 1) and attributed to Cavarozzi was sold in London in 1970[54] and sold again there in 1971, attributed to Gramatica.[55] It is now in a private collection in England. In the painting, an angel plays with a pick on an Italian cittern, a splendid example of a type of this instrument developed in the 1570s.[56] It has six double courses, the lowest four wound with wire, as was customary. A grotesque head caps the pegbox. On a decorative table covering are a rose, a violin and bow, two partbooks in oblong format (one open, the other closed), and a wicker basket. The basket contains a small bound book with clasps (perhaps a prayer book), an embroidered napkin (perhaps a communion-cloth) and an unidentified object (perhaps the box for a pyx).

The folded verso of the open partbook is headed: "MORALES Cum quatuor v[ocibus] SE[CUNDI TONI TENOR 8]" (the bracketed material is obscured by the fold). After a small majuscule Roman E, the verso presents four staves of music and text. The recto, hanging over the table, is easier to read, even though a fold masks its first half. Headed "[MORALES Cum quatuor vocibus] QUARTI TONI TENOR 17," it is followed by four staves of music and text. At the lower right-hand corner appears "C ii."

The verso exposes some 22 breves of excerpts from the tenor part of the *Magnificat secundi toni* by Cristóbal de Morales (c.1500–1553), and the recto 17 breves from the tenor of his *Magnificat quarti toni*.[57] By painting on the recto the number 17 and the gathering indication C ii, and by carefully spacing text and music, the artist persuades us that we are looking at a printed edition.

Of the fifteen extant editions containing both *Magnificats*,[58] only two of them present the tenor part on page 17 and signed C ii. Both editions are from Venice in 1545: one by Gardane, the other an unsigned reprint, probably by Scotto. There are, however, five important differences between these two virtually identical printed editions and the painting. First, both Venetian prints have six staves per page, whereas the painting has four. Second, neither these editions nor any others juxtapose portions of Morales's second and fourth *Magnificats* on facing

[54]Sotheby's sale, October 28, 1970, lot 6: canvas, 114.3 x 86.3 cm.

[55]Christie's sale, November 26, 1971, lot 86: from the collection of the Honorable Dominic Elliot; bought by Rossi for 2400 guineas (annotation in the Getty copy held by the J. Paul Getty Museum, Malibu).

[56]See Ian Harwood and James Tyler, "Cittern," *New Grove*, IV, pp. 418–19 and figure 7.

[57]Cristóbal de Morales, *Opera omnia*, IV, ed. Higinio Anglés, Monumentos de la Música Española, XVII (Rome, 1956), pp. 28–30: mm. 83–88, 94–98, 105–116, and pp. 61–62: mm. 88–95, 101–2, 109–11, 119–21, 128–30, respectively.

[58]Ibid., pp. 38–43.

folios. Third, the painting's version lacks the opening six breves of "Sicut locutus est"; the artist continues directly with "ad patres nostros" after the double bar. Fourth, breves 86/2–88 in the painting are a third too high. Fifth, there is an incorrect semibreve B in the painting, instead of C (breve 119) as in all printed sources.

These discrepancies suggest that the artist used a presently unknown edition, although likely one by Gardane or copied from him. At least four editions have not survived: one from Rome (1541),[59] two by Gardane (1547 and 1552), and one by Alessandro Vincenti (1619).[60]

Not only the Magnificat text for the Annunciation scene itself, but the rose also, refers to the Virgin,[61] as does perhaps the small closed volume (in the basket) resembling a Book of Hours. The box for the pyx and the communion-cloth strengthen the associations of purity. Even though the Virgin herself is wanting in the painting, Gramatica is apparently invoking a long iconographical tradition of including music-making and, in some cases, even scores in Annunciation scenes. Examples occur in a thirteenth-century embroidery,[62] in a fifteenth-century tapestry, [63] in an early sixteenth-century Magnificat window,[64] and in a painted French enamel,[65] as well as in paintings and engravings of the sixteenth and seventeenth centuries.[66]

Gramatica's choice of music, though perhaps fortuitous, seems especially apt for a plucked string instrument. While no instrumental settings of these two Magnificats are known, Morales's countrymen Fuenllana (1554) and Valderrabano (1547) set others of Morales's Magnificats for vihuela, and Henestrosa (1557) set one for "tecla, harpa y vihuela."[67]

[59]Cited by Lewis, "Antonio Gardane," I, 425.

[60]Morales, Opera omnia, nos. 5 and 7, p. 40; no. 16, p. 43.

[61]See H. Colin Slim, "An anonymous twice-texted motet," in Words and Music, The Scholar's View, ed. Laurence Berman (Cambridge, Mass., 1972), pp. 295–96.

[62]Heinrich Detzel, Christliche Ikonographie, I (Freiburg im Breisgau, 1894), p. 161.

[63]Gertrud Schiller, Iconography of Christian Art, I, trans. Janet Seligman (Greenwich, Conn., 1971), Plate 127.

[64]Margaret Rickert, Painting in Britain: The Middle Ages (Baltimore, 1954), Plate 200.

[65]Mardon Penicaud (op. 1510–1540): Louis XII Triptych in London, Victoria and Albert Museum, no. 522–1877.

[66]See, for example, Cornelis Verdonck's Magnificat a 5 in a painting by Martin de Vos at Cannstatt, engraved by Johannes Sadeler in 1585, in Max Seiffert, ed., "Niederländische Bildmotetten," Organum, first series, 19 (1929), 16, no. 4; and a four-voice Magnificat in an engraving by Crispijn de Passe de Oude of 1603, reproduced in F. W. H. Hollstein, Dutch and Flemish Engravings and Woodcuts, XV (Amsterdam, c.1957), 155, no. 196.

[67]Howard M. Brown, Instrumental Music Printed Before 1600, A Bibliography (Cambridge, Mass., 1965): 1547[5], no. 112; 1554[3], nos. 3, 10, 21; and 1557[2], no. 48.

The artist's extraordinary juxtaposition of two folios from Magnificats two and four is difficult to explain. Possibly he had a mutilated edition at hand. Because many of the same phrases appear on both folios, the message from the painting seems to be: "The hungry he has suffered . . . the rich sent away. As he spoke to our father . . . and to his seed forever." Its significance for the painting remains elusive.

Lodovico Lana (1597–1646) painted but one work that is "remotely Caravaggesque."[68] This canvas, whose present location is unknown, portrays three figures: a theorbist on the left, the head only of a central figure, and a transverse flute player on the right. On a table lies open a book, in oblong format, of lute and theorbo tablature, facing the player. Next to it is a quill pen in an inkpot. At the verso's outer edge is "Corrente per il lauto del Signor Geronimo Valeriani lautinista del Signor Duca del Modena." On the recto's inner edge is "Corrente per la tiorba."

Born near Ferrara in 1597, the year before it was incorporated into the Papal States, Lodovico Lana studied at Bologna with Guido Reni. He settled in Modena in 1619, by then the capital of the Estense Dukes. Aside from a brief visit to Rome to work for Prince Pamphilio Pamphili (1563–1639), Lana remained in Modena and its environs for the rest of his days. He painted altarpieces for churches at Modena and Ferrara, as well as religious canvases and portraits in ducal residences at Modena and nearby Sassuolo. Duke Francesco I appointed him court painter and director of his Academy. Lana died in Modena in 1646.[69]

As a young man working in Rome for Prince Pamphili, Lana came briefly under Caravaggio's sway. Prince Pamphili, who owned Caravaggio's *Rest on the Flight into Egypt*,[70] also could have brought him into contact with such paintings by Caravaggio as Cardinal del Monte's *Boy Lutenist* and Marchese Giustiniani's *Love as Conqueror*.

While under the ownership of Professor Mariano Rocchi in Rome, Lana's painting first surfaced in 1911 at an exhibition in Florence, where it was attributed to Caravaggio.[71] In reviewing the exhibition, Hermann Voss changed the attribution to Lana, both for stylistic reasons and on the strength of a monogram that appears on the upper body of the theorbo.[72] Nicolson challenges Voss's reading of the monogram

[68]Nicolson, *International Caravaggesque Movement*, p. 63: canvas, 111 x 100 cm.

[69]I. Kunze, "Lana," in Ulrich Thieme and Felix Becker, *Allgemeines Lexikon der Bildenden Künstler*, 22 (1928), 280–81.

[70]Friedlaender, *Caravaggio Studies*, pp. 239 and 247.

[71]*Mostra del ritratto italiano* (Florence, 1911). The painting is reproduced in the *Gazette des Beaux-Arts*, 6 (1911), 69.

[72]"Ein Konzertbild der Florentiner Porträtausstellung und sein Meister," *Der Cice-

as containing each letter of Lodovico Lana. Instead he reads it as A M within a C, and suggests that the monogram was the signature of an instrument maker, possibly one from Cremona.[73] I believe Voss correct and Nicolson wrong, notwithstanding that at least one other Caravaggesque, Theodoor Rombouts (1597–1637), also depicted a monogrammed theorbo (albeit with a different inscription).[74]

Having obtained an export license in 1915 for his painting—"non ritiene ch'esso rivesta tale estreme di importanza artistica"[75]—Rocchi sold it. It went to England, where it remained until 1957 in the collection of the Duchess of Wellington.[76] Sold that year, it went on exhibition the following July at Agnew's in London, where Nicolson studied it.[77] After shuttling back and forth among auction houses on New Bond Street, it was sold from Faerber and Maison Limited in 1965.[78] Here the trail ends.

Reproducing the painting from a Sotheby photograph in 1976, Robert Spencer identified the instrument as a theorbo with six stopped courses doubled in unison (except for the first single-strung course) and with nine single bass strings.[79] Though he gave the correct tuning, Spencer did not augment the small solo repertoire for theorbo by transcribing the corrente in the painting.

The instrument, the tablatures with their music, and the composer Valeriano all merit further attention. From the space it occupies in front of the player, Lana's theorbo, with its three rosettes, seems very large in body size and neck length. It has one more bass string than either the 170-centimeter Tieffenbrucker theorbo made at Venice in 1608[80] or the 168-centimeter theorbo illustrated by Praetorius in

---

rone, 3 (1911), 736–38, illustrated p. 737 and the monogram drawn on p. 736. In *Mostra del ritratto italiano* (see previous fn.), the monogram is read as "C A V A."

[73]"Pictures from Hampshire Houses," *The Burlington Magazine*, 99 (August, 1957), 274 and Plate 33: canvas, 110 x 100 cm [sic].

[74]*The Five Senses* at Ghent, Museum voor Schone Kunsten; reproduction in Richard D. Leppert, *The Theme of Music in Flemish Paintings of the Seventeenth Century*, II (Munich and Salzburg, 1977), p. 241, Plate XXIII.

[75]"Cronaca delle belle arti," *Bollettino d'Arte*, 9 (1915), supplement 2, no. 5 (May, 1915), 32.

[76]Nicolson, *International Caravaggesque Movement*, p. 63.

[77]"Pictures," p. 274.

[78]See Sotheby's sales of November 29, 1961, lot 118 and December 2, 1964, lot 96 (both illustrated). A photograph was made for Faerber and Maison on March 11, 1965 (courtesy A. C. Cooper Ltd., London).

[79]"Chitarrone, Theorbo and Archlute," *Early Music*, 4 (1976), 410–11 and Plate 6.

[80]Ibid., Plate 3 and in Harwood and Spencer, "Chitarrone," *New Grove*, IV, p. 288, Plate 2.

1619.[81] Lana's instrument seems closer in size (and perhaps in date) to the three-rosetted instrument on the left in a *Concert* from the late 1620s by Pietro Paolini (1603–1681).[82] It is probably a little larger than Rombouts's monogrammed theorbo in his *Five Senses*, which dates perhaps from the 1630s.[83]

In addition to the theorbo and transverse flute actually shown in the picture, a third instrument is implied by the lute tablature on the verso of the open book. However, the tablature is unclear, because Lana painted it in undulating perspective to represent folds in the page. Several numerals remain legible, including a "ij" for a bass string, which indicates the need for at least an eleven-course lute.[84] But even if the folds in Lana's verso did not obscure the pitches, accurate transcription of Valeriano's lute corrente would be impossible, since the tablature lacks rhythmic signs.

Because the theorbo dominates the canvas, Lana appropriately painted the recto folio of tablature with great realism. Virtually all the numerals for pitches are still legible. The tablature requires the theorbist to use only the first five of his nine single bass strings as depicted. Hence the corrente goes no lower than C. However, by calling for numeral "X" (10) on the third and highest-pitched upper pair of strings, which thereby takes the player up to a, the tablature requires one more fret than the nine that Lana depicted. This discrepancy is easily resolved: the theorbist could finger the high a off the neck and onto the body.

The first line of tablature has rhythmic signs above it; the remaining three lines have none. Even by extrapolating from the few rhythmic signs present and by taking advantage of the regularly placed vertical lines in all four staves (except in mm. 19–20), one cannot be secure about the rhythms Valeriano intended. The following transcription is thus offered with some reservations.[85]

The music reveals itself as typical corrente style of the early seventeenth century:[86] mostly two-voice texture, with several idiomatic descending scale fragments (mm. 5 and 9); a little hemiola (mm. 17–18); few sequences (mm. 16–18); and only rudimentary imitation, following the double bar at m. 23. This double bar presumably signals the custom,

[81]*Syntagma musicum,* II, Plate V; facsimile ed. by Willibald Gurlitt (Cassel, 1958–59).

[82]*Concert with five figures;* two versions listed in Nicolson, *International Caravaggesque Movement,* p. 77.

[83]See above, fn. 74.

[84]See, for example, the lute depicted in Paolini's *Bacchic Concert,* cited in Nicolson, *International Caravaggesque Movement,* p. 77.

[85]I am indebted to Nigel North for aid in the transcription.

[86]Meredith Ellis Little and Suzanne G. Cusick, "Courante," *New Grove,* IV, pp. 875–76.

Example 2. Girolamo Valeriano, *Corrente per la tiorba* from Lana, *Triple Portrait* (c. 1625?)

(continued)

Example 2, continued

Notes:
  mm. 1¹ and 23¹, string 2: [1] added
  m. 7, last eighth, string 2:5
  m. 28³, string 1:7; string 3:8
  m. 29¹, string 1: [5] added

frequent in some correntes, of repeating the first, but not the second, section.[87]

Theorbist, instrument, and tablatures dominate the picture space. Presumably the transverse flautist improvises, but the function of the fat-faced central gentleman remains obscure. While both figures could be absent without diminishing the force of the portrait of the theorbist, the unavailability of the original painting for examination makes hazardous any assumption that Lana did not originally include them in it. Even so, because Lana assigned the theorbist such a commanding position, we may surely conclude that in him the artist was portraying Valeriano.

By including a quill pen and inkpot, Lana perpetuated a tradition already established in Renaissance portraits of composers. Several paintings of Palestrina with music paper and quill pen are well known.[88] Another portrait, by Cariani (Giovanni de Busi; c.1485–c.1547), represents an unidentified composer who for some reason has just finished copying the same piece onto facing pages.[89] As in the Renaissance, Lana eloquently reminds us of the compositional act.

Valeriano composed not only the lute corrente, but presumably also the theorbo corrente on the facing page. The verso inscription further states that he is lutenist to the Duke of Modena. But when was Valeriano so employed, and by which duke?

[87]See Girolamo Frescobaldi, *Il primo libro* (Rome, 1637), ed. Pierre Pidoux (Cassel, 1961), pp. 70–75 and 91.

[88]See, among others, portraits reproduced in MGG, X, Plate 47, no. 2; in the *Enciclopedia della musica*, III, Plate CLXXXI; in Karl Michael Komma, *Musikgeschichte in Bildern* (Stuttgart, 1961), p. 101, Plate 240; and in Heinrich Besseler, *Die Musik des Mittelalters und der Renaissance* (Potsdam, 1931), p. 293, figure 141.

[89]Bergamo, collection Nino Zucchelli; reproduction in *Giorgione e i Giorgioneschi*, ed. Pietro Zampetti (Venice, 1955), Plate 99.

Account books belonging to the Dukes of Modena are now kept in the Archivio di Stato at Modena. Unfortunately, there is a huge gap in the *bollette dei salariati*, from 1627 until 1644, and there are significant losses in other kinds of account books between 1635 and 1645— ironically, just the decade to which Nicolson assigned Lana's painting. Beginning in 1624, the *bollette* record Valeriano for three years as one of several musicians employed by Duke Cesare d'Este, who died in 1628. The earliest *bolletta* to include Valeriano's name shows that the musician, having accepted employment by Cesare, started receiving a salary on July 26, 1624, at a monthly rate of 60 lire.

> Signore Girolamo Valeriano sonatore di Sua Altezza Serenissima deve havere per sua provigione dell'Anno presente, cominciando a 26 luglio a lire 60 il mese per tutto decembre. Lire 210.[90]

For each of the next two years, 1625 and 1626, "Signore Girolamo Valeriano sonatore" receives 720 lire, at the same monthly rate of 60 lire.[91] This rate continues during 1627, the last year his name appears before the gap in the Archivio's records.[92] When the records resume in 1644, they make no mention of him.

This new information means that Lana could have portrayed Valeriano as the theorbist as early as July 1624. Nor need we now necessarily assume, as Nicolson does, that Lana painted him in Modena. Both painter and musician traveled within the duchy, probably with Cesare. In October 1622, for example, Lana was painting at nearby Scandiano.[93] And payments to Valeriano through an intermediary suggest that at times he too was away.[94]

With the gap in archival documents from 1627 until 1644, nothing further can be said about whether Valeriano continued to serve Cesare d'Este until 1628, or about whether Valeriano then worked for Cesare's successors, Alfonso III and Francesco I, as did Lana.

After Cesare moved the Estense court to Modena in 1598, artistic patronage continued on much the same scale as previously at Ferrara. For example, he commissioned a painting by Caravaggio in 1605.[95] However, modern scholars do not always realize the extent and diversity of Cesare's musical interests. Two of his composers are well known: Ora-

---

[90]Modena, Archivio di Stato, bollette dei salariati (henceforth MAS, BS), registro 144, p. 33. I am indebted to Angelo Spaggiari, Director of the Archivio di Stato, and to Jessie Ann Owens and Linda Bauer for help with this and the following entries.

[91]MAS, BS, registri 151, p. 33 and 152, p. 93; and 153, p. 33, respectively.

[92]MAS, BS, registro 149, p. 131.

[93]Giuseppe Campori, *Gli artisti italiani e stranieri negli stati estensi* (Modena, 1855), p. 238.

[94]MAS, BS, registro 152, p. 93.

[95]Friedlaender, *Caravaggio Studies*, p. 199.

zio Vecchi (1550–1605), the Duke's maestro di musica and teacher of his children from 1598 to 1605;[96] and Sigismondo d'India (c. 1582–c. 1629), who in 1624 described the Estense court singers as the best in Europe.[97]

However, except for Salomone Rossi (1570–c.1630), who dedicated a collection of instrumental music to Cesare in 1608 and who, with a group of musicians, entertained Cesare at Mirandola in 1612,[98] Cesare's instrumentalist-composers are less well known. Gemignano Capilupi (1573–1616) taught Cesare's sons to play the lute in 1603 and, after Vecchi's death, was maestro del corte until 1616.[99] Don Nicolò Rubini (1584–1625), a cornetto and organ virtuoso as well as a composer, succeeded Capilupi as Cesare's maestro di musica.[100] During Rubini's last six months as Cesare's maestro (the musician was murdered on January 21, 1625), he would have had as colleagues not only the newly recruited Valeriano, but also three otherwise unknown musicians listed with Valeriano in the archival documents. They are: "Signor Lucha Salvatori musico"; "Messer Giovanni Padovano sonatore"; and "Messer Francesco Maria Belordine sonatore."[101]

Then as now, salaries reflect substantial differences in status—here, between Signor Salvatori and Signor Valeriano on the one hand and Messer Padovano and Messer Belordine on the other. Salvatori and Valeriano each receive 60 lire per month; Padovano and Belordine receive less than 10 lire each per month.

Although the gap in the archives at Modena prevents us from knowing whether Valeriano and his companions served Cesare d'Este's successors after 1628, surviving notices demonstrate that Cesare had a considerable retinue of instrumentalists and composers at his court in the 1620s. With Lana then in Modena and its environs, the chances are good that he painted Valeriano during the last years of Cesare's reign, that is, between 1624 and 1628. Moreover, the other two figures in Lana's triple portrait may very well be two of Cesare's musicians cited above.

[96]William R. Martin, "Vecchi, Orazio," New Grove, XIX, p. 584, and Gino Roncaglia, La cappella musicale del duomo di Modena (Florence, 1957), p. 56.

[97]Elvidio Surian, "Modena," New Grove, XII, p. 450.

[98]Iain Fenlon, "Rossi, Salamone," New Grove, XVI, pp. 225 and 223.

[99]Jerome Roche, "Capilupi, Gemignano," New Grove, III, p. 752, and Roncaglia, "La cappella musicale," pp. 82–86.

[100]Nigel Fortune, "Rubini, Nicolò," New Grove, XVI, pp. 296–97.

[101]They appear in the registri cited above, fnn. 90–92 and 94. A "Giulio Bellordine, violinista (1594–1603)," cited by Giancarlo Casali, "La cappella musicale della cattedrale di Reggio Emilia all'epoca di Aurelio Signoretti (1567–1631)," Rivista italiana di musicologia, 8 (1973), 195, was presumably a relative of Francesco Maria at Modena.

If one may generalize from only the ten paintings discussed in this essay, it appears that Caravaggio (except for his *Rest on the Flight*) and Magnone chose music (or had it chosen for them) for their paintings that was neither written by their contemporaries nor particularly relevant to the subject matter of their canvases. Crescenzi, Cavarozzi, Gramatica, and Lana, however, chose up-to-date compositions that contribute substantially to the iconography of their paintings. Only further investigation will determine the correctness of this generalization.

Orpheus in Britannia

CURTIS A. PRICE

Opera was born when Orpheus was permitted to sing his own story in the theatre. The elevation of the Thracian musician—already the most developed of the mythological figures depicted in the sixteenth-century *dramma mescidati* and *intermedi*—from emblematic character to full-blooded protagonist sparked a new theatrical genre; for the perfect singer could hardly enact the fable without recourse to his art. The beginnings of opera in Italy are thus inseparable from the Orphic tradition. In England, of course, opera did not evolve at "that wonderful moment" when "Jonson and Shakespeare might have collaborated with Douland and Wilbye,"[1] yet throughout the seventeenth century English dramatists and composers, like their Italian cousins, were often drawn to the Orpheus legend. This essay surveys the most important appearances of the myth in Restoration drama. The quintessential singer surfaces in comedies, tragedies, farces, and in a musical extravaganza, but always helplessly surrounded and fettered by plain, spoken dialogue—an ironical acknowledgment of English resistance to opera during the period when much of the rest of Europe bowed to the Italian lyre.

Seventeenth-century English playwrights typically viewed the Orpheus myth with a jaundiced eye, rarely presenting it in its unadulterated, classical form; rather, the idyll becomes a debauch, Euridice's second death is trivialized as rape, and the hero is depicted as an ineffectual lover, insane, tiresome, and forlorn. In Act V of Thomas Durfey's comedy *A Fool's Preferment* (1688), for example, Lyonel delivers a song while impersonating Orpheus—without disrupting the naturalistic setting, since the character is feigning madness. In Elkanah Settle's *The Empress of Morocco* (1673) and Charles Davenant's *Circe* (1677), which include the most important Orpheus scenes before Purcell's time, the legend is grotesquely transformed so as to ridicule the apotheosized version favored by early Italian opera composers. And the underworld

---

[1] Edward J. Dent, *Foundations of English Opera* (New York, 1965), p. 2.

masque in *The Empress of Morocco* was itself frequently parodied in plays of the 1690s; on one occasion it was reshaped into a satire of the alleged love affair between the celebrated actor-singers William Mountfort and Anne Bracegirdle—the former becoming, through his bizarre death, an Orphic martyr.

The earliest extended appearance of Orpheus in an English play is in Fletcher's tragicomedy *The Mad Lover* (c. 1617). General Memnon, driven insane by unrequited love, is entertained by Stremon, "a soldier that can sing," on the pretext that the general in his distracted state has invoked Orpheus to describe the joys of lovers. In the fourth-act masque, Stremon, who portrays Orpheus, tries to bring Memnon to his senses by showing the folly of killing oneself for love.[2] But the *scena* does not appreciably ease the madman's condition, nor does it exploit the inherent operatic qualities of the legend.[3] Fletcher's concern that the entertainment not assume a life of its own is firmly underlined by the dialogue between Orpheus and Charon, which bears no resemblance to the traditional confrontation at the River Styx. The Thracian hero is simply an interlocutor who prompts the ferryman to warn Memnon not to condemn his soul by committing suicide.

Why did Fletcher include these classical characters, yet eschew the compelling dramatic conflict of the myth? In a recent discussion of the scene, Mary Chan notes that "Memnon is himself a kind of Orpheus figure in his desire to be the ideal lover," but she admits that in Fletcher's hands the "legend has become distorted and debased," the masque being included not for allegorical or satirical purposes, "but merely for melodramatic and sensational effect."[4] The Charon dialogue was widely imitated, obviously influencing the Orpheus scenes in Restoration plays, in which the myth is also perversely interpreted.

The fourth-act masque of Orpheus and Euridice in Settle's heroic play *The Empress of Morocco* is the most elaborate representation of the legend in the whole of seventeenth-century English drama. Set by Matthew Locke, it is a self-contained miniature opera wherein Orpheus descends to Hades and sues Pluto and Proserpine for the release of his beloved. While reducing the story to its bare essentials and offering little development of the dramatis personae (Euridice, for example, does not sing), the masque has an ingenious, perhaps over-

[2]The attempted cure for madness recalls the antimasque of Thomas Campion's *The Lords' Masque* (1614), in which Orpheus frees Entheus (Poetic Fury) from unjust confinement in a cave for common lunatics.

[3]John P. Cutts discusses the play in "Music and *The Mad Lover*," *Studies in the Renaissance*, 8 (1961), 236–48.

[4]"Drolls, Drolleries and Mid-Seventeenth-Century Dramatic Music in England," *RMA Research Chronicle*, 15 (1979), 124.

elaborate, allegorical role in the play. The villain, Crimalhaz, while holding prisoner the young king of Morocco, Muly Labas, and his queen, Morena, entertains the captive audience with a court masque. The queen mother, who pretends to plot her son's escape, privately arranges for him and Morena to take the title roles in the opera, advising Muly Labas that at the end of the entertainment he and "Euridice," still in costume, can slip past the guards. But the queen mother, secretly determined to destroy her son, falsely informs Morena that Crimalhaz, not Muly Labas, will act Orpheus, and that the villain intends to rape her at the end of the revels.

The masque, which is a novel variation on a traditional disguise plot, has the same function as the similarly contrived ballet in the last act of *The Revenger's Tragedy* (1607), namely to provide a spectacular setting for the climactic catastrophe. But echoes of *The Mad Lover* reverberate, especially in the distortion of the legend. According to the queen mother's announced scenario, "Euridice" is to escape the underworld, but tragedy ensues when Morena stabs "Orpheus." The young king's murder is thus a metaphor of the maenads' destruction of the hero, and Euridice's second death, while omitted from the script, is nevertheless symbolized both by the threatened rape and by Morena's swoon at the revelation that she has killed her husband. Whereas in *The Mad Lover* the dramatic conflict of the myth is entirely untapped, in *The Empress of Morocco* it is ingeniously exploited. Muly Labas is an Orphic figure who is destroyed while attempting to free his wife from a fantastic and hostile world. The protagonist's final speech, delivered immediately after the masque, is laced with ironic allusions, as if the young king in his death throes were still half in the character of Orpheus.

Locke's music, which survives nearly intact, deserves to be better known.[5] In an uncharacteristically conservative style, declamatory and almost entirely unrelieved by tuneful passages, it pays homage to early seventeenth-century Italian dramatic monody. The depiction of Orpheus is particularly effective, as the hero makes a direct and, for Locke, highly sentimental plea for Euridice's release, with no Monteverdian display of vocal pyrotechnics (see Example 1). But the music does not enhance the allegorical role of the masque within the play, such sophistication being beyond Locke's ability to express (or, at least, ours to detect). The play drew a vicious attack from John Crowne, Thomas Shadwell, and John Dryden,[6] yet emerged as one of the most successful dramas of the 1670s. And the masque, which largely escaped the critics' wrath, was imitated by later playwrights.

The next appearance of a singing Orpheus is in Charles Davenant's

---

[5]Briefly discussed in my essay "Music and Drama," *The London Theatre World, 1660–1800*, ed. Robert D. Hume (Carbondale, 1980), pp. 214–19.

[6]See *Notes and Observations on the Empress of Morocco* ([London,] 1674).

Example 1. Matthew Locke, from "The Masque of Orpheus," in Elkanah Settle's *The Empress of Morocco* (1673), Act IV Oxford, Christ Church, Mus. MS 692

my martyred saint, brings me a pilgrim here, my fair Eu- ri- di-

-ce, my fair Eu- ri- di- ce

semi-opera of 1677, *Circe*, a liberal redaction of the Iphigenia in Tauris story. John Banister, much less gifted than Locke, supplied most if not all of the music for the first production. At a later, undetermined date, Henry Purcell reset the verses accompanying the conjuration of Pluto near the end of Act I.[7] Orpheus appears not in this scene, but in the fourth act, where Circe entertains Orestes, an Argive youth whom she has just saved from sacrifice. As the scene opens in her enchanted palace, Orpheus is accompanying Circe's women as they sing first a pastoral love song and then an explicitly erotic verse designed to aid in the youth's seduction. Finally, Orpheus himself sings a lament for Euridice, "Give me my Lute, in thee some ease I find."[8] The lyric seems incongruous to the stage action; bitterness pervades the first stanza ("All Women now are false, and few are fair"), while in the second, Orpheus finds an arrogant solace in his art ("The Young shall sigh no more,/But all my noble Verse adore;/It has more Graces than the Queen of Love"). As Circe and the bewitched Orestes dally in dumb show, Cupid descends to chide Orpheus for his mourning and abstinence, calling upon some bacchants to raise the Thracian's spirits. Unable to penetrate his grief, *"they fling their darts at Orpheus, who falls dead."*

The masque is a savage allegory of Circe's seduction of the Greek youth, and anticipates his metaphorical death, soon to occur in the enchantress's private grotto. By its very fidelity to the myth, however, the scene departs paradoxically from the Orphic theatrical tradition, and

[7]For testimony of Banister's authorship, see John Downes, *Roscius Anglicanus* (1708), pp. 36–37. Music for a revival is found in *The Works of Henry Purcell*, vol. XVI, ed. Alan Gray (London, 1906), pp. 95–119, and is discussed in Curtis A. Price, *Henry Purcell and the London Stage* (Cambridge, 1984), pp. 97–105.

[8]Printed in Henry Playford's *Choice Ayres & Songs*, vol. II (1679), p. 14.

should be counted among the handful of dramatic renditions ending with the violent death of the protagonist. It is a pity that Purcell did not compose new music for this scene.

Banister's two surviving songs in the masque reveal a flair for the dramatic and little else. "Give me my Lute," with its chromatically descending bass and heavy reliance on diminished melodic intervals, aims at pathos but is spoiled by pedestrian word-setting and several awkward harmonic progressions. It is strophic, but near the beginning of the second strain, three extra beats throw off the phrasing by half a measure, apparently the result of Banister's mispronunciation of "Euridice" (see Example 2). Consider Locke's more Italianate rendering in the masque in *The Empress of Morocco* (Example 1).

The plays discussed above each include snatches of the legend, for quite different effects. The fourth-act serenade in *The Mad Lover* might as well have been delivered by Apollo or Juno, for all that Fletcher makes of the myth's inherent operatic qualities; Settle seems to have been guided to the story specifically because it was an ideal miniature opera that could be fashioned into a warped image of the main plot of *The Empress of Morocco*; and the fourth-act masque of *Circe*, though on a smaller scale, is more skillfully integrated into the drama. But these scenes, while designed as unflattering allegories of the action of the spoken part of each play, do not in themselves poke fun at contemporary classicized drama. One is not meant to laugh at Morena because she is dressed like Euridice; and the bacchants' destruction of Orpheus during Circe's love-making may be bizarre, but it is not funny. All the appearances of Orpheus in later Restoration plays are, however, lampoons of the classical mode.

The part of Lyonel in Durfey's 1688 comedy *A Fool's Preferment*, a reworking of Fletcher's *The Noble Gentleman*, was created for Will Mountfort. In the earlier play this character (called Shattillion) is driven mad after being coyly denied by his betrothed, a favorite of the king. Durfey altered the role in two important ways. First, while Fletcher only hinted at the king's philandering, Lyonel is now explicitly made the victim of royal promiscuity, since his beloved Celia has in fact been the king's unwilling mistress. Throughout the later play, Lyonel's ex-

Example 2. John Banister, song from Charles Davenant's *Circe* (1677), Act IV

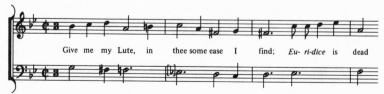

travagant behavior exhibits a fine balance between outrage and insanity. Durfey's second major change is that his madman is allowed to sing several songs, thereby exploiting Mountfort's "clear Countertenour."[9] The lyrics were set by Purcell and published in the first edition of the playbook.[10] The songs are brief, tuneful, and technically easy—perhaps a reflection of the actor's modest musical abilities. Yet taken together, they reveal the core of Lyonel's personality: while Fletcher's Shattillion is shown to be truly mad through soliloquies, Durfey's Lyonel is ambiguously portrayed, and we wonder whether he is feigning madness up to the final song.

Near the end of Act V, while a dance is performed to celebrate the resolution of the main plot, Lyonel enters *"in a mad posture,"* thinking he is in the underworld: "Hah! here they are! and in the height of Revelling[,] *Pluto, Minos, Radamanthus,* the King of the Infernals, and the Judges. . . . Great *Pluto*—know that I am *Orpheus,* and through the dismal shades of direful night, am come to seek my long lov'd *Proserpine.*" That Lyonel confuses Euridice with the Queen of the Shades would seem to confirm his lunacy. But this speech has a deeper meaning. He still bitterly resents Celia's royal affair; by seeking his "long lov'd *Proserpine,*" Lyonel would make Pluto—that is, the king—a cuckold. He continues the impersonation of Orpheus: "I'le charm thee God, with Musick, my soft Aires shall lull the Pow'rs of thy barb'rous Empire, and set my Love at liberty." And in the ensuing song, "If thou wilt give me back my love," his ire abates as he restores the dramatis personae of the legend to their proper roles. Purcell's setting is a hauntingly beautiful minuet in F major. Through its utter simplicity, Lyonel attains an apotheosized peace of mind. But the other speaking characters, interpreting the little charade as full proof of dementia, carry him off to a doctor.

Durfey is a much underrated dramatist, most of whose comedies have complex satirical designs. And he, almost alone among the playwrights of the 1680s and 1690s, learned how to exploit actor-singers such as Mountfort. Though obviously indebted to the fourth-act masque in *The Mad Lover,* the episode in *A Fool's Preferment* is more appropriate to the drama and better attuned to the musical possibilities of the Orphic myth. Lyonel (as Orpheus) enters a Hades of fools, retrieves Celia's affection, and soothes his own savage breast, only to be seized by maenad-like supernumeraries.

Several plays produced in the early 1690s have scenes reminiscent of the masque in *The Empress of Morocco;* they are not so much parodies

[9]See *An Apology for the Life of Colley Cibber,* ed. B. R. S. Fone (Ann Arbor, 1968), p. 76. Mountfort also played the recorder (see, for example, Dryden's *Don Sebastian,* II.ii, III.ii) and was an amateur composer.

[10]See *The Works of Henry Purcell,* vol. XX, pp. 11–22.

of Locke's embryonic opera as borrowings of Settle's disguise stratagem with its classical trappings.[11] Perhaps the clearest example is in Durfey's *The Marriage-Hater Match'd* of 1692; though Orpheus does not appear, the fifth-act masquerade is closely linked to a later play in which the myth has a very important role. Compared to other comedies of the period, the plot is simple. Phaebe, a cast-off mistress who appears in breeches for most of the action, tricks her former lover, Sir Philip Freewit, an ultimately benign rake, into an agreeable marriage. The main attraction of the play is a gallery of fools and knaves, most of whom hope to marry Berenice, "A witty . . . Brisk, Humorous, Freakish Creature." One must admire Durfey's skill in maneuvering the large and potentially unwieldy cast, giving each of the suitors a distinctive personality and narrowly averting total chaos in the final scene. Berenice wants to marry Darewell, a bluff sea captain, but must devise a plan to keep her other admirers, particularly Solon, from interfering. The latter is informed that the evening's masquerade will afford him an opportunity to spirit Berenice away from his rivals. And a plotting maid tells Solon, "Rely upon me; I'll give an account of her Habit, and you shall steal her off and Marry her in spite of" Captain Darewell. Of course, Solon is misinformed about Berenice's costume, and marries the maid instead—one of seven weddings performed in masquerade. Sir Philip laughs at Solon, until the rake discovers that he himself has been tricked into marrying Phaebe.

In light of his indebtedness to the masque of Orpheus in *The Empress of Morocco,* one might wonder why Durfey did not take the plunge and allow the dramatis personae to sing, especially since six actor-singers had been cast in the main roles: Mountfort (Sir Philip Freewit), Mrs. Bracegirdle (Phaebe), Mrs. Lassells (Berenice), John Bowman (Lord Brainless), Charlotte Butler (La Pupsey), and Thomas Doggett (Solon). Instead, the main musical feature of the scene is Purcell's sophisticated drinking song, rendered by nameless attendants: "As soon as the chaos was made into form," a vaguely apropos commentary on the resolution of the plot.[12] Some knowledge of the theatrical background of *The Marriage-Hater Match'd* is necessary to explain this seemingly missed opportunity and to understand the position of the play in the English Orphic tradition.

Throughout the Restoration, but perhaps most consistently during the early 1690s, typecasting was observed by most comic dramatists.

---

[11]In addition to the comedies discussed below, see Southerne's *The Wives Excuse* (1691), Act V, and Thomas Scott's *The Mock-Marriage* (1965), Act V.

[12]*The Works of Henry Purcell,* vol. xx, pp. 84–88, and Price, *Henry Purcell,* pp. 160–64.

They wrote for specific actors portraying stylized characters or "lines."[13] Two of the most popular comedians were Mountfort, who, despite creating the role of the madman in *A Fool's Preferment*, was typically cast as a witty, often artistically accomplished rake, and Mrs. Bracegirdle, who regularly took the part of a clever heiress, lightheartedly thwarting all assaults on her virtue. *The Marriage-Hater Match'd* was therefore unusual because she was cast against type, since Phaebe is not only Sir Philip's erstwhile lover but the mother of his illegitimate child. Mountfort was more comfortable in the role of Philip, the "marriage hater."

In their private lives, some of the Thespians assumed the personalities they displayed on stage. Bowman, for example, gradually became the indolent fop he often acted. Others let it be known that their off-stage behavior was not unlike that which they habitually showed in the theatre. Notable among them was Mrs. Bracegirdle, who never married. Her self-professed virginity became a cause célèbre and was an important issue in the death of her colleague Mountfort.

The circumstances of the actor's murder on December 9, 1692, are so well documented and discussed in the secondary literature that only a sketch of the facts is needed here.[14] Captain Richard Hill, a violent young gentleman of the sort often caricatured on the stage, became infatuated with Mrs. Bracegirdle. Repeatedly rebuffed, he concluded that she was Mountfort's lover, the only evidence for this supposition being that the two were often cast as romantic leads. (The quality of their acting apparently convinced the hotheaded soldier of an offstage affair.) Like Solon in the play, Hill decided that to win her heart he would have to abduct her, and brought his friend, the notorious teenage rake-hell Lord Mohun, into the design. They botched the kidnaping, however, and, heated by humiliation and a bottle of canary, the profligates spent much of the night in the street before Mrs. Bracegirdle's lodgings, ostensibly trying to offer an apology, but—as was rumored at the time of the trial—probably also lying in wait for Mountfort, who lived nearby. The actor finally arrived and greeted the young men. Without warning, Hill stabbed Mountfort, who died the next day. The assailant escaped, while Mohun was later tried in the House of Lords and acquitted of murder.

The report of the trial was published in 1693, and manuscript copies of the depositions of several witnesses survive.[15] Though they provide a

---

[13]The importance of actors and casting to the interpretation of plays of the period is discussed by Peter Holland, *The Ornament of Action* (Cambridge, 1979), chap. 3, esp. pp. 70 ff.

[14]The best account remains Albert S. Borgman's *The Life and Death of William Mountfort* (Cambridge, Mass., 1935), part 2.

[15]The latter documents are published in Borgman, *William Mountfort*, Appendix C.

wealth of largely corroborated evidence about the case, the primary sources offer no proof of anything other than a professional relationship between Mountfort and Mrs. Bracegirdle; among the doggerel rhymers, however, a sexual liaison was treated as common knowledge. The most detailed popular account of the sad affair is *The Player's Tragedy, Or, Fatal Love, a New Novel* (1693), in which the names have been slightly changed. A piece of anonymous hack journalism this may be, but the pamphlet was obviously penned by someone with well-placed informants, and the sensitive description of the chaste Mrs. Bracegirdle's succumbing to Mountfort's charm is entirely convincing.

The scandal passed, the Drury Lane theatre company recovered from the loss of Mountfort, and Mrs. Bracegirdle soon resumed acting the kinds of characters that had inflamed Captain Hill's passions. In fact, a mere five months after the murder she appeared in the title role of Durfey's comedy *The Richmond Heiress* (April 1693), a part conforming to her witty virgin "line." The play is rich in allusions to contemporary events; and in the first act, during a discussion of various Theatre Royal actors, Sir Quibble Quere mentions Mrs. Bracegirdle herself:

Well, I'll say't she Acts *Statira* curiously.
　　From every Pore of him a Perfume falls.
　　He kisses softer than a Southern Wind:
　　Curles like a Vine; and touches like a God.[16]
When I was last at the Play, and she was saying of this, my Mouth, I'll say't, went to-and-agen, to-and-agen, as fast as hers, and repeated it after her so loud, that all the People in the Pit thought I was bewitch'd.

The satire on the actress's admirers surely included the bewitched Captain Hill, who is said to have attended the theatre daily, standing on stage or behind the scenes to hang on Mrs. Bracegirdle's every word. Yet a far more extraordinary attack on her would-be suitors is found in Act V. To reduce the complex and convoluted plot to its essentials, Fulvia, the Richmond heiress, outwits her guardian, Sir Charles Romance, who has arranged for her to marry his booby son, Tom. She rather inclines to the rakish Frederick, who employs Quickwit as a go-between. In the last act Cunnington, a villain whom Sir Charles has hired to further his son's chances with Fulvia, informs Quickwit of a plan to abduct the heiress during a ball at Sir Charles's house later that evening: "I wait here for some Masquerading Habits, that I have sent a Messenger to borrow at *Twickenham*; there's to be a little Ataque too of *Pluto*, *Orpheus*, and *Euridice*, of my Composing, and the Musick of Mr. *Purcels*." Cunnington explains that he will sing Pluto, and Fulvia (Mrs.

---

[16]Statira's speech in Nathaniel Lee's *The Rival Queens*, I.ii.42–44. The play was revived a week before Mountfort was murdered.

Bracegirdle), whom he wants to ravish, will be Euridice. This is another, even more audacious, borrowing of *The Empress of Morocco* stratagem, but Durfey adds a remarkable twist.

Having gained intelligence of the devious plan, Quickwit has Cunnington hauled safely out of the way and arranges for Frederick to act Orpheus, while he, Quickwit, will stand in as Pluto. The entertainment is in two parts, the first a dance of mummers, who, as Sir Charles explains, are "some of the young fry of the Neighbour-hood that having a frolick this Evening, desire to give us a share on't." Although the choreography is not described in the stage directions, it was obviously designed to foreshadow events in the masque itself, since Sir Charles, approving Cunnington's scenario, says, "the Subject is the stealing an Heiress, and the Figures are Love, Desire, Youth, and Avarice, that all Court Lady *Pecunia*." These emblematic dancers represent Fulvia and her four principal suitors: in order, Quickwit, Frederick, Tom Romance, and Sir Quibble Quere. Following the dance and a ballad unrelated to the action, Frederick, Quickwit, and Fulvia enter in costume, apparently ready to perform Purcell's masque; but the two men, having forcibly replaced Cunnington and another conspirator, have not had time to learn their parts. Fulvia's waiting woman suggests that the masquers withdraw to an adjoining room to rehearse, thereby giving the heiress a chance to escape.

Although Purcell's masque of Orpheus is never performed, the ensuing action closely parallels the fourth-act entertainment of *The Empress of Morocco*. In a doubly symbolic gesture, "Fred. *takes one of* Fulvia's *hands*, Quickwit *the other, and as they are leading her off she turns back.*"

> *Fulvia.* Hold, hold, are ye mad? why, Sir *Charles*, and you Squire Small-Brains, you will not suffer me to be carried off thus before your faces, will ye?
>
> *Sir Charles.* But into the next room to practice a little, Madam.
>
> *Tom Romance.* You are to act *Euridice*, you know, Madam, and they will only see if you are perfect in your cue; Mr. *Cunnington* there, has shewn me the whole design.
>
> *Fulvia.* And Mr. *Quickwit*, the witty Player here, has shewn it me, Sir. Come, *Pluto*, you must unmask.
>
> [*Unmasks* Quickwit.]
>
> *Quickwit.* 'Dsdeath, Madam, what d'ye mean, you wont discover us, and undoe all?
>
> *Fulvia.* Yes faith, Sir, I've a fancy in my head that 'tis not lucky to be stolen to day; therefore you *Orpheus*, otherwise call'd *Frederick* the constant, you must uncover too, your singing will hardly get ye a Mistress to night, I can assure ye.
>
> *Frederick.* She discovers us—Death and Confusion! what new turn's this?

Seeing the plan subverted, Sir Charles draws his sword, but Fulvia intervenes: "Nay, no fighting, good Gentlemen." She then breaks loose from Sir Quibble, who tries to pull her into a waiting coach. This scene is a stinging allegory of the attempted rape of Anne Bracegirdle, who, with her mother's help, saved herself from being bundled into a coach hired by Captain Hill.[17] Rather than ignore the scandal, Durfey and the theatre company apparently hoped to exorcize it with a public airing, allowing the actress to speak for herself. With the unscrupulous Sir Charles and Cunnington exposed, Fulvia pours scorn over all her suitors, even Frederick, a former paramour, by disclosing his marriage contract to Sophronia. In her final speeches, Mrs. Bracegirdle stepped out of character to address the town:

> Since such a general defect of honesty corrupts the Age, I'll no more trust Mankind, but lay my Fortune out upon my self, and flourish in contempt of humane Falshood. . . .
>   My eyes in contradiction to the World, have ever (scorning Interest) fix'd on Merit, and led by Love and Generous Inclination, have strove to make that Sentiment appear by a free present of my Heart and Fortune to one I thought as nobly had deserv'd 'em. But, oh! the Race of Men are all Deceivers, and my relief, is my resolve to shun 'em. . . .

It is tempting to see Sir Quibble and Sir Charles as reflections of Captain Hill and Lord Mohun. Charles, who encourages assaults on Fulvia's virtue, resorts to violence when his plans go awry. Quibble's final speech contains an acerbic allusion to Mohun's trial in the Peers: "Why then a Plague of all Intrigues: I'll go and get drunk, and despite all Womankind, for I'll say't, I'll ne're hang my self about the matter, but I'll have my Money again if there be Law in *England*. . . ." The most puzzling aspect of this scene is the dismissal of Frederick, on whom Fulvia is earlier prepared to bestow her fortune and affection. Could he have represented the late Will Mountfort?

Fulvia rejects the rake only after learning of his engagement to Sophronia. His predicament reminds me of the moralistic remark in *The Player's Tragedy* that Mountfort's alleged adultery with Mrs. Bracegirdle earned him "a great many Enemies, and those of the most dangerous kind, Despairing and Neglected *Lovers*, who cou'd not but be provok'd to see him bear off that Prize from them, for which, as a

---

[17]According to the article on Mrs. Bracegirdle in *A Biographical Dictionary of Actors, Actresses, Musicians . . . in London, 1660–1800*, ed. Philip H. Highfill, Jr., Kalman A. Burnim, and Edward A. Langhans, II (Carbondale, 1973), p. 273, the attempted abduction in the play forms "an obvious parallel to the events of the previous December" (that is, the foiled rape and subsequent murder); but no closer reading of the drama is proffered.

Marry'd Man, he seem'd so very ill qualified."[18] Most telling of all, Frederick was to have taken the part of Orpheus in the aborted masque. In light of Durfey's fondness for satirical designs and the delight he took in self-borrowing, one should recall that Mountfort made his final appearance in *A Fool's Preferment* as Orpheus. Fulvia seems to allude to Lyonel when she unmasks the dumbfounded Frederick ("your singing will hardly get ye a Mistress to night"), while Orpheus's musical silence symbolizes the actor's death.

The unfulfilled promise of music by Purcell in the fifth act of *The Richmond Heiress* is highly ironic. The "lost" masque was probably intended as a humorous acknowledgment of the missed opportunity to create a miniature opera for the actor-singers assembled at the end of *The Marriage-Hater Match'd*. But Durfey's most remarkable achievement—yet another debt owed to *The Empress of Morocco*—is that despite the collapse of the elaborately prepared masque, he retains the outlines of the legend in the brilliant climax. While attempting to retrieve Fulvia from a Hades of deceit and confusion, Frederick is destroyed. But the allegory is in most other respects a deliberate perversion of the myth. "Euridice," not "Orpheus," fails the test of faith by turning to look back. And Fulvia's public declaration of chastity is a strange apotheosis.

The Richmond Heiress was not the end of the affair; as *The Player's Tragedy* shows, Mrs. Bracegirdle's presumably innocent role as *provocatrice* in Mountfort's death continued to dog her. And the final scene of the play, though sailing very close to the wind, did not address the central question of whether the thespians were romantically attached, as Captain Hill had believed. Furthermore, Mrs. Bracegirdle's cry of a plague on both your houses would appear to dishonor the memory of the late actor. If Mountfort had been only a victim of Hill's mad infatuation, surely she would have shown him more respect.

Durfey tackled this suspicion head on in his next play, the first part of the *Don Quixote* trilogy (May 1694), of which Act II, scene ii, is a fairly straightforward rendering of the goatherd's story (in the novel, Part 1, Chapters 12–14). In this scene in a *"Deep Grove,"* Don Quixote attends the funeral of Chrysostome, a young man who died of a broken heart after being rejected by Marcella. She is a wealthy heiress, disillusioned by fawning and mercenary suitors, and living in the mountains as a shepherdess. Ambrosio, the dead man's friend, delivers the eulogy, which degenerates into an abusive gloss on Marcella's perfidy. After a dirge is performed,[19] the "cruel Tygress" herself makes a dramatic ap-

---

[18]Borgman, *William Mountfort*, p. 163.

[19]Set by John Eccles and discussed in my essay "Music and Drama," pp. 229–30, and in *Henry Purcell*, pp. 209–10.

pearance to defend her reputation. Casting Mrs. Bracegirdle as the remorseless Marcella was at once daring and natural, but, astonishingly, Durfey also altered the attributes of the late Chrysostome to reflect Mountfort. Cervantes's character is handsome and passionate, a gifted poet and writer of plays for Corpus Christi.[20] Durfey's Chrysostome is similarly accomplished and, departing from the novel, a musician as well. But above all, he is made an Englishman.

Ambrosio is disgusted that Marcella should disrupt the funeral of the man whose ardent advances she scorned, but she offers a spirited self-defense: "Pity's the Child of Love; and I ne'er yet Lov'd any of your Sex, I might have some Compassion for his Death; but still the Occasion of it moves my Mirth." Ambrosio asks disbelievingly, "Have you no Remorse?" Her reply has a cutting double edge: "I rather look on him as a good Actor; that Practising the Art of deep deceit, as Whining, Swearing, Dying at your Feet, Crack'd some Lite Artery with an overstrain, And dy'd of some Male Mischief in the Brain."[21] As Marcella, Mrs. Bracegirdle eloquently protested her innocence in the Mountfort affair. To act a scene of love convincingly, as they had often done on stage, did not necessarily imply a behind-the-scenes romance; "male mischief," that is, adolescent misadventure, killed the "good actor." Only in the second of the *Don Quixote* plays, in which Marcella (again portrayed by Mrs. Bracegirdle) is abducted and nearly ravished, does one realize that Durfey was exploiting the actress's notoriety rather than trying to repair her reputation.

The allusions to the tragedy of Will Mountfort in *The Richmond Heiress* and the aftershocks in *Don Quixote* brought together the two main strands of the Orphic tradition in seventeenth-century English drama: the enactment of the myth as a ritualistic cure for madness induced by unrequited love, as Stremon attempts in *The Mad Lover* and Lyonel accomplishes in *A Fool's Preferment*; and "Orpheus and Euridice" as opera-within-play, invented by Settle in *The Empress of Morocco*, where the legend is mingled with a stock disguise plot. Both kinds of scene stem from the Italian operatic tradition. The "lost" masque in *The Richmond Heiress* is thus a metaphor of the contemporary resistance to all-sung opera in England.[22] At the same time it is a

---

[20]Mountfort was, coincidentally, a playwright.

[21]Much of the scene was cut in performance, but all of the dialogue quoted above was untouched.

[22]The legend was set to music twice in the decade or so after Purcell's death. In October 1697 a masque of *Orpheus and Euridice* was performed at a girls' boarding school near Oxford. Four songs survive (three by Richard Goodson and one by John Weldon), but the libretto is lost; see Neal Zaslaw, "An English 'Orpheus and Euridice' of 1697," *The Musical Times*, 118 (1977), 805–8. In the February 1707 issue of *The Muses Mercury* is printed John Dennis's six-page text of "The Masque of Orpheus and Euridice,"

ringing affirmation of the power of native spoken drama; the Thracian bard remains silent because the masque, jostled violently by a complicated and highly allegorical plot, has not even been rehearsed. Orpheus, "distorted and debased" in *The Mad Lover*, double-crossed in *The Empress of Morocco*, ridiculed and then slain for singing a lament in *Circe*, was in Durfey's play deprived of his lyric voice and, perhaps equally humiliating, accused of leading his beloved Euridice down the garden path. Finally, the little opera was to have been set by Purcell, the Orpheus Britannicus. The music is tantalizingly offered and then withdrawn, cruelly frustrating our expectation, while underscoring the irony that the great dramatic composer lived during an era when true English opera was a rare thing.

---

with singing roles for Pluto, Proserpine, and several spirits, as well as the title characters. The verses owe much to Settle's entertainment in *The Empress of Morocco*, yet the ending is genuinely happy, as the grand chorus shows: "Let Hell have Universal Jubilee./And let it in this charming Song agree,/*Orpheus* returns with his *Euridice.*/ And thus th'Infernal Pow'rs to Mortals tell/That Constancy can conquer Hell." The libretto was supposed to be set by Daniel Purcell, but no music survives; the production may have been subverted by play-house politics. See my article, "The Critical Decade for English Music Drama, 1700–1710," *Harvard Library Bulletin*, 26 (1978), 60. Despite the impression conveyed by the couplets quoted above, neither work would appear to be satirical.

Terpsichore at the Fair:
Old and New Dance Airs in Two
Vaudeville Comedies by Lesage

DANIEL HEARTZ

Le Sublime n'est pas plus difficile à attraper, que l'art d'amuser l'esprit en badinant.

—Lesage, Preface to *Théâtre de la Foire* I (1721)

LEOPOLD MOZART, WHEN VISITING Paris with his family in early 1764, was astonished to learn that people danced at the carnival balls to menuets so old they had already been danced to as long ago as the reign of Henri IV (1594–1610). Other dances were also current: "above all, Contredanses or what we call English dances are danced."[1] The contredanse represented a slightly newer fashion than the menuet. Both descended from the old family of round dances known as branles in the sixteenth century. The continuity with which some sixteenth-century dance patterns persisted into the eighteenth century can be demonstrated by examples drawn from two vaudeville comedies written by Alain-René Lesage for the Parisian trade fairs, works that have significance in the history of theater as well as musical delights: *Arlequin Roi de Sérendib* of 1713 and *Les Couplets en procès* of 1729–30.

From its beginnings vaudeville comedy was a spectacle for the less favored classes of urban life, although it was not without patrons and partisans from the upper strata of society. It had to compete for attention with acrobats, tightrope walkers, marionettes, animal acts, and the many other diversions that seem to have been a part of trade fairs every-

---

[1] Letter of March 4, 1764, addressed to Lorenz Hagenauer, Salzburg. *Mozart: Briefe und Aufzeichnungen. Gesamtausgabe*, I, ed. Wilhelm A. Bauer and Otto Erich Deutsch (Kassel, 1962–75), p. 134: ". . . und was für Menuet?—Menuets, die zur Zeit Heinrich des 4.ten schon getanzet worden, und in der ganzen Stadt sind etwa 2. oder 3. favorit Menuet, die immer müssen gespiellet werden, weil die Personen keinen anderen Danzen können, ausser den ienigen Menuet, bey dessen Abspielung sie das Danzen gelehrnet haben. Am meisten aber werden Contra dances, oder die bey uns so genannten englischen Tänze getantzet!"

where, at all times. William Hogarth best captured this atmosphere of boisterous pleasure-seeking in his festive "Southwark Fair" of 1733, depicting an annual institution that took place on the banks of the Thames south of London during September.[2] In this delightful and famous assemblage of theatrical lore, the trestle stage upon which Cibber and Bullock play "The Fall of Bajazet" literally falls, along with the actors and a violin, into the neatly arranged display of pottery wares beneath. There are also a bagpiper and walking dog, a fire-eater, a lady drummer, tightrope artists, a Harlequin disporting under "Punches Opera," a waxworks displaying "the whole court of France," an equestrian fighter, and a peep show, to name but a few of the entertainments. There is no similar visual documentation for the equivalent summer fair in Paris, held on the northern outskirts in the parish of St. Laurent (approximately in the present location of the Gare de l'Est). But for its twin, the late-winter fair held in the suburb of St. Germain south of the Seine, there is the well-known miniature painting by Nicholas van Blarenberghe of the Foire St. Germain, dated 1763.[3] Its scale is tiny but the central event is clear: Harlequin and other comedians in their traditional costumes give a specimen of their antics on a balcony above the entrance to the theater, towards which one of the troupe beckons the milling crowd while another plays a side drum. On the left, instead of pottery for sale, there is a gallery crammed with paintings; to the right, instead of a waxworks, there is a marionette show. A dog act engages the attention of a few spectators in the middle foreground (or is it only a stray dog barking?). All events take place in a covered courtyard, appropriately to the season.

Humble as were the origins and early history of the genre that came to be known around 1715 as opéra comique, its main creator took pains to document that history and collect the best and most original plays in ten illustrated volumes in octavo, Le Théâtre de la foire.[4] Alain-René Lesage (1668–1747) was not an unknown literary talent when he turned to writing vaudeville comedies in 1712. He had scored a resounding success with his Crispin rival de son maître for the Comédie Française

[2]Reproduced in Engravings by Hogarth, ed. Sean Shesgreen (New York, 1973), Plate 27.

[3]It is reproduced most recently in James R. Anthony, "Théâtres de la Foire," New Grove, XVIII, pp. 728–29.

[4]LE THEATRE DE LA FOIRE, OU L'OPERA COMIQUE, CONTENANT LES MEILLEURES PIECES qui ont été représentées aux Foires de S. Germain & de S. Laurent. Enrichies d'Estampes en Taille douce, avec une Table de tous les Vaudevilles & autres Airs gravez notez à la fin de chaque Volume. PAR MRS. LE SAGE & D'ORNEVAL (Paris, 1721–34). The last volume (X) is edited by Carolet. There is a modern edition, with critical notes, of Lesage's Arlequin Roi de Sérendib by Jacques Truchet, Théâtre du XVIIIᵉ siècle, 2 vols. (Paris, 1972), I, 165–90.

in 1707, the same year that saw the publication of his immensely popular novel *Le Diable boiteux*.[5] *Turcaret* followed two years later on the stage of the august royal troupe, and was equally successful. Yet Lesage had a falling-out with the players over it that was to have lasting consequences. Perhaps it was inevitable that the arrogance of the royal players would upset an author such as Lesage—a lifelong enemy of hypocrisy, exaggeration, and pomp, a throwback to an older and more earthy French civilization before the Sun King, an heir to the *gauloiserie* of Rabelais.[6] Gargantua's clear-sighted view of life, with all its warts as well as its joys, found a spiritual descendant in Lesage, who abandoned the Comédie Française for good when he embraced the freer, albeit more risky, platform of the fair theaters. At the same time, his novelistic career continued apace with the brilliant *Gil Blas de Santillane*, the first installment of which came out in 1715. Between 1712 and 1736 he wrote a hundred-odd comedies for the fair theaters, alone or in collaboration with others, but always as the dominant partner, it has been claimed.[7]

A critic writing for the *Mercure de France* in January 1719 complained about writers of reputation who did not fear to cheapen their pens by drawing the public to the fairs. Lesage was the main such writer. The anonymous critic complained further: "One can say, to the shame of the century, that bad taste has so prevailed in favor of these sorts of plays, that the ambiguous and farcical in which they revel is preferred to the best tragedies and comedies played in the regular theaters."[8] We shall presently see what passed for ambiguity ("l'équivoque") and farce ("le bas comique") in Lesage's vaudeville comedies. But first it will be helpful to have his summary of how opéra comique evolved.

[5]Joseph Haydn's first opera, in the 1750s, was but one of many stage works descended from *Le Diable boiteux*. For a consideration of Haydn's contacts with Parisian opéra comique, see D. Heartz, "Haydn und Gluck im Burgtheater um 1760: *Der neue krumme Teufel, Le Diable à quatre* und die Sinfonie 'Le Soir,' " *Bericht über den Internationalen Musikwissenschaftlichen Kongress Bayreuth 1981* (Kassel, 1983), pp. 120–35.

[6]Vincent Barberet, *Lesage et le Théâtre de la Foire* (Nancy, 1887; facsimile reprint Geneva, 1970), p. 36. See also Ardelle Striker, "A Curious Form of Protest Theatre: The *Pièce à Écriteaux*," *Theatre Survey*, 14 (1973), 55–71, on Lesage's relationship to his immediate predecessors at the fair theaters.

[7]Barberet, *Lesage*, p. 213. He argues this point by showing the relative lack of success that Lesage's collaborators were able to achieve on their own. Marcello Spaziani questions this view in "Per Una Storia della Commedia 'Foraine': Il periodo 1713–1736," *Studi in onore di Carlo Pellegrini*, pp. 255–77. See also Spaziani's *Il teatro della Foire* (Rome, 1965).

[8]Nicole Wild, "Aspects de la musique sous la Régence—les Foires," *Recherches sur la musique française classique*, 5 (1965), 129–41. The quotation, on page 135, is as follows: "On peut dire, à la honte du siècle, que le mauvais goût avait tellement prévalu

La Muse de la Comedie rassemble la Poësie, la Musique, et la Danse pour composer ses petits divertisemens, sous le nom d'Opera Comique.

Plate 1. Frontispiece to Vol. I of *Théâtre de la foire* (1730), engraved by Picart

A frontispiece engraved in 1730 by Picart and added to the first volume of the *Théâtre de la foire* shows poetry, music, and dance brought together by the Muse of Comedy, Thalia, to form opéra comique (Plate 1). In the background, on a balcony outside their theater, Pierrot (with his hat off), Harlequin, and other players entice the crowd below, while Scaramouche gestures toward a banner showing a ropedancer and an acrobat. Lesage relates in his preface that at first the fairs were content with farces played by ropedancers in between their acrobatic acts. Then fragments of the old Italian comedies (from the Gherardi troupe, banished by Louis XIV in 1697) were spoken; these were successful, but the Comédie Française managed to put a stop to them because they drew crowds. Dialogues and monologues were banned successively. Forbidden to speak, the Forains resorted to placards ("écriteaux"), with speeches written large, as a backdrop against which the characters mimed their rôles. The inscriptions were first in prose, later in verse, set to popular vaudeville tunes that the orchestra played and the audience became accustomed to singing. Since the placards cluttered the stage, the actors devised a system of rolled banners bearing the speeches above the stage. Children dressed as Cupids, suspended by counterweights, unfurled the banners as the action progressed. This account, told in Lesage's typically terse and direct manner, takes us up to 1713 and the first three works in Volume I, belonging to the category of "pièces par écriteaux": *Arlequin Roi de Sérendib, Arlequin Thétis*, and *Arlequin invisible*. An illustration from the first comedy shows the suspended Cupids holding a verse describing Harlequin, who is in the middle with his typical mask and motley (Plate 2).

The spectacle with popular songs pleased the public, continued Lesage in his preface, and the players thought it might do so even more if the actors themselves sang the vaudevilles. Permission was sought of the Opéra, which alone held the privilege of singing dramas on stage, and was granted in 1714 (on payment of a large fee). The three plays of 1714 in Volume I, all by Lesage, illustrate the type consisting entirely of sung vaudevilles; they are the Prologue *La Foire de Guibray* and the two independent acts *Arlequin Mahomet* and *Le Tombeau de Nostradamus*, for which the Prologue provided a link. The decisive moment was at hand. As described by Lesage: "One gradually mixed a little [spoken] prose with the verses, in order to link the couplets better, or to avoid making overly banal verses, with the result that, imperceptibly, the plays became mixed." And indeed, there are a few lines that are not

en faveur de ces sortes de pièces, que l'on préférait souvent l'équivoque et le bas comique qui y était répandu, aux meilleures tragédies et comédies que l'on jouait sur les théâtres réglés. Les auteurs de réputation ne craignaient pas d'avilir leur plume pour y attirer le public. . . ."

ARLEQUIN

C'est lui (plaignez ses malheurs)
C'est lui qui le sort balote.
Reconnoissez-le à ses pleurs,
Encor plus à sa culote.

MEZZETIN. ARLEQUIN. PIERROT.

Plate 2. Scene from *Arlequin Roi Serendib Théâtre de la foire*, Vol. I (1730)

sung in the four plays of 1715 that conclude Volume I, Letellier's *Arlequin Sultane favorite* and Lesage's *La Ceinture de Vénus, Télémaque,* and *Le Temple du destin.*

Opéra comique assumed its classic form with the mixed genre, consisting mostly of sung vaudevilles with some prose dialogue. The term describing it became current at about the same time—1715. Squabbles with one or more of the privileged theaters (including the Italian comedians, reïnstated by the Regent in 1716) led to many suppressions of the fair theaters in the decades that followed, but the form assumed by opéra comique remained unchanged in essentials until the inroads made upon it by the visiting Buffoni and the Italian ariette in the 1750s. It is a quirk of history that in prohibiting speaking at the fair theaters, the Comédie Française unwittingly promoted the ingenious dodge of a comedy sung to popular songs, which then became a far more potent rival than what had preceded it. With *Arlequin Roi de Sérendib* for the Foire St. Germain in 1713, Lesage made the breakthrough from sketchy dramas using a handful of vaudeville tunes to a three-act, well-constructed drama using over a hundred melodies. The huge anthology of airs needed for opéra comique gave the old vaudeville tunes a renewed lease on life.

ARLEQUIN ROI DE SÉRENDIB

Harlequin has been shipwrecked off the savage isle of Sérendib (an old name for Ceylon, which Horace Walpole later coined into "serendipity"). The stage represents a solitary spot with steep cliffs. Harlequin has managed to rescue a purse he has stolen from another passenger, as the first vaudeville explains. It is sung to "Je laisse à la fortune Matelots, Galions" (Air 144 in the appendix of tunes to Volume I of the *Théâtre de la foire;* airs from this source will be identified hereafter only by a number in parentheses). The chosen "timbre" (i.e. the title by which the tune is known) is quite appropriate, with its allusion to sailors and galleons. To those in the know it provided a commentary as soon as the orchestra struck up the jolly tune in G, even before the public, helped by several members of the company planted in the audience, began to sing the text suspended above the stage:

Auprès de ce rivage
Hélas! notre vaisseau
Avec tout l'équipage
Vient de fondre sous l'eau!
Un Procureur du Maine
Dans la liquide plaine

A trouvé son tombeau;
Moi, grace à mon Génie,
J'ay sçû sauver ma vie,
Et l'argent du Manseau.

Lesage's skill at epigrammatic construction is immediately apparent: the comic point arrives only with the last word "Manseau" (the attorney from the province of Maine).

Lesage's descriptions of the pantomime scenes take up as much space as the sung verses, perhaps necessarily so, since they must furnish the dramatic thread. The first scene continues with Harlequin counting his money as a new character arrives, a gun on his shoulder and a patch on one eye. Harlequin is properly terrified and expresses his fear to the air "Quand le péril est agréable" (5), after which the armed man places his turban on the ground, gestures to Harlequin to drop some coins into it, and cries out "Gnaff, Gnaff." Harlequin obliges. Another brigand appears, his arm in a sling, peglegged, with a broad sword at his side. The ritual is repeated, except that this bandit says "Gniff, Gniff"; a third says "Gnoff, Gnoff." (Without recourse to spoken French, Lesage could still resort to jargon.) The scene is concluded with dancing and feasting by the brigands, while poor Harlequin is put in a barrel and left as a feast for wild animals. He describes his plight in an air sung to "Grimaudin" (54), the scabrous significance of which will become clear below in connection with Les Couplets en procès. A wolf attacks Harlequin, who catches it by the tail. The barrel is dragged around the stage until it breaks in two; the wolf flees in one direction and Harlequin in the other.

The scene changes to the capital of Sérendib. Two popular masks of the commedia dell'arte, as developed in France, appear: Mezzetin, dressed as a High Priestess, and Pierrot as his confidante. They have dressed as women because of the local custom decreeing that a male stranger be sacrificed monthly after having been made "King for a Day." The dramatic exposition is accomplished by two airs mimed by Mezzetin, "Menuet de M. de Grandval" (6) and "Je ne suis pas si diable" (43), and one by Pierrot, "Du Cap de Bonne Espérance" (20). The last of these, given below as Ex. 1, was particularly favored by Lesage for purposes of exposition.

The three-bar phrases that mark this tune identify it as a descendant of the old branle simple, whose step pattern led to a phrase structure of $3 \times 4/4$. The rhythmic and melodic plainness of the tune and its mainly conjunct motion also suggest great age. Its singsong quality makes an oddly satisfying match with the deadpan terseness of Lesage in telling a tale that is at once complicated and piquant: the Grand Vizir made Mezzetin High Priestess after having been smitten with her (his) charms. Lesage plays upon the ambiguous nature of the situation by his

Example 1. Air: "Du Cap de Bonne Espérance"

next choice of timbre, "Ne m'entendez-vous pas" (19), conveying something like "But don't you understand the possible consequences?" Mezzetin's fears lead him to wish he had fewer charms (Ex. 2). Here we encounter another dance pattern from the Gallic past, the 3 x 3/4 phraseology of the branle de Poitou, one of the sixteenth-century ancestors of the seventeenth-century menuet (several early examples of which show the same phraseology). There follow an air for Pierrot, "Le fameux Diogenes" (22)—a reference to the Greek cynic philosopher that may have had any number of levels of meaning when applied to Mezzetin's plight—and a dialogue air for both to "Reveillez-vous, belle Endormie" (1), an apparently ancient gaillard-like tune in G that begins like the British national anthem.

Next the Grand Vizir himself arrives to continue his ardent wooing of Mezzetin, which he threatens to carry to term within a day. This leads to more fear and trembling on the part of Mezzetin and Pierrot in Scene 4, expressed to the air "Les Trembleurs" (61) from Lully's *Isis*, a useful descriptive piece with many quick notes. Exit Mezzetin and Pierrot. Enter Harlequin, carried on the shoulders of four men in a triumphal march, followed by the Grand Vizir, the Head Eunuch, palace officers, and executioners. Harlequin is delighted to be received as King. His first act is to order a meal. The Chief Executioner reads a jargon prayer over it, certain words of which are echoed by his followers: "Basileos, alisii, agogi, aformi." This vaguely Greek nonsense is pursued

Example 2. Air: "Ne m'entendez-vous pas"

through the alphabet to "Tragizo, trapeza, porphyra, kécaca." Harlequin takes the last word as a request for action. The act ends as he takes off his turban and proposes to use it as a chamber pot, raising cries of indignation from all. This too is quite in keeping with Hårlequin's traditional character, described by Riccoboni as "insolent, railleur, plat, bouffon, et surtout infiniment ordurier."[9]

Harlequin as King is fêted in various ways in Act II. The pleasures of the table count more with him than the pleasures of the harem. In Scene 6 his lady, La Favorite, complains about his priorities. Harlequin sings his reply to the lovely air "Quel plaisir de voir Claudine" (9), which was used once before in Act II, Scene 3, and seems to convey sensual anticipation. The tune (Ex. 3) is cast in the rhythmic pattern of a branle gay, a rural dance from Brittany that is perhaps the oldest of all the branles. The couple swear eternal fidelity on the cloth-covered altar of the table, described as fearsome for chickens, and cement their vow with the knife, the terror of shoulders of mutton:

Sur ces couverts, sur cette nappe blanche,
Sur cet autel redoutable aux poulets,
Par ce couteau la terreur de l'éclanche,
Je fais serment d'être à vous à jamais.

This giddy vow is sung to the minor strains of "Folies d'Espagne" (16), which is nothing other than the melody of the old sixteenth-century dance "La Folia." (The tune will return in the sacrificial scene in Act III when Harlequin, at another altar, is about to be knifed.) A doctor interrupts their revels and remonstrates with Harlequin, who refuses to stop eating and drinking; Harlequin's gluttony is one of the traditional *lazzi* associated with this mask, and furnishes the main theatrical ancestor of the banquet scene in Mozart's *Don Giovanni*. For his efforts the doctor receives a plate of cream in the face, and this, says Lesage, in his usual deadpan descriptive prose, "finishes the meal and the second act." But not before Harlequin has a song scornful of the doctor, whom he compares to Sancho Panza—a reference, duly footnoted by Lesage, to

Example 3. Air: "Quel plaisir voir Claudine"

[9]Luigi Riccoboni, *Histoire du Théâtre italien*, II (Paris, 1730–31), p. 315.

a recently failed play of the same name at the Comédie Française. Here the appropriateness (if any) of the timbre, "Ma Mère, mariez-moi" (146), eludes us (Ex. 4). The phrase structure of 4 x 4/4 in cut time, taken together with the rather doleful and mainly conjunct melody, resembles many specimens of the old branle double, whereas the two quarter-note upbeats point to a particular variety, the gavotte.

Example 4. Air: "Ma Mère, mariez-moi"

Harlequin opens Act III with a song asking the Head Eunuch if he must be faithful to La Favorite. What a horrid thought! It would enrage him, especially because in such matters his nationality is clear (Lesage takes care to save it for the last word):

> Mon cher, dois-je, toujours fidele,
> Ne cajoller que même Belle?
> Ventrebleu! j'en enragerois
> Moi qui suis là-dessus François.

This is sung, appropriately, to the timbre "Ah! vraiment, je m'y connois bien" (143). The Head Eunuch replies with an air that saw frequent use in Parisian vaudeville comedies, "Faire l'amour la nuit et le jour" (39). The timbre in this case comes not at the beginning but at the end (in a few cases it comes in the middle); Lesage incorporates its words into his verse (Ex. 5). Putting the point at the end, in the most memorable musical phrase, parallels Lesage's frequent epigrammatic constructions. The tune in this case offers another specimen of the odd phrase struc-

Example 5. Air: "Faire l'amour la nuit et le jour"

ture peculiar to the branle de Poitou and certain early menuets, and there is some reason to believe that these dances had amorous connotations.[10] Given a new lease on life, Harlequin takes a liking to a female slave who has been brought to him. She is Greek (giving Lesage a chance to use more pidgin Greek), and more of his class than La Favorite. But before the dalliance proceeds very far the Grand Vizir and his priests appear. Informed of his imminent sacrifice, Harlequin laments and addresses his tears: "Coulez, hâtez vous de couler"—a silly line that Lesage duly annotated as coming from *Callirhoé* (by Destouches), which was then playing at the Opéra.

The climactic scene in the temple offered further opportunities to spoof the Opéra. Mezzetin as High Priestess is supposed to sacrifice Harlequin; only gradually does she (he) come to recognize his identity. The situation is the same, although Lesage does not say so here, as the recognition scene between Orestes and Iphigenia in *Iphigénie en Tauride* by Desmarets and Campra, put on at the Opéra in 1704 and revived in 1711. Both Mezzetin's and Harlequin's speeches are sung to "Folies d'Espagne," used before at the mock-altar of the table.

MEZZETIN

Dans quel climat avez-vous pris naissance?
Jeune Etranger, parlez, dites-le nous.
Je veux ici prendre votre défense,
Et vous sauver moi-même de mes coups.

ARLEQUIN

Vous demandez le nom de ma patrie,
Je vais parler avec sincerité.
C'est à Bergame, hélas! en Italie
Qu'une Tripière en ses flancs m'a porté.

Mezzetin recognizes Harlequin, as does Pierrot, after Harlequin sings a lament to "Monsieur Lapalisse est mort" (77), the main "tragic" tune of the vaudeville repertory. Its timbre refers to the death of the Chevalier de La Palisse at the battle of Pavia in 1525. The piece should be intoned in a slow and dirgelike way, i.e. without dance connotations (Ex. 6). At the last words, "Recognize him by his tears, even more by his trousers," Harlequin must show the motley he wears under the sacrificial robe (see Plate 2).

The comedy is brought to a quick conclusion as the three scoundrels

---

[10]D. Heartz, "The Chanson in the Humanist Era," *Current Thought in Musicology*, ed. John W. Grubbs (Austin, 1976), 202–3. The pattern turns up often in the romance, which is amorous by definition; see D. Heartz, "The Beginnings of the Operatic Romance: Rousseau, Sedaine, and Monsigny," *Eighteenth-Century Studies*, 15 (1981–82), 149–78.

Example 6. Air: "Monsieur Lapalisse est mort"

C'est lui, (plai- gnez ses mal- heurs) C'est lui que le sort ba-

lot- te. Re- con- nai- sez— le̯ à ses pleurs, En-core plus à sa cu- lot- te.

embrace, steal what they can from the temple, and depart for Paris. Mezzetin is given an air (Ex. 7) appropriate for happy conclusions, as is apparent from its one-word timbre "Joconde" (13). Its square cut (4 × 4/4) suggests dance, and its peculiar upbeat structure corresponds with the famous rigaudon in Lully's *Acis et Galatée*.[11] Harlequin rejoins with "Lon lan-la, derirette" (52), a lively triple-meter piece notated in the same key of G, providing a kind of after-dance to "Joconde" and saying little more, with its nonsense syllables, than that the show is over.[12]

Arlequin Roi de Sérendib embraces a wide spectrum of humor from the broadest kind of slapstick farce, through the ambiguous—as in the

Example 7. Air: "Joconde"

J'ai fait pré- pa- rer un vais- seau, Pour nous sau- ver en Fran- ce.

Le jour a per- du son flam- beau, Par- tons en di- li- gen-

-ce. Que nous al- lons boi- re̯ à Pa- ris De fla- cons de Cham-pa- gne.

[11]Quoted in the article "Rigaudon" in *MGG*, XI, p. 506.

[12]Is it mere coincidence that the first airs in Act I are also noted in G? The tunes could be transposed, of course, in performance, but there were advantages to keeping them at their traditional pitches, which best suited the compass of untrained voices. Since they were accompanied by a small orchestra, and scores were used, transposition would be an inconvenience. There is the matter of long ingrained habit as well. Tunes in the appendices of the *Théâtre de la foire* were modified in rhythm to accommodate particular textual demands, but they never were changed in pitch. If "Reveillez-vous belle endormie" always appears in G, and nowhere else—like its related melody, "God save our gracious King (Queen)," which is always sung in G—it is because people demanded and expected to sing it there from the first notes of the orchestra, just as they do today with the national anthem. Even after the public stopped singing the tunes, I believe that the pitch remained an important element in getting the audience to recognize the tune and timbre.

questions of gender—to a fairly sophisticated parody. Looked at another way, it has something to offer to both the sophisticated public in their expensive loges and the more numerous groundlings in the pit. Lesage calls on a wide spectrum of vaudeville types as well, and many of them display the characteristics of traditional dances going back a couple of centuries.

LES COUPLETS EN PROCES

Lesage continued to be the leading poet of the fair theaters during the two decades after his first vaudeville comedies. There emerged at the same time two successful younger poets to rival him, in the persons of Piron and Pannard. Whereas Lesage and his collaborators remained faithful to the traditional airs when constructing his comedies, and admitted only a few new or newly fashionable airs, the younger writers sought more musical novelty. Little by little, the newer airs gained prominence, to the point where they began to dispossess the "fredons," as the old tunes were called. The struggle furnished Lesage the subject of the prologue *Les Couplets en procès*, which also bears Dorneval's name as a collaborator. It was written for the Foire St. Germain in 1729, given again at the Foire St. Laurent the following year, and printed in Volume VII of *Le Théâtre de la foire* (Paris, 1731). Only a portion of the required tunes are printed in the appendix to Volume VII, and the source of the others in the previous volumes is not indicated; but I have identified them, citing the volume by a Roman numeral, and the air by number, in parentheses. The shorter length of this one-act prologue enables us to describe all the tunes actually sung (as opposed to those merely cited in the text), at least to the extent of their key and meter.

Turning the art of vaudeville comedy inward upon itself for subject matter produced not only a charming work but also a most instructive one. The characters include judges, lawyers, and the two quarreling parties. The old airs are led by Flon Flon, who is dressed "en vieux Grivois" ("as an old smut-monger") and La Comère Voire, dressed "en Harangère" ("as a fishwife"); they are described in the list of characters as "Vieux Couplets Chantans." "Flon, flon, larira, dondaine" (I, 118) is a simple old air in G, structured like a branle double of the gavotte type and showing its age by being restricted entirely to the tonic and the three steps above it. The timbre comes near the end of the tune, as is true of many of the older airs. "Oüida, ma Comère" (I, 168) shares the same rhythmic structure but vacillates tonally between G and e. Six airs make up the "Vieux Couplets Dansans." They are: "Le Mitron de Gonesse" (I, 112); "Marotte Mignonne" (III, 153); "Pierre Bagnolet" (I,

86); "La belle Diguedon" (IV, 82); "Le Traquenard" (III, 149); and "Grisellidis" (I, 92).

How old are these "old couplets"? "Le Mitron de Gonesse" deploys the rhythmic pattern of the branle gay, and, like so many dances of this type from around 1500 on, it is in the key of G and restricted in range. Gonesse was a village near Paris famous for its bread; "mitron" means "journeyman baker." Features of the branle family are prominent in the other couplets as well. "Pierre Bagnolet," for example, has melodic traits in common with certain branles de Bourgogne of the midsixteenth century (Exs. 8a–c). All three tunes are structured like the gavotte and play melodically around the third degree, but eventually climb to the fifth and sixth degrees in their second strains. The little repeated eighth-note figure bracketed in "Pierre Bagnolet" recalls a

Example 8a. Air: "Pierr' Bagnolet"

Example 8b. Bransle XII de Bourgogne

Example 8c. Bransle III de Bourgogne

similar recurring figure in Claudin de Sermisy's well-known setting of
Clément Marot's chanson "Tant que vivray."[13]

The first décor represents a street, probably a painted drop curtain
near the front of the stage. Flon Flon and La Comère Voire enter, search-
ing for a lawyer, whom they find in M. Grossel ("Big salt"). He opens the
first vaudeville with the line "Que demandez-vous vieux Soldats?" It is
sung to "Mon père, je viens devant vous" (I, 10), which is a branle gay
type in g. La Comère Voire identifies herself and her companion in the
next air, "Je ne suis né, ni Roi, ni Prince" (I, 15), another branle gay type,
this one in D:

Nous sommes de vieux Vaudevilles
A la critique fort utiles,
Et qui sont en très-grand renom
Depuis fort long-tems à la Foire . . .

In spoken dialogue Flon Flon explains that they and all the other old
Airs du Pont Neuf insist upon their rights to deliver the goods at the
Opéra Comique. And who questions your rights? asks Grossel. La
Comère Voire responds:

C'est toute la maudite Engeance
	Des Airs Nouveaux:
C'est le *Menuet*, la *Contre-danse*
	Quelques *Rondeaux*,
Le *Tambourin*, le *Rigaudon*,
La *Musette*, & le *Cotillon*.

Of the six dances named, Le Menuet and La Musette will later appear as
"Couplets Nouveaux chantans et dansans," the others as "Couplets
nouveaux Dansans" (except that Le Rigaudon, which was needed for
purposes of rhyme and meter here, is replaced by La Loure). The scorn
and malice with which La Comère Voire sings about the newcomers is
conveyed by the timbre, "Grimaudin" (I, 54). It is a simple triple-meter
tune in D, but in fact harbors an obscenity, as may be gathered from the
following verse, directed to "La Florence, danseuse de l'Opéra, à Paris,
1697":[14]

[13]First printed by Pierre Attaingnant in *Chansons nouvelles en musique* (Paris,
1528). The repeated ascending thirds in eighth notes in the second strain of the vaudeville "Quand la Mer-rouge apparut" (V, 91) are inherited from a sixteenth-century
chanson "Au joly bois," in which these notes were associated with the words "Baisez-
moi tant tant." For the chanson melody see D. Heartz, "Les Goûts réunis or the Worlds
of the Madrigal and the Chanson confronted," *Chanson and Madrigal 1480–1530*, ed.
James Haar (Cambridge, Mass., 1964), p. 100, note 18, and Example 34.

[14]Paul Lacroix, *Notes et documents sur l'histoire des théâtres de Paris au xviie siècle* (Paris, 1880), p. 103.

La Florence est jeune et jolie.
  Je voudrois bien
Pour contenter mon envie:
  Soir et matin
Loger mon petit Grimaudin
Dans son château de Gaillardin.

La Comère Voire continues in spoken prose, saying that the rascals wish to throw them out of a shop they had occupied for twenty years. Flon Flon explains further that their adversaries have already gone to get an expulsion order. The thought irks him so much that he sings an angry air about settling the dispute with the blows of a club, which seem to be described by the timbre, cited at the end of his song: "Hé flon, flon! . . ." Grossel restrains Flon Flon. He boasts of his long experience as an orator and actor, of his stentorian lungs and his command of rhetoric, in "Lucas se plaint que sa Femme" (VII, 162), an air in G mixing duple and triple meters. Grossel seems on the point of becoming a caricature of the lawyer as a pompous old fool; the next air (Ex. 9), sung to "En tapinois, quand les nuits sont brunes" (VII, 163) makes him even more ridiculous. He will succeed, or else consent to be treated like an ass. The leaps at the beginning suggestively convey the braying of the very animal in question. Grossel's proposal that the new airs be condemned to remain in balls and concerts indicates their main origins. The most famous of the new tunes was the contredanse "Cotillon" (alias "Ma Comère quand je danse" [I, 140], and it emerged in the ballrooms around 1705.[15]

Example 9. Air: "En tapinois, quand les nuits sont brunes"

Scene 2 brings the troupe of "Vieux Couplets dansans" on stage. Each is introduced in turn in a dialogue between Grossel and La Comère Voire (Ex. 10), sung to "Les Cordons-bleus" (VII, 164). Some manipulation is needed to make the text and music agree, which is unusual

---

[15]It is exemplified in music and steps as "Branle. Le Cotillon. Danse à quatre" in R. A. Feuillet, *Quatrième recueil de danses de bal* (Paris, 1705); the relevant page is given in facsimile by Jean-Michel Guilcher, *La Contredanse et les renouvellements de la danse française* (Paris and The Hague, 1969), p. 76.

Example 10a. Air: "Les Cordons-bleus"

with Lesage—the more so when the air is printed in the same volume. Once again the rhythmic structure is that of the branle double, gavotte type. There is a little dance, in the same key of C and with the same ending at the first cadence, in *Le Balet comique de la Royne* (1581), entitled "Le son de la clochette" (Ex. 10b). More modest and square-cut than most of the music in that courtly ballet, "Le son de la clochette" may have already been old when printed in 1582; in its context it impresses listeners as a borrowing from popular dance music. At the end of Scene 2, Grossel boasts of his rare eloquence to the possibly ironic timbre "Je suis malheureuse en Amant" (VII, 165), set as a 6/8 air in the key of a. Then he leads the old airs off stage as they all sing "Allons à l'Audiance" to the air "Allons à la Guinguette, allons" (V, 125). ("Guinguette" refers to a small suburban tavern.) The air is short, only four bars in 2/2, and little more than a descending scale in G.

Example 10b. "Le son de la Clochette"

Scene 3 introduces the new couplets and their lawyer, M. Gouffin ("fine taste"). Gouffin begins with a 6/8 air in G, "Philis, en cherchant son Amant" (VII, 101), telling "Seigneur Menuet" that he understands their cause fully and will give them satisfaction. The tune lacks any salient characteristics, and is perhaps for this reason chosen as a foil for the stunning reply of Menuet, sung to "Qu'elle est belle?" (VII, 166). "Balance, novelty, beauty, gaiety, and lightness" are not only extolled by Le Menuet, but embodied by this menuet, and by its verse as well, providing an exemplary case of matching style and content. The tune (Ex. 11), made up of two eight-bar strains, is more triadic and tonal than most. Its broadly conceived outlines and elegance of detail set it quite apart from the old airs; so does its consciously strong harmonic basis, which is evident from the small number of common chords—scarcely exceeding I, V, and V⁷—needed to support it.

Example 11. Air: "Qu'elle est belle?"

The menuet represented the epitome of eighteenth-century ideals of beautiful movement. Hogarth drew its floor patterns and motions in his *Analysis of beauty* (1753) to demonstrate grace of line. With this he contrasted the jerky and more primitive motions characteristic of the country dance—equivalent to the French branles and the older airs of the vaudeville repertory. The movement patterns of the country dance are represented in the top panel of Plate 3, the smoother lines of the menuet in panels 123 and 122.

La Musette follows Le Menuet. She proposes sending the old airs back where they came from, singing to a catchy 3/8 air in G, "Et pourquoi donc dessus l'herbette" (VII, 19):

Fi donc! fi donc! sur notre Scene
Pourquoi souffrir des Airs si vieux?
Le Public les trouve ennuyeux,
   Ils donnent la migraine.
Renvoyez-les au nom des Dieux,
   A la Samaritaine.

Plate 3. Floor patterns of dances from Hogarth, *Analysis of Beauty* (1753)

The last word designated a pump house in the Seine at the north end of the Pont Neuf, and thus referred to the old airs' origins as Pont Neufs.

In Scene 4 it is the turn of the Nouveaux Couplets dansans to make their appearance, which they do as La Musette describes in her air "Les Sept sauts" (VII, 167). It is one of the older airs and had appeared in earlier volumes, but was included in Volume VII in a form specially adapted to the text used here (Ex. 12a). Instead of the usual "seven leaps" at the end, as the timbre indicates, there are only three. Leaps of a fifth as in this ending are not a new thing in French dance music; Ex. 12b, a branle de Bourgogne of the mid-sixteenth century, provides a good comparison. It is possible that the suggestion of braying derision attached to Ex. 9 above pertained to other occurrences of the figure as well. Gouffin addresses the newcomers and promises them that the old couplets, of which he names four, will be banished for good. He sings to "Je vais toujours le même train" (VII, 168), another air in G; it is in 3/8 time and has the characteristics of a fanfare. An epigrammatic twist at the end of the verse suggests less than perfect confidence in the new airs on the part of the authors:

> Suivez moi tous. Je vous promets
> De vous renvoyer satisfaits.
> Sur votre Scene pour jamais
>   Vous régnerez en paix.
> Plus de *Lampons*, de *Triolets*,
> De *Zons-zons*, de *Branles de Mets*.
> Amis enfin je vais

Example 12a. Air: "Les sept sauts"

Example 12b. 8ᵉ Branle de Bourgogne

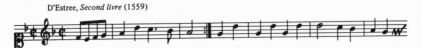

Banir les vieux Couplets.[16]
Et vous n'aurez plus désormais
Rien à craindre que les sifflets.

Exit Gouffin and the Nouveaux Couplets dansans, leaving Le Menuet and La Musette to do the short Scene 5, consisting of one vaudeville. Le Menuet sings the praises of Gouffin to "Il étoit un Avocat" (VII, 120), an attractive gavotte in C, and they too dance off, singing the refrain. We are at the midpoint of the show; and, assuming that the airs were sung at the pitches notated in the *Théâtre de la foire* volumes, the several airs in G in Scenes 3 and 4 have prepared for Scene 5 as if they were in a dominant-to-tonic relationship.

Having emptied the stage, the authors can change the scene, which they do. The curtain lifts to reveal several magistrates, with Mount Parnassus and a winged Pegasus in the background; this is the scene illustrated in the title vignette engraved by Demarne (Plate 4). Le Bazoche du Parnasse, i.e. the Court of Apollo and the Muses, first hears a plea from an unnamed poet (Piron) who claims his tragedy *Calisthène* was unjustly sentenced by the parterre (at the Comédie Française).[17] He is represented by M. Babillary ("prattler"), who sings to the ancient air we have encountered above, "Reveillez-vous, belle Endormie" (I, 1). The presiding judge responds that he has full knowledge concerning the good taste of the parterre, and thus denies the appeal. He sings this to a short gavotte-like air in G, described as "de la *Ceinture,*" meaning the Vaudeville finale composed by Jean-Claude Gillier for Lesage's *La Ceinture de Vénus* of 1715 (I, 69). The choice thus underscored Lesage's success, to the further detriment of Piron.

The recorder next announces the case of the new airs versus the old. Gouffin and Grossel step forward, as pictured in the illustration. Gouffin begins, claiming that the old couplets are not only boring to the public but are also an affront to decency (which indeed many of them were). This is sung to "de l'Horoscope accompli" (VII, 124), a

---

[16]The old couplets mentioned by name display some noteworthy features: "Lampons" (I, 64) has a second strain that begins like "Yankee Doodle"; "Triolets" (III, 181) wavers between 6/8 and 3/4 like a gaillarde, and in fact closely parallels the entire sixteenth-century gaillarde melody known in France as "Puisque vivre en servitude," about which see D. Heartz, "Voix de ville: Between Humanist Ideals and Musical Realities," *Words and Music: the Scholar's View. A Medley of Problems and Solutions Compiled in Honor of A. Tillman Merritt,* ed. Laurence Berman (Cambridge, Mass., 1972), p. 121.

[17]*Calisthène* opened on February 18, 1730, the same day as the successful opéra comique *La Reine du Barostan* by Lesage and Dorneval, which "killed" the tragedy according to Henri Lagrave, *Le Théâtre et le public à Paris de 1715 à 1750* (Paris, 1972), p. 401, note 84.

Plate 4. Title vignette from *Les Couplets en Proces* engraved by Demarne in Vol. VII of *Le Théâtre de la foire* (1731)

lengthy 3/4 tune in g of a menuet character, with strains of eight and sixteen bars which in truth are rather boring. Grossel replies by asking his adversary to be more delicate because "je suis un avocat"—a line recalling the timbre "Il étoit un Avocat" in the previous scene. He sings this to "Je ferai mon devoir," which is not present in the ten volumes of the *Théâtre de la foire* but may be found in Favart's *Cythère assiegée* (Brussels, 1748), No. 227.

The exchanges between the two lawyers become more heated. Gouffin asks Grossel not to interrupt him because he pleads in good faith; his tune, "Robin, turelure lure" (I, 47), is an old air in G alternating duple and triple meter. The timbre, which comes at the end, is sung by Grossel, who conveys something equivalent to the English expression "poppycock." Gouffin argues that the new airs have revived opéra comique; if the old ones were replaced altogether, it would be in even better shape. He sings his response to "Quand on a prononcé ce malheureux oui" (IV, 58), an attractive 2/2 air in g; its single upbeat and its downward leaps are characteristic of the bourée. Grossel, coughing and spitting as the stage directions specify, rejoins with another catalogue of old airs, including such frequently used ones as "Allons-gay" and "Ramonez-ci ramonez-là." His gavotte-like air in g, "N'aurai-je jamais un Amant?" (VII, 169), ends with the lines "Et tout le reste/Des gaillards Couplets,/Faits/Pour rendre les coeurs gais." "Gaillard" means "lusty" as well as "cheerful," and it is the libertine meaning that Gouffin seizes, interrupting Grossel to insist that indeed the old airs are all too lusty. The new airs were received as brothers but have now turned into vipers, claims Grossel, singing to "Or écoutez petits & Grands" (I, 78), a branle simple type in D. Furthermore, they pretend to be sufficient for all and worth all our airs, he continues in "Oüistan-voire" (VII, 170), an air in G that begins with the same upbeat pattern as "Joconde" (Ex. 7). The timbre appears in the middle of the verse, where Grossel has worked up to his main point: the utility of the old airs as against the new ones in expressing the drama.

The new airs, asserts Grossel, are only good in opéra comique for relaxing the mind from the attention given to the old airs, which are charged with the essential task: the important mission of expressing the passions. *"Hoc opus, hic labor est."* (Grossel often includes a Latin tag to enhance his point, as in this quotation from Vergil.) Gouffin takes vigorous exception to this view, claiming that the new airs can express the passions equally well when they so choose. He thus provokes the climactic speech of Grossel, in which it is difficult to mistake the practice of Lesage himself.

> I defy you, Master Gouffin, on this point. Can a *Menuet* or a *Contredanse* expose a subject? Which of your new couplets is as apt to tell a tale as *Le Cap de Bonne Espérance?* [He sings the beginning, which he also does for

the three following airs as he cites them.] And the old *Joconde!* To express joy have you the equivalent of *Allons-gai, Toujours-gai, D'un-air gai!* How would you paint desolation if you did not have the Air *Lapalisse! Et sic de coeteris.*

Gouffin responds to this declaration by saying we have a hundred couplets to express joy; and as for sad airs, when they are needed the grand Opéra will furnish them. He sings his retort to the menuet from *Les Fêtes grecques et romaines* by Collin de Blamont, first put on at the Opéra in 1723; the air (VII, 171) is in G, and bears similarities to the song sung by Le Menuet (Ex. 11). Mark his words well, admonishes Grossel, and imagine the consequences. We already have all the little geese ("Petite-oye") of the Opéra: *"Venienti occurrite morbo!"* ("Flee the approaching disease!") If you do not put your affairs in order, the Opéra's recitative will come plant its stake in our territory!

Grossel concludes his case for the old airs with an admonition to let them live out their lives with peace and honor, sung to "Les Folies d'Espagne" (I, 16). The dialogue then shifts to speech. Grossel says to remember that we are the founders of opéra comique. We are the restorers of it, exlaims Gouffin. We shall see if the court will favor traitors, says Grossel, to which Gouffin replies that it was the old airs that were disloyal by serving the Italian comedians in their parodies. But do not couplets from the Italian troupe sometimes come to us in exchange? Do not confound gratitude with treason, says Grossel. The last exchange between the two lawyers before the pronouncement of sentence is a vaudeville in dialogue, sung to "Hé, bon, bon, bon! Je t'en répond" (VII, 58; Ex. 13), which has some features of the famous cotillon

Example 13. Air: "Hé, bon, bon, bon! Je t'en repond"

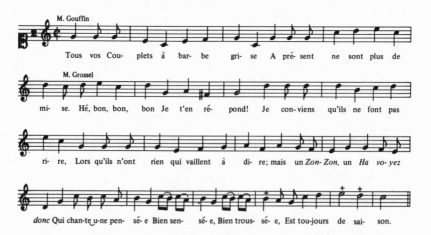

from Mouret's *Les Fêtes de Thalie* (1714). Lesage had first used this air in his parody of *Télémaque* in 1715 (I, 141); he was not one loath to take quick advantage of a really good tune.

The sentence, as might be expected, consigned the old and new couplets to live together in peace. Each is valuable if well positioned—a conclusion worthy of summing up Lesage's long career at the fair theaters.

> A bien vivre avec leurs Rivaux
> Nous condamnons les Airs Nouveaux.
> Les Couplets, tant Jeunes qu'Antiques,
> Les Grands ainsi que les Petits,
> Tendres, Gaillards ou Flegmatiques,
> Chacun bien placé vaut son prix.

The presiding judge sings this to an appropriate timbre, "Voulez-vous sçavoir qui des deux" (I, 14), a triple-meter tune in D. When Gouffin protests such a mélange, the judge insists that the old couplets must remain, but a wise author should guard against their too frequent use; he sings this advice to "Vous qui vous moquez par vos ris" (I, 55), also in triple meter, but in d. Even a "Flon Flon" can be used without giving offense, if it is covered with a certain "je ne sçai-quoi," he sings to "Un certain je ne sçai quoi" (VII, 69), a 6/8 air in a. Grossel issues a final warning: if you new couplets chase out your papas you will soon shut up shop. His air, triple meter in C, is sung to "Vive Michel Nostradamus" (VII, 104), which is Gillier's vaudeville finale for Lesage's *Tombeau de Nostradamus* (1714). The judge dismisses the parties with the last two lines of the previous vaudeville, and then starts up another air, "Toque mon Tambourinet" (I, 172):

> Qu'ici chacun danse,
> Puisque tout Couplet
> Doit de la Sentence
> Etre satisfait:
> Toque le Tambourin, toque,
> Toque le Tambourinet.

The refrain, repeated in chorus (Ex. 14), is all that survives in the *Théâtre de la foire* volumes. Other music is necessary to clothe the shorter lines 1–4. For all its brevity, the refrain demonstrates yet again how en-

Example 14. Air: "Toque mon Tambourinet"

To- que le Tam- bou-rin, to- que, To- que le Tam-bou- ri- net.

demic was the three-bar phrase in triple meter. Inherited from the bran-le de Poitou, this curious Gallic pattern persisted here and there throughout the eighteenth century. Who is to say whether some of the old dances that Mozart heard in France did not, at some unconscious level, help form the strange three-bar phrases of the minuetto in his pe-nultimate symphony?

Les Couplets en procès ends with general dancing. The stage direc-tions are explicit, as is characteristic for Lesage, perhaps because when he began writing for the fair theaters much of the story had to be told in pantomime. All the couplets, old and new alike, dance alone and in pairs, each according to his character. Then they all unite and finish the divertissement with a *Balet général*. It says something about the vital-ity of the work that thirty years later Favart, the greatest poet of vaude-ville comedy after Lesage, could model one of his own works, *Le Procès des ariettes* (1760), very closely on *Les Couplets en procès*. Without the vaudeville comedies of Lesage to stand upon, in the most general sense, there could have been no Favart.

Had not Lesage fled the Comédie Française for the fairs, there would be no vaudeville comedy as we know it. He created it almost at a single stroke with the wickedly funny *Arlequin Roi de Sérendib*. Thanks to him an old Gallic strain of humor, of song and dance in particular, con-tinued to flourish. The advantages of using old airs in a form of comedy that depended on audience recognition and association were evident to Lesage. Yet he did not slight some of the most beautiful recent crea-tions inspired by Terpischore.

The *Balagany* in *Petrushka*

ROLAND JOHN WILEY

ASK A STUDENT OF BALLET WHAT "balagan" means, and the answer (if one is forthcoming) will probably be a description of the setting of *Petrushka*. To the extent that the first and fourth scenes of this ballet were inspired in part by the *balagany* of the Shrovetide carnival in St. Petersburg, such a response would have merit, though a Slavist might find it wanting in awareness—of the connotations of "balagan" and the place of *balagany* in Russian thought. In this case the Slavist's complaints are not the mere quibbles of a specialist: understanding the word and the object it denotes will clarify our perception of what Diaghilev and his collaborators were doing.

Etymologists believe that "balagan" came into Russian from Turkish, in which it means "wooden structure or building," and that the word originated in the Persian bālāḥānä or "balcony" (made up of bālā, "high," and ḥānä, "home").[1] The use of "balagan" in Russian is found as early as 1672–73 in one source of the vibrant *Life of Archpriest Avvakum, Written by Himself:* after the intrepid cleric dragged a sledge through the Siberian winter, he set up camp near his persecutor Pashkov and constructed a small *balagan* in which to live.[2] In addition to dwellings, *balagany* were used for storehouses and places of trade and manufacture.

In time "balagan" came to be associated with theatrical entertainments, especially those attended by the commonfolk at fairs, "a temporary building (constructed in the open air) for theatrical performances of the masses, with a little square for the appearance of clowns, comic scenes, etc., to the accompaniment of simple music."[3] (See Plates 1 and

---

[1]On the history of "balagan," see N. M. Shanskii, *Etimologicheskii slovar' russkogo yazyka*, I, 18–19; D. N. Ushakov, ed., *Tolkovyi slovar' russkogo yazyka*, vol. I, col. 80; Vladimir Dal', *Tolkovyi slovar' zhivogo velikorusskogo yazyka*, 3rd. ed., vol. I, col. 104.

[2]N. K. Gudzii, ed., *Zhitie protopopa Avvakuma im samim napisannoe i drugie ego sochineniya* (Moscow, 1960), pp. 73–74, fn. 1.

[3]Academy of Sciences of the USSR, *Slovar' sovremennogo russkogo literaturnogo yazyka*, 17 vols. (1950–1965), I, col. 251. See also the discussion of "balagan" in Aleksei

Plate 1. Swings and *balagany* (from an engraving by John Atkinson)

2.) By the time Alexandre Benois came to write about the *balagany* in St. Petersburg, "balagan" referred not just to the wooden structures, but to the entire fairground, the midway. In this meaning the word could have connotations of coarseness, primitiveness, and bad taste. Thus Konstantine Skalkovsky criticized the first production of *Sleeping Beauty*, which he found to be inordinately lavish and lacking in dramatic values, by calling it a large *balagan*, and pointing out that such spectacles do not attract educated adherents.[4] "Balaganit'," a verb derived from "balagan," also has pejorative connotations: to behave in an affected manner, to play the fool, to behave foolishly.

The first *balagan* used for theatrical spectacles was constructed in Moscow in 1702.[5] It was operated (folklorists speculate) by *skomorokhi*, Slavic counterparts to Western jongleurs, minstrels, and *Spielmänner*. These entertainers in the popular tradition

> . . . became puppeteers, who showed the famous "Petrushka," or leaders of "learned" bears; they entertained the public with a humorous and sometimes sharp, satirical word. At fairs they took jobs as callers at the carousels and the *balagany*; one could see them in the *balagany* themselves, acting out short satirical and comic scenes.[6]

Soviet folklorist Nina Savushkina points out that "the Petrushka

---

Yakovlevich Alekseev-Yakovlev, *Russkie narodnye gulyan'ya po rasskazam A. Ya. Alekseeva-Yakovleva v zapisi i obrabotke Evg. Kuznetsova* (Moscow and Leningrad, 1948), pp. 86–87. In a footnote to these pages, the editor points out that until the second half or even the last third of the nineteenth century, the pre-eminent connotations of "balagan" were of a building that was temporary and collapsible. The building's function was not an issue until the 1880s; by then the word was associated almost exclusively with theatrical performances.

"Balagan" continued to be a versatile word in Russian after the *balagany* as here described had disappeared from St. Petersburg. In 1907 Andrei Belyi referred to the cinema as "the democratic theater of the future, a *balagan* in the noble and elevated sense of this word" (*Arabeski* [Moscow, 1911], p. 351). And as recently as September of 1982 an advertisement in a Russian-language newspaper published in New York City could exhort taxicab drivers to stop at a kiosk at Broadway and 42nd Street and to purchase a new stereophonic recording, "In the Noisy Balagan," the title no doubt a reference to the city (*Novoe russkoe slovo*, September 9, 1982, p. 8).

[4]"Theater and Music," *Novoe vremya*, January 5, 1890, p. 3. "In the [*balagany*] performances most of the attention is paid to crude effects, namely beating the bass drum, gunshots, Bengal Lights, etc. . . . The very concept of 'balagan-like' became an adjective for something 'coarse' and 'raucous' " (F. A. Brokgaus [= Friedrich Arnold Brockhaus] and I. A. Efron, *Entsiklopedicheskii slovar'*, vol. IIA, 781).

[5]According to the compilers of the dictionary published by the Academy of Sciences of the USSR, cited above in fn. 3. Brockhaus and Efron state that in 1700 Peter the Great ordered a "large hall of comedy," made of wood, to be constructed on Red Square; ready by December 25, 1702, it was staffed by German actors recruited from abroad (*Entsiklopedicheskii slovar'*, vol. IIA, p. 781).

[6]Anatolii Alekseevich Belkin, *Russkie skomorokhi* (Moscow, 1975), p. 109.

Plate 2. The *ded* (caller) of a *balagan* (from *Vsemirnaya illustratsiya*, 14 Feb. 1881)

performances were the art of the cities and their environs and suburban villages, especially Petersburg and its surroundings." "The *balagan* and the peepshow were the absolute property of the city festivals," she continues a few pages later, describing a typical setting:

> The *gulyan'ya* [popular festivals celebrated in the open air], like the fairs, coincided with holidays (Shrovetide, Easter, etc.).[7] Besides

[7]Normally the *balagany* were put up for the Shrovetide fair, taken down for Lent, and put up again six and one-half weeks later, in anticipation of Bright Week, on exactly the same sites (*Russkie narodnye gulyan'ya*, p. 50). "In the last decade [report

balagany—temporary buildings made of planking, with a canvas roof with flags on it—swings [similar to Ferris wheels] and carousels were constructed on the squares. On the program of *balagany* performances were circus numbers (jugglers, tightrope walkers), the exhibition of all kinds of "wonders" (mermaids, dwarfs, giants, strongmen, monsters), and pantomimes on subjects of a popular cast ("The Battle of the Russians with the Kabardinians"), songs, dances. . . . The urgings of the *balagan's dedy*, the callers, constituted the principal dramatic genre which determined the success of the entire show. They were given out before the beginning of a performance in a special little balcony built onto the *balagan*. Rather, they were not spoken but acted out. One *ded*, turning directly to the public—or two, a caller and a hustler—attract the spectators by leading a dialogue. . . . And next to them the *dedy* from the carousels and swings were performing, advertising their enterprises. The whole holiday atmosphere of the festival was infused with the carnival mood of the people, with its freedom and familiarity, with jokes aimed in equal measure at oneself and at those around one. In the urgings of the *dedy* of the *balagany* and the swings there was much improvisation on the most varied and often topical themes. . . . The *dedy* were able to use simple but colorful theatrical costume and makeup. They normally came out in a caftan, bast sandals, with a beard and moustache of oakum, and a pasted-on nose. Supplementing their colorful discourse with humorous gesticulations and movements of the body, they either talked about themselves or "bullied" someone in the public.[8]

The offerings of the fairs changed in the last half of the nineteenth century as competition among the entrepreneurs intensified. The pre-eminently funloving, perhaps debauched festivities were leavened by attractions of greater cultural pretensions. With the 1880s, Alexandre Benois noted, a period of *kvass* nationalism began [that is, a time characterized by admiration of traditional (sometimes backward) aspects of the national heritage], and

> . . . in the *balagany* theaters this change was very marked. The light-hearted, diverting pantomimes and harlequinades disappeared, but to make up for them the cumbersome Gromoboi, Bova-Korolevich, and Ilya Muromets [heroes of Russian legend] reigned; melodramas from the history of the homeland started booming forth and droning on; dramati-

---

Brockhaus and Efron in 1891], *balagany* are always built in January, remain dismantled until 15 May (the coronation day of Emperor Alexander III, who reigns in God's grace), after which the place must be cleared, but performances in the *balagany* are given only during the weeks of Easter and Shrovetide and on 15 May" (*Entsiklopedicheskii slovar'*, vol. IIA, p. 781.

[8]Nina Ivanovna Savushkina, *Russkii narodnyi teatr* (Moscow, 1976), pp. 126, 129–31. Alekseev-Yakovlev, who operated a "temporary theater of the people," pointed out that the made-up *ded* was often an expedient forced on the proprietors of the *balagany* by the shortage of "true masters of the craft" (*Russkie narodnye gulyan'ya*, p. 63).

zations of Pushkin and Lermontov came into fashion which profaned the originals. Other theaters, catering to the fashion of the times, began to be called "Amusement and Benefit" or "Enlightenment and Amusement." And already the spirit of pedagogy, the guardianship of mores, the wish to replace the primitive, more sincere people's art with some kind of surrogate of a more *recherché* order, breathed in everything.[9]

When the Director of the Imperial Theaters relinquished the state's monopoly on theatrical performances in the capitals—another change dating from the 1880s—the most important *balagany* were officially renamed "temporary theaters of the people." The new title, which emphasized the departure of leading entrepreneurs from the modest traditions of the fairgrounds, seems to have stimulated the use of "balagan" to refer to theatrical performances that were simple-minded and pretentious at the same time.[10]

As their businesses grew more complex, entrepreneurs vied with one another for the most desirable locations on the fairground. The proprietors of the most prominent theaters enjoyed preferential treatment from civic authorities who assigned the sites; as a result the smaller *balagany*, those in which the Petrushka shows were given, were relegated to a street behind the privileged ones.

Throughout their history the "people's entertainments" had no doubt drawn criticism because standards of public behavior at the fairgrounds during carnival were relaxed. In the 1890s the complaints lodged against them increased, as a result of which the fairs in St. Petersburg were discontinued altogether. Benois associated their downfall with opposition from the Temperance Society;[11] Alekseyev-Yakovlev claimed that the government closed them down, concerned that they might be centers for subversive activity. Whatever the immediate cause, the municipal governor in charge of the Field of Mars, a large parade ground in St. Petersburg where the fairs had been held since 1873,[12] issued a ruling in December 1896 that prohibited the construction of the *balagany* there after Shrovetide the following spring.[13]

[9]Aleksandr Nikolaevich Benua [= Alexandre Benois], "Shrovetide," *Rech'*, February 10, 1917, pp. 2–3.

[10]Alekseyev-Yakovlev, whose book is critical of Tsarist bureaucracy throughout, claimed that the derisive use of "balagan" originated in the belittling of the people's theaters by government officials (*Russkie narodnye gulyan'ya*, p. 86).

[11]See *Aleksandr Benua razmyshlyaet . . .* (Moscow, 1968), p. 182, and Benois's *Moi vospominaniya v pyati knigakh*, 2 vols. (Moscow, 1980), I, 296–97; II, 521.

[12]Before 1872 the *balagany* had been put up in the Admiralty Square, next to the Winter Palace, but a fire that year during Shrovetide destroyed some of the *balagany* and posed a threat to the imperial residence. The fair was moved to the Field of Mars the next year. After 1835, when a fire killed many spectators, *balagany* were required to have aisles of a specified width and a number of emergency doors (*Bol'shaya sovetskaya entsiklopediya*, 2nd ed., vol. IV, p. 100).

[13]*Russkie narodnye gulyan'ya*, p. 100. For a discussion of the negotiations between

The entrepreneurs appealed, but to no avail. And although the government made new locations available and offered to place the people's theaters under the supervision of one of its ministries, the *balagany* soon died out. The Field of Mars was used for the last time during Shrovetide of 1897; and at a new location, the Semenovsky Square, "an unsuitable, remote, unhappy place, uninteresting in its ... architectural surroundings," the St. Petersburg fair was given for the last time in 1898.[14]

Only after we know this much about the *balagany* does their significance in Diaghilev's era become apparent. When they disappeared from the Field of Mars a tradition ended, but images of the *balagany* soon began to stir in the memory of some artists. Benois's essays on the Shrovetide fair are familiar and eloquent proofs of this,[15] as are Alexander Blok's two short poems about *balagany*. In the first, a vignette written in July 1905, a little girl and boy respond to the puppet show of a *balagan:*

Here a little balagan is open
For merry and nice little children,
The little girl and boy
Are watching the ladies, kings and devils.

And the infernal music sounds,
The doleful bow howls.
The frightening devil seized the little guy,
And the cranberry juice trickles down.

The second, written in November of 1906, conveys a profound sadness by means of the image of an uprooted *balagan* in which a harlequinade had played:

Above the black slush of the road
The fog hangs heavy.
The dray cart, groaning,
Hauls my faded balagan.

---

the municipal governor and the entrepreneurs, see "Theater and Music," *Novoe vremya*, March 11, 1897, p. 4.

[14]*Russkie narodnye gulyan'ya*, p. 100. According to the compilers of the *Bol'shaya sovetskaya entsiklopediya*, 3rd ed., vol. II, cols. 1650–1651), *balagany* continued to be used for variety shows [*estradnye divertismenty*] until the 1930s.

[15]The first, "Shrovetide" (cited above, fn. 9) was published at the height of the privations of war in 1917—circumstances that might produce a strong sense of nostalgia— and reprinted, with changes and additions, in *Aleksandr Benua razmyshlyaet . . .*, pp. 176–84; see also his *Zhizn' khudozhnika; vospominaniya*, 2 vols. (New York, 1955), vol. II, 15–29; reprinted in *Moi vospominaniya v pyati knigakh*, vol. I, 289–98. In English see his *Reminiscences of the Russian Ballet*, trans. Mary Britnieva (London, 1941), pp. 26–36; *Memoirs*, trans. Moura Budberg, 2 vols. (London, 1960), I, 112–129.

Harlequin's face in the daylight
Is paler than Pierrot's.
And Columbine hides in the corner,
Rags sewn together in a motley way.

In 1906 Blok also wrote a play, "The Little Balagan" [Balaganchik],
in which he draws on the images of the fairground again, but with very
different purposes.[16] Nostalgia for the Shrovetide festivities is perceived (if at all) only in the transformed stereotypes of the harlequinade,
which return here, juxtaposed with enigmatic mystics and an "author"
whose protestations of everyday normalcy intrude into the larger context of artifice in such a way as to make everyday normalcy seem incongruous. Pierrot pines for Columbine, but the woman whom he sees as
his lover is claimed by the mystics to be the personification of death.

Blok dedicated his play to Vsevolod Meyerhold, who mounted it in a
stark production, set on a stage within a stage where the normally unseen mechanical apparatus responsible for illusion—cables, lights,
scaffolds—made up the decoration.[17]

Whatever the diversity of interpretations they offer, Blok's works
demonstrate the vitality of the *balagan* as a stimulus to artistic creation. In the poems the *balagan* is a reality lovingly recalled; in the play
it is a temporary dwelling of intense, bizarre visions, a setting for exper-
iments in staging and language. The play, moreover, is syncretic in that
Blok reconciles or unites his sensitivity to native traditions—the
balagany—with his perception of the tendencies of the avant garde.

In the summer of 1910, four years after Blok's play was produced,
Alexandre Benois withdrew his services from the Diaghilev enterprise
after the impresario had attributed the story of the ballet *Schéhérazade*
to Léon Bakst in wanton disregard of Benois's authorship. While the
collaborations of the *saisons russes* were often contentious, this break
was especially serious: Benois resolved to stay away permanently, and
Diaghilev, for the moment, was content to let him.[18] (Perhaps the artist's deep-rooted conservatism prompted Diaghilev to precipitate a crisis at this time, sensing that Benois's departure would at some point be
inevitable.) Then, when the impresario heard Stravinsky's new *Kon-
zertstück*, "Petrushka's Cry," along with the Russian Dance intended
as its companion piece, he resolved to use the music for a ballet. He

[16]For the original texts of the poems and the play, see Aleksandr Blok, *Sochineniya v
dvukh tomakh*, vol. I (Moscow, 1955), pp. 146–47, 198, 537–50.

[17]In connection with the significance of the production, see Dzh. Boult [= John E.
Bowlt], "Constructivism and the Stage," *Novyi zhurnal*, No. 126, March 1977, pp.
108–18.

[18]According to Richard Buckle, citing a letter of Stravinsky to Roerich (*Diaghilev*
[London, 1979], p. 173).

effected a rapprochement with Benois, who was put in charge of the scenario and decorations. Who else but Benois, wrote Diaghilev to his old friend, could assist them in creating a ballet about the Petersburg Shrovetide? For the answer we may turn to the painter himself, who wrote more eloquently about the collaboration than any of his colleagues, and in the course of his writings assessed them all.

According to Benois, Diaghilev himself could not be expected to assist in the creation of a ballet. Making artistic contributions had never been his part, but rather, "having believed in us and being the only one among us who did not feel squeamish about business matters, who was not frightened at the thought of rough clashes with people of a different mind, made it his goal to promote the realization of our dreams."[19]

To Benois, Fokine, though born and raised a Petersburger, was more provincial than Diaghilev. A prisoner in the theater school, the choreographer lacked sufficient knowledge and appreciation of the Shrovetide festivities in his own city to produce a scenario. The painter made no attempt to conceal this opinion, which led to an acrimonious exchange in the Petersburg press.[20]

---

[19]*Aleksandr Benua razmyshlyaet . . . ,* p. 506. Benois continues in a later passage (pp. 510–11):
> There was something in Diaghilev's character—an irresistible attraction to the last word—which had been displayed even earlier [that is, when he was still in Petersburg]. That trait assuredly played a role in the fact that for all his education he was nevertheless a provincial, and that, no sooner had he come to Petersburg as an 18-year-old youth and joined a circle of people themselves still young, still a long way from any kind of "completeness of culture" and yet more developed and more experienced in questions of art [than Diaghilev] than he very painfully sensed this *infériorité* of his, and then strove not only to catch up with his friends, but to overtake them. This "running start", this striving to outdistance all, remained after that a characteristic feature of all his later activity; when from the "provinces" of Petersburg he found himself in a true capital, the City of Lights, a concern not to disgrace himself in front of the local savants and arbiters of artistic matters who impressed him, this concern began to take on more and more painful nuances. And then, ever more frequently arguments and disagreements broke out among us.
>
> Personally, I not only loved Seriozha warmly, but also stood in awe of him; I had a feeling toward him which is encountered in a person who lacks certain talents toward a person who possesses them in full measure. In this case business ability, Diaghilev's courage, and his inclination toward sometimes perilous daring were his talents and "advantages"—qualities absolutely lacking in me. But for all my worship of my friend, I did not forgive him his foibles, and most of all among these his inclination toward *mondanité,* toward snobbishness, in which I saw something frightfully unworthy and, at times, just plain pitiful.

[20]"It is necessary to give Fokine his due," wrote Benois in his review of *Petrushka,* though the choreographer had been too distracted by details and "was not successful with typical Russian scenes either. This Petersburger, a student of the theater school, knows the people's merriment more from the tasteless nonsense of *The Hunchbacked*

Stravinsky he did not dismiss so peremptorily. Benois began his discussion of *Petrushka* in the memoirs by taking most of the credit for the
scenario himself, then yielded to the composer:

> My rapture over Stravinsky was so great that I was quite ready to ef-
> face myself out of piety before the unquestionable genius of his music—
> since to him, of course, belonged the very *initiative* of the whole
> undertaking—I "only helped" produce concrete images for the stage. To
> me belonged almost all of the composition of the subject of the ballet,
> the composition and character of the *dramatis personae*, the denoue-
> ment and the development of the action, the majority of the various de-
> tails, but all this seemed to me trifles compared with the music.[21]

Two points emerge from Benois's remarks. First, he seems to belittle
his own contribution to *Petrushka* as a means of expressing his esteem
for Stravinsky. The credits that he takes for himself at the end of the
quotation are hardly trifles. Second, if the composer's own recollections of the Shrovetide fair are any measure,[22] he was not equipped to
supply the information that Benois commanded, which in wealth of detail and graphic vividness is decidedly of a higher order. As a practical
matter, there is no reason to doubt that Stravinsky welcomed this

---

Horse and wares manufactured 'in the Russian style' than from personal experience"
("Art Letter," *Rech'*, August 4, 1911, 2).

"Is it possible to write this way about one's principal collaborator?" an angry and
astonished Fokine retorted, answering Benois's points and going on to declare *Sadko*—
for which Anisfeld, not Benois, painted the decorations—his favorite creation ("With
M. M. Fokine," *Peterburgskaya gazeta*, August 24, 1911, p. 3).

"It is very dangerous for an artist motivated by ambition to think himself capable of
everything to the same degree," answered Benois. "It was clear to me and to many who
worked on *Petrushka* and who saw Fokine that this work was not a pleasure, but something alien to him" ("Art Letter," *Rech'*, 8 Sept. 1911, p. 2).

The two men were reconciled and worked together producing *Petrushka* after leaving Diaghilev. In 1923 Benois came to write about Fokine again, and again expressed
reservations about his superficial education and his level of culture, while maintaining
that the choreographer was a man of exceptional endowments (*Aleksandr Benua razmyshlyaet . . .* , pp. 165–66).

[21]*Moi vospominaniya v pyati knigakh*, vol. II, 527. Benois's willingness to efface
himself was also evident in his review of *Petrushka*:

> On the *affiche* it indicates that I am half-author of the libretto, but in fact my
> participation in its creation (besides production: decorations and costumes) may
> be expressed only in that I helped Stravinsky work out the subject for the stage,
> helped him to illustrate with corresponding actions one or another situation in
> his music. The very thought, initiative, and all the color of the thing, to say
> nothing of the music, belong totally to him ("Art Letter," *Rech'*, August 4, 1911,
> p. 2).

[22]Igor Stravinsky and Robert Craft, *Expositions and Developments* (New York,
1962), p. 35. Stravinsky the musician remembered the sounds of St. Petersburg, Benois
the painter its visual images.

source of lore about the fairgrounds from which to draw the inspiration he needed to convert his concert pieces into a ballet.

This leaves Benois himself, whose nostalgia for the Petersburg fairs stood ready to be tapped:

> As for the personality of Petrushka himself, I immediately felt my own kind of "duty of an old friend" to immortalize him on a real stage. But the idea of representing "Shrovetide," those dear *balagany*—this great delight of my childhood which had been the delight of my father before me—on a real stage tempted me even more. It was especially tempting to erect some kind of monument to the *balagany*, these *balagany* which had already been abolished for some ten years.[23]

If Benois, for whom the past was a matter of such concern,[24] was in charge of *Petrushka*, one wonders why he placed a story that bears so little resemblance to its authentic prototypes in a setting so faithful to life. The scenario of *Petrushka* departs in outline and detail from Benois's own descriptions of the harlequinades and Petrushka shows at the Shrovetide fairs. And the Petrushka of the ballet owes little to the Petrushka of the puppet shows, a first cousin of Til Eulenspiegel who outwits his foes and is mischievous when not aggressive or even bellicose. The conjurer of the ballet is not based on any clearcut historical model (among those which Benois described), and bears a closer resemblance to the Astrologer in *Le Coq d'or* than to the earthy *dedy* of the fairs.

These observations are not criticisms but evidence of a modernizing hand that helped shape the story. It could have been Benois's, but one cannot discount the possibility that Diaghilev—not the genuine creator but the dabbler, the adjuster, the remaker of old things—may have played a part. After only twelve years the Shrovetide fairs were enough of the past to be refurbished, made current: Diaghilev's ballet, like Blok's play, unites popular tradition with avant-garde theater. In both, the popular tradition is represented by the *balagan*. In both, a sense of alienation from society, of the psychological suffering of the individual,

---

[23]*Moi vospominaniya v pyati knigakh*, vol. II, 521.

[24]Reflecting in 1939 on his place in the Diaghilev enterprise, Benois wrote:

In general I am an incorrigible *passé*-ist; I profess the belief that only one thing in the world is actual and real—this is the past. The present is a passing moment, the future simply does not exist, and all attempts to "throw oneself in front of time", to outstrip time, are absurd self-deceptions, worthy only of the most lightminded people, such as the Italian futurists. What remains is the past, the one sphere of our observation, our appreciation, our sympathies and our condemnation. *All* phenomena of the past attract and interest me but, of course, nothing excites and interests me like my own past. Ah, if one could only find oneself again in the time of one's childhood, one's youth, could only re-live one's enthusiasms of that time in the atmosphere of that time!" (*Aleksandr Benua razmyshlyaet . . .*, pp. 501–2).

brings the work into contact with issues of early twentieth-century thought. In both, the striking contrast between the fairground show in history and in its stylized setting places the message of the work in high relief. Diaghilev's transformed puppet show is a companion piece of Blok's transformed harlequinade.

As regards the *saisons russes*, the importance of the *balagany* in *Petrushka* is easily missed in efforts to ferret out the subtleties of Diaghilev's accomplishment. To notice it we need but pause to recall what was Russian about the Russian seasons: the collaborators and the dancers—at least some of them. And what of the settings and the stories of the ballets? There were works such as *Les Sylphides*, *Le Spectre de la rose*, *Midas*, *Narcisse*, *L'Après-midi d'un faun*, *Jeux*, *Josephslegende*, and the like, which were not Russian in any sense; there were Oriental potboilers such as *Cleopatra*, *Les Orientales*, and *Schéhérazade*, which appealed to audiences of the time who associated with Russianness the blandishments of the East, particularly the fabricated orientalisms of a composer such as Rimsky-Korsakov; there were works such as *Firebird* and *Le Sacre du printemps*, which as theater pieces could lay some claim to Russian subject matter but that were nevertheless artistic conjurations of a Russia that none of their creators had ever seen. And there was *Petrushka*, which presented a picture of Russia that was part of the life experience of its creators and performers. It was to this extent the only Russian ballet of the early seasons with any claim to historical authenticity. And the *balagany*, not the fable, made it so.

The Parody Chansons of Certon's *Meslanges**

EDWARD KOVARIK

A NUMBER OF SCHOLARS IN RECENT YEARS have compiled source lists that attempt to account for all the settings of a given chanson text. Examples include Howard Brown's catalogue of theatrical chansons, Hubert Daschner's chanson bibliography, Frank Dobbins's Moderne study, and my own (much smaller) listing of fricassee fragments.[1] Anyone perusing these lists of multiple settings will be struck by the frequent occurrence of one relatively late source, *Les Meslanges de Maistre Pierre Certon* (1570). Investigation of the source itself confirms one's suspicions: the table of contents yields many text incipits familiar from the first half of the century, and a look at the music shows that in many cases not only the text but also the musical substance of an earlier work has been incorporated into Certon's setting.

It should be emphasized at the outset that these are not two- and three-part chanson arrangements of the kind that have been explored at some length in recent years,[2] but are instead chanson expansions for five or more voices—larger new works created out of the substance of the old. Certon is by no means the only composer to have written

---

*This study has been funded in part by a grant from the Social Studies and Humanities Research Council of the University of Windsor (Ontario).

[1]Howard Mayer Brown, *Music in the French Secular Theater, 1400–1550* (Cambridge, Mass., 1963), pp. 183–282; Hubert Daschner, *Die gedruckten mehrstimmige Chansons* (Bonn, 1962); Frank Dobbins, "Jacques Moderne's 'Parangon des Chansons,' " *Royal Musical Association Research Chronicle*, No. 12 (1974), 1–90; and Edward Kovarik, "Apropos of the Fricassee," *Studies in Music* (Adelaide), 12 (1978), 1–24.

[2]See, for example, Lawrence F. Bernstein, "The Cantus-Firmus Chansons of Tylman Susato," *JAMS*, 22 (1969), 197–240, and Daniel Heartz, "*Au pres de vous*—Claudin's Chanson and the Commerce of Publishers' Arrangements," *JAMS*, 24 (1971), 193–225. A list of prints containing 3-voice arrangements is in Heartz, p. 222; for a list of sources containing 2-voice arrangements, see Bruce Bellingham and Edward G. Evans, Jr., eds., *Sixteenth-Century Bicinia*, Recent Researches in the Music of the Renaissance, vols. XVI & XVII (Madison, Wisc., 1974).

works of this kind, but the concentration of such works in his oeuvre—indeed, in a single printed source—is a matter of some significance.[3]

Despite its size (about 160 pages), the nature of its repertoire, and its position as Certon's last publication, *Les Meslanges* has never been scrutinized very thoroughly, because it is incomplete: only five of the original six partbooks survive in the unique set at the University of Uppsala (the quintus is lost).[4] Various methods exist for restoring portions of this voice,[5] but even without the quintus much can be learned about the nature of Certon's parody technique. Moreover, the topic is particularly appropriate in this forum, because it touches upon the work of John Ward.[6]

A description of the print and a list of its contents may be found in the catalogue of DuChemin prints prepared by Lesure and Thibault.[7] Here also may be found a transcription of the title page and of Certon's rambling introduction, a disquisition on the powers of music as extolled by numerous ancient and modern authors. Certon addresses the introduction to Nicholas LeGendre, "Seigneur de ville-roy, et Prevost des marchans de la ville de Paris," and concludes by dedicating the book to him "comme à celuy qui l'a mieulx merité par vertu & erudition, & auquel je suis plus obligé & tenu par juste occasion." An attractive speculation by Aimée Agnel is that the works in *Les Meslanges* may have been written for musical events held at the Chateau LeGendre near Corbeil.[8]

Printed at the front of the superius partbook just after Certon's intro-

[3]Examples were written by Gombert and Willaert, among others. Important collections include LeRoy and Ballard's *Livre de Meslanges Contenant Six vingtz Chansons* (1560)—now lost—and a much altered reissue of that collection by the same printers, *Mellange de Chansons* (1572). The contents of this print are transcribed in Stephen M. Curtis, "Mellange de Chansons: Transcribed and edited," PhD. diss. (Washington Univ., 1975).

[4]*Repertoire Internationale des Sources Musicales*, A/I/2: *Einzeldrucke vor 1800*, vol. II, ed. Karlheinz Schlager (Kassel, 1972), p. 95.

[5]Two concordances with the *Mellange de Chansons* (see fn. 7 below) yield complete quintus parts ("Regret soucy" and "Reviens vers moy"); elsewhere portions of the voice can be restored by the comparison of repeated segments involving voice exchange, and occasionally by the logic of antiphonal passages—three voices answered by three, or four voices answered by four (see Ex. 5).

[6]In addition to Professor Ward's well-known articles "The Use of Borrowed Material in 16th-Century Instrumental Music," *JAMS*, 5 (1952), 88–98, and "Parody technique in 16th-Century Instrumental Music," *The Commonwealth of Music*, ed. Gustave Reese and Rose Brandel (New York, 1965), pp. 208–28, references to the chanson literature turn up on occasion in his other writings.

[7]François Lesure and Geneviève Thibault, "Bibliographie des Editions Musicales publiées par Nicolas du Chemin," *Annales musicologiques*, 1 (1953), 343–45. A facsimile of the title page appears in Lesure's article on Certon in *Die Musik in Geschichte und Gegenwart*, ed. Fr. Blume, vol. II (Kassel, 1952), cols. 977–78.

[8]*Pierre Certon: Chansons polyphoniques publiées par Pierre Attaingnant*, restituées par Henry Expert et Aimée Agnel, vol I (Paris, 1967), viii.

duction is an epigrammatic Latin poem, sixteen lines in hexameters, addressed to LeGendre by Léger DuChesne: "ad eundem, Epigramma Leodegarij a Quercu." DuChesne (d. 1588) was a Parisian professor and minor literary figure[9] who had connections with the printing establishment of Attaingnant—a series of his commentaries on classical authors was published by Attaingnant's widow—and he may have come to know Certon through this connection (Certon, Master of the Children at the Sainte-Chapelle, had stood as godfather to one of Attaingnant's grandchildren).[10] DuChesne was probably responsible for editing the texts in Les Meslanges. It is difficult to explain his presence in the volume otherwise, and the texts are printed in a careful, not to say fussily precise, manner: the first word of each line is always capitalized, punctuation and diacritical marks abound, pedantic latinizations (faict, dict) and hyphenations (des-heritée) are employed, and parentheses—not a common occurrence in chanson texts—sprout everywhere at the slightest provocation.

Although the title page proclaims ninety-eight works, the print actually contains ninety-six, arranged as follows: forty works à 5 at the beginning, then forty-seven works à 6, two à 7, and five à 8, plus two canons printed at the end of the bassus partbook. All the texts are in French, but Latin tags are attached to two of the works: the "Oraison Dominicale: Père de nous"[11] at the beginning of the collection and a "Da Pacem des Laboureurs" near the end. A table of contents at the end of each book describes the collection as "Chansons et Cantiques"; the title page has the slightly fuller description "tant Cantiques que Chansons Spirituelles & autres." In addition to the chansons, which number eighty-four, the collection includes three psalms (in the French translations of Marot and Bèze),[12] the two Latin-tagged works mentioned above, two noëls,[13] a lament on the death of Claudin de Sermisy,[14] and

[9]Dictionnaire de Biographie Française, ed. Roman D'Amat et R. Limouzin-Lamothe, vol. XI (Paris, 1967), col. 1241.

[10]Daniel Heartz, Pierre Attaingnant: Royal Printer of Music (Berkeley, 1969), pp. 166–67 and 184.

[11]The text is the rhymed French translation by Clément Marot, first printed in 1533. See P. Leblanc, La Poésie religieuse de Clément Marot (Paris, 1955), pp. 135–40.

[12]The psalms are "Pourquoy font bruit" (Ps. 2), "Resveillez vous chascun fidèle" (Ps. 33), and "Dès ma jeunesse" (Ps. 129); the texts are printed in O. Douen, Clément Marot et le Psautier Huguenot (Paris, 1879), I, 498; I, 493; I, 651. Certon's music for the first two is unrelated to the arrangements for lute and voice in Guillaume Morlaye: Psaulms de Pierre Certon, reduits en tablature (1554), ed. F. Lesure and R. de Morcourt (Paris, 1957), hence also unrelated to Certon's Cinquante pseaulmes de David (1555). All three of the settings in Les Meslanges incorporate the standard tunes of the Genevan psalter.

[13]"Reveillez vous Pastoureaulx" and "Or est venu Noël." The latter is a ballade from Marot's L'Adolescence Clementine; modern edition in C. A. Mayer, Clément Marot: Oeuvres diverses (London, 1966), pp. 157–58.

[14]"Musiciens, chantres melodieux"; the complete text is in Heartz, Attaingnant, p. 104.

two additional "spiritual" texts, one of them the popular "Susanne un jour."[15]

The two canons "Le roy boyt" at the end of the bassus book represent a Christmas morning scene, with shepherds gathered to observe the Christ Child imbibing his mother's milk—this evidently being a justification for the drinking of wine. The first canon, six parts in one over a three-part pedal, has the following text:

Jesus Christ Le Roy des Roys
Pour boire vin en ce monde
Il beut des fois plus de trois
Du laict de la vierge munde*   *[pure]
Un berger qui le voyoit
Crioit tant hault qu'il pouvoit:
      Le Roy boyt.

The second canon, twelve parts in one plus a repeated high pedal note, urges those still sleeping to arise and see "le roy qui boys." The first canon is preceded by four lines of verse, which set the scene:

Neuf bergers sont icy tous en ce lieu
Pour adorer nostre grand Roy & Dieu
Chascun s'apprest' ainsi comme l'on doit
A bien chanter & crier le Roy boyt.

The whole may well represent the remnants of a Christmas tableau once staged at LeGendre's chateau.

Listed in the appendix to this study are the eighty-four chansons of *Les Meslanges.* For all but one ("C'est ma mignonne"), earlier settings of the same texts have been located. In a few cases Certon's music has nothing to do with the earlier setting; these entries are coded with a ° in the Appendix. In a few other cases I have been unable to check the earlier setting; these are coded with a question mark. In all the remaining works there is at least some similarity between Certon's setting and the earlier version, ranging from the quotation of a few notes at the beginning to the use of similar material throughout. Works that show a substantial degree of similarity are marked with asterisks.

Within this body of music, a primary division can be made on the basis of the early versions. Most of these first appear as polyphonic chansons printed by Attaingnant (or printed at a later date by some other northern printer). A few, however, first appear elsewhere, usually prior to the beginning of Attaingnant's career, as outlined below:

---

[15]See Kenneth Jay Levy, "Susanne un jour: the History of a 16th Century Chanson," *Annales musicologiques*, 1 (1953), 375–408. The other text begins: "Humaine creature, Plorer dois & gemir."

Antecedents in Monophonic Chansonniers

The French manuscripts F-Pn 9346 and F-Pn 12744,[16] thought to date from the end of the fifteenth century, evidently preserve a monophonic repertoire (tunes and strophic texts) that was otherwise transmitted orally. The two manuscripts contain early versions of four of Certon's works.

Canti Firmi in Polyphonic Settings

Three types of cantus firmus can be distinguished: (1) tenors of four-voice settings in Petrucci's chansonniers (three examples); (2) upper parts (altus/superius) of double-canon settings in Antico's *Motetti Novi*, 1520³ (two examples);[17] and (3) tenors of three-voice *chanson rustique* settings, a chanson type that has been associated with the court of Louis XII in the first decade of the sixteenth century.[18] Such settings appear in a group of early sixteenth-century manuscripts and in a series of Italian prints ranging from Antico's *Chansons a troys* (1520⁶) to Abbate's *La Courone* (1536¹).[19]

Text Collections Printed Before 1528

For purposes of the present investigation, these consist of the *Jardin de Plaisance*, c. 1501,[20] and a series of miniature chansonniers (c. 1512–1527) edited by Brian Jeffery, chiefly in the first volume of his *Chanson Verse of the Early Renaissance*.[21] That these texts were sung to monophonic tunes is a logical assumption supported by a number of concordances with the works in two categories above. All three categories,

---

[16]Manuscript abbreviations follow the system employed in the *Repertoire Internationale des Sources Musicales* (RISM). F-Pn 9346 is edited in Théodore Gérold, *Le Manuscrit de Bayeux* (Strasbourg, 1921); F-Pn 12744 is edited in Gaston Paris and Auguste Gevaert, *Chansons du XVe Siecle* (Paris, 1875).

[17]Dates followed by a small superscript number refer to catalogue entries in RISM [B/I,1]: *Recueils Imprimés, XVIe–XVIIe Siècles*, I: *Liste chronologique* (München-Duisburg, 1960).

[18]See Howard Mayer Brown, "The Genesis of a Style: The Parisian Chanson, 1500–1530," in *Chanson & Madrigal: 1480–1530*, ed. James Haar (Cambridge, Mass., 1964), pp. 21–24, and the same author's "The *Chanson rustique*: Popular Elements in the 15th- and 16th-Century Chanson," *JAMS*, 12 (1959), 16–26.

[19]See Lawrence F. Bernstein, "*La Courone et fleur des chansons a troys*: A Mirror of the French Chanson in Italy in the Years between Ottaviano Petrucci and Antonio Gardano," *JAMS*, 26 (1973), 1–68; the manuscripts are listed and described on pp. 8–14.

[20]Antoine Vérard, *Le Jardin de plaisance et Fleur de rhetorique*, I: *facsimile*; II: *Introduction et notes*, par E. Droz et A. Piaget (Paris, 1910–15).

[21]London, 1971; a second volume appeared in 1976.

then, contain works for which Certon's source was probably a monophonic "popular tune" or "chanson rustique" rather than some specific polyphonic setting. This must surely be so in those instances where no polyphonic setting was ever printed by Attaingnant, and it seems also to apply in a few cases even where such settings were printed. The works involved are listed in Table I.

When different settings of the same fundamental material are compared, it becomes apparent that the works listed here differ as a group from the works to be discussed later. Text variation in these works often involves not the simple inversion of a phrase or substitution of a word, but rather the recasting of substantial portions of the stanza, perhaps with a change in meaning.[22] Alterations in the musical substance are sometimes equally great. All this applies as well to Certon's settings, which relate more or less closely to the corresponding early versions, but in no case with the consistent similarity of some of the works to be examined later.

One could assume that in working with a familiar tune Certon might exercise his fancy more freely than in other circumstances. He evidently did so in the case of "Sus le pont d'Avignon," for in the third line Certon introduces a variant form of the theme—a descending arpeggio—which is unlike the form he uses in his *Missa Sus le pont d'Avignon.*[23] In most cases, however, a more likely explanation is that Certon is working with a form of the tune that has changed in oral transmission. The case of "L'amour de moy" is typical. This tune, one of the most attractive in the monophonic repertoire, is also one of the most stable. Four versions dating from around the turn of the sixteenth century preserve the melody with only minor differences of detail.[24] Certon's setting, a half-century later in date, represents a significant departure from this group (compare Exx. 1a and 1b). Of the four lines set by Certon, only the first and fourth, which are identical, remain relatively unchanged. The second line has been transposed down a fourth (with some change of detail), and the beginning of the third line is substantially altered.[25]

[22]See the comments in Table I. In sources with multiple stanzas, the differences become even greater after the first stanza.

[23]*Missae tres Petro Certon* (LeRoy & Ballard, 1558), ed. Henry Expert, *Pierre Certon: Messes à quatre voix*, Monuments de la Musique Française, II (Paris, 1924).

[24]The sources used for this comparison are those listed in Table I. The monophonic chansonniers pitch the melody on C and preserve only two sections of music; the polyphonic settings, pitched on F, extend the virelai form (Abba) and are presumably to be completed by a repeat of the opening section. Certon sets only the four-line refrain, which he also pitches on F.

[25]I have derived the shape of the melody chiefly from the superius and tenor of Certon's 6-voice setting.

Table I: Early versions prior to Attaingnant's prints

Text	Early versions	Later versions in prints	Comments
Adieu soulas	a) 2c: 3v setting by Févin, ed. Brown in *Chanson & Madrigal*, p. 161 b) 3b: Jeffery I, 86		Certon's first two lines are similar to Févin's; the last two are less similar in both text and music. Jeffery's text varies from both in lines 2 and 3.
A quoi tient-il	a) 3a: JP, no. 564	b) Anon., 4v At 32.Ch (1528[5]) c) Gombert, 4v At 28.Ch (1531[1]) Ed. CE XI, 20	4-line rondeau in JP; (b) and Certon have refrain and next 2 lines; (c) has only refrain plus return of opening at end. Certon quotes only the first few notes of (b); Gombert varies.
A tout jamais	a) 2c: Anon. 3v setting in An Ch.à3 (1520[6]) b) 3b: Jeffery I, 74–75 c) 2c? 3v setting by Jacotin or Richafort in An-A Courone (1536[1]) d) 2c? Anon. 3v setting in Egenolff I, no. 39	e) Crecquillon, 4v Sus 2.L (1544[10])	The poem is a rondeau cinquain by Jean Marot, father of Clément. Certon has only the first 4 lines, plus a return of the opening words at the end. The various settings share a general melodic similarity in the opening phrase.
Au joly bois je rencontray	a) 2c: two 3v settings by Willaert in An-A Courone (1536[1]) b) 2c? 3v setting by Clemens in At 42.Ch.à3 (1529[4]) c) 2c? Hypothetical 3v setting; basis of KyBd arr. ed. Seay AtKb (CMM 20), p. 105	d) 5v setting by Willaert in L&B Mellange (1572[2]), and others	Hypothetical monophonic version ed. Heartz in *Chanson & Madrigal*, p. 243; bibliography ibid., p. 100, n.18. The various versions show greater similarities in the refrain ("Baisez moy, tant, tant") than in the opening section. Certon's 4v setting (with bowdlerized text], ed. Lesure, *Anthologie*, no. 18, is not the model for the 5v setting in *Les Meslanges*.

(continued)

Table I, continued

Text	Early versions	Later versions in prints	Comments
Bon temps	a) 2a: *Canti B*, no. 14		Various forms of the tune are discussed in H. Hewitt, "A *Chanson rustique* of the early renaissance: Bon temps," *Aspects of Medieval and Renaissance Music*, ed. Jan LaRue [New York, 1966], pp. 376–91. Certon's c.f. resembles Hewitt's version E with the 2nd and 3rd lines interchanged.
C'est mal-encontre	a) 2c: Anon. 3v setting in An *Ch.à3* (1520[6])		Certon's opening phrase is identical with (a); later phrases are vaguely similar or different. The texts vary substantially after first 2 lines.
Ceste fillette	a) 3a: JP fol. 120[v]	b) Coste, 4v in Mod *Par.6* (1540[16])	Coste's text varies substantially from Certon and JP. Certon and Coste share only certain rhythmic similarities.
J'ay un mary	a) 1: 12744, no. 133 b) 2b: Anon 4v in An *Mot Nov* (1520[3])		Musically, (a) and (b) are closely related; Certon's music is different, but his form is the same (abba). All 3 texts vary somewhat in lines 3 and 4 (Antico is intermediate).
L'amour de moy	a) 1: 9346, no. 27 b) 1: 12744, no. 27 c) 2a: Anon 4v in *Canti C* and elsewhere, ed. Brown *ThCh*, no. 48 d) 2c: Anon 3v in GB-Lbm 5242 and elsewhere, ed. Brown *ThCh* no. 47 etc.		See Ex. 1. Extensive text variation in lines 2 and 3.

Reconfortez le petit cueur	a) 1: 9346, no. 21 b) 1: 12744, no. 54 c) Janequin, 4v in At *Ch.nou* (1528³) and elsewhere	The text in Certon and (c) is an expanded version of the texts in (a) and (b). Certon and (c) have in common only what is already present in (a) and (b)—a few repeated notes at the beginning and repetition of the opening syllable, "Re-."
Reveille toy franc cueur	a) 1: 12744, no. 49 b) 3v setting by Compère in E-Seg, ed. CE (CMM 15), V, 46 c) 4v setting by P. de Cornets in F-CA 125-8, ed. Coussemaker, *Notice sur les collections* (1843), Appendix, no. 3	No text in Compère; supplied from (a). The other 3 texts all vary somewhat after the first 2 lines. Musically, (a), (b), and Certon are all fairly close; (c) is distantly related.
Sus le pont d'Avignon	a) 2a: *Canti C*, fo.62 b) Claudin, 4v in Ms. frag (see Appendix)	No text in *Canti C*. Four-line stanza in Certon and Claudin; line 3 varies.
Tout d'un accord	a) 2b: 4v setting by Vassoris in An *Mot Nov* (1520³)	Certon's text is similar to (a); musically the two share only a few isolated motives.

Example 1a. "L'amour de moy" after Brown, *ThCh*, no. 47; tenor of 3v setting

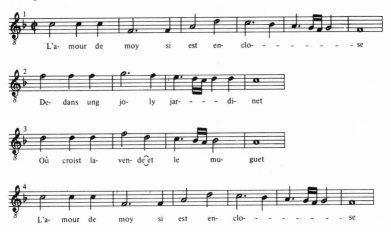

Example 1b. Melody of "L'amour de moy" in Certon's setting

Not included in Table I are three works in which oral transmission played at best a minimal role. All three texts were set by an earlier generation of composers (two by Josquin, one by Mouton), but the musical settings had little or no influence on Certon and his immediate source. "Vray dieu d'amours" was a popular catchphrase used as the starting point for many different texts and associated with a number of musical settings. Mouton's text is the only one that approaches Certon's—they are quite similar at the beginning, less so later—but there are no similarities in the music.[26] The tune used by Certon (and Mouton as well) to set the first three words (Ex. 2) was evidently part of the popular tradition, however, for variants of it turn up in connection with other text continuations and in otherwise unrelated musical settings.[27]

Example 2

Vray dieu d'a- mours

The text of the second work, Josquin's "My lares vous," is very similar to the text set by Roquelay and Certon.[28] Musically, Josquin's setting has nothing in common with the later works except its opening notes, the punning solmization syllables *mi la re*. The figure occurs on a different pitch level in the later composers, but its rhythm is the same in Roquelay as in Josquin; Certon changes it. The first line only of Certon's text for the third piece, "Ma bouche rid et mon cueur pleure," appears in the *Jardin de Plaisance*, as part of a textual quodlibet; this single line also constitutes the entire text of Josquin's six-voice setting.[29] Presumably the text derives from Ockeghem's famous bergerette: the rhyme scheme is similar, and the connection is emphasized by Josquin's quotation of Ockeghem's superius. Certon and his sources (two four-voice settings printed by Attaingnant) are melodically unrelated to either Ockeghem or Josquin.[30]

The issue of an oral tradition having been raised, it must be pursued, for among the works yet to be mentioned—works for which models exist in the printed chanson repertoire—some give evidence that they may incorporate a monophonic tune. This evidence may be in the nature of the text—the use of refrains and nonsense syllables, the popular

[26]Mouton's setting is edited in S. M. Curtis, "Mellange de Chansons," no. 15, and in Jean Bonfils, ed., *Chansons françaises pour orgue (vers 1550)*, Le Pupitre, 5 (Paris, 1968), where it is attributed (after D-Mbs 1508) to "Jo. Descaudin." A variant form of the text, closer to Mouton than to Certon, appears in Jeffery, *Chanson Verse*, I, pp. 132–33.

[27]One such is an anonymous 4-voice setting in I-Bc Q.17, fol. 71v–72; another is an Italian piece beginning with this French incipit in Pasoti and Dorico's *Libro Primo de la Croce (1526)*, ed. William Prizer, Collegium Musicum: Yale Univ., 2nd Series, VIII (Madison, Wisc., 1978), p. 39. Perhaps the figure derives from the rising fourth found in versions in the monophonic chansonniers.

[28]*Josquin des Pres: Wereldlijke Werken*, ed. Albert Smijers (Amsterdam, 1924–25), no. 34.

[29]JP, no. 18; *Josquin des Pres: Wereldlijke Werken*, no. 19.

[30]Ockeghem's text reappears in a 5-voice setting by Wildre in the *Mellange de Chansons* (1572²), but with no reference to Ockeghem's music.

narrative element, the ironic or naive treatment of a conventional scene[31]—but it is also in the short-winded and repetitive (not to say "cliché-ridden") nature of the music. A tentative list of such works is given in Table II. Many of the early versions appear to be settings of tenor melodies, a striking aberration in a genre that is generally considered to be superius-dominated.[32] The tenor was of course the traditional place to put a cantus firmus, and such may be the case here. Worthy of a special note is "J'ay veu le cerf," purportedly a popular drinking song.[33] Manchicourt's setting of this text consists of variations on two melodic phrases heard over and over; Certon's setting teases the listener by presenting only bits and pieces of the two phrases until the very end, where they are heard complete.

Table II: Polyphonic settings that may incorporate a monophonic tune

En entrant (Clément Marot)	Tenor melody
Il est jour	Tenor melody
J'ay veu le cerf	Ornamental treatment of two phrases
L'autre jour	Two tenor settings by Certon
Ma peine n'est pas grande	Two settings of the same tune (in superius), each with two stanzas
O vin en vigne	Setting by Orlando di Lasso (*Sämtliche Werke*, XII: *Kompositionen mit französischem Text*, ed. A Sandberger, I, no. 16) uses same theme for the nonsense syllables "et dehet, dehet" as Certon's setting; the settings are otherwise different.
Un jour Robin	Tenor melody
Vignon vignon	Tenor melody; same tune used in the setting by Orlando di Lasso (*Sämtliche Werke*, XVI: *Kompositionen mit franzosischem Text*, ed. A. Sandberger, III, no. 17)
Vos huis	Two settings of the same tune

At the opposite pole from the works that hint at the incorporation of a monophonic tune are certain others where the evidence points in the opposite direction. Such, for example, are works whose texts exhibit a sophistication of thought or language that places them outside the popular tradition. Perhaps the best example in *Les Meslanges* is the follow-

---

[31]See Brown, *French Secular Theater*, pp. 109–10.
[32]Brown, "The Genesis of a Style," p. 33.
[33]Gustave Reese, *Music in the Renaissance*, rev. ed. (New York, 1959), pp. 351–52.

ing, delicately erotic and displaying a sophisticated imagery far removed from the popular mind:

M'amye un jour de Dieu Mars des-arma
Comme il dormoit soubs la verde ramee;
Et de l'armet & cuyrasse s'arma,
Tenant en main sa hache envenimee.

Mars s'esueillant luy dict "ma bien aymee,
J'ay de tes yeulx la puissance cogneüe.
Pourquoy t'es-tu encontre moy armee?
Veu que tu peux me vaincre toute nüe?

Also to be included in this category are settings of texts by contemporary poets such as Clément Marot and Mellin de Saint-Gelais. In such cases there had not been time for a real oral tradition to accumulate. Even if we assume, for the sake of argument, that the poets wrote (or caused to be written) tunes to accompany their poems—a thesis put forward with considerable vigor by Jean Rollin[34]—these tunes were not yet either oral or popular, and in many cases polyphonic settings appeared so closely upon the heels of the poetry that they came to be inseparably linked with it.[35] Of course it is entirely possible that such works, even without popular antecedents, may have later passed over into oral tradition. This must have happened to some of the works used later in the century as *timbres* for noëls and, with altered texts, as sacred chansons. In such works, however, the monophonic version is very much a secondary phenomenon, ultimately to be referred to a polyphonic original, and there is no compelling reason to assume that oral tradition played a role in Certon's settings.

Among the texts by Marot, however, two in particular may have been associated with a monophonic tune: "En entrant" and "Longtemps." The first text is very much in the folksong vein; the second is more sophisticated. Both appear first as polyphonic settings based on a tenor, but in both cases Certon's version is modeled not only on the tenor but also on Claudin's setting of it.

The whole issue is a difficult one, and not likely to be resolved to everyone's satisfaction. Certainly there are some among the settings of *Les Meslanges* in which the possible quotation of a monophonic tune

[34]Jean Rollin, *Les Chansons de Clément Marot* (Paris, 1951). Rollin's views have been received with considerable skepticism; see, for example, François Lesure, "Autour de Clement Marot et de ses musiciens," *Revue de musicologie*, 33 (1951), 109–19.

[35]In some cases the polyphonic settings preceded the first appearance of the poetry in print; see Heartz, *Attaingnant*, p. 103.

must remain an open question. One thing that does seem clear, however, is that it is not necessary to assume the existence of an oral tradition in order to account for that unique phenomenon of the chanson repertoire, the proliferation of dependent settings. On the contrary, a great deal of the borrowing must be looked upon as a purely literary activity. This must surely be the case, for example, where different dependent settings quote different voices of the same well-known model,[36] or when a whole string of dependent settings arises from a model which is itself newly written and independent of all earlier versions.[37]

I do not intend to dwell upon the existence of dependent settings; indeed, to keep the Appendix down to manageable size I have omitted mention of most such settings, even those written by Certon himself. However, in addition to the few-voiced chanson arrangement and the many-voiced chanson expansion, there is a third type, which should at least be mentioned here. A typical example is a four-voice reworking of a four-voice original, the two works appearing only a few years apart among the early prints of Attaingnant. Sometimes the later work served as Certon's model, sometimes the earlier one (see Table III).

As mentioned earlier, the works marked with asterisks in the Appendix are those most closely related to the earlier settings. Very often they exhibit passages of direct parody: in several works Certon reproduces exactly the imitative opening of his model—pitch level and order of entries as well as the actual shape of the imitated motives.[38] He also quotes simultaneously from two voices of the model: thematic line plus bass, or an imitated motive and its countersubject.[39] In "Quant j'ay beu" (pitched, exceptionally, a fifth below its model), Certon expands upon the repeated V-I bass movement at the end of the first line, showing that he is not simply taking over a monophonic original (Ex. 3). Perhaps the most common kind of parody is one of texture: antiphonal duo passages in the model become antiphonal trios in Certon's setting, a device that can reproduce the effect of the original even without direct quotation.[40]

---

[36]Dependent settings derived from Roquelay's "Grace, vertu" are based variously on his tenor (Heurteur's 3-voice setting in Moderne's *Parangon.3*, 1539[19]), on his bassus (Gardane's 2–voice setting, ed. Bellingham, *Sixteenth-Century Bicinia*, no. 98), and on his superius (Nicholas's 5-voice setting in *Mellange de Chansons*, 1572[2], ed. Curtis, no. 63). Gardane's 2-voice setting of "Las voulez vous" (ed. Bellingham, no. 90) is based on the superius of Vermont's chanson; Certon's 6-voice setting is based on the tenor.

[37]A good example is Lasso's "Las voulez vous" (ed. A. Sandberger in *Orlando di Lasso: Sämtliche Werke*, XII, 3), which is unrelated to Vermont's earlier version and which gave rise to dependent settings by Nicholas, Castro, Faignient, and Turnhout; see Brown, *French Secular Theatre*, p. 251.

[38]"Ell'a bien ce ris," "Le Content," "Quant j'ay beu," and "Si par fortune."

[39]See "Contentez vous," "Le Content," and "Veu le grief mal."

[40]See "Amour partez," "Ell'a bien," and "Le Content."

Table III: Double four-voice settings

		Sources	Commentary
Longtemps y'a	a) Anon, 4v	At-2 Ch.nou (1528[3])	Claudin sets the tenor of (a) in his superius (with variants) and accompanies it with three new voices in imitation; Certon's setting is based on Claudin's, since he refers to the imitated motive not present in (a). Further: (a) and (b) vary in line 4, and Certon follows (b).
	Ed. Seay, AtKb (CMM 20), p. 121	At-6 35.Ch (1528[7])	
	b) Claudin, 4v	At-19 36.Ch (1530[4])	
	Ed. CE (CMM 52), IV, no. 102	At-71 2.esl (1536[3])	
Ma bouche rid	a) Anon, 4v	At-2 Ch.nou (1528[3])	Duboys uses the superius of (a) as his superius (with slight variation) but precedes the first phrase with pre-imitations; the two texts vary appreciably. Certon follows the text of (a) and does not adopt the imitative beginning of (b).
	b) Duboys, 4v	At-9 37.Ch (1528[8], 1531[2])	
	Ed. Seay, AtKb (CMM 20), p. 184	At-71 2.esl (1536[3], etc.)	
Par fin despit	a) Anon, 4v	At-8 30.Ch (1528[4])	Claudin uses the superius of (a) as his superius, introducing a pause in the middle of line 2. This pause does not appear in (c) or in Certon's setting; hence the assumption that both are based on (a) rather than (b). The 4-line text is identical in all versions. Certon makes a freely canonic duo for superius and tenor out of the original superius.
	b) Claudin, 4v	At-54 31.Ch (1534[14])	
	Ed. CE (CMM 52), IV, no. 119	At-79 3.esl (1537[4])	
	c) Claudin, 3v	At-65 31.Chà3 (1535)	
	Ed. CE (CMM 52), IV, no. 120	Mod 4.L (1539[18])	
Regret soucy	a) Anon, 4v	At-7 32.Ch (1528[5])	I have not seen version (b). Concerning the relationship between (a) and (b), Heartz reports (JAMS, 24, 224) "imitative subjects [of a dependent 3v setting] are related to (a) but still more closely related to (b)." In Certon's setting the last line is set apart, preceded by final longas and a barline. This does not occur in (a) but may perhaps derive from (b).
	b) Jacotin, 4v	At-79 3.esl (1537[4])	
Vray dieu d'amours	a) Anon, 4v	At-8 30.Ch (1528[4])	Jacotin uses the superius of (a) as his superius, adding some embellishment and rewriting the last phrase. Certon's setting does not resemble either version very closely, but is more similar in text to (a) than to (b).
	b) Jacotin, 4v	At-70 1.esl (1536[3])	

Example 3a: Anon, *Quant j'ay beu*

Example 3b. Certon, *Quant j'ay beu*

The works marked with two asterisks are those most closely dependent: every line of text (or almost every one) is set to material taken from the model, wholly or in part. Works marked with a single asterisk are relatively less close to their models; they contain a greater proportion of free material, and the parody relationship is less obvious.

Of course this one- and two-star system is an oversimplification, for Certon actually employs a wide range of procedures. The following general remarks, then, are an attempt to deal in orderly fashion with an essentially unruly situation. For the present study, a sampling of the works (twelve examples) was transcribed in full. The others were partially transcribed and then examined in the original notation. The discussion below is based chiefly on the sample of twelve, but I have not hesitated to draw in other works to reinforce a particular point.

Certon expands upon his models in various ways, most obviously in length. His settings are often one-half to two-thirds again as long as the originals. There is also an expansion of range, most often downward. This happens because in many of the models the bassus lies relatively high, descending no lower than Bb or A (all the V-I cadences resolve upward). Certon's bassus normally descends to F or G, and thus often fills out the bass register by as much as a fourth; V-I cadences resolve downward. Expansion at the top of the ensemble is less common; Certon's superius is usually written in the same clef as the model—either soprano or treble. In a few works Certon extends the range by as much as a third up ("Ell'a bien," "Si par fortune"), but in one work ("Par fin despit") he actually avoids the high f' of the model.

Certon's settings adopt the mode and "key signature" of their models, as they also do (with a few exceptions) the pitch level of internal cadences. Irregular cadence forms in the models, however, are not preserved. Beyond the cadence pitches, no particular effort seems to have been made to preserve the harmony of the model; in numerous cases directly corresponding passages differ in their choice of chords. Melodic phrases are sometimes transposed away from their original pitch, either for variety in successive statements or for other reasons. In "Si par fortune," an irregular cadence in the model (of a type not uncommon in the early Parisian chanson) is changed by Certon into a regular V-I; to preserve the level of the cadence on D, Certon transposes the superius line up a fifth (Ex. 4). In several works Certon changes the opening sonority of the model. In one case ("Contentez vous"), the change brings about a unity of opening and closing harmonies, but in other works it either has the opposite effect ("Tant que vivray") or no effect at all ("En entrant").

Small changes in text are common, even among the works most closely related to their models. Very often these are minor indeed, involving the substitution of one word for its near equivalent: "en" for "à," "un" for "le," "pas" for "point." Sometimes they involve the inversion or recasting of short phrases: "Et puis apres" for "Mais apres deul," or "Aller m'y fault" for "M'y fault aller." In what may be a touching concession to Father Time, Certon revised the first word in his own model "Fuyons tous d'amours le jeu" to read "Fuyez tous." In another

Example 4a. Certon, *Si par fortune* (4v)

Example 4b. Certon, *Si par fortune* (5v)

of his own models, "Si par fortune," he changed the original fourth line "Au temps premier . . ." to "Autant premier." This particular change is carried through in all the voices; but changes such as this, involving the substitution of a word or phrase similar to the original not in meaning but in sound, were sometimes inserted in just one voice as a kind of private joke. Two examples: in place of the correct reading "D'un si amer malheur . . ." Certon's bassus has "D'ainsi aymer . . ." (in "Amour ne scauriez vous"); and in place of the correct reading "C'est que de son corps gay," Certon's superius has "*cueur* gay" (in "Ce joly mois de May").

The kinds of changes described above do not affect the overall length of the text, which is normally the same in Certon's setting as in the model.[41] Expansion occurs, rather, chiefly within the individual segments that correspond to a single line of text. Symptomatic of this is the frequent repetition, often several times, of phrases or even whole lines of text within each voice. The space between phrases of text may be expanded as well: segments that in the model are contiguous or overlapping may in Certon's setting be well separated, the music "marking time" for a measure or more after a cadence before the introduction of new material.

Almost all of the chansons in *Les Meslanges* are expanded at their conclusion by a cadential extension, a device not found in the models. Usually the extension is plagal: one or more voices sustain the final note while the other parts continue to move, eventually reaching a IV-I cadence. Another possibility is for each voice to reach its conclusion within the final chord at a different time, the sense of movement being thus gradually reduced until all voices come to rest. These extensions are only a few bars long, but they are present in such numbers that they become a significant stylistic feature.[42] Something similar occurs in several works at internal cadence points, where a I-IV-I progression is used to prolong the cadence and delay the entry of the next segment.

In a few cases Certon tightens up the rhythm of his models (Ex. 5). More often he will slow down the rhythm by stating the borrowed material in longer values—semibreves instead of minims—and surrounding it with faster-moving voices. A favorite device is to begin a phrase in normal values and then continue it (or restate the whole thing) in longer notes. Very often the voice holding the long notes is the superius or the tenor, for borrowed material is more likely to turn up in these voices than elsewhere. Motives found in the tenor of the original are routinely transferred by Certon to the superius, and vice versa. Closely interacting superius/tenor duos, however, are not always preserved in Certon's version; sometimes the thematic material appears in the superius but is abridged or omitted in the tenor ("Ayez pitié"; "Je suis desheritée").

Individual vocal lines are frequently broken up by rests or held notes

[41]Exceptionally, lines 3 and 4 of Claudin's "Mon cueur est sourvent bien marry" are omitted in Certon's setting.

[42]Although not found in the Parisian chanson, such cadential extensions occur in numerous works of Josquin des Prez, among which are some of the chansons printed at mid-century by Susato (1545[15]) and Attaingnant (*Trente sixiesme livre*, 1550). Perhaps this is where Certon got the idea.

Example 5a. Claudin, "Il est jour dit l'alouette"

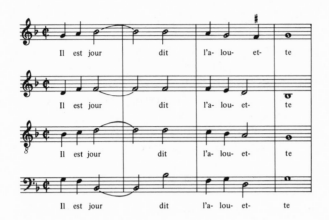

Example 5b. Certon, "Il est jour dict l'Alouette"

extending to a length of several breves, but apart from this Certon's rhythms do not differ appreciably from those of his models. Texture and melodic line are another matter. Certon's settings lack the delicate balance of homophonic and imitative styles that we think of as characteristic of the Parisian chanson (not all of the models exhibit this balance either: some are homophonic throughout). As a rule Certon's settings are continuously contrapuntal. Homophony, if it appears at all, appears within passages for a reduced number of voices, usually in an antiphonal arrangement of three against three or (in the eight-voice works) four against four. Isolated homophonic passages in the models are often rewritten, with one voice (superius or sometimes tenor) extracted and treated imitatively. Certon's melodic lines are short and constricted in movement and range; the pre-cadential melismas that grace the earlier chanson are routinely omitted. Indeed, ornamental figures found anywhere in the phrase may be trimmed away (Ex. 6).

Never is a line of text treated as a single musical phrase, as is the normal procedure in the earlier works, instead, each line becomes the basis of a larger segment of music. It is taken apart (when the grammatical structure permits) and its parts are treated separately, articulated by internal cadences, reiterated, or repeated antiphonally from one group

Example 6a

Example 6b. *Par fin despit*

Example 6c

of voices to another. Individual words may be dwelt upon, and motives stated once in the original may be heard two or three times in succession in Certon.

Although Certon will sometimes mimic the opening measures of his model, he cannot sustain the deception for long, since he seems unable to resist writing additional entries or new accompaniment motives. Indeed, the idea of supplementing or developing given material is always part of Certon's thinking. His points of imitation contain more entrances than their models, and they are usually more closely spaced. In "Que n'est elle," a reworking of his own four-voice chanson, Certon actually changes the shape of the imitative answer so that it will work in close overlap.

Not infrequently Certon will alter a given line, either by changing the rhythm to make it more distinctive or by changing the melodic shape. At times he will suppress the original entirely in favor of new, more interesting material of his own devising. He may take up a suggestion in the original and carry it further. In one case, for example, he replicates the descending third of the borrowed theme to produce a descending arpeggio (Ex. 7).

On a few occasions Certon supplies text-illustrative figures not present in the model, such as a brief melisma on "ramage" in "Reveillez vous" or downward fifth and octave leaps on the words "haut et bas" in "Ramonez moy ma cheminée." Another text-related technique that occurs often enough to be called a mannerism involves delaying the final syllable of a phrase, so that instead of coinciding with the cadence it comes afterwards, on a repetition of the cadence note.

Certon's handling of the sectional repeats in his models is variable. Literal repetition of the last line, a common feature of the models, does not occur in Certon, because the final segment in its expanded form already includes a great deal of repetition. However, the initial repeat,

Example 7a

La, la   mais- tre Pier-   re

Example 7b

La, la,   la,   la   mais- tre   Pier-   re

another common feature, does occur. In most of the models the music of the opening two or three lines of text is repeated for the next two or three lines. Normally this repetition is exact, and often it is indicated in the original prints by the use of double text and repeat signs. In Certon the repeated music is always written out, and occasionally the whole second statement is varied. More often, however, only the first part of the repeat is varied, the remainder eventually turning into an exact restatement. Much the same thing happens when opening material recurs at the end: Certon usually sneaks into the repeat by treating the themes afresh at the beginning of the segment and gradually merging them into a literal restatement.

Who wrote the models that Certon used? A tabulation of the works listed in the Appendix shows that Claudin de Sermisy is by far the most popular composer (twenty-one examples), a fact not surprising in light of Certon's avowed respect for the older man.[43] The works derived from Claudin are not only the most numerous, as a group they are also among the works most closely related to their models—no doubt another token of Certon's esteem. Lagging quite a way behind Claudin are two other figures, Janequin (nine examples) and Certon himself (six examples). A few of these works are closely modeled, but many are more freely treated than Claudin's settings. Beyond these three figures no composer contributes more than two or three models, though the total number of composers represented, twenty-two, is surprisingly large.

A tabulation of the sources containing Certon's models reveals that most of the prints were issued by Attaingnant, a finding that reinforces the picture drawn by Heartz of a close relationship among Claudin, Certon, and the printer.[44] What is noteworthy is that the models do not occur haphazardly within Attaingnant's oeuvre, but are concentrated in a relatively few books, these perhaps representing well-thumbed volumes in Certon's library. Among the books that appear most often as sources are: *Trente et sept chansons musicales (37.Ch)*, At-9 (1528[8]) and At-32 (1531[2]); *Premier livre contenant xxxi. chansons musicales esleves de plusieurs livres (1.esl)*, At-70 (1536[2]); and *Tiers livre contenant xxi. Chansons musicales a quatre parties composeez par Jennequin & Passereau (3.L)*, At-73 (1536[6]). The first of these (37.Ch) contains ten of the models, the second (1.esl) eight, and the third (3.L) six.

It has been the intention of the present study to expose a facet of Certon's creative activity hitherto largely unrecognized. The large-scale and intricate chanson settings in *Les Meslanges* function, in our thinking, as a counterbalance to those products of Certon's later career which

---

[43]In addition to writing the deploration printed in *Les Meslanges*, Certon also dedicated his book of motets (1542) to Claudin; see Heartz, *Attaingnant*, pp. 182–84.

[44]Heartz, *Attaingnant*, pp. 103–4.

are perhaps better known: the simple homophonic settings of the *Premier Livre* (1552).[45] More than a counterbalance, indeed, since in size and sheer numbers the works of *Les Meslanges* far outweigh the contents of the earlier print. Perhaps it is possible to draw an analogy with Certon's celebrated younger contemporary, Claude LeJeune, who is known chiefly for his homophonic chansons in *musique mesurée*, but who also contributed a magnificent parody chanson to LeRoy & Ballard's *Mellanges de Chansons* of 1572. Certon, like LeJeune, had more than one string to his lyre.

[45]See Daniel Heartz, "*Voix de ville:* Between Humanist Ideals and Musical Realities," *Words and Music: The Scholar's View,* ed. Laurence Berman (Cambridge, Mass., 1972), p. 117.

Sigla for 16th-century printers

An	Antico
An-A	Antico-Abbate
An-S	Antico-Scotto
At-	Attaignant; catalogue of works in Daniel Heartz, *Pierre Attaingnant: Royal Printer of Music* (Berkeley, 1969).
D-	DuChemin; catalogue of works in François Lesure and Geneviève Thibault, "Bibliographie des Editions Musicales publiées par Nicolas du Chemin," *Annales musicologiques*, 1 (1953), 269–373.
Gar	Gardane
L&B	LeRoy & Ballard; catalogue of works in F. Lesure and G. Thibault, *Bibliographie des éditions d'Adrien LeRoy et Robert Ballard* (Paris, 1955).
Mod	Moderne; catalogue of works in Samuel F. Pogue, *Jacques Moderne: Lyons Music Printer of the Sixteenth Century* (Geneva, 1969).
Sus	Susato; catalogue of works in Ute Meissner, *Der Antwerpener Notendrucker Tylman Susato*, 2 vols. (Berlin, 1967).

Sigla for modern editions

Arcadelt CE	*Jacobi Arcadelt: Opera Omnia*, ed. Albert Seay (Corpus Mensurabilis Musicae, 31), VIII: Chansons, I (1968).
Brown *ThCh*	Howard Mayer Brown, ed., *Theatrical Chansons of the Fifteenth and Early Sixteenth Centuries* (Cambridge, Mass., 1963).
Claudin CE	*Claudin de Sermisy: Opera Omnia*, ed. Gaston Allaire and Isabelle Cazeaux (CMM 52), III and IV (1974).
Certon	*Pierre Certon: Chansons polyphoniques publiées par Pierre Attaingnant*, restituées par Henry Expert et Aimée Agnel, 3 vols. Maitres Anciens de la Musique Française, II–IV (Paris, 1967–68).
Curtis	Stephen M. Curtis, "Mellange de Chansons: Transcribed and edited." Ph.D. diss. Washington Univ., 1975.
CW	*Das Chorwerk* (Wolfenbüttel, Möseler Verlag).
Eitner *60 Ch*	Robert Eitner, ed., *60 Chansons zu vier Stimmen aus der ersten Hälfte des 16. Jahrhunderts*. Publikation älterer praktischer und theoretischer Musikwerke, XXIII (1899).
Gombert CE	*Nicolas Gombert: Opera Omnia*, ed. J. Schmidt-Görg (CMM 6).
Janequin	*Clement Janequin: Chansons Polyphoniques*, ed. A. Tillman Merritt and François Lesure, 6 vols. (Monaco, 1965–71).
Lesure *Anth*	François Lesure, et al., *Anthologie de la Chanson Parisienne au XVIe Siècle* (Monaco, 1953).
Manchicourt	*Pierre de Manchicourt: Twenty-nine chansons*, ed. Margery A. Baird. Recent researches in the music of the Renaissance, XI (Madison, Wisc., c. 1972).
Mittantier CE	*French Music of the Sixteenth Century, I: Collected Works of Mittantier & Vassal*, ed. Albert Seay. CMM 66 (1974).
Passereau CE	*Passereau: Opera Omnia*, ed. Georges Dottin. CMM 45 (1967).
Seay *AtKb*	*Pierre Attaingnant: Transcriptions of Chansons for Keyboard*, ed. Albert Seay. CMM 20 (1961).
Whisler	Bruce A. Whisler, "Munich Mus. Ms. 1516: A Critical Edition." Ph.D. diss. Eastman, 1974.

Appendix

The 84 chansons of *Les Meslanges* and their models. (NB. Only the earliest printed sources are cited.) Asterisks mark the works that are surely (**), or probably (*), parody chansons; ° indicates early works that bear no relationship to Certon's settings.

<table>
<tr><td></td><td align="right">Page in
superius book</td></tr>
<tr><td>A cent diables la verolle (6v)</td><td align="right">130</td></tr>
<tr><td>   Heurteur, 4v</td><td>At-83 *4.L* (1538[13])
"Bon voisin"
At-96 *4.L* (1540[11])
"Heurteur"</td></tr>
<tr><td>   Ed. Eitner *60 Ch*, no. 28</td><td></td></tr>
<tr><td>Adieu soulas, tout plaisir & liesse (6v)
    monophonic tune; see Table I</td><td align="right">71</td></tr>
<tr><td>Amour ne scauriez vous apprendre (5v)
    poem by Mellin de Saint-Gelais</td><td align="right">31</td></tr>
<tr><td>   °Arcadelt, 4v
    Ed. CE (CMM 31), VIII, no. 45</td><td>L&B *3.L* (1554[27], etc.)</td></tr>
<tr><td>*Amour partez, je vous donne la chasse (6v)</td><td align="right">82</td></tr>
<tr><td>   Claudin, 4v</td><td>At-14 *31.Ch* (1529[2])
At-71 *2.esl* (1536[3], etc.)</td></tr>
<tr><td>   Ed. CE (CMM 52), III, no. 6</td><td></td></tr>
<tr><td>A quoy tient-il, d'ou vient cela (5v)
    monophonic tune(?); see Table I</td><td align="right">23</td></tr>
<tr><td>   Anon, 4v</td><td>At-7 *32.Ch* (1528[5])</td></tr>
<tr><td>A tout jamais d'un vouloir immuable (6v)
    poem by Jean Marot (father of Clément)
    monophonic tune; see Table I</td><td align="right">98</td></tr>
<tr><td>**Au joly bois a l'umbre d'un soucy (5v)</td><td align="right">26</td></tr>
<tr><td>   Claudin, 4v
    Ed. CE (CMM 52), III, no. 12</td><td>At-14 *31.Ch* (1529[2])</td></tr>
<tr><td>Au joly bois je rencontray m'amye (5v)
    monophonic tune; see Table I</td><td align="right">14</td></tr>
<tr><td>*Ayez pitié du grand mal que j'endure (5v)
    poem by Chappuys or Heroiet</td><td align="right">20</td></tr>
<tr><td>   Claudin, 4v</td><td>At-30 *33.Ch* (1532[12])
At-70 *1.esl* (1536[2])</td></tr>
<tr><td>   Ed. CE (CMM 52), III, no. 18</td><td></td></tr>
</table>

Bon temps ne viendras-tu jamais (6v)   68
    monophonic tune; see Table I

*Ce joly moys de May (6v)   108

    Passereau, 4v   At-83 *4.L* (1538[13])
    Ed. CE (CMM 45), no. 20

Ce sont gallans qui s'en vont resjouyr (5v)   25

    Janequin, 4v   At-55 *28.Ch* (1534[12])
                                  At-73 *3.L* (1536[6])
                                    Gar *25cf* (1538[19])
                                    Gar *2.L* (1548[5])
    Ed. Janequin, II, no. 57

Ceste fillette a qui le tetin point (5v)   22
    monophonic tune; see Table I

    G. Coste, 4v   Mod *Par.6* (1540[16])

C'est ma mignonne Qu'amour me donne (5v)   61

    no other settings found

C'est mal-encontre que d'aymer (5v)   42
    monophonic tune; see Table I

**Contentez vous amy de la pensée (5v)   17

    Claudin, 4v   At-69 *1.L* (1536[4], etc.)
                                      At-161 *1.esl* (1549[17])

    Ed. CE (CMM 52), III, no. 33
*Ell'a bien ce ris gracieux (6v)   128

    Claudin, 4v   At-101 *11.L* (1541)
                                      At-107 *11.L* (1542[14], etc.)
                                    Mod *Par.10* (1543[14])

    Ed. CE (CMM 52), III, no. 45

*En ce moys delicieux (6v)   116

    Arcadelt, 4v   L&B *16.L* (1565[8], etc.)
    Ed. CE (CMM 31), VIII, no. 117

*En entrant en un jardin (8v)   156
    poem by Clément Marot

    Claudin, 4v   At-14 *31.Ch* (1529[2])
    Ed. CE (CMM 52), III, no. 48

*En languissant je consomme mes jours (5v)   46

    Cadeac, 4v   At-82 *3.L* (1538[12])
                                      At-95 *3.L* (1540[10])

**Entendez vous qu'un autre je seconde (5v)   24

    Certon, 4v   At-44 *30.Ch* (1534[13])
                                                      At-79 *3.esl* (1537[4])
                                                      D-86 *4.rec* (1567)
    Ed. Certon, I, 10

**En un lieu ou l'on ne voit goutte (6v)   94

    Certon, 4v   L&B *5.L* (1556[14])

**Faict elle pas bien d'aymer qui luy donne (6v)   89

    Santerre, 4v   At-69 *1.L* (1536[4], etc.)

*Fortune helas, m'as-tu mis en oubly? (6v)   90

    Anon, 4v   At-6 *35.Ch* (1528[7])
    Ed. Whisler, II, 227

*Fuyez tous d'amours le jeu (6v)   118

    Certon, 4v   L&B *2.L* (1554[26], etc.)

**Grace & vertu, bonté, beaulté, noblesse (5v)   33

    Roquelay, 4v   At-7 *32.Ch* (1528[5])
                                                      At-71 *2.esl* (1536[3], etc.)

*Hors envieux il est temps de partir (5v)   50

    Gombert, 4v   At-41 *Ch.mus* (1533)
                                                      At-71 *2.esl* (1536[3], etc.)
                                                      D-85 *1.rec* (1567)
    Ed. CE (CMM 6), XI, no. 17 (a fourth lower than as printed by At-
    taingnant)

*Il est jour dict l'Alouette (8v)   154

    Claudin, 4v   At-2 *Ch.nou* (1528[3])
                                                      At-9 *37.Ch* (1528[8], 1531[2])
    Ed. CE (CMM 52), III, no. 59

*Il n'est plaisir ne passe-temps (6v)   106

    Janequin, 4v   At-55 *28.Ch* (1534[12])
                                                      At-73 *3.L* (1536[6])
                                                      Gar *25cf* (1538[19])
                                                      Gar *2.L* (1548[5])
    Ed. Janequin, II, no. 46

**J'ayme le cueur de m'amye (6v)   72
    poem by Clément Marot

    Claudin, 4v   At-19 *36.Ch* (1530[4])
                                                      At-71 *2.esl* (1536[3], 1537[3])
                                                      D *4.L* (1551[7])
    Ed. CE (CMM 52), III, no. 71 (Claudin's 3v setting uses a different
    theme, not taken up by Certon, in lines 2 and 4)

•Ma peine n'est pas grande (6v)   120
   monophonic tune(?)

      a) Janequin, 4v   At-123 *16.L* (1545[8])
         Ed. Janequin, III, no. 110
         Lesure *Anth*, no. 13

      b) Maillard, 4v   L&B *2.L* (1554[26])

••M'amye un jour le Dieu Mars des-arma (5v)   18

   Certon, 4v   At-109 *12.L* (1543[8])
                                 D-6 *2.rec* (1549[28])
                                 L&B *1.rec* (1554[25])

   Ed. Certon, II, 56

•Mon cueur est souvent bien marry (6v)   121

   Claudin, 4v   At-2 *Ch.nou* (1528[3])
                                 At-9 *37.Ch* (1528[8], 1531[2])
                                 At-79 *3.esl* (1537[4])

   Ed. CE (CMM 52), IV, no. 106

•My lairrez vous tousjours languir (5v)   16

   Roquelay, 4v   At-30 *33.Ch* (1532[12])
                                 At-70 *1.esl* (1536[2])
                                   D-22 *4.rec* (1551[8])

••N'auray-je jamais reconfort (6v)   78

   Jacotin, 4v   At-2 *Ch.nou* (1528[3])
                                 At-9 *37.Ch* (1528[8], 1531[2])
                                 At-70 *1.esl* (1536[2])

   Ed. Seay *AtKb* (CMM 20), p. 194

•On en dira ce qu'on vouldra (6v)   103
   poem by Clément Marot

   Claudin, 3v   At-65 *31.Chà3* (1535)
                                 etc.

   Ed. CE (CMM 52), IV, no. 115

O vin en vigne (5v)   44
   monophonic tune(?)

   ?Lupi, 4v   At-92 *9.L* (1540[14])—not
                                 seen

•Par fin despit je m'en iray seulette (5v)   40

      a) Anon, 4v   At-8 *30.Ch* (1528[4])

      b) Claudin, 4v   At-54 *31.Ch* (1534[14])
                                 At-79 *3.esl* (1537[4])

     Ed. CE (CMM 52), IV, no. 119

**Pleust a Dieu que fusse arondelle (5v)   38
    response to "Si Dieu vouloit"

    Janequin, 4v   L&B 7.L (1569)
    Ed. Janequin, VI, no. 233

**Quand j'ay beu du vin claret tout tourne (6v)   80

    Anon, 4v   At-6 35.Ch (1528[7])
                                    An-S 1.L (1535[8])
    Ed. Whisler, II, 291

Quand je vous ayme ardamment (5v)   63
    poem by Clément Marot

    a) ?Alaire, 4v   At-84 5.L (1538[14])—not
                                       seen

    b) °Arcadelt, 4v   At-149 25.L (1547[12])
                                    L&B 3.L (1561[2])

        Ed. CE (CMM 31), VIII, no. 12
        Eitner, 60 Ch, no. 4

*Que n'est elle aupres de moy celle que j'ayme (5v)   28

    Certon, 4v   At-92 9.L (1540[14], 1542[13])
                                    Mod Par.8 (1541[7])
    Ed. Lesure, Anth, no. 11

*Que t'ay-je faict desplaisante fortune? (5v)   12

    Anon, 3v   At-10 42.Chà3 (1529[4])
                                    Rhau Tric (1542[8])

*Ramonez moy ma cheminee (6v)   86

    Hesdin, 4v   At-69 1.L (1536[4], etc.)
    Ed. Eitner, 60 Ch, no. 27

Reconfortez le petit cueur de moy (5v)   32
    monophonic tune(?)

    Janequin, 4v   At-2 Ch.nou (1528[3])
                                    At-9 37.Ch (1528[8], 1531[2])
                                    An-S 2.L (1535[9])
    Ed. Janequin, I, no. 1

*Regret soucy & peine me font de vilains tours (5v)   13

    a) Anon, 4v   At-7 32.Ch (1528[5])

    b) ?Jacotin, 4v   At-79 3.esl (1537[4])—not
                                       seen

Reveille toy franc cueur joyeux (5v)   15
    monophonic tune; see Table I

•Reveillez vous c'est trop dormy (5v)   10

    Janequin, 4v   At-81 2.L (1538[11], 1540[9])
    Ed. Janequin, II, no. 69

Reviens vers moy qui suis tant desolée (7v)   138

    °Lupi, 4v   At-89 7.L (1539[17], 1540[13])
                                   L&B 1.rec (1554[25])
                                   D-85 1.rec (1567)
    Ed. Eitner, 60 Ch, no. 35

••Si Dieu vouloit que je feusse arondelle (5v)   36
    cf. "Pleust a Dieu"

    Janequin, 4v   L&B 7.L (1569)
    Ed. Janequin, VI, no. 232

•Si j'ay du mal maulgre moy je le porte (5v)   62
    (the first line is a quotation from Rondeau #25 of Clément
    Marot; the remainder is different)

    Claudin, 4v   At-82 3.L (1538[12], 1540[10])
    Ed. CE (CMM 52), IV, no. 141

•Si j'ay eu du mal ou du bien (6v)   124

    Claudin, 4v   At-30 33.Ch (1532[12])
                                     At-70 1.esl (1536[2])

    Ed. CE (CMM 52), IV, no. 142

••Si mon mal-heur m'y continüe (6v)   70

    Claudin, 4v   At-30 33.Ch (1532[12]) "Pele-
                                      tier"
                                     At-71 2.esl (1536[3]) "Pele-
                                      tier"
                                     At-76 2.esl (1537[3])
                                       "Claudin"
    Ed. CE (CMM 52), IV, no. 146

••Si par fortune avez mon cueur acquis (5v)   9

    Certon, 4v   At-41 Ch.mus (1533)
                                     At-71 2.esl (1536[3], etc.)
                                     L&B 2.rec (1555[23])

    Ed. Certon, I, 4

•Sur la rousée fault aller (6v)   84

    Passereau, 4v   At-69 1.L (1536[4], etc.)
    Ed. CE (CMM 45), no. 16
    Lesure, Anth, no. 6

Sus le pont d'Avignon (6v)   125
    monophonic tune

    Claudin, 4v   F-Pm Res 30345A(6), fo. 7ᵛ
                          (ms. frag. attached to At-73)

    Ed. CE (CMM 52), IV, no. 149

**Tant que vivray en aage florissant (5v)   8

    Claudin, 4v   At-2 *Ch.nou* (1528³)
                          At-9 *37.Ch* (1528⁸, 1531²)

    Ed. CE (CMM 52), IV, no. 150

Tous bons pions commencez de trotter (5v)   34

    ?Maillard, 4v   At-88 *7.L* (1539¹⁷)—not
                          seen

*Tout ce qu'on peult en elle voir (6v)   122

    C. Rore, 4v   L&B *8.L* (1557¹⁵, etc.)
                          D-79 *3.rec* (1561)

    Ed. Lesure, *Anth*, no. 23

Tout d'un accord passant melancolye (5v)   51
    monophonic tune; see Table I

**Un jour Robin alloit aux champs (6v)   92

    Claudin, 4v   At-2 *Ch.nou* (1528³)
                          At-9 *37.Ch* (1528⁸, 1531²)
                          At-70 *1.esl* (1536²)

    Ed. CE (CMM 52), IV, no. 157

*Un vieillard amoureux Est souvent mal content (5v)   41

    Janequin, 4v   At-40 *24.Ch.mus* (1533)
                          At-73 *3.L* (1536⁶)
                          Mod *Par.7* (1540¹⁷)

    Ed. Janequin, II, no. 35

**Veu le grief mal que longuement j'endure (5v)   30

    Villiers, 4v   At-84 *5.L* (1538¹⁴, 1540¹²)
                          Mod *Par.3* (1538¹⁷)
                          L&B *1.rec* (1554²⁵)
                          D-85 *1.rec* (1567)

Vignon vignon, vignon vignette (8v)   146
    monophonic tune(?)

    a) Anon, 4v   At-6 *35.Ch* (1528⁷)
        Ed. Seay, *AtKb* (CMM 20), p. 106

    b) Claudin, 3v   At-65 *31.Chà3* (1535)
                          etc.

    Ed. CE (CMM 52), IV, no. 161

Vos huis sont ils tous fermez (6v)   67
    monophonic tune(?)

      a) Goddard, 4v   At-147 *24.L* (1547[11])
                                                           etc.

        Ed. Brown, *Th Ch*, no. 159

      b) Nicholas, 6v   L&B-68 *L.Mesl* (1560)—
                                                           lost
                          L&B-165 *Mel* (1572[2])

        Ed. Curtis, no. 124

Vray dieu d'amours mauldict soit la journée (6v)   110
      a) Anon, 4v   At-8 *30.Ch* (1528[4])

      b) Jacotin, 4v   At-70 *1.esl* (1536[2])

A Letter from Melchior Newsidler

ARTHUR J. NESS

IN A LETTER DATED DECEMBER 23, 1577, the Augsburg lutenist Melchior Newsidler (1541–c. 1590) sent the future Wilhelm II, Duke of Bavaria, his wishes for a "radiantly good and peaceful New Year," and mentioned that, as in previous years, he was enclosing some of his lute pieces, a few "gar guette" German dances.[1] The letter reads (also see Plate I):[2]

> Durchleuchtiger hochgeborner Fürst Genediger herr / Eure Fürstlichen Genaden / sendt mein vnderthenigste dienst / sampt wunschung eines Glückseligen guetten vnd fridlichen Newen Jars Jederzeit beuor / demnach sich E. F. G. Genedigst zuerinneren wissen / das ich derselben wie Jar her / ettliche stuck auff die lautten Zum Newen Jar vnderthenigst presentiert / hab ich denselben brauch ihst / auch nachkhumen wollen / vnd derwegen etlich gar guette deüsche thentz zusamen geschriben / welche ich (dieweil ich selbst zu E. F. G. nicht khumen khinden) E. F. G. hiemit vnderthenigst pressentieren thue / mit vnderthenigster bitt E. F. G. wöllen dieselben mit Genedigem willen ohn

---

[1] Newsidler, son (not brother) of the Nuremberg lutenist Hans Newsidler (c. 1508–1563), may have been hinting for employment, since in 1576 he had applied for (but did not receive) a position at the Stuttgart court. In 1580 he became lutenist to Ferdinand II at Innsbruck, but was dismissed a year later (ironically, perhaps, in view of his later infirmity) for eating meat during Lent. He was regularly in the service of the Fuggers, who had commissioned his portrait for 61 gulden in 1574, and who employed him "bey der Tafel," at banquets and while sledding. Through the intercession of the music-loving Marcus Welser, Newsidler received a pension from the Fuggers to see him through his gouty old age. Adolf Layer's essay, "Melchior Neusiedler," *Lebensbilder aus dem Bayerischen Schwaben*, 5 (1956), 180–97, provides the most thorough biography. Also see the articles by Kurt Dorfmüller in *MGG*, vol. IX, pp. 1407–11, and Hans Radke in *New Grove*. vol. XIII, pp. 156–58.

[2] Munich, Bayerisches Hauptstaatsarchiv, HR I Fasz. 470/734. The letter reads in translation:

Most serene, honorable Prince, kind Lord, Your princely Grace: Sent is my most humble pledge, as well as wishes for a radiant, good, and peace-filled New Year. Always before, when wanting to be remembered by Your princely Grace, I have (the same as this year) humbly presented some pieces for the lute. To that end I also want to comply

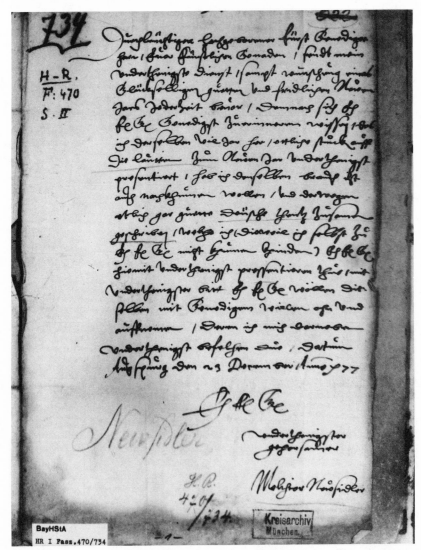

Plate 1. Munich, Bayerisches Hauptstattsarchiv, HR I Fasz. 470/734: Letter from Melchior Newsidler to Wilhelm II, Duke of Bavaria, dated December 23, 1577. Reproduced with permission of the Bayerisches Hauptstattsarchiv.

and therefore have compiled some quite good German dances, which (since I am unable to appear personally before Your princely Grace) I do herewith humbly present with a most humble request that Your Grace will be pleased and receptive of that which I moreover most humbly submit. Dated Augsburg, 23 December [15]77. Your princely Grace's most humble, dutiful Melchior Newsidler.

Vnd auffnemen / deren ich mich darneben vnderthenigst befolchen due
/ datum Augspurg den 23 December Anno 77

E.F.G.
vnderthenigster
gehorsamer
Melchior Newsidler

[Addressed in another hand:]
Dem Durchleuchtigen Hochgebornen Fürsten vnnd Herrn Herrn
Wilhalm, Pfalzgraffen bey Rein / Herzog in Obern vnd Nidern Bayern /
Meinem genedigem fürsten vnnd Herrn.

Melchior Newsidler is one of the most important and prolific German lutenists of the sixteenth century.[3] His compositions survive in
numbers greater than those of any of his contemporaries, and, because
they were so widely disseminated, must have exerted important influences on other lutenist-composers of his day. Some even appear in
English sources alongside works by John Dowland.[4] Moreover, several
books were prepared under his supervision, a rare occurrence in
sixteenth-century lute publications: two in Italian tablature (the usual
system used in southern Germany) published by Gardano at Venice in
1566, and the *Lautenbuch* in German tablature published at Strassburg
by Jobin in 1574.[5] Newsidler's output totals at least two hundred extant
pieces, although the full count is not yet in:

[3]Few of his works have appeared in modern editions; for some, see Howard M.
Brown, *Instrumental Music printed before 1600* (Cambridge, Mass., 1965) [hereafter
BrownI], item 1574/5. Of all Renaissance instrumentalists whose works have not yet
appeared in complete critical editions, Melchior Newsidler is deserving of the highest
priority. In the 1960s Thomas Binkley started a complete edition, which was announced in Dormüller (see fn. 1 above), but his manuscript was destroyed. Being aware
of the particularly knotty editorial complexities of Newsidler's output, Mr. Binkley
has apparently decided not to resume his projected edition.
The Hungarian lutenist-musicologist Daniel Benkö has recently told me of his
plans to edit a complete edition of the lute music of all the Newsidlers (Hans, Melchior,
and Conrad), and has started with the works of Hans.
[4]For some concordances in English sources, see John M. Ward and friends, "The
Lute Books of Trinity College, Dublin," *Lute Society Journal*, 9 (1967), 17–40; 10
(1968), 15–32 (with "additions," 12 [1970], 43–44); Cambridge, University Library,
Add. Ms 3056 (The Cozens Lute Book); and Edinburgh, University Library, Ms DC
5.125.
[5]To the surviving and lost sources cited in *BrownI* should be added the *Teutsch /
Lautenbuch schoener neuer Lautenstück* published posthumously (as the title page
acknowledges) at Strassburg in 1597; the reference to "neuer" suggests that its contents differed from those of the 1574 book. (See Albert Göhler, *Die Messkataloge* [Leip-
zig, 1901; repr. Hilversum, 1965], items 1.673–76.) Important manuscript sources for
his music, in addition to the Paris and Munich sources discussed here, are Donau-
eschingen, Fürstliche Fürstenbergische Hofbibliothek, Ms G.I.4/11–13 (3 vols.);
Wolfenbuettel, Herzog August Bibliothek, Ms Guelf. 18.7 Aug. and 18.8 Aug. (The
Hainhofer Lute Books); and Berlin (ex-Wollfheim; now in Cracow), Mus Ms 40598 (the
incorrectly called "Nauclerus-Bakfark Codex": the pieces attributed to "MN" are by
Newsidler, not Nauclerus).

23 fantasias and ricercars (including parodies on Clemens non Papa's "Rossignolet qui chantez," Cipriano de Rore's "Anchor che col partire," Josquin's "Cueur langoureaux," Verdelot's "Dormendo un giorno," and doubtless others still awaiting identification);
34 German and 38 Italian dances;
104 intabulations.[6]

His original fantasias and ricercars show him to be an excellent composer. Many use full three- and four-part textures, and he is particularly fond of exploiting the instrument's upper reaches, gradually soaring into higher and higher positions, thus demanding of the player great virtuoso skill. The intabulations, in particular, wear a patina of brilliant ornamentation, "mit fleiss ausgesetzt, auch artlich und zierlich Coloriert," as he advertises on his 1574 *Lautenbuch*.[7] A work may sometimes be traced through successive encrustations of ornamentation. For example, in Munich, Bayerische Staatsbibliothek, Mus Ms 1627, Newsidler's "Fantasia sopra Anchor che col partire" (dated 1572) is fairly unadorned; but in the 1574 *Lautenbuch*, it appears with added ornamentation.[8] (See Ex. 1.)

Since the fantasia exists in a "pre-publication" manuscript version, the question arises: do some of Newsidler's New Year's pieces for Wilhelm survive in the Bayerische Staatsbibliothek among the so-called Herwarth lute tablatures? The evidence is strong. The Herwarth collection does not include "etlich gar guette deüsche thentze," to be sure, but of the published lute books from the Herwarth acquisition, more than half have disappeared; and, certainly, popular German dances of the day are more likely to have been used (and lost) than the

---

[6]His intabulations include works by Lasso (32), Crecquillon (9), Anonymous (8), Clemens non Papa (7), Josquin (6, at least three now lost), Rore (5), Verdelot (4), Arcadelt (4), Sandrin (4), Senfl (3), two each by Meiland, Lupus, Lupi Didier II, Scandellus, Regnart, Berchem, Sermisy, Appenzeller, and Willaert, and one each by Hofhaimer, Mouton, C. Festa, Brack, Godard, Cadeac, Canis, Hollander, Pathie, D. Ferabosco, Zirler, Gosse, Azzaiola, Dressler, Morell, Ivo de Vento, and Eccard.

[7]His father had used the term "nach organisticher Art" on his books of 1536. That a content of "colored" intabulations might be featured in a lute book is particular to German publications, some by lutenists who seem to have made a specialty of the art, and may not have otherwise contributed original works for the lute, such as ricercars and fantasias. A few come to mind, including Bernhard Jobin, an engraver by profession (*BrownI* 1572/2), Sebastian Ochsenkhun (*BrownI* 1558/5). Matthaeus Waissel, a minister (*BrownI* 1573/3, 1591/13, 1592/12), and Sixt Kargel, an editor for Jobin after 1574 (*BrownI* 1586/5); all were essentially compilers of anthologies. Intabulations with stylistic ornamentation must have been an attractive feature for potential purchasers.

[8]The beginning, with examples of fantasias by others on the same madrigal, is published in John M. Ward, "Parody Technique in 16th-Century Instrumental Music," *The Commonwealth of Music*, ed. Gustave Reese and Rose Brandel (New York, 1965), pp. 214–15.

Example 1a. Fantasia sopra Anchor che col partire (Newsidler)

Mus Ms
1627,
No. 12

Example 1b. Teutsch Lautenbuch (1574): Fantasia super Anchor MN

Newsidler intabulations of motets, chansons, and madrigals that do survive.[9]

Prime candidacy must be given to pieces copied by a hand that I have labeled elsewhere *Scribe A* of the Munich tablatures.[10] Most of the pieces copied by him are, as we shall see, concordant with works in

[9]See Louise Martinez-Göllner, "Die Augsburger Bibliothek Herwart und ihrer Lautentabulaturen," *Fontes artis musicae*, 16 (1969), 45–48, for a 16th-century list of printed instrumental music thought to have come from the Herwarth collection. It includes the Newsidler and Kargel books, but listed as separate volumes.

[10]The Munich lute tablatures are the subject of my doctoral dissertation (a topic suggested by John Ward), "The Herwarth Lute Tablatures at the Bavarian State Library, Munich: A Bibliographical study with emphasis on the works of Melchior Newsidler and Marco dall'Aquila" (New York University, 1984). Not all of the 16th-century lute manuscripts now at Munich stem from the library of the Augsburg patrician, financier, and bibliophile Hans Heinrich Herwarth (1521–1583), as is sometimes suggested. The complex is best described as a miscellany of sheet music for lute; it contains over 350 pieces of diverse provenance in both time and place, copied by some 26 scribes on papers carrying some 40 different watermarks. Until the 19th century, most were stored, unbound, in envelopes, which became a catchall for a variety of materials. (The envelope with Mus Mss 1511 materials, for example, at one time even contained some 17th-century keyboard pieces and instrumental parts for a ballet dated 1671.) Since

Newsidler prints. He is responsible for distinct fascicles in the following manuscripts:

Mus Ms 1627
folios 1–16ᵛ (Nos. 1–12)

This fascicle was bound with lute prints by Newsidler (1566) and Kargel (1574), which were sent in October 1861 as "Dubletten" to the then Königliche Bibliothek in Berlin and lost during World War II.[11] The manuscript is expertly copied on paper bearing an Italian watermark,[12] and the final piece is signed "Melchior Neusidler [the Italian form of the name], 1572."

Mus Ms 266
folios 1–16ᵛ (Nos. 1–14)

The fascicle was part of "Bruckstücke" stored in an envelope until bound in the mid-nineteenth century, and rebound in 1968. The paper bears an Augsburg watermark of c. 1565.[13] The use of fairly expensive paper and the careful layout (pieces are arranged so that they appear on facing pages) suggest a presentation copy.

Mus Ms 2987
folios 12–13ᵛ (Nos. 37–38)

These pages, according to the "Altes Repertorium," were found loose and uncatalogued around 1860 in one of the large Lasso choirbooks (Mus Ms 2750), although some question remains as to whether all of the

---

some of the fascicles and sheets have the scribblings of a *Nebenschreiber*, who has sometimes dedicated pieces to Herwarth, these may be the fascicles that were logged into the ducal library in 1586 as "Ein Pintl oder fasciculus darinnen lautter gescribne vnd zum Tayl getrückte Tabulaturen auf die Lutten, lauten Kinderwerckh vnd nichts werth," a description that hardly passes with the fascicles copied by Scribe A. Those fascicles contain none of the scribblings of the Herwarth associate, who seems (like a graffito artist) to have been unable to resist the temptation of an empty space, at times even defacing what had been a beautifully and perhaps professionally, copied fascicle. The Scribe A pieces may have reached the ducal library independently, perhaps from Newsidler, as I intend to argue.

[11]The original state of the manuscripts and their later disposition may be traced in the "Altes Repertorium," an uncatalogued shelflist in the Musikabteilung, prepared in the 1820s by Joseph Schmidbauer and updated in the mid-19th century by Julius Josef Maier. The second part of Mus Ms 1627 was originally bound with Schmid's keyboard tablature of 1607. The librarian who prepared the list mentioned in fn. 9 above was accustomed to grouping the contents of bound volumes in one entry, so the lost Newsidler and Kargel books sent to Berlin may not have come from the Herwarth collection, or at least the present first fascicle of Mus Ms 1627 may not have been bound with them originally.

[12]Papers bearing the watermark of an anchor are interleaved with those of a crossbow. The marks and others mentioned here are reproduced in my dissertation (see fn. 10 above).

[13]See Charles Briquet, *Les filigranes* (Geneva, 1901; repr. with additional bibliography, Leipzig, 1923; repr. New York, 1968), No. 9001.

sheets now comprising this signature actually came from the choir-book.[14]

Paris, Bibliothèque nationale,
Ms Rés 429
folios 1–48[v]

This *Sammelhandschrift* consists of two distinct fascicles, bound to-gether in the late sixteenth century. The section (hereafter Paris I) pre-pared by Scribe A is copied on paper bearing an Augsburg watermark with printed six-line staves.[15] The manuscript, which was purchased from the estate of Professor F. Gehring of Vienna around 1882,[16] has an original parchment binding with references to St. Ursula, a figure ven-erated in Cologne and Strassburg.

The relationships among pieces copied by Scribe A and their printed concordances are complex, but may be illustrated with a few short ex-amples. A passamezzo by Newsidler appears in a fairly simple version in Munich, Mus Ms 266, No. 8, but with more ornamentation in New-sidler's 1566 Venetian print (the British Library copy of that print has numerous handwritten corrections, many of which agree with readings in the Munich manuscripts):

Example 2: Passage in 1566 print compared with Munich, Mus Ms 266

14For a discussion of this point, see my dissertation, vol. I, pp. 40–41. The bifolium contains no watermark.

15Cross of St. Anthony above the letter *P* (the letter identifies a fairly good grade of paper; see my dissertation, page 92, note 6). Stanley Boorman tells me that these are the earliest examples of printed tablature paper known to him.

16See Albert Cohen firm, *Katalog der Musikalischen Bibliothek des Herrn Dr. F. Gehring, Privatedocent an der Universität Wien* (Berlin, 1880).

Three versions of the intabulation of Ferabosco's "Io mi son giovinett'e" suggests a hierarchy, with a version published by Jobin in the middle:[17]

Example 3: Intabulation of "Io mi son giovinett'e," No. 11 in Munich, Mus Ms 266, compared with Jobin print and Mus Ms 266, No. 134

The Jobin version retains the ornamentation of measures 1 and 4 from Mus Ms 266, but, in the second half of measure 3, takes on an encrustation of 64th notes (perhaps the differences in the first part of the 32nd-note figure are due to misplaced ciphers). In Mus Ms 266, No. 134, all three figures receive further embellishment.

Similar relationships are evident in many of the concordances between the pieces copied by Scribe A and the printed sources of music by Newsidler. If successive layers of encrusted ornamentation signal a later reworking of an intabulation, then Scribe A's pieces come from the bottom layers of Newsidler's output.[18] The relevant concordances are shown below.[19] The sign > ("greater than") indicates a concordance

---

[17]If it was Jobin who made the arrangement.

[18]For details, see my dissertation, chapter V.

[19]Unique pieces copied by Scribe A are Mus Ms 1627, No. 3, "Je ne puis tenir" (Appenzeller), No. 4, "Jouissance" (Willaert), No. 7, "Como t'haggio" (Azzaiola), No. 8, "Tu mi far star" (Azzaiola?), No. 9, "La ferarese" (Newsidler), No. 10, "Se dire je lo soie" (Appenzeller); Mus Ms 266, No. 1, "Alla dolce ombra" (Rore), No. 14, "Sancta Maria" (Verdelot); Mus Ms 2987, No. 38, "Per su [sic] hospiti boschi" (C. Festa); Paris I, No. 7, "Chi passa per questa strada," No. 11, "Stabat mater" (Josquin), and No. 13, another "Chi passa."

with encrustations of embellishment; < ("lesser than"), one with less embellishment; and =, little or no change.

Title	1566 prints (Venice)	1572 print (Jobin)	1574 print (Strassburg)	1586 print (Kargel)	Other manuscripts
Mus Ms 1627					
1. Gustate et videte (Lasso)	= II, No. 6			No. 20 = 1566, No. 6	
2. Benedicam (Lasso)	> II, No. 5			No. 17 = 1566, No. 5	
5. Toutes les nuicts (Crecquillon)					> Ms 266, No. 164
6. Je fille (Gosse)					> Paris I, No. 14
11. Anchor che col partire (Rore)			< No. 21		> Ms 266, No. 125
12. Fantasia super Anchor (dated 1572; attr. to Newsidler)			< No. 46		
Mus Ms 266					
2. Signor mio caro (Rore)	< I, No. 7	No. 18 = 1566, No. 7			
3. Carità di Signor (Rore)	< I, No. 8				
5. Pis ne me peult venir (Crecquillon)		< No. 16			
6. Vray dieu disoit (Lasso)	< I, No. 15	No. 20 = 1566, No. 15			
7. Suspirs ardans (Arcadelt)	< I, No. 10				< Ms 266, No. 136
8. Passa mezo MN	= I, No. 13A				
9. Saltarello	= I, No. 13B				
10. Bewar mich Herr (Zirler)		< No. 24	< No. 23		
11. Io mi son giovinette (D. Ferabosco)		< No. 10			< Ms 266, No. 134
12. Helas, quel jour (Lasso)	< II, No. 12	< No. 21			

13. Sussana ung jour   = II, No. 7   >Ms 266,
    (Lasso)   No. 149

Mus Ms 2987[20]

37. Susanna ung jour   = No. 34
    (Lupi Didier II;
    attr. "MN")

Paris I[21]

2-6. Five passamezzos anticos with Saltarellos

[No. 8 = a galliarda added in 17th century]

 9. In te domine   = No. 5
    (Lupus)

10. Vita in ligno   <No. 3
    (Senfl)

12. Benedicta es   <No. 1
    (Josquin)

An examination of Newsidler's handwriting, as shown in his letter to Duke Wilhelm, seems essential. The letter is almost certainly in his hand, since it shows little sign of being the work of a professional scribe, particularly when compared with a letter by the Italian "bassiste" to the Munich court, Agostino Persei (Plates II and III).[22] The latter's letter, with its well-formed, scribal uniformity, must be the work of a professional *Briefmaler*. (That an Italian would have mastered German script so well seems unlikely.) Anomalies between the two may assist in defining the characteristics of Newsidler's handwriting. There are a number of features common to both letters:

German lowercase *r*'s resemble our lowercase *w*.[23] Melchior's hand is, however, bilingual, as one might expect of a musician who traveled to Italy. He does not always use the German form of the letter *r*, but rather he mixes it with an Italic one resembling our lowercase *v*. The

[20]The folios may be reversed, and perhaps the dedicatory-like Festa madrigal should precede the signed intabulation of the Didier II chanson.

[21]Versions of items 1 through 6 appear in Waissel's print of 1573 in the same order as in Paris I, although Waissel acknowledges that pieces in his anthology were collected from the best lutenists in Germany and abroad (including Padua), making it questionable that these works should be attributed to him rather than to Melchior Newsidler. The first one does, in fact, bear very close resemblances to one in Newsidler's 1574 print (No. 41).

The order of gatherings in Paris I may also have been disturbed; the gatherings of motets and the second "Chi passa" may have preceded the dances.

[22]Munich, Bayerisches Hauptstaatsarchiv, Kurbayern Äusseres Archiv 4854, fol. 239–239[v].

[23]For example, in the Persei letter, the words "Hochgeborner" (l. 1), "Jaren" (l. 2), "erzaignung" (l. 3), and "mir" (l. 11), and in Newsidler's letter, "beuor" (l. 5) and "vnterthenigste" (l. 3).

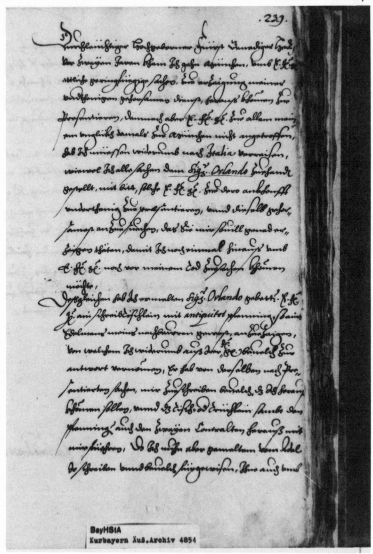

Plate 2. Munich, Bayerisches Hauptstattsarchiv, Kurbayern Äusseres Archiv 4854 ("Libri antiquitatem"), fol. 239: Letter from Agostino Persei to Wilhelm II or Albrecht V, undated. Reproduced with permission of the Bayerisches Hauptstattsarchiv.

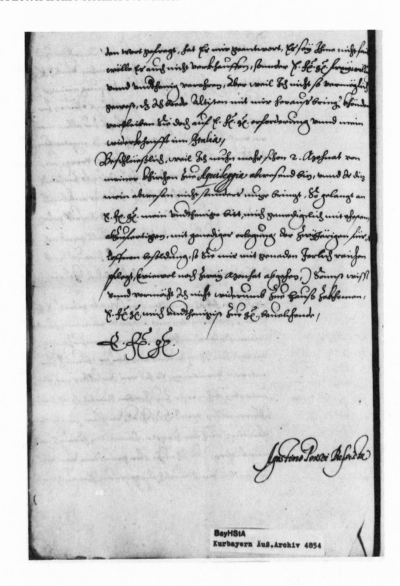

Plate 3. Ibid., fol. 239ᵛ. Reproduced with permission of the Bayerisches Hauptstattsarchiv.

word "December" (line 19) uses the Italic form, but the r's in "Hochge-borner" (line 1) and in "herr" (line 2) use both forms, as does his signature, "Newsidler" using the Italic form and "Melchior" the German.

Lowercase e in German script resembles our lowercase n or printed lowercase r.[24] Newsidler also uses the German form, as in the words "herr" and "Genaden" (line 2), "ettlich" (line 7), and the last e in "Pressentieren" (line 14). But again, Newsidler's hand is bilingual, since he mixes the Italic with German e.[25]

The conventional lowercase m in German script is expanded, so that the upstroke does not retrace the downstroke. That is, the letter has two dips in its midst, as in the m's in the Persei letter.[26] Newsidler's m's are, however, closer to ours, and sometimes have the second hump a bit higher than the first.[27]

German lowercase h's are made of two loops, usually joined to the following letter in a continuous stroke. Newsidler's are frequently not connected to the following letter.[28]

The German lowercase letters ch represent the c with a pen-twist that resembles a cresting wave attached to the lopped h.[29] See Persei's and Newsidler's formation of the word "hochgeborner" (line 1, in both letters), Newsidler's "Ich" (line 7), and his signature (line 23)—he would certainly want his name to be recognized. On other occasions, however, Newsidler's c in the formation ch is hardly a swell, let alone a cresting wave, particularly in the middle of the letter, when he may have allowed his attention to lapse. The Persei h in the ch formation slants properly from left to right, whereas Newsidler's slants right to left, and the bottom loop is not completed. Sometimes the downward portion of Newsidler's h intersects the swell representing the c.[30]

Newsidler's w's are also different from those in Persei's letter.[31] Frequently Newsidler also indicates a w or u with a small half-circle left open on the right, as in "Zum neuen" (line 8) and "Augspurg" (line 19).

[24]See, for example, in Persei's letter the words "-em" (l. 6), "meinem" (l. 13), "ettliche" (l. 3), "erzaigung" (l. 3), "Presentieren" (l. 5), etc.

[25]See the other e's in "pressentieren" (l. 14), in "beuor" (l. 5), and "Melchior" (l. 23).

[26]See "mein" (l. 5), "mit" (l. 9), "mir" (l. 11), and "meinem" (l. 13).

[27]See Newsidler's "meins" (l. 2), "demnach" (l. 5), "nachkhumen" (l. 10), "khumen" (l. 13), "Genedigem" (l. 16), "auffnehmen" (l. 17), and "December" (l. 19).

[28]See Persei's word "hab" (l. 7, etc.), and Newsidler's "nachkhumen" (l. 11), "ettlich" (ll. 7 and 11). Compare Newsidler's "her" (l. 7), "nachkhumen" (l. 10), "welche" (l. 12), and many other places.

[29]See Persei's words "Ich" (l. 2), "sachen" (l. 8), and "nicht" (l. 6), and Newsidler's "ich" (ll. 7 and 9), "nachkhumen" (l. 10), and "welche" (l. 12).

[30]See "fridlichen" (l. 4), "demnach sich" (l. 5), and (significantly, towards the end of the letter, when he may have been tired) "auch" (l. 10), "ich" (l. 12), and "ich mich" (l. 17).

[31]Compare Persei's words "wiewol" (l. 8), "welchem," and "widerumb" (l. 18, and Newsidler's "wie" (l. 7), "welche" (l. 12), "wöllen" (l. 15), and "Newsidler" (l. 23).

(In Persei's, the large flourishes of the pen, bordering on the decorative, are left open at the bottom.)

The capital *D* in Newsidler's "December" (line 19) is made by combining what we would call an *L* and a reversed *C*, leaning heavily forward. In the same line, the capital *A* of "Augspurg" and "Anno" are formed with three strokes, an upward one with a loop before the upstroke is made, a downstroke that bends to the right, and then the cross-stroke.

Only a few numerals appear in Newsidler's letter: two 7's, a 2, and a 3 (line 19). The 2 is a German type, fallen forward, one might say. The 3 is narrower in its upper part than its lower, and the 7's seem to have been made with the pen grazing the paper before and after the numeral, creating a nib at their beginnings and ends.

Some of the features of Newsidler's letter are found in the tablatures copied by Scribe A (see Plates IV, V and VI): the small circle above *U*'s and *W*'s (throughout), and the three-stroke *A*'s with loop.[32] The toppled numeral 2 does not always appear in the tablature in the same form as in the letter, but does occasionally, perhaps during lapses in copying (see Plate IV, "1572," etc.). The German-type numeral 2 may be inappropriate to Italian tablature.[33] The 7 with nibs at the beginning and end appears often, as well (see especially Plate V).[34]

Of course, the titles and even Newsidler's name at the end of the Mus Ms 1627 fascicle are written in italics. Fortunately, German script is used in one title, "Bewar mich herr," coming at the end of the piece, presumably when the scribe may have been tired and anxious to continue with the next piece (see Plate VI). German manuscripts commonly use script for titles in German, and Italic for pieces with French or Italian titles.

The B in this title consists of an *L* with superimposed and forward-leaning 3, similar to the *D* of "December"; the *e* is the Italic type; the *w* has a final loop; and the *r* is about halfway between the German and Italic types. The *m* resembles ours, rather than the German type, and has a second hill higher than the first; the *c* of *ch* is of the swelling, rather than "cresting wave" type; and the *h* slants right to left. The *h* is not connected to the following *e* in "herr"; and that word has an Italic *e*, and *both* the German and the Italic types of *r*: compare the same word in the letter (see Plate 1, line 2), also the two types in Newsidler's full signature, and the *r*'s in his name on Plate IV. There should be little doubt that Scribe A and Melchior Newsidler are one and the same.

The pieces copied by Scribe A in the Munich and Paris manuscripts

---

[32]Also see Mus Ms 266, Nos. 1, 12, and 13; Ms 2987, No. 38; and Paris I, fol. 4ᵛ and fol. 37ᵛ.

[33]Also Mus Ms 266, No. 4 (measure 2), 266, No. 3 (fol. 4, line 4).

[34]See also Paris I, fol. 37ᵛ; Ms 266, Nos. 1, 12, and 13; and Ms 2987, No. 38.

Plate 4. Munich, Bayerische Staatsbibliothek, Mus Ms 1627, fol. 15ᵛ:
Title, "Fantasia super anchor che col partire di M: Melchior Neusidler
1572."

Plate 5. Munich, Bayerische Staatsbibliothek, Mus Ms 266, fol. 14: Conclusion of Lasso's "Susanna ung jour."

Plate 6. Ibid., fol. 11: Conclusion of Zirler's "Bewar mich Herr."

are, therefore, important resources for the study of sixteenth-century music, and may actually be the most extensive collection of autographs by any composer of the Renaissance. They provide a vivid and authentic example of how a lutenist might vary the embellishments applied to an intabulation. Since Newsidler was active when lutenist ornamentation served to define polyphonic lines, his style may have valid application to ensemble music as well, permitting us to abstract the processes of embellishment as found in a practical musical source.

Newsidler's intabulations also supply abundant models for further examination of *musica ficta* as one lutenist applied it to several versions of the same piece. He is fairly consistent, but his afterthoughts may reveal much, and deserve our attention. Above all, since Newsidler copied the pieces in the Munich and Paris manuscripts and supervised the 1566 and 1574 prints, he has left us an accurate yardstick against which to measure critically how music by other composers of the Renaissance has come down to us.

Da Pu: The Recreative Process for the Music of the Seven-String Zither

THE SEVEN-STRING ZITHER *(gu qin)* of China has a large repertory preserved in a tablature notation, which consists of symbols representing instructions for finger positions, plucking methods, and various ornamental techniques. It gives, however, little apparent rhythmic direction. To perform a piece from notation is therefore not simple. *Da pu* is the process of deciphering and interpreting the tablature, whereby mute music in notation is converted to live music to be experienced. This paper is a preliminary investigation of the process and its significance.

Like any other musical genre with a long history, that of the seven-string zither has developed its individual characteristics and set of traditions, among which is *da pu.* An investigation of the process requires an understanding of the tradition as a whole, some features of which are briefly summarized as follows:[1]

1. *Long History.* The music of the seven-string zither has a long and uninterrupted history from antiquity until the present day, as attested by archeological and literary evidence. The instrument existed, with a construction similar to the one found today, as early as 200 B.C. Its predecessors, with the same basic features but with some variations (of which the most important was the number of strings—originally five), can be traced back several centuries to the Zhou dynasty (eleventh to fifth century B.C.).[2]
2. *Social Context.* The zither's intimate and exclusive association with

---

[1]An excellent introduction to the history, social context, lore, and sources of the seven-string zither is Robert H. Van Gulik, *The Lore of the Chinese Lute,* 2nd ed. (Tokyo, 1968).

[2]There also existed zithers with ten or more strings during its early history. See Lin Youren, "Qixuanqin yu Qinqu Shen, Yun Fazhan de Wojian" [My Views on the Historical Relationship Between the Seven-String Zither and the Tones of its Music] in *Yinyue Yishu* [Arts of Music], 8 (1982), 48–56.

China's small and elite class of literati is unique: no other instrument is so closely identified with the refinement and sophistication of this social class. The great majority of China's population had little chance to hear this music, although many would have heard of the name of the instrument, because it is often mentioned in popular performing genres such as storytelling and theater.

3. *Lore.* A rich lore concerning the instrument and its music has been accumulated and preserved, both orally and in writing. Physical parts of the instrument and many of the individual finger techniques have symbolic significance; individual pieces in the vast repertory are laden with extramusical content. The symbolism and the extramusical content are closely related to the history, philosophy, cosmology, and religion of China, especially as cultivated and transmitted by the literati.[3]

4. *Literary Sources.* A large amount of writing throughout Chinese history bears on the instrument, its music, its technique of performance, and its lore and philosophy.[4]

5. *Repertory in Tablature.* There exist today about sixty to seventy major collections of notation, with approximately two thousand pieces in all.[5] Most of them date from the fifteenth century, with a small number of pieces preserved from earlier periods. The earliest extant piece is from the sixth century A.D.

6. *Performance Practice.* During various periods of its long history, the instrument has been used as part of an ensemble for ritual music, and as an accompanying instrument for songs. However, its outstanding role in performance is, and has been throughout history, as a solo instrument. Historical writings suggest that its solo music has been played not so much for an audience as for the performer's own enlightenment and enjoyment. Occasionally, performers may play for each other, but zither players have predominantly been "amateurs," in the sense that one would not depend upon performance as a means

---

[3]See James Watt, "The Qin and the Chinese Literati," *Orientation,* 12 (1981), 38–49.

[4]An important and useful bibliographical work on this matter is *Zhongguo Gudai Vinyue Shumu [A Bibliography of Musical Monographs from the Past],* compiled by Zhongyang Yinyue Xueyuan [Central Conservatory of Music] (Beijing, 1961). It lists 179 items of major literary sources on the seven-string zither dating from A.D. 170 to 1840. Some are mainly collections of pieces in tablature notation. Others are essays on the history, philosophy, and lore of the instrument and its music, and manuals on playing the instrument.

[5]These figures are according to Zha Fuxi in his privately printed memoir *Sou Bo Bie Ji [A Second Collection of Sou Bo's Articles]* (n.p., 1959), p. 61. Minor collections are not included in this survey. The total number of pieces, which depends upon the criteria in judging whether two items are versions of the same piece or different pieces, is often taken to be higher by other scholars.

of living.[6] This private mode of performance may have had a critical role in the shaping of many of the musical characteristics of this instrument, among which, for example, is its extremely low dynamic level.

The zither is basically a flat and elongated wooden box with seven strings. The hollow body is about three and one half feet long; about seven inches wide on one end, tapering to about four inches on the other; and one to two inches thick. The upper surface, with the strings stretched lengthwise across it, is slightly convex in its width-wise dimension, while the lower surface is flat with two sound-emitting holes. The whole elongated body is a resonating chamber, with its upper face also serving as the fingerboard (see Plate 1). The player plucks the strings with the right-hand fingers, while the left-hand fingers move along the board to make stopped notes and harmonic notes, and occasionally also pluck the strings. Thirteen studs, or markers, run lengthwise along one side of the upper surface, to help the left hand find its place. The strings have traditionally been made of silk. During the last two or three decades, musicians have experimented with other materials, including steel and nylon.

Plate 1. Yao Bing-yan playing the seven-string zither.

[6]Professional zither players are rarely mentioned in the literature. This century, however, has seen a few outstanding players who perform and teach professionally.

Each finger movement of the right and left hands has a name and a written symbol corresponding to it. These symbols, and what they represent, are shown as *zhi fa,* or finger techniques. For example, the symbol 大 , which stands for 抹 , pronounced *mo,* indicates plucking the string inward with the right index finger. Other symbols indicate which string to pluck, and which position and in what manner the left-hand finger is to stop the string. The notation consists of a sequence of these symbols, or a combination of them written in clusters. They derive from, and are closely related to, Chinese written characters.

A large number of manuals explaining the meanings of these symbols are preserved from historical times. According to a survey of these manuals, there are over a thousand symbols representing finger techniques, some for the right hand alone, some for the left, others for combinations of both hands.[7] Many are variations of a basic technique. The meaning of some symbols has changed over time: the same symbol may refer to different finger techniques depending on when it was used.

Figure 1 reproduces the first page of notation of a piece from the fifteenth-century collection called *Shenqi Mipu* [The Fantastic and Secret Repertory].[8] Reading from right to left by columns, the first column gives the title of the piece: *Wu Ye Ti* [Crows Cry in the Night]. The next nine columns provide the collector's remarks on the piece, followed by the notation proper: clusters of symbols representing the finger techniques.

The following is a translation of the collector's note.

> Qu Xian [the collector's name] writes: this is an ancient piece. According to the Chapter on Music in the Standard History of the Tang dynasty, "Crows Cry in the Night" was composed by Prince Yi-qing of Linchuan. In the 17th year of the reign of Yuan Jia (A.D. 441), Prince Yi-kang of Peng Cheng was demoted to serve in Yi-Zhang. Prince Yi-qing at the time was serving as the local governor of Jiangzhou. When the two brothers met in the provincial capital, they wept. The Emperor Wen heard of this incident and was offended. Yi-qing was ordered to return to his native town, which caused him great fear. One night his concubine heard crows crying. She went to his study and told him that this was a good omen, that he would receive pardon soon. That year, he was appointed governor of Southern Zhi-zhou. He therefore composed a piece called

---

[7]See Zha Fuxi's privately printed memoir *Sou Bo Ji* [*A Collection of Sou Bo's Articles*] (n.p., 1959), p. 124. Zha wrote that, according to a survey by Gu Meigeng, there are 1036 techniques (with names) corresponding to 1393 symbols. Among them, 122 named techniques have no symbols; 34 symbols have no names.

[8]Compiled by Qu Xian and first printed in 1425. Two copies of the work are known to exist in this century: one is an edition from the Jia Jing reign of the Ming dynasty (1522–1566), the other from the Wan Li reign (1573–1620). The latter was reprinted and published by Yinyue Chubanshe [The Music Publishing Company] (Beijing, 1956). See Zha Fuxi, *Sou Bo Ji,* supplementary volume, p. 71.

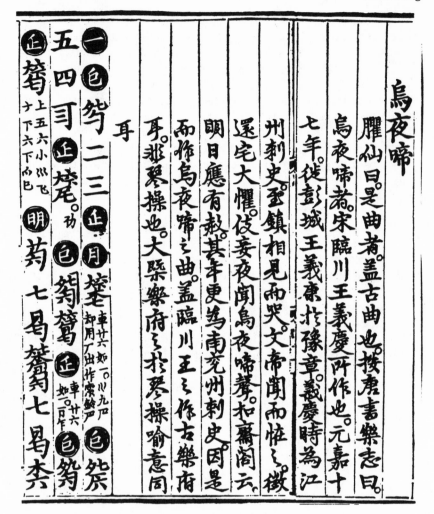

Figure 1. Notation of *Shen qi mi pu*

"Crows Cry in the Night." Note that the piece with the same name by the Prince [Yi-qing] of Lin-chuan was a song, not a piece for the zither. It is probable, however, that both the song and the zither piece have the same meaning.

This beginning page for "Crows Cry in the Night" is representative of the majority of pieces in the collections: the notation proper is preceded by a programmatic title and a paragraph of explanation. In this example, the title "Crows Cry in the Night" suggests a natural scene, or an activity in nature. The accompanying note describes a historical incident that presumably motivated the creation of the music. Both the title and the preface give extramusical meaning to the piece.

This page can also be used to illustrate several aspects of the notational symbols. These observations are necessary before the discussion of the *da pu* process.

1. The meanings of some of the notational symbols are unambiguously transmitted from generation to generation without change. For example, the symbols for the numerals one through seven, when placed at the lower portion of the cluster of symbols, refer to the string to be plucked; on the other hand, the symbols for the numerals one through thirteen, when placed at the upper portion of the cluster of symbols, refer to the positions (studs) where the left hand is to stop the string. Another example is the symbol called *mo* (mentioned above), which means "plucking the string inward with the right index finger."

2. The meaning of some of the symbols has changed through the centuries. In order to read the symbol correctly, one must refer to manuals published around the time of the collection. For example, in the fifteenth century, the symbol of two closely spaced numerals, for example, "67," refers to a stud position somewhere halfway between 6 and 7; the exact location depends on which string and studs are involved and which scale is used. In the twentieth century, the same symbol refers to a position beyond 6, seven-tenths of the distance towards 7: in other words, 6.7.

3. The meanings of some of the symbols are not quantitatively explicit: the manuals explain them in vague terms. For example, the symbol called *zhuo* 綽 means that the left-hand finger glides to the designated stud position from the left as the right hand plucks the string. How far to the left of the designated stud position the left hand should begin the slide is not spelled out. Another example is the symbol called *ru man* ⼊ 慢, which means "begins to slow down." There is, however, no indication of how slowly the music should go or the rate of slowing down.

4. For someone used to reading Western staff notation, the most conspicuously missing symbols are those that give explicit temporal instructions: there is no symbol to indicate the relative duration of the individual pitches produced by various finger techniques. There are, however, several symbols that give general, impressionistic description rather than specific, quantitative rhythmic instructions. The symbol called *ru man* has already been mentioned. Another example is a symbol called *ji* 急, which means "quickly" in this context. It is used as a prefix to other symbols such as *shang* 上, meaning "moving up [that is, toward the right]." Thus, *ji shang*, which usually appears after the right hand plucks a stopped note, means "[the left hand

then] moves up quickly." Another example is a small circle that appears from time to time to mark the end of a musical phrase. The performer usually rests a little at those points. These marks appear in only some of the collections.

5. Other kinds of temporal instructions are not spelled out, but only implied in the instructions for the right-hand plucking techniques. Thus the symbol called *li* 搖 instructs the performer to pluck two or more neighboring strings outward in quick succession with the index finger. The pitches thus produced are temporally very close to each other. If the performer is to pluck neighboring strings successively but slowly, other symbols are used.

The above discussion should make it clear that performing a piece from notation is not a matter as simple and straightforward as sightreading from a score for piano. The notation allows some flexibility, and demands that the performer carry out a process of reading and interpretation requiring a considerable amount of research, reflection, and experimentation. Such a process is known as *da pu*.

During the summers of 1980, 1981, and 1982, I studied *da pu* with Yao Bingyan, the foremost contemporary performer and, if I may coin the term, *dapuist* in China.[9] He was a zither performer for forty years and an active *dapuist* for almost thirty. True to the tradition of zither players in history, he was not a musician by profession, but was an accountant in a factory all his life until he retired in 1980. The following discussion of *da pu* will be presented in two parts: first, a model of the process, which I constructed from my observation of Yao's activities, our discussion, and analysis of his music; second, Yao's own verbalization of what he does.

My model of the process consists of three stages of activity, which the *dapuist* carries out: the research into the literary content of the music; the deciphering of the technical content of the notation (that is, the finger techniques); and his creative input.

It has already been mentioned that each piece in the zither repertory has a title that may paint a picture, suggest a mood, or tell a story. Many of these titles are closely associated with the history, myth, and philosophy of China. Most pieces have explanatory notes as prefaces, which further elucidate the programmatic content of the music. "Crows Cry in the Night," for example, alludes to certain historical figures and gives a possible reason for the composition of the piece.[10] "Dialogue be-

[9]Yao Bingyan died of cancer on March 18, 1983, at the age of 63.

[10]Xu Jin questions the appropriateness of the above-quoted literary preface for "Crows Cry in the Night," and argues that a different story should be attached to this piece. See his *Qinshi Chubian [A Preliminary Study of the History of the Seven-String Zither]* (Beijing, 1982), 45–49.

tween the Fisherman and the Woodcutter" alludes to the Taoist ideals of a simple life in nature, free from worldly intrigues and complexities. "Mist over the Rivers Xiao and Xiang" alludes to the story of the historical figure Guo Wangchu of the Southern Song dynasty (thirteenth century), who lived at a time when half of China was occupied by foreign invaders. On one level, that piece paints the picture of the mist over the rivers; but on another level, it expresses Guo's rage and sorrow over the incompetence of the government and the loss of his country to foreign invaders. This feeling has been shared by many in subsequent historical periods, and could very likely have contributed to the popularity of this piece. For some pieces, the mere title alludes to historical figures, incidents, and moods that a literate Chinese should know, so that a preface is not even necessary.

The first stage of *da pu* is, therefore, the recognition of the literary content, or extramusical meaning, of the piece. The *dapuist* must have a broad exposure to Chinese culture, history, and philosophy. He may have to conduct a certain amount of literary and historical research in order to identify the meaning of the title and accompanying preface, and to recognize the event they allude to.

The second stage is the deciphering of the technical content of the notation: to know the meaning of the symbols and clusters of symbols that are instructions for the two hands. The problem can be complicated because, as mentioned previously, the meaning of some of the symbols has changed in history. A *dapuist* must know the historical context of the symbols through research before he can determine the proper meanings. There exist today manuals on finger techniques from various historical periods.[11] A proper study of the notation and the manuals, including correct dating, choice, and verification of editions, and a critical examination for possible mistakes, such as misprints and copying errors, form an important part of this stage of work. A *dapuist* is also expected to have a certain amount of technical proficiency in order to perform the finger techniques.

After clarifying the meaning of the symbols, the performer still has a great deal of latitude in the actual execution of the music. In particular, the absence of explicit temporal instructions in the notation leaves much of the rhythmic aspects of the music to the discretion of the *dapuist*. A few instructions for the left-hand movement that do not specify the extent of the movement also give the *dapuist* a certain degree of

[11]One of the earliest such manuals containing a substantial number of symbols and explanations is the lost *Datang Zhengsheng Qinpu,* 10 vols., by Chen Zhuo (b. A.D. 904), part of which was reproduced in *Qinshu Daquan [A Complete Compendium of Zither Literature],* 22 vols., by Jiang Keqian (1590). The latter was recently reprinted and published in full as vol. 5 of *Qinqu Jicheng [A Compendium of Zither Music]* (Beijing, 1980).

freedom in the choice of pitches. Some of the major decisions he has to make are: Which are the important melodic motifs? How are they to be treated rhythmically? What are the phrase patterns? For a technique such as *chuang*, in which, after a stopped note is plucked by the right hand, the left-hand finger is to "move to the right a little and then quickly move back," how much to the right is the finger to move, and how quickly is it to move back? Should there be a meter? If so, what should it be? What is the tempo? How should the dynamic levels vary? The answers to these questions, which may affect the music quite drastically, involve musical decisions based upon two considerations:

1. The musical vocabulary must conform to a certain extent to that of the "living" repertory, some of which the *dapuist* has already acquired through oral transmission from his teacher. While he may not know exactly what he should do, he knows what he should not do.
2. The personal feelings, or state of mind (*yi jing*), he obtains upon producing the music should match the literary content of the piece. Prerequisites to proper matching are the correct understanding of the literary content and the symbols for finger technique, and the proper execution of these techniques to produce the music. The *dapuist's* ability to judge matters such as proper matching and correct understanding depends, of course, upon his literary and musical sensitivity, nurtured through years of playing the "living" repertory that he learned by oral transmission.[12]

To summarize, the first stage involves research on literary material; the second stage involves research on technical matters. Given ideal notions of scholarship, all *dapuists* should arrive at the same, or similar, conclusion after these two stages. The third stage, however, is where personal judgment is crucial. What is the correct musical sense? More important, what is considered correct matching between the musical sound and the literary content? These are judgments that arise from the *dapuist's* personal experience and individuality. It is at this stage that the *dapuist's* role is closest to that of a Western composer.

When Yao Bingyan was asked "what is *da pu*?" he answered by proposing a metaphor to illustrate his idea: the *da pu* process can be likened to a traveler visiting a new land. It also consists of three stages,

---

[12]The relationship between the music and the literary content seems to be far less specific than, say, that between the Wagnerian leitmotives and what they mean. Yao very seldom points to specific phrases and relates them to specific extramusical meanings. Occasionally, Yao does point out certain phrases that have onomatopoeic meanings.

which Yao calls *dong ji* [motivation], *fang fa* [method], and *xiao guo* [result]. He explained them as follows:[13]

To Yao, the title, preface, and other literary sources relating to a piece are verbal abstractions on the meaning of the music. They are likened to words in a guidebook for a traveler, which describe scenery, relate anecdotes, and highlight attractions. By reading the guidebook, the traveler is led by the words into a realm of imagination or state of mind (*yi jing*). He may be inspired to actually visit the new land in order to achieve this state of mind by experiencing the real physical world rather than an imaginary one. Analogously, when the *dapuist* studies the title, preface, and other literary sources related to the piece, the words supply him with stories, pictures, and moods, putting him in a state of mind induced by the imagination. He may be inspired to actually experience the musical terrain in order to achieve this state of mind through real music rather than through verbal abstractions on the meaning of the music. The reading and understanding of the literary sources relating to the piece in order to induce the state of mind are what Yao considered the first stage. He called it "motivation."

The second stage, "method," refers to the execution of the music, which is analogous to taking the actual journey—the physical act of traveling and the experience of the sights and sounds of a new land. Similarly, the *dapuist* journeys through the musical terrain. Through the physical act of making the music, which includes aural, visual, and tactile experiences, the third stage, the "result," will be achieved.

As the traveler journeys through the new land, his state of mind is what Yao called the "result." It is a state of mind that the voyager anticipated through the verbal description of the guidebook and his own imagination. Now he is actually experiencing that state through the physical contact with the sights and sounds of the land. Analogously, the *dapuist* experiences a state of mind as a response to the physical experience of the music.

The state of mind naturally depends upon the physical experience. For a traveler, it depends upon his itinerary, his means of transporta-

---

[13]Yao published several articles on the subject. See his "Qixuanqinqu 'Jiukuang' Dapu Jingguo" [The Process of Dapu for the Zither Piece 'Wine Madness'], *Yinyue Yishu [Arts of Music]*, 5 (1981), 26–31; " 'Quyuan Wendu' Houji" [Notes after Working on 'Quyuan Asking for Direction'], *Qinlun Juexin [New Studies on Zither]*, 5 (March, 1981), 51; " 'Guguan Yushen' Houji" [Notes after Working on 'Meeting the Spirits in a Deserted House'] ibid., pp. 59–62; "Qinqu Gouchen: 'Wu Ye Ti' " [The Resurrection of Zither Music: 'Crows Cry in the Night'], *Yinyue Yanjiu [Studies in Music]*, 21 (1983), 82–90. After mulling over his metaphors for some time and presenting them here in English (which in itself is a form of interpretation), I find it difficult not to instill, intentionally or not, some of my own ideas into his original metaphor.

tion, and his activities along the way, all of which determine the sights and sounds he would experience. For the *dapuist* it depends upon the musical terrain he travels, a terrain he creates from the notation.

If the traveler dislikes what he experiences, he can rechart his itinerary and change his activities; likewise, a *dapuist* can create different kinds of terrain by manipulating the musical material provided by the notation. This brings him back to the second stage: the method. The notation allows him a certain flexibility. Guided by the verbal abstraction on the meaning of the music (motivation), he exercises this flexibility by manipulating the musical terrain (method) until he achieves the prescribed state of mind (the result).

After many attempts, the *dapuist* arrives at a version in which he experiences a state of mind prescribed by the verbal description. The *da pu* process is then complete. Even though the state of mind that he experiences in making music seems to agree with the prescription, they are in fact different, because the former is a musical experience, the latter a literary experience.

Yao noted that, on rare occasions, there are pieces for which, regardless of how he manipulates the musical material derived from the given notation, the "result" never seems to fit the prescription. One example is a piece called *Gu feng cao* [Song of Antiquity], from the same fifteenth-century collection mentioned earlier. After he carried out the *da pu* process on that piece, he wrote in his notes:

> I had not tried to work on this piece because from the title [and the accompanying notes], it seems to be another of those plain and uninteresting pieces about ancestral shrines. [Here Yao is referring to the pieces in the zither repertory that are influenced by ritual music for the worship of sages, kings, and ancestors.] Recently I started playing it, and discovered that its content was completely different from what I had imagined it to be. I therefore begin to wonder:
> 1. Could the music of antiquity [ritual music] really have sounded like this?
> 2. Could it be that [Song of Antiquity] is not its original title? The compiler of this collection did write in the preface that he changed the titles of some of the pieces in the collection because the original ones were vulgar.
> 3. Perhaps my interpretation of the musical material is wrong?

In this case, Yao eventually disregarded the original title and literary notes, and supplied his own extramusical meaning to the piece based upon his response to the music sound.[14]

Each *dapuist* creates his own state of mind as a response to the liter-

---

[14]He believed that "Song of Antiquity" was in fact dance music from Western China, a far cry from ritual music, and understandably disturbing to the compiler.

ary content of the piece; and each *dapuist* has his own criteria for judging whether the musical terrain that he has created matches the prescribed state of mind. Therein lies the individual creativity of the *dapuist.* This also explains why the tradition of zither music has always been personal and private.[15] The aim of the player, according to the philosophy of zither music, is an inner state of mind, which can never, or hardly ever, be truly shared by a second person.[16]

The *da pu* process also illustrates the close relationship between notation and performance practice. The tablature notation is sometimes· criticized as "inadequate" and "immature" because of a lack of explicitness in its instructions on rhythmic and other matters. This "lack" of explicitness could be interpreted as a strength rather than a weakness. It may be the result of a deeper purpose: to allow a certain degree of individual creativity on the part of the performer. It follows that, in treating the repertory of the seven-string zither, one has to redefine one's concept of the identity of a piece of music. Meter, rhythm, and phrasing, taken for granted in Western art music as important factors of identity (as they are, in most cases, quite explicitly and unambiguously notated by the composer), are, in the music of the seven-string zither, allowed a more flexible interpretation from one performer to another, and from one performance to another by the same performer. Furthermore, because the performance is mainly a personal and private activity, a rigid consensus on what *should* and *should not* be done becomes, understandably, less meaningful. This explains why a large number of pieces appeared in many versions, sometimes drastically different from one another, in collections from different historical periods. The performers in different periods were allowed, if not encouraged, to reinterpret a preexistent piece. They sometimes modified the finger techniques so that notes, phrases, even whole sections, might be added or deleted from the original version that they learned. This kind of activity has, of course, gone beyond the *da pu* process described here. It is nevertheless another important subject for research, especially in the light of the vast amount of notations available for study.

Yao's model of *da pu* puts heavy emphasis on the "meaning" of the

[15]The private nature of zither music has been investigated from another perspective. See Bell Yung, "Choreographic and Kinesthetic Elements in Performance on the Chinese Seven-String Zither," *Ethnomusicology,* 28 (1984), 505–17.

[16]Among the rich lores of the zither tradition, one of the best known and probably most quoted is the story about the friendship between the legendary zither master Bo-ya (believed to have lived some time between the 8th and 5th century B.C.) and Zi-qi, the only person who could understand his music. When the latter died, Bo-ya smashed his zither, and never touched the strings again, because no one else in the world could understand his playing. Their friendship has always been the symbol of the truest and greatest of friendships in China.

music and the state of mind of the *dapuist*. He emphasizes the "result" only in terms of the literary, or extramusical, meaning; the matching of the "result" and the "motivation" is the only criterion for this "method." However, from my observation, Yao and other zither performers (including myself) are also concerned with the behavior of musical sound independent of literary meaning.[17] It is my opinion that Yao's denial of purely musical thinking is due to two factors. First, zither players, as scholars, are by definition literarily oriented. Second, a traditional scholar in China is heavily indoctrinated in Confucian philosophy, which tends to de-emphasize, if not censor outright, the non-literary, purely sensual, elements in the performing arts. From a Western musicologist's point of view, however, the repertory of zither music contains highly sophisticated structures in musical sound, which deserve careful study for their own sake, independent of literary associations.

In conclusion, I would like to address two questions in relation to *da pu*. First, how old is the process? While the term itself seems to have first appeared in print only in the early twentieth century,[18] activities similar to Yao's must have been carried out quite regularly throughout history. In the fifteenth-century collection *Shenqi Mipu* under discussion, the compiler wrote in a note appearing at the end of volume one: "The last few pieces originally had no phrase marks. During the last few days in my leisure hours, I put down phrase markings based upon my personal feeling and understanding of the meaning of the music. Musicians please note."[19] Similar references can be found in other historical documents.[20]

---

[17]When I raised this issue in the form of a question, I was not able to get a direct answer from him.

[18]Yang Shibo, in his *Qinxue Wenda [Questions and Answers in Zither Study]* (1923), writes: "To play a piece [of zither music] according to ancient tablature is commonly known as *da pu*" (p. 12). Shi Yinmei has also mentioned the term in her "Duiyu Changming Qinxue zhi Wojian" [My Views on an Enlightened Approach to Studying the Zither" in *Jinyu Qinkan [Publication of the Jinyu Zither Society]* (Shanghai, 1937), p. 52. A systematic survey of literature may likely uncover earlier usage of the term.

[19]This note appears only in the edition of *Shenqi Mipu* from the Jia Jing reign of the Ming dynasty (1522–1566). See fn. 8.

[20]For example, Shi Yinmei, "Duiyu Changming Qinxue," wrote "The old collections of notation should be studied and interpreted [*zhengli*] in detail. . . . The most difficult part of *dapu* is to add the different kinds of vibrato [*yinnao*]. . . . Beat and meter are the skeleton of a piece of music. The notation did not generally indicate them clearly. Therefore, to play a new piece [from notation] is like dealing with a tray of sand. Each *dapuist* has to go his own way." Zha Fuxi wrote: "*Da pu* is likened to the arrangements of furniture in a room." (*Sou Bo Ji*, p. 83). The appearance of many versions of the same piece in different editions, some of which may be centuries apart, is another indication that it was common practice for a zither player to "interpret" the notation in his own way. A study of different versions and editions should shed more light on *da pu*.

What is the significance of *da pu*? In view of the fact that only about twenty percent of all zither notation is today heard as live music, the *da pu* process should be extremely important in the reincarnation of a vast amount of music in China. Furthermore, this preliminary study has shown that *da pu* is a creative process that involves an individual who must carry out scholarly research, be literarily and musically knowledgeable and sensitive, possess technical proficiency on the instrument, and be creative. In other words, a *dapuist* has to be a scholar, a performer, and a composer. It is an example of a complex human creative process that deserves attention, both in the context of Chinese culture and in the general context of human creativity.

Table of Chinese characters for terms and names in the text.

da pu   打譜

dong ji   動機

fang fa   方法

Gu Feng Cao   古風操

gu qin   古琴

Guo Wangchu   郭望楚

ji   急

li   攊

mo   抹

ru man   入慢

shang   上

Shenqi Mipu   神奇秘譜

Wu Ye Ti   烏夜啼

xiao guo   效果

Yao Bingyan   姚丙炎

yi jing   意境

zhi fa   指法

zhuo   綽

Béla Bartók and Text Stanzas in Yugoslav Folk Music

ALBERT B. LORD

In HIS BOOK ON YUGOSLAV folk songs, Béla Bartók listed several ways in which Serbo-Croatian folk music might be distinguished from other Central and East European folk songs. After commenting on various melodic characteristics and before dwelling on the importance of heavy ornamentation in the mode of performance, he stated: "As for *text structure*, there is no stanza structure. Ten-syllable lines are preponderant."[1] In this paper I address myself to the question of text-stanza structure in Yugoslav folk songs, as presented in the seventy-five songs from the Milman Parry Collection analyzed by Bartók in *Serbo-Croatian Folk Songs*, and in one epic song from Bihać published in Volume XIV of *Serbo-Croatian Heroic Songs*.

Bartók's description of text stanza is found in his study of morphology in *Serbo-Croatian Folk Songs*:

> The texts of folk songs in the first-mentioned two countries [Slovakia and Hungary] present almost without exception decided stanza structure (that is, a more or less symmetrical recurring structure of two, three, or four text lines) connected with the use of rhymes.[2]

Coming from the background of Slovak and Hungarian folk music, where four-section melodies are the most common and where "the text stanzas are predominantly composed of four lines, corresponding to the four sections of the melody," Bartók found that in the Balkans two- and three-section melodies were the rule, and that four-section melodies were comparatively rare. He discovered that "in Rumania, suddenly, the text-stanza structure disappears (except in songs of urban or semi-rural origin) though rhymes are still in use," and that on "Bulgarian and

---

[1]Béla Bartók and Albert B. Lord, *Serbo-Croatian Folk Songs: Texts and Transcriptions of Seventy-Five Folk Songs from the Milman Parry Collection* (New York, 1951), p. 85.

[2]Ibid., pp. 34–35.

Serbo-Croatian territory . . . there are no more text-stanza structures
and no rhymes (except in songs of urban or semi-rural origin). . . ."[3]

A little further on he was more specific:

> When we use the expression "text stanzas" or "absence of text stanzas,"
> we refer to the form of the texts stripped from the melody. If the lines of
> the song text keep a symmetrical, recurring arrangement, then obvi-
> ously there exists a text-stanza structure (which generally tallies with
> the melody stanza). But if, stripped from their melodies, they present no
> regular arrangement and only structurally independent text lines re-
> main, it would be senseless to call them text stanzas. In the latter case
> the single text lines will be adapted to the melody stanzas in various
> ways, being originally probably only one text line in various forms of re-
> peats to a given melody stanza.[4]

Bartók elaborates on these statements in great detail in the pages
that follow in his book, and I owe much to them.

Let me illustrate what Bartók has said about the adaptation of a single text line to two- or three-section melodies. As he has remarked, it
would not be appropriate to call these instances "text stanzas." In Bartók's book Nos. 2, 5, 6c, 8a, 8b, 9, 10a, 10b, 11, 12c, 12d, and 15 are good
examples of adaptation by simple repetition of the line:

Example 1

Now my beloved is building a tower,
Now my beloved is building a tower.

It is symptomatic that the single line of text may have to be adapted in
some further way as well to the two-section or other melodic structure.
I say symptomatic, because it seems to indicate the importance of melodic structure over text structure. Thus in No. 4:

[3]Ibid., p. 35.
[4]Ibid., pp. 35–36.

Planino moja starino, lele,	O my ancient mountain, lele,
Planino moja starino!	O my ancient mountain!

"Lele" is added to the first appearance of the line to fit it to the musical structure.

In other cases the adaptation is done by various kinds of repetition of parts of the line. For example, in No. 14 the first four syllables are repeated:

Sitna travo, sitna travo, zelena,	O little grass, little grass, green,
Sitna travo, sitna travo, zelena!	O little grass, little grass, green!

Or the last four syllables may be repeated, as in No. 17:

Razbolje se Zorna Zorka, Zorna Zorka,	Fell ill Zorna Zorka, Zorna Zorka,
Razbolje se Zorna Zorka, Zorna Zorka.	Fell ill Zorna Zorka, Zorna Zorka.

Or there may be a strange arrangement of text as in No. 16a, in which the last four syllables of the line are repeated, or, perhaps better, stated at the beginning of the line:

Example 2

16a

Little letter, of sorrow is the little letter.
Little letter, of sorrow is the little letter.

There are also several three-section melodies in Bartók's book to which a single line of text is adapted by various repetitions. Such are Nos. 16b, 22, 25, and 26. In No. 16b the octosyllabic line is repeated twice; after its first repetition, its last four syllables in turn are repeated, followed by a rest before the second repetition of the whole line:

Što nam piše beg Lakišić,	What writes us Bey Lakišić,
Što nam piše beg Lakišić, beg Lakišić	What writes us Bey Lakišić, Bey Lakišić,
Što nam piše beg Lakišić?	What writes us Bey Lakišić?

In No. 22 the line is repeated, followed by the repetition of the last five syllables:

Kraj mora Džeha zaspala,   Džeha fell asleep beside the sea,
Kraj mora Džeha zaspala,   Džeha fell asleep beside the sea,
Džeha zaspala.   Džeha fell asleep.

In No. 25 the first four syllables of the line are presented, followed by "ago"; then the same four syllables are repeated, followed by "bego"; and finally the line is stated:

Example 3

The wind a blossom, agha,
The wind a blossom, bey,
The wind carried a blossom down along the plain.

And in No. 26 we find:

Poskočiće trava potrvena,	Will leap up the grass that's trodden down,
Trava potrvena,	Grass that's trodden down,
Poskočiće trava potrvena.	Will leap up the grass that's trodden down.

Such are some of the ways in which a single line may be adapted to a two- or three-section melodic structure, as illustrated from songs in Bartók's transcriptions of Yugoslav folk songs from the Milman Parry Collection. In none of these cases, indeed, do we have a text stanza.

Nevertheless, text stanzas do exist in Serbo-Croatian folk song. We find that, together with the single line, the couplet is also a strong structural element in that tradition. When it is used with a two-section melodic stanza, it forms a bona fide text stanza. In Bartók's book Nos. 6a, 6b, 12a, 12b, 12e, and 13 are examples. No. 6a, for example, shows a two-section melody to which two text lines are sung:

Razbolje se Djerdjelez Alija	Djerdjelez Alija fell ill
U planini pod jelom zelenom.	On the mountain under a green fir tree.

Couplets like this are the clearest examples of text stanzas, and I will return to them shortly; but we should look briefly at the adaptation of couplets to melodies of three sections, such as we find in Nos. 18, 19, 21a, 21b, 24, 27a–e, and 28a–c. In Nos. 18 and 19 the second line of the couplet is repeated to fit the third section of the melody; in Nos. 21a and 21b the first line is repeated to form the second melody section.

No. 18

Knjigu piše dva Ćirića,	The two Ćirići wrote a letter,
A na ruke Pivodiću,	To the hands of Pivodić,
A na ruke Pivodiću.	To the hands of Pivodić.

No. 21a

Pivo pije Selim beže,	Selim Bey is drinking beer,
Pivo pije Selim beže,	Selim Bey is drinking beer,
Pivo pije, podvriskuje.	He drinks beer and shouts.

In Nos. 27a–e and 28a–c the second melody section corresponds in the text to the last six syllables of the first line, as in No. 27a:

Example 4

27a

Bey Alibey asked his love,
Asked his love,
What is that, my dear love?

This is simply a variant of the repetition of the first line, as in No. 21a above. Strangely enough, in spite of the fairly large number of three-section melodies in the Bartók volume, there is only *one* three-line text stanza, a bona fide one! This is the heterometric No. 53—and it is sung to a melody of *four* sections; the first line is repeated:

Example 5

53

A fir branch blossomed by the sea,
A fir branch blossomed by the sea,
Ah, Marica, lovely barmaid,
Come sit beside me.

Although four-section melodies are rarer than two- or three-section melodies in our area and were considered by Bartók to be of urban or semi-rural origin, four of them in this book will serve as examples of the relationship of their text stanza to the melody stanza. They are Nos. 37, 39a, 42, and 50. In Nos. 37 and 50 text couplets are simply repeated (in the case of No. 37 each line is extended by the repetition of its last three syllables):

No. 37

Odbi, odbi, ladjo, od kraja, od kraja,	Depart, depart, O ship, from the shore, from the shore,
Sad se dragi z dragom pozdravlja, pozdravlja.	Now dear one to dear one says farewell, says farewell.
Odbi, odbi, ladjo, od kraja, od kraja,	Depart, depart, O ship, from the shore, from the shore,
Sad se dragi z dragom pozdravlja, pozdravlja.	Now dear one to dear one says farewell, says farewell.

No. 50

Šta je uzrok, moj dragane,	What is the reason, my dear one,
Što me mladu ne voliš?	That you do not love me, young as I am,
Šta je uzrok, moj dragane,	What is the reason, my dear one,
Što me mladu ne voliš?	That you do not love me, young as I am?

As in the case of the adapting of couplets to three-section melodies, and of the one triplet to a four-section melody, the question arises as to whether these form text stanzas. I shall return to that in a moment, but first let us look at the remaining two four-section melodies, Nos. 39a and 42. They are made up of a rhymed couplet, two long lines of thirteen syllables, with a rest, or caesura, after the eighth. Four sections are formed by splitting each line into two. The rhyme clearly betrays their urban origin.

Example 6

O Almasa, heavenly soul,
Beautiful is your glance.

All because of you I lost
My young life!

No. 42

Na prestolju sultan sjedi,	On his throne sits the sultan,
Abdulah Džemil,	Abdulah Džemil,
A do njega mlad vezire,	And next to him a young vizier,
Abdul Alidah.	Abdul Alidah.

It is now time to discuss whether the adaptation by repetition of couplets or triplets to melodies of three or four sections creates a text stanza. It certainly is in a somewhat different class from the couplets fitted to two-section melodies, or the four-section melodies that we have just seen (Nos. 39a and 42), in which a split couplet forms four sections of text. These procedures do create stanzas.

However, the textual tradition and the musical tradition do not seem at times to be ideally matched. Sometimes the textual riches are more than the music can take, and sometimes the textual tradition is not rich enough for the particular task at the moment. Perhaps what is available is not of the right kind to meet the requirements of the music, and the text-maker must improvise. Bartók said that a heterometric style is characteristic of Serbo-Croatian folk song. On the line level, the textual tradition is basically isometric, and must repeat phrases in order to accommodate the heterometric rhythm of the music.

I think that a case may be made for calling "text stanzas" those comparatively numerous couplets in which the last six syllables of the first line are repeated to fill the second section of a three-section melody, as in No. 27a:

Beg Alibeg ljubu pitijaše,	Bey Alibey asked his love,
Ljubu pitijaše,	Asked his love,
"Šta je ono, moja ljubo mila?"	"What is that, my dear love?"

If one strips the text of everything required by the melody—the repetition of "ljubu pitijaše" falls into that category—what remains is a good "text stanza," namely the basic couplet itself.

When one whole line of a couplet is repeated to fill a second or a third melody section, or, as in the case of No. 53, to form the second section of a four-section melody, the question of whether it is a "text stanza" or not is a more difficult one. Even more problematic is the repetition of a full couplet to accommodate a four-section melody. This is like repeating a single line to fill a two-section melody. Is the textual stanza tradition so bankrupt that it could not satisfy the rather simple demands of three- or four-section melodies? In order to attempt to answer that, I propose to return to the case of No. 6a, which has a couplet and a two-section melody, and to observe the syntactic and semantic makeup of its textual stanzas and their relation to one another.

Example 7

6a

Djerdjelez Alija fell ill
On the mountain under a green fir tree.

2) Na njemu se bijeli košulja,   His shirt shone white,
   Kaj no gruda u planini snjega.   As a ball of snow on the moun-
                                        tain.
3) Nit' ga pere majka ni sestrica   Neither his mother nor his sister
                                        wash him,

   Ni vjerena skoro dovedena.   Nor his newlywed true love.
4) Siv mu soko vode donosaše,   A gray falcon brought him water,
   Djerdjelezu rane ispiraše.   Washed Djerdjelez's wounds.

Although stanza four is a rhymed couplet, there is no attempt to use
rhymed couplets throughout.

Each couplet is an independent unit, so that the pause between melody stanzas does not interrupt a textual sentence. In the first two couplets above, the second line either adds an idea of location (stanza one) or
ornaments the first line with a simile (stanza two). The verb in both
cases is in the first line. The same general comment applies to the third
stanza, except that the second line adds a third subject to the two gov-
erning the verb in the first line of the couplet, forming a progression:
"mother" (majka), "sister" (sestrica), "true love" (vjerenica).

There is a tension between the third and the fourth stanzas, but no
grammatical connection. The fourth stanza could have begun with
"but"; it did not, and thus the syntactic integrity of the couplet has
been preserved. No. 28a is another variant of this song; it bridges the
gap between the family and the bird very skillfully in its fourth and fifth
stanzas:

4) Kiša pere, žarko sunce suši,   The rain washes him, the hot sun
                                         dries him,
   Njem' dolazi siv zelen sokole,   There comes to him a gray, green
                                         falcon,

5) Pa mu nosi u kljunu vodice,   And brings him water in its beak,
   I pod krilom bijele pogače.   And under its wing white cakes.

In this case (No. 28a, stanzas four and five), the stanzas are joined easily
by the conjunction *pa* ("then"), but each stanza still has its own unity.
Stanza four has the logical sequence *pere* ("washes") and *suši* ("dries")
in the first line, and the action moves forward with *dolazi* ("comes")
and the appearance of the bird. Stanza five is unified by the verb *nosi*
("carries") and what the bird carries and how. In short, stanzas can be
readily joined by a conjunction to form four-line syntactical units; the
stanzas themselves, however, still maintain their own integrity.

Similarly, in No. 6a, the two lines of the fourth couplet form a para-
tactic construction, which is made more emphatic by the end rhyme.
These four stanzas provide the setting for the conversation between
bird and hero, which should constitute the central substance of the ballad. In reality the ballad veers off into another ballad shortly after this,
though not before the conversation begins. In No. 6a, stanzas 5 and 6
open the question-and-answer sequence between Alija and the falcon.

5) Govori mu Djerdjelez Alija: Djerdjelez Alija spoke to him:
   "Aj, Boga ti, siv sokole beli!   "By God, gray falcon!
6) Kakvo sam ti dobro učinijo,   What good thing have I done for
                                         you,
   Te me pojiš tihom vodom lad-   That you bring me cold water?"
   nom?"

Here are two more stanzas, each with an integrity of its own, but at
the same time together forming a unit. In both cases two couplets
joined make a quatrain syntactically and semantically perfect. The first
couplet here (5) gives speaker, verb of speaking, and vocative; the second poses the question. The same can be said for the parallel stanzas in
No. 28a (6 and 7), although the speaker and the verb of speaking are absent.

6) "A Boga ti, siv zelen sokole,   "By God, gray, green falcon,
   Kakvo sam ti dobro učinijo,   What good thing have I done for
                                         you,
7) Pa mi nosiš u kljunu vodice,   That you bring me water in your
                                         beak,
   I pod krilom bijele pogače?"   And under your wing white
                                         cakes?"

In No. 6a we have, then, six couplets, each sung to a two-section melody. Another way of looking at it, of course, would be to say that we have three quatrains (i.e. stanzas 1–2, 3–4, 5–6) each divided into two melodic sections; in other words, each quatrain has two two-section melodies. In sum, a textual four-line stanza structure is clear from the analysis of syntactic and semantic units; but four-section melodies are lacking, so the two-section melody has to be repeated in order to accommodate the quatrain.

One might, indeed, extend the syntactic and semantic unit beyond the quatrain. No. 28a, for example, begins with a clear quatrain in stanzas one and two:

1) U gori se zelen bajrak vija,	On the mountain a green banner waves,
Pod njim' leži ranjen bajraktare.	Under it lies a wounded standard-bearer.
2) Na njemu se bijeli kosulja,	On him his shirt shone white,
Baš k'o gruda u planini snjega.	As a ball of snow on the mountain.

But the next syntactic-semantic unit might well be thought of as including three stanzas (3–4–5).

3) Nit' ga pere majka ni sestrica,	Neither his mother nor his sister wash him,
Ni 'jubovca skoro dovedena.	Nor his newlywed true love.
4) Kiša pere, žarko sunce suši,	The rain washes him, the hot sun dries him.
Njem' dolazi siv zelen sokole,	A gray, green falcon comes to him.
5) Pa mu nosi u kljunu vodice,	And brings him water in its beak,
I pod krilom bijele pogače.	And under its wing white cakes.

The same is true in No. 6a, which might be thought of as beginning with three quatrains, as we saw; but they are followed in stanzas 7, 8, and 9 by a syntactic-semantic unit of six lines:

7) "Velko si mi dobro učinijo.	"You did me a great service,
Jako moji 'tići polećeli,	My little birds were flying,
8) U zelenu travu popadali,	They fell to the green grass,
A ti sjaha sa konja vilena,	And you dismounted from your wondrous horse,
9) Pokupijo moje tice lude	Gathered up my helpless little birds,
Bacijo hi u jelovo granje."	And put them on the branches of a fir tree."

Looked at from the point of view of syntactic-semantic units, the stuff of text-stanza structure is there beyond any doubt, but the melodic structure has not been developed beyond three sections.

One expects that all the stanzas in a song will have the same basic format, i.e. they will all be couplets, or triplets, or quatrains, or whatever. The flexibility of the songs in the Bartók book of Yugoslav folk music in this regard, and their lack of rigidity in actual performance, is worth noting, because it is so unexpected. It is not uncommon, in the performance of a melody of two sections, to have an alternation of text stanzas of a single line repeated and couplets. No. 12b, for example, consists of three stanzas of couplets, followed by thirteen stanzas of a single line repeated, and is capped by a final couplet.

No. 27d also has a strange mixture of lines and couplets:

1 couplet
3 lines
1 couplet
1 line
2 couplets
1 line
1 couplet
2 lines
2 couplets
2 lines

Nos. 27b and 27c also contain a mixture of couplets and single lines repeated, but in a different combination from that of 27d above.

Thus No. 27b:

2 couplets
4 lines
2 couplets
1 line
1 couplet
2 lines
3 couplets
1 line
2 couplets
6 lines

and No. 27c:

2 couplets
10 lines

Yet No. 27a has twenty-eight stanzas, all of which consist of couplets, except stanzas 16 and 28, which have a single line repeated.

While it is true that in performance there is a looseness of stanza structure, even a somewhat cavalier treatment of such formations, it cannot be truly said that there is no stanza structure in the texts of Serbo-Croatian folk songs. Moreover, I hope to have shown that the potential for a rather sophisticated grouping of stanzas was present in the material considered, and that on occasion it was realized.

There is a similar phenomenon of text-stanza structuring in the singing of epic to the gusle or tambura in Yugoslavia, as demonstrated in Volume XIV of *Serbo-Croatian Heroic Songs*, edited by David E.

Bynum.[5] Some of the texts that were recorded on phonograph records or on tape have been published indicating the pauses not only between lines but also between groups of lines. For the first time, the student of South Slavic oral traditional epic can see the way in which the singer assembles his lines into units in performance. In analyzing folk music Bartók paid considerable attention to pauses, or rests, and their length, including the final pause at the close of a stanza.

In the epic presentations of Murat Žunić in Bihać, northern Bosnia, in the spring of 1935, we note that he begins each unit with an extra-metrical "He," thus marking it off very clearly. He opens the song "Sila Osmanbeg and Pavišić Luka" with six single lines, each introduced by "He." Lines seven and eight form a couplet, followed by three triplets: 9–11, 12–14, and 15–17; lines 7, 9, 12, and 15 are preceded by "He." Lines 18–21 give us a quatrain; 22–24, a triplet; this is followed in 25–28 by another quatrain. Then come two triplets: 29–31 and 32–34; four quatrains: 35–38, 39–42, 43–46, and 47–50; and for the first time, a quintet: lines 51–55. The series, beginning at line 7, reads: 2, 3, 3, 3, 4, 3, 4, 3, 3, 4, 4, 4, 4, 5. From here to line 129 the following sequence emerges: 4, 3, 3, 3, 5, 5, 3, 3, 3, 3, 3, 3, 3, 3, 5, 4, 4, 3, 3. Between lines 7 and 129 there are 19 triplets, 9 quatrains, 4 quintets, and 1 couplet; triplets seem to be predominant. A change occurs after line 129. Murat settles down to a long series of couplets, interrupted at line 156 by a quatrain and at line 220 by a triplet. Finally, at line 316 we have a single line, followed in line 317 by another single line, and then comes a break as Murat announces: "I'd like some lunch, heroes!"

After Murat has had some stew (čorba), he continues to line 833, when he stops again "to rest a little." Between lines 318 and 833 the same general pattern emerges as in lines 1–317. First comes a series of single lines, four this time; then 2 couplets and another single line; then a triplet, a quintet, a quatrain, 2 quintets, and 2 couplets. From here (line 354) to line 756, in other words for about 400 lines, Murat sings predominantly in triplets, with a sprinkling of couplets. Then at line 757 he changes to couplets, which he maintains unbroken until line 833, when he breaks to rest again.

In sum, Murat begins with several single lines; proceeds to a section that includes quatrains and quintets; follows with a section primarily of triplets; and ends with couplets. The progression is in descending number of lines per unit. But each unit is permissive of an occasional variation.

I must stress that this is Murat's pattern, and it should not be generalized. Each singer has his own arrangements. For greater detail, I refer

[5]David Bynum, ed., *Serbo-Croatian Heroic Songs*, vol. XIV (Cambridge, Mass., 1979).

the reader to Volume XIV of *Serbo-Croatian Heroic Songs*, which contains the original texts edited with commentary by Bynum, and to its forthcoming companion, Volume XIII, with English translations by Bynum and others and with musical transcriptions and commentary by Stephen Erdely of the Massachusetts Institute of Technology.

At this point two questions arise, which must be addressed before we conclude. The first is the correlation, if any, between the syntax and semantics, on one side, and the stanza units, as outlined above for epic song, on the other. We have touched on this subject in discussing syntactic-semantic units in folk song, and it is incumbent on us to say something about it in Murat's material. The second question is that of the relationship, if any, between the lyric and the epic text-stanza structures.

Some of Murat's "stanzas," as I shall call them tentatively, are syntactic units held together semantically. The first couplet, lines 7–8, is a good example:

He, ja, beg Osmanbeg iz Osika bil-	Bey Osmanbey of Osik the white
a, Nej' izidje gradu i bedemu.	Went out onto the city wall.

And the following triplet (lines 9–11) is also self-contained:

He, uz leden beden pleća prislonijo,	He leaned his back against the icy wall,
A bojali čibuk zapali —.	And lit his painted pipe.
Odbija beže na čekrk dimove.	The bey blew out rings of smoke.

On the other hand, the next two "stanzas", two triplets, are less clearly defined as triplets, syntactically or semantically:

Lines 12–14

He, jaze pogleda gradu niz tećiju,	He looked down at the *tekija* [dervish monastery]
A niz tećiju na novu sedej —	And past the *tekija* to the new[?].
Uzdiše beže o' srdašca svoga,	The bey sighed from his heart.

Lines 15–17

He, neg' proliva suze niz obraze.	And wept tears down his cheeks,
A pogleda preko osičkog —.	And looked across the plain of Osik.
Već je žarko rodilo se sunce,	Already the bright [hot] sun had risen,

Lines 12 and 13 form an excellent couplet, syntactically and semantically. Line 14—the last line of the first triplet—and the first line of the second triplet also make a natural couplet, syntactically and semantically. In fact, these two lines are frequently joined together, making a two-line formula. Or one might add line 16, the second line of the second triplet, and create another triplet in which the conjunction *a* forms a close semantic connection between lines one and two of the second triplet. We would thus, following the syntax and the meaning, have discovered a couplet and a triplet, perhaps more natural to our minds than the two triplets of Murat, as follows:

Lines 12–13

> He, jaze pogleda gradu niz tećiju,   He looked down at the *tekija*
> A niz tećiju na novu sedej—   And past the *tekija* to the new[?]

Lines 14–16

> Uzdiše beže o' srdašca svoga   The bey sighed from his heart,
> Neg' proliva suze niz obraze,   And wept tears down his cheeks,
> A pogleda preko osičkog—.   And looked across the plain of Osik.

However, this leaves the last line of the second triplet isolated. But not for long, because it belongs properly, according to syntax and semantics, to the first line of the following quatrain:

Lines 17–18

> Vec je žarko rodilo se sunce,   Already the bright [hot] sun had
>   risen,
> Ja ogrijalo strmce i ravnic —   And warmed the steeps and level
>   plains.

The remainder of the quatrain, minus its first line, forms a good syntactic and semantic triplet:

Lines 19-21

> A kad je begu oči utekoše,   When the bey's eyes looked further,
> Pa on vidi jednog konjenik —   He saw a horseman,
> a, Dje jaše preko osičkog —   Riding across the plain of Osik.

That is a fine triplet, but when one moves on to the next of Murat's triplets, one finds that its first line really belongs with the last line of Murat's quatrain; let us put it there:

Lines 19–22

> A kad je begu oči utekoše,   When the bey's eyes looked further,
> Pa on vidi jednog konjenik —   He saw a horseman,
> a, Dje jaše preko osičkog —   Riding across the plain of Osik
> Ja na sijahu baš k'o na zviretu. On a horse just like a wild beast.

Syntactically and semantically, that is a thoroughly satisfactory quatrain, and to separate any part of it from the rest is to do it a syntactic and semantic injustice. Obviously, however, Murat did not feel that way about it, and the reason for the discrepancy in our two judgments is that Murat's triplets and quatrains and couplets were not intended to follow syntactic and semantic patterns, but existed on their own on the level of performance rather than on the level of syntax and meaning. These groupings, therefore, are not really textual stanzas at all, although they look and even sound as if they were.

Let us return to Murat's song and follow it a little further. We ended at line 22, with the bey seeing a horseman riding across the plain on a horse like a wild beast. The next line (23) could be a single line, or it could go with the quatrain we have just constructed, as an added comment to the riding on a horse like a wild beast, thus making the quatrain into a quintet. It could also introduce a new triplet:

Lines 23–25

Oštro jaše uz polje zelen —	He rode sharply along the green plain.
Poznaje ga silen Osmanbeže,	Osmanbeg the mighty strove to recognize him,
He, poznaje ga, poznati ne mere.	Strove to recognize him but could not.

Thus the last line of Murat's triplet (22–24) should not be separated from the first line of his quatrain (25–28).

However, once we have used the first line of Murat's quatrain in the preceding triplet, the triplet that remains is syntactically and semantically coherent:

Lines 26–28

Sve to bliže kad se prikuči —	As he came ever nearer,
Pozna beže Silić Nasufbeg —	The bey recognized Silić Nasufbeg,
Svog sestrica sa ravna Pozdrav — Pozdravlje—	His sister's son from level Podzdravlje—

The next two of Murat's triplets are syntactically and semantically sound. We shall end our sample here.

In Murat's performance we have gone from a good couplet and a satisfactory triplet through problematic groupings to land safely with two triplets (lines 29–31 and 32–34), which were again well integrated. In between we did some regrouping according to syntactic and semantic principles, thus creating a new text-stanza structure. Here are the old and the new side by side, schematically:

Murat's performance	Syntactic groupings
lines 12–14 triplet	lines 12–13 couplet
lines 15–17 triplet	lines 14–16 triplet
lines 18–21 quatrain	lines 17–18 couplet
	lines 19–22 quatrain
lines 22–24 triplet	lines 23–25 triplet
lines 25–28 quatrain	lines 26–28 triplet

This chart shows that Murat interrupted, or separated, two lines that went properly, that is, syntactically and semantically, together. In two cases (lines 14 and 17), the line at the end of a group should have gone with the following group; or, put another way, the break should have come before lines 14 and 17 rather than after them. In the other three cases, the line at the beginning of Murat's groups should have gone with the preceding group.

In analyzing the units in epic, we have been concerned with pauses entirely apart from any consideration of melodic sectioning, as was the case with our investigation of folk song. For details about the musical aspects of epic performance, see Vol. XIV and the forthcoming Vol. XIII of *Serbo-Croatian Heroic Songs*, as noted above.

Before I conclude this section, which obviously needs further investigation, I must remark that it is a regular practice in stanza formation—not only in Serbo-Croatian but also in Bulgarian, Romanian, Old French, and elsewhere—for the first line of a laisse or a stanza to repeat in one form or another the last line of the preceding laisse or stanza. A close look at Murat's practice in this passage shows that that is not the case with him. These are real interruptions, not repetitions or echoes.

Interruptions of this sort, which have something of the effect of syncopation, bring to mind one of the characteristics of Serbo-Croatian and Bulgarian folk melodies remarked on by Bartók:

> The line-, word-, and syllable-interruptions effected by shorter or longer rests [are] not for articulation's sake, but for decorative—one might also say for expressive—purposes. . . . This astonishing custom will invariably deceive even the best-trained musicians when they first listen to this kind of interruption. They will without fail interpret the rests erroneously, that is, as section caesuras.[5]

It seems doubtful that this phenomenon in the folk song is directly related to the interrupting of syntactically and semantically related lines in epic by a pause. But I feel that the similarity is worthy of note. The presence of such pauses indicates, as I said earlier, that in performance

[6]Bartók and Lord, *Serbo-Croatian Folk Songs*, p. 74.

Murat's rhythm of presentation in grouping lines often takes precedence over the syntactic and semantic units we associate with true stanzas.

Murat's example teaches us, or at least suggests to us, that in folk song the text stanzas are syntactic and semantic units as well as units of length, but that this is not so in epic. In this way, it would seem that we can note a formal differentiation between the two genres in an aspect that at first it appeared they shared.

Regional Song Styles:
The Scottish Connection

ANNE DHU SHAPIRO

THE BASIC PREMISE OF THIS ESSAY is simple: the place a person comes from can shape the style of his music—its creation as well as its performance. On the surface, this premise is self-evident. We can all detect regional accents in speech. We know also that Javanese musical style is easily distinguishable from that of the neighboring isle of Bali. The concept of regionality is part of the heritage of Western musicology. In the Aquitanian, Germanic, and Sarum chant repertoire, for example, there is evidence in manuscripts of strong regional styles. What is constantly amazing, however, even to scholars of ethnic musics, is the persistence of some of these regional traits, lasting through generations of change and even through the transplantation and intermingling of cultures. For instance, though nobody is surprised to find African music different from British-American, the survival of some of its distinctively African features through two centuries in American culture is remarkable enough to have fueled scholarly controversies down to the present day.

This essay presents another case of regional persistence that is also found in American folk song—that of Scottish song style. By examining certain melodic and rhythmic traits of Scottish music, the effect of regional origin on the creation and performance of songs can be shown at three increasingly detailed levels: 1) Scottish song style in general within the British-American tradition, as it has continued in the United States; 2) the musical styles of the two Scottish regional languages and cultures, Gaelic and Lowland Scots; and 3) a local style on a single island within the Gaelic song-style area.

The examples in this paper are all drawn from a vocal repertoire that for the most part has been transmitted orally, and which, for lack of a more universally accepted term, we call folk song or traditional song. This is to distinguish it from the repertoires of popular and art song, which depend more upon written transmission and on a degree of professional expertise in their composers. Yet this is in many ways an artificial line, and at least some of the findings about the effects of region on style may apply to popular and art genres as well, though perhaps with less clarity.

Level I: The Scottish Strain in British-American Folk Song

On the most general level, the "regional style" under consideration is that of British-American folk song, a repertoire of many thousands of tunes and texts created and re-created over a period of more than three centuries, largely by English-speaking people of Britain and North America. That this rather large area is in some sense a single region is supported by the wide dispersal of a common repertoire of tunes and texts throughout. A song such as "Lord Randal," to name but one of many instances, was collected in Scotland in the eighteenth century and has indisputable relatives collected in America in the latter half of the twentieth century.[1]

Within the British-American folk-song region are clearly distinguishable subregions, which have been noticed ever since folk songs began to be collected. The late seventeenth- and early eighteenth-century London publications of Purcell, Playford, and others reveal a vogue for the "North Countrie" or Scottish tune.[2] Later, with the rise of nineteenth-century nationalism, collectors of folk song began to dispute the origin of certain tunes held in common between two or more regions (the printed polemics of Stenhouse, Chappell, and Glen are prime examples in the British-American field).[3] Early twentieth-century collecting was done chiefly by region: members of the English

---

[1]See Bertrand H. Bronson, *Traditional Tunes of the Child Ballads*, 4 vols. (Princeton, 1959–72), vol. I, pp. 191–236. Other Child ballads from Scotland with related text versions found in the U.S. include: Earl Brand (Child 7), Edward (13), The Twa Brothers (49), Sir Patrick Spens (58), Fair Annie (62), Sweet William's Ghost (77), The Twa Corbies (26), Mary Hamilton (173), The Bonnie House o' Airlee (199), Lady Maisry (68), The Gypsy Laddie (200), Lizzie Lindsay (276), Lord Thomas and Fair Annet (73), The Trooper and the Maid (299), and Our Goodman (294). See Herschel Gower, "The Scottish Palimpsest in Traditional Ballads Collected in America," in *Reality and Myth*, ed. William E. Walker and Robert L. Welken (Nashville, 1964), pp. 117–44.

[2]For example, Henry Purcell's "New Scotch Tune" in *Musick's Handmaid* (London, 1689) and Henry Playford's *Collection of Original Scotch Tunes* (London, 1700). See also Claude Simpson, *The British Broadside Ballad and its Music* (New Brunswick, N.J., 1966), which lists fourteen ballads with "North" in the title and 38 with "Scotch," "Scotland," or "Scots" in the title.

[3]In particular, William Chappell in his *Popular Music in the Olden Time* (London, 1853–59) criticizes the Scottish attributions of William Stenhouse in *Songs of Scotland* (Edinburgh, 1848–49). John Glen, in *Early Scottish Melodies* (Edinburgh, 1900), in turn refutes Chappell's arguments. The controversy is summarized in Henry George Farmer's introduction to the 1962 facsimile reprint of the *Scots Musical Museum*, 2 vols. (Hatboro, Pa., 1962), vol. I, pp. vii–xiii. The original *Museum*, edited by James Johnson, was published in four volumes (Edinburgh, 1853).

Folk-Song Society collected in various counties of England, and Americans such as Barry, Belden, Cox, Flanders, Lomax, and Scarborough collected in different parts of the United States. However, most twentieth-century collectors placed less emphasis on the *differences* between songs of various regions than on what they had in common, especially in terms of the repertoire of Child ballads, which was often the focus of such collections.

The settlement of North America by successive waves of immigrants from various regions of the British Isles and other areas of the world makes the U.S. a natural place for the study of the persistence of regional traits. Philipps Barry, in the early twentieth century, noted the pervasive influence of Irish folk-song style in the Northeast and isolated what he felt were three elements of Irish style: the "Irish sixth," the "Irish cadence," and the "Irish Come-All-Ye" tune shape. These traits were readily identifiable as Irish since many of Barry's informants were from Ireland themselves or were but one generation removed.[4]

The persistence of distinctive regional traits in the music of areas of the U.S. where Scottish immigration has occurred is more remarkable, as many more generations have passed since the original settlements. Immigrants began to come from Scotland at the time of the Jacobean uprisings in 1715, and increased in number after the Battle of Culloden in 1745, when the clans' power was finally broken by the English. Even greater numbers were driven out by general economic conditions or specific pressures such as the Highland Clearances, in which whole regions were emptied to make way for sheep farming.[5]

The Scottish immigrants settled primarily in three areas: the coastal and piedmont areas of the Carolinas, New York State, and Nova Scotia.[6] The Carolinas and New York were settled earliest; by 1825, the New York settlements had dispersed, and the bulk of new immigrants from Scotland went to the Canadian provinces of Nova Scotia, Prince Edward Island, and New Brunswick, where they formed a sizable unassimilated minority.

Most nineteenth-century Scottish immigrants to America were Gaelic-speaking Highlanders. In fact, as late as 1866 there was a Gaelic-

---

[4]Philipps Barry's references to Irish style are scattered throughout his works, but are found most prominently in "Notes on the Ways of Folk-Singer with Folk-Tunes," *Bulletin of the Folk-Song Society of the Northeast*, 12 (1937), 2–6, and in his *Folk Music in America*, National Service Bureau, Federal Theatre Project, WPA (New York, 1939), p. 10.

[5]The effect of the clearances is summarized in a pamphlet, *The Highland Clearances*, published by The Gaelic Society of Scotland (n.p., n.d.), and in a lengthier book by John Prebble, *The Highland Clearances* (Harmondsworth, England, 1963).

[6]Immigration patterns are discussed in Ian Charles Cargill Graham, *Colonists from Scotland: Emigration to North America, 1707–1783* (Ithaca, N.Y., 1956) and Duane Meyer, *The Highland Scots of North Carolina, 1732–1776* (Chapel Hill, 1957).

speaking parish in North Carolina.[7] The Gaelic-speakers gradually assimilated into American life and learned to speak English. Their song texts became English as well, although certain distinctively Scottish turns of phrase remained in some of them.[8] The tunes themselves also retained certain melodic and rhythmic characteristics that mark them as Scottish. For example, one melodic trait that distinguishes many Scots tunes from English, Irish, or American tunes is the unusual frequency of large intervals, especially leaps of major and minor sixths, octaves, or even tenths. A distinctive rhythmic feature is the use of the short-long pattern, recognized as a regional peculiarity of Scotland by writers on music as early as the eighteenth century; Burney and Quantz both mentioned it, and dubbed it the "Scots Catch" or "Scotch Snap."[9]

An example of how large intervals can mark a tune as Scottish, even though it is closely related to other non-Scottish tunes, may be found in a version of "The Demon Lover" sung by Mrs. Ef Chrisom of Burnsville, North Carolina, collected there by Cecil Sharp in 1916–18 (Ex. 1a). When compared phrase by phrase with another common variant of the

Examples 1a and 1b. Two versions of "The Demon Lover" from Sharp, *English Folk Songs from the Southern Appalachians*, vol. I, p. 256. 1a = 35-N, sung by Mrs. Ef Chrisom, Burnsville, North Carolina; 1b = 35-O, sung by Mrs. Francis Carter, Proctor, Kentucky.

[7]Charles Dunn, *Highland Settler* (Toronto, 1953), pp. 138–39.

[8]See Herschel Gower, "The Scottish Palimpsest," cited in fn. 1 above.

[9]Johann Joachim Quantz (*Versuch einer Anweisung die Flöte traversiere zu spielen*, ed. Arnold Schering [Leipzig, 1906], repr. of orig. ed. Berlin, 1752) writes in Chap. XVIII, par. 58, of the "Lombardic style" of rhythm, but points out that "it appears to be rather similar to Scottish music" ("der Schotländischen Musik etwas ähnlich zu sein"). Charles Burney (*A General History of Music*, 2 vols., vol. II [London, 1782], p. 847) calls the rhythm a "Scots catch" and complains of its overuse in Italian opera.

same song (Ex. 1b), this tune (as well as four other variants collected in the same part of North Carolina) stands out by virtue of the large intervals in phrases 1, 2, and 4. While matching general contour and range with the common variant, it consistently uses larger intervals where the other tune uses stepwise motion or small leaps.

The last phrase of Ex. 1a, in particular, shows a peculiarly Scottish melodic turn: an upward leap of a sixth from the third degree of the scale is followed by a cadence with its final on the perceived second degree. This cadence is akin to those melodic phrases which Francis Collinson in his book *Traditional and National Music of Scotland* calls "thumbprints," or "brief but unmistakable melodic turns" that mark tunes as Scottish.[10] (A selection of his examples is given in Ex. 2.) Each one has both frequent leaps of large intervals and a final cadence that creates a pleasant tension through the failure to return to the expected note—the note that in a tonal system would be termed the "tonic" of the scale. This kind of cadence might be added to the two characteristics already mentioned that distinguish Scots melody from that of other regions.

Collinson also discusses the characteristic "Scotch snap" rhythm, which he renames the "Scots" snap. Countering arguments against its authenticity in traditional Scots music, he concludes emphatically that it is "the very lifeblood of Scots musical rhythm."[11] This feature is also found in several other Sharp examples (see Ex. 3), especially in combination with the large intervals.

If we accept that the traits described above, and the songs in which they appear, do indeed represent a distinctly Scottish strain in the broader British-American tradition, the question then remains: why are these traits found so frequently in Scottish song? Why, in short, does Scottish song sound Scottish?

Example 2. Some "thumbprints" of Scottish melody from Collinson's *Traditional and National Music of Scotland*, pp. 23–24.

[10]Francis Collinson, *Traditional and National Music of Scotland* (London, 1966), pp. 23–24.
   [11]*Ibid.*, p. 29.

Example 3. "Lord Randal" version 7-E, sung by Miss Florence McKinney, Habersham Cty., Georgia; from Sharp, *English Folk Songs*, vol. I, p. 41.

O where have you been, Lord Ran-dal my son? O where have you been, my on-ly son? I've been a-court-ing, moth-er, O make my bed soon, For I'm sick at the heart And fain would lie down.

Level II: The Relationship Between Gaelic and Lowland Scots Folk Song

The answer to this question must in part be sought in the relationship between the music of the two language groups of Scotland, Gaelic and Lowland Scots. Scholars of Scottish traditional music have usually treated the songs and singers of the two language groups as belonging to two totally separate traditions. They have assumed that these two groups utilize not only differing texts and poetic forms, but also essentially different music. Collinson, for example, in a chapter entitled "Gaelic and Lowland Scots Song," holds that the linguistic division of the country "has the same effect of dividing the song melodies of Scotland into two separate streams largely independent of each other."[12] Although he cites cases of tunes of one culture being used by the other, he dismisses these incidents as "desultory borrowing," due either to the activities of song-writing poets such as Ramsay, Burns, and Scott or to the incidental exchange of tunes during times of war.

As further evidence of this divided treatment, collecting in Scotland has largely been the task of two separate groups: the Gaelic-speaking collectors, who are often more interested in finding evidence of the survival of ancient Gaelic poetic forms than in describing their present-day transformations, and those who know only English, who exhibit a similar tendency to look for the supposedly oldest layers of Lowland Scots songs in their search for ballads related to the Child canon.

There are, of course, undeniable differences in the total text and music complex of Gaelic and Lowland songs. The rhythm, syntax, and accentuation of the two languages are different; the poetic and conceptual

[12]*Ibid.*, p. 32.

heritage of the two linguistic traditions differs as well.[13] Nonetheless, it cannot be overlooked that the singers themselves, those through whom the traditions have survived, have intermingled, and, since at least the eighteenth century, have shifted from one culture to the other, sometimes in the space of one generation. The question then arises: what happens to the music of the Gaelic speaker when he becomes English-speaking—a frequent event in the eighteenth and nineteenth centuries, both in Scotland and the New World? Does he stop singing his Gaelic songs once he learns English? Do his English-speaking children stop singing Gaelic tunes? On the contrary; it is my contention that the Gaelic melodic repertoire, far from having disappeared when the language was dropped, has been one of the decisive influences on the English-language Lowland Scots tunes, which, as we have seen, form a distinctive stylistic group within the British-American repertoire.

Some support for this theory is found in the relationship between tunes with Gaelic and English texts in the repertoire of a present-day bilingual singer, John "Skipper" Nicolson of the Isle of Skye, in the Inner Hebrides. He may be taken to represent the singer in transition between his native Gaelic and his second language, English—a stage shared by many immigrants to America in the eighteenth and nineteenth centuries.

John Nicolson is a lively, engaging seventy-seven-year-old crofter who lives with his wife and several grown children on a seaside farm in South Cuidraich, near Uig, Skye. He is Gaelic-speaking but also fluent in English, with only an occasional hesitation in finding a word. His children are also bilingual. He sings, in a baritone range with a clear, relatively unwavering tone, a repertoire of over one hundred Gaelic songs. Many of these he composed himself for use at local Ceilidhs, family entertainments, or as entries in the annual Gaelic Mod festivals in the category of unaccompanied composed song. In addition, he has recently composed two songs in English for a newcomer to Skye, a Dutchman named John Hellinga, who bought property on the island and instituted some much-needed land reforms. The first English song, a historical account of the Highland Clearances and their effect on the "patient men of Skye," was composed at Mr. Hellinga's request; the second, Skipper Nicolson's own idea, is a song in praise of "the noble Dutchman," in the same vein as traditional Gaelic songs routinely composed in praise of chieftains or other important personages.[14] A complete text of the song follows Ex. 4.

[13]For an overview of these differences see Charles Dunn, "Highland Song and Lowland Ballad, a Study in Cultural Patterns," *The University of Toronto Quarterly*, 18 (1948), 1–19.

[14]James Ross ("A Classification of Gaelic Folk Song," *Scottish Studies*, 1 [1957], 95–151), in categorizing Gaelic song types, singles out the praise song as a distinct type.

Mr. Nicolson claimed the tune to "The Noble Dutchman" (Ex. 4a) to be his own creation. When asked if he knew any tunes like it in his Gaelic repertoire, with very little hesitation he sang the Gaelic song "Clachan Ghlinn-da-ruadhail" (Ex. 4b).

The resemblance between the two tunes (only the first two stanzas of each are given) might lead us to question Mr. Nicolson's claim to have composed the music for "The Noble Dutchman," since the Clachan song, by his own admission, uses an older Gaelic tune.[15] Yet in the aesthetic world of the traditional singer, this is indeed composition; refashioning the Gaelic tune to fit the new text makes a completely new entity. In fact, the use of old tunes with new texts may well be one of the principal means by which, over time, whole families of related tunes are spawned.[16]

The small variations Nicolson made in the melody as he changed languages shed some light on the influence of Gaelic style on Lowland style. In the first phrase of the Gaelic version, for example, the word for "beautiful eyes," *mheal-shuiteach* (pronounced myel shutyech), requires a quick, accented slide—an unavoidable Scots-snap rhythm. At the same point in the English version, the place-name "Waternish" requires no such rhythm, but the singer's idea of the tune seems to include it; and at "echoed," the next available place where an English word could benefit from such a rhythm, he puts it in. He also makes good use of it for the Dutchman's first and last names, Jonny Hellinga, which, with typical Gaelic pronunciation, he elides into something resembling "Johnnis Hellingar." And, though he makes several changes in the tune's contour (most notably at the middle cadence of the first stanza), he faithfully reproduces the last phrase—one of Collinson's "thumbprint" types, with a downward leap of a sixth, and an emphasis on $\hat{2}$ before the final descent to $\hat{1}$.

Another important point of resemblance between the two tunes, not discernible on the written page, is the similarity of vocal style in performance despite the change in language. Skipper Nicolson's voice wavers slightly because of age, but he uses it in an easy manner, not seeming to strain to reach the higher notes. There is little deliberate use of vibrato, though enough natural vibrato is present to give each tone penetration without a narrow, reedy quality. Nasality is practically

---

[15]Nicolson dates it to the eighteenth century because of the text references to King George, but the text itself is a nineteenth-century creation, found set to a tune similar to Nicolson's in many Gaelic songsters. One such songster, which Nicolson himself owns, is *A'Choisir-chiuil, the St. Columba Collection of Gaelic Songs* (London and Glasgow, n.d.), in which "Clachan Ghlinn-da Ruiadhail" is found on p. 27.

[16]See Samuel Bayard, "Prolegomena to a Study of the Principal Tune Families of Folksong," *JAFL*, 63 (1950), 1–44, and Anne Dhu Shapiro, "The Concept of Tune Families in the British-American Folksong Tradition," Ph.D. Diss., Harvard University, 1975.

Example 4. John "Skipper" Nicolson's "The Noble Dutchman" compared with his version of "Clachan Ghlinn-da Ruaidhail."

1. The news we've heard from Wa-ter-nish has e-choed through the High-lands;

1. Mo chail-eag mhin-gheal mheal-leach, A dh'fhas gu fal-lain fuas-gailt,

That the No-ble Dutch-man has bought part of our is-land.

Gur trom mo cheum o'n dhea-laich sinn, Aig Cla-chan Ghlinn-da-ruadh-ail

2. His name is Jon-ny Hel-lin-ga His fame has gone be-fore him,

2. Cha suaimh-neas oidch' air lea-baidh dhomh, 'Gad fhai-cinn ann am brua-dar

From all that I have seen and heard Both young and old ex-tol him.

'Sam Bio-bull-fein cha laimh-sich mi, Gun t'iom-haigh ghraidh gam bhuai-readh.

nonexistent, except as a part of the Gaelic language. Most striking is the singer's treatment of rhythm. While keeping a fairly steady overall beat, Mr. Nicolson shapes each phrase with a pairing of notes, almost eliding some (e.g. Johnnis Hellingar) while audibly separating others; this gives the performance a swinging but somewhat choppy character.

The relaxed, easy tone and flexible rhythm are typical of Scots singing in general, and they offer one possible explanation for the presence

Text of "Skipper" Nicolson's "The Noble Dutchman"

1. The news we've heard from Waternish
   Has echoed through the Highlands;
   That the Noble Dutchman
   Has bought part of our island.

2. His name is Jonny Hellinga
   His fame has gone before him;
   From all that I have seen and heard
   Both young and old extol him.

3. He sailed across from Holland
   With Dollars and with Guilders;
   He bought from the MacDonald laird
   His land, his stock, his buildings.

4. The crofters now are full of joy
   The laird is on their side now;
   He gave them land as they desire
   No tax, no rent will bind them.

5. From Sgor a'Bhaigh to Gearraidh
   From Faisach up to Trumpan;
   Of land the finest anywhere
   From Hallain down to Guibeg.

6. Here the crops are heaviest
   The cattle are the finest;
   And when they go to market
   They're unequaled in the Highlands.

7. When Jonny comes to Faisach
   There will be celebrations;
   The taverns will be drained quite dry
   As he receives ovations.

8. In Dutch he'll drink a toast to them
   And they'll reply in Gaelic;
   And though their drams were one foot high
   They'll drain them dry in Gearraidh.

9. I end my song and wish him well
   May peace and joy attend him;
   His stay with us content and long
   Ceud mile failt, we send him.

of large intervals in the tunes of both language groups: the intervals do not present a problem for this relaxed vocal technique; they may not even seem large to a singer raised in such a style.

Skipper Nicolson is an example of the Gaelic-speaking singer-composer in transition between two cultures. More such cases could probably be found, and should be before firm conclusions are drawn. However, it seems probable that there were in the eighteenth and nineteenth centuries many like Nicolson who, pressed by economic conditions, ventured further afield—to Glasgow, Nova Scotia, or North Carolina. Some of their melodies surely came with them and weathered the change from Gaelic to English without losing their distinctive flavor. Gaelic performance style may also have influenced the way the common British-American stock was to be sung in a particular family or locality—hence the differences we find in intervallic and rhythmic content in our North Carolina examples 1a and 1b. Thus Highland regional traits persist in Lowland song—and the resulting Scottish song style in turn persists in the larger British-American repertoire.

Level III: Regionalism at the Local Level: An Isle of Skye Contour?

Skipper Nicolson knows many songs. Some of them he has made up and some he has learned from others. In his acquired repertoire, he distinguishes between songs he learned from Skye singers and those that come from elsewhere—the Isle of Mull to the south, Harris and Lewis to the west, or the Mainland to the east. In creating songs, as we have seen with "The Noble Dutchman," he may use the skeleton of a learned song as the basis for his new one.

Preliminary investigation of Nicolson's repertoire together with the singer indicates that he differentiates the Skye tunes from those of other places on the basis of overall shape or contour. A catalogue of the shapes of six of his own composed tunes (Table 1) shows a definite preference for the overall arch-shaped contour—low-high-high-low, best exemplified by "The Noble Dutchman" and "Farewell to Stornoway." He also identifies tunes that he feels originated in Skye and which are now in the common Gaelic repertoire (some of which are represented in the widely circulated Gaelic songster A'choisir-chiuil). These are tabulated by contour in Table 2. In contrast, the tunes identified by Nicolson as being from Lewis or Mull have different contours, as seen in Table 3.

It is premature to conclude that there is a single preferred tune contour for the Skye singer, as there has not been much investigation of other singers of Skye for comparison. Mr. Nicolson's delineation of a "Skye contour" may in fact be his own personal preference. Many singers of the British-American tradition have so-called "service tunes," which they use over and over in variant forms for different texts. However, Nicolson's identification of a typical "Skye sound," even in tunes from a larger repertoire, points to the possibility that the differentiations

Table 1: Overall contour of Nicolson's compositions (titles in English)

1) "The Noble Dutchman"

2) "Farewell to Stornoway"

3) "The Highland Clearances"

4) "Uig Song"

5) A song to commemorate the closing of the pubs

6) A song in praise of his wife

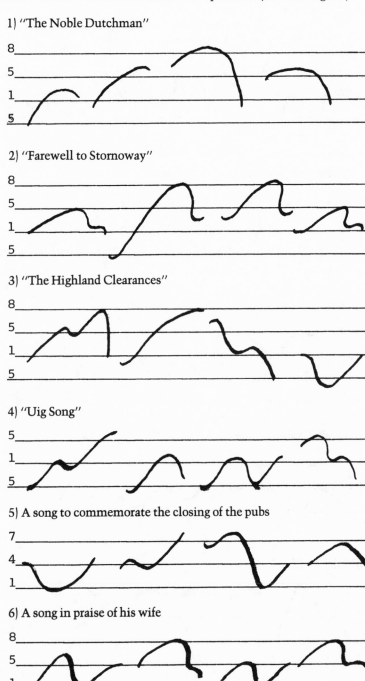

Table 2: Contour of some traditional tunes sung by Nicolson and thought by him to be from Skye

1) Unidentified song no. 1 by Mrs. MacPherson

2) Unidentified song no. 2 (MacPherson)

(chorus)

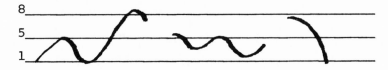

3) "Crodh Chailein" (verse)

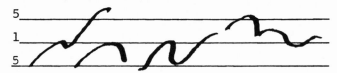

4) "Eilean a Cheo"

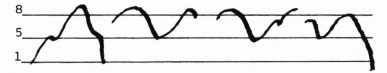

Table 3: Contours of some traditional songs sung by Nicolson and thought by him to be from other locales

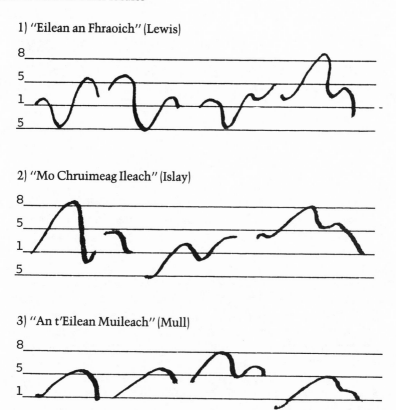

1) "Eilean an Fhraoich" (Lewis)

2) "Mo Chruimeag Ileach" (Islay)

3) "An t'Eilean Muileach" (Mull)

by region that we have seen operating in the larger arenas of British-American and Scottish folk-song traditions may also be found in various local traditions within these larger regions.

Preferences for particular tune contours, habitual vocal techniques, and language or dialect-related rhythms may certainly combine to make a distinctive sound, identifiable by the singers themselves as belonging to a locality. While some of its components may undergo change when language and cultural context change, there is a remarkable persistence of that distinctive sound through years of tradition. The Scottish connection is but one instance of many that could and should be investigated in British-American folk song.

Interplay of Tonality and Nontonal Constructs in Three Pieces from the *Mikrokosmos* of Bartók [*]

IVAN WALDBAUER

MUCH MUSIC OF THE TWENTIETH CENTURY, AND even more of its music theory, is permeated by intellectually or mechanically conceived and operated nontonal or atonal constructs and processes. Schoenberg's twelve-tone row, other musical sets and series, and artificial scales such as the whole-tone or the octatonic are only the most conspicuous examples. A great deal of Bartók's music poses a particular theoretical problem in this respect, increasingly so after 1926: what happens when music that is basically tonally conceived makes use of nontonal or atonal intellectual-mechanical constructs and processes? In the present essay, I will address in three cases the narrower question of how Bartók deals with the actual or potential conflict between expectations raised by intellectual-mechanical constructs and artifices, on the one hand, and by centuries-old musical practice, on the other.[1] The three pieces from the *Mikrokosmos* (1926–1937) chosen here for investiga-

---

[*]The contents of sections III and IV of this study were presented in a different form at the International Bartók Conference, Budapest, September 28–30, 1981, published in *Studia Musicologica Academiae Scientiarum Hungaricae*, 24 (1982), 527–36. Section I forms the basis of a paper given at the Bartók-Kodály Conference co-sponsored by the Departments of Music and Ural-Altaic Studies of the University of Indiana, Bloomington, April 4–8, 1982.

[1]In his second and third "Harvard Lectures," Bartók uses the term "polymodal chromaticism" to denote the phenomenon that occurs when two or more different melodic expectations operate simultaneously, as when a given melody makes use of diatonic motives belonging to different modes based on the same tonic (Béla Bartók, *Essays*, ed. Benjamin Suchoff, (London, 1976), pp. 361–75 and 376–83). Although Bartók does not mention artificial scales and other constructs in this context, their presence often produces sharper and more enduring conflicts than polymodality. The first study dealing with the conflict between artifice and tonality is Milton Babbitt, "The String Quartets of Bartók," *MQ*, 35 (1949), 377–85.

tion, Nos. 140, 144, and 143 (in that order), should represent a fair selection, in that the answers they yield may have a wider application to much of the entire Bartók oeuvre.

The selection of these pieces is based on three considerations. First, they have at least three features in common with each other: (a) the pitch content in each is derived from a nontonal basic set of notes that is presented as a single motive; (b) whatever the length of these motives, they are short enough to be instantly grasped; and (c) in each piece the motive appears in conjunction with its symmetrical inversion, which adds to the nontonal character of the sets. In addition, the three particular sets share yet one more common trait: their potential (in case of No. 143, actual) emphasis on that favorite Bartók chord, the major-minor-triad in its first inversion (e.g. e–g–c–e♭ ').[2]

Second, the interrelation between such symmetrical nontonal or atonal constructs and inherited tonality will, I believe, be fairly represented by these three pieces. In No. 140, construct and overall tonal construction are very nearly one and the same thing. In No. 144, tonality is imposed upon the unfoldings of the construct almost entirely from without. And in No. 143, the demands of, and expectations raised by, construct and tonality play approximately equal roles, each influencing the operations of the other. This creates the illusion that these two disparate entities are merely indivisible and inseparable facets of a single principle, i.e. they shape a work of art that appears, to use Schoenberg's term, as the unfolding of a unitary principle.

The third consideration of selection is that at least two of these pieces show an immediately perceptible resemblance to certain characteristically Bartókian families of pieces. No. 140 belongs in the family of pieces in Bartók's percussive style, often intensified by insistently repeated notes (e.g. "Bear Dance" of 1910, "Allegro Barbaro" of 1911, Sonata for Piano of 1926, etc.); and No. 144 is yet another example of the slow-moving, seemingly disjointed mood pieces—perhaps "heterogeneous noise music" would be a more vivid label for these—such as the "Night Music" of 1926, the second movement of the Piano Concerto No. 1 of 1926, and many others. With No. 143 the situation is different, but only in external appearance. On first hearing, it strikes one

[2]The chord is usually referred to as the "α chord" in the more recent literature on Bartók, e.g., in László Somfai, "Bartók," New Grove, II, p. 207. The usage originates with the theorist Ernö Lendvai, whose most important contributions are "Bevezetés a Bartókmüvek elemzésébe" (Introduction to the Analysis of Bartók's Works), Zenetudományi Tanulmányok, 3 (1955), 461–506 (French version in Bartók: sa vie, son oeuvre, Budapest, 1956, 2nd ed., 1968); "Bartók und der goldene Schnitt," Österreichische Musikzeitschrift, 21 (1966), 607; and Béla Bartók: An Analysis of his Music (London, 1971).

as unique in the Bartók oeuvre, for the texture consists mostly of wide-ranging slow arpeggios, and the subtle chord changes these broad arpeggios contain are perceived as having a noticeable (and intended) time lag. It is almost as if No. 143 were some kind of an homage to Brahms, specifically to that family of Brahmsian music to which belong the Intermezzi Op. 117, No. 2, Op. 119, No. 1, and many others. Yet that relation between construct and tonality described earlier make No. 143 of the *Mikrokosmos* a close relative to perhaps the greatest number of his other pieces, of which I should like to mention here only the first movement of the Fifth String Quartet.[3]

My investigation will proceed with the aid of charts made up basically along the principles of Heinrich Schenker.[4] In each piece, the constructs and artifices, and the intellectual processes by which they are operated, will be exposed first. Analyses of the overall tonal direction will follow, with occasional forays into the details of local harmonic events. For Nos. 140 and 144, a single chart will serve both purposes, but the two steps of the procedure will require two separate charts for No. 143.

[3]This quartet movement is chosen for the comparative ease with which its crucial features can be seen. The overall tonal plan of the movement consists of each subsequent section's being based on the ascending steps of the whole-tone scale on B♭, with a significant halt on the passing F (mm. 126 ff.) signaling the recapitulation. This appears to parallel the outline of the first theme through mm. 1–10 and 12. Although the ascent of the latter passes through all chromatic notes between the second and fourth degrees, C and E, and then between E and A♭, thus establishing the notes B♭–C–E–A♭ as pivotal, the notes D and G♭ do emerge in the next rank of importance, with F in the following rank and the remaining passing notes merely ephemeral.

[4]Five comments concerning these charts are in order. First, save for note- and phrase-repetitions, all notes are included on these charts in their original sequence. Second, no attempt has been made in Examples 2a and 3a to represent a structural discant *(Urlinie)*. The one appearing in Ex. 3c is offered only to show the reason for departing from orthodox Schenkerian theory in this respect: the melodic element in these compositions is too often not an outgrowth and intensification of the triad; rather, it originates from outside the tonal system, with which it is made to coexist. Third, in examples 1a–c, 1e, and 2a, fully drawn noteheads in the middle and upper voices indicate chord-tones; small noteheads indicate neighbor-notes of one kind or another. In Ex. 1d, large noteheads show those notes of the octatonic scale segment that actually sound; small notes signify the implied notes of the set. Fourth, in Ex. 2a the special symbols ♮♯♭ and ♯♮♭ are used for certain simultaneously sounding half-steps. Fifth, the reader may compare these charts to earlier attempts at representing Bartók's music in voice-leading charts, such as Felix Salzer, *Structural Hearing* (New York, 1952, rev. ed. New York, 1962), Examples 186, 241, 441, 452, 480, and 504; Roy Travis, "Toward a New Concept of Tonality?," *Journal of Music Theory*, 3 (1959), 257–84, containing a chart of *Mikrokosmos*, No. 124; and Travis, "Tonal Coherence in the First Movement of Bartók's Fourth String Quartet," *The Music Forum*, 2 (1970), 298–371.

I. No. 140, "Free Variations"

The chart (Ex. 1a) shows both that the mechanical aspects of "Free Variations" (No. 140) are in potential conflict with the requirements of tonality, and also that Bartók treats those mechanical elements in a way that allows him to sidestep this conflict. The first of these artifices is the octatonic scale. In mm. 1–7 the interval of a fifth is filled out by it, in descending motion from a to d, i.e., a–g♯–f♯–f–e♭–d, in additive rhythms. The second artifice is seen in mm. 7–9 and 10–13. This is the contraction and transposition of the six-note octatonic scale motive into a fully chromatic six-note motive; it first fills out the a–d' interval of a fourth. Then from m. 10 on, an extended form of this chromatic variant outlines the ascending d–a fifth in the tenor (however, the bass A added at this point is *not* a direct derivation of either artifice). This much constitutes the thematic statement. The first variation (mm.13–33) exposes the third artifice, the process of inversion. In mm. 13–19 the ascending form *(inverso)* of the octatonic scale fills out the a'–e" fifth in the treble, against which the lower voices make a few tentative attempts to present at least a part of the earlier *recto* motive. What follows at this point, however—in mm. 19–24, where the second artifice of chromatic contraction is expected—is that Bartók does not follow the already established third artifice of literal inversion. Had he done so, the result would be, as shown in Ex. 1b, the filling out of the e–a fourth by the bass and tenor (cf. m. 7). It is, then, a modification of the established procedure that is presented here; in other words, mm. 19–24 show a semblance of inversion, but not the manifestation of it. A similar but even more thoroughgoing modification is seen in mm. 34–51, the second variation. Now it is the two octatonic scales that are distorted. What the literal form would be is shown in Ex. 1c. Further, this variation makes use only of the first and third of the artifices; the chromatic contraction is left off. However, a fourth artifice, only hinted at in the first variation, is joined here to the two remaining ones: the *inverso* and *recto* forms of the octatonic scale motive now imitate one another at the distance of one ²⁄₄ measure.

Only one artifice remains in the next pair of variations (mm. 52–57 and 58–64): the use of the octatonic scale motive, this time without distortion. First the treble presents the motive at its original place, between d and a, in a new rhythmic-melodic guise. This is accompanied by a transposed and fragmented derivation of the octatonic motive (mm. 52–55), as shown in the large notes of Ex. 1d. Next the roles of treble and bass are reversed, and more transpositions of the fragmented basic set are heard in the treble. This leads, at m. 65, to the last variation. All four artifices are brought together here—octatonic scale mo-

Example 1a

Example 1b   Example 1c   Example 1d

tive, chromatic contractions, inversion, and imitation, in their original *locus* and rhythmic shape—in the spirit of a true recapitulation and finale, ending the piece with a *strepitoso* cadential extension.

Tonally, the piece presents little difficulty. Since the opening octatonic scale segment is enclosed by the d–a fifth and its contraction by the a–d′ fourth above, the first nine measures clearly establish a major-minor chord on D. The addition at m. 10 of the bass note A (from outside the artifices) turns this into a D$^6_4$, which duly resolves in mm. 13–19 to an A chord. As was the D chord before, this A chord is also outlined by an octatonic scale segment enclosed by root and fifth. It is at this point that the alteration in the literal inversion of the contracted form can be seen in its true significance. By cutting short the descent of the contraction at f, Bartók averts a harmonic change from an A to an E chord (as would be implied by the literal form, given in Ex. 1b); the A harmony remains undisturbed. Further reinforced by the bass notes c (m. 20) and c♯ (m. 22)—added from outside the artifices—and with f and f♯ sounding as added sixths, this A$_6$ chord continues through the next variation, mm. 34–51. Modifying the octatonic scale segments in this variation further stabilizes the A$_6$ meaning, for it averts the possibility of hearing these measures as a return to the opening D chord, or even as an oscillation between the A$_6$ and D chord (compare Ex. 1c). Both of these modifications, however, as well as the addition of controlling bass notes, are in the nature of clarification of harmonic meaning rather than an absolute necessity. They avert potential conflicts, thereby enabling an easier and smoother comprehension of, rather than a change in, the overall tonal meaning.

Thus, at m. 52 this steadily hammered A and A$_6$ chord resolves to what is easiest to hear as a B$_7$ chord. In this B$_7$ chord, the upper chromatic neighbor of the root is heard in the bass, and the resolution of this appoggiatura is in the alto. In m. 56 the B chord moves to an analogous C chord; then from m. 58 on, a return to the D chord begins, first with the e♭ appoggiatura prominent. Eventually this appoggiatura loses its prominence, and the harmony settles into the already familiar shape of the D chord at mm. 63 and 65. This final D chord is sounded either in conjunction or in alternation with the A chord to the end of the piece.

The interpretation of the overall harmonic movement given in Ex. 1a outlines a rather simple set of progressions in the key of D, one that is a natural and organic outgrowth of the first three, or even of all four, of the artifices:

I	V	Passing VI	Passing VII	Modified I$_6^4$$_3$	I$_6$	I
(1–9)	(10–51)	(52–56)	(56–57)	(58–62)	(63–64)	(65 ff.)

According to this analysis, the final a pitch is the fifth of the tonic D chord, and not the root of the dominant.[5]

There should be no dispute over the basic progressions: D–A— passing motion–D. The passing motion itself is, however, somewhat ambiguous, especially if one views it outside of the context of the entire piece. Example 1e gives an alternative interpretation. But this only serves the purpose, first, of showing that this other possible interpretation amounts to much the same thing as the one given in Ex. 1a; and second, of showing that whatever ambiguities exist in this passage are

Example 1e. Another interpretation of *Mikrokosmos* No. 140, mm. 62–65

[5]No. 140 could, possibly, be viewed as being in the key of A. This would imply a mode defined by the primary relationship between its first and fourth degrees, the alternation between I and IV beginning in this instance with IV. Even if such a mode is assumed, it must be noted that no precedent in Hungarian folklore can be found for it. The body of Hungarian tunes that could possibly be viewed as implying such a I–IV alternation is mostly in the Mixolydian mode. (See Nos. 144 and 148–50, in Bartók, *The Hungarian Folksong* (Budapest, 1924; English translation, London, 1931). However, the alternation in these and similar tunes does not usually begin with IV, nor do the tunes resemble the "Free Variations" in any other way. Thus it is more convincing to view the D–A alternation here as between tonic and dominant, in accordance with common practice.

caused in part by the many tritones contained in it, and even more by the absence of clearly established, controlling bass notes. Controlling bass notes obviate all ambiguity in the opening portions as well as in the final section of the piece, whether they come from within the artifices themselves or from outside. The clarity of the passages that frame the middle section permits the ambiguity. And in all similarly ambiguous passages that may come up in other pieces, it is a methodological necessity to look for, and interpret according to, such larger contexts. There are two additional reasons for preferring the interpretation given in Example 1a. The first is its simplicity. The second and main reason is that the implied bass progression a–b–c–d is in fact the continuation of the a–e♭–f–f♯–g♯–a octatonic scale, that is to say, the one heard at the beginning, and thus a logical and organic outgrowth of it.

To sum up the relation between artifice and tonal direction in No. 140, it can be said, first, that the role of the artifices is absolute in controlling local events with consistency within, as well as between, these events. The artifices have strong, but not absolute, control over tonal direction. When any conflict between these two elements arises—to be sure, Bartók manages to sidestep most of these in this piece—artifice is made to yield to the demands of tonal clarity. Further, although such conflicts are slight, the potential for bigger conflict is nevertheless sensed, and thus the music is heard as being doubly determined, or double-coded, by the two fundamentally disparate elements.

II. No. 144, "Minor Seconds, Major Sevenths"

Example 2a shows both the operations of the ruling intellectual construct, or artifice, and the overall tonal direction in piece No. 144, "Minor Seconds, Major Sevenths." Here, however, unlike before, tonal direction is determined *entirely* by controlling and clarifying bass notes, most if not all of which come from *outside* the ruling artifice. They are the more welcome because the artifice itself, exposed in mm. 1 and 2, is so rich in implications that it could be used virtually with any tonal or harmonic meaning.

In Ex. 2b some of these implications, mainly those actually used by Bartók, are shown. Most important among these is the a'–a'♭ minor second, opening gradually into an e♭'–d" major seventh. But four more minor seconds, two from a up to c♭ and two more symmetrically downwards from a♭ to f♯, are there as well. In fact, all but two of all possible minor seconds between e♭' and d" are exposed; yet almost the only influence this artifice exerts on the tonal-harmonic vocabulary of this piece is that the e–f and c–d♭ minor seconds (or their inversions) hardly

Example 2a. Intellectual construct and overall tonal direction in *Mikro-kosmos* No. 144

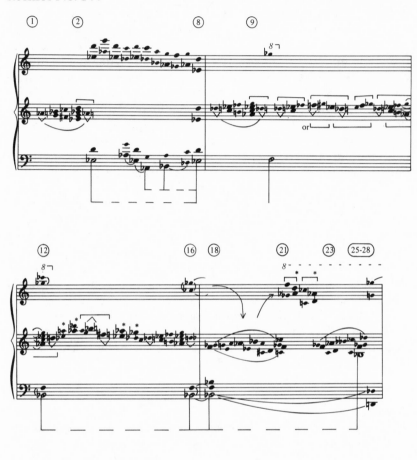

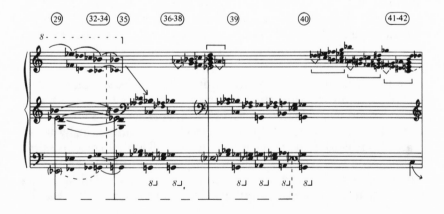

Example 2a, continued

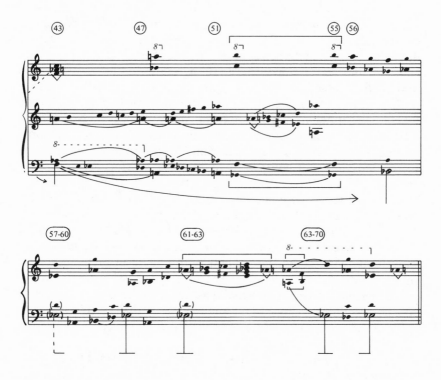

* $\textbf{\textit{3}}$ or $\textbf{\textit{3}}$ = chromatic tone cluster

ever occur later on in the piece (and even when they do, they assume a passing character, as for instance the last major seventh in m. 7, d♭–c′, or m. 18, where the f′–e′ that seems to be the bass is actually the tenor). The exposed minor seconds do, however, raise the expectation that they will play a role in their inversions as major sevenths. In addition, the artifice conspicuously exposes perfect fourths and the tritone, giving rise to the expectation that these will be brought into relation with each other, as shown in the second staff of Ex. 2b.

A certain limit is nevertheless evident from what Bartók actually does in the first eight expository measures. It seems that the expanding and piled-up minor seconds first exposed in m. 1 actually circle the g′–

Example 2b

etc.

bb' minor third, which is then immediately established as the third and fifth of an Eb major seventh chord, sounding together with the chromatic neighbor notes enclosed by the g'–bb' minor third. The remainder of these eight expository measures confirm Eb as the tonal center. But these events might better be described as further material exposed and brought into relation with the ruling artifice, rather than as either new artifices or actual organic outgrowths of the first artifice. A pentatonic tune is heard in the twin lines of the extreme high treble. Its perfect fourths, inherent in pentatonicism, may well be perceived as being related to the artifice; but now they appear in a "diatonicized" form, offering as much contrast as connection. The occurrence of each note of this melody, and its accompaniment, together with its upper major seventh, provides another relation to the artifice. But rather than having a restricting effect on the pitch content of the piece, it has a liberating one. It tells the listener to accept the interval of the major seventh, with or without a tonal-harmonic context. In other words, this interval is a constant and unvarying color element, regardless of its effect on tonal movement. The accompanying bass twin line injects yet another element. It outlines a I–IV–V–(bVII)–I cadential progression, neither inherent in Bartók's music nor normally associated with the kind of pentatonicism found in the discant melody. Nonetheless this bass progression, too, reinforces the Eb tonality already indicated by the two other elements.

The rest of the piece outlines a rather straightforward tonal movement in Eb as follows:

I	II	V & V$_6$	I$_6$	V of II i.e. VI$_\natural$	V of V i.e. II$_\natural$	V	I
(1–8)	(9–11)	(12–28)	(29–40)	(41–42)	(43)	(56)	(57 ff.)

The last I chord is cadentially extended. Over these bass-determined harmonies, the opening construct of the first two measures appears in a dizzying variety of positions, with a corresponding variety of tonal meanings. An enumeration of all of these minutiae in the order of their occurrence would become repetitious; a few characteristic instances will be enough to support the point. At mm. 8–9 the artifice outlines an Ab major seventh chord, in exact analogy to mm. 1–2, where it outlines an Eb major seventh chord. The addition of the bass F (from outside the artifice) makes this, however, a clear II chord; and a little later, at m. 12, when the bass moves to Bb against the very same chord (plus the previous f, now in the tenor), the whole sound-complex becomes an equally clear V chord. At m. 18 the bass remains bb, but the construct (now in an insignificantly altered form) changes venue. Starting from the f–gb minor second, it first opens into the c'–cb" major seventh;

then, carrying this motion one step further, at m. 25 it opens into the bb–db″ minor tenth. The tonal meaning all along remains that of the Bb dominant chord. To reinforce the chord's function, the D–db major seventh is added to this sound in the bass (V₆, the first inversion of the Bb major-minor triad). In counterpoint against this low bass major seventh, another major seventh is added three octaves and a perfect 4th higher: g″–gb‴. The function of the latter becomes clear only later, at mm. 29–32. Here the bass D–db of the V₆ passes to G–gb, the bass of the I₆ chord; thus it turns out that the high g″–gb‴ in the treble merely anticipates this V₆–I₆ resolution and continues, from mm. 29 through 32, to outline the eb minor triad downward from its third, gb‴, to the root and stepwise down to the fifth. Moreover, this happens now in a comparatively novel way: it is now the upper members of these major sevenths that carry tonal significance, rather than the lower ones, as was most often the case before.

Two further points demonstrate unusual flexibility in the opening construct. First is the use of the C major seventh chord (made richer by the addition of both of its ninth, d″ and db″) in mm. 41–42. In analogy with the cases in mm. 8–9, 12, and 18, discussed in the preceding paragraph, this chord, being supported by the bass c′ (and c), sounds clearly as a V of II (or VI♮) chord. But at mm. 51–55, the same seventh, c‴–b‴, forms part of that climactic piling-up of major sevenths that is shown as the last configuration in Example 2b. Since the last clearly defined bass before m. 51 was f′ (m. 43), and the next one, Bb, will not come until the end of m. 56, one may interpret this c‴–b‴ seventh either as part of the prolongation of the F chord itself or as part of the prolongation of the *progression* from the F to the Bb chord. The other point concerns that very F chord in m. 43. Here the already exposed symmetrical chromatic expansion around the ab–a minor second omits the two chromatic pitches below ab, so that the listener perceives a clear F major-minor triad. Thus these measures (43 ff.) serve as yet another example of the artificial construct's enforced yielding to tonal requirements.

I hope that the contrast between the two pieces has been made manifest. In contrast to its function in No. 140, the role of the artificial nontonal construct in No. 144 is almost entirely restricted to controlling local events of the piece. Tonal direction is the exclusive function of bass notes added from outside the construct. They may or may not clash with the pitches of the construct itself; but in either case the net effect is nil, for the artifice itself has been so constructed as to maximize the sense of conflict. All this is not to belittle the significance of the construct. On the contrary; aesthetically, the piece owes everything to it. The unfoldings of the construct create the general sound of the piece; its consistency, intensity, and condensed quality all result from the construct as it goes through variations in motion-form, register, and musical character. But the overall tonal structure of the piece is as independent of the artificial construct as it could conceivably be. Thus No. 144 demonstrates an altogether different case of the double-coding that was noted in connection with the previous example, No. 140.

III. No. 143, "Divided Arpeggios," and Its Mechanical Elements

"Divided Arpeggios" represents a middle position between the two extremes of Nos. 140 and 144. It does not have the relatively simple and transparent harmonic scheme that, in No. 140, was the organic outgrowth of equally simple and transparent constructs, providing a mere backdrop to the main event of that piece, which was the rhythmic unfoldings of its harmonic-melodic materials; neither does it display, as did No. 144, a plethora of sound images generated from a basic set, upon which a tonal scheme is imposed *from without* to facilitate orientation and to keep the proliferating and diffuse sound elements within bounds, much as the isorhythmic *taleae* of fourteenth-century motets keep the endlessly burgeoning motivic material within bounds. No. 143 is the product of Bartók's blending of two disparate and divergent entities, construct and tonality, mainly by setting up artificial parallels between the two.

Example 3a provides a chart for the demonstration of both the basic set and the mechanical operations of it in No. 143. Both this chart and the chart in Ex. 3c below show the three main sections of the piece— exposition, development, recapitulation. Each section is made up of two segments. After five measures of introduction, a basic set of eight notes is exposed in mm. 6–7, as two major-minor triads in first inversion:

This doubly symmetrical set is arpeggiated (first up, then down); in addition, its two halves are treated in a kind of spatial antithesis throughout the entire piece. The mechanical procedure, exposed in mm. 6–13, is based on the whole-tone scale: two moves up by major thirds (at mm. 8 and 10) followed by three moves down by whole steps (mm. 11–12). At m. 14, where the second segment of the exposition begins, both set and process are altered. But before continuing with their further course, it will be helpful to consider the possible tonal implications of both the set and the process. The eight-note set has no clearcut tonal implications in itself. Only the diminished seventh chord (bracketed in the ex-

Example 3a

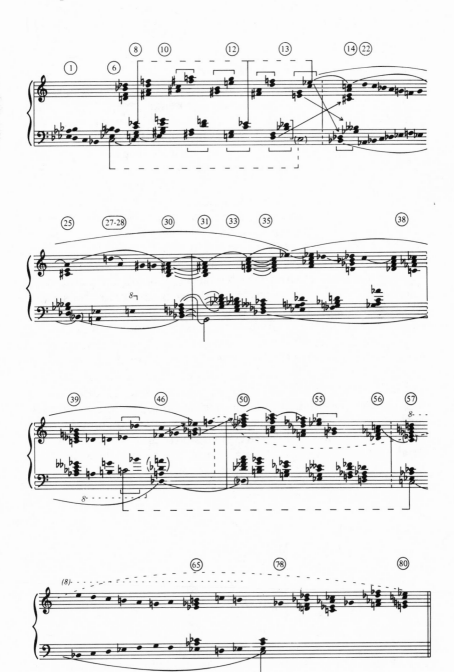

ample above) has that potential, but this chord is by its very nature too indeterminate for such a purpose.[6] The whole-tone based procedure is an outright threat to diatonic tonality—a threat, one may add, soon to be realized.

Let us return now to the further fate of these mechanical elements. At m. 14 the distance between the two halves of the set is increased from a minor to a major third, whereby the procedure too is altered: the lower half-set descends by the already exposed major third (from d, m. 12, to B♭, m. 14), but the upper half is moved down by a minor third. The resulting new, yet familiar, sound-complex lasts through mm. 25–26, but a new element is added to it in m. 21. The two melodic lines entering here above and below the sound-complex successively outline parts of both possible whole-tone scales (a♭–b♭–c–d, and d♭–e♭–f–g–a, respectively). However, these as well as the melodic tritones of mm. 25–26 are only *references* to the mechanical procedure, not a technically or mechanically definable organic *outgrowth* of them.

At the beginning of the development (m. 31), even this tenuous connection with the exposed artifices ceases. For the duration of this section, up to m. 49, the exposed pitch relations of both set and procedure are entirely abandoned. Intervals within each half-set are constantly changing; the two halves are symmetrical neither in themselves nor in relation to each other; and the distance between the two halves changes without any mechanical regularity, as does the distance from one presentation of the complete set to the next. All that remains here from the exposed regularities is the spatially antithetical use of the two half-sets within the characteristically wide-ranging arpeggiated texture.

At the recapitulation, m. 50, both set and procedure return, but they appear now with a new mechanical twist: the contents of mm. 6–13 are presented here in mirror-inversion. Inversion of the first six measures is literal; in the seventh (m. 56), set, procedure, and literal inversion all leave off. Example 3b shows that a literal continuation of the inversion

Example 3b

[6]It should be noted that assuming the first half of the set as complete in itself and considering the second half merely as a recurrence of the first a major ninth higher

would lead to the same chord-complex as does, in fact, the altered form. Reasons for the alteration will be dealt with below, when the tonal analysis of the piece is discussed.

In the remaining part of the recapitulation, mm. 56–67 are an almost literal version of mm. 14–24; 68–77 extend this segment and combine it with brief references to mm. 6–7; and finally the piece is concluded with a new and hitherto unused procedure applied to the half-set: in mm. 79–80 the half-set is moved up by a perfect fourth and then down by a minor second.

IV. No. 143: Tonal Analysis

Example 3a has shown the mechanics of the construct and its operations. To the eye its meaning is clear and unequivocal. To the ear, however, Example 3a represents only half of what is heard, and quite possibly the lesser half. I believe that what the listener actually perceives is much closer to what is shown in the chart in Example 3c.[7] This chart is based on a peculiarity of No. 143 almost unique in Bartók's oeuvre from at least 1911 on. This is that the sequence of its pitches, and the chords these pitches add up to, can be interpreted throughout in terms of a nineteenth-century harmonic vocabulary that stays for the most part within the bounds established by composers such as Schumann or Brahms, with only an occasional foray into the realm of Wagner and R. Strauss (for instance, in mm. 14–25 and 31–38). In Ex. 3c, the overall tonal movement of the piece can be seen as follows. The opening segment (mm. 1–13) establishes and prolongs a C chord. This has at first the appearance of an Ab sixth chord with its third delayed in the bass (mm. 1–4), the whole Ab chord being enriched by the ninth, bb; but by m. 8, the note ab is heard as a neighbor note of g and the first member of a 6–5 suspension. The second segment (mm. 14–30) contains basically the single chord a–c–eb–f♯, i.e., the first inversion of the diminished seventh of the dominant. Soon eb is replaced by e♮, but the chord's function remains the same. This segment is a prolongation of the progres-

---

would only further reduce its potential for tonal definition. The α chord by itself is even more indeterminate than the diminished seventh chord, for every member of it can be an appoggiatura capable of several resolutions.

[7]The chart in Ex. 3c needs two comments in addition to those given in note 4. First, groupings of the notes in simultaneously sounding chords constitute my understanding of the chord-grammar of this piece. And second, the score contains many shifts in octave register between adjacent chords. In some passages, as in mm. 14–30 and 57–78, where these shifts seem irrelevant to harmonic interpretation, they are not shown. All other register shifts appear in the chart, but transpositions (in parentheses) to a single octave register are also provided to make voice-leading more readily apparent.

Example 3c

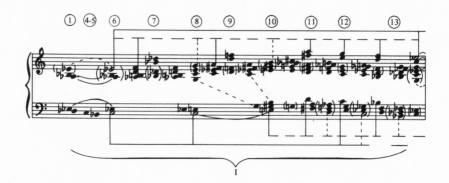

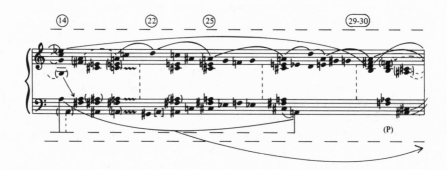

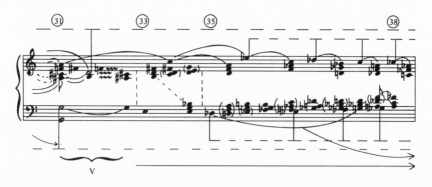

(continued)

Example 3c, continued

sion from the tonic to the dominant. The third segment, beginning the development, starts at m. 31 with a dominant ninth chord. This is followed by a prolongation of the progression from this chord back to the opening tonic chord. The tonic chord, reached at m. 39—just halfway through the development—again appears in the guise of an A♭ chord, but further enriched in comparison with the opening. It now contains not only its ninth, b♭, but also f♯ (spelled as g♭); and, as before, it will in the end (m. 79) resolve to the tonic by the now familiar and expected 6–5 suspension. The repetition of this suspension produces the first of the three most important parallelisms in the entire composition.

Before this happens, however, one more harmonic event takes place throughout the rest of the development and the entire first segment of the recapitulation (mm. 46–57). The very same prolonging chord that was used earlier (mm. 35–38) to reach the enriched tonic is once more established and prolonged here (from m. 46 on) for the same purpose. The chord is d♭–e♭ (or f♭)–g–b♭: the diminished seventh chord of A♭, alternating occasionally with the functionally identical V⁴₃ of A♭ (Ex. 3d shows the prolongation at mm. 35–38 in a somewhat more detailed form). The return of this enriched tonic chord anticipates the recapitulation of the material by eleven measures; it is absent during the first segment of the recapitulation (except for the treble anticipating it in an arpeggio between mm. 51 and 57), and returns only at mm. 57–58 for the final segment. Both times it is reached from the diminished seventh chord over the d♭ bass note; this constitutes the second of the three principal tonal-harmonic parallelisms of the piece. The concluding segment (measures 57 to the end) holds this enriched tonic (with f♯, but also with b♮ instead of b♭) until m. 78, where it resolves in just two measures to the pure form of the tonic C chord by passing briefly through the Neapolitan sixth.

A brief glance at Examples 3d and 3e, two different charts of mm. 31–39, may at this point provide a better understanding of the passage. The prolongation of the progression from dominant to tonic begins at m. 33 and becomes so ambiguous, due to its chromatic passing motion from

Example 3d

Example 3e

m. 35 on, that final interpretation of the relative importance of its details becomes possible only in retrospect—after its goal, the A♭ chord of m. 39, has been reached. Ex. 3d shows the interpretation that I judge most persuasive in itself, and which is the only convincing one in relation to the A♭ goal. Example 3e represents another possible interpretation, but in this interpretation measures 33–38 lead back to the G ninth chord. This second interpretation derives a degree of authority from Bartók's own first draft of the piece, in which a G ninth chord is actually reached in m. 39.[8] Bartók himself may have felt that the passage in question pointed more convincingly towards A♭ (as shown by the chart in Example 3d) than to G. At any rate, sometime after completion of the first version, he raised the contents of mm. 39–44 by one half-step to the present A♭ ninth chord, making the appropriate changes in mm. 44–45 in order to reach the diminished seventh of A♭ in second inversion at mm. 46 ff. Apart from clarifying the tonal meaning of mm. 35–39, the change brings into sharper focus not only the two already discussed parallelisms of the piece, but a third one as well.

V. The Conflict and its Resolution

The third parallelism, perhaps the most conspicuous among the three important ones, consists in that tonic-dominant-tonic tonal plan that is found on the highest level of organization of the entire piece. It is in close parallel with the harmonic content of the local events exposed in mm. 6, 7, and 8; at the same time, the phenomenon also directs attention to the most important paradox of this method of composition. The local event is perceived as the product of intellectually and mechanically conceived constructs, which operate independently of the

[8] I should like to express my thanks to Dr. Benjamin Suchoff, Trustee of the Estate of Béla Bartók and Director of the Bartók Archives (Stonybrook, N.Y.) for providing me with photostat copies of all manuscript materials relating to No. 143.

demands of inherited tonality. In contrast, the overall tonal plan is executed through the disparate route of traditional tonality—at times in disregard of, at other times in direct contradiction to, those very mechanical constructs.

True, a whole plethora of local details are formed, or at least informed at one remove, by those constructs, and these details stamp the entire piece with their own consistent and characteristic sound. But the role of the constructs themselves is restricted to the creation of certain local expectations in the mind of the listener, and these expectations produce tension throughout the piece precisely by their coming into various conflicts with the ultimately ruling tonal expectations. The fact that other mechanically engendered entities receive confirmation by the disparate route of tonally directed movement, possibly in contravention of the mechanical constructs, further underlines this point. The two main parallelisms of the piece earlier discussed show this clearly. The basis for the presentation of the tonic as a 6–5 suspension over a stationary root and third is merely one of many possibilities offered by the mechanical constructs. For it to become replete with tonal implication, the addition of a note from *outside the constructs* is necessary, and Bartók duly adds the bass note c at m. 8 to turn the possibility into an explicitly stated tonal reality. And the other two occurrences of this form of the tonic chord (at mm. 39 and 57–58) come into being entirely without benefit of the mechanical constructs. The same can be said of the remaining main parallelism, the prominent role given to the two diminished seventh chords over the d♭ bass. The note d♭ is prominently featured in the set, as well as in the first three introductory measures, and so is the diminished seventh *per se*; but the two diminished sevenths at mm. 35–38 and 46–56 merely refer to these. Their existence in both instances comes about by tonally directed movement, which is separate from and in contravention of the original mechanical constructs. Nor is the final appearance of this important d♭ in measure 79, accompanied by the Neapolitan sixth, the result of artifice; rather, it comes about by fiat of the composer.

To conclude this inquiry, let us return once more to the voice-leading chart (Ex. 3c) to see what exactly Bartók does to resolve conflicts between the two kinds of expectations. These fall into two categories. The first is the addition, from outside the construct, of a note or notes to those dictated by the construct, for the purpose of establishing tonal direction. Characteristically, there is only a single example of this in our piece, the already discussed bass note c in measure 8 (also the analogous e two measures later). Outside of No. 144, this device is only a little more frequent in the other similarly constructed pieces in the *Mikrokosmos.* The other category is modification or abandonment of the construct to accommodate the dictates of tonality. A closer study of five more instances of this reveals five specific points that will further support the already stated argument.

First, in considering mm. 14–25, it can be easily seen that continuation of the previously established set and procedure would lead to chords on a♭, g♭, and so forth down the whole-tone scale, but not to the chords required by tonality, i.e., the diminished seventh chord on a at m. 14 and the dominant ninth chord on g at m. 31. Second, the change to the diminished chord at m. 14 creates a sort of twentieth-century trill, measured and staggered, as it is embedded in the arpeggiated texture. With only the note f♯ remaining stationary, the other notes of the chord, a, c, and e♭, alternate with their chromatic neighbors. Here and in the recapitulation at mm. 57 ff., this trill is still related, even if only tenuously, to the original constructs; but duplication of these trills at mm. 31–32 and 39–43, a motivically and formally significant feature, comes altogether from outside the construct. Third, the already mentioned melodic whole-tone scale fragments at mm. 22–25 and 63–66 are not organic outgrowths of the mechanical procedure, but are a mere reference to it. In fact, their presence is possible only because they fit (or are made to fit) into the previously described trill, which is itself the result of modification in the set. Fourth, in m. 56, the mechanical process of presenting the material in inversion is changed. Had it not been altered, the desired goal of the enriched A♭ chord would not have been reached from the tonally required diminished seventh chord on d♭, but from the first inversion of a dominant seventh chord on f, as was shown in Ex. 3b. Clarity of tonal design would have suffered, and one of the important parallelisms of the piece would have been obliterated. The fifth and perhaps most significant point can be made, finally, by comparing the respective tonal meanings of the parallel passages at mm. 14–25 and 56–57 ff. One whole step apart, they are identical as to their interval structure; yet they do not represent chords one whole step apart, because their respective tonal contexts require that we interpret the first one as a–c–e♭ (or e♮)–f♯, the second as c–e♭–f♯–a♭. This points once more to the tonal significance of the trill, for that is what makes it possible to hear these chords as the same and yet so different in their differing contexts.

VI. Conclusions

The foregoing analyses afford three conclusions. First, the recognizable elements of all three pieces are produced and defined by two separate processes, one directed by tonality, the other by mechanical construct. Second, in case of conflict arising from this double-coding, tonality takes precedence. These two conclusions offer an analogy with older practice, as a fleeting glance at, say, the artifice fugues of the *Well-Tempered Clavier* will readily show.

But a third conclusion points to a specifically Bartókian style characteristic. By paralleling, in the tonal construction, several entities contained in the intellectual construct, and doing this sometimes in outright contravention of the literal form of the construct itself, Bartók creates a synthesis between disparate elements. This synthesis is a one-time occurrence in each piece and is entirely the product of the creator's will and sensibilities. And this synthesis, brought into existence and maintained by will, reveals Bartók's aesthetic standpoint. The immediately perceptible illusion of organic interrelations is of greater importance to him than any narrow, technically defined integrity of the means employed in achieving it.

Drumming in Korean Farmers' Music:
A Process of Gradual Evolution

ROBERT C. PROVINE

THERE IS A CONSIDERABLE GRAY AREA between the conservative Western notion of a finished composition and that of extemporized music. Charles Ives found himself in between with his Concord Sonata, of which varying versions were published, left in manuscript, and played by Ives himself in a recording studio. Other twentieth-century compositions also fall into the gray area, with parameters that were formerly notated now either left to the performers' discretion or omitted entirely, so that the pieces exist in no fixed form.

The concept of a dynamic, evolving piece of music such as the Concord Sonata is well supported by examples from outside the Western art music tradition, especially in the oral transmission of complex music. The present study examines aspects of a dynamically conceived drum piece in one type of Korean "Farmers' Music" (nongak). The piece is constantly evolving, but is considered at any point in the course of its evolution to be fixed, reproducible, and teachable as an entity.

Kim Pyŏng-sŏp,[1] the composer/performer of the piece under study, thinks of his piece as fixed in nearly all details and describes any deviation in performance (whether by himself or his students) as a mistake. Nevertheless, he feels free, outside the performance context, to subject his piece progressively to a variety of carefully conceived modifications, arriving each time at a new version that then remains fixed until he finds a reason to change it further.

This essay is based on my observation and active study of the piece as it existed at three times: early 1975, late 1979, and late 1982. Mr. Kim taught it to me entirely by oral means, and I made no attempt at transcription until after I had the music thoroughly under my fingers in

---

[1] Mr. Kim was born in 1922. He has taught Farmers' Music part time (in addition to his farming) since 1957, and as a full-time professional in Seoul since 1974. He has received numerous awards, including the Presidential Prize in the 1964 National Folk Arts Competition.

1975. My transcriptions were the first description of Mr. Kim's piece in any written notation.[2]

Context, Style, and Instrumentation

Korean Farmers' Music of the southwestern Chŏlla provinces is played and danced by a band of about twenty to thirty performers. Nearly all the instruments employed are percussion (gongs and drums); the sole melodic instrument, a conical oboe called a *hojŏk*, is considered dispensable. Notably loud, Farmers' Music is traditionally performed outdoors, for a variety of shamanic rites, work support rhythms, and pure entertainment. While it has long enjoyed popularity with the common man, educated and socially higher Koreans have tended to disdain it, preferring more dignified forms of professional music derived from folk sources.

A typical performance of Farmers' Music for entertainment lasts for an hour or more and consists of group dances by the full band, solo dances by the leading performers, and acrobatics or earthy skits. The drum piece discussed here is an unaccompanied solo played and danced by Mr. Kim. Although it occurs as a part of a full performance of Farmers' Music, it is musically complete in itself.[3]

Predictably, comments on musical style in Farmers' Music deal primarily with rhythm. Korean folk rhythm is metrical; but the chief factor in the Korean concept of meter is not the recurrence of a beat structure but rather of a standard length of time, coupled with a sense of consistent speed. Hence one bar may have four beats (12/8) and the next three beats (3/2), but they will have the same duration and thus be considered to belong to the same metric category. The Korean term for this metrical structure is *changdan*; it is usually rendered in English as "rhythmic pattern," but refers literally to the recurring length of time.

---

[2]Privately printed as *Drum Rhythms in Korean Farmers' Music* (Seoul, 1975). An earlier attempt to transcribe a similar piece by a different performer may be found in Chŏng Hoe-gap, "Kim Yun-dŏk yŏnju Chŏng Hoe-gap ch'aebo 'Sŏlchanggo' " ["Sŏlchanggo," played by Kim Yun-dŏk and transcribed by Chŏng Hoe-gap], *Ŭmdae hakpo* [Bulletin of the College of Music, Seoul National University], 2 (1964), no pagination. A more recent transcription of Mr. Kim Pyŏng-sŏp's piece, with choreography, may be found in Chu Yŏng-ja, "Han'guk changgo ŭmak ŭi nat'anan rhythm kwa movement yŏn'gu" [A Study of Rhythm and Dance Movement in Korean Drum Music], *Han'guk munhwa yŏn'guwŏn nonch'ong* [Essay Collection of the Korean Culture Institute, Ewha University], 38 (1981), 217–290.

As this article was in press, an important essay on Kim Pyŏng-sŏp and his music appeared: Keith Howard, "Nongak, the *Changgu* and Kim Pyŏng-sŏp's *Kaein Changgu Nori*," *Korea Journal*, 23, no. 5 (May 1983), 15–31, and 23, no. 6 (June 1983), 23–34.

[3]Occasionally, a gong player will play along during the final section of a drum piece, less as an accompaniment than as a signal to the rest of the band that the piece is coming to a close.

In Mr. Kim's drum piece, as in numerous other types of complex "folk" music in Korea, two beat structures dominate: a four-beat bar with duple subdivision (4/4), in which rhythmic interest tends to center on syncopation; and a four-beat bar with triple subdivision (12/8), in which interest often focuses on what the Western analyst might consider alternating meters of uniform duration. In the latter case, for instance, one might encounter a normal 12/8 alternating with 6/4, 3/2, 6/8 + 3/4, or even 5/8 + 5/8 + 2/8.

The performer of the drum piece dances while playing. Foot patterns have a strong tendency to complement beat patterns; the typical four-step pattern associated with a rapid 12/8, for example, tends to become three-step for 3/2 and two- or six-step for 6/4. This correlation is an obvious blessing to the transcriber.[4]

Mr. Kim's drum piece lasts about fifteen minutes. It is in three substantial sections (each normally named by the rhythmic pattern used in it), sandwiched between a short, virtuosic prelude and a short coda:

Prelude: fast pattern *samch'ae*, typically 12/8 (♩. = 104–120)
1. very fast pattern *tumach'i*, 4/4 (♩ = 144–168)
2. moderate pattern *kutkŏri*, typically 2 x 6/8 (♩. = 52–60)
3. *samch'ae*
Coda: *samch'ae*

The instrument used is a lightweight version of the standard Korean hourglass drum, *changgo* (see Plate 1). The paulownia-wood body is

Plate 1. *Changgo* from In-hak Choe, *Hankuk Minsok (Korean Folklore)*, 1974, p. 179

[4]While the interaction of dance and rhythm is extremely useful in deciphering

completely hollow, even in the narrow middle portion. Large, over-hanging drumskins are stretched over the open ends and laced to each other with cord. For dancing, the drum is strapped to the performer with sashes around the shoulder and waist. The right hand strikes the right drumhead (usually in the center, rather than along the border as is common in most other types of *changgo* playing) with a slender strip of bamboo, producing a crisp, high-pitched sound. The left hand plays with a mallet on either drumhead, producing a lower-pitched and more resonant sound. These two basic sonorities (called *ttak* and *kung* by Mr. Kim) range sufficiently in pitch and timbre so that performers tend to describe this percussive music in terms usually applied to melody in other Korean genres.

Types of Modification

1. Accretion

Mr. Kim has often enlarged his piece by inserting new material. Example 1 shows how three bars (that is, recurrent time lengths) in 1975

Example 1. *samch'ae*, as played in 1979 and 1982

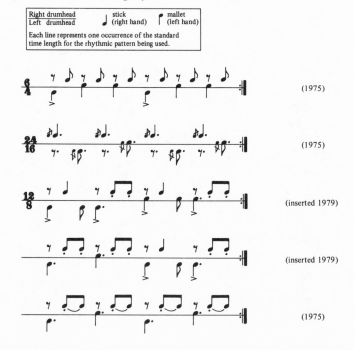

rhythmic structure for transcription, I shall be able to consider dance only tangentially in this essay.

grew to five by 1979 (and remained there in 1982). In cases of accretion, one must often modify the choreography; in this case, the performer moves forward during the first inserted segment and back to his original position during the second.

2. Omission and substitution

Occasionally in a later version Mr. Kim has simply dropped whole passages which, for one reason or another, he found unsatisfactory.[5] More often, he has replaced an earlier passage with a new one. The first three bars of the 1975 version, all in straightforward 12/8, were replaced in 1979 by a concise two-bar flourish of 3/2 and 12/8 (see Example 2).

3. Variants

Small variants occur more frequently in the evolution of Mr. Kim's piece than the radical changes described above. In the continuation of

Example 2. *samch'ae*

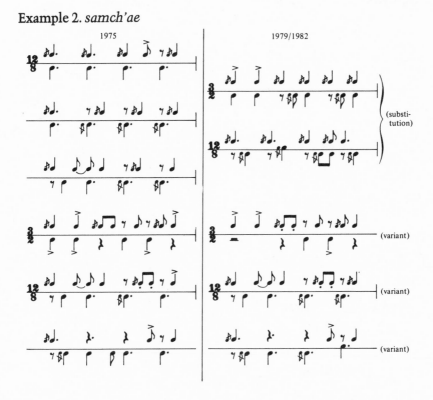

[5]For example, the beginning of the *kutkŏri* section in the 1975 version; see *Drum Rhythms*, p. 26, nos. 110–115.

Example 2, the three remaining bars of the 1979/82 version are all minor variants of the 1975 version. In the first variant bar, the omission of the initial two sharp mallet strokes makes an attractive contrast to the heavy use of the mallet in the preceding bars. The second variant bar shows increased activity on the fourth beat. The third variant is primarily visual: on the fourth beat the mallet is struck on the right head rather than the left.

Example 3 shows a two-bar phrase that differs in all three transcriptions. The 1975 version is difficult to play, and Mr. Kim may have bowed to student pressure to modify it. The 1979 version is less challenging, and also less interesting, with its regular thumping of the mallet. The 1982 version, a good compromise, demonstrates the gradual tightening found in many of Mr. Kim's modifications.

Some of Mr. Kim's changes border on the imperceptible, such as the simple omission of a grace note (Example 4) and the alteration of only two beats in an extended passage (excerpted in Example 5). In many cases, the presence or absence of a grace note is considered optional, but

Example 3. *tumach'i*

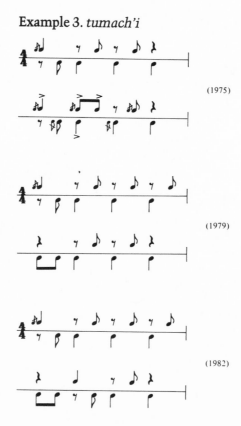

Example 4. *tumach'i*

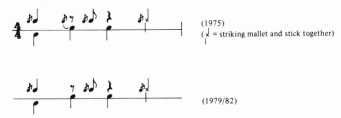

(1975)
(= striking mallet and stick together)

(1979/82)

Example 5. *tumach'i*

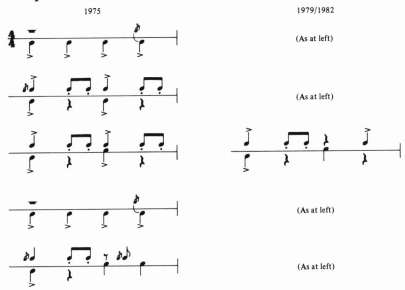

it happens that Mr. Kim habitually played the grace note in Example 4 in 1975 and no longer did so in 1979 or 1982. When asked about this sort of variant, he would usually respond that either way was entirely satisfactory; but subsequently I could observe that he habitually performed only one alternative. Slight though such modifications might be, Mr. Kim and his students observe them faithfully.

I must re-emphasize that the modifications described above are not capricious or extemporaneous. In 1975, Mr. Kim *always* played those versions marked "1975" in the transcriptions (apart from mistakes). In short, the piece was fixed and reproducible from day to day and even week to week. However, he felt free to make periodic revisions, which in turn became fixtures in the piece and were passed on to current students.

The extended passage (about fifty seconds' duration) in Example 6 shows how all these gradual changes may fit into a larger musical context. The excerpt is taken from the first large section of the piece, in the

Example 6. *tumach'i (obangjin)*, 1982 version

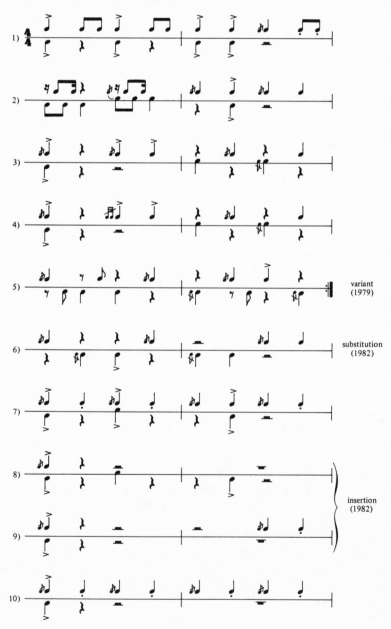

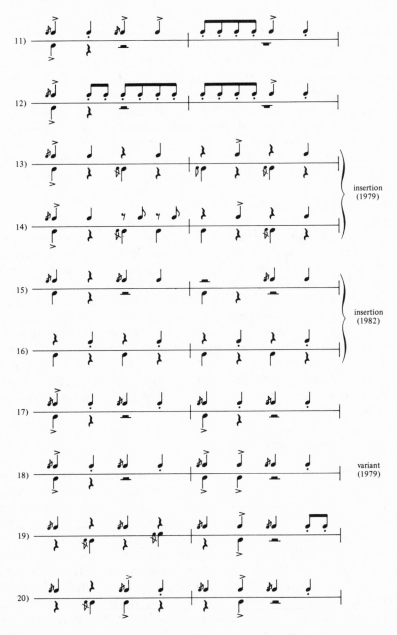

rhythmic pattern *tumach'i,* and it derives in part from music played during a group dance called *obangjin* ("five directions formation"). Although the tempo remains the same throughout the *tumach'i,* the pattern length of this extract is two bars rather than one (cf. Exx. 4 and 5).

Mr. Kim claims to be the only player to have an *obangjin* subsection in a solo drum piece, and he has taken pains to ensure its musical quality and suitability for dancing.

Of the twenty lines of music in the 1982 transcription, six are simple insertions of new material (four from 1982, two from 1979), one is a substitution (1982), and two are variants (1979). The 1975 version of line 5 was just like the 1975 phrase in Example 3. Line 6, in 1975, was identical to line 2. Line 18 was identical to line 17 at the time of my first transcription. The various changes have resulted in an overall expansion of the passage, yet with less repetition of material than before. Rhythmic vitality and interest have been heightened with no loss of cohesion.

Sources of New Material

It is a long-standing practice among Korean folk musicians to listen to other performers and compliment them by borrowing useful material. Mr. Kim has obtained material in this way, as well as creating his own. There is no copyright arrangement, formal or informal.

I have seen Mr. Kim ask elderly musicians to demonstrate their renditions of certain passages or special realizations of particular rhythmic patterns, in an attempt both to retrieve older ways of playing and to gather fresh material for use in his own piece. His sources are not always older performers, however; Mr. Kim is even willing on occasion to adopt students' suggestions, if the material is not too stylistically disruptive (one of the phrases in the *tumach'i* section, for example, is mine).

Effects of the Modifications

The gradual evolution of Mr. Kim's piece has generally brought about greater cohesiveness in both the musical and visual components. After learning his piece in 1974 and 1975, I felt (and in hindsight still feel) I had acquired a collection of individually through-composed passages that were loosely, if elegantly, connected by transitions that consisted of an indefinite number of repetitions of a single phrase.[6] But in succeeding years, Mr. Kim has reduced the amount of transitional material, specified the number of repetitions for virtually all phrases throughout the piece, and generally avoided excessive recurrence of material. As each of the three main sections of the piece has grown more seamless and integrated, he has revised the choreography to reflect the musical changes.

The length of the piece has not changed significantly, since inser-

[6]As explained in *Drum Rhythms*, p. 8.

tions in one place have often been balanced by omissions elsewhere and by a decrease in repetitions. In 1975, the piece lasted about twelve and a half minutes; in 1982 it was closer to fourteen minutes. Because of the physical stamina needed to perform the work, it is unlikely that Mr. Kim (sixty years old in 1982) will ever enlarge it beyond fifteen minutes.

Concluding Observations

I sense that Mr. Kim's piece changes less as time goes by. During my extended period of study with him in 1974–75, the piece was modified frequently. In 1979, I observed many additional changes, but in 1982, comparatively few changes; in both cases, however, two weeks' practice was sufficient to get the new material well in hand.

Economics and the frantic pace of life in modern Korea have had their effects on Mr. Kim and his teaching. Almost no one is willing to spend the time and money required to learn the complete drum piece properly, and so Mr. Kim finds himself teaching simplified excerpts and arrangements to schoolchildren and a few university extra-curricular groups. He has fashioned pieces of three, four, and five minutes' duration, emphasizing the dance elements and omitting the most technically difficult musical passages. The piece in its entirety is kept aside for the dedicated few.

It might be hypothesized—wrongly, I think—that Mr. Kim has only recently brought his piece to a relatively fixed state, for the sake of his pupils; a student usually finds it easier to learn a piece in fixed form than one that varies unpredictably. In former decades Mr. Kim might have taught his students a number of discrete passages, which could be variously bound together with extemporized transitions. But since Mr. Kim only took up teaching full time in the early 1970s, this hypothesis would need to be checked against the practices of other performers and teachers. My own inclination is to believe that the piece has evolved as a whole, according to Mr. Kim's personal artistic vision, and that at age sixty he is comparatively satisfied with his work and finds less reason to tamper with it.

Mr. Kim knows both what he is doing and what he has done. He remembers, to the last detail, what he was playing and teaching in 1975 and 1979, as well as the problems or strengths of particular students. When I went to him in August, 1982, he could recall and play passages from the piece as he taught them to me in 1975 and 1979; then he would demonstrate his current renderings.

The composer's piece evolves because of his continuing urge for improvement. It is nevertheless necessary that the modifications of the piece occur within stylistic constraints, lest alien materials be incorporated. Mr. Kim insists on doing things "the old way" and therefore frequently asks aged musicians for information on how things used to be done. Yet he finds no contradiction (nor should we) in making changes, if he feels no damage has been done to stylistic norms. As long as he perceives continuity in the tradition, he welcomes new and interesting material.

I suggest that the dynamic concept of this piece of drum music is essential to the tradition of Korean Farmers' Music (and of much other Korean folk music). Aspects of the musical tradition are not lost when Mr. Kim changes his piece; rather, the flexibility essential to the overall tradition is preserved. To freeze the piece in the name of "authenticity" or "correctness" would be to violate its very nature.

"Oh, I Never Will Forget You":
A Samoan Farewell

JACOB WAINWRIGHT LOVE

Everyone who has a heart has echoed Goethe's Faust in an urgent wish: "Verweile doch! Du bist so schön!"[1] The sentiment that touches us at grand, happy, fatal moments prods us to hold the hour fast, and beg Time to "tarry a while"; for the instant is beautiful, and we know the beauty will fade: at the height of emotion, we prepare to remember. The need to hold on, and then to mark the moment, manifests itself when we think to fix our feelings in mind; it springs naturally, privately, from a foreboding of change.

In Samoa, where private yields to public at events that threaten change, the impulse to create a memory arises in song, as one element in the rituals of departure. Before a person embarks on a major journey, friends and relatives gather, to share oratory, prayers, and perhaps 'ava (a beverage consumed with ceremony). When they can put off the departure no longer, they rush to adorn the traveler with necklaces of flowers and shells: they reach out to clasp and kiss, and many shed tears; some begin singing, and the throng joins in.

Several songs can serve to mark the moment,[2] but one of them has

---

[1]Johann Wolfgang von Goethe, *Faust*, line 1700 (recapitulated in 11581–86). The concept of the "moment"—the transcending of time, through the union of action and feeling—burns at the center of the drama, which turns the well-worn tale of a professor's search for experience into a universally appreciable parable.

[2]Perhaps the most frequently heard of these today—a signal of the beginning of journeys and the ending of funerals—is " 'Ia fa'atasi pea Iesu ma 'oe," text 317 in the Protestant hymnal, *O Pese ma Viiga i le Atua* (Malua, W. Samoa; 1909); it is a version of "God be with You!" (words, J. E. Rankin; music, W. G. Tomer), found in many hymnals, including Ira D[avid] Sankey, James McGranahan, and George C[oles] Stebbins, *Gospel Hymns[:] Nos. 1 to 6 Complete* (Cincinnati, 1894), no. 340. According to the American sailor Hugo Evon Frey (b. 1883), seamen being transferred home from the naval station in American Samoa in 1904–06 departed to the accompaniment of a band's rendition of "Home! Sweet Home!" (*Hugo's Odyssey* [Los Angeles, 1942], p. 143), for which Samoan words appear in the Protestant hymnal (text 286).

In the days the Germans governed Western Samoa (1899–1914), their music some-

stood paramount for nearly a century: "the farewell song of every island lover, the melody that soars above the melancholy rattling of anchor chains on every outward-bound schooner that spreads her white wings upon the breast of the great South Seas"[3]—a song whose text promises abiding remembrance.

By 1906, foreigners had noticed it in the principal ports of the arch·pelago. Isobel Field heard it in 1892, at Apia, the capital of Western S; moa:

> It was a very moving sight[,] for the harbor was filled with boats, canoes, and rafts, and all along the beach people were waving hats, handker-chiefs, flags, tablecloths. The *Curacoa* [sic] steamed twice round the two other men-of-war in port (the *Buzzard* and *Walleroo*), her homeward bound pennant flying, her band playing . . . Samoa's poignant song of farewell, *To Fa My Feleni*.[4]

---

times prevailed. Karl Rudolf Indra (b. 1861) recalls: "Rings um das Schiff schwärmten eine Menge von Booten, unaufhörlich stiegen feingeputzte Herren und Damen (vorzugsweise der Half-Caste) die Schiffstreppe hinauf, während die uns schon bekannte uniformierte Musik von Apia auf dem Oberdeck tragische, jämmerliche Weisen auf-spielte. 'Muss' i denn, muss i denn zum Städtle hinaus, und Du mein Schatz bleibst hier', erklang es im Angesichte des Waiaberges [Mt. Vaea], der verwundert über solche, noch nie gehörte Musik sein ehrwürdiges Haupt schüttelte" (*Südseefahrten* [Berlin, 1903], p. 205). Paul Ebert heard the band of S.M.S. *Planet* play the same music, "ein letzter Gruss der unvergesslichen Südsee" (*Südsee-Erinnerungen* [Leipzig, 1924], p. 237). On board the cruiser *Bussard* during the early 1890s, another traveler, Otto Ehrenfried Ehlers (1855–95), heard the ship's band play it (*Samoa*, 5th ed. [Berlin, 1900], p. 192). Augustin Friedrich Krämer (1865–1941) observed a few years later that the same "Schiffskapelle spielte 'Muss i denn zum Städtle hinaus' und 'Talofa Samoa', während der weisse 'Bussard' majestätich durch den Riffeinlass auf die blaue See hinausfuhr" (*Hawaii, Ostmikronesien[,] und Samoa* [Stuttgart, 1906], p. 193).

[3]Beatrice [Ethel] Grimshaw, *In the Strange South Seas* (London, 1907), pp. 336–37. An indomitable traveler, Grimshaw (1871–1953)—"the first white woman to ascend the notorious Sepik and Fly Rivers" (New York *Times*, July 1, 1953, p. 29)—also recorded her experience in *Isles of Adventure* (New Guinea, Solomon Islands, New Caledonia), *Fiji and its Possibilities* (Fiji, New Hebrides), *The New New Guinea*, and, indirectly, in many works of fiction, of which one of the cleverest, *Victorian Family Robinson* (London, 1934), by reviving interest in its model—[Johann David Wyss (1743–1818)], *Der Schweizerische Robinson*, ed. Joh[ann] Rudolf Wyss (1781–1830), 2nd ed. (Zurich, 1821),—may have invited productions of a film, *Swiss Family Robinson* (RKO, 1940; Disney, 1960).

[4]*This Life I've Loved* (New York, 1937), p. 339; Field (1859–1953) was the daughter of Fanny Van de Grift (1840–1914), whose second husband was Robert Louis Stevenson (1850–94). The band also played *Home! Sweet Home!*—the song that, in Hawai'i nine years before, had closed King Kalākaua's coronation-ball (Field, p. 167). About twenty years later, Frank Burnett heard the song when he left Apia: "The vessel was thronged with natives of both sexes, decorated with garlands of tropical flowers, who, when the ship was ready to sail, left us to our great regret, singing the . . . Samoan farewell song, *Tofa mai Feleni*, known all over the South Pacific" (*Summer Isles of Eden* [London, 1923], p. 132); Burnett wrote books of adventure, including *Ruined Cities of Ceylon*

Lewis Ransome Freeman heard it on leaving Pagopago, the chief town of Tutuila, American Samoa:

> A crowd of our native friends on the dock began singing the plaintive half Samoan, half English farewell song, *"Tuta-pai, mai feleni"*—{"Goodbye, my Friend["]}[;] and the oft repeated refrain, "O Ai neppa will fa-get you," followed us till the yacht passed out of hearing around the point.[5]

Even at Manu'a, that "most isolated and primitive section of American Samoa,"[6] the song found an audience, among which a member of Jack London's entourage observed: "As we heaved anchor that afternoon, the boat bearing the king and queen circled the *Snark* three times, its occupants singing 'Tofa-Mai-Feleni,' the native song of farewell."[7] The

---

and *Exploring and Fishing in British Columbia.* Otto Riedel (b. 1867), merchant of Hamburg, provides another account of departure from that harbor (apparently in 1906): "Die Native-Kapelle spielte rührende deutsche Weisen und das schöne samoanische Abschiedslied *'Tofa mai feleni!'* (Leb wohl, mein Freund!)[.] Es war eine Situation, von der man sagen konnte, dass ein Eisblock dabei auftauen müssen" (*Der Kampf um Deutsch-Samoa* [Berlin, 1938], p. 204).

[5]*In the Tracks of the Trades* (New York, 1920), p. 283; his departure occurred in or before 1910. A member of the Explorers Club, Freeman (b. 1878) wrote books of travel, including *Afloat and Aflight in the Caribbean, Discovering South America,* and *Down the Grand Canyon;* he provided photographic illustrations for the first edition of Rudyard Kipling, *The Feet of the Young Men* (Garden City, NY; 1920). Frey recalls that as he stood weeping on the deck of the *Ventura,* c. 1906, his hostess "sang that most wonderful of all farewell songs, *'Tofa Maflegi'* (Goodbye my Friend). Her rich contralto voice carried far out to the echoing hills. And then [from seemingly hundreds of canoes and longboats] a thousand voices joined in" (p. 145). The English poet Rupert Brooke (1887–1915), who voyaged to Pagopago on the *Ventura* in 1914, fancies that for later travelers, as for him, "the crowd on shore would be singing them that sweetest and best-known of South Sea songs, which begins 'Good-bye, my Flenni' ('Friend,' you'd pronounce it), and goes on in Samoan" (*Letters from America* [London, 1919], p. 169). The Polish pianist (later President) Ignacy Jan Paderewski (1860–1941), who passed through Pagopago in 1904 (Frey, p. 86), was too preoccupied with his pet parrots to have noticed human vocalizing (*The Paderewski Memoirs,* written with Mary Lawton [New York, 1938], pp. 353–60).

[6]Margaret Mead, *The Social Organization of Manua* [sic] (Honolulu, 1930), p. 4. A student of Oceania, Mead (1901–78) was best known for the publications of her youth, which have recently been reviewed in [John] Derek Freeman, (b. 1916), *Margaret Mead and Samoa* (Cambridge, Mass.; 1983).

[7]Martin Johnson, *Through the South Seas with Jack London* (New York, 1913), p. 240. Charmian Kittredge London corroborates his description: "There they go, the grave King, the motherly Queen, Viega [= 'Vienna'] and his gorgeous wife, all singing, they and the brown oarsmen: 'I nev-ver will for-ge-ett you!'.... Three times they have circled us in the long whaleboat, singing and waving" (*The Log of the Snark* [New York, 1915], p. 241). Jack [=John] [Griffith] London (1876–1916), socialist and author, got material for sketches and stories from the voyage of the *Snark,* a 55-foot ketch-rigged yacht, which left San Francisco in 1907, and arrived (via Hawai'i, the Marquesas, Tahiti, Samoa, Fiji, and the Solomons) the next year in Australia, where the venture was abandoned in early 1909. Johnson (1884–1937), a jeweler's apprentice (of Indepen-

song likewise decorated a departure from Fanning Island, a lonely Polynesian outpost located closer to Hawai'i than to Samoa.[8]

Performances were not limited to commemorating departures by
sail or steam. Sydney Greenbie heard the song after a party in a "little
Sunday-school shack" in Apia, while several foreigners took a ferry to
their lodgings:

> With the first dip of their oars into the sea the swarthy oarsmen began
> the song which, exotic and sentimental as it was, left every heart as ach-
> ing for the shore as it did those of the simple half-caste maidens for their
> casual lovers of the colder Antipodes. 'Oh, I neva wi' fo-ge-et chu,'
> drawled the oarsmen, and they on shore joined in with the softer voices
> of that gentler world.[9]

On another occasion, one woman sang the song to an American sailor,
while they lingered adrift at leisure in a canoe, anticipating his shipping
out (Frey, 133). Nor did the song apply only to departures by water: Beatrice Grimshaw reports that after a feast in 1907, "we climbed back to
the road, and drove home, six buggies full of laughing brown and white
humanity, crowned and wreathed with green ferns, and singing the
sweet, sad song of Samoa—'Good-bye, my flennie' " (pp. 336–37).

During the last few decades, the rituals have changed with the circumstances of embarkation, and Samoans perform the song less often
than before, because airplanes have become the principal means of ex-
trainsular travel. In the past, the image of the voyager faded slowly from
view, while the boat slipped out of the harbor: now, the link between
staybehinds and traveler snaps at once, when the passenger steps beyond the boarding-gate; and at the moments of departure, measured in
seconds rather than minutes, the traveler stays quarantined, not on a
deck, but in a capsule, separated from friends by sight and sound.

---

dence, Kan.), served as the *Snark*'s cook and photographer. As a wildlife-
cinematographer, he circled the globe six times. His first film was *Trailing African
Wild Animals* (1922); in 1929–31, he documented in sound and pictures the lives of
Pygmies of the Belgian Congo. For a recent appreciation of his work, see Douglas J.
Preston, "Shooting in Paradise," *Natural History* (December 1984), 14–19.

[8]Burnett recalls: "The Greig family, sitting upon the shore at the entrance to the
lagoon, bade the party adieu by singing the beautiful, though somewhat sad, Samoan
Farewell Song, known wherever the Polynesian race is found on the isles of the Pacific"
(*Through Tropic Seas* [London, 1910], pp. 57–58).

[9]*The Pacific Triangle* (New York, 1921), p. 242. Greenbie (1889–1960) was a journal-
ist, travel-writer, and historian; with his wife, the poetess Marjorie Latta Barstow
(1891–1976), he composed dramas and biographies. During World War II, the American
author James Albert Michener (b. 1907), sitting in a corner of Aggie Grey's bar in Apia,
would watch as the proprietress "sang *Tofà, ma felangi* (Farewell, my friend) at the
sunrise conclusion of some memorable brawl" ("Memories of a Pacific Traveler," *Saturday Review* [June 1980], 46).

HISTORY

The Samoan farewell of today consists of two units, each of which has a separate history, both as a foreign song, and as a Samoan contrafactum. The first unit received its local stamp early in the 1890s, probably in the aftermath of the great hurricane of 1889; the second joined it at about the turn of the century, possibly as early as 1899.

Recalling a sojourn in the islands in 1895–96, Edward Reeves terms the first unit "evidently modern," a song "composed in honour of a departing European guest."[10] In 1902, the wife of the Consul General of the United States adds that the first unit was "written by a native poet in honor of Admiral Kimberly when he sailed home after the hurricane which wrecked his flotilla."[11] Five years later, Grimshaw reiterates that the song was "written by a native" (p. 337). In 1915, Charmian Kittredge London calls the song "the 'Farewell to Admiral Kimberly' that has become farewell to every one in Samoa" (p. 241). In 1930, Thomas Henley, probably reporting a tradition current among the European denizens of Apia, attributes the "original version" to "Manila, a Samoan, who composed it shortly after the great hurricane of 1889."[12] Albert (later Sir Albert) Fuller Ellis[13] also connects the song with the admiral:

> [He] must have had the gift of dealing with coloured people. During the stay ashore of himself and his officers, the Samoans became so attached to him that a farewell song was composed in his honour, and sung on their departure. . . . It is still [in 1936] used as a farewell song by the Polynesians and, at times of parting, is sung so feelingly that few can listen to it unmoved.[14]

[10]Brown Men and Women (London, 1898), p. 132. His title for it—"the Samoan song of greeting"—errs consistently with his mistranslation of its first words: "Good morning, my friend" (instead of "Goodbye, my friend"). As employed in Oceania, the term "European" is a racial descriptor; it could refer, as well to an American of European descent, as to a traveler from Europe.

[11]Llewella Pierce Churchill, Samoa 'Uma (New York, 1902), p. 294. In a letter pasted into a copy of the book in the Tozzer Library (Harvard University), she writes: "My plan was in the book, as in my life out there, to withdraw from the petty annoyances of the beach [= Apia] and its politics and humbugs, to take to the woods[,] where things are sweeter, and out of the jungle to bring some simple accounts of bird and beast" (to Harvard Prof. William McM. Woodworth, December 4, 1902).

[12]A Pacific Cruise (Sydney, 1930), p. 89. He adds that Manila, "with his brother, Toloa'i (afterwards Chief Vaotogo)[,] were responsible for many of the native songs of that period"; no chiefly title "Vaotogo" appears in the Samoan book of honors (M. K. Le Mamea, O le Tusi Faalupega o Samoa [Apia, 1971]).

[13]He became a trader in the Pacific in 1878, at the age of eighteen; trained as a chemist, he recognized the importance of phosphate-deposits on the island of Nauru, whose commercial development he oversaw into the 1940s.

[14]Adventuring in Coral Seas (Sydney, 1936), p. 235. Ellis recalls the song in confusion. He quotes, as he correctly states, "the refrain"; but that section constitutes the

This naval figure was the American Rear Admiral Lewis Ashfield Kimberly (1830–1902), a veteran of 43 years' service at the time the song honored him.[15]

The hurricane of March 15–16, 1889, marked a turning-point in Samoan colonial history.[16] To support rival policies, the German Empire, the British Empire, and the United States, had sent warships to the area: before the storm, the vessels rode uneasily at anchor in the harbor of Apia; afterwards, all but one rested on the bottom or the beach, having been caught in vicious crosscurrents and smashed against the reefs. About two hundred sailors drowned.[17]

Helplessly facing the destruction of his fleet, hopelessly confronting the end of his mission, his career, and his life, Kimberly made a gallant gesture toward his British compeers, in demonstration of a generosity that shall ever grace the annals of friendly interchange. H.M.S. *Calliope*, struggling to gain the safety of the open sea, had to pass within a few yards of his flagship, *Trenton*. Both ships were pitching violently in a boiling sea, *Trenton* powerless to maneuver. The British vessel bore down on the American, and Kimberly's "extreme anxiety at this supreme moment" made him "feel as rigid and as cold as a harpstring."[18] The ships came so close, men on opposed yard-arms could have touched: and then *Calliope* cleared. In relief, Kimberly waved,[19]

---

refrain of the modern song, which was first heard about a decade after the departure of the "gifted" admiral. He then quotes the first line of the refrain of the original song. His second lines ("When you go to your home" and "I do love you") are apparently unique.

[15]He entered the navy in 1846, and first sailed in the sloop *Jamestown*, on a mission to suppress the slave-trade along the African coasts (1847–50); during the War of the Rebellion, he served as Lieutenant Commander on Captain (later Admiral) David Glasgow Farragut's flagship, *Hartford*; he retired in 1892, to West Newton (Mass.), where he succumbed to heart-disease (obituary, New York *Times*, January 29, 1902, p. 9). His account of the storm, reprinted as *Samoan Hurricane* (Washington, DC; 1965), does not mention the song allegedly "composed in his honour."

[16]Robert Louis Stevenson would give it a greater significance: "[it made] a marking epoch in world-history; directly, and at once, it brought about the congress and treaty of Berlin; indirectly, and by a process still continuing, it founded the modern navy of the [United] States" (*A Footnote to History* [London, 1892], p. 267). Contemporaries understood it to be the worst peacetime-disaster to have befallen the American Navy.

[17]The hurricane supplies the background for the narrative in Edwin P[almer] Hoyt (b. 1923), *The Typhoon that Stopped a War* (New York, 1968); however, as may be expected in a work by an author who has produced no less than 112 books in twenty years (1962–81), details pass breezily, more in the style of a newspaper than in that of a history.

[18]Lewis A[shfield] Kimberly, "Samoa and the Hurricane of March, 1889," in *Naval Action and History 1799–1898* [Papers of the Military Historical Society of Massachusetts, 12] (Boston, 1902), 331.

[19]Henry Pearson (navigating officer of the *Calliope*), letter to his wife, March 28, 1889; printed in *Winchester Cathedral Record*, 1978, p. 21 (personal communication, Ian Graham).

and his men saluted their rivals,[20] with, as Captain Henry Coey Kane remembers, "three such ringing cheers that they called forth tears from many of our eyes, they pierced deep into my heart."[21] The British crew responded in kind.[22] *Trenton* soon sank, luckily losing just one man; *Calliope* escaped.[23]

On shore after the storm, Kimberly worked to establish order in the town; he earned praise for tactful conduct in consideration of local needs and customs. Within seven weeks, he had managed to charter a steamer, by which to repatriate most of his men. The New York *Times*

[20]Hence the sailor's rime: "Blood is thicker than water,/ And long will England hold it dear,/ And long be told in fo'castle song,/ Of the flagship 'Trenton's' parting cheer" (quoted in Henley, p. 103). The first line echoes Kimberly's citation of Anglo-American unity, in acknowledging Kane's gratitude: "Our cheers came with sincerity and admiration for the able manner in which you handled your ship. We could not have been gladder if it had been one of our ships, for in a time like that I can truly say, with old Admiral Josiah Latnall, 'that blood *is* thicker than water' " (quoted in Stevenson, p. 266). (Though Kimberly writes of "cheers," the New York *Times* notes but one "ringing cheer.") In 1859, Josiah Tattnall (1795–1871)—not "Latnall," or Henley's "Tatnall" (p. 102)—commander of the American squadron in the Far East, aided a British fleet, in violation of his nation's neutrality; he achieved renown by citing this proverb to explain his action. During the War of the Rebellion, he commanded the Confederate naval forces; his flagship was the ironclad *Merrimac* (renamed *"Virginia"*).

[21]Quoted in Kimberly, p. 331. The admiral may have ordered *Trenton*'s band to play "God Save the Queen": so his obituary in the New York *Times*; but the *Illustrated London News* avers that the band played "The Star-Spangled Banner" (April 27, 1889, p. 519). Edward Rowe Snow alleges that the band of U.S.S. *Vandalia* played the latter music (*The Vengeful Sea* [New York, 1956], p. 204). None of these accounts explains how musicians could have played together on the deck of a wildly tossing ship, amidst noise, wind, rain, and saltspray.

[22]Pearson recalls that "the Americans gave us three cheers. Then our fellows cheered back[,] and I found the tears pouring down my cheeks and mixing with the horizontal rain, which struck like hail, and the salt foam." Thomson Murray MacCallum confirms that *Trenton*'s men gave "a hearty cheer, which was answered from the other ship" (*Adrift in the South Seas* [Los Angeles, 1934], p. 204). George [Egerton] [Leigh] Westbrook (who was not present) reports that the Americans "stood at attention" as they cheered (*Gods Who Die*, as told to Julian Dana [New York, 1935], p. 319). W. C. Cartwright, a gunner on *Calliope*, remembers that "our men immediately jumped into the rigging and returned the cheer," but that Kane called them down, saying "I would rather lose the ship than lose a single man" (Henley, p. 103). The *Illustrated London News* gives a full-page illustration of the cheering (April 27, 1889, p. 517).

[23]Returning the next day, it found *Trenton* "resting on the bottom of the harbour with the stumps of her masts rising above the surface, still flying the flag of the American admiral" (*Winchester Cathedral Record*). Kimberly recalls: "There being no doubt in my mind in regard to our final fate, I said to the captain, 'If we have to go down, let us do so with our flag flying' " (p. 353). Annie Bronson King puts this decision into verse: " 'If we must die'—the leader's voice/ Outswelled the voice of thunder—/ [']It is our own[,] our solemn choice/ To die our dear flag under[']" (1890; quoted in Kimberly, p. 362). *Calliope* survived to serve in the Great War, notably at the Battle of Jutland (1916); several of its officers of 1889 died in action during that war.

took note of no music on the occasion of their departure, but did record that "for a few minutes loud cheering was heard in every direction," when the steamer slipped out to sea: "The crews of the men of war *Nipsic* and *Rapid* and hundreds of people on the beach cheered the departing steamer, and the *Trenton* and *Vandalia* men on the decks of the *Rockton* returned the cheers with a will" (May 21, 1889, p. 1; italics added). Apparently, no eyewitness-account of Rockton's departure specifies the verbal content of the cheering; but, as during the hurricane, two shouts conventional in hailing friends—*hurrah*[24] and *hip*[25]—are almost certain to have been cried out, in the form of "three cheers,"[26] a triple "Hip, hip! Hurrah!"[27]

Three transcriptions of music for the first unit of the song appeared in the nineteenth century. In 1898, Reeves published a three-voice version in C major, "noted down [by an unspecified transcriber] during the

[24]This interjection (also *hurray* and *hooray*) is first encountered in English writing in 1716, as a substitute for *huzza* (accent on ultimate), which originated (before 1573) in "the shouts the seamen make when friends come aboard or go off" (*Oxford English Dictionary*, s.v. *Hurrah* and *Huzza*). It was well known to sailors of the late nineteenth century: in place of "away," it enlivens the second section of the seaman's *Dixie*, which was, of recent American songs, "the chief favourite with the sailor, as a shanty" (W. B. Whall, *Sea Songs and Shanties*, 6th ed. [Glasgow, 1927], p. 141). Stated three times, it begins each of the (nine) stanzas that comprise John Malone's poem "To the Men of the Trenton" (1890; quoted in Kimberly, p. 360). Perhaps its phonetic influence causes the shout *hoodah* to replace *doodah*, in one of the most famous of shanties, "Sacramento" (c. 1850), the seaman's version of the minstrel-song "Gwine to Run All Night, or De Camptown Races" (1850), by Stephen Collins Foster (1826–64). On December 8, 1914, when New Zealand took Western Samoa from Germany, "das Gebrüll der Engländer in Apia [included] . . . 'Hurrahs' und 'God Save the King' usw." (Frieda Zieschank, *Ein Jahrzehnt in Samoa* [Leipzig, 1918], p. 137).

[25]This interjection first appears in 1818, when it is already associated with *hurrah* ("They hipped and hurraed me"); in its only cited independent use, the English poet Thomas Hood (1799–1845) writes of "Three times three and hip-hip-hips!" (*OED*).

[26]I have not found evidence to support Hoyt's statement that "the sailors of the *Nipsic* gave three cheers for their lucky comrades who were going home" (p. 227). A triple shout seems to have been an English nautical invention. The *OED* quotes: "three Hussaws, Seamen like" (1679), and "[saluting ships with] 3 Huzzas" (1712). Felix Count von Luckner (1881–1966) writes of nineteenth-century sailors' use of "drei Hurras," or " 'three sheers' [sic] in der Sprache der Engländer" (*Im Segelschiff um die Welt* [Köln, 1935], p. 36). After a party in Samoa (September 11, 1893), the band of H.M.S. *Katoomba* "gave three cheers" for their hosts, Stevenson and his wife (*The Letters of Robert Louis Stevenson*, ed. Sidney Colvin [New York, 1911], 4:252). When Queensland annexed New Guinea (April 4, 1883), "three cheers were given for Her Majesty the Queen" (Richard Lovett, *James Chalmers* [New York, n.d.], p. 239). Even the word "cheer," in the sense of "a shout of encouragement," owes its existence to sailors, with whom the first known use in English (1720) associates it: "We gave them a cheer, as the seamen call it."

[27]Cheering that "lasted a few minutes" must have included other, less organized, shouts, exclaimed sporadically (and perhaps handclapping, whistling, and singing); in addition to the cheering, *Rapid*'s band played "Auld Lang Syne" (Hoyt, p. 227).

actual performance." In September of that year, Adolf Heilborn produced a monophonic version in D major, transcribed from what he called a performance à 3.[28] The third version, also monophonic, was published in 1899 by Benedikt Friedländer, in a German magazine.[29] In these transcriptions, Reeves poorly underlays the text, which he spells atrociously; both Germans have good control over underlay, word-division, and spelling (Friedländer's is better).

The later addition to the song, Henley says, "was first written by the Hon. O. F. Nelson in 1899 for an amateur band, which he then conducted, and the two songs were combined on that occasion."[30] Since Nelson worked in or near Apia, it is reasonable to suppose that he had the unified song first performed there. By about 1906, it had reached Pagopago, for Frey, recalling his departure from that port, quotes the last line of the new section (p. 145).[31] A German planter includes the new section in a reminiscence of his leaving Apia, in the period 1910–14:

Und jetzt stimmt der Vorsänger, der auf seinem Bootshatzen gestützt auf der kleinen Plattform am Bug des Bootes steht, mit hoher Stimme ein Lied an; nach den ersten Tönen bin ich im Bilde, es ist das schöne samoanische Abschiedslied, das ich so oft gehört. 'Tofa mai fileni' (Leb wohl, mein Freund). Mehrstimmig fällt der Chor der Ruderer ein, zum Takt des Ruderschlages singen sie, fahren im grossen Bogen eine Abschiedsrunde um das vor Anker liegende Schiff. . . . Nach jeder Strophe singen sie den Refrain des Liedes: 'Niemals will ich dich vergessen'. Auch ich werde nie diese Insel mit seinen Bewohnern vergessen, niemals.[32]

[28]*Allgemeinde Völkerkunde in Kurzgefasster Darstellung* (Leipzig, 1898), pp. 177–78. He reprints it in *Die Deutschen Kolonien* (Leipzig, 1912), p. 162; where he notes, "Die Männer singen zur Melodie Terz und Quinte, der Schluss verhallt in der Oktave." A folklorist early in life, Heilborn (1873–1941) later turned to biography (Charles Darwin, Käthe Kollwitz, Otto Sommer, Paul Unger, Henrich Zille).

[29]*Westermanns Monats-Hefte für das gesamte geistige Leben der Gegenwart,* 86 (1899), 97–117, 200–227; where Georg Raphael's assistance in preparing the music is acknowledged. A philosopher of Berlin, Friedländer (1866–1908) studied socialism and the cultural manifestations of friendly intercourse.

[30]Olaf Frederick Nelson, an able musician still remembered warmly, was a half-caste ('afakasi) businessman, whose defense of native rights and customs led to his exile in the 1920s, during the days of the *mau,* a rebellion against the rule of New Zealand. He collected folktales: see his "Legends of Samoa," *Journal of the Polynesian Society,* 34 (1925), 124–45. The Nelson Memorial Library, in Apia, is named for him.

[31]He misspells "*atu*" as "*alu.*" Otherwise, the earliest recollections were published in 1920 by Lewis Ransome Freeman (recording travels in or before 1910), and in 1921 by Greenbie (recording travels c. 1914).

[32]Hubert Schneidersmann, *Als Pflanzer in der deutschen Südsee* (Magdeburg, 1939), pp. 105–6. He traveled on the interisland steamer *Tofua.*

Like the first line of the English refrain, the German one has eight syllables, and therefore fits the tune perfectly; but whether that "chorus of
oarsmen" sang in German is not known.

An account of music in Samoa during the Great War, when soldiers
from New Zealand occupied the islands, reviews the song sympathetically:

> The regimental band took up the air. Bandmaster Cole wrote the score,
> and the band, whose playing, by the way, reached a high degree of finish
> on the island, took delight in playing this tune to the natives at their fort-
> nightly Sunday concert. The Samoans came from far and near to these
> open-air concerts on the water-front, and their appreciation was dis-
> tinctly marked of this little tribute the white-man band made to their
> national music.
>
> The air is a plaintively haunting one, suggestive of sorrow at parting.
> Really to appreciate its beauty one should hear the Samoans sing it
> themselves. . . . A goodly concourse of these dusky musicians could get
> more meaning out of these simple little harmonies than could forty regi-
> mental bands—however great their skill.[33]

The band's "open-air concerts on the water-front" probably took place
in and around a bandstand on Beach Road, not far from Main Street.[34]
The account continues, by noting that, when the soldiers prepare to
leave Samoa, and "the band reaches the water-front and breaks forth
into the strains of 'Tofa ma Faleni,' the disconsolate natives, tears
streaming down their brown cheeks, join in the music and wave fare-
wells to the troops" (p. 247). To the Samoans, it must have made a dis-
consolating sight indeed: a foreign band, playing a local song, in farewell to itself.

The song seems to have been printed separately but once, in Fiji,
where a version arranged by Arthur Levy, with English words by W. F.
Wyatt, was published, probably in the late 1920s, by Alport Barker, pro-
prietor of the *Fiji Times and Herald*; Henley reproduces an excerpt
from it (facing p. 88).[35] (The publication is dedicated to the Governor of
Fiji, Sir Bickham Sweet-Escott, and his Lady.) Only this print, and an
edition prepared by the German traveler Ernst von Hesse-Wartegg,[36] include music for the second unit of the song.

---

[33]L[eonard] P[oulter] Leary (b. 1891), *New Zealanders in Samoa* (London, 1918), p.
243.

[34]Photographs of this bandstand appear in Schneidersmann, facing p. 42; and in
Erich Scheuermann, *Samoa* (Horn in Baden, [1926]), no. 124.

[35]The musical style as arranged is more strictly four-part than Samoan custom de-
crees; the parallel fifths in the outer voices (measures 10 and 14) may owe more to
Levy's arranging than to his transcribing.

[36]*Samoa[,] Bismarckarchipel[,] und Neuguinea* (Leipzig, 1902), p. 244. His edition,

SOURCES

The Samoan farewell reflects foreign styles of music. The former unit shows several possible influences: Victorian hymnody,[37] Anglo-American balladry,[38] and American minstrelsy.[39] The model for the latter is the first half of the hymn-tune *Erie*, commonly known by the beginning of the usual text: "What a friend we have in Jesus."[40]

The music of *Erie* was composed about 1868, by Charles Crozat Converse (1832–1918), an attorney of Warren, Mass.[41] The publication that most effectively promoted the popularity of the words and the tune, and ultimately the Samoan development of the music, was one of a se-

---

in B♭ major, specifies only 2 voices (in the treble-clef), and provides no text except the title, "Tofa, mai Feleni"; Henley's, in G major, is a 4-voice harmonization with text-underlay.

[37]The melodic contour of its first phrase resembles that of the beginning of *Lux Benigna*, the hymn-tune composed in 1865 by John Bacchus Dykes (1823–76) for the text "Lead, kindly Light," drafted in 1833 by John Henry (later Cardinal) Newman (1801–90); but the structures of the tunes do not match. No model for the music appears in the collected *Gospel Hymns*.

[38]The contour and implied harmonies of the tune resemble those of "Thomas O'Winsbury," in Bertrand Harris Bronson (b. 1902), *The Traditional Tunes of the Child Ballads*, vol. II (Princeton, 1962), no. 100, variant 4. The contour of the first phrase resembles that of "John of Hazelgreen," in Bronson, vol. IV (Princeton, 1972), no. 293, variants 5b and 11; but the structures of the tunes do not match.

[39]The beginning of the first phrase slightly resembles that of Will S. Hays's end-song "Susan Jane," in anon., *Minstrel Songs, Old and New* (Boston, 1882) pp. 18–20. Minstrel-shows were not unknown in Samoa: in Apia, on September 30, 1879, sailors of U. S. S. *Lackawanna* presented "a negro minstrel and variety entertainment[,] and the white men playing there and imitating the darkies, set the native audience perfectly wild" (Laulii and Alexander A. Willis, *The Story of Laulii, Daughter of Samoa*, ed. W[illia]m H. Barnes [San Francisco, 1889], p. 218). In the 1880s, there was a "celebrated old darkey fiddler, known as 'Uncle Bruce,' at Apia" (p. 228).

[40]*Erie* first appeared in anon., *Silver Wings* (Boston, [1870]). The author of the words was Joseph Medlicott Scriven (1819–86), a graduate of Trinity College, Dublin (B.A., 1842), who emigrated to Canada in 1844. He worked as a teacher and private tutor; but when his fiancée drowned (on the eve of the wedding), he dedicated his life to serving the poor. About 1855, he penned these verses, which seem to have been first published in 1865; he too died by drowning.

[41]A former student at the Leipzig Conservatory, and a graduate of the Albany Law School (LL.B., 1861), he composed chamber-music, overtures, symphonies, oratorios, and hymns. He probably conceived the tune for Scriven's text (anon., *The Hymnal 1940 Companion* [New York, 1949], p. 266). His (59-word) obituary in the New York *Times* cites "What a friend we have in Jesus" as his principal accomplishment (October 19, 1918, p. 15). By a quirk of fate, another of his hymns, "The Rock Beside the Sea" (1852), became the *Hawai'ian* farewell, "Aloha 'Oe" (1878)—a valedictory that acquired a greater significance in 1932, when its performance ended the closing ceremonies of the first Los Angeles Olympic Games. (*Hawaiian Music and Musicians*, ed. George S. Kanahele [Honolulu, 1979], pp. 11–13).

ries of *Gospel Hymns*.[42] "What a friend we have in Jesus" appears in *Gospel Hymns No. 2*, edited by P. P. Bliss and Ira D. Sankey (New York, 1876), number 57.[43] It swept the hymn-singing world: "very few hymns have been more widely published or more frequently sung."[44] That it speaks pointedly of a "friend" probably struck Nelson, the putative adaptor, as a useful bit of allusion for a song that would address "friends" (*feleni*); but present-day Samoans, knowing only Nelson's trope ("Oh, I never will forget you"), miss that point.

Persons acquainted with the style of music favored by the editors of the *Gospel Hymns* have recognized its similarity with the style of the modern music of Polynesia—religious and secular works alike. In the 1880s, one visitor calls Samoan singing "a sort of half-chant, half-hymn."[45] Observing a Samoan entertainment for tourists, Greenbie notes: "In the barbaric, unmetered strain of some wild native song would suddenly appear the unmistakable relics of a gentle Moody and Sankey hymn—and over the faces of Christian ladies in the audience would creep involuntary smiles at this reminder from the old home town" (p. 32). As in this passage, music published and popularized by Bliss and Sankey is often attributed to "Moody and Sankey":[46] the con-

---

[42]The term "gospel hymn" was coined, or at least established in common use, by Ira David Sankey (1840–1908), the best known evangelistic singer of the late nineteenth century; before his time, such hymns had been called "Sunday school songs." George Coles Stebbins (1846–1945), a collaborator of Sankey's, credits the first of the *Gospel Hymns* (1875) with setting the style: the term was "such an appropriate designation in the popular mind that the name has remained" (quoted in Charles H. Young, "Ira D. Sankey, a Product of Lawrence County," in *The Ira D. Sankey Centenary* [New Castle, Penn.; 1941], p. 28).

[43]The text receives wrongful attribution to Horatius Bonar (1808–89); the tune, dated 1868, is printed "by per[mission]." Philip Paul Bliss (1838–76) was an evangelical singer, who participated in many revival meetings, mainly those led by Major Daniel Webster Whittle (1840–1901); one of their campaigns covered Mobile, Atlanta, Nashville, Louisville, Peoria, Kalamazoo, and Chicago. A jolly man, who closed his letters "Gospelsongfully yours," Bliss was burned to death in the "Ashtabula disaster," a train-wreck in Ohio.

[44]Sankey, *My Life and the Story of the Gospel Hymns* (Philadelphia, 1906), p. 333. It is one of the musical elements of the collective American consciousness that Connecticut insurance-executive Charles Ives (1874–1954) taps, through quotation in his *Symphony 3*, "The Camp Meeting" (1904) and *Piano Sonata 1* (1902–09) (John Kirkpatrick, *A Temporary Mimeographed Catalogue* [New Haven, 1960]). A political cartoon of 1924 also exploits its currency, by showing fat businessmen singing "The Cash Register Chorus": "What a friend we have in [President Calvin] Coolidge" (reprinted in *Harper's*, July 1984, 37). Among Blacks in the United States, it ranks as one of the three best-liked hymns of its type (Wyatt Tee Walker, *"Somebody's Calling My Name"* [Valley Forge, Penn.; 1979], p. 119).

[45]Alfred P. Maudslay (1850–1931), *Life in the Pacific Fifty Years Ago* (London, 1930), p. 209.

[46]Within months of Bliss's death, Sara J. Timanus (Mrs. Wilber F. Crafts) protests

fusion arises from the unforgettable presence and preaching of the evangelist Dwight L. Moody, at whose revival-meetings after 1870 Sankey directed the music.[47]

American vessels took copies of the *Gospel Hymns* around the world. The whaler *Fleetwing* (of Martha's Vineyard, Mass.), Captain Hoopingstone, visited the western Pacific in 1879–80; George Westbrook, a Samoan trader then resident on Pingalap Atoll,[48] reminisces (p. 96):

> Aboard the *Fleetwing* was a harmonium[,] and both . . . [Hoopingstone's wife] and daughter played. The hymns of Moody and Ira D. Sankey were favorites then; I used to lie at ease on the settee in the Captain's cabin and listen to the lovely girl play and sing such hymns as "There's a Land that is Brighter than Day," "Safe in the Arms of Jesus," and "Hold the Fort, for I am Coming."

The first of these hymns (composed in 1867, in Elkhart, Ind.) stands as number 80 in *Gospel Hymns No. 2;*[49] the last appears there as number

---

the error of this pattern of attribution, in anon., *Song Victories of "The Bliss and Sankey Hymns"* (Boston, 1877), p. 152; however, it is not inaccurately that Will H. Houghton, President of the Moody Bible Institute, calls the *Gospel Hymns* "Moody and Sankey Hymnbooks" (*The Ira D. Sankey Centenary*, p. 35.)

[47] A shoe-salesman of Massachusetts, Dwight L[yman] [Ryther] Moody (1837–99) removed in 1856 to Chicago, where he opened a Sunday-school two years later; his efforts expanded to include gospel-campaigns in England (1873–75, 1881–84, 1891–92) and the United States. He founded the Northfield Seminary for Young Women (Mass., 1879), the Mt. Hermon School for Boys (Northfield, 1881), and the Bible Institute (Chicago, 1889). Contemporaries regarded him as "the central figure of his generation in the religious history of his country" (Stebbins, *Reminiscences and Gospel Hymn Stories* [New York, 1924], p. 321). He first met Sankey in Indianapolis, at a convention of the Young Men's Christian Association (YMCA).

[48] The atoll now constitutes part of the Ponape District, Federated States of Micronesia. Westbrook spent four-fifths of his life in the South Pacific. Born in 1861 in England, he dined and conversed there as a boy with both Moody and Sankey, plus: Robert Moffatt (1795–1883), Scottish Congregationalist missionary, and father-in-law to ["Dr."] David Livingstone (1813–73), missionary and explorer in Africa; George [later Sir George] Williams (1821–1905), founder of the YMCA (London, 1844); Charles Haddon Spurgeon (1834–92), English nonconformist divine, author of fifty volumes of sermons; and Anthony Ashley Cooper, seventh Earl of Shaftesbury (1801–85), philanthropist, sponsor of foreign missions, and president of the Ragged School Union for forty years. Westbrook carried excellent credentials as an observer of hymnody: in addition to his acquaintance with many evangelical personages, he had had as a boy in London the practice of singing regularly in choirs at revival-meetings (p. 6).

[49] No. 110 in the collected *Gospel Hymns* (words, S. Fillmore Bennett; music, Joseph P. Webster), it bears the title "Sweet Bye-and-Bye," recalling the refrain ("In the sweet by-and-by,/ We shall meet on that beautiful shore"); as printed, the text reads "fairer" for Westbrook's "brighter." MacCallum records that on his ship in the Pacific in the 1890s, sailors sang the hymn for an islander's funeral (p. 315). To its tune, Samoans sing a text beginning *O Iou suafa, Iesu e* 'O Jesus, your name' (*O pese ma Viiga i le Atua*, text 58).

130 (words only);[50] "Safe in the Arms of Jesus" is found elsewhere.[51] "Hold the Fort" attained immediate influence. Four years after its composition, it ended a comic act at a circus in Dublin: one clown punned, "I am rather Moody tonight; how do you feel?"; another responded, "I feel rather Sankey-monious": the audience hissed, and then arose and sang "Hold the Fort" until the clowns withdrew (Sankey, pp. 73–74). By 1877, it had reached southern Africa, set to a text in the Zulu language (Song Victories, 153). It must have traveled to Samoa with similar speed, for Thomas Powell, the missionary who translated it for the hymnal (O Pese ma Viiga i le Atua, text 175), quitted the islands in 1885. The first of the Gospel Hymns provided the source from which a missionary identified as "Mr. Walkup" led services on a small vessel trading in the Pacific in the 1890s; he was remembered to have favored "Beautiful River," known usually by its first line, "Shall we gather at the river" (MacCallum, 310).[52] The musical style these hymns convey serves as a matrix from which the style of modern Samoan music springs.

STRUCTURE

The original Samoan version of the song consisted of a series of stanzas alternating with a refrain set to the same music. A second section,

---

[50]Words and music appear in Bliss, Gospel Songs (Cincinnati, 1874), no. 79; and as no. 11 in the collected Gospel Hymns. Bliss composed the hymn in May 1870, and first performed it that month in YMCA meeting-rooms in Chicago. The text recalls a wartime-signal: on October 5, 1864, the Confederate army under Gen. John Bell Hood (1831–79) attacked the supplies of Gen. William Tecumseh Sherman (1820–91), who by semaphore sent the defenders the message "Hold the fort; I am coming": encouraged, they fought on, until reinforcements relieved the siege (Sankey, p. 169). (Sherman's message has a colon, rather than a semicolon, in Song Victories, p. 47; Stebbins reduces that to a comma, p. 190; the message is "Hold fast. We are coming" in Hezekiah Butterworth, The Story of the Tunes [New York, 1890], p. 56.) The text begins: "Ho! my comrades, see the signal,/ Waving in the sky!/ Reinforcements now appearing,/ Victory is nigh!"

[51]First published in Songs of Devotion (1868), it is no. 6 in the collected Gospel Hymns. The blind poetess Fanny Jane Crosby (1820–1915) composed the text, to a tune by William Howard Doane (1834–1915). Sankey notes: "It has become very famous throughout the world, and was one of the first American hymns to be translated into foreign languages" (p. 270); its performance was prohibited in the Turkish Empire (p. 150).

[52]It became "one of the most famous Sunday School songs ever written" (Stebbins, p. 233). No. 669 in the collected Gospel Hymns, it has words and music composed in 1864 by Robert Lowry (1826–99), who after 1868 edited an authoritative series of Sunday-school songbooks published by Biglow & Main. For its music, Samoan words devised by Samuel James Whitmee, a missionary who worked in the islands in 1863–76 and 1891–94, appear in O Pese ma Viiga i le Atua (text 376).

equal in length to the first, was later added as a new refrain, while the old refrain became the first stanza. With the original stanza designated as *a* and the original refrain as *A*, the first structure can be described as *aAaAaA;* with the addition of the new refrain, *B*, the structure became *ABaBaB*.

Identifying cognate stanzas with subscript numbers, we find the following evidence for the textual structure of the song.[53]

a_1Aa_2A	Reeves, 1898
a_2	Heilborn, 1898
a_2	Friedländer, 1899
A	Churchill, 1902
$Aa_1a_3a_2$	Krämer, 1903
A	Burnett, 1910
$a_1Aa_2Aa_3A$	Burnett, 1923
AB	Henley, 1930
BA	Ellis, 1936
ABa_1Ba_2B	Churchward, 1951
ABa_1B	Falealupo, 1972
ABB	Aggie's, 1979

As might be expected in a non-narrative text, which does not recount an inevitable chain of events, the order of stanzas is variable. Two stanzas (a_1 and a_2) may be regarded as standard, but the third (a_3) failed to sustain its popularity; and there may well have existed other stanzas, composed for specific events or persons, which did not attract the notice of foreign writers.[54] In today's version of the song, the old refrain still appears at the beginning, where Krämer first puts it.

---

[53]Burnett's text of 1923, garbled throughout, quotes two lines of *A*, meshed with other lines as a "chorus"; his text of 1910 gives the "chorus" (*A*) in full. Several passing references to the words include excerpts quoted in Grimshaw (from *A*), Lewis Ransome Freeman (from *A* and *B*), Frey (from *A* and *B*), and Greenbie (from *B*). Churchill calls *A* "the chorus" (p. 294). The fifth item is found in Krämer, *Die Samoa-Inseln*, vol. II (Stuttgart, 1903), p. 350; the antepenultimate item, in Spencer Churchward, *A Samoan Grammar*, 2nd ed. (Melbourne, 1951), p. 139. The form *ABa₁B* represents the version of a band of young men (discussed below); the last form represents that sung in the *fiafia* 'floor-show' at Aggie's [Hotel], Apia.

[54]Churchill confirms that, "while the verses are frequently altered to suit other occasions [than the original], the chorus remains the same" (p. 294). In the performance of any song in Samoa, three stanzas seem to be the normal upper limit: at Aggie's in 1971–74, most performances of songs presented as entertainment followed the forms *aBaB* and *aBaBaB* (sometimes the final refrain was repeated); at informal occasions in the villages, most performances indulged in for casual amusement followed the same plans; some songs recorded for broadcast on radio do have more than three stanzas, and a few have more than five.

WORDS

A recension of the most carefully collected version of the text—Krämer's, with the stanzas rearranged to conform with the order assumed above—is given in Example 1; it comprises only the first unit of the song. The text of the second unit is a simple affair, just a repeated pair of lines: the first is the English "Oh, I never will forget you" (pronounced by Samoans in various ways); the second, either a nonsensephrase ("La, la, la, la, la, la, la, la"), or the clause *Sāmōae lē galo atu!* 'O may you not forget Samoa!'.[55]

Example 1: Recension and translation of Krämer's text. The term *susana* 'wild flower' (a_1, line 3) is not in any Samoan dictionary: it may indicate a '(black-eyed) susan', a plant that is not indigenous to the islands. *Tāupou* are ceremonial hostesses, chosen and invested in office by high chiefs. Stanza a_3 is obscure, and its application uncertain; Krämer glosses its third line, "Unterdrückt, macht ein Ende euerem Schmälen."

A   Tōfā, mai feleni; 'o le 'ā 'ou te'a.
        Folau i le va'a i le pule Meleki.
        Ne'i galo mai Apia, si ota 'ele'ele;
        E manatua mai pea le 'au pāsese.

a_1 Fa'afogafoga mai, Sāmoa 'uma,
        Se'i fai atu 'o la'u fa'atusa:
        Pei 'o le susana i totonu o mauga,
        Fa'apea la'u pele 'i tāupou 'uma.

a_2 Fa'ato'a-a-iloa se mea faigatā,
        Pe 'ā tēte'a ma uō fa'apēnā.
        E mutimutivale le alofa tīgā,
        Pe 'ā tūla'i e fa'atōfā.

a_3 Ne'i 'e te'e pe to'atāma'i,
        Ina ta le'i tusa ma le māsani.
        Tatao lea pito 'i le fa'alagilagi;
        Fa'amolemole fai vave sou tali.

A   Goodbye, my friend; I'll be left behind.
        Sail in the boat under American command.

[55]In the performance of 1972, the clause changes to "*Sāmōae ne'i galo atu!*," whose dehortative particle *ne'i*, by replacing the simple negative *lē*, adds force to the thought.

Don't forget Apia, my cherished soil;
The passengers will always remember me.

a₁ Harken unto me, all you Sāmoans,
While I tell you my comparison:
Like a wildflower deep in the mountains,
So is my dear one among all *tāupou*.

a₂ One first knows a difficult thing,
When separating from friends like that.
A heartfelt love is deeply stirred,
When arising to say farewell.

a₃ Don't you be offputting or wrathful,
For I'm not yet equal or accustomed.
Suppress this tendency toward scolding;
Please make haste with your response.

In one important respect, the text violates traditional norms of style: it gets to the point. To admit that "I never will forget you" gives my game away, by allowing nothing to your fancy—no metaphors to enjoy, no intimations to ponder, no revelations to await. Since verbal play means everything to a people who revel in language, the text fails to conform to an aesthetic principle that ordinarily controls the composition of Polynesian poetry—a requirement for a poet to maneuver circumspectly about a subject, to approach it "repeatedly in different ways from different points of view to convey symbolic hidden meanings."[56] The straightforwardness of the diction likely targets the stylistic expectations of the foreigners whom the song first addressed.

In the extant versions of the text, the usual sorts of distortion due to oral transmission appear. These often include the substitution of one word for another of identical syntactical function: *Fa'alogo* 'Listen' for *Fa'afogafoga* 'Harken', and *Sāmoa* for *Apia*. The first of these examples trades an ordinary, informal term for a polite, formal one; the second exchanges the land of the singers for the principal town of the archipelago. The distortion of texts may sometimes involve inappropriate variation, as in the shift from *Oh* (an exclamation) to *Or* (a conjunction, found in the text as sung in Falealupo in 1972). It may otherwise bear no

---

[56]Adrienne Kaeppler, "Polynesian Art and Aesthetics," manuscript (1984). Similar conclusions about the norms of style, in relation to the use of metaphor, are reached in my "Samoan Variations" (Ph.D. dissertation, Harvard University, 1979), chap. 1; the usual sorts of distortions due to oral transmission are discussed in pp. 234–67. By indulging in simile, stanza *a₁* manages to approach traditional verbal style.

semantic significance, as in the substitution of *"Kutipai"* for "Good-bye," and "my friend" for *"mai feleni."*

The most complicated distortions affect the line that refers to Admiral Kimberly. Since few Samoans apprehend his name, character, and achievement, alteration of the phrase that alludes to him is not surprising. Here follow four versions of the line, with translations.[57]

(1) *'A e folau le va'a o le ali'i-pule o Meleki.*
When the boat of the commander of America sails.

(2) *'Ā folau le va'a o le ali'i-pule Meleke.*
The boat of the American commander will sail.

(3) *Folau i le va'a i le pule Meleki.*
Sail in the boat under American command.

(4) *'A e i luga o le vasa le ali'i e pule i Meleke.*
When the gentleman in command of America is on the ocean.

Apart from one example of the usual sort of change (*le vasa* 'the ocean' for *le va'a* 'the boat'), in which a small phonemic substitution (/s/ for /ʔ/) engenders a large semantic shift, these lines tell different stories with kindred material. The key-word is *pule* 'command, power, authority'. In the first text (as in the second), this word modifies *ali'i*, which may be glossed 'gentleman, fellow, chief'; the phrase *o Meleki* 'of America' specifies his origin. The second text makes the word *Meleke* (equivalent to *Meleki*) work as an adjective, 'American'.[58] In Krämer's text, the gentleman has disappeared, leaving an 'American command' behind. In the modern version, the gentleman returns, having attained power in (or over) America. To performers of the present, Kimberly's identity is unimportant, since the man serves merely as a figure for the traveler: the sound of the words is the thing; and any apposite sense they bear is fine, so long as the syntax makes it intelligible.

MUSIC

The music of the song looks in two directions, sacred and secular: it scans the world of nineteenth-century religious expression, particu-

---

[57]The versions are edited here. The first is that of Reeves. The second is Churchill's, glossed "And the ship is sailing/ Of the American ruling chief" (p. 295). The third is Krämer's, glossed "Und reist auf dem Schiff auf Amerikas Befehl"; Krämer also gives a variant, *'A e folau le va'a o le ali'i pule meleki,* "Es geht fort das Schiff des amerikanischen Admirals" (p. 350, fn. 3). The fourth is that performed in Falealupo in 1972; it matches that of a performance on the audio-disk *Motu Pasefika* (Apia, n.d.), side 1, band 6.

[58]In current Samoan usage, the terms *Meleke* and *Meleki* are obsolete, having been replaced by *Amerika.*

larly American evangelistic hymnody of 1860–80; and it faces also that of American popular music, the minstrel-songs and sentimental ballads that entertained great numbers of people. Aware of the latter affinities of the style, one observer went so far as to assert that the Samoan farewell was adapted "nach eines schwermutigen, amerikanischen Niggerweise."[59] Citation of the musical preferences of "Black Tom" Tilden, a trader on Pingalap in 1876,[60] will show the secular context in which the song appeared: his favorite pieces of music were the minstrel-song "Wait for the Wagon" (1851), the abolitionists' anthem "John Brown's Body" (1860), the political taunt "Poor Old Jeff,"[61] and the military triumph "Marching Through Georgia" (1865).[62] Notwithstanding the intermixture of nationalities among the crews plying the Pacific, and a predominance of the British and the Germans as settlers and tourists in Samoa, the musical styles the islanders borrowed—and not only for this song, but for most of their music—possess a distinctively North American flavor.

Example 2 collates the tunes of the published transcriptions of the first unit of the song, in a score normalized for key and meter. Despite the effects of time, personality, and circumstances of performance, comparison confirms the essential identity of these versions: they exhibit similar contours, expressed in similar rhythms, governed by similar metrical constraints. The most interesting of their differences occurs at the beginning: the two earliest versions treat the G as an upbeat to the C, while the others treat that G as a downbeat; the three latest introduce a new upbeat. Some of the other differences may be due more to the transcribers than to the performers.[63]

---

[59]Max Fleck, *Mit S.M.S. "Seeadler" in der deutschen Südsee[,] 1899–1900* (Leipzig, 1925), p. 138. He entitles the song *"Tofa lau filengi"*; his Samoan word *lau* 'your' is a misspelling of *la'u* 'my'. He remembers wistfully: "Dies Lied, das uns die lieben, kleinen Samoamädchen zum Abschied sangen, lag uns noch lange in den Ohren" (p. 138).

[60]He was Westbrook's partner (p. 35). Born a slave in Delaware, he claimed he had escaped to Boston, had shipped as a cook on whalers, and had settled in Samoa, whence he had been exiled for robbery.

[61]"Jeff" represents Jefferson Davis (1808–89), President of the Confederate States (1861–65), about whom George Frederick Root (1820–95) includes two songs in *The Bugle-Call* (Chicago, 1863): "Call 'Em Names Jeff" (pp. 14–15), and "Jefferson D----, Sir" (pp. 44–45); other candidates for Tilden's favorite are "Jeff in Petticoats" (1860s) and "Hang Jeff Davis on a Sour Apple Tree" (a contrafactum of "John Brown's Body").

[62]Henry Clay Work (1832–84) composed the words and music, to honor Sherman's march from Atlanta to the sea (1864); the refrain begins with a double "Hurrah." J[ohn] [Whetham] Boddam-Whetham (b. 1843) records that by 1871, the song had become so widely known, that one adventurer could sing it merrily, while helping massacre 66 natives of the New Hebrides (*Pearls of the Pacific* [London, 1876], p. 191).

[63]Grimshaw's rhythms in the second halves of measures 1–5 surely fail to catch the

Example 2. Collation of the tunes of the first unit of the Samoan farewell.

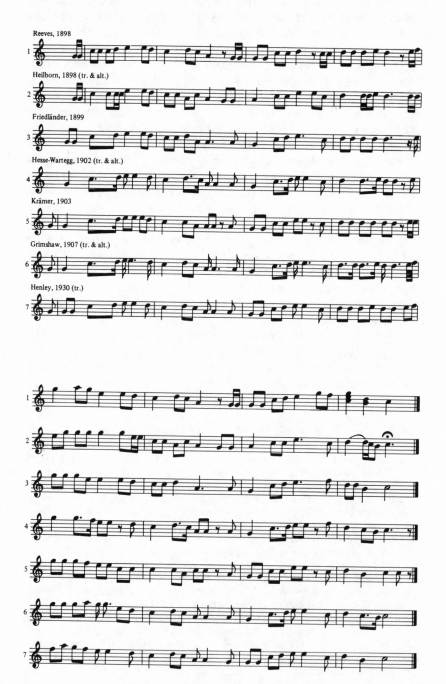

Example 3 transcribes a performance given impromptu in 1972 by several young men of Falealupo, the westernmost village of Western Samoa. Here and there throughout the performance appear chromatic passing-tones, which might be taken for ports of call on a voyage between diatonic tones; they are perhaps as much artifacts of Western notation as signs of concepts in the minds of the singers. Sliding between diatonic tones characterizes Samoan renditions of music in all styles; it probably occurred in the performances transcribed in Example 2, although the transcriptions fail to show it. Example 3 also reveals a tendency for the melody to lie embedded in the middle of the texture, in the tenor, rather than in the highest part (where Reeves, Hesse-Wartegg, Krämer, and Henley, write it). When Polynesians perform Western idioms, their improvising often hides the melody in a tonal crowd, which can support the illusion of its disappearance among strangers.[64]

The harmonizations of the tunes (including evidence not shown in Example 2), reveal that both musical units employ a severely restricted harmonic vocabulary: chords of I, IV, and V, in root-position only. (The melody of the first unit of the song, by adding a sixth to the subdominant, implies a first-inversion ii-chord). No secondary dominants intrude: in all voices, nonchordal notes appear only as passing-tones and auxiliaries; suspensions and appoggiaturas do not occur.

Both musical units realize the same harmonic pattern, one common in Western popular music: a sequence of chords that amount in the aggregate to the ground of the *passamezzo moderno*, a dance whose music flourished in Italy in the sixteenth century.[65] This pattern, which has many historical implications, underlies music so widely different in style and function as: the sixteenth-century English air "John, Come Kiss Me Now"; the seventeenth-century tune now sung to the words "Fair Harvard"; the eighteenth-century Methodist Episcopal hymn "Amazing Grace"; Foster's sentimental ballad "Old Folks at Home" (1851); and the American rock-'n'-roll song "Listen to the Rhythm of the Falling Rain" (1960s). The ground of the *passamezzo moderno* has undergone countless evolutionary changes, including a metrical trans-

---

syncopation correctly, although her rhythms in 6 and 7 may succeed. Other differences may have come from the use of various stanzas (defined by text) for a model.

[64]Major R. Raven-Hart observes: "It is often difficult to recognize the melody unless one already knows it; and when a group is singing on a boat or a verandah, the listener often discovers that no one at all is singing the melody. As a Tongan lad put it: 'But everyone *knows* that tune: no fun to sing it!' " ("Musical Acculturation in Tonga [and Samoa]," *Oceania*, 27 [1955], 110–17).

[65]For a brief history of this and related grounds, see John M[ilton] Ward, "Passamezzo," *MGG*, 10 (1962), cols. 877–880; for detailed information on grounds and their music, see others of his works, bibliographed in this volume.

Example 3: Transcription of the first stanza of the Samoan farewell, as performed in 1972. The singers, in descending order, are: Ropati Onofia (b. 1954), Sosaiete Tāi'i (b. 1952), Mū Seumanutafa (b. 1948), and Lutia Solia (b. 1944). An accompaniment (not transcribed) consists of one homemade 3-string 'ukulele, played by Ropati; and one guitar, played by Mū. (In the last chord, the guitar supplies the bass C.) Since the original recording is of low fidelity, some passages—particularly in the soprano, where Ropati tends to hum—are partly conjectural. The absolute pitch-level of the performance is a major third lower.

(continued)

Example 3, continued

Oh,   I nev-er will for-   get   you;   Sā   mō ae ne-'i ga-lo a-   tu.

formation that made it the basis of the blues.[66] Its genius embraces a tonal and temporal simplicity that has endeared it to different ages and cultures, vastly separated in space and time.[67]

ENVOY

A traveler to the islands writes of the special meaning the song bears for all who have heard it in a Polynesian setting:

For those who have known the moonlight nights of those enchanted shores, have smelt the frangipani flower, and listened to the soft singing girls in the endless, golden afternoons, and watched the sun go down upon an empty, sailless sea, behind the weird pandanus and drooping palms—the sweet song of the islands will ring in the heart for ever. In London rush and rain and gloom, in the dust and glitter of fevered Paris, in the dewy cold green woods of English country homes, the Samoan air will whisper, calling, calling, calling—back to the murmur of the palms, and the singing of the coral reef, and the purple tropic night once more.[68]

[66]Otto Gombosi first pointed this out, in "The Pedigree of the Blues," *Proceedings of the Music Teachers National Association,* 40 (1946), 382–89. On the *passamezzo* and popular American music, see his "Stephen Foster and 'Gregory Walker'," *MQ,* 30 (1944), 133–46.

[67]From the nineteenth century, a contrafactum of the first unit of our song survives: a "healing-song" recorded by Richard Michael Moyle, and published on his audio-disk *The Music of Samoa* (Wellington, New Zealand; 1973), side 2, band 1. The tune of the second unit, known to servicemen by the text "Just before the battle, Mother" (originally set to its own tune, composed, like these words, by Root [Chicago, 1863]), during World War II took on the text "When this bloody war is over," which Edgar A. Palmer edits decorously in *G. I. Songs* (New York, 1944), p. 239.

[68]Grimshaw, pp. 336–37. Her "purple tropic night" does not necessarily betoken purple prose: persons accustomed to temperate latitudes find that by being brighter, sunlight in the tropics heightens the perception of color, and thereby intensifies the experience of the senses; the vista seen from the ocean during departure from a tropical island, outstandingly in the liminal luminescence of twilight, can vitally affect the perceived meaning of associated events, such as the performance of music: hence the im-

But we need not have seen Samoa to sense this air. It calls to each of us, always: everyone reserves eternal moments, "golden afternoons" when no clock runs true, with intimates who give us cause to gaze and sigh, "Oh, I never will forget you."

Hence for us disciples, whose guide in studies and study's guard are one (while our oneness of will hangs on his fame), the song embodies a happy figure of homely fondness: for like the storm-tried Samoan companies who warmly hailed a wise-hearted friend, eyes wet with valedictory tears, we cannot freeze the date; nor shall we halt the voyage, or set the traveler's course: but we can try to seize the moment for the sake of memory; with Faust, we may dare sue for sympathy's hour to stall its pace. We pledge inwardly to remember, and thus merge, Time's boundaries: outwardly, we sing our traditional songs, fostered as testimonial effigies, tendered to display temporal designs,—which, as the future dotes on friends who dream, although the fire of history still refines, will risk all defilements Care shall afford, to stand festive in token of esteem: we confer, in one of JOHN MILTON's lines,[69]

The public marks of honour and reWARD.

---

portance of hue in the context surrounding our song. In a Samoan sunset of the 1870s, Boddam-Whetham found that "a brighter gold was on the waves, a deeper purple in the distance" (p. 203); at sea near the islands, Marie Fraser saw the twilight render the ocean "regal in its colouring of purple and gold" (*In Stevenson's Samoa* [New York, 1895], p. 3); in 1891, the American artist John LaFarge (1835–1910) saw "the lavender of the rain clouds . . . made gold by the sunset" (*Reminiscences of the South Seas* [New York, 1912], p. 239). Alva Carothers watched the dusk turn Tutuila "to blue, then purple" (*Stevenson's Isles of Paradise* [San Diego, 1930], p. 281); Louis Becke discerned "purpling shades of the setting sun" (*Pacific Tales* [London, 1914], p. 145); Lewis Ransome Freeman saw the waves "glimmering purple" (p. 284). Half a world away, in Brazil, Claude Lévi-Strauss could feel that the tropical "night began to deny the sky its golds and purples" (*A World on the Wane,* tr. John Russell [London, 1961], p. 72). The splendor of sunset informs the Samoan proverb *pūlapula a lā goto* 'radiant like a setting sun' which is applied to a respected individual in the fullness of life, when culminating
:ments transcend prior accomplishments, as the sky's final brilliance crowns

nson Agonistes, A Dramatic Poem (London, 1671), verse 992.

Bibliography of the Works of John Milton Ward

[Items are listed in order of publication.]

"Trumpets in the Elizabethan and Early Stuart Theatre (1584–1642)." Master's thesis. University of Washington, 1942.

"Trumpets in the Elizabethan and Early Stuart Theaters (1585–1642): A Study of the Use of Sound Formulae and of the Omission of Music Directions in the Play-Texts," *Abstracts of Theses and Faculty Bibliography, 1942–1943* (Seattle, University of Washington, 1944), pp. 49–50.

"Trumpets and the Tudor Theater" (abstract), *BAMS*, 8 (1945), 32–33.

Untitled notes to *Ballads*, album of three audio-disks (Asch Records, #560).

"Richard Dyer-Bennet," notes to *Richard Dyer-Bennet*, album of three 12" audio-disks (Stinson-Asch Records #461).

"Richard Dyer-Bennet," notes to *Richard Dyer-Bennet*, album of three 10" audio-disks (Stinson-Asch Records #364).

"The Lute in 16th-Century Spain," *Guitar Review*, 9 (1949), 27–28.

"The 'Dolfull Domps'," *JAMS*, 4 (1951), 111–121.

"The Editorial Methods of Venegas de Henestrosa," *Musica Disciplina*, 6 (1952), 105–113.

"The Use of Borrowed Material in 16th-Century Instrumental Music," *JAMS*, 5 (1952), 88–98.

Untitled review [of Francsico Correa de Arauxo, *Libro de Tientos*, ed. Santiago Kastner, Monumentos de la Música Española, XII (Barcelona, Instituto Español de Musicología, 1952)], *MQ*, 40 (1954), 244–247.

Untitled review [of Banchieri, *Festino*, perf. by The Primavera Singers, cond. Noah Greenberg, Esoteric ES–516], *MQ*, 40 (1954), 275–276.

"The Folia," *IMSCR*, 5 (Utrecht, 1952), 415–422.

"The Vihuela de Mano and its Music (1536–1576)." Ph.D. dissertation. New York University, 1953.

The Dublin Virginal Manuscript [ed.]. Wellesley, Mass.; 1954. The Wellesley Edition, 3. [2nd ed. (corrected, revised, and augmented), 1964.]

Untitled review [of Franciscus Bossinensis, *20 Recercari da sonar nel Laùto*, ed. Benvenuto Disertori (Milan, Zerboni, 1954)], MLA *Notes*, 2nd ser., 12 (1955), 317–318.

"Les Sources de la musique pour le clavier en Angleterre," in *La Musique instrumentale de la renaissance*, ed. Jean Jacquot (Paris, CNRS, 1955), pp. 225–236.

Untitled review [of W. Thomas Marrocco, *The Music of Jacopo da Bologna*, University of California Publications in Music, V (Berkeley, University of California Press, 1954)], *JAMS*, 8 (1955), 36–42.

"Otto John Gombosi (1202–1955)," *Acta Musicologica*, 28 (1956), 57–59.

Untitled notes to Guillaume de Machaut, *Motets, ballades, virelais, rondeaux*, performed by the Collegium Musicum of the University of Illinois, cond. George Hunter (audio-disk Westminster LP XWN 18166), 1956.

"Music for *A Handefull of Pleasant Delites*," *JAMS*, 10 (1957), 151–180.

"Le Problème des hauteurs dans la musique pour luth et vihuela au XVIe siècle," in *Le Luth et sa musique*, ed. Jean Jacquot (Paris, CNRS, 1958), pp. 171–178.

"The Lute Music of MS Royal Appendix 58," *JAMS*, 13 (1960), 117–125.

Contributions to *MGG*, 1961–66:

   "Milán, Luis," IX, col. 289–292.

   "Mudarra, Alonso," IX, col. 843–844.

   'Narváez, Luis de," IX, col. 1268–69.

   "Passamezzo," X, col. 877–880.

   "Pisador, Diego," X, col. 1297–98.

)manesca," XI, col. 778–779.

      ggiero," XI, col. 1086–88.

"Spanien: Die Vihuelisten des 16. Jh.; Die Gitarristen des 17. Jh.," XII, col. 1001–04.

"Urrede (= Wrede), Juan," XIII, col. 1176–79.

"Valderrábano, Enriquez de," XIII, col. 1215.

"Parody Technique in 16th-Century Instrumental Music," in *The Commonwealth of Music, in Honor of Curt Sachs*, ed. Gustave Reese & Rose Brandel (New York, 1965), pp. 208–228.

"Joan qd John and Other Fragments at Western Reserve," in *Aspects of Medieval and Renaissance Music: A Birthday Offering to Gustave Reese*, ed. Jan LaRue (New York, 1966), pp. 832–855.

"The Lute Books of Trinity College, Dublin," *Lute Society Journal*, 9 (1967), 17–40. In collaboration with members of Music 200, Harvard University.

"Apropos *The British Broadside Ballad and Its Music*," *JAMS*, 20 (1967), 28–86.

Untitled review [of Claude M. Simpson, *The British Broadside Ballad and Its Music* (New Brunswick, NJ; 1966)], *JAMS*, 20 (1967), 131–134.

"The Lute Books of Trinity College, Dublin, II: Ms. D.1.21 (The so-called Ballet Lute Book)," *Lute Society Journal*, 10 (1968), 1–18.

"The Fourth Dublin Lute Book," *Lute Society Journal*, 11 (1969), 1–22.

"Spanish Musicians in Sixteenth-Century England," in *Essays in Musicology in Honor of Dragan Plamenac*, ed. Gustave Reese & Robert J. Snow (Pittsburgh, University of Pittsburgh Press, 1969), pp. 353–364.

"Barley's Songs Without Words," *Lute Society Journal*, 12 (1970), 1–22.

"Curious Tunes for *Strange Histories*," in *Words and Music: The Scholar's View . . . in Honor of A. Tillman Merritt*, ed. Laurence Berman (Cambridge, MA; 1972), pp. 339–358.

"Additions to the Inventory of TCD MS. D.3.30/I," *Lute Society Journal*, 12 (1970), 43–44.

"Tessier and the Essex Circle," *Renaissance Quarterly*, 29 (1976), 378–384.

"The maner of dauncynge," *Early Music*, 4 (1976), 127–142.

"The So-called 'Dowland Lute Book' in the Folger Shakespeare Library," *Journal of the Lute Society of America*, 9 (1976), 5–29.

"A Dowland Miscellany," *Journal of the Lute Society of America*, 10 (1977), 5–153. Dowland issue.

"A Dowland Miscellany: Errata & Addenda," *Journal of the Lute Society of America*, 11 (1978), 101–105.

"In Memoriam *Gustave Reese* (1899–1977)," *Renaissance Quarterly*, 31 (1978), 48–49.

"The Hunt's Up," *Proceedings of the Royal Musical Association*, 106 (1980), 1–25.

Contributions to *The New Grove* (1980):

"Crane, William," V, 23.

"Daza, Esteban," V, 288.

"Farthing, Thomas," VI, 410.

"Fuenllana, Miguel de," VII, 6.

"Golder, Robert," VII, 500.

"Heywood, John," VIII, 545.

"Memo, Dionisio," XII, 130.

"Ripa, Alberto da," XVI, 49.

"Tailer, John," XVIII, 526–527.

"Wilder, Philip van," XX, 414–416.

"Changing the Instrument for the Music," *Journal of the Lute Society of America*, 15 27–29. [= Revised version of "Le Problème des hauteurs. . . ."]

"Sprightly and Cheerful Musick[:] Notes on the Cittern, Gittern & Guitar in 16th- & 17th-Century England," *Lute Society Journal*, 21 (1983 for 1979–81), 1–234.

"The Relationship of Folk and Art Music in 17th-Century Spain," *Studi Musicali*, 12 (1983), 281–300.

The Dublin Virginal Manuscript. A new edition. London: Schott, 1983.

Afterword

John Ward and Japanese Culture

MASAKATA KANAZAWA

THE DAY I ARRIVED IN BOSTON for the first time was memorable for its beautiful weather, with a clear blue sky, mild climate—so unusual for a late summer day—and pleasantly fresh air. As I was stepping down on-to the platform of South Station, I felt half relieved, from the long train trip across the continent after a fifteen-day voyage on the Pacific, and half uneasy about what I should do next. I had then no idea of how far Cambridge is from Boston, or how to get there. But before I had time to think about the problem, a stout gentleman approached me and said, "Are you Mr. Kanazawa from Japan? I am John Ward. My wife is wait-ing for us in the car outside." For a moment I was speechless, as I never imagined the possibility of a prospective professor meeting an un-known, newly arriving student at a train station. But he was quite indif-ferent to my reaction and, saying "Is that all you have?" picked up my trunk. Later on, he repeatedly told me that he had never carried a heavier trunk in his life. It was no wonder, for half of its contents were books and manuscripts. Out on the street, I met Mrs. Ward, who said, "Well, you finally arrived," shaking hands. She then drove us on Stor-row Drive, giving me explanations and introductions about the things on the way. When we crossed the Charles and came into Cambridge, another car approached ours and a bespectacled young man, sticking his head out from his driver's seat, started shouting at us. I had no idea what was the matter, but the Wards were both all smiles; giving a loud cheer, they shouted back at him. He then smiled broadly, waved his hand, and drove away in a different direction. "That was Nick Eng-land," said Mr. Ward. "His wife just had a baby, and he is on his way back from the hospital."

That was the way I arrived at Cambridge and met John and Ruth Ward for the first time. I still remember very vividly everything that happened on that day. Right away Professor Ward started asked me questions—questions about Japan, that is. At first I thought he was ˙ trying to be friendly or was perhaps just curious about the ˙nd of his new student, but soon I realized that his motivation

482

was quite serious and deep-rooted. Did I play some Japanese instruments? No, unfortunately. Did I sing in a traditional style? No. But at least I must be familiar with some specific examples of Japanese music; do tell him about them. Silence. Being eager to learn about "Western" music, I was not prepared for these questions—at least not on the first day of my arrival. Furthermore, the questions were not limited just to music; they included anything on Japan. And I am afraid I disappointed him greatly from the start. But then he came out with an even more unexpected question: "Are you by chance related to the royal family? You have a physiological resemblance to the crown prince." I stammered and was just barely able to answer: "All the Japanese are blood relations in one way or another, although one may have to trace that back more than ten centuries to prove it." "That's true," he said in a grave tone of voice, "and that is why you Japanese have such a unique culture, so different from others. You can hear it in your music." (The words may not be accurate, but that is the way I have always remembered them.)

Later I did a lot of thinking about what he said and began to realize there can be a much deeper meaning behind that statement. In fact, I believe he was giving me his first lesson: In music one can hear the culture to which it belongs. Of course that is true with any culture and its music in the world, not just Japanese. And at that point I realized that the musical interests of John Ward are not limited to the so-called "Western" styles, but that it covered all nations. His extremely popular course, "Music and Ritual," taught in collaboration with Rulan Pian, is exactly the fruitful outcome of such a worldwide interest of his thinking. At the same time it was he who made me realize that I did, in fact, know something about the music of my own country. To my own surprise, I could answer some of his more specific musical questions. Without being much aware of it, I had some experience of traditional music in my family background. My grandfather was an amateur *noh* singer, and one of my uncles is a semi-professional. One of my aunts was a skilled *koto* and *shamisen* player and appeared on radio programs in her girlhood. I was often taken to *kabuki* performances and in fact made a rather extensive field study of Japanese folk music when I was a college student. All these experiences came back to me as Professor Ward kept asking me questions, and I was encouraged to study Japanese music as a whole in due time.

Actually, the Wards had already been in close contact with Japanese music and culture before my arrival. One of his treasures is a lacquer box of Japanese origin, which was given to him by his teacher. He also had a marvelous collection of Japanese folk art, particularly earthenwares, which his art-historian friend collected for him in Japan. Furthermore, he and his wife had an extensive introduction to Japanese music and its culture-at-large from Professor Shigeo Kishibe of Tokyo University, who was a visiting professor at Harvard in the year prior to my arrival. Still his curiosity had not been saturated, and a shower of questions kept falling on me. So, I finally told him that he should visit Japan to find out the answers to all those questions of his, and he said he would. Yet it took ten more years before the Wards set foot on Japanese earth in person.

They arrived at Haneda Airport on March 18, 1969, and stayed in Japan until April 19. They chose the season well, as the cherry blossoms were in full bloom. I made a reservation for them at a quiet hotel behind the Imperial Palace, with a room facing onto the picturesque moat of the palace. The place was literally covered with flowers, and the atmosphere could not have been better for mediating on Japanese culture. The first thing they did was to visit the Mingei-kan, a famous museum of Japanese folk art that used to be the private home of Sōetsu Yanagi, the great scholar on the folk arts. Together we went to various performances of *gagaku, noh,* and *kabuki,* and at the same time we experienced various other Japanese adventures, eating at an old restaurant that specialized in bean curd cooking or wandering around in a traditional garden. The most memorable of these adventures was a ten-day visit to Kyoto and Nara, including excursions to Katsura and Shigakuin Palaces. We were also lucky to have a wonderful taxi driver, who took us around various places during our stay in Kyoto. Downtown one day we visited Satake Music Shop, specializing in traditional Japanese instruments, and stayed there for hours to enjoy Mr. Satake's eager explanatory talks and demonstrations of the instruments. But equally interesting to John Ward, I am sure, were the noisy folk festival of Kitano Shrine and the shopping at potters' stores around the Gojōzaka area. One thing he wanted very much was the experience of staying at a traditional Japanese inn overnight. So one day we got permission from Mrs. Ward, who was happier at the Western-style Miyako Hotel, and moved to the Tawara-ya, one of the most famous traditional inns in the town. The experience was quite new to me, too. It was as if we were visiting a rich friend's house to stay, rather than finding shelter for a night at a commercial inn. Our room was quite impressive, with a private garden, and the dinner, served by a well-mannered maid, consisted of a series of fancy dishes. After serving us the first round, she left the room to fetch another fresh bottle of *sake,* closing the paper screen behind her. John Ward then turned to me and said: "Now what we need is a *jiuta* dancer with her *shamisen* player." And he was exactly right.

Another adventure the Wards had in Kyoto was a *kagura* performshinto ritual dance) at Fushimi Inari Shrine which took place on st day in Kyoto. It happened that I had work to do in Tokyo, and m to their own plan. Actually, we had visited the shrine two days earlier and overheard the concluding passage of a *kagura* performance, which someone had asked to be performed for a reason we did not know. Evidently the Wards were fascinated about the idea of asking for a performance for themselves, although I was not aware of their interest. But being Christians, they did not know how to ask, and I was not around to help them. So they found a wonderful solution: they persuaded their friendly taxi driver to arrange a memorial performance for his forefathers. The taxi driver was evidently quite happy with the idea and agreed to do so, while the Wards could experience another cultural event with Japanese music.

John Ward made his second visit to Japan in 1975, this time without Ruth. He arrived on September 18 and stayed as long as seven weeks. As a result he has had a chance to enjoy two ideal seasons of Japan: spring and fall. He repeated his memorable experience at a Japanese inn by staying at the Fukuda-ya, the most exclusive establishment in Tokyo. In fact, he was assigned to the favorite room of Yasunari Kawabata, the Nobel Prize-winning author of "Yukiguni" (Snow Country) and "Sembazuru" (Thousand Cranes). John Ward invited Prof. Kishibe and myself for a memorable dinner there on the first evening. While we were enjoying the traditional dishes and exchanging bottles of *sake*, I kept imagining the famous novelist appearing from the next room to join us. Such was the atmosphere of that evening.

This time again I tried to take him to various musical events day after day. We attended a *koto* concert at which Mrs. Kishibe was one of the leading performers. We visited Ono Teruzaki Shrine near Ueno, where we watched Mr. Masatarō Tōgi, the retired director of the Imperial Household Musicians, giving a lesson of *gagaku* ensemble. Actually, I tried my best for him not to miss any interesting performance of traditional music, particularly *noh* and *kabuki*. And what impressed me the most was the fact that he could always identify a good performance from an inferior one, in spite of his inability to follow the language. I felt it quite remarkable, since Japanese music depends so much on its text.

During his second stay in Japan, Professor Ward did not remain a mere visitor to enjoy the country; he also participated in musicological activities and met a number of Japanese scholars. He gave a talk at Kunitachi Music College on the tradition of the English ballad and its influence on Canadian and American folksongs, taking "Greensleeves" as his example, and another discussion on "Hunt's Up" to a group of scholars and students specializing in European early music. But probably the most fruitful accomplishments for him during his stay was his visit to the workshop of a famous *noh* mask maker, from whom he acquired a mask of a young woman. I was quite surprised, as it was hardly possible to buy a mask from him, unless you were an accomplished *noh* performer yourself. In fact, the mask in question was to become the main feature at an exhibition held by the maker, who agreed to sell it to John Ward after the event. Later I was told that a number of *noh* players were interested in getting that mask, but the maker explained to them: "I have already made my mind to marry my daughter and send her off to America." And John Ward meanwhile explained to me why he dared to ask to have her: "She was really alive—not one of those masks which are pretty and yet merely retain a copy of a woman's face. And I thought it rather a good idea to keep one real *noh* mask in Cambridge, Massachusetts, so that a good *noh* performer might learn about its existence and perhaps make a long trip all the way to the East Coast to give a performance with it." As far as I know, the mask is still in his possession, waiting for the appearance of a real *noh* performer who can bring the beauty of its womanhood to life.

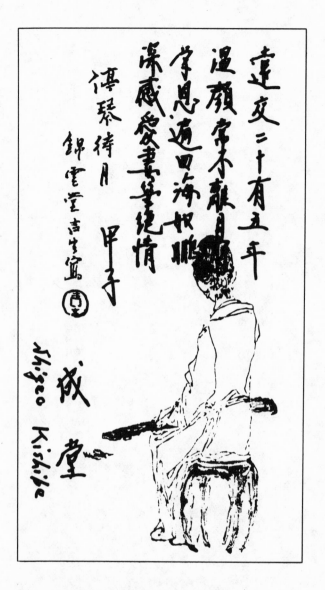

Our friendship across the miles has
    lasted over twenty-five years

Your kind countenance is always
    before my eyes

Your scholarly influence is like the
    Peng eagle that reaches the Four Seas

Your dear wife has won my admiration, which
    cannot be fully expressed with mere words

                    —Shigeo Kishibe